Foundations of Behavior Genetics

Foundations of Behavior Genetics provides a forward-looking introduction to this fascinating field. Written by an experienced teacher and researcher, this text focuses on concepts, methods, and findings that inform our understanding of heredity–behavior relations.

The book's neuroscience perspective asks students to think about potential neural mechanisms involved in pathways from genes to behavior. While the text is primarily focused on human behavior genetics, it also emphasizes the importance of non-human animal models in experimental studies, as well as their evolutionary connections to humans.

Part I covers the history of behavior genetics and the basics of non-molecular genetics; Part II discusses molecular genetics and neurogenetics; Part III addresses various behavioral disorders; and Part IV explores health, social behavior, and ethical implications.

The text includes detailed chapter summaries, several "Check-up" questions after major sections that test student understanding, and recommended readings. Instructors are provided with a test bank of multiple-choice items and hi-res JPEGs of the many illustrations created for the book.

Professor Scott F. Stoltenberg has taught and conducted research at the University of Nebraska since 2009. He has previously taught at Black Hills State University and done research at the University of Michigan. He earned his BS from Saint John's University (MN) and his Ph.D. in Psychology from the University of Illinois at Urbana-Champaign. He has conducted behavior genetic research for more than three decades, first with fruit flies and then with human participants. He teaches courses in behavior genetics, addiction, and neuroscience.

Foundations of Behavior Genetics

SCOTT F. STOLTENBERG

University of Nebraska–Lincoln

CAMBRIDGE
UNIVERSITY PRESS

CAMBRIDGE
UNIVERSITY PRESS

University Printing House, Cambridge CB2 8BS, United Kingdom

One Liberty Plaza, 20th Floor, New York, NY 10006, USA

477 Williamstown Road, Port Melbourne, VIC 3207, Australia

314–321, 3rd Floor, Plot 3, Splendor Forum, Jasola District Centre, New Delhi – 110025, India

103 Penang Road, #05–06/07, Visioncrest Commercial, Singapore 238467

Cambridge University Press is part of the University of Cambridge. It furthers the University's mission by disseminating knowledge in the pursuit of education, learning, and research at the highest international levels of excellence.

www.cambridge.org
Information on this title: www.cambridge.org/highereducation/isbn/9781108487979
DOI: 10.1017/9781108768412

First published 2023

Printed in the United Kingdom by TJ Books Limited, Padstow Cornwall 2023

A catalogue record for this publication is available from the British Library.

Library of Congress Cataloging-in-Publication Data
Names: Stoltenberg, Scott F. author.
Title: Foundations of behavior genetics / Scott F. Stoltenberg.
Description: New York, NY : Cambridge University Press, 2023. | Includes bibliographical references
    and index.
Identifiers: LCCN 2021035044 (print) | LCCN 2021035045 (ebook) | ISBN 9781108487979 (hardback) |
    ISBN 9781108768412 (epub)
Subjects: MESH: Genetics, Behavioral | Genetic Variation | Mental Disorders–genetics
Classification: LCC QH443 (print) | LCC QH443 (ebook) | NLM QU 450 | DDC 572.8/77–dc23
LC record available at https://lccn.loc.gov/2021035044
LC ebook record available at https://lccn.loc.gov/2021035045

ISBN 978-1-108-48797-9 Hardback

Additional resources for this publication at www.cambridge.org/stoltenberg

To Jerry Hirsch, for giving me an opportunity, providing unwavering support, and for leading by example.

Brief Contents

List of Figures xiv

List of Tables xviii

List of Boxes xix

Preface xxi

Acknowledgments xxiii

Part I Fundamentals

1 **Introduction to Behavior Genetics** 3

2 **Mendelian Genetics** 25

3 **Heritability** 46

Part II Molecules and Cells

4 **Genes** 73

5 **Genetic Variation** 94

6 **Neurogenetics** 117

Part III Behaviors and Behavioral Disorders

7 **Serious Mental Illness** 145

8 **Learning and Memory** 169

9 **Emotion and Depressive Disorders** 194

10 **Fear and Anxiety** 222

11 **Addiction** 248

Part IV Health, Social Behavior, and Implications

12 Eating and Exercising   **279**

13 Social Behavior   **306**

14 Behavior Genetics in Real Life   **331**

15 Eugenics   **351**

Glossary   372
Index   394

Contents

List of Figures   xiv

List of Tables   xviii

List of Boxes   xix

Preface   xxi

Acknowledgments   xxiii

Part I Fundamentals

1 Introduction to Behavior Genetics   3

   1.1   A Brief History of Behavior Genetics   3

   1.2   Behavior Genetics Focuses on Understanding Individual Differences
         in Behavior   10

   1.3   Pathways from Genes to Behaviors Cross Levels of Analysis   13

   1.4   Non-Human Animal Models Are Essential in Behavior Genetics   16

   1.5   Ethical Oversight of Behavior Genetic Research Is Necessary   20

   1.6   Summary   22

   Recommended Reading   22

   References   23

2 Mendelian Genetics   25

   2.1   Developments in Science, Agriculture, and Medicine Set the Stage
         for Understanding Heredity   25

   2.2   Early Thinking about Generation   26

   2.3   Gregor Mendel: Early Depression and Failures   29

   2.4   Experimental Hybridization Was the Key   30

   2.5   Mendel's Law of Segregation Describes Inheritance of a Single Locus   32

   2.6   Mendel's Law of Independent Assortment Describes Inheritance
         of Multiple Loci   35

   2.7   Mendel's Laws Are Used to Map Relative Positions of Genes
         on Chromosomes   36

   2.8   Mendelian Disorders in Humans Are Caused by Variants in Single Genes   42

   2.9   Summary   44

   Recommended Reading   45

   References   45

3 Heritability   **46**

3.1 Genetic Factors That Affect Quantitative Traits Are Inherited in
     Mendelian Fashion   46

3.2 Phenotypic Variation in a Population May Be Due to Genetic and
     Environmental Sources   48

3.3 Genetic Variance May Be Due to Polygenes, Dominance, and
     Epistatic Interactions   52

3.4 There Are Many Sources of Environmental Variance   53

3.5 Heritability Indexes Degree of Phenotypic Variance Due to Genetic Effects   58

3.6 Beware of the Potential for Misunderstanding and Bias   66

3.7 Summary   67

Recommended Reading   68

References   68

Part II Molecules and Cells

4 Genes   **73**

4.1 Chromosomes Carry Hereditary Material   73

4.2 The Structure of DNA Determines Its Functions   77

4.3 DNA Replication Involves Making Copies   80

4.4 DNA Sequence Specifies Amino Acid Sequence in Proteins   81

4.5 Epigenetic Processes Regulate Gene Expression   85

4.6 What Is a Gene?   89

4.7 Summary   92

Recommended Reading   93

References   93

5 Genetic Variation   **94**

5.1 There Are Different Types of Genetic Variation   94

5.2 How Genetic Differences Play a Role in Phenotype Differences   99

5.3 Assessing Genetic Variation   102

5.4 Non-Experimental Methods: Testing Associations between Genetic Variants
     and Behavior   107

5.5 Experimental Methods: Generating Genetic Variation   110

5.6 The Human Genome Project Changed Biomedical Science   113

5.7 Summary   115

Recommended Reading   115

References   116

6   Neurogenetics   **117**

  6.1   Neurons Are Cells Specialized for Communication   117

  6.2   Genetic Variation for Neural Components Is Common   122

  6.3   Formation and Maintenance of Synapses and Circuits Depends on Genes   126

  6.4   Genetic Variation Affects Neural Activation Patterns   131

  6.5   Genetic Variation Can Moderate the Impact of Drugs on Neural Activity   136

  6.6   Summary   140

  Recommended Reading   140

  References   141

Part III   Behaviors and Behavioral Disorders

7   Serious Mental Illness   **145**

  7.1   Mental Illness and Its Impact   145

  7.2   Risk for Developing Mental Illness   147

  7.3   How Should Behavior Genetics Researchers Think About Mental Illness?   149

  7.4   Schizophrenia Signs, Symptoms, and Diagnostic Criteria   154

  7.5   Neurobiology of Schizophrenia   155

  7.6   Schizophrenia Genetics: Heritability   157

  7.7   Schizophrenia Genetics: Molecular Genetics   159

  7.8   Schizophrenia Genetics: Non-Human Animal Models   163

  7.9   Summary   165

  Recommended Reading   165

  References   166

8   Learning and Memory   **169**

  8.1   Intelligence Is Indexed by IQ Tests   169

  8.2   Intellectual Disability Is a Developmental Disorder with Multiple Causes 171

  8.3   Learning Disorders Are Not Considered Intellectual Disabilities   177

  8.4   Memory Is a Crucial Aspect of Cognitive Ability   179

  8.5   Alzheimer Disease Is a Common Cause of Neurocognitive Disorder   184

  8.6   Summary   189

  Recommended Reading   190

  References   190

9   Emotion and Depressive Disorders   **194**

  9.1   Emotions Prepare for Action and Communicate   194

  9.2   There Are Many Ways to Measure Emotion   196

  9.3   Emotion Regulation Difficulties May Lead to Psychopathology   199

  9.4   Mood Disorders Are Common, and Symptomatically Heterogeneous   201

9.5   Prevalence and Symptoms of Depressive Disorders   204

9.6   The Genetic Epidemiology of Depressive Disorders   206

9.7   Efforts to Characterize Genetic Mechanisms of Depressive Disorders
        Are Ongoing   208

9.8   Genetic Evidence from Non-Human Animal Models   212

9.9   Summary   216

Recommended Reading   217

References   218

10   **Fear and Anxiety**   **222**

10.1   Fear and Anxiety Are Defensive Responses to Threats   222

10.2   The Genetics of Fear and Anxiety in Mice   225

10.3   Anxiety-Related Personality Traits as Phenotypes for Genetic Analysis   229

10.4   Anxiety Disorders Are Common   231

10.5   Anxiety Disorders Run in Families and Are Polygenic   234

10.6   Obsessive-Compulsive and Related Disorders   237

10.7   Trauma- and Stressor-Related Disorders   240

10.8   Summary   243

Recommended Reading   244

References   244

11   **Addiction**   **248**

11.1   Addiction Is Characterized by Impaired Control Over Substance Use,
        Tolerance, and Withdrawal   248

11.2   The Neurobiology of Addiction   254

11.3   Non-Human Animal Models of Alcohol Use Disorder Genetics   257

11.4   Alcohol-Related Traits and Alcohol Use Disorder Run in Families   262

11.5   Alcohol Metabolism Genes Affect Risk for Alcohol Use Disorder   265

11.6   There Are Many Genes That Contribute to Risk for Alcohol Use Disorder   269

11.7   Summary   273

Recommended Reading   273

References   273

Part IV Health, Social Behavior, and Implications

12   **Eating and Exercising**   **279**

12.1   Eating and Exercising in Context   279

12.2   Genetic Variation Partially Explains Risk for Obesity   284

12.3   Genetic Variation Partially Explains Risk for Eating Disorders   289

12.4   Exercise Motivation and Benefits Show Genetic Influence   296

12.5   Summary   301

Recommended Reading   302

References   302

13   Social Behavior   306

13.1   Individual Differences in Social Behavior Are an Important Part of Life   306

13.2   The Neurobiology of Social Behavior   309

13.3   Individual Differences in Social Cognition and Sociability   311

13.4   Affiliation and Attachment   314

13.5   Sexual Behavior Circuits   320

13.6   Aggression: Harming Someone Else   324

13.7   Summary   326

Recommended Reading   327

References   327

14   Behavior Genetics in Real Life   331

14.1   Direct-to-Consumer Genetic Testing   331

14.2   Precision Medicine for Mental Illness   337

14.3   Behavior Genetics and the Justice System   340

14.4   Designer Babies   343

14.5   What Use Is Behavior Genetics?   345

14.6   Summary   348

Recommended Reading   349

References   349

15   Eugenics   351

15.1   Social Darwinism   351

15.2   Galton's Theory and Its Reception   354

15.3   The Eugenics Records Office in the United States   356

15.4   Involuntary Sterilization Laws and Immigration Policies   359

15.5   America Exports Eugenics to Nazi Germany   364

15.6   Race and Its Place in Behavior Genetics   366

15.7   Summary   369

Recommended Reading   370

References   370

Glossary   372

Index   394

Figures

1.1	Familial resemblance	4
1.2	Locke and Darwin	4
1.3	Francis Galton	6
1.4	Morphological variation in dog breeds	7
1.5	Thomas Hunt Morgan	8
1.6	Logo of the Second International Congress of Eugenics, 1921	9
1.7	Three commonly used behavioral measures	11
1.8	Levels of analysis	14
1.9	Three main questions in behavior genetic research	15
1.10	Key model organisms in behavior genetics	18
2.1	Breeds of sheep	26
2.2	Homunculus	27
2.3	Qualitative and quantitative traits	27
2.4	Bakewell's New Leicester sheep	28
2.5	Gregor Mendel	30
2.6	Traits of the garden pea	31
2.7	Monohybrid cross of pea shape	32
2.8	Theoretical model of a monohybrid cross of pea color	33
2.9	Punnett squares for a monohybrid cross of pea shape	34
2.10	Dihybrid cross	35
2.11	Sex-linked white eye mutation	38
2.12	Dihybrid cross with mutants for sepia eye and vestigial wings	38
2.13	Backcrossing vestigial wings and black body mutants	39
2.14	No recombinant types produced when male F_1 generation males are backcrossed to parental line females	40
2.15	Crossing over and map distance	40
2.16	Hypothetical pedigrees showing different inheritance patterns	43
3.1	Height is normally distributed in populations	47
3.2	Polygenic inheritance can approximate the normal distribution	48
3.3	Partitioning phenotypic variance	49
3.4	Variance partitioning in a hypothetical study of depression-like behavior	50
3.5	A laboratory mouse and a standard cage	51
3.6	Dominance and epistasis	52
3.7	Patterns of G×E interaction	55
3.8	Genotype–environment correlations	57
3.9	Pedigree indicating genetic relatedness to a proband	59
3.10	Heritability estimates of temperament traits in cattle	60
3.11	Types of twins	61
3.12	Selection for depression-like behavior in rats	65
4.1	Human karyotype	74
4.2	Meiosis	75
4.3	Mitosis	76
4.4	Watson and Crick's double helix model of DNA	78

4.5   Genetic information is contained in the nucleotide bases of the DNA double helix   79
4.6   Semiconservative DNA replication   80
4.7   Transcribing DNA into mRNA   82
4.8   Alternative splicing and translation of mRNA into proteins   83
4.9   Translating mRNA sequence into a protein   84
4.10 The genetic code   85
4.11 Epigenetic regulation of gene expression   86
4.12 Maternal care impacts stress responsivity in adult offspring   88
4.13 What is a gene?   91
5.1   The Great Pyramid of Giza   95
5.2   Types of DNA sequence variation   96
5.3   The Genome Data Viewer   98
5.4   Examples of DNA sequence variations and their impact on mRNA and amino
      acid sequence   100
5.5   Thermalcycler   103
5.6   Gel electrophoresis   104
5.7   Polymerase chain reaction   106
5.8   Genotyping bead array   107
5.9   Population stratification   109
5.10 CRISPR-Cas9   112
5.11 Cost of sequencing   114
6.1   Cell membrane and organelles   118
6.2   Basic structure of a neuron   120
6.3   Synaptic activity   122
6.4   Serotonergic pathway in the brain   123
6.5   Pathway of serotonin synthesis and metabolism   124
6.6   Neurexins and neuroligins   127
6.7   Structure of the 5-HT1B receptor   129
6.8   Structure of the serotonin transporter   130
6.9   Magnetic resonance imaging   134
6.10 Potential impact of drugs on neural activation   137
6.11 The 5-HTTLPR polymorphism of the serotonin transporter gene   139
7.1   Share of population with mental health and substance use disorders, 2017   146
7.2   Mental and substance use disorders as a share of total disease burden, 2017   147
7.3   Models for understanding genetic and environmental risk   148
7.4   Levels of analysis   150
7.5   Qualitative diagnoses as a function of endophenotypes   152
7.6   Research Domain Criteria   153
7.7   Enlarged ventricles associated with schizophrenia diagnosis   156
7.8   Hypofrontality associated with schizophrenia diagnosis   156
7.9   Risk for developing schizophrenia-related psychoses   157
7.10 Microcephaly in 3q29 microdeletion   160
7.11 Schizophrenia endophenotypes   161
7.12 Synaptic plasticity and neural circuitry genes harboring private damaging mutations   162
8.1   Standardized IQ score distribution   170
8.2   *FMR1*   173
8.3   Trisomy 21 karyotype   175
8.4   Synteny of human chromosome 21 and three mouse chromosomes   176
8.5   *In utero* RNAi affects response of auditory cortex neurons to speech sounds in rats   179

8.6   KIBRA protein regulates dendritic growth in hippocampus   181
8.7   Olfactory conditioning in fruit flies   182
8.8   Mutations that affect learning and memory   184
8.9   Alzheimer disease pathology   186
8.10 Mechanism of amyloid plaque production   186
8.11 Genes associated with early onset Alzheimer disease   188
8.12 APOE genotypes   188
9.1   Emotion in dogs and cats   195
9.2   Amygdala activation in response to facial expressions of threat   197
9.3   The process model of emotion regulation   200
9.4   Genetic correlations across psychiatric disorders   203
9.5   Prevalence of an episode of depressive disorder around the world as well as sex
      and age differences   205
9.6   The top 20 leading causes of DALYs worldwide   206
9.7   Heritability estimates for depressive disorder   207
9.8   Candidate gene association studies for depression 1991–2016   209
9.9   Action of selective serotonin reuptake inhibitors   211
9.10 Depression-like behavior paradigms   213
9.11 Hypothalamic-Pituitary-Adrenal Axis   215
10.1 Public-speaking anxiety   222
10.2 Rodent assays for fear- and anxiety-like behavior   224
10.3 Two mouse strains that differ on anxiety-like behaviors   226
10.4 Diazepam modulates GABA$_A$ receptors   227
10.5 Silver fox domestication study   229
10.6 Self-report items from the Big Five Inventory   230
10.7 Prevalence of anxiety disorders around the world as well as sex and age differences 233
10.8 Anxiety score distribution for European American and African American veterans 236
10.9 Obsessive-compulsive disorder runs in families   238
10.10 Self-destructive grooming behavior of *Sapap3* knockouts   240
10.11 Witnessing trauma   242
11.1 Past month substance use in the US   249
11.2 Alcohol use   250
11.3 Alcohol or drug use disorders   252
11.4 Reward pathway   255
11.5 Alcohol preference in two inbred lines of mice   258
11.6 Mating scheme to develop recombinant inbred lines   260
11.7 Heritability estimates for addictive disorders   264
11.8 Ethanol metabolism   265
11.9 Genotype frequency of rs671   268
11.10 Voluntary alcohol consumption in rats with different *Aldh2* genotypes   269
11.11 Genes most studied for association with alcoholism   270
11.12 Manhattan plot of GWAS findings for alcohol dependence   272
12.1 Food availability worldwide   280
12.2 Nutrition transition   281
12.3 Obese mice   282
12.4 Appetite control circuits   283
12.5 Body mass index chart   285
12.6 Worldwide obesity rates   286
12.7 Twenty-five genes associated with BMI   289

12.8	Number of females and males with anorexia nervosa or bulimia nervosa from 1990 to 2017	290
12.9	Manhattan plot of anorexia nervosa GWAS	295
12.10	Rates of insufficient physical activity across the globe for men and women	298
12.11	Twenty-five genes associated with physical activity	299
12.12	Endocannabinoid system	301
13.1	Relations among genes, brains, and social behavior	307
13.2	Agonistic behavior	309
13.3	Social interaction dynamics	310
13.4	Brain circuits for social behavior in mice	311
13.5	Williams syndrome critical region on chromosome 7	313
13.6	Non-allelic homologous recombination	313
13.7	Oxytocin receptor	315
13.8	Autism spectrum disorder	318
13.9	Autism spectrum disorder risk genes	320
13.10	Female Satin Bowerbird inspects bower	321
13.11	Courtship behavior in *D. melanogaster*	322
13.12	Aggression in other non-human animal models	325
14.1	Direct-to-consumer genetic testing kit	332
14.2	23andMe genetic weight report	335
14.3	Precision Medicine Initiative	337
14.4	Precision medicine in psychiatry	338
14.5	Selective serotonin reuptake inhibitors	339
14.6	Genetic genealogy	341
14.7	Views on human genetic engineering	343
14.8	CCR5 receptor and the HIV replication cycle	345
14.9	Three main questions in behavior genetic research revisited	346
14.10	Weak and strong genetic explanations	347
15.1	Thomas Malthus	352
15.2	Herbert Spencer	353
15.3	Karl Pearson and Francis Galton	355
15.4	Kallikak's pedigree	357
15.5	Carnegie Library, Luverne, MN	358
15.6	Field worker training at the ERO	359
15.7	*Buck v. Bell*	361
15.8	Army mental tests	363
15.9	Nazi extermination camps	365
15.10	Lebensborn Program	366
15.11	Scientific racism in the 1960s	368

Tables

3.1 Realized heritability after one generation of divergent selection for depressive-like behavior   64

5.1 Genomes of species important in behavior genetics   95

5.2 Median autosomal variant sites per genome   96

6.1 Serotonin receptor genetics   125

7.1 Endophenotype criteria   151

11.1 *ADH1B* single nucleotide polymorphisms and relative reaction rates of three genotypes   266

11.2 *ADH1C* single nucleotide polymorphisms and relative reaction rates of two genotypes   266

Boxes

1.1 Critical Concept: Measuring Behavior   10
1.2 Critical Concept: Model Organisms   17
2.1 Sheep Breeders Make Their Mark on Genetics   28
2.2 Bloomington Drosophila Stock Center   41
3.1 Species Spotlight: *Mus musculus*   51
3.2 Critical Concept: Twinning   61
4.1 Critical Concept: *Homo sapiens* Chromosomes   74
4.2 Critical Concept: Transgenerational Epigenetic Inheritance   88
5.1 NCBI Genome Data Viewer   97
5.2 Critical Concept: CRISPR-Cas9   111
6.1 Critical Concept: Neurotransmitter Systems   122
6.2 Critical Concept: Neuroimaging Genetics   133
7.1 Critical Concept: Research Diagnostic Criteria (RDoC)   152
7.2 ICD-11 Diagnosis: Schizophrenia   154
7.3 Environmental Risk Factors for Schizophrenia   158
8.1 ICD-11 Diagnosis: Disorders of Intellectual Development   171
8.2 Mouse Models of Trisomy 21   175
8.3 ICD-11 Diagnosis: Developmental Learning Disorder   177
8.4 Species Spotlight: Dissecting Learning and Memory in Fruit Flies   182
8.5 ICD-11 Diagnosis: Dementia Due to Alzheimer Disease   185
9.1 Genetic Differences in Amygdala Activation in Response to Facial Expressions
of Threat   197
9.2 ICD-11 Diagnosis: Mood Disorders   201
9.3 ICD-11 Diagnosis: Bipolar Type I Disorder, Current Episode Manic, without
Psychotic Symptoms   202
9.4 ICD-11 Depressive Disorders   204
9.5 Non-Human Animal Models for Investigating Depression-Like Behaviors   212
10.1 Selection for Tameness in Silver Foxes   228
10.2 ICD-11 Diagnosis: Anxiety or Fear-Related Disorders   232
10.3 ICD-11 Diagnosis: Obsessive-Compulsive or Related Disorders   237
10.4 ICD-11 Diagnosis: Disorders Specifically Associated with Stress   240
11.1 ICD-11 Diagnosis: Alcohol Dependence   253
11.2 Recombinant Inbred Lines   259
11.3 Alcohol Dehydrogenase (ADH)   266
12.1 Appetite Control Circuits   283
12.2 ICD-11 Diagnosis: Feeding and Eating Disorders   290
12.3 ICD-11 Diagnosis: Anorexia Nervosa and Bulimia Nervosa   292
12.4 The Role of Puberty in Disordered Eating   293
13.1 Non-Allelic Homologous Recombination   313
13.2 ICD-11 Diagnosis: Autism Spectrum Disorder   319
13.3 Measuring Aggressive Behavior in Non-Human Animal Models   325
14.1 ClinVar   332
14.2 5-HTTLPR Genotype and SSRI Treatment Response   339
15.1 The Kallikak Family   356
15.2 Army Mental Tests   362

Preface

Behavior genetics addresses one of the most complex questions in science: What causes behavior? Specifically, researchers in behavior genetics seek to understand the role of *genetic differences* in *individual differences* in behavior. The complexity of this problem cannot be overstated, especially when the most informative experimental approaches may be ethically off-limits.

In this book I focus on the basic concepts and methods in behavior genetics, warts and all, and try not to oversell the findings. In the last thirty years we have seen unprecedented advances in biotechnology and computing that have been put to good use in behavior genetics. Such technological advances seem to generate recurring cycles of optimism and disappointment as new avenues of inquiry reveal unexpected complexity. We tend to extol the virtues of the new approaches, sometimes bash the old approaches, and hope to learn from our mistakes. It is important to recognize that the details of some of today's most exciting findings will likely fall short under future scrutiny. That is how science progresses. Students must learn to appreciate how science works in a way that strengthens their confidence in the process. This book focuses on concepts and methods that have been historically important and will hopefully engender some humility when considering how much we know about one of the most complex problems in science.

We live in an era when editing the human genome is not only possible but has been accomplished. We also live in a time when survivors of state-sponsored forced sterilizations still walk among us. We cannot permit the same scientific hubris concerning heredity–behavior relations that justified wholesale human rights abuses to permeate the next generation of scientists and citizens. It seems that the time is ripe for a book in behavior genetics to embrace the twenty-first century without ignoring the twentieth.

I have conducted behavior genetic research since the late 1980s and have been teaching it for nearly as long. In graduate school my research focused on geotaxis in fruit flies. As a postdoctoral fellow, in the mid-1990s, I began conducting candidate gene association studies in humans. This book covers methods used in both animal and human behavior genetic studies and emphasizes the crucial role of *convergent evidence* throughout.

This book contains:

- Boldfaced key terms (defined in glossary)

- Interim review questions (i.e., "Check-ups") for each main section

- Boxes with additional detail in each chapter

- A list of recommended readings in each chapter

- Bulleted summaries of each chapter

The perspective of this book is that while it is important to describe statistical associations between heredity and behavior, it is imperative that we consider the biological mechanisms through which those associations are manifest. Accordingly, this book relies more on neuroscience than on advanced statistical models for understanding pathways from genes to behavior.

The chapter lineup in *Foundations of Behavior Genetics* covers four major themes. The first three chapters (Fundamentals) cover the history of behavior genetics and the basics of non-molecular genetics. The next three chapters (Molecules and Cells) discuss molecular genetics, and neurogenetics. The next five chapters (Behaviors and Behavioral Disorders) discuss topics such as schizophrenia, learning and cognition, emotion, depression, anxiety, and substance use disorders. The final four chapters (Health, Social Behavior, and Implications) discuss topics such as obesity, social behavior, behavior genetics in real life, and eugenics. The material in the first six chapters should be covered in sequence before moving on to material in the final nine chapters. However, the final nine chapters could be covered in whatever order suits the reader.

The intended audience for this book is advanced undergraduate psychology majors. Courses such as Introduction to Psychology, Research Methods & Statistics, and Biopsychology, or their equivalents should be considered prerequisites to a Behavior Genetics course taught with this book. Other courses such as Developmental Psychology, Social Psychology, and Abnormal Psychology would be desirable, but should not be considered prerequisite.

Supplementary material included in the Instructor's Package includes a Test Bank with at least twenty multiple choice items per chapter, and all artwork as JPEGs or PNGs (many in color) for use in lectures.

Acknowledgments

This book would not exist if not for the mentoring that I have received from Doug Bernstein over several decades. His enthusiasm and support for effective teaching has always been an inspiration. His experience in and knowledge about writing textbooks coupled with his readiness to help have been invaluable to me.

A debt of gratitude is owed to my colleagues who served as reviewers. Their thoughtful perspectives were critical in the organization, tone, and contents of the book. Although I did not always take their advice, I always appreciated it, fully considered it, and found it valuable. Any mistakes or awkward sentences in the book are my responsibility.

A similar debt is owed to my students, who have helped me across the semesters to think more clearly about behavior genetics. Their enthusiasm for the topic keeps me motivated.

Thanks to the editorial staff at Cambridge. Stephen Acerra has been and continues to be a champion of the book. Maggie Jeffers and Nicola Chapman kept me on task and moved things along. Thanks for being so easy to work with.

Finally, thanks to my life-partner, Shelley Jennifer Creeger Stoltenberg. None of this would have been possible without you by my side. Here's to the future!

Cheers,

Scott F. Stoltenberg

Part I Fundamentals

1 Introduction to Behavior Genetics

Behavior genetics – the scientific study of heredity–behavior relations – has come of age. Since the middle of the twentieth century, accumulating scientific evidence has shown that genetic differences between individuals play a significant role in behavioral differences between them. In fact, it is now generally accepted that genetic variation is an important contributor to individual differences in behavior. Although the fundamental question about the role of inheritance in behavioral resemblance is not new, recent technological advances provide new ways to peek behind nature's curtain. It is easy to get excited about the potential for discoveries in behavior genetics. We appear to be entering a new era in which it may be possible to understand the biological mechanisms responsible for familial behavioral resemblance. However, we should enter this era with humility. The history of behavior genetics is full of periods of excitement followed by disappointment. It also contains sobering lessons of scientific hubris and state-sponsored human rights violations. There is a lot to be excited about, but it is important to remember history, and to understand the limitations of behavior genetics, especially when considering the application of behavior genetic findings to human beings.

This chapter provides a brief look at the history of behavior genetics and introduces some of its early influential thinkers. It goes on to discuss modern dog breeds because they are the outcome of applying practical knowledge about heredity–behavior relations. Dogs also provide a personal touchpoint to the material because many of us have had extensive interactions with them. Further, it introduces the use of non-human animals to understand human problems, which is an important feature of much behavior genetic research. This chapter considers our shared evolutionary history with other animals, which is the basis of their ongoing contributions to improving human health. It also sets the stage for the rest of the book by introducing the main behavior genetic research questions. Finally, the role of ethics oversight in the conduct of behavior genetic research is discussed. This chapter provides the context in which to consider behavior genetics concepts, methods, and findings.

1.1 A Brief History of Behavior Genetics

Officially, the field of behavior genetics was established in 1960, when its first textbook was published (Fuller & Thompson, 1960). Prior to that, efforts to understand the role of genetic differences in individual differences in behavior were mostly non-systematic, anecdotal, literary, philosophical, or focused on animal breeding, or evolution.

1.1.1 Familial Resemblance for Behaviors Has Been Observed Throughout History

It is likely that throughout human history people have noticed that some traits tend to "run in families." It is easy to see familial resemblance for physical traits, such as ear and nose shape, or

Figure 1.1. **Familial resemblance.** It is easy to see that members of families share physical similarities. Source: The Good Brigade / DigitalVision / Getty Images.

(a)   (b)

Figure 1.2. **Locke and Darwin.** (a) John Locke (1632–1704) developed the idea that humans are born as "blank slates" and experience is the main factor in individual differences in behavior. (b) Charles Darwin (1809–1882) focused on biological causes of behavior. He appreciated the role of behavior as a driving force of evolution and that behavioral traits can be the targets of selection. Source: (a) Hulton Archive / Staff / Getty Images. (b) Bettmann / Contributor / Bettmann / Getty Images.

eye and hair color (see Figure 1.1). You may have also noticed that some behavioral characteristics in children may resemble the behavior of their parents, such as having an outgoing personality, or suffering from anxiety, or even showing a tendency to abuse substances. Such resemblance is commonly recognized, and has inspired familiar phrases, such as "like mother, like daughter," or "the apple doesn't fall far from the tree."

Familial resemblance for behavioral traits has long been noted by writers, such as William Shakespeare, in lines like "Her dispositions she inherits" (*All's Well That Ends Well*, Act I:1) (Loehlin, 2009). Or when describing the character Caliban, "A devil, born a devil, on whose nature, nurture can never stick" (*The Tempest*, Act IV:1, Prospero) (Berg, 2001). In fact, this passage appears to have been the inspiration for a phrase that has long been used to characterize efforts to understand whether heredity or experience is more important in shaping behavior: "nature versus nurture."

Generally, philosophers have held that behavior is a result of some combination of nature and nurture, although there have been those who have taken stronger positions favoring one or the other. Contrasting views in this controversy are consistent with those of philosopher John Locke and naturalist Charles Darwin (Loehlin, 2009). Locke (see Figure 1.2(a)) developed the position that nearly all our capacities are produced by experience and suggested that we enter the world as "blank slates" on which experience writes. Darwin (see Figure 1.2(b)), on the other hand, made the argument that human beings are part of the biological world, which is shaped by the forces of evolution, and that many of our capacities are rooted in biology. Darwin's argument was buttressed with systematic, data-driven observations that he had collected over decades of intensive study as a naturalist.

1.1.2 Behavior Is a Driving Force in Evolution

Charles Darwin's contribution to behavior genetics should not be ignored. Of course, his primary contribution to science was his development of and support for the theory of evolution via natural selection. Let us consider his oft used example of the finches of the Galapagos Islands that emphasizes morphological (i.e., physical structure) change made possible by the available genetic variation in populations and driven by niche specialization.

After returning home from his voyage on the HMS *Beagle* (1831–1836), Darwin studied the birds that he had collected on the trip and noted that on different Galapagos Islands there were finches that had substantially different beak morphology. On one island, ground finches had rather small beaks, whereas on another island, there were ground finches that had substantially larger beaks. In fact, he had collected many birds during his time on the Galapagos Islands, and kept careful records of where he collected them. It appears that Darwin collected approximately fifteen different species of finch on the Galapagos Islands. He postulated that at some point in the past, a small number of finches from the mainland (i.e., South America) arrived on a previously finch-less island, and subsequently spread out to colonize the other islands. He also hypothesized that the different islands provided different food sources, such as plants that produce either small or large seeds. On islands where small seeds predominated, finches with small beaks were better able to feed, and were therefore at an advantage in terms of both survival and reproduction. Similarly, on islands where large seeds were most plentiful, finches with larger beaks were more likely to thrive and multiply.

An important aspect of Darwin's finch example is that it shines a light on how *behavior* is a driving force in evolution (Thierry, 2010). Different islands provided different food supplies (e.g., small vs. large seeds), and it was differential success in feeding *behavior* that drove morphological change and the divergence of Galapagos finch species. Finding and consuming food has obvious implications for survival and successful reproduction. Even if a finch had a specialized beak, they would be an evolutionary dead end if they were not successful in finding and consuming the appropriate food (i.e., without appropriate behavior). In other words, it is behavior in combination with morphology in variable environments that drives evolution.

In addition, Darwin's theory of evolution provided a strong argument for shared evolutionary history across species, which is an important justification for the use of non-human animal models to investigate aspects of human behaviors and disorders (Thierry, 2010). We address the use of non-human animal models in behavior genetics later in this chapter.

1.1.3 Galton Studied the Inheritance Patterns of Mental Qualities and Talent in Families

Francis Galton (see Figure 1.3) is sometimes called the "father of behavior genetics" because of his contributions to the study of the inheritance of traits in families, and for his focus on "mental qualities" and "talent." He published his first analysis of the transmission of such traits in families in a two-part article in 1865 (Galton, 1865a, 1865b), and later in books such as *Hereditary Genius: An Inquiry into Its Laws and Consequences* (Galton, 1869), and *English Men of Science: Their Nature*

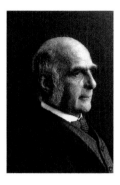

Figure 1.3. **Francis Galton.** Galton made contributions to many scientific areas including behavior genetics. Source: adoc-photos / Contributor / Corbis Historical / Getty Images.

and Nurture (Galton, 1874). In these works, Galton set out to show that talented people were found in higher proportions in some families than in others. Of note, Galton had a half-cousin named Charles Darwin. They were both grandchildren of Erasmus Darwin, who was a physician and natural philosopher in his own right. Quite a talented family, to be sure. Galton conceded that it is impossible to completely isolate the effects of heredity and environment by studying families because typically in families both are shared.

Galton attempted to disentangle nature from nurture by studying twins (Galton, 2012), and was the first to do so (Burbridge, 2001). Although he did not pioneer the comparison of identical and fraternal twins that has been a methodological standby for modern behavior genetics (see Chapter 3), he recognized that twins could be studied to address whether trait similarity changed across development. Galton stated that "nature prevails over nurture when the differences of nurture do not exceed what is commonly to be found among persons of the same rank of society and in the same country," which is a pretty strong statement given the flaws in his study design (i.e., the confounding of heredity and environment).

Galton coined the term eugenics to refer to "the science which deals with all influences that improve the inborn qualities of a race" (Galton, 1904), and was an outspoken proponent of its practice. We discuss eugenics in some detail in Chapter 15. But for now, let us just say that Galton's imprint on behavior genetics is still visible. His work is still with us more than a century later in other areas too, spanning from meteorology (e.g., weather maps), to statistics (e.g., regression), to forensic science (e.g., fingerprints), and even to cutting cakes (see Galton, 1906).

1.1.4 Modern Dog Breeds Are Largely the Result of Breeding for Behavioral Traits

An important type of evidence for the role of heredity in behavior has come from our relations with domesticated animals, especially dogs. Modern breeds of *Canis lupus familiaris* (the common dog) are the result of thousands of years of association with humans that has dramatically affected morphological and behavioral traits. No other land animal displays as much morphological and behavioral diversity as dogs. The modern concept of the dog breed, a line of dogs that share similar physical and behavioral traits maintained by selective breeding, formally originated in England in 1859 at the first modern dog show, and was subsequently institutionalized at the creation of the Kennel Club in 1873 (Pemberton & Worboys, 2015). The Fédération Cynologique Internationale (FCI), the world governing body of dog breeds, recognizes about 350 different breeds. It is easy to spot substantial physical variation in breeds of dogs from the small breeds like the Maltese that

HUNDE I.

1. Bernhardiner. — 2. Neufundländer. — 3. Mastiff (Bullenbeißer). — 4. Deutsche (Tiger-) Dogge. — 5. Bulldogge. — 6. Dalmatiner. — 7. Deutscher Schäferhund. — 8. Schottischer Schäferhund (Collie).
9. Pudel. — 10. Bullterrier. — 11. Black and tan Terrier. — 12. Deutscher rauhhaariger Pinscher (Rattenfänger). — 13. Spitz. — 14. König Karls-Hündchen. — 15. Malteser. — 16. Japanisches Chin-Hündchen.
17. Zwergaffenpinscher. — 18. Windspiel. — 19. Mops. — 20. Nackter Hund. — 21. Zwergpinscher (Black and tan Toy-Terrier).

Figure 1.4. **Morphological variation in dog breeds.** This illustration was first published in 1895 and shows substantial variation in height, weight, body conformation, muzzle shape, and other characteristics of 21 dog breeds. Source: THEPALMER / DigitalVision Vectors / Getty Images.

weigh about 6 to 8 pounds (2.7 to 3.6 kg), to the large like the Mastiff that can easily weigh over 200 pounds (90.7 kg; see Figure 1.4). Similarly, astonishing variability can also be seen in behavioral traits, with dogs that can be trained to herd other animals, use their sense of smell to track or find things, dig holes, run in races, hunt, fetch, fight, pull sleds, and so on.

Humans and dogs have been living in close proximity for hundreds of thousands of years, but true domestication of dogs is likely to have begun around 20,000 years ago. In that time, certain canine behavioral traits have been considered advantageous, and have been the targets of intentional selective breeding efforts. Behaviors that have been useful in hunting, farming, protection, and other areas in life, have been favored. Dogs that displayed the favored behaviors were nurtured and bred, whereas those that did not display them were not. In other words, humans have selectively bred dogs for *behaviors*. For the most part, the breeding efforts were not coordinated or systematic. But dogs that were useful and friendly were actively favored over those that were not. The selective breeding efforts became more systematic in the late 1800s when "dog fanciers" standardized descriptions of different breeds, began the practice of dog shows and keeping pedigrees, and codified the focus on "pure bred" dogs (Pemberton & Worboys, 2015).

Restricting mating between dog breeds reduces genetic variation within breeds, which has led to rather high prevalence rates of genetic disorders in certain breeds. On the bright side (for humans), the appearance of diseases in dogs that are also found in humans means that canines have an opportunity to serve humans in yet another way. Namely, certain canine genetic disorders serve as non-human animal models for diseases such as cancer, obsessive-compulsive disorder, narcolepsy, Alzheimer disease; or for behaviors such as aggression or anxiety (Ostrander, Wayne, Freedman, & Davis, 2017).

Breeding dogs *for* certain behaviors does not require a detailed understanding of heredity–behavior relations. It only requires a basic understanding that behavioral traits run in families and that mating together the animals that show the desired behavior increases the chances that the behavior will be expressed in later generations. There was, however, great interest in better understanding genetics in the late nineteenth and early twentieth century, primarily driven by those interested in agricultural applications.

1.1.5 Behavior Genetics Was Established in the Twentieth Century

Although Gregor Mendel delivered lectures describing his model of inheritance in 1865, which were later published (Mendel, 1866), his insights into heredity were not widely known or appreciated until they were "rediscovered" around 1900. Mendel's Laws were a scientific breakthrough that provided a framework for understanding the inheritance of any trait, including behavior. We cover Mendelian genetics in Chapter 2.

Early experimental work in heredity involved the examination of traits first in parents and then in their offspring, as Mendel had done. Thomas Hunt Morgan's group used Mendel's Laws and the common fruit fly, *Drosophila melanogaster*, to map the location of genes associated with specific mutations affecting eye color, wing shape, and other morphological traits (see Figure 1.5). The first quarter of the twentieth century also saw the genesis of systematic behavior genetic research, such as work by Edward Chace Tolman and Robert Choate Tryon into the inheritance of maze learning in rats (see Innis, 1992).

Enthusiasm for Mendelian genetics was also evident in those who were focused on human behavior. Francis Galton's ideas on eugenics were especially influential when Mendelian genetics represented the cutting edge of science (see Figure 1.6). The application of Mendelian genetics in combination with behavioral science, which was also in its infancy at the start of the twentieth century, produced an overly simplistic view of heredity–behavior relations that was ripe for misuse by those with a racist agenda (Chase, 1980). Such "scientific racism" was used to justify the legalization of involuntary sterilization across the United States, to restrict immigration into the

Figure 1.5. **Thomas Hunt Morgan.** T. H. Morgan won the Nobel Prize in Physiology or Medicine in 1933 for his contribution to the understanding of chromosomal inheritance. Source: THEPALMER / DigitalVision Vectors / Getty Images. Used with permission of Archives, California Institute of Technology.

Figure 1.6. **Logo of the Second International Congress of Eugenics, 1921.** The meeting held at the American Museum of Natural History in New York had 53 scientific presentations on topics in sessions titled: "Human and Comparative Heredity," "Eugenics and the Family," "Human Racial Differences," and "Eugenics and the State." Source: Harry H. Laughlin, The Second International Exhibition of Eugenics held September 22 to October 22, 1921, in connection with the Second International Congress of Eugenics in the American Museum of Natural History, New York (Baltimore: William & Wilkins Co., 1923). Image in the public domain.

United States, and inspired Nazis in Germany to carry out the Holocaust. We tackle eugenics in Chapter 15. We mention it here to acknowledge that behavior genetics has had a profound and disturbing impact on world history, and to urge caution and careful consideration in any potential application of behavior genetic findings to human beings.

The twentieth-century horrors conducted in the name of eugenics have cast a long shadow on the field of human behavior genetics. Efforts to understand the role of genetic variation in human individual differences in behavior were also limited because of the dominant role in psychology played by behaviorism, which focused on the primacy of environmental influence and learning and de-emphasized the role of biologically based individual differences in behavior. In addition, the potential toolbox of genetic methods was relatively bare thereby limiting scientific inquiry into human behavior genetics. The technological barrier persisted until the end of the twentieth century when the breakthrough technology of polymerase-chain reaction (PCR) was developed (see Chapter 5).

Through much of the twentieth century, important advances in behavior genetics were achieved in research using non-human animals. Fruit flies (*D. melanogaster*), mice (*Mus musculus*), and rats (*Rattus norvegicus domesticus*) were the species that made the largest contribution, although dogs, monkeys, zebra fish, honeybees, roundworms, and other species have been and continue to be used to investigate heredity–behavior relations. Although the state of genetic methods was also a limiting factor to progress, more experimental genetic methods will always be available to those who work with non-human animals compared to those who work with humans. For instance, it is ethically unacceptable to conduct controlled breeding experiments or to induce genetic change in humans, but such approaches are routine in studies using non-human animals.

Check-up

- Who were the two cousins who made important contributions to understanding heredity–behavior relations in the late 1800s, and what were their contributions?
- What can dog breeds reveal about heredity–behavior relations?
- What is eugenics and how was science used to advance eugenic policies in the early twentieth century?

1.2 Behavior Genetics Focuses on Understanding Individual Differences in Behavior

The focus of behavior genetics is on understanding the role of genetic *variation* in *individual differences* in behavior. Researchers do not seek to identify genes that "cause" behaviors, or to find genes "for" behaviors.

It is easy to see that in a population not everyone behaves the same. Researchers also recognize that individuals are genetically unique, except for identical twins. In other words, there are genetic differences between people. So, the focus is on understanding how genetic differences between people are associated with behavioral differences between them. In that sense, behavior genetics focuses on diversity. Without both genetic and behavioral diversity, there would be no need for the field of behavior genetics.

1.2.1 Reliable and Valid Measures of Behavior Are Necessary

The importance of properly measuring behavior in behavior genetic research cannot be overstated. To be useful in behavior genetic research, behavioral measurements must be both reliable and valid. Reliable measures are those that show consistency. If you step on a scale and it indicates that you weigh 155 pounds (70.3 kg), and then you step on it a second time a minute later and it indicates that you weigh 160 pounds (72.6 kg), then it is not a reliable scale. Valid measures are those that measure the intended construct. If you are interested in measuring height, you should use a ruler with inches (or centimeters), not a scale with pounds (or kilograms). Although it is true that on average taller people tend to be heavier than shorter people, weight is not a valid measurement of height.

Psychologists have developed and tested quite a large toolbox of reliable and valid behavioral measures to study human and non-human animal behavior. Commonly used types of behavioral measures to study human behavior in behavior genetics include self-report questionnaires, reaction-time tasks, and neuroimaging. Commonly used behavioral measures to study non-human animal behavior in behavior genetics include spontaneous activity (e.g., running wheel), beverage preference (e.g., two-bottle choice), and attack latency (e.g., resident-intruder paradigm). This text focuses significant attention on reliable and valid behavioral measurement because without it, genetic analysis is meaningless (see Box 1.1).

Box 1.1 Critical Concept: Measuring Behavior

Although it is easy to get excited about the spectacular technological advances in molecular genetics, it is important to keep in mind that the goal of behavior genetics is to understand the causes of individual differences in *behavior*. Therefore, in addition to being experts in genetics, behavior genetics researchers must also be experts in measuring behavior. Behavior genetics is a subfield of psychology that uses the tools and methods of genetics to better understand individual differences in behavior.

Psychologists have been diligently developing tools for measuring behavior for over a century. In some cases, the best way to learn about a person's behavior is to ask them questions. Such self-report can be done verbally during an interview or in writing by using a questionnaire.

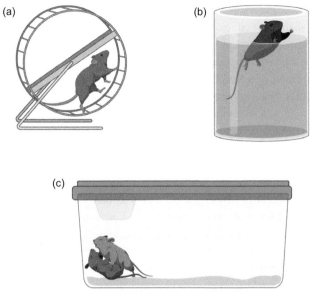

Figure 1.7. **Three commonly used behavioral measures.** (a) The running wheel indexes spontaneous activity in rodents. (b) The forced swim test indexes depressive-like behavior by measuring amount of time the rodent spends passively floating in a container of water. It is widely used in the pharmaceutical industry to test the effectiveness of drugs as antidepressants. (c) The resident-intruder test places an unfamiliar mouse into the cage of another mouse (i.e., the resident) and then observers record encounters and count the frequency of various behaviors (e.g., biting, attack latency). Source: Created with Biorender.com.

For example, information about a person's past experiences or attitudes may be obtained in this way. In other cases, the behavior of interest may be better measured by assessing reaction times or by tracking a person's gaze, or any number of methods developed in cognitive psychology. It might also be of interest to examine neural activity patterns or hormonal responses to specific stimuli. All these methods, and many more, have been developed and refined by psychologists and are routinely used in behavior genetic research with human participants.

Although it is not possible to collect self-report information from non-human animals, there are many tools available to measure behavior in non-human animals for behavior genetic research (see Figure 1.7). Automated methods for behavioral observation are common in such work. The running wheel for rodents is a good example of how researchers have automated behavioral data collection. Each turn of the wheel can be counted and automatically recorded as an index of activity. Depression-like behavior can be measured in the forced swim test. Rodents can also be observed in specific social situations such as the resident-intruder test that assesses aggressive behavior. Each of these behavioral measures will be described in more detail in subsequent chapters.

Throughout the text, measures of behavior are described in detail to emphasize the importance of proper behavior measurement in behavior genetics. The long-recognized importance of quantitative behavioral measurement in behavior genetics can be illustrated by Francis Galton's motto: "Whenever you can, count" (quoted in Newman, 1956).

The advances in molecular genetics that made it possible to sequence genomes are largely responsible for the recent surge in interest in behavior genetics. The ability to directly characterize genetic differences between people revitalized human behavior genetic research, which had been languishing because of the shadow of eugenics and the limitations of the available methods. Each of us is genetically unique. Identical twins are an exception to this rule, but they share genetic identity only with each other. They are still genetically unique from everyone else. On average, there are about 6 million genetic differences between any two unrelated individuals. It is now possible to investigate how genetic differences between people are statistically associated with behavioral differences between them. The cost to conduct such genetic tests has been dropping rapidly since the start of the twenty-first century, which has facilitated behavior genetic research.

In addition to genetic uniqueness, individuals are exposed to different environments throughout their lives. Some combination of genetic and environmental differences is responsible for individual differences in behavior. In non-human animal experiments, it is possible to carefully control both genes and environment to investigate pathways to behavior. Human behavior genetic studies, on the other hand, make use of existing genetic and environmental variability in correlational study designs. The ability to directly examine genetic variation in human populations has ushered in a new era in behavior genetics that may lead to important breakthroughs in our ability to explain, predict, and control behavior.

1.2.2 Population Thinking Focuses on Differences

In your introductory psychology course, you learned about the basic structure of the human brain. For example, you learned that the human brain is split into two hemispheres. When describing anatomy, it makes sense to focus on typical structures. Such an approach is quite useful when there is little to no variation in the population for the trait. Nearly all humans have a brain that consists of two cerebral hemispheres. Having two hemispheres is considered to be normal, whereas having some other number of hemispheres is considered to be abnormal, a deviation from the type. Typological thinking assumes that there is a proper type and that individual differences are errors. It is a categorical approach that can sort individuals into groups based on their similarity to the type.

Behavior genetics, on the other hand, assumes that individual differences in heredity and experience contribute to individual differences in behavior, and that differences are normal. Such differences are both the raw material for evolution, and its product. Accepting individual differences as normal is called population thinking. To be fair, anatomists recognize that individual differences in structure exist and can be considered normal. But it is important for all of us to recognize the tendency to prefer simple categories over more complex descriptions. Population thinking tends to be better suited to traits that vary on some dimension rather than on discrete categories.

Contrasting categorical and dimensional traits may seem familiar to you from other psychology courses you have taken. In statistics, it is important to know whether your data is categorical or continuous to select the proper type of analysis to conduct. If you have data measured on a continuous scale, you might want to use a t-test to compare the means of your groups, whereas a chi-square independence test would be inappropriate.

One type of categorical data of interest in behavior genetics has to do with someone who meets criteria for a diagnosis of a psychiatric disorder. Medical diagnoses are purposefully designed to determine whether someone is in one category or another, specifically, whether they have an illness or not. In each chapter of the book that addresses mental illness, we will consider whether the current diagnostic system categorizes people in a way that facilitates understanding of the role of genetic variation in risk for that disorder. In other words, do diagnostic categories reflect underlying biology? Are mental illnesses categorical, or are they continuous? The success of our efforts to understand the role of genetic variation in risk for mental illness may hinge on the answers to these questions.

Pointing out the distinction between typological and population thinking is intended to emphasize the importance of behavioral and genetic variation to the field of behavior genetics. It is not intended to stake out a position in the historical "debate" about these terms in the philosophy of science (Witteveen, 2015, 2016). The focus in behavior genetics is on understanding the role of genetic differences between individuals in behavioral differences between them. For behavior genetics, variability is axiomatic. In addition, population thinking avoids the value-laden terms of normal and abnormal when describing differences. Therefore, population thinking is the proper perspective for understanding heredity–behavior relations.

Check-up

- Describe reliability and validity in the context of measuring behavior.
- What is population thinking, and why is it important in behavior genetics?

1.3 Pathways from Genes to Behaviors Cross Levels of Analysis

The heart is the organ of blood circulation, the lungs are the organs of respiration, and the brain is the organ of behavior. To begin to understand the role of genetic variation between individuals in behavioral differences between them, it makes sense to focus attention on brains, their molecules, proteins, cells, circuits, and systems. In addition, because most of the genes that humans carry are expressed in the brain, there are many potential targets to investigate. Of course, other biological systems are also involved in behavior. For example, the execution of behaviors requires motor systems that involve muscles and neurons in the peripheral nervous system. However, the behaviors of primary interest to psychologists are not those that involve only muscles and local neural circuits like basic reflexes. Therefore, many examples in this book illustrate the role of genetic differences in brain structure or function.

A foundational assumption in psychology is that it is possible to identify specific factors that contribute to individual differences in behavior. We must assume that individuals do not behave randomly, but that their behavior is a product of their biology, history of experiences, developmental stage, and the current social and cultural context (see Figure 1.8). The causes of behavior can be numerous. Although researchers recognize that behavior is determined by many factors, they aim to reduce that complexity by focusing on a subset of potential causes. Understanding factors that influence behavior at one level of analysis may be sufficient to address a particular behavioral problem, although it might not provide a comprehensive understanding of the behavior. For example, if your car is getting poor gas mileage, it might need new spark plugs. Changing the spark plugs will make the engine run better, but your mileage may not improve much if your driving behavior includes rapid acceleration and exceeding the speed limit. Spark plugs and driving behavior are at different levels of analysis, and they independently affect gas mileage. Researchers understand that choosing to address questions at certain levels of analysis does not imply that other factors are unimportant, but that such reductionism is necessary for research questions to be tractable.

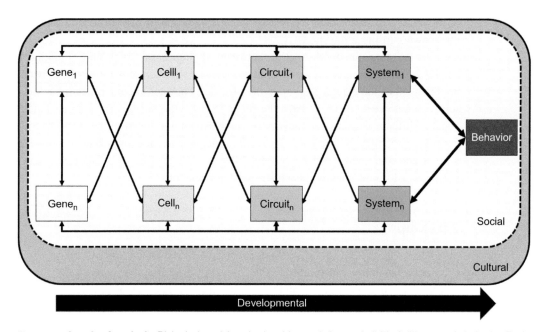

Figure 1.8. **Levels of analysis.** Biological, social, and cultural factors influence individual differences in behavior. Each of these broad levels may be further reduced into additional levels that contain component parts or concepts that may be used to construct the next level. For example, genes code for proteins, which are used to build cells.

In behavior genetics, researchers ask three basic types of questions: (1) Are genetic differences associated with individual differences in behavior? (2) Which genetic differences are associated with individual differences in behavior? (3) What are the mechanisms by which genetic differences are associated with individual differences in behavior? Broadly speaking, these questions can represent three different eras of research in behavior genetics. The questions also provide a theoretical framework for investigating heredity–behavior relations.

The first question dominated behavior genetic research in the twentieth century. A primary focus of such research was to examine whether genetic similarity was statistically associated with behavioral similarity (see Figure 1.9(a)). If genes play a role in behavioral similarity, then individuals sharing more genes should be more similar to each other behaviorally than are those who share fewer genes. Such studies were crucial in demonstrating that genes play some role in behaviors, but they did not provide insight into specific biological pathways from genes to behavior.

The second question seeks to identify specific genetic variants that are statistically associated with behavioral differences. For the most part, this question represents the current era of behavior genetic research. Multiple approaches are used to identify such gene–behavior associations in a very active area of research. It is important to note that although identifying gene–behavior associations is a valuable next step in understanding the role of genetic differences in behavioral differences, isolating the effects of single genetic variants on behavior also tends to oversimplify paths from genes to behavior (see Figure 1.9(b)). But on the bright side, the identification of specific genetic variants that are statistically associated with behavior can be used to identify biological pathways for further study.

The third question seeks to characterize the specific molecular mechanisms that impact biological function in relevant pathways from gene to behavior. A significant amount of research is currently investigating such pathways with work in non-human animals leading the way. If genetic

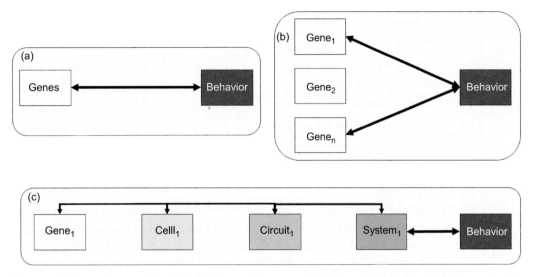

Figure 1.9. **Three main questions in behavior genetic research.** (a) Is genetic similarity statistically associated with behavioral similarity? (b) Which genetic variants are associated with behavioral similarity? (c) What are the molecular mechanisms by which genetic similarity produces behavioral similarity?

variants are associated with individual differences in behavior, they may do so by affecting the functions of cells, which in turn affects the function of biological circuits, which can then alter the functioning of biological systems (see Figure 1.9(c)). The effects of such pathways may differ according to environmental context, developmental stage, and may interact with other pathways. Answering the "mechanism question" will occupy behavior genetics researchers for the foreseeable future and will be interdisciplinary by necessity.

1.3.1 Genes Do Not Code "for" Behaviors

You have probably read a news headline that said something to the effect of "Researchers have discovered the gene for [insert your favorite behavior here]." It is important to recognize that the job of headline writers is to grab your attention so that you read the article. Headlines do not always accurately represent the information contained in the article. Headlines are simple because we prefer simplicity. In general, we prefer simple explanations of causes. The problem is that causal pathways from genes to behavior are not simple. Saying that a gene is "for" some trait, implies that the gene has a single function, namely, to affect that particular trait. When I say that my shovel is for moving snow, you can see the direct one-to-one connection. I specifically purchased the shovel to do a particular job, and I only use it for that job. Although, to be honest, snow shovels can be used to do other things. Decades of behavior genetic research have shown that genes and their products do not have a simple one-to-one relation with behaviors. As we will see, one important role that genes play is in producing proteins, which are used to build cells and to perform biological processes that comprise circuits and biological systems. Statistical effects of genetic variation on behavioral differences between people are typically small, indirect, and are combined with other effects. Although it may be tempting to use simple language to describe pathways from genes to behaviors, we should do our best to avoid oversimplification, and we should avoid using the phrase "gene for behavior."

Check-up

- What are the three basic types of questions asked by researchers in behavior genetics?
- Explain the concept of levels of analysis and the challenges it poses for understanding heredity–behavior relations.

1.4 Non-Human Animal Models Are Essential in Behavior Genetics

As you learn more about behavior genetics, you will see that non-human animal models have been and continue to be important in efforts to understand heredity–behavior relations. Typically, the term non-human animal model refers to the use of animals in experiments that are intended to generate knowledge about diseases or conditions that are experienced by human beings. Because of the shared biology between mice and humans, for example, it is possible that the biological mechanisms that underlie a condition like obesity are also shared. In such cases, the animals are used in the place of humans to answer questions relevant to human conditions because of experimental and ethical considerations. Findings from studies with non-human animal models should be considered alongside findings from studies with human participants to identify patterns. The use of such convergent evidence is important because it recognizes that all empirical approaches have some limitations, and that when findings are consistent across different approaches, we can have more confidence in them.

The ultimate goal of much of the animal research conducted in behavior genetics is to help human beings. However, there is a substantial amount of animal behavior genetic research conducted that is not directly relevant to human health but is focused on understanding the animal and its place in nature. For example, research into orientation with respect to gravity (i.e., geotaxis) in fruit flies (*D. melanogaster*), or food-seeking behavior in roundworms (*Caenorhabditis elegans*) can help to better understand niche selection and foraging in an evolutionary context. Learning more about the universe is a good thing. Such research can help to illuminate basic gene–behavior pathways, although it may not address issues directly relevant to humans.

For more than 2,500 years, scholars have been using non-human animal models in biomedical research (Franco, 2013). Nearly every medical advance was facilitated using animal models, and human life expectancies have increased as a result. Life expectancy in the United States in 1900 was 46.3 years for men and 48.3 years for women. In 2018, it was 80 years for men and 84 years for women. The average world life expectancy rose from 31 years in 1900 to 71 years in 2014. A large share of the credit for these dramatic increases is due to biomedical advances that depended on non-human animal models such as antibiotics, sterile surgery techniques, blood transfusions, vaccines, and heart bypass surgeries. We all benefit from biomedical research that uses animals.

1.4.1 Some Behavior Genetic Methods Cannot Be Ethically Conducted with Human Participants

One of the important reasons for using non-human animals in behavior genetic research is that it would be unethical to conduct certain types of genetic research with human participants. For example, it is routine for researchers to specify mating partners in genetic studies with non-human animals. In studies designed to understand the inheritance of traits across generations, it is vitally important to choose which animals will produce offspring. Furthermore, in studies where it is advantageous to have animals that are genetically identical, or nearly so, strains of animals produced by generations of brother to sister matings can be used. Obviously, it would violate human rights to control human reproduction in this way, but it is a standard experimental control in non-human animal studies.

For decades, genetic researchers have induced genetic change (i.e., mutation) in animals and then observed its effect on traits of interest. The approach is called mutagenesis. X-rays and chemicals were first used to cause mutations, but precise control over the location of the mutation was not possible until recently with the development of molecular genetic techniques. But regardless of the method of mutagenesis, researchers routinely make changes to genes in non-human animals to better understand heredity–behavior relations. Obviously, it is not ethically permissible to change the genes of human research participants.

It is clear that non-human animals such as fruit flies and mice confer important advantages over human participants in behavior genetic research. Methodologies that involve controlled matings and mutagenesis are foundations of genetic research. It is difficult to imagine the state of genetic knowledge if these methods were not available for researchers to use with non-human animals. But it is equally difficult to imagine a world where those methods were available for researchers to use with human participants. However, it is clear that we are entering an era where the tools exist to make changes in human genes. It is critical that the public be educated about the potential for genetic manipulation so that there can be a discussion about what limits should be in place. In Chapters 14 and 15 we discuss these and other ethical issues facing behavior genetics.

1.4.2 Humans and Non-Human Animals Share an Evolutionary History

How can we understand anything about human diseases or traits by studying animals that are not human? This important question is best answered by borrowing the title from Theodosius Dobzhansky's oft cited article, "Nothing in biology makes sense except in the light of evolution" (Dobzhansky, 1973). I encourage you to read this delightful paper. In it, Dobzhansky argues that both the diversity and unity of life on earth can be explained by evolution via natural selection. Without going into all the details here, the relevant arguments for using non-human animal models to study human conditions is based on a shared evolutionary history, which produced biology that is shared among species (see Box 1.2). In the context of this book, we focus on shared genetics and shared nervous systems. Humans shared an ancestor with fruit flies 794 million years ago, and with mice a mere 88 million years ago (Hedges, 2002; Kumar, Stecher, Suleski, & Hedges, 2017). So, while there has been a lot of time for divergence between the species (i.e., diversity), much of the biology has been conserved (i.e., unity).

Box 1.2 Critical Concept: Model Organisms

The use of non-human animal model organisms to investigate diseases or behaviors relevant to humans is widespread (Figure 1.10). The main reason to use model organisms instead of humans in research is that they offer experimental advantages. First, ethical prohibitions about certain experimental procedures in humans are not relevant to model organisms. For example,

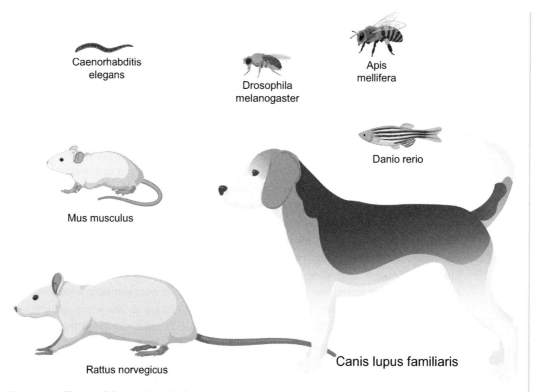

Figure 1.10. **Key model organisms in behavior genetics.** Many non-human animal species have made important contributions to our understanding of heredity–behavior relations. Although most commonly used model organisms in behavior genetics today are the fruit fly (*D. melanogaster*) and the laboratory mouse (*M. musculus*), a substantial amount of behavior genetic research has been conducting using roundworms (*Caenorhabditis elegans*), honeybees (*Apis mellifera*), zebra fish (*Danio rerio*), Norway rats (*Rattus norvegicus*), and dogs (*Canis lupis familiaris*). Source: Created with Biorender.com.

experimental designs that involve breeding are commonplace in model organisms but are out of the question for humans. In addition, genetic studies that involve genetic engineering (i.e., making changes to genetic material) are routine in non-human animals but are prohibited in humans.

Next, animal models offer the opportunity to more precisely control factors that may influence the behavior under study. Such factors can include genes and environments. Inbred lines of animals reduce genetic variability and careful control of housing and testing conditions reduces environmental variability. In studies with human participants, such control is often not possible.

Finally, because of a shared evolutionary history of humans and other animals, sufficient biological similarity exists to provide the basis for comparisons across species. It is important to note that a particular finding in one species does not automatically mean that it will generalize to another species, even when they are closely related. However, model organisms provide a starting point from which research questions that shine a light on biological mechanisms of diseases or behaviors important to humans can be addressed.

Even though it has been nearly 800 million years since we last shared an ancestor with fruit flies, most of the genes that are thought to play roles in human diseases are found in fruit flies. The genetic relationship is even closer between humans and mice. Virtually all genes found in humans can be found in mice. Therefore, if we are interested in studying the role of a particular gene in a specific behavior, it is likely that we can study it across species. When we study something in different species using different methods, and find similar results, such convergent evidence can enhance our confidence in whatever is found. For example, variations in genes that code for proteins involved in the breakdown of alcohol play a role in individual differences in alcohol drinking behavior across species. In fruit flies, mice, and humans, genetic variants that interfere with alcohol metabolism are associated with reduced alcohol drinking behavior. Because of this convergent evidence across species, we can be confident that genetic variation in the alcohol metabolism pathway plays a role in alcohol drinking. We will take up this example again in Chapter 11.

At first glance, the central nervous systems (CNS) of humans and fruit flies appear to have little in common. On average, human brains weigh just over 3 pounds (approximately 1.35 kg), whereas an entire fruit fly weighs less than a milligram. So, an average size human brain weighs about as much as 1.5 million *D. melanogaster*. In addition, there is substantial divergence between human and fruit fly CNS anatomy, although fundamental molecular pathways are conserved. For example, many of the same neurotransmitter systems are found in both species, such as serotonin, dopamine, glutamate, and acetylcholine (Martin & Krantz, 2014). A mouse (*M. musculus*) brain weighs about 0.4 g, which means that it would take 3,375 mouse brains to weigh as much as an average human brain (1,350 g). But even though the mouse brain is much smaller than the human brain, the two have many anatomical similarities, and share basic circuits and systems. Therefore, because of the shared biology between *D. melanogaster*, *M. musculus*, and humans (*Homo sapiens*), fruit flies and mice have been and will continue to be very useful organisms in behavior genetic research.

1.4.3 Non-Human Animal Models Have Limitations

Although there are many reasons to continue using non-human animals in behavior genetic research, there are also some important limitations of such models to consider.

There have long been debates about whether and to what extent animals should be used in research based on (1) the ethics involved in subjecting animals to research procedures, and (2) the extent to which the results of non-human animal studies generalize to humans.

The use of animals in medical experiments, or at least in certain procedures such as vivisection (i.e., exploratory surgery on live animals), has had vocal critics for centuries. Such opposition has helped to produce the current structure of regulations and strict oversight, especially in biomedical research using vertebrates that is funded by government entities. There is still room for improvement in how we treat animals, but one must also consider the millions of lives that have been saved using non-human animals in research. It is not obvious how to balance the equation, but it is something on which everyone should reflect.

The findings of behavior genetic research do not necessarily generalize from one species to another. For example, even though there is strong evidence that genetic variation in alcohol metabolism affects alcohol drinking behavior across species, there are also many other factors that play a role in that behavior. Taste is a critical factor in mouse alcohol drinking, whereas in humans it is less so. In addition, mice tend not to drink to intoxication, whereas humans do.

Human behavior genetic research is often focused on behavioral problems, such as psychiatric disorders, but non-human animals may not exhibit analogous behavioral disorders. Therefore, it is not possible to directly study alcohol use disorder in non-human animals, because they do not experience it. However, it is possible to study specific behaviors that contribute to the disorder, or behaviors that seem to represent expressions of the behavioral problem in animals. For example, a model of drinking has been developed in mice, called drinking in the dark (Crabbe, Phillips, & Belknap, 2010) that has contributed substantially to our understanding of human binge drinking. Attempts to generalize knowledge derived from one species to another should be done cautiously and require rigorous verification.

Check-up

- What are the advantages and disadvantages in using non-human animal models when trying to understand human problems?
- What is convergent evidence and why is it important in behavior genetics?

1.5 Ethical Oversight of Behavior Genetic Research Is Necessary

There was little to no ethics oversight of research conducted prior to the middle of the twentieth century. The researcher was the sole arbiter of whether the procedures violated participant rights. Such lax oversight led to many abuses by researchers, and eventually to the establishment of rules and regulations to govern research with the goal of protecting the rights of non-human animal subjects and human research participants. Most behavior genetic research is conducted at academic institutions, and much of it is funded by government agencies such as the National Institutes of Health (NIH) in the United States or the Research Councils in the United Kingdom. Such agencies require research oversight by local organizations whose members include research experts and members of the community. The focus of these organizations is to protect non-human animal subjects and human research participants.

1.5.1 Oversight of Research on Non-Human Animals Is Comprehensive

In the United States, every institution that conducts non-human animal research is required to have a local Institutional Animal Care and Use Committee (IACUC) that is charged with oversight of all research conducted with vertebrate non-human animal subjects. IACUCs must have a minimum of five members, who typically include researchers, a non-scientist, and someone from the community not affiliated with the institution. All IACUCs must also include a veterinarian with experience or training with experimental animals. All research study protocols need to be approved by the IACUC before the research project can begin. In addition, research protocols need to be reviewed at least once every three years. The IACUCs also inspect all animal research and housing facilities every six months.

The IACUC is responsible for the welfare of non-human animal subjects for all research conducted at its institution. They follow regulations developed by the NIH Office of Laboratory Animal Welfare (OLAW), and report violations to it. Substantial and repeated violations can lead to a loss of funding to the researcher or even a halt to research funding to an entire institution in egregious cases of non-compliance.

Research protocols need to justify the number of animals used, and that the species is appropriate for the research question. Research procedures need to limit the discomfort to the animals to the extent possible, including the use of anesthetics or analgesics when appropriate. One of the goals is to avoid or minimize the amount of pain, discomfort, and stress experienced by the animals. Housing and testing conditions must be appropriate to the species and reasonably comfortable and healthy. All study personnel must be appropriately trained in proper techniques and procedures. Medical care by a veterinarian must be available. Methods of euthanasia must be consistent with best practices in the field to minimize suffering.

As you can see, there is currently a great deal of concern for the welfare of non-human animal research subjects, and the primary goal is the reduction of animal suffering. There are situations in which some exceptions to the regulations are made, like in pain research, but the current situation is much more ethically acceptable than it was before the 1970s when there were few rules and little to no oversight.

1.5.2 Oversight of Behavior Genetic Research Protects Human Participants

Research that involves human participants is regulated by government agencies and locally overseen by committees, called Institutional Review Boards (IRBs) in the US. In other parts of the world, the bodies may be called ethics committees, but they have a similar charge: to protect human research participants. As with IACUCs, IRBs are a response to a history of unethical research practices that drew attention to the lack of research oversight. There were certain cases that served to illustrate the extent to which research could potentially harm human participants. Several physicians in Nazi Germany during World War II conducted experiments on concentration camp prisoners which sometimes resulted in the death of the prisoner. In the Tuskegee Syphilis Experiment, physicians of the US Public Health Service left syphilis untreated in African American men for decades after it was known that penicillin would cure it. Other work, done by psychologists, used deception in ways that led participants to believe that they had harmed someone when they had not (e.g., Milgram's Obedience Study [Russell, 2011]), or that they had become prisoners (e.g., Stanford Prison Experiment [Carnahan & McFarland, 2007]). These studies, and many more, led to the development of regulations and IRBs that serve to protect human research participants today.

In the United States, IRBs are governed by Title 45 Code of Federal Regulations Part 46, which specifies its membership and responsibilities for institutions that receive any federal funding for the conduct of research with human participants. IRBs must have at least five members, with at least one scientist and one non-scientist among them. IRBs are required to approve and annually review all protocols for the conduct of research with human participants at that institution.

For an IRB to approve a research project, risks to participants must be minimized, and any risks need to be reasonable when considering the potential benefits of the research. In addition, selection of the subjects for research must be equitable and should not take advantage of vulnerable populations like children or those with impaired decision-making ability. Potential participants should also be given the opportunity for informed consent, and have it documented. In other words, they need to be given information about what will occur during the study and have the option to decline participation. Participants should also have an expectation of privacy and confidentiality, when appropriate. Essentially, participants should be treated as individuals with agency, and who have a right to be treated with respect and dignity, and not be forced into doing things against their will. They should also have the right to end participation in the study at any time. Researcher non-compliance with IRB policies can result in studies being shut down, and loss of funding.

We no longer live in a time when someone with an MD or a PhD can do whatever they think best with non-human animal research subjects, or to human research participants. But it is important to appreciate that we are only about forty years into the IACUC and IRB era, which is about the length of a researcher's career.

Check-up

- What are the responsibilities of IACUC and IRB?
- Why is ethical oversight of research necessary?

1.6 SUMMARY

- Behavior genetics is an area of psychology that seeks to understand the role that genetic differences between individuals play in behavioral differences between them. The field of behavior genetics has only been around officially since about 1960.
- Researchers in behavior genetics do not seek to identify genes that "cause" behaviors, or to find genes "for" behaviors. Fundamental assumptions in behavior genetics are that not everyone in a population behaves the same and individuals are genetically unique, with the exception of identical twins. Population thinking expects diversity and considers it the norm.
- To begin to understand the role of genetic variation between individuals in behavioral differences between them, it makes sense to focus attention on brains, their molecules, proteins, cells, circuits, and systems. As the heart is the organ of blood circulation, the brain is the organ of behavior. If genetic variants are associated with individual differences in behavior, they must do so by affecting the functions of cells, which in turn affects the function of biological circuits, which can then alter the functioning of biological systems.
- Because genes and their products do not have a simple one-to-one relation with behaviors, the phrase "genes for behaviors" is an oversimplification and should be avoided.
- Non-human animals have been and continue to be important in efforts to understand heredity–behavior relations. Experimental and ethical constraints in human behavior genetics do not constrain research using non-human animals. An important rationale for using non-human animal models to learn about human conditions and disorders is that we have a shared evolutionary history and biology.
- Behavior genetic research is closely regulated to ensure ethical conduct. Local Institutional Animal Care and Use Committees oversee all research conducted with vertebrate animals at institutions that receive government funding with a goal of enhancing animal welfare. Local Institutional Review Boards oversee all human subjects research conducted at institutions that receive government funding with a goal of protecting the rights of research participants.

RECOMMENDED READING

- Black, E. (2003). *War Against the Weak: Eugenics and America's Campaign to Create a Master Race*. New York: Four Walls Eight Windows.
- Darwin, C. (1859). *On the Origin of Species by Means of Natural Selection, or Preservation of Favoured Races in the Struggle for Life*. London: John Murray.

- Dobzhansky, T. (1973). Nothing in biology makes sense except in the light of evolution. *American Biology Teacher, 35*(3), 125–129.
- Galton, F. (1869). *Hereditary Genius*. London: Macmillan.
- Galton, F. (1906). Cutting a round cake on scientific principles. *Nature, 75,* 173.
- White, B. H. (2016). What genetic model organisms offer the study of behavior and neural circuits. *Journal of Neurogenetics, 30*(2), 54–61.

REFERENCES

Berg, J. M. (2001). Shakespeare as a geneticist. *Clin Genet, 59*(3), 165–170.

Burbridge, D. (2001). Francis Galton on twins, heredity and social class. *Br J Hist Sci, 34*(122 Pt 3), 323–340.

Carnahan, T., & McFarland, S. (2007). Revisiting the Stanford prison experiment: Could participant self-selection have led to the cruelty? *Pers Soc Psychol Bull, 33*(5), 603–614. doi:10.1177/0146167206292689

Chase, A. (1980). *The Legacy of Malthus: The Social Costs of the New Scientific Racism*. Urbana, IL: University of Illinois Press.

Crabbe, J. C., Phillips, T. J., & Belknap, J. K. (2010). The complexity of alcohol drinking: Studies in rodent genetic models. *Behav Genet, 40*(6), 737–750. doi:10.1007/s10519-010-9371-z

Dobzhansky, T. (1973). Nothing in biology makes sense except in the light of evolution. *American Biology Teacher, 35*(3), 125–129.

Franco, N. H. (2013). Animal experiments in biomedical research: A historical perspective. *Animals (Basel), 3*(1), 238–273. doi:10.3390/ani3010238

Fuller, J. L., & Thompson, W. R. (1960). *Behavior Genetics*. New York: Wiley.

Galton, F. (1865a). Hereditary talent and character: Part 1. *Macmillan's Magazine, 12,* 157–166.

Galton, F. (1865b). Hereditary talent and character: Second paper. *Macmillan's Magazine, 12,* 318–327.

Galton, F. (1869). *Hereditary Genius: An Inquiry into Its Laws and Consequences*. London: Macmillan and Co.

Galton, F. (1874). *English Men of Science: Their Nature and Nurture*. London: Macmillan & Co.

Galton, F. (1904). Eugenics: Its definition, scope and aims. *Nature, 70,* 82.

Galton, F. (1906). Cutting a round cake on scientific principles. *Nature, 75,* 173.

Galton, F. (2012). The history of twins, as a criterion of the relative powers of nature and nurture (1, 2). *Int J Epidemiol, 41*(4), 905–911. doi:10.1093/ije/dys097

Hedges, S. B. (2002). The origin and evolution of model organisms. *Nat Rev Genet, 3*(11), 838–849. doi:10.1038/nrg929

Innis, N. K. (1992). Tolman and Tryon: Early research on the inheritance of the ability to learn. *Am Psychol, 47*(2), 190–197.

Kumar, S., Stecher, G., Suleski, M., & Hedges, S. B. (2017). TimeTree: A resource for timelines, timetrees, and divergence times. *Mol Biol Evol, 34*(7), 1812–1819. doi:10.1093/molbev/msx116

Loehlin, J. C. (2009). History of behavior genetics. In Y.-K. Kim (Ed.), *Handbook of Behavior Genetics* (pp. 3–11). New York: Springer.

Martin, C. A., & Krantz, D. E. (2014). Drosophila melanogaster as a genetic model system to study neurotransmitter transporters. *Neurochem Int, 73,* 71–88. doi:10.1016/j.neuint.2014.03.015

Mendel, G. (1866). Versuche über Pllanzen-hybriden. *Verhandlungen des naturforschenden Ver-eines in Brünn, Bd. IV für das Jahr 1865, Abhand-lungen,* 3–47.

Newman, J. R. (1956). Commentary on Sir Francis Galton. In *The World of Mathematics* (p. 1169). New York: Simon & Schuster.

Ostrander, E. A., Wayne, R. K., Freedman, A. H., & Davis, B. W. (2017). Demographic history, selection and functional diversity of the canine genome. *Nat Rev Genet, 18*(12), 705–720. doi:10.1038/nrg.2017.67

Pemberton, N., & Worboys, M. (2015). The invention of the basset hound: Breed, blood and the late Victorian dog fancy, 1865–1900. *European Review of History/Revue européenne d'histoire, 22*(5), 726–740. doi:10.1080/13507486.2015.1070124

Russell, N. J. (2011). Milgram's Obedience to Authority experiments: Origins and early evolution. *Br J Soc Psychol, 50*(Pt 1), 140–162. doi:10.1348/014466610x492205

Thierry, B. (2010). Darwin as a student of behavior. *C R Biol, 333*(2), 188–196. doi:10.1016/j.crvi.2009.12.007

Witteveen, J. (2015). "A temporary oversimplification": Mayr, Simpson, Dobzhansky, and the origins of the typology/population dichotomy (part 1 of 2). *Stud Hist Philos Biol Biomed Sci, 54*, 20–33. doi:10.1016/j.shpsc.2015.09.007

Witteveen, J. (2016). "A temporary oversimplification": Mayr, Simpson, Dobzhansky, and the origins of the typology/population dichotomy (part 2 of 2). *Stud Hist Philos Biol Biomed Sci, 57*, 96–105. doi:10.1016/j.shpsc.2015.09.006

2 Mendelian Genetics

To understand heredity–behavior relations it is important to first understand the mechanisms of heredity. The gains in knowledge about genetics in the twentieth century are stunning. An obscure scientific paper that was published in the late nineteenth century and rediscovered at the beginning of the twentieth laid the foundation for identifying the molecule of heredity about fifty years later, and for the project to map all human genes about fifty years after that. Basic principles of genetics are taught in middle schools today and it is generally accepted that genetic variation plays a role in individual differences in behavior. In this chapter we discuss some ideas about heredity that predate our modern understanding. We also examine the life of two important figures in the history of genetics and describe their contributions.

2.1 Developments in Science, Agriculture, and Medicine Set the Stage for Understanding Heredity

It is safe to say that 1822 was an important year in the history of behavior genetics because during that year both Francis Galton and Johann (Gregor) Mendel were born. In the previous chapter we discussed Galton's contributions to behavior genetics, and in this one we present the work of a humble Augustinian monk who provided the foundation for understanding heredity.

As we creep ever nearer the middle of the twenty-first century, it becomes increasingly difficult to imagine what life was like in the nineteenth century. But nearly everything we take for granted today, like cars, airplanes, antibiotics, electric light, telephones, and even indoor plumbing either did not exist or was not available to most people living in the 1820s. In much of the nineteenth century, many children were expected to work on farms or in factories and received little education. It was legal to own slaves in the British Empire until 1833 and in the United States for another thirty years after that. The state of science did not generally include careful experiments and statistical analysis of large data sets, although the first instance of a controlled experiment was conducted in 1753 to identify the cause of scurvy. The nineteenth century saw dramatic developments in scientific methods and their application to important questions.

The state of knowledge regarding heredity was rather primitive in the early 1800s (Russell, 2006). Farmers, however, were motivated to understand heredity for its practical application in the improvement of crops and livestock (see Figure 2.1). The goals were to enhance traits that had economic value, to eliminate traits that were problematic, and to make the improvements stable across generations (see Box 2.1). These were businesspeople seeking ways to grow their businesses by harnessing the power of generation, a broad term that was used at the time to describe the combined concepts of reproduction, heredity, and development whereby organisms produce offspring like themselves.

For the most part, European farmers in the 1800s did not carry out large-scale, systematic, data-driven, multi-generational breeding schemes to improve their livestock. Instead, most had rather small-scale operations and implemented breeding strategies with an aim to prevent the degeneration of their stock in terms of fertility or traits of economic interest, often by breeding the best and by not breeding the worst animals (Russell, 2006).

Figure 2.1. **Breeds of sheep.** Illustration of early sheep breeds that shows extensive variety in wool type and body conformation. Sheep were, and continue to be, bred for wool to be used in the textile industry, or for meat.
Source: Nastasic / DigitalVision Vectors / Getty Images.

It is easy to see that some traits run in families, but some of the evidence can appear to be contradictory. Some characteristics are clearly shared between parent and offspring, while others are not. The expression of some traits in offspring appear to be combinations of the parental traits. Whereas others may skip generations and reappear later. Farmers in the 1800s were more focused on developing practices that improved their livestock, thereby increasing profit, but were not focused on developing theories of heredity (Cobb, 2006; Wood & Orel, 2005).

Check-up

- Describe the state of knowledge about genetics in the 1800s.
- Why were farmers interested in understanding heredity?

2.2 Early Thinking about Generation

For much of human history, the female was assumed to be the one responsible for generating life. When it became clear that both males and females were required for sexual reproduction, alternative views developed about which parent's contribution was the most important. Typically, it was thought that one sex contributed the key components of life, while the other's contribution was merely to activate the process, or to provide sustenance.

2.2.1 Heredity Derives from One Parent (Ovists and Animalculists)

Alternative versions of preformationist theories suggested that a single parent was primarily responsible for producing offspring. Ovists argued that ova (i.e., eggs) in females contained preformed embryos and that males either contributed nothing to offspring or that their contribution was merely to initiate the development of the embryo. Animalculists argued that spermatozoa found

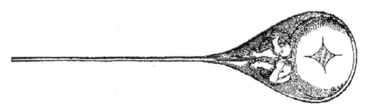

Figure 2.2. **Homunculus.** A tiny person inside a sperm cell illustrates the animalculist view of generation. Source: Preformation, drawn by N. Hartsoecker 1695. Image in the public domain.

in male seminal fluid contained preformed embryos and that the female's contribution was to provide nutrition and to generally support development (see Figure 2.2).

Such preformationist theories were focused on the reproductive and developmental aspects of generation. They either ignored the well-known fact that offspring can resemble both parents, not just one; or argued that deviations of offspring appearance from the parent of record were "accidental monstrosities" (Russell, 2006).

2.2.2 Qualitative versus Quantitative Traits

Explanations of heredity in theories of generation tended to focus on certain traits and to completely ignore others. As just noted, some traits in offspring, like eye color in humans, seem to be exact copies of one of the parents. For example, if mother has brown eyes and father has blue, then the children are likely to have brown eyes that appear identical to mom's. Such traits are now referred to as qualitative traits because the alternative forms can be classified into discrete categories based on certain qualities. In our example, eyes are either brown or blue, they are not a mixture of the two colors. Preformationist theories of generation focused on examples of qualitative traits in parents and offspring as supporting evidence, especially when the trait in the parent of origin fit the theory.

However, preformationist theories sometimes ignored examples where expression of a trait in offspring appeared to be some combination of the father's and the mother's traits. Height, for example, is one trait where offspring are often intermediate to their parents (see Figure 2.3).

Figure 2.3. **Qualitative and quantitative traits.** Individual characteristics can be measured on scales that reflect either categories or amounts. (a) When the characteristic is best measured as a category (e.g., eye color), it is referred to as a qualitative trait because it represents a difference in kind. (b) When the character is best measured along a dimension (e.g., height), it is referred to as a quantitative trait because it represents a difference in amount. Source: Created with Biorender.com.

Such traits are now referred to as quantitative traits because they are expressed along some dimension that can be quantified (i.e., counted). Such quantitative traits were difficult to explain in a preformationist framework, and in retrospect make it easier to understand why progress in understanding heredity depended on adopting an empirical approach.

Box 2.1 Sheep Breeders Make Their Mark on Genetics

In the eighteenth century, natural philosophers, and medical doctors with an interest in generation were mostly focused on reproduction and development. Animal breeders were beginning to systematically breed their livestock to maintain and improve health and other economically valuable traits. Sheep breeders were at the forefront of efforts to use breeding strategies, and Robert Bakewell (1725–1795) is perhaps the best known for his development of the New Leicester (aka Dishley) breed of sheep (see Figure 2.4), although he also applied his techniques to horses, pigs, and cattle. Bakewell's farm in Dishley (near Leicester), England, was a well-known center for innovative farming practices (Wykes, 2004).

Bakewell's strategy focused on a program of breeding animals for "beauty," quality of meat, and quick maturation by practicing "in-and-in breeding" of closely related animals. His early maturing breed could be sent to slaughter for the mutton market at 2 years of age, rather than 4 years of age for competing breeds. This represented an enormous profit for farmers whose investment in each animal would be halved.

Bakewell sold the services of his breeding stock at high prices and did not allow animals that he judged inferior to breed. He focused his attention on the improvement of specific traits with

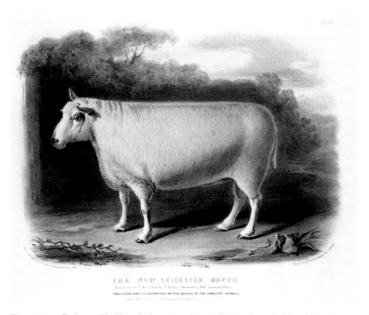

THE NEW LEICESTER BREED.

PROFESSOR LOW'S ILLUSTRATIONS OF THE BREEDS OF THE DOMESTIC ANIMALS.

Figure 2.4. **Bakewell's New Leicester sheep.** Illustration of a New Leicester ram. Robert Bakewell selectively bred sheep for their mutton. Also known as New Dishley sheep the animals were bred for a stocky "barrel" shape and had a small head and short legs. They were fast maturing and produced abundant, fatty meat. Source: Photo 12 / Contributor / Universal Images Group / Getty Images.

economic importance and strictly controlled the mating of his livestock to that end. He also hosted many visitors from around Europe who were interested in learning his techniques so that they could adopt them in their home countries.

His success in using selective breeding to improve economically important traits in an economically important animal encouraged others to follow his strategies, and more importantly to seek to understand the mechanisms of heredity. In Central Europe, the sheep breeding industry was gearing up to satisfy demand for wool and mutton. In Moravia (now part of the Czech Republic), the Sheep Breeder's Society was established in 1814 by sheep breeders and university professors to serve as a forum for the generation and exchange of ideas and practices to further the industry. They held annual meetings and published a weekly journal (Poczai, Bell, & Hyvonen, 2014). Frequent topics of discussion included the inheritance of traits, inbreeding, and practical breeding strategies with an eye toward improvement. At the annual meeting in 1836, Cyrill Napp, Abbot of St. Thomas Abbey in Brünn tried to change the focus from practical sheep breeding to understanding general mechanisms of inheritance, "What we should have been dealing with is not the theory and process of breeding. But the question should be: what is inherited and how." Seven years later, Napp welcomed a new monk named Gregor Mendel to the monastery and provided him the opportunity to answer that question.

Check-up

- Explain the alternate versions of preformationism.
- How do qualitative and quantitative traits differ?
- Discuss Bakewell's strategy for breeding sheep.

2.3 Gregor Mendel: Early Depression and Failures

Johann Mendel was born into a farming family on July 20, 1822 in a small rural village called Heinzendorf bei Odrau (Hynčice in Czech) in what was then the Austrian Empire and is now the Czech Republic (De Castro, 2016). He did so well in grammar school that at age 11 he was sent to a college-prep school (i.e., gymnasium) about 28 miles (46 km) away in Troppau (Opava). During his time there he experienced his first bout of what might now be diagnosed as major depressive disorder, which he struggled with throughout his life. During these episodes he was bedridden for months at a time. He graduated from gymnasium in 1840 with honors and was then sent to the Philosophical Institute at the University of Olmütz (Olomouc) for a two-year program in practical and theoretical philosophy and physics. He did well in the program, although it took him an extra year to complete because of recurrent episodes of depression.

In 1844 Mendel joined an Augustinian monastery in Brünn (Brno) and took the name Gregor. Becoming a monk allowed Mendel to continue his education and kept him from returning home to become a farmer. St. Thomas monastery had a large library and many of the monks were scientifically active. It was relatively common in the nineteenth century for men of the cloth and/or wealthy gentlemen (e.g., Darwin) to engage in scientific research. They were educated, had enough free time, and because there was no profession of "scientist" at the time it was quite acceptable for gentlemen to engage in research.

By 1848 Mendel had progressed through the ranks of the priesthood and was given his own parish. However, he proved ill-suited for the work of parish priest, and again experienced an incapacitating bout of depression.

2.3.1 Success and Failure in Teaching

Abbott Cyrill Napp recognized Mendel's scientific interests and abilities and assigned him to be a part-time substitute secondary school teacher in 1849. Mendel did well as a teacher, but in 1850 he failed the oral component of the teaching certificate examination. The following year he was sent to study science at the Royal Imperial University in Vienna. His science education up to that time had been rudimentary, and this additional exposure to leading thinkers of the day was critical in his intellectual development and his understanding of the scientific method (De Castro, 2016). He completed his studies in 1853 and became a substitute teacher in natural history and physics in Brünn. In 1856 he took the teaching certificate examination for the second time, and for the second time, he failed. On the bright side, by not becoming a certified teacher he remained a part-time substitute teacher, which provided him with sufficient time to conduct scientific experiments.

Check-up

- Describe Mendel's teaching career.
- How did Mendel's mental health impact his life?

2.4 Experimental Hybridization Was the Key

Mendel (see Figure 2.5) became interested in understanding the mechanism of heredity and spent eight years designing, conducting, and analyzing the data from his now classic experiments. It is likely that Abbott Napp played an important role in directing Mendel's research given his own long interest in understanding the mechanisms of heredity. After a brief foray into the heredity of coat color in mice, Mendel settled on the garden pea (*Pisum sativum*) as his model organism because it met his criteria for a good experimental plant (Abbott & Fairbanks, 2016). The experimental plants must necessarily

1. Possess constantly differing characters.
2. At the time of flowering, their hybrids must be protected from the action of all pollen from other individuals or be easily protected.
3. The hybrids and their progeny in the succeeding generations must not suffer any noticeable disturbance in fertility.

Figure 2.5. **Gregor Mendel.** This photograph of Mendel was taken around 1865, the year his paper on hybridization was published. Source: Universal History Archive / Contributor / Universal Images Group / Getty Images.

He also noted that peas were easy to raise in pots or on open ground, they developed quickly, and artificial fertilizations were usually successful. For the first two years of his study, Mendel made sure that the varieties he chose produced "constant progeny" generation after generation. In other words, he verified that each variety bred true for whichever traits were characteristic for that variety. He started with thirty-four varieties of *P. sativum* and determined that twenty-two bred true for their characteristics and were therefore suitable for use in crosses. From those twenty-two varieties, he found that some traits did "not permit certain and sharp separation because the difference rests on a 'more or less' that is difficult to determine." In other words, some varieties exhibited quantitative traits, which he found to be unsuitable for his purpose. Rather, he sought traits that appeared "clearly and decidedly" in the plants. In other words, he sought qualitative traits. He settled on seven "constantly differing characters" (see Figure 2.6).

After establishing the true breeding variety for each trait, Mendel began to perform hybrid crosses by collecting pollen from a male plant that exhibited one form of the trait (e.g., round pea) and using it to fertilize a female plant that had the alternative form of the trait (e.g., wrinkled pea) by dusting its stigma with the pollen. He also conducted reciprocal crosses in which the sex of the parent plants from the two lines were reversed (i.e., wrinkled pea male × round pea female). For the traits that Mendel studied, the results of the reciprocal crosses did not differ, so he combined their data for reporting.

When only a single trait is under consideration, as in our example, it is known as a monohybrid cross (see Figure 2.7). Individuals of the parental generation from different varieties (or lines) are generally denoted as P_1 and P_2, and their offspring are known as the first filial generation, or F_1. The second filial generation, or F_2, consists of the offspring of mating F_1 generation individuals. In

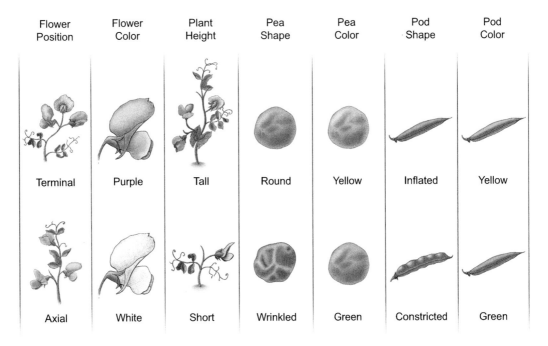

Flower Position	Flower Color	Plant Height	Pea Shape	Pea Color	Pod Shape	Pod Color
Terminal	Purple	Tall	Round	Yellow	Inflated	Yellow
Axial	White	Short	Wrinkled	Green	Constricted	Green

Figure 2.6. **Traits of the garden pea.** Mendel chose to study seven qualitative traits in *Pisum sativum* that produced clearly alternative forms regarding flower position, flower color, plant height, pea shape, pea color, pod shape, and pod color. Source: Field Museum Library / Contributor / Premium Archive / Getty Images.

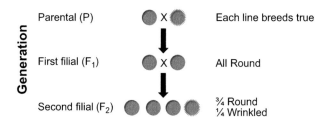

Figure 2.7. **Monohybrid cross of pea shape.** Monohybrid crosses involve a single trait of interest, such as pea shape. Pollen from a P_1 (round pea) male fertilizes a P_2 (wrinkled pea) female which produces only round peas in the F_1 generation. F_2 generation offspring produce round and wrinkled peas in a 3:1 ratio.

Mendel's case, he allowed F_1 plants to self-fertilize. Mendel reported that over the course of eight years, he made multiple crosses of each set of differing traits and examined over 10,000 plants.

Check-up

- How did Mendel determine which experimental organism to use to study heredity?
- Explain a monohybrid cross.

2.5 Mendel's Law of Segregation Describes Inheritance of a Single Locus

In Mendel's first experiment he crossed lines that differed on pea shape, either round or wrinkled. The offspring plants of crosses between true breeding plants for round peas (P_1) and wrinkled peas (P_2) produced all round peas. That is, all the F_1 generation offspring produced peas that resembled only one of their parents. This result does not support the notion of blending inheritance, where the traits of the offspring are intermediate to those of the parents. If Mendel had only conducted this cross, his data would have supported the notion of preformationism, where the traits of one parent determine the traits of their offspring. However, he also conducted the reciprocal crosses and found *identical results*, therefore his results did not support the preformationist position. The fact that all the F_1 generation offspring produced round peas provided evidence against both the notion of blending inheritance and preformationism. Even if Mendel would have stopped right there, these findings advanced the understanding of heredity. This is a strong result that is made even stronger because Mendel's design included making another generation of crosses to produce F_2 generation progeny.

In describing the results of his first crosses, Mendel indicated that one parental trait was transmitted unchanged to offspring, which he defined as dominant to the alternative in the F_1 hybrids. Subsequent crosses showed that the alternative trait re-emerged unchanged in later generations. Therefore, in the F_1 hybrid, the alternative trait (defined as recessive) was latent.

Mendel made 253 crosses in the F_1 generation, and subsequently obtained 7,324 peas representing the F_2 generation. Of these, 5,474 were round and 1,850 were wrinkled, a ratio of 2.96 to 1. Examination of the six other traits in subsequent monohybrid crosses also provided evidence

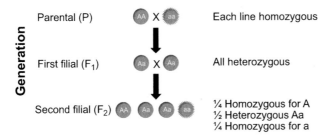

Figure 2.8. **Theoretical model of a monohybrid cross of pea color.** Mendel hypothesized that each trait was due to a pair of units of inheritance. Using current terminology, true breeding parents are homozygous, F_1 generation hybrids are heterozygous, and individuals in the F_2 generation can have any of the three genotypes. Phenotypes (i.e., round or wrinkled) are observed, whereas genotypes (i.e., AA, Aa, or aa) are inferred from phenotype.

for dominance/recessive relationships among alternative traits, and a 3:1 ratio of the expression of dominant to recessive traits in the F_2 generation.

In addition to providing strong evidence against blending inheritance and preformationism, the extensive data that Mendel collected and analyzed from monohybrid crosses carried out to the F_2 generation provided a foundation for his theoretical model of particulate inheritance (see Figure 2.8). Mendel hypothesized that two units of inheritance are carried by each individual for each trait. Let us call these units of inheritance genes. Alternative forms for a trait can be labeled with an upper case "A" for the dominant version and a lower case "a" for the recessive version. We now refer to alternative forms of a gene (i.e., A or a) as alleles. The pair of alleles for a given individual (i.e., AA, Aa, or aa) is their genotype for that trait. In addition, we now refer to a genotype that consists of two copies of the same allele (i.e., AA, or aa) as homozygous, and a genotype carrying a copy of each alternative allele as heterozygous (i.e., Aa). Observable traits, such as pea shape and color are now referred to as phenotypes.

When gametes (i.e., sperm cells within pollen grains for male plants, and eggs [ova] within ovules for female plants) are produced, each individual gamete receives only one allele for a trait. Thus, when sperm fertilizes an egg the single allele carried by the sperm is combined with the single allele carried by the egg into a fertilized zygote carrying the full complement of two alleles. Mendel hypothesized that for a given heterozygote individual, gametes containing the alternative alleles are generated at equal frequency.

A simple way to visualize the inferred genotypes in crosses was developed by Reginald Crundall Punnett (1875–1967). To construct a Punnett square, it is important to hypothesize the genotypes of both parents, which then allows the determination of the types of gametes that each would produce. In Figure 2.9 we present Punnett squares for each cross in the monohybrid cross for pea shape that we have been using as an example.

Mendel proposed what we now call the Law of Segregation to explain the pattern of results that he obtained in his monohybrid crosses (see Figure 2.9(b)). It assumes that for a given phenotype, each individual's genotype comprises two alleles. However, when an individual produces gametes the two alleles are segregated such that each gamete receives only one allele. Equal numbers of gametes are produced for each allele in the parent's genotype. At fertilization, parents each contribute one allele at random to their offspring's genotype. Gamete production in the male and female parents are independent events, as is the pairing of alleles at fertilization, which allows the simple estimation of the frequency of different genotypes in offspring by multiplication of the frequencies of each gamete. In the case of the F_1 cross, where each parent is heterozygous (i.e.,

(a) Parental Generation Cross

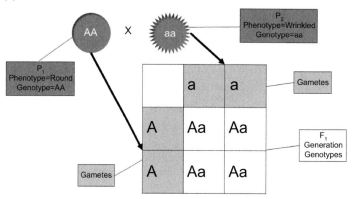

(b) F$_1$ Generation Cross

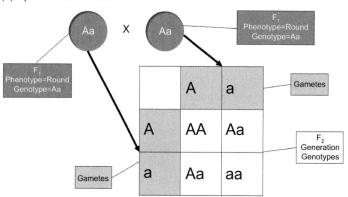

Figure 2.9. **Punnett squares for a monohybrid cross of pea shape.** (a) Pure breeding parents each produce only one type of gamete, either A-carrying gametes or a-carrying gametes. At fertilization, gametes combine at random to produce F$_1$ generation heterozygous offspring. (b) Heterozygous F$_1$ generation parents each produce approximately equal proportions of A-carrying gametes and a-carrying gametes. Those gametes combine randomly at fertilization to produce F$_2$ generation offspring with three possible genotypes: AA, Aa, and aa.

Aa × Aa), one can assume that each parent produces 50% A-carrying gametes and 50% a-carrying gametes. Therefore, in the F$_2$ generation offspring we expect genotypes to occur at the following frequencies: 25% AA (i.e., $0.50 \times 0.50 = 0.25$), 50% Aa (i.e., $0.50 \times 0.50 \times 2 = 0.50$), and 25% aa (i.e., $0.50 \times 0.50 = 0.25$). If A is dominant to a, one would expect that the distribution of F$_2$ generation phenotypes in this example would conform to the 3 to 1 ratio that Mendel observed for each of the pea phenotypes because those carrying AA and Aa genotypes are phenotypically indistinguishable.

Check-up

- What is "blending inheritance" and how did Mendel's work impact it?
- What does it mean for a trait to be recessive?
- Explain Mendel's Law of Segregation.

2.6 Mendel's Law of Independent Assortment Describes Inheritance of Multiple Loci

Mendel's theoretical model of inheritance with its Law of Segregation would have been a tremendous scientific advance on its own. But the fact that he extended his research to investigate the simultaneous heredity of pairs of traits and defined another law of heredity clinched his scientific immortality. Although conducting crosses that investigated the heredity of two traits (i.e., dihybrid crosses) was a simple extension of his monohybrid cross study design, he was the first to do it. And his results not only supported his theoretical model, they provided the tools that were later used to map the relative locations of genes on chromosomes.

Mendel reported that his first dihybrid cross involved pea shape (round and wrinkled) and pea color (green and yellow) (Abbott & Fairbanks, 2016). He crossed female round and yellow (P_1) plants to male wrinkled and green (P_2) plants (see Figure 2.10). All the resulting F_1 generation offspring were phenotypically round and yellow. When the F_1 generation plants were allowed to self-fertilize, they produced four different offspring phenotypes, often found in the same pod. Two of the F_2 generation phenotypes resembled the P generation parents (i.e., round and yellow, or wrinkled and green). The other two phenotypes observed in the F_2 generation were novel combinations of those two traits (i.e., round and green, or wrinkled and yellow). He reported that out of the 556 seeds that were produced by 15 plants, 315 were round and yellow (57%), 101 were wrinkled and yellow (18%), 108 were round and green (19%), and 32 were wrinkled and green (6%).

The genotype for round and yellow P generation parents are hypothesized to be AABB where AA represents the pure breeding round trait genotype and BB represents the pure breeding yellow trait genotype. The genotype for the wrinkled and green P generation parents is hypothesized to be aabb where aa represents the pure breeding wrinkled trait genotype and bb represents the pure breeding green trait genotype. Of course, these parents produce gametes carrying either AB or ab alleles, respectively. F_1 generation offspring are all phenotypically round and yellow, and are all hypothesized to be genotypically double heterozygotes (i.e., AaBb). Each of the F_1 generation plants are hypothesized to produce four types of gametes AB, Ab, aB, and ab at equal frequency.

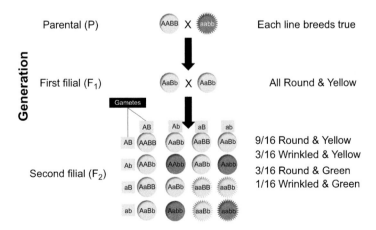

Figure 2.10. **Dihybrid cross.** In a dihybrid cross two traits are examined. In this example, pea shape (round or wrinkled) and pea color (yellow or green) are examined by first breeding parents who breed true for round/yellow and wrinkled/green peas. All first filial generation (F_1) plants produce round/yellow peas. When they self-fertilize to generate second filial generation (F_2) offspring four phenotypic classes are produced in a 9:3:3:1 ratio.

These gametes each carry a single allele for each trait. With the aid of the Punnett square, it is easy to see how the F_2 generation genotypes are a product of simply combining gametes from the two parents. This approach can be extended to examine crosses with additional traits.

Mendel applied the theoretical model that he developed for the monohybrid cross to each of the two traits in the dihybrid to derive the Law of Independent Assortment, which states that alleles for one trait are distributed to gametes without respect to alleles from other traits. The result of this principle is that gametes of all possible combinations of alleles will be present at equal frequency, and that the frequencies of F_2 generation genotypes are the product of the corresponding gametes. Essentially, in the dihybrid cross two separate and statistically independent monohybrid crosses are occurring simultaneously.

The probability of each of the four phenotypic classes observed in the dihybrid F_2 generation is a product of the probabilities of the phenotypic classes observed in the F_2 generation of each monohybrid cross. As a reminder, in the pea shape monohybrid cross, the F_2 generation phenotypes were observed in a 3 to 1 ratio (round to wrinkled). So, ¾ of the progeny were round and ¼ were wrinkled. Similarly, in the pea color monohybrid cross, the F_2 generation phenotypes were observed to be ¾ yellow and ¼ green.

In the dihybrid cross, the ratio of phenotypes observed in the F_2 generation was 9:3:3:1 (i.e., round, yellow : round, green : wrinkled, yellow : wrinkled green). The probabilities of those combinations of traits are the product of the probabilities of each of each of the traits when considered alone.

The probability of round, yellow peas is ¾ × ¾ = 9/16.
The probability of round green peas is ¾ × ¼ = 3/16.
The probability of wrinkled yellow peas is ¼ × ¾ = 3/16.
The probability of wrinkled green peas is ¼ × ¼ = 1/16.

Mendel's theoretical model provides a powerful tool to understand heredity. His insights were made possible by his careful experimental design that made use of reciprocal crosses, was bred to the F_2 generation, and was extended to include multi-hybrid crosses. His success also depended on his careful and fortuitous selection of model organism and traits, and on his efforts to ensure true breeding parental stock. Mendel's contribution to genetics cannot be overstated, although it was not recognized in the scientific community until 1900, over thirty years after its publication and sixteen years after his death.

Check-up

- What is a dihybrid cross?
- Explain Mendel's Law of Independent Assortment.

2.7 Mendel's Laws Are Used to Map Relative Positions of Genes on Chromosomes

In the first few years of the twentieth century, Mendelian genetics was "rediscovered" after being ignored for decades. An important focus of research was on unifying Mendelian principles with Darwinian evolution. Thomas Hunt Morgan was awarded the Nobel Prize in Physiology and Medicine in 1933 for his work on genetics using *Drosophila melanogaster*.

Morgan used many different non-human animal models early in his career to study evolution. However, in the early 1900s he and a small number of researchers started to use *D. melanogaster* for genetic research because of its well-known advantages. The *D. melanogaster* is a cosmopolitan species, meaning that they live in a wide range of habitats, and are often found around humans. Because they readily adapt to a wide variety of environments, they are reasonably easy to raise in the laboratory. Fruit flies are small and inexpensive to feed and house. A single pair of *D. melanogaster* can produce hundreds of offspring within a couple of weeks. It is this tremendous fecundity that enabled Morgan and his students to dramatically scale up breeding experiments so that they were able to identify relatively rarely occurring mutations that produced identifiable morphological changes. By the time Morgan's lab produced the standard genetic map of *D. melanogaster* in the early 1920s, they had generated and examined somewhere between 13 and 20 million fruit flies (Kohler, 1994). No other experimental organism at the time, even Mendel's peas, could compete with the brute force productivity of *D. melanogaster* in terms of advancing the understanding of heredity (see Box 2.2).

Although Morgan's group was not the first to report the identification of a mutation in *D. melanogaster* – that honor goes to Frank Lutz in 1908 – they were the most prolific mutant hunters. Once they started finding mutant flies, they kept at it for more than a decade and eventually found more than one hundred. It became clear to Morgan and his students that the mutations that they were finding were inherited in four groups. The number of these so-called linkage groups corresponded to the number of chromosomes in *D. melanogaster*, and their existence helped to confirm the chromosomal theory of inheritance, which identified chromosomes as the location of genetic material. *Drosophila melanogaster* have four pairs of chromosomes, three of the chromosome pairs are relatively large and one is relatively small. One of the large chromosome pairs differ for males and females and are therefore known as sex chromosomes. Females carry two X-chromosomes whereas males carry one X and one Y chromosome. It is the ratio of X-chromosomes to autosomes (i.e., non-sex chromosomes) that determines a fruit fly's sex. Normal females have two X-chromosomes and two large autosomes (chromosomes 2 and 3, ignoring the small chromosome 4) for a ratio of 1.0. Normal males have one X-chromosome and two large autosomes for a ratio of 0.5.

One of the first mutations identified by the Morgan group is perhaps the most famous. In 1910 they reported the discovery of a *D. melanogaster* male that had white eyes instead of the red eyes that are considered the wild-type for the species. The *white* mutation is abbreviated as *w*, and the wild-type is indicated as +. By crossing white-eyed males to red-eyed females, Morgan found that in the F_1 generation, white eyes were recessive to red and that in the F_2 generation, white eyes reappeared, but only in males (see Figure 2.11). No white-eyed females were found in the F_2 generation. In the reciprocal cross with white-eyed female and red-eyed male parents, the F_1 generation consisted of all red-eyed females and all white-eyed males. When the F_1 generation individuals were mated to each other they produced F_2 generation offspring with each sex having half white eyes and half red. This sex-linked pattern of inheritance had not been previously described. Morgan hypothesized that the mutation that produces white eyes is found on the X-chromosome.

As you can see, Morgan's approach was the same as Mendel's: investigating the inheritance patterns of categorical traits with reciprocal monohybrid and dihybrid crosses with pairs of traits carried out to the F_2 generation. Both types of crosses provided evidence that was consistent with Mendelian inheritance. For example, data from crosses with the wing mutant vestigial and the eye color mutant sepia conformed to Mendelian expectations of independent assortment. This was

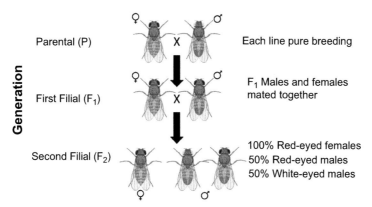

Figure 2.11. **Sex-linked white eye mutation.** Mating a white-eyed male (*w*/Y) to a pure breeding red-eyed female (+/+), the offspring of the F₁ generation all have the wild-type red eyes. Because male parents can only donate their X-chromosome to female offspring, only those female offspring will therefore carry the *white* mutation (+/*w*). Male parents give their Y-chromosome to their sons, so male F₁ progeny from this cross cannot carry the mutation (+/Y). Female parents have only X-chromosomes, which are given to both sons and daughters. When individuals from the F₁ generation are crossed, the X-chromosome carrying the *white* mutation will be passed to half of the female F₂ generation progeny (+/*w*) as well as to half of the male progeny. Because males have only one X-chromosome, if it carries the *white* mutation, they will have the white-eyed phenotype (i.e., *w*/Y), otherwise they will have red eyes (i.e., +/Y). All females will have red eyes although half will carry the recessive *white* mutation (i.e., +/+ and +/*w*). Source: Created with Biorender.com.

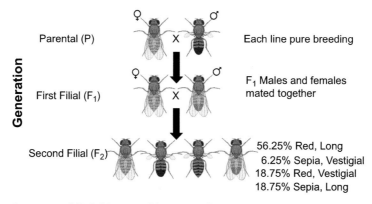

Figure 2.12. **Dihybrid cross with mutants for sepia eye and vestigial wings.** Evidence that the mutations for sepia eyes and vestigial wings are independently assorting can be obtained from a dihybrid cross. First, pure breeding wild-type (i.e., long wings, red eyes) flies are mated to flies doubly homozygous for the vestigial (*vg*) wing mutation and the sepia (*se*) mutations. Offspring from the F₁ generation, all of which have long wings and red eyes (i.e., +vg/+se), are mated to each other. The 9:3:3:1 phenotype ratio seen in Mendel's dihybrid F₂ generation crosses is observed. Source: Created with Biorender.com.

interpreted by Morgan and his team to indicate that the mutant genes responsible for those two phenotypes are located on different chromosomes (see Figure 2.12).

In other cases, Morgan and his students noted that the observed frequency of F₂ generation offspring of dihybrid crosses did not conform to expectations based on Mendel's Law of Independent Assortment, a phenomenon that they called linkage (Morgan, Sturtevant, Muller, & Bridges, 1915). As you will recall from the dihybrid cross example of pea shape (round or wrinkled) and pea color (yellow or green), four phenotypic classes were observed in the F₂ generation. Two of the classes represented the same combination of traits seen in the parental generation, that is, round and yellow peas, as well as wrinkled green ones. These are called the parental types. The other two phenotype combinations that occurred were new combinations of the phenotypes: round green and wrinkled yellow. These are called recombinant types. The frequencies of observed phenotypes were 9:3:3:1 (dominant parental [56.25%]: recombinant [18.75%]: recombinant [18.75%]: recessive parental [6.25%]) for pea shape and color.

It occurred to Morgan and his students that if one assumed that the mutations were on the same chromosome then observed deviations from the expected frequencies of recombinant types could be used to estimate the distance between the positions of mutations on the chromosome. To experimentally isolate the effects of linkage to a single parent, it is best to use a backcross design. Backcrosses involve the crossing of two parental lines to generate F_1 generation offspring. One parental line is true breeding for the wild-type expression of both traits (e.g., brown body and long wings; ++/++). The other parental line is true breeding for the mutant forms of the traits (e.g., black body [b] and vestigial wings [vg]; bb/vgvg). But rather than mating F_1 generation offspring to each other as is done to generate F_2 generation offspring, in a backcross design F_1 generation offspring (+b/+vg) are mated to individuals from the phenotypically double recessive parental line. Those double homozygous recessive individuals can contribute only one type of gamete (b/vg) and because they are recessive the type of gamete contributed by the F_1 individual can be ascertained (see Figure 2.13).

Interestingly, Morgan and his students discovered that when male F_1 generation flies were mated back to the double homozygous recessive parental line a completely unexpected distribution of phenotypes was observed in their B_1 generation offspring (see Figure 2.14). In those reciprocal crosses only parental type offspring were observed. None were of either recombinant type. Based on their findings, they hypothesized that recombination does not occur in male *D. melanogaster*.

Morgan and his students developed a theoretical model to connect the observations that they had made of Mendelian inheritance using backcrosses with the notion that the hereditary material was made up of chromosomes. They imagined genes as discrete beads on a string that were

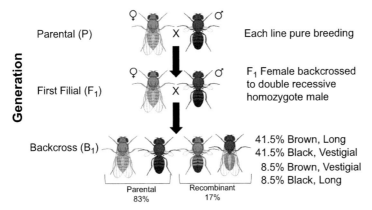

Figure 2.13. **Backcrossing vestigial wings and black body mutants.** Evidence of the linkage of mutations can be derived from the results of a backcross. In this example, pure breeding wild-type (i.e., brown body, long winged) flies are mated to double homozygous recessive mutant flies with black bodies (b) and vestigial wings (vg) in the parental generation. Their F_1 generation offspring are all phenotypically indistinguishable from their wild-type parents. F_1 generation females are mated back to double homozygous recessive mutant flies to produce B_1 generation offspring. Under independent assortment, the expectation is that the four phenotypic classes are represented equally (i.e., each at 25%). However, when fewer than expected recombinant types are observed the interpretation is that the mutant genes under investigation are located on the same chromosome. Source: Created with Biorender.com.

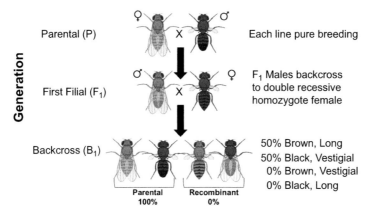

Figure 2.14. **No recombinant types produced when male F₁ generation males are backcrossed to parental line females.** When F₁ generation males are backcrossed to females of the double homozygous recessive line, only parental type offspring are produced in the B₁ generation. This suggested to Morgan and his students that the F₁ generation males were producing only two types of gametes. In other words, they were essentially passing on the chromosomes that they inherited intact. No recombination occurs in male *D. melanogaster*. Source: Created with Biorender.com.

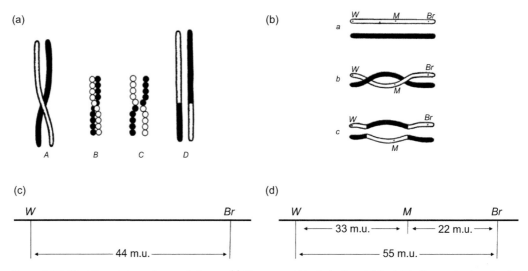

Figure 2.15. **Crossing over and map distance.** (a) Morgan and his students published this diagram to describe the reciprocal exchange of material between homologous chromosomes called crossing over. Genes were hypothesized to lie in a linear series along chromosomes like beads on a string. (b) Three-point crosses can be used to estimate recombination rate. Here Morgan diagrams such a cross with X-linked mutants white (*W*), miniature (*M*), and bar (*Br*). (c) When only white and bar are investigated in a dihybrid backcross, recombinant types make up 44% of the observed progeny and an estimation of 44 map units between them. (d) When miniature is also included in a trihybrid cross design, the distance between white and bar is estimated by summing the observed recombinants between white and miniature, and bar and miniature. The difference between the estimate of 55 map units and the dihybrid estimate of 44 map units suggests that double recombination events in the dihybrid cross reduce the observed number of recombinant types. Source: Morgan et al. (1915). Image in the public domain.

located in a linear series (see Figure 2.15). Their model described a process called crossing over that explained the recombination of phenotypes that were observed in the dihybrid crosses. Crossing over occurs during gamete formation when homologous chromosomes (i.e., chromosome pairs, one from each parent) pair up and physically exchange material. The differential rates of recombinant types that were observed in various dihybrid crosses were explained by theorizing that the mutant loci that recombined at higher rates were physically farther away from each other on the same chromosome, and that those that combined at low rates were physically closer together. Therefore, the chromosomal map distance between two loci could be estimated by their recombination rate. A unit of measurement to be used in genetic mapping was proposed by Alfred H. Sturtevant, one of Morgan's students, called the centimorgan (cM), which represented one map unit and was defined to equal to a recombination rate of 1 percent.

By conducting dihybrid and trihybrid backcrosses and then counting the number of recombinant offspring Morgan and his students were able to generate a genetic map for each of the four chromosomes of *D. melanogaster* that estimated the location of each of the recessive mutants that they had identified. When the frequency of recombinant types observed in backcrosses is less than 50 percent it indicates linkage.

Two-point crosses can be used to establish the relative locations of mutations on a chromosome. However, as we see in Figure 2.15, three-point crosses are more accurate estimates of recombination rate. Double crossovers, where an initial crossover event is undone by a second crossover event, are more common over long distances. Therefore, the three-point crosses are more accurate because they combine the information from two shorter distance estimates, which reduces the likelihood of double crossover events.

Check-up

- What are the advantages of using *Drosophila melanogaster* to study heredity?
- What is a backcross?
- What is the relation between recombination rate and map distance?

Box 2.2 Bloomington Drosophila Stock Center

Evolutionary biologist Theodosius Dobzhansky often referred to *D. melanogaster* as "the queen of species" (personal communication to me from my PhD adviser Jerry Hirsch, who worked with Dobzhansky while on the faculty at Columbia University). Dobzhansky apparently admired *D. melanogaster* for the ease with which it can be raised in a laboratory, and for its seemingly endless capacity for genetic variation. Both traits are on display at the Bloomington Drosophila Stock Center (BDSC) in Bloomington, Indiana. The BDSC currently holds around 71,000 genetically different pure breeding stocks of flies and distributed nearly 223,000 subcultures to researchers around the world in 2018. It is supported by the National Institutes of Health, by Indiana University and by modest user fees (around $20/stock). The stocks represent well-characterized mutations that are of scientific value for their use in breeding studies.

The BDSC is a direct descendant of the original stocks of flies studied by T. H. Morgan and his students at Columbia University in 1913. They provided stocks for free to those who requested them. When Morgan took a position at Cal Tech in 1928, he, Alfred Sturtevant, and Calvin Bridges took the stocks to Pasadena and established the original Drosophila Stock Center. In the late 1980s it was moved to Indiana University. At that time, it consisted of 1,675 stocks. Now with nearly 71,000 stocks there are over 60 people employed by BDSC as "stock keepers."

Of course, the BDSC maintains a user-friendly website that enables potential users to search or browse the available stocks. Stocks can also be ordered online. The web page also contains basic information about *D. melanogaster* and its care. Although there are other important non-human animal models in behavior genetics, *D. melanogaster* still appears to be the queen of species.

2.8 Mendelian Disorders in Humans Are Caused by Variants in Single Genes

The mapping of Mendelian traits in *D. melanogaster* was an important demonstration that genes reside in linear series on chromosomes and that it is possible to create such a map. It took about a century, but the linear sequence of genes along human chromosomes has been mapped and is serving to advance biotechnology, biomedicine, and knowledge of the human genome that previously was not possible. In fact, prior to the completion of the Human Genome Project, one of the most important kinds of information about the genetics of traits in humans was the observation that certain traits tended to run in families. Patterns of familial inheritance of traits were most clearly seen in rare medical conditions or disorders. Of course, the breeding designs that were used so effectively to understand the inheritance of Mendelian traits in plants and non-human animals are not available for use in humans.

Pedigrees provide a way to visualize the transmission of traits across generations in a family by graphically representing phenotypes and genetic relationships (Bennett, French, Resta, & Doyle, 2008). Although most behavior traits run in families they do not exhibit the simple patterns exemplified by single-gene Mendelian inheritance. In the next chapter we examine the inheritance of such traits. Some traits do, however, run in families and exhibit patterns of inheritance across generations that provide information about their underlying genetics. These conditions are determined by the inheritance of single genes that follow Mendelian patterns that can reveal whether the disease-causing genetic variant (1) acts in a dominant or recessive fashion, and (2) whether it is located on a sex chromosome (i.e., X or Y) or an autosome.

Ideally, a pedigree includes the sex, phenotype status (e.g., affected or not affected), and genetic relationships for every individual across multiple generations of a large family (see Figure 2.16). In practice, complete information for every individual is not available. Some family members may be deceased or may not have available phenotype information. Some families do not have many members or may have incomplete or inaccurate information about genetic relationships.

Let us consider a hypothetical disease that is caused by a dominant rare allele. Alleles are considered rare in the general population if their frequency is less than 1 percent. As in the previous examples that we have seen for Mendelian traits, dominance describes a situation where having only one copy of an allele is enough for it to determine the phenotype. In the case of single-gene disorders, individuals with the affected phenotype (i.e., those having the disease) carry either one or two copies of the dominant allele. One can assume that if the disease is rare and caused by a dominant allele, those unaffected do not carry a copy of the disease-causing allele. In the case of a rare allele, one can also assume that most affected individuals are heterozygous for it. Autosomal dominant inheritance is shown in the hypothetical example in Figure 2.16(a). In this example, an affected female in generation I mates with an unaffected male and produces an unaffected female and an affected male offspring. The male offspring mates with an unaffected female, which produces

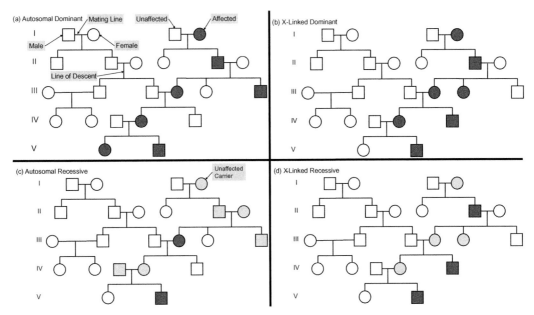

Figure 2.16. **Hypothetical pedigrees showing different inheritance patterns.** (a) Autosomal Dominant, (b) X-Linked Dominant, (c) Autosomal Recessive, and (d) X-Linked Recessive.

three offspring in generation III, two of whom are affected. Because the generation II affected father has both an affected daughter and an affected son the likely hypothesis is that of a dominant disease-causing allele that is not located on the X-chromosome (i.e., is autosomal). Fathers pass their X-chromosome only to their daughters, not to their sons. The inheritance pattern of the hypothetical disease is consistent with a single dominant allele that is located on an autosome. Huntington's disease is an example of an autosomal dominant disorder. Huntington's disease is a rare progressive neurological disorder that impacts movement, emotion, and cognition. The most common form of Huntington's disease has adult onset, with symptoms beginning in a person's thirties or forties.

Figure 2.16(b) shows a hypothetical case where a rare dominant allele located on the X-chromosome causes a disease. Affected females can pass on the disease to sons and daughters but affected fathers can only pass on the disease to daughters. Sons inherit a Y-chromosome from their fathers, not an X-chromosome. Daughters inherit an X-chromosome from each parent. Rett's syndrome is an example of a rare X-linked dominant disorder. The inheritance pattern in Rett syndrome, however, is not typical because males who inherit the dominant disease-causing allele on their X-chromosome usually die in infancy. Therefore, nearly all cases of Rett syndrome are female. The disorder is characterized by severe deficits in language development, learning, coordination, and other areas of function, potentially including microcephaly (i.e., small head) that develop in infancy.

Figure 2.16(c) shows a hypothetical case of the inheritance of an autosomal recessive disorder. To develop the disease (shown on the pedigree as darkly shaded symbols), homozygosity for the disease-causing allele is necessary. Heterozygous carriers of the disease-causing allele (shown on the pedigree as lightly shaded symbols) do not develop the disorder. Phenylketonuria (PKU) is an example of an autosomal recessive disorder. PKU is a rare disorder due to a mutation that abolishes metabolism of the dietary amino acid phenylalanine. PKU develops upon exposure to phenylalanine in food and can produce profound intellectual disability. Testing of newborns can identify those at genetic risk for developing PKU and lifelong dietary management (low phenyl-alanine diet) can prevent the development of the disorder or reduce the severity of symptoms.

Figure 2.16(d) shows a hypothetical case of the inheritance of an X-linked recessive condition. Affected males carry a copy of the recessive allele on their only X-chromosome (i.e., are hemizygous). Affected females carry two copies of the recessive allele. Unaffected female carriers (shown on the pedigree as lightly shaded squares) carry one recessive allele. The presence of a single copy of the dominant allele is sufficient to prevent the condition. The most common type of color vision deficiency (i.e., red-green color vision defect) is an example of an X-linked recessive condition. This condition is found in approximately 1 in 12 males and 1 in 200 females. Those with the condition have difficulty distinguishing between some shades of red, green, and yellow.

As you can see, although the kind of genetic mapping of Mendelian traits in *D. melanogaster* cannot be used to map genes for genetic disorders in humans, pedigrees provided important genetic information before the human genome was sequenced. Pedigrees can differentiate between dominant and recessive alleles and between autosomal and X-linked patterns of inheritance for qualitative traits such as diseases. Pedigrees also provided strong evidence that Mendelian inheritance played an important role in human genetics.

Check-up

- What is a pedigree and how is it used to study heredity?
- What kinds of traits show Mendelian inheritance patterns in human families?

2.9 SUMMARY

- Early thinking about heredity often combined it with embryology and development. Preformationism held that only one parent contributed to offspring traits and that the other parent either activated the process or provided sustenance.
- Gregor Mendel suffered from bouts of depression and was unable to pass the certification exam to become a high school teacher. He also laid the foundation for understanding genetics by conducting eight years of experimental crosses of pea plants.
- Mendel's Law of Segregation is demonstrated in monohybrid crosses. It assumes that for a given phenotype, each individual's genotype comprises two alleles. However, when an individual produces gametes, the two alleles are segregated such that each gamete receives only one allele.
- Mendel's Law of Independent Assortment is demonstrated in dihybrid crosses. It states that alleles for one trait are distributed to gametes without respect to alleles from other traits.
- Morgan and his students used Mendelian principles to investigate genetics in *Drosophila melanogaster*. They mapped genes in a linear series along chromosomes and provided support for the chromosomal theory of inheritance.
- Pedigrees provide a way to visualize the transmission of traits across generations in a family by graphically representing phenotypes and genetic relationships. Although most behavior traits run in families they do not exhibit the simple patterns exemplified by single-gene Mendelian inheritance.

RECOMMENDED READING

- Henig, Robin M. (2000). *The Monk in the Garden: The Lost and Found Genius of Gregor Mendel, the Father of Genetics*. Boston: Houghton Mifflin.
- Kohler, R. E. (1994). *Lords of the Fly: Drosophila Genetics and the Experimental Life*. Chicago, IL: University of Chicago Press.
- Zimmer, Carl (2018). *She Has Her Mother's Laugh: The Powers, Perversions and Potential of Heredity*. New York: Dutton.

REFERENCES

Abbott, S., & Fairbanks, D. J. (2016). Experiments on plant hybrids by Gregor Mendel. *Genetics, 204*(2), 407–422. doi:10.1534/genetics.116.195198

Bennett, R. L., French, K. S., Resta, R. G., & Doyle, D. L. (2008). Standardized human pedigree nomenclature: Update and assessment of the recommendations of the National Society of Genetic Counselors. *J Genet Couns, 17*(5), 424–433. doi:10.1007/s10897-008-9169-9

Cobb, M. (2006). Heredity before genetics: A history. *Nat Rev Genet, 7*(12), 953–958. doi:10.1038/nrg1948

De Castro, M. (2016). Johann Gregor Mendel: Paragon of experimental science. *Mol Genet Genomic Med, 4*(1), 3–8. doi:10.1002/mgg3.199

Kohler, R. E. (1994). *Lords of the Fly: Drosophila Genetics and the Experimental Life*. Chicago, IL: University of Chicago Press.

Morgan, T. H., Sturtevant, A. H., Muller, H. J., & Bridges, C. B. (1915). *The Mechanism of Mendelian Heredity*. New York: Henry Holt and Company.

Poczai, P., Bell, N., & Hyvonen, J. (2014). Imre Festetics and the Sheep Breeders' Society of Moravia: Mendel's forgotten "research network." *PLoS Biol, 12*(1), e1001772. doi:10.1371/journal.pbio.1001772

Russell, N. (2006). *Like Engend'ring Like: Heredity and Animal Breeding in Early Modern England*. Cambridge: Cambridge University Press.

Wood, R. J., & Orel, V. (2005). Scientific breeding in Central Europe during the early nineteenth century: Background to Mendel's later work. *Journal of the History of Biology, 38*(2), 239–272. doi:10.1007/s10739-004-5427-3

Wykes, D. L. (2004). Robert Bakewell (1725–1795) of Dishley: Farmer and livestock improver. *Agric Hist Rev, 52*(1), 38–55.

3 Heritability

Mendel's theoretical model provided a powerful framework for understanding inheritance. However, traits that do not fit neatly into categories, but instead vary along some dimension (e.g., height), present a challenge to the Mendelian genetic model. This chapter discusses how this conundrum was resolved and how the solution led to the establishment of the field of quantitative genetics. Most behavioral traits vary along a dimension, so this issue is particularly relevant to behavior genetics. Next, the chapter introduces the concept of variance partitioning and discusses approaches commonly used in behavior genetics to investigate the roles of genetic and environmental variation on individual differences in behavior. Finally, the chapter discusses what has been one of the most important, and sometimes misunderstood, statistics in behavior genetics: heritability.

3.1 Genetic Factors That Affect Quantitative Traits Are Inherited in Mendelian Fashion

Early in the twentieth century, there was a heated debate about whether Mendelian genetics applied to traits that did not fall neatly into categories. It was the battle of the Mendelians (led by William Bateson) versus the Biometricians (led by Karl Pearson and W. F. R Weldon) (Gillham, 2015), and it began a marriage between the newly named field of genetics and the budding field of statistics from which quantitative genetics was born. Unfortunately, it also appeared to provide a scientific basis for eugenics, which is discussed in Chapter 15.

As the Biometricians noted, many traits in populations vary continuously along some dimension instead of falling into discrete categories. A good example of this is height. It is easy to see that human adults are not just short, medium, and tall, but they range from quite short (21.51 inches [54.64 cm]) to quite tall (107.10 inches [272.03 cm]), with most people being somewhere in the middle. In the US, the average height of men is 69.00 inches (175.30 cm), and the average height of women is 63.50 inches (161.50 cm). When the heights of individuals in a population are plotted on a histogram, the distribution approximates a normal distribution, which is sometimes called a bell curve (see Figure 3.1). For a normally distributed trait, approximately 68 percent of individuals fall within 1 standard deviation (s.d.) of the population mean, 95 percent of individuals fall within 2 s.d., and nearly everyone falls within 3 s.d. of the mean. Many of the traits of interest to psychologists, like motivation or impulsivity, vary continuously in populations and are typically measured using numerical scales, and are often referred to as quantitative traits. Quite often, but not always, the score distributions in populations for quantitative psychological traits approximate normal distributions.

The Biometricians observed that these quantitative traits did not appear to be inherited in Mendelian patterns in families. This conundrum was formally resolved when R. A. Fisher presented

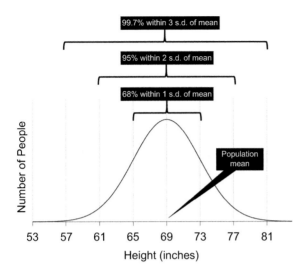

Figure 3.1. **Height is normally distributed in populations.** When men's height is plotted on the x-axis, and the number of men at each height is plotted on the y-axis a normal distribution is approximated. The curve shown here is a normal distribution with a mean of 69 inches and standard deviation of 4 inches.

a model whereby Mendelian inheritance of genetic factors was operating, but that instead of a single Mendelian locus there are a large number of Mendelian factors involved, each having a small cumulative effect on the trait (Fisher, 1918). Fisher showed that there was no need to envision a new mode of inheritance to explain quantitative traits. The extension of Mendelian genetics to include Fisher's polygenes brought the two sides of the debate together.

The power of Fisher's model was in summing the effects over multiple genetic factors (i.e., polygenes) that are each inherited in Mendelian fashion. For example, consider a hypothetical trait that is influenced by four separate genetic loci identified as A, B, C, and D for simplicity. If each of these loci has one allele that is associated with more of the trait (i.e., an increasing allele) identified with uppercase letters (A, B, C, D), and another associated with less of the trait (i.e., a decreasing allele) identified with lowercase letters (a, b, c, d), an individual's score on the trait is a function of their cumulative score across the four loci.

As the number of contributing loci increases, the distribution of the trait in the population more closely approximates the normal distribution. When four loci are considered, there are 81 potential genotypes where individuals have two alleles at each locus (e.g., aabbccdd). The number of increasing alleles for each 4-locus genotype represents that genotype's genetic score. When each potential genotype is plotted according to its number of increasing alleles it is easy to see how such polygenic additive effects can produce normally distributed traits in populations (see Figure 3.2).

Over half (i.e., 44) of the potential genotype combinations in the population have an intermediate number (i.e., 3, 4, or 5) of increasing alleles. Whereas only two genotypes represent the extreme cases of either all decreasing (i.e., aabbccdd with a cumulative score of 0) or all increasing alleles (i.e., AABBCCDD with a cumulative score of 8). The distribution of such polygenes provides a way to think about the role of genetic influence on quantitative traits in populations. Fisher's polygenic model provides the foundation for the field of quantitative genetics, has largely been supported by recent findings in molecular genetics, and continues to guide our thinking about heredity–behavior relations.

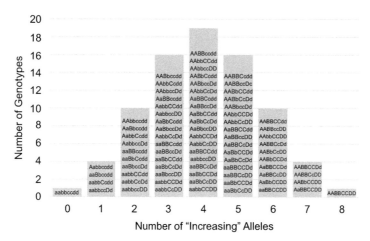

Figure 3.2. **Polygenic inheritance can approximate the normal distribution.** Eighty-one potential genotypes resulting from all possible combinations of four hypothetical loci are shown on the x-axis in order of the number of their "increasing" alleles. The number of genotypes containing a given number of increasing alleles is shown on the y-axis. Most of the genotypes have an intermediate number of "increasing" alleles, and few genotypes have all "increasing" or "decreasing" alleles.

Check-up

- Describe the main point of contention between the Mendelians and the Biometricians.
- Describe Fisher's polygenic model and the role it played in the debate between the Mendelians and the Biometricians.

3.2 Phenotypic Variation in a Population May Be Due to Genetic and Environmental Sources

Of course, individual differences in quantitative traits in a population are not solely due to polygenic effects. In fact, much of psychology is devoted to better understanding non-genetic factors that influence individual differences in behavior. Such non-genetic factors can be considered together as environmental factors. Fisher's model (Fisher, 1918) showed that quantitative trait variation in populations could be broken down into variation due to environmental and genetic sources. In fact, a major focus of quantitative genetics is to estimate how much of the variation on a quantitative trait in a population is due to environmental variation and how much is due to genetic variation.

Variance is a statistical term that quantifies individual differences in a population. Going back to our example of height, if *everyone* in a population is 69 inches tall, the variance equals zero (0). On the other hand, if the average height in the population is normally distributed with a mean of 69 inches, and nearly everyone falls somewhere between the range of 57 inches and 81 inches (as seen in Figure 3.1), then the standard deviation is 4 inches. The standard deviation is the square root of the variance, therefore the variance in our example is the standard deviation squared (s.d.^{2}) or 16. The main point for our purposes is that more variation in the

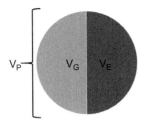

Figure 3.3. **Partitioning phenotypic variance.** In a population, overall phenotypic variance (V_P) in a trait can be assigned to that due to genetic (V_G) and that due to environmental (V_E) variance components, where $V_P = V_G + V_E$.

population produces a higher variance estimate than when there is little or no variation. Variance is an index of the spread of the distribution.

In quantitative genetics, we focus on variance, rather than the mean of the distribution, because we are interested in understanding the source of individual differences in the population. We want to know why individuals are different from each other. We want to be able to partition the overall phenotypic variance (V_P) in the population into that due to genetic variance (V_G) and that due to environmental variance (V_E). If we use a pie chart, where the entire pie represents all the variance of the trait in the population, then we can slice the pie into two parts, one representing variance due to genetic differences between individuals, and one representing variance due to environmental differences between them (i.e., $V_P = V_G + V_E$; see Figure 3.3).

Let us consider an interesting rodent behavioral model that often is used by pharmaceutical companies to test drugs for their antidepressant effects, and by researchers to study depression-like behavior. We are not able to interview or give a self-report questionnaire to mice to ask them how they feel, so we need to devise tests to directly measure depression-like behavior. The most commonly used test for depression-like behavior in mice is called the forced swim test (Porsolt, Le Pichon, & Jalfre, 1977). When a mouse is placed in a container full of water, it will initially swim vigorously and try to escape. Eventually, it stops swimming and just floats. When mice are given drugs that are effective for treating depression in humans, they tend to swim for a longer time before giving up than do mice that are not given the antidepressant. Therefore, in the forced swim test the amount of time that a mouse spends just floating (i.e., not swimming) is the operational definition of depression-like behavior.

Testing strains of mice that have different genetic backgrounds enables researchers to assess the contribution of genetic variation to individual differences on a trait in a population. Inbred strains typically have been maintained by mating brother to sister for at least twenty generations and consequently are considered to be isogenic (i.e., having little to no within-strain genetic variation). Individuals from inbred lines are homozygous at nearly all loci. Outbred strains, on the other hand, are maintained by mating together individuals that are not related to each other. The genetic variability in outbred lines is more like that found in naturally occurring populations. Regardless of the precise levels of genetic variability, the assumption is that outbred populations contain more genetic variation (i.e., heterozygosity) than do inbred populations.

To demonstrate how researchers might attempt to partition the variance of depression-like behavior in mice into that due to genetic and environmental sources let us consider two populations of mice and two environments in which to raise them. One of the mouse strains should be inbred and the other outbred. One environment should be a standard laboratory cage that contains only the necessary bedding, food, and water. The other environment should be enriched with a running wheel, obstacles to climb, and other materials with which the mice can interact and explore.

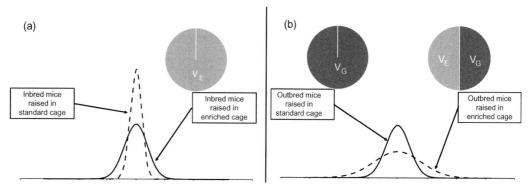

Figure 3.4. **Variance partitioning in a hypothetical study of depression-like behavior.** Individuals in an outbred population of mice vary genetically, whereas individuals from an inbred population do not. Standard laboratory conditions can be kept similar, whereas enriched conditions (e.g., running wheel, other novel items) provide opportunity for environmental variability. (a) The graph shows hypothetical data of depression-like behavior of two groups of inbred mice, the dashed line shows little behavioral variance of mice raised in a standard cage, compared to the solid line that shows somewhat greater behavioral variability of mice raised in an enriched environment. Because the individuals are isogenic, any variability is attributed to environmental sources. (b) The graph shows hypothetical data of depression-like behavior of two groups of outbred mice, the solid line (standard cage) shows less variance than the dashed line (enriched cage). All the variation can be attributed to genetic sources for those raised in the standard cage, whereas both genetic and environmental variation contribute to behavioral variance in outbred mice raised in enriched conditions.

Many individuals from each of the groups representing the four possible combinations of the two lines and the two environments ([1] inbred/standard, [2] inbred/enriched, [3] outbred/standard, and [4] outbred/enriched) should be tested in the forced swim test.

When the inbred mice raised in standard conditions are tested, some individual differences in depression-like behavior should be expected and can be interpreted as the result of error in the measurement of the behavior, lack of complete homozygosity, and non-systematic differences in environment and development. In Figure 3.4(a) a hypothetical score distribution (dashed line) is presented that shows tightly clustered scores (i.e., low variance). This distribution is not used in partitioning variance per se, but it is instructive to see that one should not expect every individual in the tested sample to have identical scores on the trait. The solid line shows the hypothetical distribution of inbred mice raised in an enriched environment. The means of the two distributions are the same, but the variance is greater in the score distribution of inbred mice raised in an enriched environment. All the trait variance in that group is attributed to the environment because all of the tested mice in that group are genetically the same, but the environment in which they were raised varied.

When outbred mice raised in the standard laboratory cage are tested, individual differences in depression-like behavior are attributed to genetics because the mice were raised in a uniform environment, but individuals were genetically different from one another (see Figure 3.4(b)). When outbred mice raised in the enriched environments are tested, both genetic variation and environmental variation contribute to the individual differences in depression-like behavior (see Box 3.1).

These hypothetical results illustrate an important point about partitioning trait variance into genetic and environmental components in a population: namely that phenotypic variance in a population is a function of the genetic variation present in the individuals tested and of the environments to which they have been exposed. The variability is not a fixed property of the trait.

Box 3.1 Species Spotlight: *Mus musculus*

Description. Mice are small rodents that are currently the most commonly studied mammalian non-human model in biomedical research (see Figure 3.5). They have been widely used in genetic research for well over a century (Russell, 1985). In fact, Gregor Mendel made a brief foray into studying the inheritance of coat color in mice before abandoning them to study traits in peas.

Adult mice weigh approximately 1.4 to 1.6 ounces (40–45 g) and measure 3.0–3.9 inches (7.5–10.0 cm) from nose to base of tail, with a tail length of 2.0–3.9 inches (5.0–10.0 cm). Female mice become reproductively mature at about 6 weeks of age (males at 8 weeks) and can produce litters of three to fourteen pups (average six to eight) five to ten times per year. Laboratory mice typically have a lifespan of two to three years.

Behaviors. Mice are mostly active at twilight (i.e., crepuscular) or at night (i.e., nocturnal). A complete list of behaviors that have been studied in laboratory mice is too long to provide here. They are used to study psychiatric disorders such as depression, anxiety, substance use, obsessive-compulsive disorder, schizophrenia, and others. They are also used to study aggression, maternal and paternal behaviors, and other social interactions. It may be easier to compile a list of behaviors that are not studied using mouse models than those that are.

Genetics. Humans and mice shared a common ancestor approximately 88 million years ago. Because of this shared evolutionary history, humans and mice share most of their genetic material and much of their basic biology. Thousands of genetically distinct strains of laboratory mice are maintained for research.

Figure 3.5. **A laboratory mouse and a standard cage.** A substantial amount of research in behavior genetics is conducted with laboratory mice.
Source: thelinke / E+ / Getty Images.

Check-up

- What is variance and why is it so important in behavior genetics?
- What does it mean to partition variance?
- What are inbred and outbred strains and how are they used to partition variance?
- Describe depression-like behavior in mice and how it is used in research.

3.3 Genetic Variance May Be Due to Polygenes, Dominance, and Epistatic Interactions

The primary reason for estimating the amount of genetic variance (V_G) that contributes to overall phenotypic variance (V_P) is to understand how *genetic differences* contribute to *individual differences* in the trait, in a population. From a different perspective, we want to understand familial resemblance: how does *genetic similarity* contribute to *trait similarity*? Whether one focuses on differences or similarity merely reflects perspective, because they represent two sides of the same coin.

Genetic variation can be partitioned into three components: additive (V_A), dominance (V_D), and interaction (V_I), so that $V_G = V_A + V_D + V_I$. Additive genetic variation is a direct result of polygenic inheritance. As previously indicated, polygenes can be thought of as locations in the genome that are associated with either a small increase or decrease in an individual's trait score. In our example, we used uppercase letters to identify increasing alleles and lowercase letters to identify decreasing alleles for relevant genotypes. Polygenes are passed from parent to offspring in sexually reproducing species and are therefore responsible for resemblance between relatives on quantitative traits.

Variation for a quantitative trait in a population due to dominance variance (V_D) is a result of dominance/recessive relations. We discussed dominance/recessive relations for categorical traits in Chapter 2. When a single locus is considered, the trait score of a heterozygote might not lie perfectly in between that of the two homozygotes as it would for additive loci. For illustration, let us consider a locus where the average trait score of increasing allele homozygotes (AA) is 2 and the decreasing allele homozygotes (aa) is 0 (see Figure 3.6(a)). If the mean score of the heterozygotes (Aa) is 1, then the locus would be considered additive. However, if the heterozygote mean score

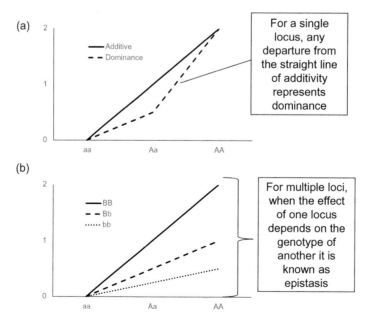

Figure 3.6. **Dominance and epistasis.** (a) Dominance describes a departure from additivity at a single locus. (b) The effect of a particular locus could depend on a genotype at another locus, termed a gene-gene (epistatic) interaction.

differs from 1, the locus would be considered to exhibit dominance. If there was complete dominance for the decreasing allele, the heterozygote score would be 0. Any deviation from a strict additive effect would contribute to dominance variation for the trait in the population.

Interaction variance (V_I) is a source of genetic variation that accounts for combinations of genotypes at *more than one locus*. When the effect of one locus depends, at least in part, on the genotype of another it is termed epistasis. As you recall from our discussion of dihybrid crosses in Chapter 2, genotypes at one locus can mask or modify the effects of another locus on a trait. There are many potential patterns of results that are possible due to epistatic interaction. The main point is that there is a departure from strict additivity such that the effect of a locus on a trait is different when it is considered jointly with another locus (see Figure 3.6(b)). In the example shown, the scores show an additive pattern across genotypes aa, Aa, and AA only when coupled with genotype BB. The presence of one or two b alleles produces a departure from strict additivity. Such a pattern of results is evidence of epistatic interaction between the A and B loci.

The combined variance due to dominance and to interactions is often referred to as non-additive genetic variance. It is important to note that non-additive genetic variance is not passed from one generation to the next. The dominance/recessive relations and the interactions among loci are a property of specific genotypes carried by individuals in a population, but because of the mechanisms of sexual reproduction, those genotype combinations are broken up when gametes are produced. For example, an individual's genotype may be AaBb, which may be subject to non-additive dominance and epistatic effects. However, the gametes that they produce would be AB, Ab, aB, and bb, any of which could couple with another set of gametes during fertilization. The presence of dominance and interaction effects are only observed in diploid genomes, not in haploid gametes.

Offspring inherit their parents' genes, but not their parents' genotypes. So, most of our focus will be on additive genetic effects because they can be passed from one generation to the next and represent the genetic contribution to familial resemblance.

Check-up

- Describe two types of non-additive genetic variance.
- Explain why non-additive genetic variance does not contribute to familial resemblance.

3.4 There Are Many Sources of Environmental Variance

Of course, not all individual differences in behavior in a population are due to genetic sources. However, because the field of quantitative genetics was developed to understand the role of genetic variation in quantitative traits and is used in agriculture to facilitate selective breeding the focus is on genetics. In fact, all non-genetic sources of variation are typically combined into a catchall category called environmental variance. Sources of environmental variance on behavior can include pre- and postnatal experiences, nutrition, life stresses, socioeconomic status, peer influences, and just about anything else studied in psychology. Another source of environmental variance is measurement error. If you have ever tried to measure someone's height with a standard tape measure, you might have noticed that it is not easy to get the exact same measurement every time. Which means that there was likely some measurement error. Similarly, when measuring behavioral traits such as personality, or cognition, or self-reported symptoms of mental illness, there is also room for error.

Environmental variance can be considered a nuisance by experimentalists because it can decrease the precision of the measurement of genetic effects. Therefore, researchers may strive to reduce it.

3.4.1 Environmental Factors May Either Increase or Decrease Phenotypic Similarity

Some environmental factors tend to make individuals more alike behaviorally, which would reduce the variance of that behavior in the population. Factors associated with an *increase* in behavioral similarity are known as shared environmental factors (Plomin & Daniels, 1987). It is important to point out here that when partitioning variance, studies do not typically assess specific environmental factors to determine if they are, in fact, shared. If any non-genetic factor is associated with an increase in behavioral similarity between relatives it contributes to shared environment. Consider, for example, investigating child depression in families in which parents divorce. It may be that the experience of parental divorce is associated with increased similarity on risk for depression in the children. In this case, the divorce would be considered a shared environmental factor.

On the other hand, some non-genetic factors are associated with behavioral differences between relatives. Those factors associated with a *decrease* in behavioral similarity are known as non-shared environmental factors. Continuing with our divorce example, if one of the children in the family experiences an increase in depression symptoms as a result of the divorce, but another does not, the divorce would be considered to contribute to non-shared environmental variance in depression symptoms. The key here is not whether the environmental factor (i.e., divorce) was *actually shared* by the children in the family, but how it was statistically associated with similarity on the trait (i.e., depression symptoms). When the factor is associated with increased behavioral similarity, it is termed shared, and if it is associated with decreased behavioral similarity, it is termed non-shared.

3.4.2 Genotype Effects May Depend on Environmental Context

The impact of genetic variation at a locus on a quantitative trait may depend on the environment in which it is found. Let us consider a single locus with genotypes aa, Aa, and AA in our hypothetical line of outbred mice (see Figure 3.7). If one were to randomly select one group of mice from this outbred line to be raised in standard cages, and another group to be raised in enriched cages it would be possible to test for a G×E interaction effect on depression-like behavior. Assume that in each group of mice, there are multiple individuals that carry each of the three possible genotypes at the target locus (i.e., aa, Aa, and AA) that we test behaviorally in the forced swim test.

Figure 3.7(a) illustrates a potential outcome of an environmental effect (i.e., a difference between the environmental conditions), but no genetic effect (i.e., a difference between groups defined by genotype), or G×E interaction effect (i.e., genotype effect depends on environmental condition). In this hypothetical example, mice raised in enriched environments displayed less depression-like behavior, on average, than those raised in standard cages, and there was no difference between scores for mice with different genotypes. There was no G×E interaction effect in this condition.

Figure 3.7(b). illustrates a potential outcome of a genetic effect, but no environmental effect or G×E interaction effect. In this hypothetical example, mice with the aa genotype displayed the most depression-like behavior, on average. Mice with the AA genotype displayed the least depression-like behavior; and heterozygotes displayed intermediate depression-like behavior scores.

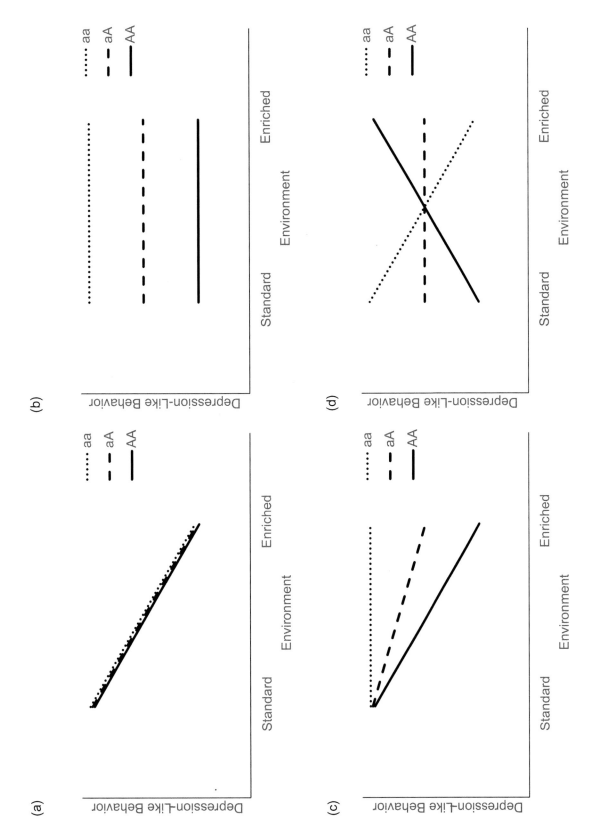

Figure 3.7. **Patterns of G×E interaction.** Each of these panels presents a potential pattern of interplay between genotypes at a single locus and two environmental conditions: (a) Environmental effect, no genotype effect, no G×E interaction. (b) Genotype effect, no environmental effect, no G×E interaction. (c) Small genotype and environmental effect, G×E interaction (fan shaped). (d) No genotype effect, no environment effect, G×E interaction (crossover).

This pattern of behavior was observed in the group raised in standard cages, as well as in the group raised in enriched cages. There is no G×E interaction effect in this condition, because the genetic effect does not depend on the environmental condition.

Figure 3.7(c) illustrates a potential outcome when a genetic effect is observed in the group raised in the enriched conditions, but not in the group raised in the standard conditions. This hypothetical example illustrates a G×E interaction effect. The genetic effect depends on the environments to which the animals were exposed. One could hypothesize that the standard (i.e., high-risk) environmental conditions are sufficient to result in maximum depression-like symptoms in the tested mice regardless of their genotype. However, when raised in an enriched (i.e., low-risk) environment, the mice with lower genetic risk (i.e., aA and AA) displayed less depression-like behavior. The main effects of both genotype and environment are likely to be significant, but small, when this pattern of results is observed.

Figure 3.7(d) illustrates a potential outcome that is a dramatic G×E interaction effect. This hypothetical example shows a crossover interaction, where the genotype displaying the least depression-like behavior in one environment, displays the most in the alternative environment, and vice versa. This pattern of G×E interaction effect has the interesting property that neither the genotype effect nor the environmental effect is statistically significant.

In the classical quantitative genetics model, if a genetic effect is manifest only in certain environments, but not in others, it cannot be directly inherited, and therefore does not contribute to additive genetic variance for the trait. When partitioning trait variance in a population, the amount due to these genetic effects that are dependent on environmental context can be assigned to $V_{G×E}$. For our purposes, this conceptualization is sufficient. However, it should be noted that sophisticated quantitative genetic models can partition some dominance and interactive effects to additive genetic variation (Huang & Mackay, 2016).

3.4.3 Genotypes and Environment Are Not Randomly Distributed

Another factor that can contribute to quantitative trait variation is that genotypes may not be distributed randomly across environments. That is, there are correlations among genotypes and environments, whereby certain genotypes that impact a trait may be found (or placed) in certain environments that also affect the trait. How do genotypes, which are located in individuals, end up in certain environments? Let us consider the three types of genotype–environment correlations that have been described (Plomin, DeFries, & Loehlin, 1977; see Figure 3.8). To illustrate GE correlations, it may be useful to think about hypothetical genotypes and environments that impact some aspect of athletic performance, like running speed.

A passive genotype–environment correlation occurs when a particular genotype tends to be found in certain environments. The correlation would be positive if the genotype and the environment affected the trait in the same direction (i.e., both increased or both decreased), and negative if one tended to increase the trait while the other tended to decrease the trait. Consider a hypothetical example where athletically inclined parents are likely to pass some genes to their offspring that are associated with increased running speed. In addition, those parents, because of their interests in sports, expose their children to athletic opportunities, such as enrolling them in soccer leagues, and encouraging them to participate in sports. The children would grow up watching and discussing sports with their parents, and they would have access to sporting equipment in the home. In this case, both the genotype and the environment are likely to increase athletic ability in the child. The children receive their genotypes and their environments, in this example, passively from their parents. The connection between the genotypes and environments was not a result of the child's

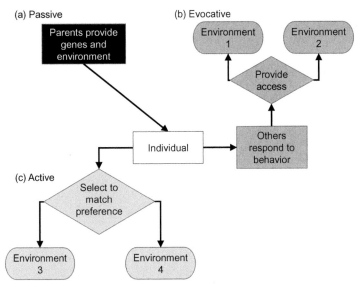

Figure 3.8. **Genotype–environment correlations.** Genotypes are not randomly distributed across environments. (a) Passive GE correlations occur when individuals receive both genes and environments from their parents. (b) Evocative GE correlations occur when a genetically influenced trait in an individual is observed by another who provides access to an environment. (c) Active GE correlations occur when genetically influenced preferences predispose an individual to choose environments that correspond to the preference.

preferences or behavior but was due to the genes that the parents contributed to their child, as well as the preferences and behavior of their parents that shaped the child's environment (see Figure 3.8(a)).

An **evocative genotype–environment correlation** occurs when an individual with a particular genotype behaves in a way that is observed by others who then provide access to a particular environment to that individual. In this case, the individual in question is not selecting the environment, but they are exhibiting some type of behavior that evokes a response in someone else that involves enabling access to an environment based on that behavior. For example, if a teacher observes a child running fast in the playground, that teacher might find a place for the child on the school's soccer team. The teacher observed a particular talent and provided an opportunity for that talent to be expressed, and perhaps enhanced through training. This situation would represent a positive evocative genotype–environment correlation (see Figure 3.8(b)). On the other hand, if a teacher observed that a student tended to act aggressively in the playground, they might assign the student to an afterschool program to reduce aggressive behavior. This example would represent a negative evocative genotype–environment correlation because the behavioral tendency due to a hypothetical "aggression" genotype was minimized by the afterschool program.

An **active genotype–environment correlation** occurs when an individual selects an environment that corresponds to their own genetic predispositions. For example, if a child recognizes that they have athletic ability and they are motivated to compete and derive satisfaction from being on teams, all of which are thought to have some basis in genetics, they may choose to pursue athletic opportunities (see Figure 3.8(c)). In this case, the individual takes an active role in selecting different environments, which contrasts with passive and evocative genotype–environment correlations. In each of the three correlation types, genotypes, and the environments in which they are found are not independent.

In practice, it is difficult to empirically quantify GE correlations for traits in humans, but it is worthwhile to note their existence. Overall, as you can see, when a quantitative trait varies in a population it is possible to estimate how much of the variation is due to genetic and environmental sources. However, the precision of those estimates may not be high, and the estimates are population-specific. It is important to point out that the coverage of partitioning variance in this text is introductory, and therefore not intended to fully prepare students to dive headlong into quantitative genetics. For a more thorough treatment of approaches to partitioning variance of quantitative traits, see the classic introduction to quantitative genetics by Falconer and Mackay (1996) or the more advanced by Lynch and Walsh (1998).

Check-up

- What is the difference between shared and non-shared environment?
- What is a crossover G×E interaction, and what does the existence of such an interaction suggest about genetic effects?
- Describe the three types of GE correlations.

3.5 Heritability Indexes Degree of Phenotypic Variance Due to Genetic Effects

By now, you may be wondering why all the fuss about partitioning variance? In the early part of the twentieth century, efforts to understand the contribution of genetic variation to trait variation in populations established the field of quantitative genetics and drove the development of fundamental statistical tools that are still widely used today, such as correlation and regression. Those involved in agriculture were especially interested in being able to determine whether selective breeding programs for economically important traits, such as milk production in dairy cattle, would be successful. It makes sense to selectively breed for a trait only if a significant amount of variance for the trait in the population is due to additive genetic factors.

The ratio of genetic variance to overall phenotypic variance is called broad sense heritability ($H^2 = V_G/V_P$) and is considered an index of the degree of phenotypic variation that is due to all sources of genetic variation, including additive and non-additive (i.e., dominance and epistasis) genetic effects. Broad sense heritability is of little interest to those desiring to alter the distribution of the trait in subsequent generations by selective breeding because the inclusion of dominance and epistatic effects in the numerator does not allow a precise estimate of additive genetic effects. It is important to focus on additive genetic effects because they represent the genetic inheritance that is passed from parent to offspring.

The ratio of additive genetic variance to overall phenotypic variances is called narrow sense heritability ($h^2 = V_A/V_P$) and is considered an index of the fraction of phenotypic variation that is due to additive genetic variation. Heritability estimates, both broad and narrow sense, range between 0 and 1. In general, when offspring closely resemble parents on a trait, narrow sense heritability estimates for the trait are high, and when offspring do not resemble parents on a trait, narrow sense heritability estimates for it are low. A program of selective breeding is likely to produce changes in the phenotypic distribution of subsequent generations if the narrow sense heritability estimate of the trait is greater than zero. Traits with higher heritability estimates are expected to attain selection gains more quickly than traits with lower heritability estimates.

Because heritability estimates are *ratios* of observed genetic and environmental variances measured in a particular population, they are not fixed features of the trait. Rather, they are dependent on the available genetic variation sampled in the population and on the environment to which members of the population have been exposed. As you may recall from our example of mice being tested for depression-like behaviors in the forced swim test, the available genetic or environmental variation was completely dependent on the experimental condition. It is entirely possible to have heritability estimates that range anywhere from 0 to 1 for the same trait depending on the populations and environments tested.

3.5.1 Genetic Relatedness and Phenotypic Similarity Are Used to Estimate Heritability

Now, let us turn our attention to how heritability is estimated. Our focus will be on concepts and will remain somewhat broad. As mentioned previously, detailed coverage of quantitative genetics is beyond the scope of this book.

Methods for estimating heritability were developed long before it was possible to collect molecular genetic data (e.g., genotypes or DNA sequence). However, as Mendel, Morgan, and others amply demonstrated, it is possible to make genetic inferences by knowing familial relatedness or by controlling it through a breeding design. Phenotypic resemblance between related individuals can result from the sharing of genes and/or environments. For resemblance due to genetic sources, those individuals who share more genetic material (i.e., are more closely related) should be more phenotypically similar. This is the basic logic that underlies heritability estimation.

We can quantify genetic relatedness in a pedigree (see Figure 3.9) because of our basic understanding of sexual reproduction. Consider a hypothetical pedigree of a target individual, also known as a proband (or index case). The proband shares 50 percent of their genetic material with each parent. In fact, during meiosis (see Chapter 4) the genetic complement of each parent is halved,

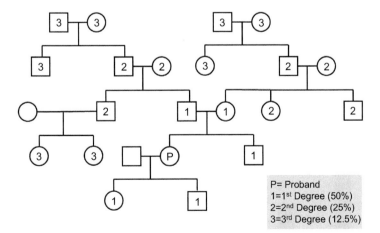

P= Proband
1=1st Degree (50%)
2=2nd Degree (25%)
3=3rd Degree (12.5%)

Figure 3.9. **Pedigree indicating genetic relatedness to a proband.** The genetic relatedness between family members can be known (e.g., by descent) or estimated based on their degree of relatedness. First-degree relatives (i.e., parents, siblings, and offspring) share 50% of their genetic material. Second-degree relatives (e.g., grandparents) share 25% of their genetic material. Third-degree relatives (e.g., great-grandparents) share 12.5% of their genetic material. Genetic relatedness is halved in each subsequent generation. The open circle and square represent individuals unrelated to the proband (P).

during gamete formation. The joining of sperm and egg at fertilization results in an offspring that shares half of their genetic material with father and half with mother. For the same reason, the proband shares 50 percent of their genetic material with their own offspring. Such genetic related-ness of the proband's direct ancestors and direct descendants is halved in each generation. The proband shares 25 percent of their genetic material with grandparents, and 12.5 percent with great-grandparents, and so on. The proband shares an average of 50 percent of their genetic material with their siblings. However, because of the randomness inherent in meiosis, siblings do not inherit the exact same set of genes from their parents (unless they are identical twins). Therefore, siblings share *on average* 50 percent of their genetic material. Modern quantitative genetic models produce heritability estimates by examining the phenotypic similarity of individuals with known genetic relatedness.

One of the important first uses of heritability estimates was to predict the potential outcome of a regimen of selective breeding for an agriculturally relevant phenotype in a given population. For example, in cattle, yearling weight is an economically relevant trait because it is a good index of the eventual weight of the animal when it will be sold for its meat. The yearling weights of parents and their offspring can be measured and used to estimate the heritability of the trait.

Of course, the same approach can be used to estimate the heritability of behavioral traits that are economically relevant as well, such as temperament in cattle. Aggressive cattle can be difficult to handle, may cause injuries to humans or to other cattle, or may damage equipment, all of which could be costly. Therefore, it is of interest to both the beef and dairy cattle industry to breed cattle with temperaments that make them easier to handle. The heritability of relevant temperament traits in cattle have been estimated by collecting data from parents and offspring (see Figure 3.10). Significant non-zero heritability estimates of economically relevant temperament traits in both beef and dairy cattle suggest that selectively breeding for these traits is likely to result in subsequent generations of cattle that are easier to handle.

Phenotypic similarity between parents and offspring is assessed by first measuring the phenotypes for each of the individuals in question. Regression analysis is typically used to assess the extent of similarity between the score of the offspring and the average score of the parents (i.e., mid-parent value), such that the estimated regression parameter (b) equals the narrow sense heritability (i.e., $b = h^2$). Similar statistical approaches that assess phenotypic similarity of individuals with known genetic relatedness have been extended to siblings and to other more distant relatives. The statistical details of such approaches are beyond the scope of this book, but they all rely on comparing the phenotypic similarity of relatives and weighting the relationships based on their genetic relatedness.

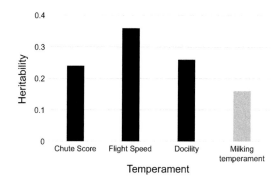

Figure 3.10. **Heritability estimates of temperament traits in cattle.** Heritability estimates of three temperament traits in beef cattle and one in dairy cattle are shown. After Haskell, Simm, & Turner (2014).

3.5.2 Twin Studies Are Used to Estimate Heritability in Humans

The most commonly used method for estimating heritability in human populations is the twin study. The basic twin study design is a special case of the approach discussed in the previous section, namely assessing phenotypic similarity for individuals with known genetic relatedness. The fundamental logic is that when individual differences in traits are influenced by genetic differences, those who share more genetic material should be more similar behaviorally than are those who share less genetic material.

Twins are siblings that result from the same pregnancy (see Box 3.2). Monozygotic (MZ) twins, also known as identical twins, share 100 percent of their genetic material (with minor exceptions such as *de novo* mutations), whereas dizygotic (DZ) twins, also known as fraternal twins, share an average of 50 percent of their genetic material.

Box 3.2 Critical Concept: Twinning

Although the biological mechanisms that lead to twinning are not fully understood, the most accepted model is that DZ twins are produced when two separate sperm fertilize two separate eggs, and MZ twins are produced when a single sperm fertilizes a single egg, which subsequently divides into two embryos (McNamara, Kane, Craig, Short, & Umstad, 2016). In this model, the timing of the splitting of the zygote determines whether the twins share embryonic membranes (chorion [outermost] and amnion [innermost]). DZ twins do not share either chorion or amnion (i.e., are dichorionic and diamniotic). Monozygotic twins can be (1) dichorionic and diamniotic, (2) monochorionic and diamniotic, (3) monochorionic and monoamniotic, or (4) conjoined (not shown on the figure), depending on when the zygotes split, early to late, respectively (see Figure 3.11).

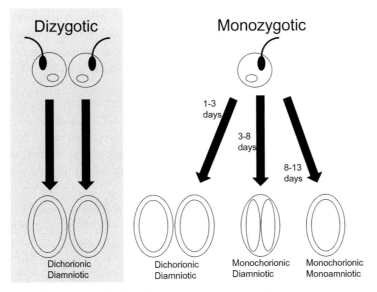

Figure 3.11. **Types of twins.** Dizygotic twins are the result of two separate sperm cells fertilizing two separate ova, and each twin develops *in utero* in their own chorionic and amniotic membranes. Monozygotic twins are the result of a single sperm fertilizing a single ovum, with a single zygote splitting and continuing development as two. The type of prenatal environment for MZ twins is thought to be determined by the timing of the zygotic split.

The degree of sharing of the prenatal environment for MZ twins may be at least partially determined by the embryonic membrane configuration. It is possible that the sharing of prenatal environment plays a role in later behavioral similarity, but at this time, the available evidence does not permit definitive statements (Marceau et al., 2016).

In a twin study, pairs of both MZ and DZ twins are phenotyped for the traits of interest. Phenotypic similarity of pairs of MZ twins and pairs of DZ twins is assessed using statistical models that can control for other variables such as age and sex. When the trait of interest is measured on a continuous scale, the correlation between the scores of twin pairs in the study sample is calculated. When the behavior of interest is a category (e.g., diagnosis of major depressive disorder versus healthy), then the probability that a twin who has the trait has a co-twin who also has the trait (i.e., the concordance) is calculated.

To estimate heritability from such data, one merely doubles the difference between the MZ and DZ correlations (or concordances): $h^2 = 2(MZ_{corr}-DZ_{corr})$. More sophisticated statistical designs are often used to estimate heritability in twin studies to allow investigation of multiple phenotypes, to control for potential confounds, to include additional family members, and so on. However, the basic idea is the same for traits with non-zero heritability: that individuals who share more genetic material are more behaviorally similar than those who share less.

This classic twin study design is also based on the notion that environmental factors associated with trait similarity are distributed similarly for MZ and DZ twin pairs. This is called the equal environments assumption. On its face, it might seem that this assumption would not hold up to scrutiny. It seems obvious that MZ twins are often dressed alike, may be given similar names, and may sometimes be confused for one another. Whereas DZ twins are usually not dressed alike and generally look no more like each other than do comparably aged siblings. It is important to keep in mind that it is entirely possible that none of those environmental factors, which seem to be similar for MZ twin pairs, are actually associated with individual differences in the behavior of interest. In fact, it seems that even though the equal environment assumption may not be "strictly valid," its impact on the precision of heritability estimates is likely modest (Felson, 2014).

Quantifying the impact of a violation of the equal environment assumption might not be possible for a given case, but if it is violated it will tend to inflate MZ similarity to some degree. It is important to note here that for most studies, heritability estimates have rather large confidence intervals. In other words, heritability estimates are not tremendously precise to begin with. Often, we are more interested in whether the heritability estimate is significantly different from zero than in estimating an exact value with high precision.

The twin study has been a mainstay of human behavior genetics for over half a century. A recent meta-analysis of all twin studies conducted between 1958 and 2012 reported an average heritability estimate of traits to be 0.49 (Polderman et al., 2015). The authors analyzed the findings of 2,748 publications that studied 17,804 traits in over 14 million twin pairs. Most of the traits studied (69 percent) fit a simple model where trait similarity was due to additive genetic variance. The twin study design has made important contributions to our understanding that individual differences in behavior are due, in part, to genetic differences.

3.5.3 Adoption Studies Are Used to Estimate Heritability in Humans

One of the drawbacks of studies that compare phenotypic similarity of people growing up in the same family is that family members share both genes and environments. In studies of non-human animals, researchers can control the environments in which subjects are raised to better understand the role of environmental variation in behavioral similarity. For example, cross-fostering designs involve purposefully placing the offspring of one set of parents with another to better understand the role of potential differences in parenting. In study designs with human participants, however, it is obviously unethical to separate parents and children for scientific purposes. But when children are adopted into other families it presents an opportunity for researchers to attempt to disentangle the roles of heredity and environment in behavioral similarity.

Adoption studies can be considered a special case of the general approach to comparing behavioral similarity of individuals with known genetic relatedness. Biological children share 50 percent of their genetic material with their biological parents, and if they are raised in the same families, they can be considered to also share 100 percent of their environment. However, when children are adopted away, they still share 50 percent of their genetic material with their biological parents, but they do not share environments. The adoptees share none of their genetic material with their adoptive families, but they do share environments. In this case, behavioral similarity between adopted away offspring and biological parents (and biological siblings who may remain with the biological parents) is considered to be due to genetic similarity. Behavioral similarity between adopted offspring and adoptive parents is considered to be environmental because they do not share genes, but they do share environments.

There are two main types of comparisons that are made in adoption studies based on the particular question of interest. First, if a biological parent has a particular disorder, like schizophrenia, what is the probability that their adopted away child will also develop the disorder (i.e., be concordant)? In this case, the biological parent is considered the proband. Second, when an adopted child develops a disorder, what are the concordance rates in biological versus adoptive parents? If a biological parent is more likely to share the diagnosis, then genetic cause is inferred, whereas if an adoptive parent is more likely to share the diagnosis, then an environmental cause is inferred. In this case, the adopted child is considered the proband. Of course, adopted away children share prenatal, and often some postnatal environment with their biological family. In addition, non-random placement with adoptive families, sometimes with relatives, can also produce some environmental similarities. Because of such limitations inherent in adoption studies, heritability estimates derived from them are unlikely to be precise.

3.5.4 Using Selective Breeding to Estimate Heritability in Non-Human Animals

Another, more direct, approach to estimate heritability is selective breeding for the trait of interest. In fact, selective breeding puts theoretical heritability estimation to the test because it enables the breeder to observe the actual change in the trait distribution from one generation to the next. The heritability estimate derived from the observed response to selection is called the realized heritability. Of course, it should go without saying that estimating heritability by selective breeding is not an option for researchers studying human populations.

Selective breeding involves controlling which individuals mate to produce offspring to make up the next generation. To determine which individuals will become parents, all eligible individuals should first be phenotyped for the trait of interest. Only individuals that score high on a trait should be mated to each other to establish the "High" selected line, and similarly, only those that score low on the trait should be mated to each other to establish the "Low" line. Most of the agricultural improvements that have been realized in economically relevant traits in both plants and animals have been the result of such directional selection.

Although selective breeding has been a mainstay in agriculture, it has also been widely used to investigate the role of genetic variation in individual differences in behaviors. Let us consider an example of selective breeding for depressive-like behavior in rats assessed using the forced swim test. In this example, divergent selection for depressive-like behavior was conducted for eighteen generations (Weiss, Cierpial, & West, 1998). In each generation, each individual rat in the study was tested in the forced swim test. During each 15-minute test session (i.e., 900 seconds), the amount of time (in seconds) spent actively struggling was recorded, as was the time spent passively floating. An "activity" score was calculated for each animal tested that represented an overall index of depressive-like behavior by subtracting the number of seconds spent floating from the number of seconds spent struggling. A negative activity score means that the rat spent more time floating than struggling. In contrast, a positive activity score means that the animal spent more time struggling than floating.

Selective breeding was initiated with eighty-four male and forty-two female Sprague–Dawley albino rats. Six pairs of males and females that had low activity scores were mated to establish the low swim activity line (i.e., SwLo), and nine pairs of males and females that had high activity scores were mated to establish the high swim activity line (i.e., SwHi). Table 3.1 presents mean activity scores for the overall sample of males and females tested prior to selection (i.e., generation 0), as well as mean activity scores for the parents and their offspring. These data can be used to estimate realized heritability for the activity index, but first it is necessary to calculate the selection differential in generation 0 (S), and the response to selection (R) in generation S1. The selection differential (S) is the difference between the mean score of those selected for breeding and the overall population mean in generation 0. For example, the mean of the males

Table 3.1 Realized heritability after one generation of divergent selection for depressive-like behavior

	N	Mean activity score	Selection differential (S)	Response to selection (R)	$h^2 = R/S$
Generation S0					
All ♂	84	-180	–	–	–
All ♀	42	-200	–	–	–
SwLo ♂	6	-479	-299	–	–
SwLo ♀	6	-277	-77	–	–
SwHi ♂	9	-7	173	–	–
SwHi ♀	9	-85	115	–	–
Generation S1					
SwLo ♂	43	-340	–	-160	0.54
SwLo ♀	56	-160	–	40	-0.52*
SwHi ♂	45	-90	–	90	0.52
SwHi ♀	41	-80	–	120	1.04*

Note: After Weiss et al. (1998). *h^2 estimates less than zero or greater than one are uninterpretable.

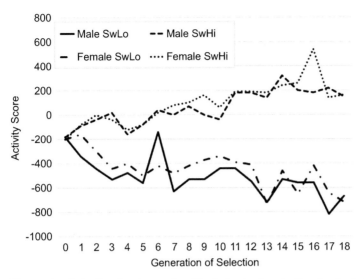

Figure 3.12. **Selection for depression-like behavior in rats.** Results of selection for high and low depression-like behavior for male and female rats across 18 generations of divergent selection. After Weiss et al. (1998).

selected as parents (i.e., $SwLo_{S0}$ males) was -479, and the overall mean of males tested in generation 0 was -180. So, for these males, S = -479 – (-180) = -299. The mean activity score of their male offspring (i.e., $SwLo_{S1}$ males) was -340. **Response to selection** (R) is the difference between the mean score of the S1 generation males and the overall male population mean in generation 0. So, for $SwLo_{S1}$ males R = -340 – (-180) = -160. Realized heritability is the ratio of selection response (R) to the selection differential (S) or h^2 = R/S = 0.54. Because selective breeding does not typically produce smooth progress across generations, it is not advisable to use data from only one generation to estimate realized heritability; however, it suffices here to illustrate the approach.

Figure 3.12 shows the selection curves for the SwLo and SwHi lines across the eighteen generations of selection. These selection curves are typical for divergent selection for behavior traits in that the response to selection continues over many generations, and that selection gains are sometimes lost in subsequent generations. The fact that selective breeding for a trait is successful provides strong evidence that genetic variation plays a role in individual differences in the behavior. In this case, it is easy to see that the program of selective breeding resulted in one line of animals that spent most of the time during the swim test passively floating (i.e., negative scores; SwLo), and another line of animals that spent the majority of the swim test time actively struggling (i.e., positive scores; SwHi). This, and other convergent evidence that is covered in Chapter 9, indicates that individual differences in behaviors associated with depression are at least partly due to genetic differences between them.

Check-up

- What is the difference between narrow and broad sense heritability estimates?
- Describe the basic logic of heritability estimation using relatives.
- Compare and contrast twin and adoption study designs.
- Why is heritability estimation important for agricultural breeding efforts?

3.6 Beware of the Potential for Misunderstanding and Bias

Although heritability estimation has been and continues to be an important tool for continued progress in agriculture, and has led to important insights in human behavior genetics, it is important to consider the term heritability and why it may lead to misunderstanding about the inheritance of quantitative traits (Stoltenberg, 1997). The scientific term heritability refers to a specific quantitative genetics statistic that indexes the proportion of overall phenotypic variance in a population that is due to additive genetic variance in that population. Such a statistic has little value to anyone other than livestock breeders and researchers. Unfortunately, to the public, the term heritability has another, more general meaning: capable of being inherited. The folk definition is without the nuance of polygenic inheritance and without the distinction between populations and individuals. Furthermore, the public's understanding of heritability is focused on the trait itself, not population variance in the trait. While this folk definition is not completely unrelated to the technical definition, they are not the same, and it is easy to conflate them. From a scientific standpoint, when traits are heritable, it means that at least some of the trait variance in the population is due to additive genetic variance. From a folk standpoint, when traits are heritable, they are genetically determined and passed intact from parent to offspring.

It is important to emphasize that when heritability estimates for a trait are non-zero it does not mean that the trait is passed down intact from parents to offspring. It means that individual differences for that trait are, at least in part, due to genetic differences between them. Traits are not passed down from parents to offspring, genes are. Using the term heritability, which has long been used in the English language to refer to non-genetic inheritance (i.e., property), to refer to a specific quantitative genetic statistic may have resulted in the misinterpretation of that statistic, and by doing so, reinforced notions of genetic determinism. We all need to be cautious when thinking about heritability estimates so that we keep in mind meiosis, polygenes, and individual differences in populations, and avoid the simplistic "traits are inherited" trap.

3.6.1 Genetic Essentialism May Lead to Deterministic Thinking

The goal of partitioning variance in quantitative traits is to understand causation. In behavior genetics we are trying to understand what causes individual differences in behaviors. The approaches outlined in this chapter focus on attributing causes of behavioral similarity to genetic sources, sometimes called nature, and to non-genetic sources, sometimes called nurture. For those adequately trained in the nuances of interpreting heritability estimates, who recognize that the estimates are somewhat imprecise, population-specific, and dependent on existing genetic variation and environmental exposure, they can be quite informative. However, heritability estimates are ripe for misunderstanding because of the commonly understood meaning of the term heritable, and because of an apparent cognitive bias in how people think about genetic causation called genetic essentialism (Dar-Nimrod & Heine, 2011; Lynch, Morandini, Dar-Nimrod, & Griffiths, 2019).

In terms of causal attributions, people appear to give genes a privileged status, such that when learning that genetic variation plays a role in individual differences in a behavior, the genetic influence tends to be considered primary. In other words, genetic causes tend to be considered more important and more powerful than other causes. It is thought that genes reflect the essence of an individual, which can be interpreted to mean that evidence of genetic causation represents outcomes that are unchangeable, fundamental, shared by all, and natural (Dar-Nimrod & Heine, 2011). Such a genetic essentialist bias can lead people to believe that if a trait like depression has a non-zero heritability estimate (which it does), it means that anyone with genetic risk for depression will necessarily develop the condition. For individuals who have a family history of a psychiatric disorder, learning about its genetic basis can seem hopeless. The genetic essentialist position places too much weight on the genetic side of the equation and undervalues the side of the environmental influences.

The variance partitioning approach, with its focus on heritability estimation, may unintentionally lead to an emphasis on genetic causation that promotes a tendency toward genetic essentialism. Thus, the nature vs. nurture debate, where one causal factor is declared the "winner" oversimplifies the causal architecture of complex behaviors, misrepresents the outcomes of variance partitioning approaches, and may inadvertently activate a fundamental cognitive bias. Behavior genetics investigators are generally well versed in the strengths and limitations of their methods, but the nuances of their findings are often not appreciated by the public. It is important to be mindful that non-zero heritability estimates for behaviors do not mean that genes cause behaviors, but that they are evidence that individual differences in those behaviors are at least partially due to genetic differences between individuals.

Genetic determinism describes a position in which genes exert strong control over traits. In this view, the environment has little influence on outcomes. It is a view that led to the eugenics movement, which included forced sterilizations in the US of those considered to carry genes for traits such as "feeblemindedness," and to the Holocaust in Nazi Germany (see Chapter 15). Those efforts were supported by leading scientists at the time. It is important to note that our current understanding of the influence of genetic variation on individual differences in behavior does not support genetic determinism.

Check-up

- Why is the term heritable ripe for confusion for non-scientists?
- What is genetic essentialism and why should students of behavior genetics be aware of it?

3.7 SUMMARY

- The debate between Mendelians and Biometricians focused on the application of an inheritance model for discrete traits to understand the inheritance of continuously varying traits. Extending the model to include polygenes established the field of quantitative genetics.
- Individual differences in quantitative traits are due to genetic and environmental factors. Variance partitioning estimates the extent to which phenotypic variation in a population is due to genes, the environment, and their interplay (i.e., interactions and correlations). G×E interaction exists when genetic effects are dependent on environmental factors. GE correlation exists when genes are not randomly distributed across environments.
- Heritability is a statistic that indexes the degree to which genetic variation explains phenotypic variation. Heritability is estimated using various approaches where phenotypic similarity is assessed for individuals with known genetic relatedness. Basic approaches include parent–offspring regressions, directional selection, and twin and adoption studies.
- The term heritable has a specific meaning in behavior genetics (i.e., non-zero heritability estimate for a trait), and a general one in the English language (i.e., capable of being inherited). This dual meaning may result in misunderstanding of the complexity of inheritance for the public.

Learning about genetic influences on a trait can activate a cognitive bias, called genetic essentialism, which can lead to overly simplistic notions of inheritance and genetic determinism.

RECOMMENDED READING

- Dar-Nimrod, I., & Heine, S. J. (2011). Genetic essentialism: On the deceptive determinism of DNA. *Psychol Bull*, *137*(5), 800–818.
- Falconer, D. S., & Mackay, T. F. C. (1996). *Introduction to Quantitative Genetics* (4th ed.). New York: Pearson.
- Fisher, R. A. (1918). The correlation between relatives on the supposition of Mendelian inheritance. *Transactions of the Royal Society of Edinburgh*, *52*, 399–433.
- Kempthorne, O. (1997). Heritability: Uses and abuses. *Genetica*, 99: 109–112.
- Lynch, M., & Walsh, B. (1998). *Genetics and the Analysis of Quantitative Traits*. Sunderland, MA: Sinauer Associates, Inc.

REFERENCES

Dar-Nimrod, I., & Heine, S. J. (2011). Genetic essentialism: On the deceptive determinism of DNA. *Psychol Bull*, *137*(5), 800–818. doi:10.1037/a0021860

Falconer, D. S., & Mackay, T. F. C. (1996). *Introduction to Quantitative Genetics* (4th ed.). New York: Pearson.

Felson, J. (2014). What can we learn from twin studies? A comprehensive evaluation of the equal environments assumption. *Soc Sci Res*, *43*, 184–199. doi:10.1016/j.ssresearch.2013.10.004

Fisher, R. A. (1918). The correlation between relatives on the supposition of Mendelian inheritance. *Transactions of the Royal Society of Edinburgh*, *52*, 399–433.

Gillham, N. W. (2015). The battle between the biometricians and the Mendelians: How Sir Francis Galton's work caused his disciples to reach conflicting conclusions about the hereditary mechanism. *Science & Education*, *24*(1–2), 61–75.

Haskell, M. J., Simm, G., & Turner, S. P. (2014). Genetic selection for temperament traits in dairy and beef cattle. *Front Genet*, *5*, 368. doi:10.3389/fgene.2014.00368

Huang, W., & Mackay, T. F. (2016). The genetic architecture of quantitative traits cannot be inferred from variance component analysis. *PLoS Genet*, *12*(11), e1006421. doi:10.1371/journal.pgen.1006421

Lynch, K. E., Morandini, J. S., Dar-Nimrod, I., & Griffiths, P. E. (2019). Causal reasoning about human behavior genetics: Synthesis and future directions. *Behav Genet*, *49*(2), 221–234. doi:10.1007/s10519-018-9909-z

Lynch, M., & Walsh, B. (1998). *Genetics and Analysis of Quantitative Traits*. Sunderland, MA: Sinauer Associates, Inc.

Marceau, K., McMaster, M. T., Smith, T. F., Daams, J. G., van Beijsterveldt, C. E., Boomsma, D. I., & Knopik, V. S. (2016). The prenatal environment in twin studies: A review on chorionicity. *Behav Genet*, *46*(3), 286–303. doi:10.1007/s10519-016-9782-6

McNamara, H. C., Kane, S. C., Craig, J. M., Short, R. V., & Umstad, M. P. (2016). A review of the mechanisms and evidence for typical and atypical twinning. *Am J Obstet Gynecol*, *214*(2), 172–191. doi:10.1016/j.ajog.2015.10.930

Plomin, R., & Daniels, D. (1987). Why are children in the same family so different from one another? *Behav Brain Sci*, *10*(1), 1–16.

Plomin, R., DeFries, J. C., & Loehlin, J. C. (1977). Genotype-environment interaction and correlation in the analysis of human behavior. *Psychol Bull, 84*(2), 309–322.

Polderman, T. J., Benyamin, B., de Leeuw, C. A., Sullivan, P. F., van Bochoven, A., Visscher, P. M., & Posthuma, D. (2015). Meta-analysis of the heritability of human traits based on fifty years of twin studies. *Nat Genet, 47*(7), 702–709. doi:10.1038/ng.3285

Porsolt, R. D., Le Pichon, M., & Jalfre, M. (1977). Depression: A new animal model sensitive to antidepressant treatments. *Nature, 266*(5604), 730–732. doi:10.1038/266730a0

Russell, E. S. (1985). A history of mouse genetics. *Annu Rev Genet, 19*, 1–28. doi:10.1146/annurev.ge.19.120185.000245

Stoltenberg, S. F. (1997). Coming to terms with heritability. *Genetica, 99*(2–3), 89–96.

Weiss, J. M., Cierpial, M. A., & West, C. H. (1998). Selective breeding of rats for high and low motor activity in a swim test: Toward a new animal model of depression. *Pharmacol Biochem Behav, 61*(1), 49–66. doi:10.1016/s0091-3057(98)00075-6

Part II Molecules and Cells

4 Genes

Gregor Mendel provided the framework for understanding genetics by systematically observing phenotypes in the context of breeding experiments even though he did not understand the underlying molecular biology. His theoretical model used the abstract notion of "factors" that we have since come to call genes. Quantitative genetics extends Mendel's theoretical model to include many genes with small effects, called polygenes, to investigate phenotypic resemblance for those with known familial relatedness. Quantitative genetics does not require knowledge of the underlying molecular processes. In this chapter, we begin to focus on the core molecular mechanisms involved in heredity. We describe the molecules of heredity, how they are passed from one generation to the next, and how they participate in a variety of biological systems and functions. By understanding genetics at the molecular level, we will be better prepared to understand the mechanisms by which familial resemblance is achieved.

4.1 Chromosomes Carry Hereditary Material

As we discussed in Chapter 2, Thomas Hunt Morgan and his students used experimental crosses of *Drosophila melanogaster* to confirm the chromosomal theory of inheritance, which stated that the hereditary material was on structures called chromosomes that are found in the nuclei of eukaryotic cells.

The first person to point out that chromosomes acted in accordance with Mendelian Laws was a 25-year-old graduate student named Walter S. Sutton just two years after Mendel's work was rediscovered (Sutton, 1902, 1903). Sutton grew up on a Kansas farm, and while in graduate school (first at the University of Kansas, and then at Columbia University) he investigated the cytology of cell division by closely observing grasshopper spermatogonia and oogonia. His work took advantage of recent developments in microscopes and dyes that made cellular structures, like chromosomes (i.e., "colored bodies"), possible to see. Sutton examined many germ cells that were in the process of dividing during the formation of gametes (i.e., sperm and eggs) to study the behavior of their chromosomes. Sutton considered most of the chromosomes in a dividing cell "ordinary" (i.e., autosomes). He noted that many of them differed in size, they appeared in even numbers, they consisted of two "limbs" joined near the middle, and that same sized chromosomes paired up at a certain stage of cell division. Sutton also described an "accessory" chromosome that did not appear to have a partner with which to pair. The accessory chromosome he identified was an X-chromosome. He did not identify the other sex chromosome (i.e., Y-chromosome) because grasshoppers do not have them. Sutton recognized that these observations and others he reported were consistent with the notion that chromosomes were the "physical basis of the Mendelian law of heredity" (Sutton, 1902). Let us consider the behavior of chromosomes during cell division in more detail (see Box 4.1).

Box 4.1 Critical Concept: *Homo sapiens* Chromosomes

There are twenty-four distinct human chromosomes. Twenty-two of them are autosomes and are labeled chromosomes 1 through 22 based on their size with chromosome 1 being the largest and chromosome 22 being the smallest. Humans also carry some combination of sex chromosomes: the large X or the small Y. Typically, females carry two X-chromosomes, and males carry an X and a Y. An individual's chromosome complement can be visualized by generating a karyotype, which are photographs of chromosomes stained during cell division, taken through a microscope, and arranged neatly for inspection (see Figure 4.1).

In diploid species, like humans, one chromosome from each pair comes from the father and the other comes from the mother. Together, the two are known as a homologous pair. During cell division each member of the homologous pair replicates into two sister chromatids that are joined by a centromere. Typically, most human cells carry a full complement of forty-six chromosomes (2n); however, gametes typically carry a haploid (n) complement.

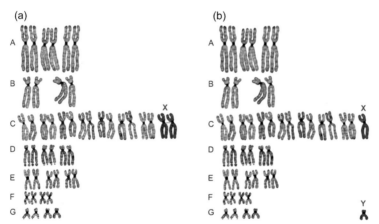

Figure 4.1. **Human karyotype.** Chromosome pairs are shown at metaphase. Twenty-two pairs of autosomes are organized by size for clarity. The chromosomal complements of females and males only differ by sex chromosomes: (a) Females typically carry two X-chromosomes. (b) Males typically carry one X-chromosome and one Y-chromosome. Source: BSIP / Contributor / Universal Images Group / Getty Images.

4.1.1 Meiosis: Producing Haploid Gametes

Typically, a sperm contains half of the father's genetic complement and an egg contains half of the mother's genetic complement. When a sperm and an egg unite in fertilization their haploid chromosome complements are combined to provide the resulting offspring with a full diploid set of chromosomes. Meiosis is the process by which those haploid gametes are produced. This reduction from diploid to haploid chromosome complement is critical in maintaining the proper number of chromosomes in the offspring. Atypical chromosome number can result in offspring that are either non-viable or have significant health-related consequences.

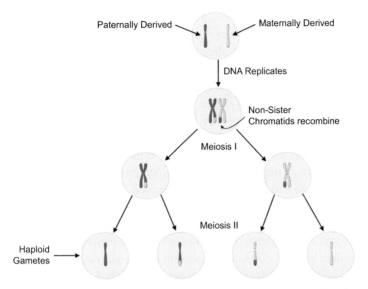

Figure 4.2. **Meiosis.** Four haploid gametes result from a germ cell undergoing meiosis. This process is the physical basis of the Mendelian Laws of Segregation and Independent Assortment. Each gamete is genetically unique. Genetic differences between gametes are due to recombination (i.e., reciprocal exchange of genetic material between non-sister chromatids in Meiosis I) and to the shuffling of chromatids into a given gamete such that any chromosome could be derived paternally, maternally, or as a result of recombination (i.e., Meiosis II). In this simplified drawing, only one of the 23 human chromosomes is shown. Haploid gametes contain a single copy of each chromosome. Source: Created with Biorender.com.

Meiosis starts with one complete diploid set of chromosomes, continues with the duplication of each chromosome, and ends with two successive rounds of nuclear divisions that produce four haploid sets of chromosomes. Meiosis is called a reduction division because the chromosome complement is reduced from diploid (2n) to haploid (n).

Before the start of meiosis, each germ cell contains its diploid complement of chromosomes that includes one paternal and one maternal copy of each chromosome. For simplicity Figure 4.2 shows the process of meiosis for a single chromosome pair. First, the chromosomes replicate to produce the familiar x-shape where the centromere holds together two identical sister chromatids. For a pair of homologous chromosomes, one member of the pair consists of two copies of the paternally derived chromosome joined at a centromere; and the other consists of two copies of the maternally derived chromosome also joined at a centromere. When a set of homologous chromosomes pair up, a maternally derived chromatid may exchange material with a paternally derived non-sister chromatid in a process called recombination, or crossing over. This is the same process that Morgan and his students hypothesized to explain departures from Mendelian independent assortment that they observed in some dihybrid crosses (see Chapter 2).

The first cell division, called meiosis I, divides the parent cell into two daughter cells. Each of the daughter cells contains a pair of sister chromatids joined at a centromere. The genetic makeup of the daughter cells differs from that of the parental cell. Chromosomes in daughter cells have undergone recombination and therefore carry a unique combination of chromosomes, some of which are paternally and maternally derived and others that are novel combinations of the two.

The second cell division, called meiosis II, divides each of the daughter cells into two more daughter cells, for a total of four gametes. Each of the gametes contains a haploid chromosome complement that is essentially genetically unique. Because of the randomness inherent in crossing over and in determining which chromatid ends up in a given daughter cell at each meiotic division across all chromosome pairs, it is statistically unlikely that any of the gametes produced carry identical mixtures of paternally and maternally derived chromosomes.

Gametes carry different combinations of genes from each parent; therefore, siblings share 50 percent of their genetic material *on average*. Each sibling shares 50 percent of their genetic material with their parents, but one sibling may have inherited more maternally derived chromosomal material than another. Perhaps you know of a family where one child resembles the father, and another more closely resembles the mother. Those children have likely inherited a different mix of chromosomes from their parents such that the first inherited more paternally derived chromosomal material and the second inherited more maternally derived chromosomal material. When you consider siblings in general, they share approximately 50 percent of their genetic material, but theoretically they could share anywhere from 0–100 percent. However, the mechanisms of crossing over and apportionment of chromosomes to daughter cells during meiosis robustly shuffles chromosomal material to produce siblings that share 50 percent of genetic material on average.

Meiosis and sexual reproduction generate genetic variability. Meiosis involves chromosomal crossing over and the assortment of chromosomes into gametes. Sexual reproduction involves the joining of gametes from different individuals. Both processes generate new combinations of genetic material that are the raw material of natural selection and are the basis of genetic individuality.

4.1.2 Mitosis: Producing Diploid Cells

Mitosis is a process of cell division that takes place in eukaryotic non-germ cells for the purpose of increasing the number of cells, as in growth. Most of the cells in eukaryotes are the product of mitosis. Mitosis should be considered a conservative process because it involves the production of daughter cells containing a chromosome complement that is identical to that of the parental cells (see Figure 4.3).

Before the start of mitosis, chromosomes are duplicated. As in meiosis, this chromosomal duplication produces sister chromatids joined by a centromere. Sister chromatid pairs are either

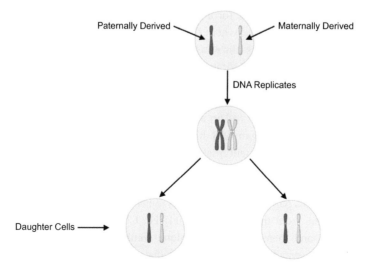

Figure 4.3. **Mitosis.** Two diploid cells are produced when a cell undergoes mitosis. The daughter cells contain the same number of chromosomes as the parent cells. Source: Created with Biorender.com.

paternally or maternally derived. Next, homologous pairs line up along the cell's midline. When the parent cell divides, one member of each sister chromatid pair is packaged into each daughter cell, which produces two daughter cells that each contain the same chromosome complement as the parental cell.

The capacity to make exact copies of the entire chromosome complement and to distribute them into daughter cells is a critical feature of eukaryotic cellular processes. Millions of cells undergo mitosis daily in a human body. Robust mechanisms of error checking and correction are in place so that mitosis is completed with high fidelity, although errors in mitosis are a common feature of cancers (Levine & Holland, 2018).

Although meiosis and mitosis both involve the duplication of chromosomes in a process of cell division, they have some key differences. Meiosis occurs in germ cells and produces haploid gametes, whereas mitosis takes place in all other cells and produces diploid copies of the parental cell. Meiosis produces genetic variability, whereas mitosis produces genetic constancy.

Check-up

- Describe Sutton's approach to studying chromosomes and what he observed.
- Why is it important for meiosis to be a "reduction division"?
- Describe the crossing over that occurs during meiosis.
- Why is mitosis considered to be a "conservative" process?

4.2 The Structure of DNA Determines Its Functions

Up to this point, we have not yet discussed what chromosomes are made of. One can learn a lot about genetics without knowing about the molecule of heredity. But of course, many people were focused on trying to identify the stuff of heredity after Mendel's work was published. Nucleic acids were discovered soon thereafter by Friedrich Miescher, a Swiss biochemist, in 1869. But neither ribonucleic acid (RNA) nor deoxyribonucleic acid (DNA) seemed to be a good candidate to carry the complex instructions thought to be necessary, because they each only used four chemical bases in their alphabets. Although their molecular structures were not known in the early decades of the twentieth century, it was known that RNA and DNA were made up of proteins and nucleic acids. RNA is composed of adenine (A), cytosine (C), guanine (G), and uracil (U), while DNA is composed of adenine, cytosine, guanine, and thymine (T). Most of the scientists at the time thought that protein was more likely than either nucleic acid to be a candidate for the molecule of heredity because it had greater potential for variety. It seemed logical that the molecule that was responsible for the amazing diversity of life on earth must require a more complex language than an alphabet of four bases could provide. The chemical alphabet that makes up proteins consists of twenty amino acids. It stood to reason that an alphabet of twenty letters would be superior to one of only four.

Most researchers were convinced that DNA was the genetic material by evidence from the study of bacteria. These studies were initiated by Frederick Griffith in the 1920s. He demonstrated that material from dead bacterial cells, called smooth (or S, for their shape), enabled a mutant form of bacteria, called rough (or R), to transform their shape to resemble the smooth form. In 1944, Oswald Avery and colleagues published a paper demonstrating that it was DNA that carried genetic

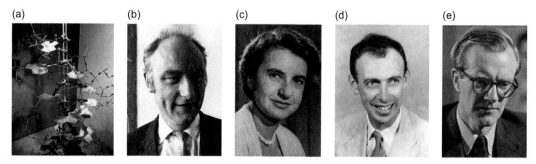

Figure 4.4. **Watson and Crick's double helix model of DNA.** (a) Physical model of the double helical structure of DNA constructed by Watson and Crick at Cambridge. (b) Francis Crick, (c) Rosalind Franklin, (d) James Watson, and (e) Maurice Wilkins. Sources: (a) Science & Society Picture Library / Contributor / SSPL / Getty Images. (b) Express / Stringer / Archive Photos / Getty Images. (c) Donaldson Collection / Contributor / Michael Ochs Archives / Getty Images. (d) Central Press / Stringer / Hulton Archive / Getty Images. (e) Bettmann / Contributor / Bettmann / Getty Images.

information that enabled the transformation from R to S. In 1952 Alfred Hershey and Martha Chase demonstrated that DNA injected into bacteria by viruses called bacteriophages was the transformative factor. Although it took around thirty years, evidence from these studies in bacteriology provided strong evidence that DNA was the genetic material.

As is often the case in science, the next advance relied on the application of the right technique and some creative thinking. In the early 1900s scientists began to shoot X-rays through crystals to investigate their molecular structure. The X-rays would diffract off the atoms and produce patterns on film that could be used to deduce the structure of the molecule. In some ways it is like shining a flashlight at an object in a dark room and then examining the shadow cast by the object to determine its shape. X-ray crystallography continues to be an important technique for investigating molecular structure and has played a role in at least twenty-five Nobel Prizes.

In 1952 Rosalind Franklin was investigating the molecular structure of DNA with X-ray crystallography with Maurice Wilkins at King's College in London, England. She had taken a particularly good photograph of an X-ray diffraction pattern of DNA which Wilkins showed to James Watson in early 1953. Watson was working with Francis Crick on the structure of DNA using physical models constructed out of metal plates and rods. The metal plates represented the nucleic acid bases (i.e., A, T, C, and G) and the rods represented the backbone of the model's double helix (see Figure 4.4(a)). In April of that same year, Watson and Crick published a one-page paper in *Nature* describing their double helical model of DNA that they hinted "suggests a possible copying mechanism for the genetic material" (Watson & Crick, 1953). Their model turned out to correctly describe the structure of DNA. As is often said, the rest is history. Watson, Crick, and Wilkins were awarded the Nobel Prize in Physiology or Medicine in 1962 for their work. Unfortunately, Rosalind Franklin died in 1958 of ovarian cancer before it was widely known how important her work was in the development of the model.

The DNA double helix looks sort of like a twisted ladder (see Figure 4.5) with a sugar-phosphate backbone as the frame of the ladder and the nucleotide bases as its rungs. For our purposes, we will essentially ignore the sugar-phosphate backbone and concentrate our attention on the bases because genetic information is contained in their sequence.

One of the first things to notice about the nucleotide bases is that A always pairs with T and G always pairs with C. Because of this complementary base pairing, if you were to unzip the double helix down the middle you can see that all the genetic information is contained on a single strand. If you know the nucleotide base on one strand, complementary base pairing enables you to determine the nucleotide base on the other strand. This is what Watson and Crick were alluding to

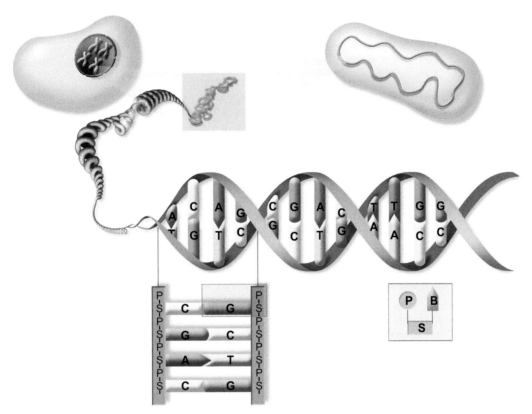

Figure 4.5. **Genetic information is contained in the nucleotide bases of the DNA double helix.** Chromosomes are in a cell's nucleus and are made of long strands of double helical DNA. The DNA is composed of a twisted ladder-like backbone of sugars [S] and phosphates [P]. The rungs of the DNA ladder are composed of a sequence of nucleic acid bases [B] (i.e., A, G, C, and T) that contains genetic information. Source: BSIP / Contributor / Universal Images Group / Getty Images.

when they mentioned that they recognized that their model suggested a copying mechanism. The nucleotide sequence found in a double helix is redundant because the sequence on one strand contains sufficient information to determine the sequence on the other strand. As we will see in subsequent chapters, this complementary base pairing feature will be utilized in molecular biology laboratory techniques to copy and manipulate genetic sequences.

Cytosine and thymine have a single-ring structure and are called pyrimidines. Adenine and guanine have a two-ring structure and are called purines. The complementary base pairing consists of a pyrimidine and a purine. The molecular distance across the structure of a complementary base pair is the same regardless of whether it is A-T or G-C and therefore provides symmetry to the double helix.

Check-up

- Why did many researchers prior to 1953 think that proteins were a better candidate to be the hereditary material than nucleic acid?
- Explain why knowing the sequence of bases on one strand of a DNA double helix enables you to know the sequence of the other strand.

4.3 DNA Replication Involves Making Copies

Both meiosis and mitosis require making copies of chromosomes. In other words, DNA replication is a critical component of an organism's capacity to produce gametes and new somatic cells. Watson and Crick hypothesized semiconservative replication as the process by which DNA is copied, wherein the new double-stranded copy contains one strand that is from the parent and one strand that is newly synthesized.

To begin replicating DNA, the double helix needs to be "unzipped" so that the molecular machinery involved in the copying has access to the nucleotide base sequence. Each strand can serve as a template to specify which nucleotide base should be added to the newly synthesized copy with complementary base pairing as the rule. For example, if the template strand has an A at a particular location, then a T will be added to that location on the new strand. Helicase is an enzyme that unzips the helix, and DNA polymerase is an enzyme that binds to a single strand of DNA and adds new bases complementary to the template strand (see Figure 4.6). Other molecules are involved in the correction of any DNA copying errors. Much more detail is known about the molecular mechanisms involved in DNA replication, but it is beyond the scope of this book. For those interested in more detail, any current molecular genetic textbook will suffice.

Check-up

- Describe the functions of helicase and DNA polymerase in DNA replication.

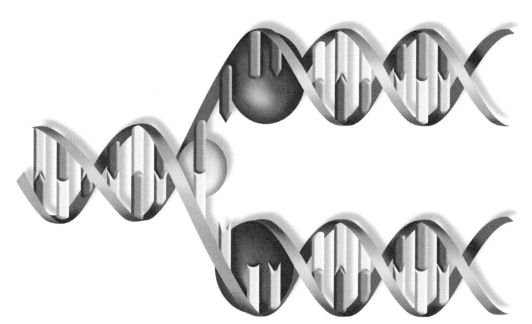

Figure 4.6. **Semiconservative DNA replication.** A double helix is "unzipped" by helicase (light gray sphere) and then DNA polymerases (dark gray spheres) make new "daughter" strands of DNA by attaching new bases that are complementary to the "parental" DNA template strand. Source: BSIP / Contributor / Universal Images Group / Getty Images.

4.4 DNA Sequence Specifies Amino Acid Sequence in Proteins

In addition to making copies of itself that are either passed to the next generation (i.e., meiosis) or put into new somatic cells (i.e., mitosis), DNA plays a critical role in making proteins. In the context of heredity, passing DNA from parent to offspring is, of course, important but it is only important because DNA participates in the production of proteins. It is proteins that build bodies, brains, neurons, and other biological components that are the raw materials of familial resemblance.

Proteins are large biomolecules comprising chains of amino acids that are involved in the structure, function, and regulation of cells. It is not known how many different proteins are expressed in humans, but it is a large number and is likely well over 20,000. Amino acids are organic compounds that are relatively simple molecules. Each contains a functional amino group (NH_2) and carboxyl (COOH) group. In addition, each amino acid has its own unique "side chain" that consists of some combination of carbon, nitrogen, hydrogen, oxygen, or sulfur atoms. For example, the chemical formula of alanine is $C_3H_7NO_2$, and for arginine is $C_6H_{14}N_4O_2$. Although approximately 500 amino acids occur in nature, only 20 are commonly found in proteins.

Constructing proteins from DNA sequence first requires the transcription of DNA into messenger RNA (mRNA) and then the translation of mRNA into protein. These processes require the coordination of several existing proteins such as RNA polymerase, and the availability of raw materials such as nucleotide bases and amino acids.

4.4.1 Transcription: Making mRNA

Cellular structure, function, and metabolism require proteins, which are produced in cells. The DNA provides the information for the construction of proteins in its sequence of nucleotide bases. DNA is rather an inert, stable molecule that is usually tightly packaged by virtue of its double helix structure and its wrapping around proteins called histones. If unwound and laid out in a continuous double helix, the DNA in one of your cells would stretch to about 6 feet (2 meters) in length. When packed into cells, it is about 50,000 times shorter than that.

To begin the process of building a protein (aka gene expression), the molecular machinery that copies a single-stranded DNA template into a single strand of mRNA needs to have access to a specific region of DNA. Several proteins are involved in a process called chromatin remodeling that sets the stage for DNA-binding proteins to commence transcription.

For our purposes, it is sufficient to begin a description of transcription at the binding of RNA polymerase to one of the DNA strands (i.e., the sense strand). Activator proteins bind to enhancer DNA sequences, and transcription factors bind to promoter DNA sequences enabling RNA polymerase to bind to the DNA and to begin transcribing it into mRNA (see Figure 4.7).

When the appropriate molecular machinery is bound to the start site, the RNA polymerase can begin making a strand of mRNA, which consists of a string of nucleotide bases that are complementary to the template strand. The same rules of complementary base pairing in DNA hold for RNA, with the exception that the base uracil (U) is used instead of thymine. So, if the DNA template strand had the following sequence, ATTGGCGTTAC, the complementary mRNA strand produced would be UAACCGCAAUG. The elongation phase of transcription continues until a terminator sequence is reached and then the transcription machinery and the new mRNA primary transcript falls away from the DNA template.

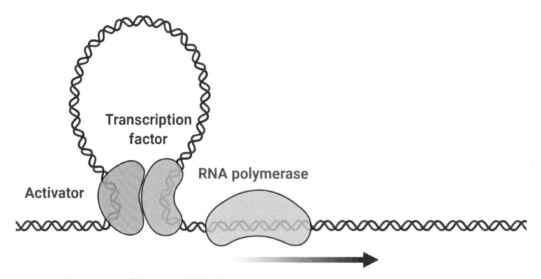

Figure 4.7. **Transcribing DNA into mRNA.** DNA sequence is transcribed into mRNA sequence by molecular machinery including RNA polymerase, activator proteins, and transcription factors. Source: Created with Biorender.com.

In eukaryotes, the mRNA primary transcript undergoes RNA processing while still in the nucleus. Such processing includes adding features to the head and the tail of the transcript that may aid in stabilizing the strand and help in its migration out of the nucleus. In addition, sections of the mRNA transcript may be cut out, or spliced, and the remaining sections joined together. A gene's DNA sequence may contain stretches that are used to specify amino acids in the next stage of processing called translation. Those stretches of DNA (and subsequently mRNA) sequence that are used to specify amino acids in translation are known as exons (i.e., *ex*pressed regions). Stretches of DNA sequence that are not subsequently encoded into the protein's amino acid sequence are known as introns (i.e., *int*ervening regions), which are spliced out during RNA processing (see Figure 4.8).

It is important to note that primary mRNA transcripts can undergo alternative splicing whereby different combinations of introns and exons can be combined to produce different mature mRNAs. This process can produce proteins that are structurally and/or functionally different from the same DNA template (see Figure 4.8).

4.4.2 Translation: Making Proteins

For the mature mRNA transcript to serve as a template for the assembly of a polypeptide chain it first needs to leave the nucleus and migrate into the cell's cytoplasm. Once in the cytoplasm the molecular machinery to take the information contained in the mRNA nucleotide sequence and use it to determine the order of amino acids needs to assemble. The components of the molecular machinery include transfer RNAs and ribosomal subunits. Transfer RNAs (tRNAs) each have a site, called the anticodon, that recognizes a complementary nucleotide sequence on the mRNA. They each also carry a single amino acid, specified by the anticodon, that they add to the growing polypeptide chain. This process takes place on the ribosome, which is composed of a small and large subunit (see Figure 4.9).

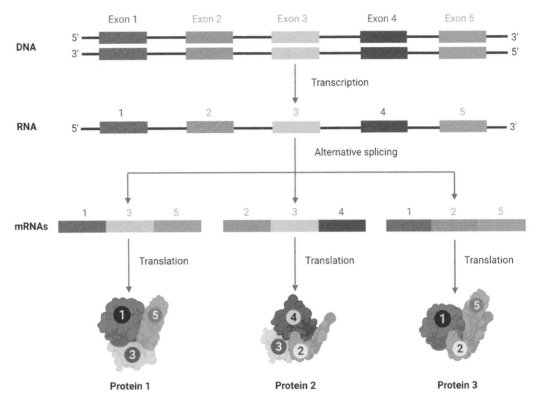

Figure 4.8. **Alternative splicing and translation of mRNA into proteins.** After DNA is transcribed into a primary mRNA transcript it may be spliced to produce different mature mRNA transcripts. Splicing involves excising the mRNA sequences that will not be translated (i.e., introns) and joining the sections that will (i.e., exons). Alternative splicing involves including some exons, while excluding others from the mature mRNA, which is then translated into protein. Source: Created with Biorender.com.

How can just four nucleotides specify twenty amino acids? The simple complementary base scheme for copying DNA into DNA or, with a minor modification, DNA into RNA will not work for amino acids. A nucleotide cannot have a one-to-one correspondence with an amino acid. Another code is needed.

If one considers that more than one nucleotide base may be used to specify an amino acid, the solution, at least theoretically, presents itself. If two nucleotides are needed to specify an amino acid, there are 4^2 combinations of A, U, C, and G possible. Of course, 4^2 is 16, which is not enough to code for twenty amino acids. However, if three nucleotides are needed in a codon to specify an amino acid, there are 4^3 possible combinations, or 64 (see Figure 4.10). Because 64 is greater than 20, this scheme allows for multiple codons to specify a single amino acid (i.e., the code is degenerate). Only tryptamine (Trp) and methionine (Met) are encoded by a single codon, UGG and AUG, respectively. The remaining eighteen amino acids are each encoded by at least two codons. Serine (Ser) and leucine (Leu) are each encoded by six codons. Three codons (i.e., UAA, UAG, and UGA) encode a signal to terminate translation and are therefore known as stop codons.

An important feature of the genetic code is that it is non-overlapping. Each set of three nucleotides on the strand of mRNA forms a single codon. Codons do not share nucleotides. For

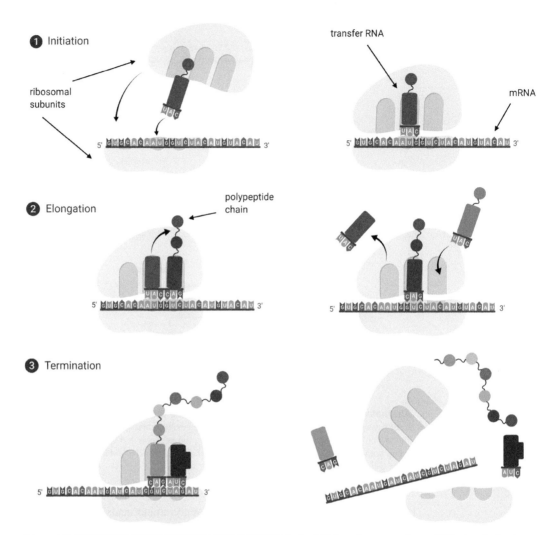

Figure 4.9. **Translating mRNA sequence into a protein.** In the initiation phase, a mature mRNA strand migrates out of the nucleus and binds to ribosomal subunits. Transfer RNA (tRNA) with complementary codons deliver amino acids to be added to the growing polypeptide chain in the elongation phase. When a stop codon binds to the mRNA in the termination phase, the resulting polypeptide chain is released, and the mRNA translation complex falls apart. Source: Created with Biorender.com.

example, the mRNA sequence UCU AAU CGC GUU ACG UGA codes for a short peptide comprised of Ser-Asn-Arg-Val-Thr, with the UGA codon serving to stop translation and therefore does not add another amino acid to the five-peptide chain. Each nucleotide in the mRNA sequence contributes information to a single codon.

The mRNA strand binds to the small ribosomal subunit and when the initiation codon (AUG) is recognized at the start of the transcript translation is initiated. The large ribosomal subunit joins amino acids together in the growing polypeptide chain brought by tRNAs that have anticodons that are complementary to the sequence specified by the mRNA during the elongation phase. During elongation about two to fifteen amino acids are added per second. Translation ends when the ribosomal complex encounters a stop codon. This process is constantly occurring in eukaryotic cells to provide the proteins necessary to sustain life.

(a)

Second Letter

	U	C	A	G	
U	UUU ⎤ Phe UUC ⎦ UUA ⎤ Leu UUG ⎦	UCU ⎤ UCC ⎟ Ser UCA ⎟ UCG ⎦	UAU ⎤ Tyr UAC ⎦ UAA ⎤ Stop UAG ⎦	UGU ⎤ Cys UGC ⎦ UGA Stop UGG Trp	U C A G
C	CUU ⎤ CUC ⎟ Leu CUA ⎟ CUG ⎦	CCU ⎤ CCC ⎟ Pro CCA ⎟ CCG ⎦	CAU ⎤ His CAC ⎦ CAA ⎤ Gln CAG ⎦	CGU ⎤ CGC ⎟ Arg CGA ⎟ CGG ⎦	U C A G
A	AUU ⎤ AUC ⎟ Ile AUA ⎦ AUG Met	ACU ⎤ ACC ⎟ Thr ACA ⎟ ACG ⎦	AAU ⎤ Asn AAC ⎦ AAA ⎤ Lys AAG ⎦	AGU ⎤ Ser AGC ⎦ AGA ⎤ Arg AGG ⎦	U C A G
G	GUU ⎤ GUC ⎟ Val GUA ⎟ GUG ⎦	GCU ⎤ GCC ⎟ Ala GCA ⎟ GCG ⎦	GAU ⎤ Asp GAC ⎦ GAA ⎤ Glu GAG ⎦	GGU ⎤ GGC ⎟ Gly GGA ⎟ GGG ⎦	U C A G

First Letter (left) · Third Letter (right)

(b)

Amino Acid	3-Letter Code
Alanine	Ala
Arginine	Arg
Asparagine	Asn
Aspartic acid	Asp
Cysteine	Cys
Glutamine	Gln
Glutamic acid	Glu
Glycine	Gly
Histidine	His
Isoleucine	Ile
Leucine	Leu
Lysine	Lys
Methionine	Met
Phenylalanine	Phe
Proline	Pro
Serine	Ser
Threonine	Thr
Tryptophan	Trp
Tyrosine	Tyr
Valine	Val

Figure 4.10. **The genetic code.** (a) Codons representing 64 combinations of three RNA bases (i.e., A, U, G, and C) specify 20 amino acids and three stop codons. The first letter of a codon represented by the four rows of letters is shown on the left. The second letter of a codon is indicated by the four rows shown on the top. The third letter of the codon is indicated by the rows shown on the right. For example, to find which amino acid is specified by the codon ACG, start by finding the A row on the left of the table, then move to the column with a C at the top. The "target box" is located at the intersection of the A row and the C column. And finally, within that box, find the row that is even with the G at the right side of the page (i.e., indicating the "third letter"). AGC, as well as the other three codons in that box encode the amino acid represented by the three-letter code "Thr." (b) Amino acids are indicated by a three-letter code. The amino acid in the example, Thr, is threonine.

Check-up

- What are amino acids and how many are commonly found in proteins?
- Explain the role of a promoter in the process of transcription.
- Discuss the types of processing that may be done to a primary mRNA transcript.
- Why does the genetic code contain 64 codons when it can only produce 20 amino acids?

4.5 Epigenetic Processes Regulate Gene Expression

Every cell in your body that contains a nucleus carries the same genetic information. How is it that cells as different as skin cells, liver cells, and neurons are constructed and maintained by the same genetic information? There may be certain genes that are expressed in all our cells, like those that code for proteins necessary for transcription and translation, but there are other genes that are expressed only in certain cell types or only at certain times. Cells therefore must have mechanisms to control gene expression so that only specific genes are expressed. In addition, such control of gene expression needs to survive mitosis so that newly formed cells express the correct suite of genes

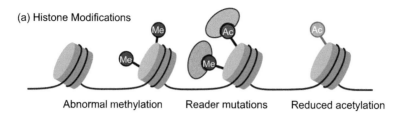

(a) Histone Modifications

Abnormal methylation   Reader mutations   Reduced acetylation

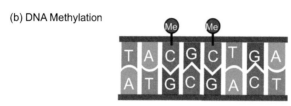

(b) DNA Methylation

Figure 4.11. **Epigenetic regulation of gene expression.** (a) Post-translational modifications of histone proteins can include the addition or removal of methyl groups, acetyl groups, or mutations in the proteins that "read" those modifications (i.e., readers). (b) DNA methylation involves the addition or removal of methyl groups to nucleotide bases.

given their type. Epigenetics is an area of study that focuses on changes in gene expression that can survive cell division and that are not the result of changes in DNA sequence (Armstrong, 2014).

In general, the mechanism of epigenetic regulation of gene expression is to limit access of the molecular machinery to a gene's DNA sequence. When chromosomes are not transcriptionally active, the double helix DNA strand is wrapped around small proteins called histones and tightly wound into chromatin, which enables packaging of the DNA into a much smaller space than would be possible for unwound DNA. Post-translational modifications of histone proteins are an important mechanism to control whether chromatin is tightly packed into heterochromatin, which is transcriptionally inactive, or into euchromatin, which is transcriptionally active. Additional control of gene expression of specific genes is achieved by the addition of methyl groups to DNA, typically in its promoter sequence (see Figure 4.11).

Histones have polypeptide tails that can be modified by the addition or removal of small chemical groups, such as an acetyl group (i.e., C_2H_3O), which is thought to be an important mechanism impacting chromatin structure (Armstrong, 2014). The addition or removal of certain chemical groups is associated with heterochromatin structure inhibiting transcription, whereas the addition or removal of other chemical groups is associated with euchromatin structure permitting transcription. Details about all the many potential post-translational histone modifications are beyond the scope of this book, but the bottom line is that such modifications affect the physical structure of chromatin, which can either impede or facilitate access to DNA for the molecular machinery of transcription.

DNA methylation and demethylation are mechanisms by which methyl groups (i.e., CH_3) are added or removed, usually to cytosines, in the promoter region of a gene. It is a common epigenetic mechanism for regulating gene expression. Methylation often occurs in areas of the genome where the DNA sequence contains many repeats of the dinucleotide CG. Such regions are referred to as CpG islands, where the "p" represents the phosphate of the DNA backbone. CpG islands are typically found in a gene's regulatory region and are 1,000–4,000 bases (1–4 kilobases [kb]) in length. When a methyl group is located on a cytosine in a CpG island it may physically impede the binding of a transcription factor to a gene's promoter and thereby inhibit expression of that gene. There are approximately 30,000 CpG islands in the human genome.

Histone modification and DNA methylation are often referred to as epigenetic marks because they are physical changes that can be observed with standard molecular biology techniques and they are considered to be indicative of genetic regulation. As such, epigenetic marks are of current interest in efforts to investigate the impact of biology on behavior (Jones, Moore, & Kobor, 2018). DNA methylation is the most studied epigenetic mark in human populations, although it is important to recognize that because DNA methylation plays a key role in cellular differentiation, patterns of DNA methylation can be highly tissue-specific. For our purposes, such tissue specificity suggests that researchers need to be cautious about generalizing DNA methylation patterns observed in readily accessible tissues (e.g., blood or saliva) to those that are less so (e.g., neurons).

Epigenetic marks are removed twice during development. In germline cells parental epigenetic marks are removed prior to the generation of gametes. Sex-specific epigenetic marks are then added to eggs and sperm. After fertilization, those epigenetic marks are eliminated, which sets the stage for a new round of epigenetic marks to be added to determine the specific gene expression patterns of different cell types. Although for some genes, epigenetic marks indicating parent of origin are maintained, thereby enabling the parent-of-origin effects.

A well-known example of epigenetic control of gene expression on a chromosomal scale is X-chromosome inactivation in mammals (Huynh & Lee, 2005). Typically, female mammals carry two X-chromosomes, of which one has been condensed into a (mostly) inactive state (i.e., most of its genes are not expressed). This is considered to be the result of dosage compensation, whereby the expression level of X-linked genes is equalized in the two sexes. An alternative approach to dosage compensation is seen in male *D. melanogaster*, where the level of transcription of X-linked genes is doubled.

In mammalian cells, a counting mechanism identifies the number of X-chromosomes present and then initiates X-chromosome inactivation when there are two or more X-chromosomes. The inactivation process relies on the generation of approximately 2,000 copies of a non-coding RNA that binds to the chromosome thereby silencing transcription. Which X-chromosome is inactivated can either be random or dependent on the origin of the chromosome. For so-called imprinted inactivation, the paternally inherited X-chromosome is inactivated. For random inactivation, the maternally derived and paternally derived X-chromosomes are inactivated at random early in embryonic development so that approximately half of the cells in the body have an active X-chromosome from the mother and half from the father. For imprinted inactivation only the paternally derived X-chromosome is silenced.

In addition, parent-of-origin dependent expression (i.e., imprinting) has been identified for approximately 100 autosomal genes in humans, some of which are associated with disorders (Monk, Mackay, Eggermann, Maher, & Riccio, 2019). One of the most well-known examples is due to parental imprinting of genes on chromosome 15, which results in different diseases, each with its own distinct cognitive and behavioral symptoms, depending on whether the paternal or maternal chromosome is expressed (Buiting, 2010). That genomic region (i.e., 15q11q13) contains several imprinted genes, which appear to be controlled via DNA methylation of the promoter regions of each gene.

Angelman syndrome (AS) produces intellectual disability, microcephaly (small head circumference), and a host of other symptoms. It is caused by imprinting of the gene *UBE3A*, which codes for a protein called ubiquitin protein ligase E3A. Both the paternally and maternally inherited copies of this gene are active in most body cells. However, in certain areas of the brain there is tissue-specific expression, whereby only the copy of the gene inherited *maternally* is active. In most cases of AS, the maternal copy of the *UBE3A* gene has some defect that results in a deficiency of ubiquitin protein ligase E3A.

(a) Licking   (b) Retrieval

Figure 4.12. **Maternal care impacts stress responsivity in adult offspring.** (a) A mother licks a newborn rat pup. (b) A mother retrieves a newborn rat pup, bringing it back to the nesting area. Source: Created with Biorender.com.

Prader-Willi syndrome (PWS) produces many behavioral symptoms that include language delay, obsessive-compulsive traits, and temper-tantrums, and often includes mild intellectual disability. There are also several physical features of PWS including short stature, small hands and feet, almond-shaped eyes, obesity, and infertility. The genetic causes of PWS are more variable but involve a deficit in *paternally* expressed genes on chromosome 15q11q13.

An important aspect of epigenetic processes is that they can be a mechanism by which our experiences impact the expression of our genes. An excellent example of this has to do with the later-life effects of maternal care in rats (Figure 4.12). A mother rat typically exhibits a substantial amount of grooming and licking behavior of her pups while in the nest. There are individual differences in the amount of such maternal care provided by mother rats. Adult offspring of mothers that provide more maternal care are less fearful and have more modest biological responses to stressors than do offspring of mothers that provide less maternal care (Francis, Diorio, Liu, & Meaney, 1999).

The mechanism that alters the stress responsivity of adult offspring is the epigenetic regulation of the expression of a gene that codes for a glucocorticoid receptor (GR) that is critical in regulating the hypothalamic-pituitary-adrenal (HPA) axis. The HPA axis is a key system in responding to stress and it appears that the maternal behavior of licking and grooming pups decreases methylation in the promoter region of a transcription factor (NGFI-A) that then acts to increase expression of the GR gene (Weaver, 2007). In other words, more maternal care increases the number of glucocorticoid receptors available, which enables better regulation of the HPA axis thereby reducing stress-sensitivity in adult offspring (see Box 4.2).

Check-up

- Explain how long DNA strands are packed into very small spaces in cells.
- What is a CpG island and what role do they play in gene expression?
- Why is it important that one X-chromosome in females is inactivated?
- Describe the epigenetic mechanism by which maternal care affects the stress response of adult offspring in rats.

Box 4.2 Critical Concept: Transgenerational Epigenetic Inheritance

When epigenetic modification is a response to environmental stimuli, can it be passed from parents to offspring? Any epigenetic marks passed on to offspring would need to be maintained through the two rounds of global demethylation and remethylation that occur during gametogenesis and embryonic development. Intergenerational transmission occurs from parent (P) to offspring (F_1 generation), whereas transgenerational transmission involves passing the modification to an additional generation (F_2) that has not been exposed to the environmental stimulus (Stenz, Schechter, Serpa, & Paoloni-Giacobino, 2018). Maintenance of acquired DNA methylation across generation would require some mechanism for protection from erasure during demethylation events.

The current evidence suggests that transgenerational epigenetic effects are not common, and that epigenetic changes acquired in life are typically not passed down to offspring. In those cases where the acquired epigenetic changes are passed to offspring, they are often lost in subsequent generations and therefore rarely become stable.

The connection between exposure to stress and DNA methylation has been investigated, at least in part because of the strong association between the experience of early life trauma and the later development of psychiatric disorders. Individuals who have experienced early life stress are at greater risk for developing substance use disorders, depression, and psychotic illness when compared to those who have not experienced such stress. Much of this work has focused on methylation levels of genes that code for proteins active in the HPA axis stress response system with the rationale that changes in capacity to respond to stress may set the stage for psychiatric illness. There is strong evidence that methylation of CpG sites in the promoter of the human GR gene (*NR3C1*) reduces its expression, but the connections to trauma or psychopathology have been inconsistent (Watkeys, Kremerskothen, Quidé, Fullerton, & Green, 2018). Investigating the potential epigenetic mechanisms mediating the impact of experience on behavior remains a promising line of research.

A mouse model that includes unpredictable maternal separation and unpredictable stress (MSUS) suggests that effects of early life stress can be transmitted from exposed fathers to their male offspring (Gapp et al., 2016). In this study, male mice were exposed to stress when they were pups. When they were adults, they fathered offspring that were not exposed to stress. When those fathers were exposed to adverse situations as adults, they were better able to cope than males who were not stressed as pups. That is, the early stress exposure increased their resilience. When their offspring were exposed to the same adverse situations they also coped well. Both the fathers and the offspring showed decreased methylation of the *Nr3c1* promoter and reduced GR expression in the hippocampus.

The increased resilience observed in the animals that were stressed as pups seems to be inconsistent with the notion of the role of childhood trauma as a risk factor for psychiatric illnesses in humans. However, it may be that the MSUS paradigm activates a level of stress in the pups that is not "traumatic" and such challenges might strengthen coping mechanisms. The main point here is that early life stressful experiences affected epigenetic mechanisms in stress response systems that persisted for at least one generation.

4.6 What Is a Gene?

Here we are, wrapping up Chapter 4, and we still have not provided a "modern" operational definition for the term gene. So far, we have discussed genes both as the hereditary material and as specific DNA sequences that are transcribed into mRNA and translated into proteins. Going forward, it is important to recognize that different definitions of genes can be used and to avoid confusion by being clear about which one is intended. Operational definitions of gene have changed substantially over the last century, primarily driven by scientific advances. In this section, we discuss different definitions of genes.

4.6.1 Genes Defined by Phenotypes

As we discussed in Chapter 2, Gregor Mendel hypothesized inherited "factors" that determined traits. These factors were passed intact from parents to offspring with each parent contributing half. He hypothesized that factors (a) were in the gametes, (b) existed in two forms for each trait, (c) were unchanged across generations, even when not expressed, and that (d) different factors were responsible for different traits. These hypothetical factors were the basis of his Law of Segregation and Law of Independent Assortment. The factors were hypothetical because Mendel observed only phenotypes across generations of controlled crosses. The actual term gene, as representing a unit of heredity, was coined in the early 1900s and, at least partly, has its origin in Charles Darwin's failed concept of pangenesis and the newly established field called genetics by William Bateson.

The gene mapping success of T. H. Morgan's fly lab relied on physically locating this hypothetical gene onto chromosomes. Morgan's work is an extension of Mendel's in that he better specified the location of genes from a rather vague "gametes" to a linear sequence on chromosomes in a cell's nucleus. However, the notion of a Mendelian gene as determining a phenotype was largely unchanged.

For decades, genes remained hypothetical units of heredity that were inferred based on observed phenotypic inheritance patterns. As discussed in Chapter 3, the field of quantitative genetics was built on and continues to investigate the effects of such unobserved genes. Heritability estimation in humans seeks to quantify the extent to which variations in such hypothetical genes account for observed phenotypic variation in a population. Clearly, the concept of a gene as a hypothetical unit of phenotypic inheritance is powerful and remains an important part of our understanding of familial resemblance.

4.6.2 Genes "for" Behaviors

One of the problems with defining a gene based on its statistical relation to an observable morphological or behavioral phenotype is that it oversimplifies the causal pathway. When Mendel hypothesized that a factor with two alleles determined pea shape, with AA and Aa producing a round pea and aa producing a wrinkled pea, it was an easy leap to say that this locus is the gene *for* pea shape. Similarly, when Morgan and his students identified the white-eyed fruit fly and mapped it to the X-chromosome, it became tempting to label that locus as a gene *for* eye color. As you can see, the shorthand expression of a *gene for* [blank] endows the gene with the power of causation. It can also imply that it is the only gene that impacts population variation in the trait, that the gene only impacts one phenotype, and that the environmental contribution is negligible.

Of course, Mendel and Morgan did not know that wrinkled peas and white eyes were the product of biological pathways that started with DNA sequence variation that produced amino acid sequence variation in an enzyme and a molecule involved in moving pigments, respectively. Subsequent research has identified the biological pathways involved in those traits, and many of the components of those pathways. The point is that by using the shorthand a *gene for* [blank] we run the risk of underestimating the complexity of biological pathways involved in phenotypes of interest, including behavior. Therefore, we should endeavor to avoid such shorthand expressions.

4.6.3 Genes Defined by Function

Beginning when Watson and Crick proposed the double helical structure of DNA and continuing to the present, genes have acquired an operational definition that relies on the relation between DNA sequence and a resulting product. In other words, the definition of the gene at the molecular level relates primarily to its function. The definition of the term gene should be compatible with previous definitions, independent of organism, represent an idea not a merely a list, and be useful across disciplines. The following definition of a gene appears promising:

> *The gene is a union of genomic sequences encoding a coherent set of potentially overlapping functional products.* (Gerstein et al., 2007)

This conceptualization of a gene considers that a gene may be composed of either DNA or RNA genomic sequence, which makes it useful for species like ours that uses DNA and for those

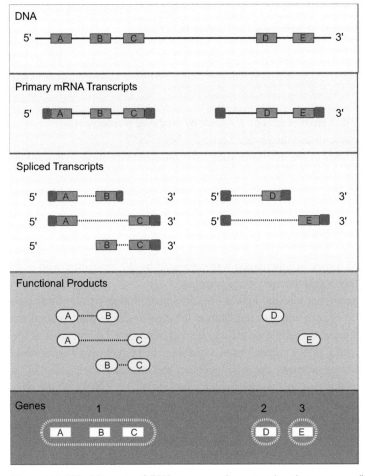

Figure 4.13. **What is a gene?** DNA sequences have stretches that are transcribed into mRNA (e.g., exons A–E), as well as those that are not translated (e.g., introns and 5′and 3′untranslated regions). Primary mRNA transcripts can be alternatively spliced to produce spliced transcripts containing different exons. Those spliced transcripts can be translated into different functional products. Because exons A, B, and C in this example produce three functional products from overlapping DNA sequence, they are considered together as a gene. Source: Created with Biorender.com. Modified from Gerstein et al. (2007).

that use RNA genomes, like viruses. It also accounts for alternative splicing that produces multiple protein products from the same initial genomic sequence. When translated DNA sequences are shared, the genomic sequence is considered one gene. When translated DNA sequences are not shared, the genomic sequence is considered different genes. In addition, when genomic sequence produces non-coding RNA it is considered a separate gene because its functional product differs from shared genomic sequence that is translated into protein (see Figure 4.13).

Behavior genetics has largely moved into the realm of molecular genetics and is therefore focused on understanding the impact of genomic sequence variation on individual differences in behavior. Genomic sequence variation can result in proteins that have different amino acid sequences, which can alter their function in biological systems. Such differences can have implications for individual differences in behavior that range from subtle to profound. Genomic sequence variation can also produce differences in gene expression. For example, a change in a single nucleotide from a C to a T could impact methylation at that site, which could affect promoter binding and therefore determine whether a promoter can bind to that location to initiate transcription. Much of the work remaining in behavior genetics is to understand how genomic sequence variation impacts biological pathways that lead to behavior.

Check-up

- Explain the logic that enables genetic research by studying phenotypes.
- Why is it problematic to use the phrase "gene for behavior"?
- Explain the importance of the functional molecular product to the modern definition of a gene.

4.7 SUMMARY

- The chromosomal theory of inheritance was suggested by Walter Sutton who examined cell divisions occurring in grasshopper spermatogonia.
- Meiosis in a sexually reproducing diploid (2n) organism produces haploid (n) gametes. When haploid sperm and egg are united at fertilization the diploid chromosome complement is restored.
- Mitosis produces daughter cells with the identical chromosome complement as the parent cells.
- Deoxyribonucleic acid (DNA) is composed of a double helix made of a sugar-phosphate backbone and nucleic acid bases: adenine, cytosine, guanine, and thymine. Each strand of the helix has a sequence of bases that pair in a complementary fashion with the bases on the other strand. The sequence of bases is the genetic information.
- DNA is copied in a semiconservative fashion whereby the new double-stranded copy contains one strand from the parent and one newly synthesized strand.
- DNA is transcribed into messenger RNA (mRNA), which is translated into protein. A codon consisting of three nucleotides on the mRNA strand specifies an amino acid according to the genetic code.
- Epigenetic processes affect gene expression primarily by physically restricting access to the DNA template for replication machinery by mechanisms such as histone modification or DNA methylation.

- Genes can be defined as hypothetical units of inheritance when studying phenotypic similarity among relatives, or in breeding studies. Genes can also be defined based on the functional product (e.g., protein) of a DNA sequence.

RECOMMENDED READING

- Mukherjee, S. (2016). *The Gene: An Intimate History.* New York: Scribner's.
- Watson, J. D., & Crick, F. H. (1953). Molecular structure of nucleic acids: A structure for deoxyribose nucleic acid. *Nature, 171*(4356), 737–738.

REFERENCES

Armstrong, L. (2014). *Epigenetics.* New York: Garland Science.

Buiting, K. (2010). Prader-Willi syndrome and Angelman syndrome. *Am J Med Genet C Semin Med Genet, 154C*(3), 365–376. doi:10.1002/ajmg.c.30273

Francis, D., Diorio, J., Liu, D., & Meaney, M. J. (1999). Nongenomic transmission across generations of maternal behavior and stress responses in the rat. *Science (New York, N.Y.), 286*(5442), 1155–1158. doi:10.1126/science.286.5442.1155

Gapp, K., Bohacek, J., Grossmann, J., Brunner, A. M., Manuella, F., Nanni, P., & Mansuy, I. M. (2016). Potential of environmental enrichment to prevent transgenerational effects of paternal trauma. *Neuropsychopharmacology, 41*(11), 2749–2758. doi:10.1038/npp.2016.87

Gerstein, M. B., Bruce, C., Rozowsky, J. S., Zheng, D., Du, J., Korbel, J. O., ... Snyder, M. (2007). What is a gene, post-ENCODE? History and updated definition. *Genome Res, 17*(6), 669–681. doi:10.1101/gr.6339607

Huynh, K. D., & Lee, J. T. (2005). X-chromosome inactivation: A hypothesis linking ontogeny and phylogeny. *Nat Rev Genet, 6*(5), 410–418. doi:10.1038/nrg1604

Jones, M. J., Moore, S. R., & Kobor, M. S. (2018). Principles and challenges of applying epigenetic epidemiology to psychology. *Annu Rev Psychol, 69,* 459–485. doi:10.1146/annurev-psych-122414-033653

Levine, M. S., & Holland, A. J. (2018). The impact of mitotic errors on cell proliferation and tumorigenesis. *Genes Dev, 32*(9–10), 620–638. doi:10.1101/gad.314351.118

Monk, D., Mackay, D. J. G., Eggermann, T., Maher, E. R., & Riccio, A. (2019). Genomic imprinting disorders: Lessons on how genome, epigenome and environment interact. *Nat Rev Genet, 20*(4), 235–248. doi:10.1038/s41576-018-0092-0

Stenz, L., Schechter, D. S., Serpa, S. R., & Paoloni-Giacobino, A. (2018). Intergenerational transmission of DNA methylation signatures associated with early life stress. *Curr Genomics, 19*(8), 665–675. doi:10.2174/1389202919666171229145656

Sutton, W. S. (1902). On the morphology of the chromosome group in *Brachystola magna. Biol Bull, 4,* 24–39.

Sutton, W. S. (1903). The chromosomes in heredity. *Biol Bull, 4*(5), 231–251.

Watkeys, O. J., Kremerskothen, K., Quidé, Y., Fullerton, J. M., & Green, M. J. (2018). Glucocorticoid receptor gene (NR3C1) DNA methylation in association with trauma, psychopathology, transcript expression, or genotypic variation: A systematic review. *Neurosci Biobehav Rev, 95,* 85–122. doi:10.1016/j.neubiorev.2018.08.017

Watson, J. D., & Crick, F. H. (1953). Molecular structure of nucleic acids: A structure for deoxyribose nucleic acid. *Nature, 171*(4356), 737–738. doi:10.1038/171737a0

Weaver, I. C. G. (2007). Epigenetic programming by maternal behavior and pharmacological intervention. Nature versus nurture: Let's call the whole thing off. *Epigenetics, 2*(1), 22–28. doi:10.4161/epi.2.1.3881

5 Genetic Variation

For evolution by natural selection to work, hereditary material must vary between individuals and such variation must cause individual differences in traits that are directly, or indirectly, involved with reproductive fitness. In other words, genetic differences between individuals are the raw material of evolution, but only if those differences produce differences in traits that are subject to natural selection. Theodosius Dobzhansky's assertion that biology only makes sense in the context of evolution makes it clear that genetic variation is a cornerstone of the entire field of biology. It is certainly the basis of behavior genetics, where we strive to understand the role of genetic differences in producing individual differences in behavior.

In this chapter, we discuss different types of genetic variation and potential mechanisms by which it may impact behavior. We also discuss the methods used to investigate associations between genetic variation and individual differences in behavior. And finally, we discuss the Human Genome Project, which has had a profound impact on the field of behavior genetics.

5.1 There Are Different Types of Genetic Variation

As we covered in Chapter 4, genes can be defined as genomic sequences that code for functional products, like proteins. A genome represents all an organism's genetic information, both coding and non-coding sequences. We will only discuss DNA genomes in this text and ignore RNA genomes (sorry viruses). Different species have different numbers of chromosomes and nucleotides in their genomes (see Table 5.1). Think of the genome as the linear sequence of nucleotide bases (i.e., A, T, C, and G) from a single strand taken from the double helix that comprises a single chromosome, and then repeat for all the remaining chromosomes. The total number of nucleotides (bases [b]) that comprise the haploid human nuclear genome (i.e., the genetic information found in a cell's nucleus) is 3,234,830,000 (or 3.2 giga bases [Gb]). Cells also contain organelles called mitochondria that contain their own mitochondrial genome comprising 16,569 base pairs (bp). Generally, when the term genome is used without specifying nuclear or mitochondrial, it is safest to assume nuclear.

To visualize how many base pairs are contained in a person's nuclear genome, consider that on a standard page with one-inch margins, approximately 2,300 characters can fit when typed in 12-point Times New Roman font. To type a person's entire nuclear genomic sequence, with no spaces, it would take approximately 1,406,448 of those one-sided pages. You would need 2,813 reams of paper for the job, which if stacked one on top of the other would stand approximately 480 feet (146 meters) tall, about the same height as the Great Pyramid of Giza (see Figure 5.1).

Within a species, each chromosome carries essentially the same linear order of genes and nucleotides. The nucleotide sequence on human chromosomes is remarkably constant across individuals. Two unrelated people are expected to have genomes that differ at approximately 4–5 million loci (Genomes Project Consortium et al., 2015). Although 5 million genetic differences

Table 5.1 Genomes of species important in behavior genetics				
Common name	Scientific name	Chromosones (haploid)	Protein coding genes	Bases (Mb)
Human	*Homo sapiens*	23	20,049	3,097
Dog	*Canis lupus familiaris*	39	20,257	2,411
Rat	*Rattus norvegicus*	22	22,250	2,870
Mouse	*Mus musculus*	21	22,515	2,731
Fruit fly	*Drosophila melanogaster*	4	13,947	144
Honeybee	*Apis mellifera*	16	15,314	250
Zebra fish	*Danio rerio*	25	25,592	1,373
Roundworm	*Caenorhabditis elegans*	6	20,191	100

Note: The prefix (Mb) stands for million.
Source: Ensembl release 99 – January 2020 © EMBL-EBI.

Figure 5.1. **The Great Pyramid of Giza.** Built around 2560 BC, the Great Pyramid of Giza stands approximately 481 feet tall (146.5 meters). It was the largest human-made structure in the world for nearly 4,000 years. The Great Pyramid is the tallest of the three pyramids located near Cairo, Egypt. Source: Kitti Boonnitrod / Moment / Getty Images.

between two people seems like a lot, it represents only 0.16 percent of the entire genome. In other words, two unrelated individuals are genetically identical for about 99.84 percent of their genomes.

Each human being is genetically unique, except for monozygotic twins. The two members of a monozygotic twin pair are genetically identical to each other at conception but can acquire genetic differences because of rare uncorrected DNA copying mistakes that occur during mitosis (Abdellaoui et al., 2015). Similarly, uncorrected DNA copying errors can occur during the production of sperm or eggs (i.e., meiosis), so that identical twins may not pass on exactly the same genome to the next generation. Such newly arising genetic changes, whether they are in the somatic tissues or gametes are known as *de novo* mutations. There are several types of genetic variation, and in the remainder of this section we describe them.

5.1.1 Single Nucleotide Polymorphisms

By far, the most common type of variant in the human genome is called a single nucleotide polymorphism, which is abbreviated as SNP and pronounced "snip" (see Table 5.2). A SNP represents the difference of one nucleotide base in a DNA sequence (see Figure 5.2(a)). For

Table 5.2 Median autosomal variant sites per genome

	Africa	Americas	East Asia	Europe	South Asia
SNPs	4.31 M	3.64 M	3.55 M	3.53 M	3.60 M
Indels	625 k	557 k	546 k	546 k	556 k
MEI	1.23 k	1.01 k	1.09 k	1.10 k	1.06 k
Large deletions	1.1 k	949	940	939	947
CNVs	170	153	158	157	165
Inversions	12	9	10	9	11

Note: SNPs = single nucleotide polymorphisms, MEI = mobile element insertions, CNVs = copy number variants, M = million, k = thousand.
Source: 1000 Genomes Project (2015).

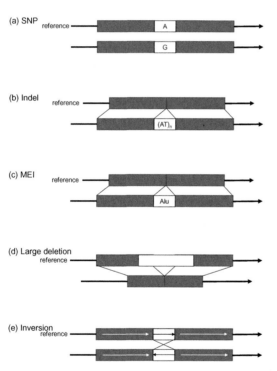

Figure 5.2. **Types of DNA sequence variation.**
(a) Single nucleotide polymorphisms. (b) Short insertion/deletions. (c) Mobile element insertions. (d) Large deletions. (e) Inversions.

example, if you compare the sequence …CTCAGGA… with …CTCGGGA…, you can see that the fourth nucleotide is "A" in the first sequence and "G" in the second. The alleles that make up the SNP can be represented within brackets …CTC[A/G]GGA… The SNP in this example is in the gene on chromosome 13 that codes for a serotonin neurotransmitter receptor (*HTR2A*).

As part of the 1000 Genomes Project the genomes of 2,504 individuals from 26 populations were analyzed to determine the frequency of different types of genetic variants. SNPs were the most common type of variant, but structural variants impact more total bases.

Each SNP in the human genome is assigned a ref SNP number that contains the letters "rs" and a unique numerical identifier (e.g., rs6313). Ref SNP numbers provide a standard approach for identifying SNPs that avoids the potential for confusion when different naming practices are used. For example, rs6313 is also known as the T102C variant of *HTR2A* (see Box 5.1). The T102C name for this variant was given by the researchers who identified it decades ago (Warren, Peacock, Rodriguez, & Fink, 1993), and it indicates the two alternative alleles and identifies the relative location of the variation (i.e., the 102nd nucleic acid in the coding sequence of the gene). You may have noticed that the alleles (T/C) are different than those we used in our example (A/G). Are we still referring to the same SNP? Yes. As you recall, DNA is double-stranded and anti-parallel with one strand oriented 5' to 3' and the other 3' to 5'. The notation 5' (pronounced five prime) indicates that a phosphate group is found on the 5th carbon on the sugar molecule of the DNA backbone. Transcription starts on the 5' end and proceeds toward the 3' end. By convention, the DNA strand that has its 5' end on the chromosome's short arm is designated the reference strand. This allows us to read DNA sequence from left to right. As you can guess from our example the A/G alleles are found when the sequence of the reference strand is used, whereas the T/C alleles are found when the sequence of the complementary strand is used. Therefore, in our example, double-stranded (i.e., including both reference and complementary strand) DNA sequence for rs6313 is shown with three nucleotides flanking the SNP.

> 5'...CTC[A/G]GGA...3' reference strand (direction of transcription →)
> 3'...GAG[T/C]CCT...5' complementary strand (direction of transcription ←)

Box 5.1 NCBI Genome Data Viewer

There are several online genomics databases that are available to the public. These services represent your tax dollars at work providing current genomics information for researchers on many species. Genome browsers assume that users are researchers who have more than just a basic understanding of genomics. So, they can seem intimidating to students. It is a good idea for new users to take advantage of the "Help" and "FAQ" pages, or other online resources, as a first step toward learning how to use these viewers.

The National Institutes of Health supports the Genome Data Viewer that is maintained by the National Center for Biotechnology Information (NCBI). The Genome Data Viewer is just one of the many valuable research tools maintained by NCBI that are too numerous to mention here. The NCBI even produces a YouTube channel to provide tutorial videos for using its resources including the Genome Data Viewer.

The Genome Data Viewer enables users to investigate the genomes of over 780 eukaryotic organisms, including all the model organisms important in behavior genetics. Users can search genomic elements by using search terms such as gene names, or ref SNP numbers, or even browse entire chromosomes.

To continue with the *HTR2A* example presented above, I typed "htr2a" into the Genome Data Viewer's search box and was quickly taken to its page (see Figure 5.3). It is simple to customize the type and amount of information provided by "configuring tracks." You can select from all the available tracks of information, or just select the NCBI recommended track sets from the "Tracks" dropdown menu. In Figure 5.3, I selected "Genetics and Variation" tracks.

I encourage you to use the NCBI Genome Data Viewer to investigate a gene or SNP in which you are interested. It is beyond the scope of this text to provide a detailed User's Guide to any

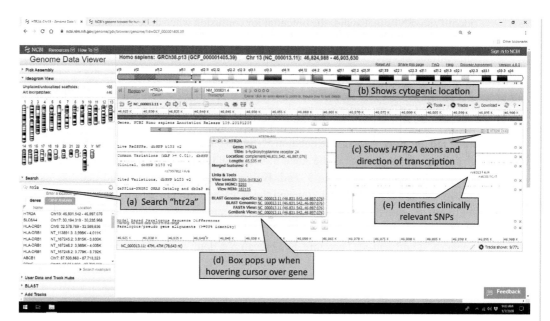

Figure 5.3. **The Genome Data Viewer.** The NCBI Genome Data Viewer provides an example of some of the information provided in a typical search. (a) The term "htr2a" was typed into the search box. Note that although the approved gene name was used, correct capitalization is not necessary. (b) The cytogenetic location of *HTR2A* on chromosome 13 is indicated by a vertical line. (c) Exons are indicated as boxes and introns are indicated as lines that connect them. Dark boxes represent coding regions and light boxes represent untranslated regions. The direction of transcription is indicated with arrows along the introns. (d) When the cursor hovers over the gene, an information box pops up that provides more detail on the gene and links to additional information. Note that the "Location" entry specifies that the gene is found on the complement (i.e., not the reference) strand. (e) Single nucleotide polymorphisms that have been associated with clinically relevant phenotypes, such as psychiatric disorders, are identified in their relative locations.

of the available online genomics databases, but it is important to note their importance to the field and to inspire you to explore them.

5.1.2 Structural Variants

Having one nucleotide instead of another at some position in the genome, as in the case of SNPs, may impact gene expression or function, but it does not change the structure of the genome. However, there are other types of genomic variation that change the number of nucleotides or their order. Such structural variants are relatively common in the human genome and in the genomes of other organisms, and many are known to be associated with important behavioral phenotypes. In this section, we describe different genomic structural variants.

After SNPs, the next most common type of genetic variant is called an indel, which stands for insertion/deletion of between 1 bp and 10,000 bp (Mullaney, Mills, Pittard, & Devine, 2010). It should be noted that there is no universally accepted definition for the upper size limit for indels, and that most indels are less than 100 bp in length. Some define any inserted or deleted genomic element between 1 bp and 50 bp as indels, and those greater than 50 bp as copy number variants (up to 3 Mb; Zarrei, MacDonald, Merico, & Scherer, 2015). The terminology is agnostic about whether the variant is due to the insertion of nucleotides into the ancestral sequence, or whether it is due to the deletion of nucleotides. Either way, the resulting polymorphism consists of alleles that contain different numbers of the repeated sequence and therefore are of different lengths (see Figure 5.2(b)). Small deletions may only impact a single gene, whereas large deletions may affect thousands (see Figure 5.2(c)). Deletions that affect many genes can have large impacts on phenotypes and may even be lethal. The potential impact on gene expression and the function of the gene's product depends on the location and size of the polymorphism. We cover the potential effects of genetic variation on gene expression and function in more detail in the next section.

Mobile element insertions (MEIs) are a specific type of copy number variant that are the result of the actions of transposable elements, which are repetitive DNA sequences that have moved from one position in the genome to another (see Figure 5.2(d)). Astonishingly, repetitive sequences due to transposable elements make up about 45 percent of the human genome (Lander et al., 2001). Actively mobile elements have the capacity to generate new genetic diversity by "jumping" from one genomic location to another, potentially disrupting the function of genes in the process.

Inversions can occur when there are two breaks in a chromosome and the genomic material between them rotates and then the breaks are repaired (see Figure 5.2(e)). Such an event does not alter the overall number of bases, but reorients genomic sequence, which may affect gene expression and recombination in the region.

Another class of genetic variation, called aneuploidy, is characterized by having an atypical number of chromosomes. Developmental processes can be very sensitive to gene dosage and therefore can be severely disrupted by aneuploidy. Recent estimates indicate that approximately 50 percent of miscarriages carry chromosomal abnormalities (Pylyp et al., 2018). Having an extra copy of most chromosomes is lethal. However, sometimes having an extra copy of a chromosome is not a sure death sentence. Trisomy 21 for example, having three copies of chromosome 21, can be lethal but it can also lead to viable births, typically causing Down syndrome. We discuss the Down syndrome phenotypes in Chapter 8. Having a single copy of a chromosome, such as in Turner syndrome, where individuals carry one X-chromosome with no other accompanying sex chromosome, is called monosomy. Aneuploidy is the result of nondisjunction during cell division where chromosomes do not sort correctly into daughter cells.

Check-up

- Describe the type of information contained in a genome.
- Explain the difference between nuclear and mitochondrial genomes.
- Describe how much variation there is between the genomes of two unrelated individuals.
- What is a SNP and why are SNPs important in behavior genetics?
- Explain the difference between an indel and a copy number variant.

5.2 How Genetic Differences Play a Role in Phenotype Differences

The mere fact that one genomic sequence differs from another does not imply that the difference plays a role in individual differences in behavior. Some genetic differences do not produce corresponding differences in biological pathways and therefore cannot cause individual differences in behavior. In this section we will discuss some of the ways in which genomic sequence differences can impact biological processes, and then we consider the notion of pathways from genetic differences to individual differences in behavior.

5.2.1 Altered Amino Acid Sequence

If a genetic variant is located within the coding region of a gene (i.e., exon) it may produce a protein with a different amino acid sequence than is produced by the gene with an alternative allele at that locus. Such a variant is considered a missense mutation. Missense mutations are those that result in a different amino acid being placed in a polypeptide chain. Silent mutations are DNA sequence variations in a gene's coding region that do not result in a different amino acid in the encoded polypeptide. Missense mutations can also be referred to as non-synonymous mutations, whereas silent mutations can also be referred to as synonymous mutations (see Figure 5.4).

As you recall from Chapter 4, the genetic code specifies how three-nucleotide codons of mRNA transcripts are translated into amino acids. The genetic code is degenerate, whereby most amino acids can be specified by more than one codon. For example, UUU and UUC code for phenylalanine. Therefore, a single nucleotide polymorphism that changes TTT to TTG would not produce a change in the resulting protein's amino acid sequence. A phenylalanine would be coded for by either sequence. Such a change would be considered a silent, or synonymous mutation. Note that this silent change occurred in the third position of the three-nucleotide codon. Most silent mutations occur at the third position, which is sometimes called the "wobble" position, because of the less precise pairing between it and the tRNA anticodon.

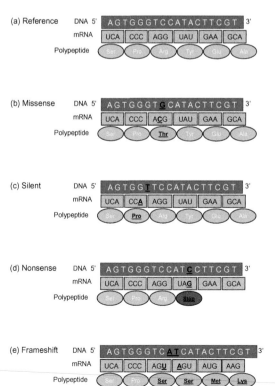

Figure 5.4. **Examples of DNA sequence variations and their impact on mRNA and amino acid sequence.** (a) An 18 bp DNA sequence, its corresponding mRNA transcript, and the resulting polypeptide. Frames b–e show alterations to this example DNA sequence and their impact on mRNA and polypeptide sequence. (b) A missense mutation that produces a change in the polypeptide (i.e., amino acid sequence). (c) A silent mutation that does not alter amino acid sequence. (d) A nonsense mutation that introduces a premature stop codon. (e) A frameshift mutation resulting from a 2 bp (AT) insertion that alters the reading frame thereby altering codons that follow.

DNA sequence variants located in the first and second positions of a codon produce amino acid substitutions (i.e., are missense). For example, AGG codes for arginine, AAG codes for lysine, ACG codes for threonine, and AUG codes for methionine (see Figure 5.4). If the substituted amino acid has similar chemical and physical properties such that the resulting protein function is unchanged, the substitution is considered conservative. If the substituted amino acid has different properties such that the function of the resulting protein is altered, the substitution is considered non-conservative.

Nonsense mutations are those that change DNA sequences in ways that specify a stop codon instead of an amino acid (see Figure 5.4). For example, changing UCA, which codes for a serine, to UAA. Such a change can produce a truncated protein, which may or may not function similarly to the protein that contains the serine at that position.

Insertions or deletions may cause frameshift mutations, which can produce proteins with completely different amino acid sequences downstream of the mutation (see Figure 5.4). This shift in reading frame occurs if the number of nucleotides inserted or deleted is not divisible by three. Such a change can dramatically alter the function of the resulting protein.

5.2.2 Altered Gene Expression or Splicing

DNA polymorphisms in non-coding regions that alter gene expression, such as promoter regions, can alter or abolish DNA transcription. Mutations can introduce or eliminate binding sites for transcription factors thereby increasing or reducing expression of the target gene. Methylation sites can be introduced or eliminated by mutation potentially impacting capacity for epigenetic regulation of the target gene.

A primary mRNA transcript contains both exons (i.e., coding regions) and introns (i.e., non-coding regions). Prior to translation, introns are removed by splicing to produce a mature mRNA transcript. Short sequences in the primary transcript identify the boundaries for splicing. Mutations that alter such splice sites can interfere with the production of a mature mRNA and may thereby halt translation.

5.2.3 Convergent Evidence to Understand Pathways from Genes to Behaviors

Given the wealth of information currently available about DNA sequence variation and its role in biological processes from gene expression to the function of cells, circuits, and systems, it is obvious that there are many steps on the pathway from genes to behavior. The domain of behavior genetics necessarily includes DNA sequence variation that leads to altered biological function and to individual differences in behavior. Investigating such pathways in humans poses significant challenges because of the ethical and practical limitations of humans as genetic research subjects. And although investigating heredity–behavior relations in non-human animal models avoids many of the challenges inherent in studying humans, generalizing across species can be problematic.

The power of convergent evidence across species and across methods must be brought to bear in behavior genetics. To advance understanding of the role of genetic variation in individual differences in behavior we cannot rely on a single approach. Instead, we must use multiple approaches across species and levels of analysis to address this complex problem. In the next sections we discuss a variety of methods used to investigate heredity–behavior relations.

Check-up

- Explain the difference between a conservative missense mutation and a silent mutation.
- Describe the potential impact of a splice site mutation.
- Explain the role of convergent evidence in understanding heredity–behavior relations.

5.3 Assessing Genetic Variation

Now that we have described different types of genetic variation, let us consider some of the methods used to measure them. The methods we describe are a triumph of molecular biology. They are based on a detailed understanding of the underlying processes by which organisms cut, copy, and paste hereditary material. They use enzymes, nucleotide bases, marker molecules, and carefully controlled conditions to manipulate DNA. Each method has practical and ethical limitations, and new methodologies are constantly being developed. We first describe some of the basic components that are used in key molecular genetic methods. Then we outline some of the key methods that are routinely used in behavior genetics to assess genetic variation.

5.3.1 Basic Components Used in Molecular Genetics

First and foremost, to assess genetic variation, it is necessary to have the DNA to examine. Genomic DNA is found in nucleated cells. In behavior genetic studies, DNA is often extracted from blood or cheek cells because they are relatively easy to collect. However, any nucleated cell can serve as a DNA source. After the cells have been collected, their membranes need to be broken down, or lysed, to gain access to the DNA. Essentially, the goal is to break open the cells, extract only the DNA, and leave the other cellular constituents behind. Detergents, salt, and enzymes are used to remove such cellular debris. Additional purification steps may be necessary to remove the detergents and other reagents used in the cell lysis step. The DNA is then typically stored in a buffered solution and kept frozen.

Assessing DNA variation often requires making copies of the DNA region of interest. Rather than inventing completely novel ways to copy DNA, researchers have instead capitalized on DNA copying methods that have been honed by millennia of evolution inside organisms. DNA polymerase is an enzyme that makes new copies of a DNA template strand and has a structure that is highly conserved across species. DNA polymerase needs to bind to a single strand of DNA template for copying. In the molecular genetic lab, the most common way to unzip (i.e., denature) double-stranded DNA is to heat it to around 90°C in a thermalcycler (see Figure 5.5). Mammalian DNA polymerase can be used in the laboratory to make DNA copies, but when it is heated to 90°C it is rendered non-functional. A real advance in molecular genetics occurred when the DNA polymerase from a bacteria that lives in hot springs, *Thermus aquaticus*, was used to make copies of DNA in a laboratory (Mullis, 1998). The DNA polymerase from *T. aquaticus*, now generally known as Taq polymerase, is thermostable. In other words, the enzyme can still function after being subjected to temperatures that boil water and unzip DNA strands.

Oligonucleotides are relatively short (i.e., around 15–25 bp) synthetic nucleotide sequences that can be designed to bind to specific complementary DNA sequences. Oligonucleotides can be used as primers, which serve as the starting point for copying a DNA

Figure 5.5. **Thermalcycler.** Polymerase chain reaction (PCR) relies on the capacity to rapidly change between temperatures, which can be done in machines called thermalcyclers. In this photo, a scientist loads a sample into a thermalcycler. Source: Monty Rakusen / Cultura / Getty Images.

template. DNA polymerase can only add nucleotides to the $3'$ end of a nucleic acid base. So, a primer serves as an anchor point for the newly synthesized DNA copy.

Oligonucleotide primers provide specificity to DNA copying because their sequence can be used to define a unique genomic sequence for binding. In other words, an oligonucleotide specifies the genomic address of a target site. Longer oligonucleotides contain more information about the target site. Consider that an oligonucleotide primer that is only 2 bp in length (i.e., a dimer), such as AT, would bind to every location in the genome containing its complementary sequence TA. However, if the primer is 25 bp in length (i.e., a 25-mer), there is likely only one genomic location with the exact complementary sequence. Adding more bases to a primer that already contains enough information to specify a unique genomic location is not beneficial. Therefore, most primers are between 18 and 25 bases in length.

Oligonucleotides can also be used as probes that bind to a complementary genomic sequence. Probes can be designed so that one will bind to a given allele (e.g., C) of a single nucleotide polymorphism and another will bind to the alternative allele (e.g., T). Such probes would differ in sequence only by a single nucleotide whereby one would contain the complementary base of the C allele (i.e., G) and the other the complementary base of the T allele (i.e., A). Both would contain the same sequences surrounding (i.e., flanking) the SNP to enable binding to the unique target site.

In addition to a DNA template, DNA polymerase, and a primer, making copies of a DNA requires nucleotide bases (i.e., A, T, C, and G). The nucleotides are collectively termed deoxynucleotide triphosphates, or dNTPs, and are added one at a time to the newly copied DNA strand. The "N" stands for nucleotide and can be replaced by A, T, C, or G to represent a specific base, as in dATP for deoxyadenosine triphosphate.

All the components routinely used in molecular genetics are available from companies that typically have sophisticated web pages to enable researchers to custom design molecular tools that can be shipped overnight to the lab. The ease of assessing genetic variation because of advances in molecular biology and the Internet has facilitated the increased interest in behavior genetics in the twenty-first century.

5.3.2 DNA Sequencing

Different approaches to determining the linear order of nucleotide bases in a DNA strand have been developed. So called "first-generation" sequencing techniques were developed in the mid-to-late

1970s (Heather & Chain, 2016). To sequence a given DNA strand using this method, it is necessary to have many copies of a DNA template, a primer to locate the sequence to copy, DNA polymerase to catalyze the reaction, and nucleotide bases (i.e., dNTPs) to make up the new strand.

The most common first-generation sequencing method is called "Sanger" sequencing after its inventor Frederic Sanger, who won the Nobel Prize for it in 1980 (along with Walter Gilbert, who developed another sequencing approach). Sanger sequencing is a chain-termination technique because it uses special dNTPs (i.e., dideoxynucleotide triphosphate or ddNTP) that once incorporated into the newly copied DNA strand interfere with the addition of more bases. In the mixture of components in which the DNA polymerase extends a fragment in a template dependent manner, newly copied fragments of different lengths are produced as the DNA polymerase stops after incorporating a ddNTP. In a reaction that contains all four regular dNTPs and a small percentage of ddATP (i.e., dideoxyadenosine triphosphate) for example, every fragment produced would end in A. Therefore, if fragments of 4 bp (i.e., xxxA), 7 bp (i.e., xxxxxxA), and 10 bp (i.e., xxxxxxxxxA) were produced, the sequence of the 12 bp target fragment would be xxxAxxAxxAxx, where x equals a non-A nucleotide, either T, C, or G. The rest of the sequence could be determined when the reaction includes all four dNTPs as well as all four ddNTPs. Such a reaction would produce many copies of each potential fragment, which then could be separated according to their lengths via gel electrophoresis (see Figure 5.6).

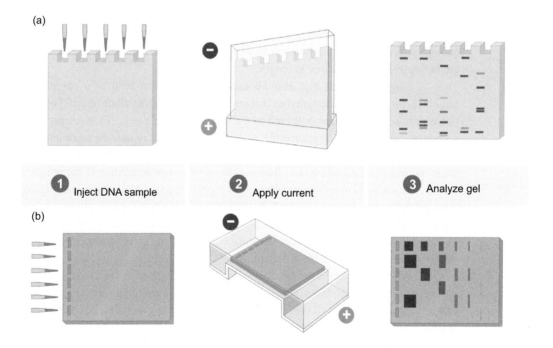

Figure 5.6. **Gel electrophoresis.** Fragments of different size can be separated by gel electrophoresis. Fragments are loaded into wells (either in (a) vertical or (b) horizontal electrophoresis rigs) and an electrical charge is applied. Because DNA fragments carry a negative electrostatic charge, they travel toward a positive charge. Smaller fragments can make their way through the gel more quickly, which over time means that the size of the fragments can be determined by the distance they travel through the gel. Source: Created with Biorender.com.

The length of DNA fragments can be determined by gel electrophoresis. This technique takes advantage of the fact that DNA strands carry a negative electrostatic charge and will therefore be repelled by a negative electrical charge and attracted to a positive one. To separate DNA fragments by length they are placed in a gel substrate that appears solid but contains many small holes through which the DNA strands travel when an electrical current is applied. Small fragments travel more easily and quickly through the gel than do large fragments, and therefore the distance traveled through the gel is a function of fragment size.

Sanger sequencing methods have been automated and were the workhorse in molecular genetics for decades. More recently, Next generation sequencing techniques (i.e., second and third generation) have been developed that have greatly increased the speed, reduced the error rate, and decreased the cost of DNA sequencing (Kulski, 2016). These Next generation techniques benefit from automation (e.g., liquid handling robots), small reaction volumes, and the development of computer software for analysis. There are at least four different types of Next generation sequencing approaches that have been developed. The technical details of the approaches are beyond the scope of this text, but each method relies on synthesizing copies of DNA templates and detecting which bases are added to the growing strand. So, the basic idea of all DNA sequencing approaches is to determine which base is added during the copying of a DNA template.

5.3.3 Polymerase Chain Reaction

DNA sequencing is not the only way to assess genetic variation. In some cases, a researcher is interested in assessing only a subset of an individual's genetic variation. Whole genome sequencing is comparatively expensive and produces a huge amount of data, much of which does not vary between individuals, and is therefore not of use in behavior genetics. Methods of assessing single nucleotide and indel variation make use of another fundamental method in molecular genetic laboratories, called polymerase chain reaction (PCR). It enables researchers to make enough copies of a specific stretch of DNA to visualize variation.

The basic components of a PCR reaction are a DNA template, a thermostable DNA polymerase like Taq polymerase, dNTPs, and primers that flank the specific region of DNA to be copied. One primer is complementary to a 18–25 bp stretch of the reference strand that is upstream (i.e., toward the $5'$ end of the chromosome) of the target sequence. This primer will bind to that location and serve as the starting point for the DNA polymerase to make its copy in the $5'$ to $3'$ direction. Another primer is also used to copy the same stretch of DNA on the complementary strand (see Figure 5.7).

Polymerase chain reactions require the rapid cycling of temperatures and are usually done in thermalcyclers. The first step in PCR unzips the double-stranded DNA so that the copying machinery can operate. This step is called denaturation because it involves heating the reaction mixture to nearly boiling (i.e., around $90°–95°C$). The second step in PCR is to reduce the temperature to approximately $50°–65°C$, at which the primers bind to their complementary sequences on the DNA template. This is called the annealing step. The third step in PCR is to increase the temperature to approximately $72°C$, which is the optimal temperature for the Taq polymerase to operate. This is called the elongation, or extension step. Repeating this cycle of three temperature steps thirty times theoretically produces over a million copies (i.e., 2^{30}) of the target sequence by doubling it each time the cycle is repeated. The exact number of copies is not important, because the goal is to make enough copies so that techniques to visualize the genetic

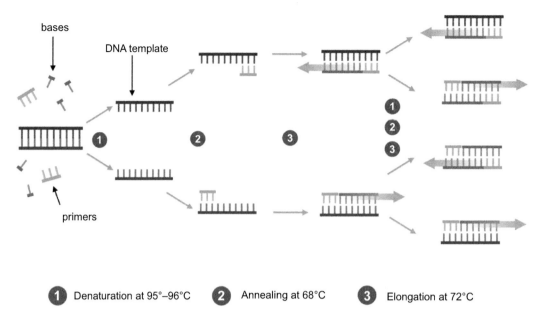

1 ⬤ Denaturation at 95°–96°C   2 ⬤ Annealing at 68°C   3 ⬤ Elongation at 72°C

Figure 5.7. **Polymerase chain reaction.** To make copies of target DNA fragments the PCR mix needs to include DNA template, primers, nucleotide bases (A, T, C, G), and DNA polymerase (e.g., Taq polymerase). The denaturation stage breaks double-stranded DNA into single-stranded DNA. The annealing phase allows the primers to bind to their complementary sequence on the DNA. The elongation phase enables the polymerase to make a copy by adding bases starting at the primer. The number of copies of the DNA target sequence is theoretically doubled after each cycle. Source: Created with Biorender.com.

variant in question can be employed. The visualization technique used depends on the type of genetic variant in question.

Single nucleotide polymorphisms can be detected in many ways. An early method of genotyping SNPs used enzymes called restriction endonucleases (aka restriction enzymes) to cut a PCR product if and only if a specific allele was present at the SNP's location. When an alternative allele was present, the enzyme would leave the PCR product intact. Therefore, alternative alleles of a SNP were identified by the length and number of the fragments present after PCR product was incubated with a restriction enzyme and separated by gel electrophoresis. Such an approach identifies restriction fragment length polymorphisms, or RFLPs.

More recently developed methods take advantage of DNA's complementary binding property. Some methods use oligonucleotide probes that bind to the target SNP. Both probes consist of complementary DNA sequence flanking the SNP, which enables them to bind to its specific location. The probes carry alternative complementary alleles to the SNP, as well as different reporter molecules so that when one of the probes binds to its complementary sequence, a specific color light is produced that is detected and analyzed to determine genotype.

Microarray genotyping methods also use oligonucleotide probes, but affix them to a solid surface, like silica beads. As before, the different probes contain sequence complementary to the alternative alleles of a SNP. Microarrays are densely packed with the silica beads carrying probes to genetic variants. Some microarrays have the capacity to genotype millions of SNPs. Genotypes at a SNP are determined by identifying the probe to which the sample DNA is bound (see Figure 5.8).

Indel and copy number variants can be detected using variants of the methods described above. Indels can be detected by simply amplifying the specific fragment of DNA that contains them using basic PCR and then separating the resulting fragments by gel electrophoresis. Different alleles contain different numbers of the insertion/deletion sequence and are therefore different in length.

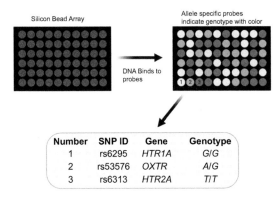

Figure 5.8. **Genotyping bead array.** A genotyping bead array consists of beads seated into wells. Each bead assays one SNP. Attached to each bead are DNA probes that bind alternative alleles for its SNP. Each probe is made of DNA sequence that is complementary to the target SNP. When sample DNA is washed over the array, fragments bind to complementary probes. When two copies of one allele bind, the laser-reader excites one color (e.g., yellow). When two copies of the alternative allele bind the laser-reader excites another color (e.g., blue). When one copy of each allele binds (i.e., heterozygosity), the resulting color is an equal mixture of the other two (i.e., green). Source: Created with Biorender.com.

Such fragment length differences can be detected by gel electrophoresis. Copy number variants can be detected using microarray techniques because alternative alleles produce different intensity of whatever signal (e.g., fluorescence) is used by the specific genotyping platform. Different companies use different technologies for the genotyping methods mentioned here. A comprehensive discussion of these techniques is beyond the scope of this book. Suffice it to say, new technologies are being developed to speed up and improve the accuracy of genotyping.

Check-up

- Describe how DNA is extracted from cells for use in genetic analyses.
- What is gel electrophoresis and why it is so useful in behavior genetic studies?
- Explain the role of different temperatures in PCR.
- Describe primers and their function in PCR.

5.4 Non-Experimental Methods: Testing Associations between Genetic Variants and Behavior

Much of behavior genetic research uses non-experimental methods to investigate heredity–behavior relations. This is especially true of human behavior genetic research because it would be unethical to experimentally manipulate the genomes of human beings to test hypotheses about the role of genetic differences in causing individual differences in behavior. That said, direct experimentation, where an independent variable is manipulated, control variables are held constant, and the dependent variable is measured, is not the only valid scientific approach. The limitations of behavior genetic research must be appreciated and considered when trying to understand heredity–behavior relations. It is important to examine evidence from different methods and populations to determine whether the findings are consistent and coherent. Considering such convergent evidence is especially important when non-experimental methods are used.

The earliest successes in identifying genetic variants that caused disorders in humans focused on diseases that are inherited in Mendelian patterns in families. The method used was linkage analysis in which genetic variants at known locations in the genome are tested for co-inheritance (i.e., linkage) with the disorder in question. Such genetic variants are often called genetic markers, which reflects that their only purpose in this study is to mark a particular region of the genome. The variants do not need to lie in a gene's coding region or be of a certain type. They simply need to vary in the population and to reside at a known location.

Linkage studies are conducted with the participation of large families with multiple generations and with multiple members affected by the disease. The goal of the study is to identify one or more genetic markers where one allele is found in those with the disorder and the alternative allele is found in those without the disorder. Such a pattern suggests that the genetic variant that causes the disease is located near the genetic marker with which it is linked. It is very unlikely that the marker is the disease-causing genetic variant, but if it is co-inherited with the disease it is likely near enough to the disease-causing variant so that recombination has not broken their connection. Once a linked region has been identified, further fine mapping of the region is typically necessary to identify the disease-causing genetic variant.

Non-human animal study designs that are similar to linkage analysis have also contributed to our understanding of heredity–behavior relations. One type, called quantitative trait loci (QTL) studies, can take advantage of the existence of different lines of a model organism, such as mice, that are homozygously fixed for alternative alleles of genetic markers distributed across the genome. In such cases, knowing the genotype at a given locus can indicate the line from which that stretch of genome was derived. In QTL studies, F_2 generation hybrids of two lines are produced and then tested for the behavioral phenotype of interest. Statistical analyses are then conducted to identify genetic markers that are associated with high or low expression of the behavioral trait. If a marker is identified that is statistically associated with high expression of the trait, then it is nominally identified as a quantitative trait locus and it is assumed that a gene located nearby is a likely candidate for contributing to the trait difference. Further mapping studies may be required to identify the gene(s) of interest. QTL studies typically provide evidence for polygenic influence on individual differences in behavior.

Linkage and QTL studies seek to identify genomic regions that harbor genetic variants that cause individual differences in behavior. Once those genomic regions are identified, genes found there become candidate genes, which can then be further investigated. The basic form of candidate gene association study used to test statistical associations between specific genetic variants and individual differences in behavior depends on whether the behavior in question is considered a categorical or quantitative trait.

When a trait is categorical, the candidate gene association test takes the form of a classic epidemiological case-control study. The allele frequencies for the candidate gene are compared for individuals with the trait (i.e., cases) to unrelated individuals without the trait (i.e., controls). The null hypothesis would be that the allele frequencies would be the same in the two groups, thereby supporting the interpretation that there is no association between variants in that gene and the trait. However, when one allele is found at higher frequency in the cases than in controls it is labeled a risk allele.

When the trait in question is quantitative, the candidate gene association test takes the form of a regression analysis. The statistical effect of having zero, one or two copies, in the case of a bi-allelic SNP, is estimated on the trait in a sample of unrelated individuals. If having more copies of the risk allele is statistically associated with an increased score on the quantitative trait, it is interpreted as evidence of association.

In an extension of the candidate gene association study, polygenic risk scores that represent a summation of multiple candidate gene allelic risk scores are tested for statistical association with a quantitative trait in a sample of unrelated individuals. This approach assumes that more than one genetic variant plays a role in causing individual differences in behavior and seeks to test a single genetic score that aggregates genetic risk across known or suspected risk alleles.

Genome-wide association studies (GWAS) take advantage of the tremendous advances in molecular biology to test statistical associations of millions of SNPs across the genome with either categorical or quantitative traits. Like linkage and QTL studies, GWAS are focused on finding locations in the genome that are statistically associated with behavioral traits. In other words, GWAS are designed to identify potential candidate genes and their variants. GWAS are typically conducted with very large sample sizes, often hundreds of thousands of participants. The Psychiatric Genetics Consortium, for example, consists of over 800 researchers from around the world and over 400,000 human participants. Behavior genetics has become big science with the advent of GWAS. Such large sample sizes are necessary for GWAS because of the typical small effect size of genetic effects coupled with the large number of statistical comparisons that are made.

Every research method has limitations. Even carefully controlled experiments run the risk of failing to control for variables that may impact the study's outcome. It is important that those who conduct research understand the limitations of their methods. Consumers of research should also be aware of such limitations.

Behavior genetic research with human participants that seeks statistical associations between genetic variation and individual differences in behavior lacks control over both genes and environment. Human populations are not genetically homogeneous but display genetic differences that are a product of different histories of ancestral populations. In other words, different populations may have different allele frequencies at loci across the genome, which can confound interpretations of genotype–behavior associations. The main problem is that observed statistically significant associations between genetic variation and the behavior of interest may be false positives due to the underlying population differences and not true associations due to differences in the pathway from gene to behavior. This issue is called population stratification, and it complicates the identification of true causal associations between genetic variants and individual differences in behavior (see Figure 5.9).

Modern human populations represent different mixtures of historical populations and it is possible that findings of statistical associations between genetic variants and traits in one population may

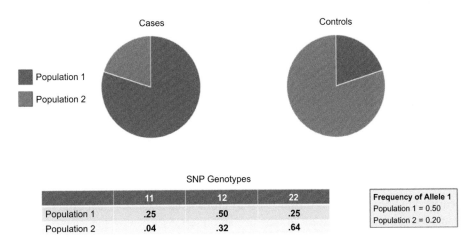

Figure 5.9. **Population stratification.** In a case-control study, the goal is to identify genetic variants that are associated with increased risk for developing some condition (i.e., being a case). This can be done by simply comparing the allele frequencies of SNPs. Risk alleles, by definition, will be found at higher frequencies in the cases than in the controls. Those SNPs that are not associated with the condition will have the same allele frequencies in the two groups. When the case and control groups comprise different proportions of two populations, allele frequency differences between the populations that are unrelated to the trait of interest falsely appear to be risk alleles. In this example, allele 1 would appear to be a risk allele because the populations differ in its frequency and population 1 makes up a higher proportion of cases.

not generalize to others and may be a function of the genetic structure of the population, not representing true causal associations. Methodological and statistical methods have been and continue to be developed to address population stratification in genetic association studies with the goal of identifying true associations between genetic variants and traits while reducing the number of false positive results that are due to genetic differences in populations that are not directly relevant to the trait.

Check-up

- Describe linkage analysis and how it is used to identify genes that cause disorders.
- What are QTL and how are they located?
- Discuss the role of hypothesis testing in different behavior genetic study designs.
- Explain why it is important to control for population stratification.

5.5 Experimental Methods: Generating Genetic Variation

Thus far, most of our discussion about genetic variation has focused on existing genomic sequence variation that was produced by spontaneous mutations. Mutations that arise in germ cells can be passed down to future generations and thereby make their way into the population's gene pool. Mutations that arise in non-germ cells cannot be passed down to offspring, but they can impact the individual's health or behavior. Depending on where they occur, the effect of mutations can be harmful, beneficial, or neutral. As the number of bases affected by the mutation increases, the greater the risk that the mutation will be harmful. Most mutations have small effects.

Ethical prohibitions against manipulating human genomes for research purposes provide a clear boundary that should not be crossed. However, that same boundary does not exist for research with non-human animal models. Mutagenesis, deliberately inducing genetic change, has been used for nearly a century in genetic research. Hermann J. Muller, who had been a student of T. H. Morgan, described using X-rays to induce mutations in *D. melanogaster* in 1928 (Muller, 1928). X-ray mutagenesis can produce point mutations (i.e., affecting a single nucleotide base) or chromosomal rearrangements at low doses, or infertility and death at higher doses.

Decades later, exposure to certain chemicals was also shown to produce mutations in fruit flies. Ethyl methanesulfonate (EMS) was found to be particularly effective at producing point mutations. It was also easy to use. Simply feeding male flies a solution containing EMS produced mutations in their sperm that were transmitted to their offspring. Changing the concentration of EMS in the food adjusts the mutation rate achieved.

Transposable elements (i.e., transposons) have also been used to induce mutations in *D. melanogaster*. Such mobile elements occur naturally in eukaryotic genomes. The transposons can be activated in lines where they already exist by crossing them to a line that expresses an enzyme (i.e., transposase) that induces them to mobilize and insert elsewhere in the genome (Kaufman, 2017). Depending on where the insertion occurs, the impact can vary greatly.

Mutagenesis by X-ray, chemical, or transposable element produces mutations at rates above the spontaneous rate and are accordingly considered valuable genetic tools. However, the locations of resulting mutations are effectively random throughout the genome and need to be mapped after the fact. More recently, other techniques have been developed to engineer genomes.

The inability to target a precise location in the genome for mutagenesis is a significant limitation of using X-rays, chemicals, and transposons. It is desirable to have the ability to target specific genomic locations for mutagenesis in common laboratory non-human animal models. The capability to selectively mutate a particular gene, or even a single nucleotide, has been developed using molecular genetic tools.

Experimental behavior genetics took a great leap forward with the development of a technique called homologous recombination that enables targeted insertion of an engineered gene into a specific genomic location. The researchers who developed it in the late 1980s, Mario R. Capecchi, Martin J. Evans, and Oliver Smithies, were awarded the 2007 Nobel Prize in Physiology or Medicine. This gene targeting technique was developed in mice and has subsequently been adapted for use in rats as well. When the targeted mutation disables the target gene, it is called a knockout. When it enhances the expression of the gene or changes its function, it is called a knock-in.

In this technique, a stretch of DNA that includes an engineered sequence (i.e., vector) that is homologous to the target gene and to the DNA sequences that flank it on both sides is introduced into embryonic stem cells. The flanking DNA sequences enable it to bind to the complementary sequence in the nucleus of the embryonic stem cells. When those cells divide, the engineered DNA sequence can be incorporated into the genome of some of the cells through homologous recombination. The process of cell division includes DNA repair mechanisms that correct potential problems that may arise. In this case, they mistakenly identify the presence of the engineered sequence as a DNA copying problem and correct it by inserting it into the genome.

Cells that contain the engineered version of the targeted gene are identified and injected into developing mouse embryos and implanted into a surrogate mother. Mouse pups that have the engineered gene incorporated into their germ cells will produce gametes containing the engineered gene. When they mature, they can be used as founders of the line of knockout, or knock-in mice, as the case may be. Efforts are underway to construct a line of knockout mice for every gene in the mouse genome and to characterize resulting phenotypes.

Typically, mice that are homozygous for a knocked-out gene live their entire lives without having a functional copy of it in any of their cells. Biological systems often can compensate for disruptions, which may moderate the impact of a knockout. To gain more control over when and in which cell types a gene's function is knocked out, so-called conditional knockout techniques were developed. Such techniques can involve engineering a tissue-specific promoter into the knockout vector, so that the engineered gene is only expressed in cells of interest. Vectors can also be engineered so that the inserted DNA sequence codes for a human gene to create so-called humanized mouse lines. Such lines can be used to investigate the impact of human genetic variation on biological systems and behavior, but with the experimental control possible with mice.

Investigating heredity–behavior relations by comparing the behavior of mice from a knockout line to that of mice from a line that is genetically identical, except for the knockout, provides remarkable experimental control over genes and environment that is impossible in humans. New techniques for making targeted changes to genomes, such as CRISPR-Cas9 (see Box 5.2) will continue to be developed and used to further advance our understanding of the role of genetic variation in individual differences in behavior.

Box 5.2 Critical Concept: CRISPR-Cas9

The construction of knockout lines of mice is expensive, time-consuming, and is not easily transferable to other species. Recently, a technology called CRISPR-Cas9 has been developed that is cheaper, faster, and more accurate than homologous recombination. Its full name is clustered regularly interspaced short palindromic repeats and CRISPR-associated protein 9, which cryptically describes its origin in a natural bacterial gene editing system.

In bacteria, this system works like an immune system to track viruses that have attacked them by taking bits of viral DNA and storing them in "CRISPR arrays" so that they could recognize and respond to future viral attacks more quickly and fully in the future. If newly attacking viruses carry DNA that is the same, or sufficiently similar to, a sequence stored in the CRISPR array, a guide RNA molecule is produced that helps enzymes like Cas9 to identify and then execute a double-stranded cut to the viral DNA thereby disabling the virus. So, the CRISPR-Cas9 system is a complex that includes both the Cas9 enzyme that can cut DNA and a guide RNA molecule (sgRNA) that can unwind double-stranded DNA and bind to a particular complementary sequence (see Figure 5.10). When the RNA guide has bound to the DNA the Cas9 enzyme can cut both DNA strands. The cell's DNA repair mechanisms are then activated to repair the break, although sometimes errors are made which can disable the target gene.

Additional enzymes can be bound to the CRISPR-Cas9 complex to catalyze specific changes to the target DNA, enabling precise gene editing with this system. It is beyond the scope of this book to describe all the CRISPR-Cas9-based techniques that have been or are being developed. Suffice it to say that the capability of this system to identify specific DNA sequences and to recruit DNA repair mechanisms suggests that it will serve as an important gene editing technique for quite some time.

No gene editing technique is error free. A recent advance called prime editing appears to be more precise than CRISPR-Cas9. Unintended gene editing errors in the research lab can be troubling and delay research advances. However, such errors in the clinic are unacceptable. Even if we disregard ethical prohibitions about genetically engineering humans, any chance of unintended genetic change must be eliminated before it should be used in humans.

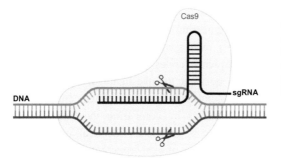

Figure 5.10. **CRISPR-Cas9.** The basic CRISPR-Cas9 system involves an enzyme that can cut double-stranded DNA and a guide RNA (sgRNA) that has a sequence that can bind to its complement, which can be engineered to enable the targeting of specific DNA sequences. Source: Created with Biorender.com.

Check-up

- Describe the methods of mutagenesis used in behavior genetics.
- Explain why a conditional knockout might be preferable to a traditional knockout.
- Discuss the advantages of using CRISPR-Cas9 over X-rays for mutagenesis.

5.6 The Human Genome Project Changed Biomedical Science

In the mid-1980s most geneticists thought that the goal of obtaining the entire sequence of the human genome was overly ambitious. At that time only the 170 kb Epstein-Barr virus genome had been sequenced, and it took several investigators years to complete (Roberts, 2001). Biologists typically worked in small labs on research projects that were investigator driven. Biological research was not considered to be especially collaborative across labs. The idea of sequencing the human genome started to gain traction after a couple of meetings devoted to its discussion brought together some leaders in the field. It became clear that to accomplish such an audacious feat would require a large-scale, publicly funded collaboration that essentially would industrialize the labor-intensive tasks required for DNA sequencing on such a scale. It would also be expensive and drain research funds away from other worthy projects. There was additional skepticism about the project because much of the genome at that time was considered to be "junk DNA" because it did not code for proteins.

Despite the controversy, support was growing for the project and in 1989 the National Center for Human Genome Research was established in the US with James Watson, co-discoverer of the double helical structure of DNA, as its director. The Human Genome Project officially began in late 1990. Genetic mapping projects in non-human model organisms were also moving forward and were helping to drive the development of techniques, software, and collaborations.

In 1991 Craig Venter, who had been director of a sequencing laboratory at the National Institute for Neurological Disorders and Stroke, started a nonprofit entity, The Institute for Genomic Research (TIGR), to compete with the government's Human Genome Project using a different sequencing strategy. The resultant controversy cost Watson his job and led to Francis Collins taking over as director of the Human Genome Project in 1993. Collins focused attention on the potential for medical applications of the project rather than on basic science advances. In 2001, the draft sequence of the human genome and initial analyses were published in joint special issues of *Science* (February 16, 2001; Volume 291, Issue 5507) and *Nature* (February 15, 2001; Volume 409, Issue 6822). Two years later, around the fiftieth anniversary of the description of the double helix, the completed human genome sequence was published, again with important papers in *Science* (April 11, 2003; Volume 300, Issue 5617) and *Nature* (April 24, 2003; Volume 422 Issue 6934). The Human Genome Project was thus declared to be completed two years ahead of schedule, with 99 percent of the gene-containing part of the human sequence finished to 99.99 percent accuracy.

Throughout its existence, the Human Genome Project was international in scope, with researchers from twenty institutions in six countries (China, France, Germany, Japan, the UK, and the US) playing important roles in the International Human Genome Sequencing Consortium. The bulk of the sequencing was done in the US and UK, primarily funded in the US by the Department of Energy and the National Institutes of Health, and in the UK by the Medical Research Council and Wellcome Trust. Craig Venter's company Celera Genomics played an important role in generating sequence data and providing motivation to the public project by competing with them.

What exactly did the Human Genome Project accomplish? For current behavior genetics researchers, it is almost impossible to think about what it would be like if the Human Genome Project never happened. It has profoundly changed the landscape of behavior genetics and a host of other scientific fields (Green, Watson, & Collins, 2015).

Without collaborations between funding agencies, institutions, and over 2,000 researchers around the world, the human genome would likely still not be sequenced. Big science such as this had never been practiced before in biomedicine, although it had been in physics for example, where multinational collaborations were necessary for particle accelerators. Biomedical science typically rewards individual primary investigators for successful projects with raises, promotions, tenure, and other types of incentives. Therefore, it can be difficult to convince researchers to join large collaborative teams. The Human Genome Project demonstrated that research consortia, where investigators work collaboratively on large-scale projects, produce results in biomedical science. Current genome-wide association studies that require large sample sizes are a direct product of the collaborative model pioneered by the Human Genome Project. Big science is here to stay in behavior genetics.

One of the most important impacts of the Human Genome Project has been on data sharing between labs and on making data publicly available. The sequence data produced by researchers was freely shared between researchers. Such openness was required so that data produced by one lab could be combined with data produced by another in a collaborative effort to construct the entire genome sequence. No longer did data stay sequestered in the lab that generated it. In fact, data was made available to the public, and it remains so today. Such data accessibility is unprecedented. Because most of the sequence data was generated by public funding, it is considered to be owned by the public. Such data sharing and accessibility has helped to change the norms in biomedical science and has played a role in the more recent open science movement. The scientific advances that have been made possible by this public model of data sharing will be an important legacy of the project.

The huge amount of data generated by the Human Genome Project and subsequent genomics research drove the development of data management and data analysis tools. Collaborations between geneticists, biostatisticians, and computer software engineers brought together people who were not typically working together to produce ways of handling and analyzing data that had not been previously imagined. Without these novel collaborations and contributions, the promises of the data set would not be realized.

At the start of the Human Genome Project, the tools and methods needed to complete it were not available. The need to scale-up the automation of DNA sequencing drove the innovation in techniques that resulted in the reduction in cost of sequencing a genome from roughly $100 million in 2001 to around $1,000 (see Figure 5.11). Note the dramatic decrease beginning in 2008 after the introduction of second-generation sequencing methods.

The Human Genome Project was the first large-scale scientific project to dedicate a significant portion of its budget (about 5 percent of its NIH funding) to the examination of its ethical, legal, and social implications (i.e., ELSI). In fact, the National Human Genome Research Institute of the NIH maintains this effort with its Ethical, Legal and Social Implications Research Program, which funds and manages research and supports workshops, consortia, and conferences on the impact of genomic research in these areas.

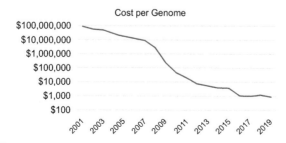

Figure 5.11. **Cost of sequencing.** Recent estimates of sequencing a "human-sized" genome given the costs at the time. Innovation fostered by the Human Genome Project dramatically reduced the cost of DNA sequencing. Note that the y-axis is on a logarithmic scale. First-generation sequencing technologies were used 2001–2007 and then second-generation sequencing technologies were used. Source: Wetterstrand KA. DNA Sequencing Costs: Data from the NHGRI Genome Sequencing Program (GSP). Retrieved from: www.genome.gov/sequencingcostsdata. Accessed January 30, 2020.

There are those who think that the Human Genome Project has not lived up to its promise, especially in the context of direct applications to improve human health. However, its impact on biomedical research and technology is ongoing and will certainly exceed its cost in time if it has not done so already. For example, the rapid development of mRNA vaccines for COVID-19 would not have been possible without the advances made by the Human Genome Project.

Check-up

- Explain why some scientists were initially against the Human Genome Project.
- Explain how the Human Genome Project has impacted how biomedical researchers work.
- Describe the types of technological advances that resulted from the Human Genome Project.

5.7 SUMMARY

- The human nuclear genome comprises 3.2 billion bases with less than 1 percent varying between people.
- Genetic variants range from single nucleotide polymorphisms to structural variants that can affect millions of bases.
- Genetic variants can have no impact or can have a dramatic effect on gene expression.
- Different study designs with different benefits and limitations have been used to identify and characterize heredity–behavior relations. Linkage analysis requires families, whereas candidate gene association studies and GWAS test unrelated individuals. QTL analyses are typically done with mice.
- Assessing genetic variants with molecular biology typically requires a DNA template, primers, DNA polymerases, dNTPs and the polymerase chain reaction.
- PCR is a widely used technique to make copies of a specific stretch of DNA by breaking it apart (denaturation), binding primers to a specific site (annealing), and then enabling DNA polymerase to make copies (elongation).
- The introduction of genetic changes is done in non-human experimental models. Early approaches produced mutations in random locations, whereas later methods enabled researchers to target specific locations.
- The Human Genome Project was an international collaboration over thirteen years to sequence the entire human genome.
- The innovations driven by the Human Genome Project have changed the ways in which biomedical science is conducted.

RECOMMENDED READING

- McEntyre, J., & Ostell, J. (Eds.) (2002–). *The NCBI Handbook* [Internet]. Bethesda, MD: National Center for Biotechnology Information. Retrieved from: www.ncbi.nlm.nih.gov/books/NBK21101/
- Mullis, K. (1998). *Dancing Naked in the Mind Field*. New York: Pantheon.

REFERENCES

Abdellaoui, A., Ehli, E. A., Hottenga, J.-J., Weber, Z., Mbarek, H., Willemsen, G., . . . Boomsma, D. I. (2015). CNV concordance in 1,097 MZ twin pairs. *Twin Research and Human Genetics: The Official Journal of the International Society for Twin Studies, 18*(1), 1–12. doi:10.1017/thg.2014.86

Genomes Project Consortium, Auton, A., Brooks, L. D., Durbin, R. M., Garrison, E. P., Kang, H. M., . . . Abecasis, G. R. (2015). A global reference for human genetic variation. *Nature, 526*(7571), 68–74. doi:10.1038/nature15393

Green, E. D., Watson, J. D., & Collins, F. S. (2015). Human Genome Project: Twenty-five years of big biology. *Nature, 526*(7571), 29–31. doi:10.1038/526029a

Heather, J. M., & Chain, B. (2016). The sequence of sequencers: The history of sequencing DNA. *Genomics, 107*(1), 1–8. doi:10.1016/j.ygeno.2015.11.003

Kaufman, T. C. (2017). A short history and description of *Drosophila melanogaster* classical genetics: Chromosome aberrations, forward genetic screens, and the nature of mutations. *Genetics, 206*(2), 665–689. doi:10.1534/genetics.117.199950

Kulski, J. K. (2016). Next-generation sequencing: An overview of the history, tools, and "omic" applications. Retrieved from: www.intechopen.com/books/next-generation-sequencing-advances-applications-and-challenges/next-generation-sequencing-an-overview-of-the-history-tools-and-omic-applications

Lander, E. S., Linton, L. M., Birren, B., Nusbaum, C., Zody, M. C., Baldwin, J., . . . International Human Genome Sequencing Consortium (2001). Initial sequencing and analysis of the human genome. *Nature, 409*(6822), 860–921. doi:10.1038/35057062

Mullaney, J. M., Mills, R. E., Pittard, W. S., & Devine, S. E. (2010). Small insertions and deletions (INDELs) in human genomes. *Hum Mol Genet, 19*(R2), R131–R136. doi:10.1093/hmg/ddq400

Muller, H. J. (1928). The production of mutations by X-rays. *Proc Natl Acad Sci USA, 14*(9), 714–726. doi:10.1073/pnas.14.9.714

Mullis, K. (1998). *Dancing Naked in the Mind Field*. New York: Pantheon.

Pylyp, L. Y., Spynenko, L. O., Verhoglyad, N. V., Mishenko, A. O., Mykytenko, D. O., & Zukin, V. D. (2018). Chromosomal abnormalities in products of conception of first-trimester miscarriages detected by conventional cytogenetic analysis: A review of 1000 cases. *J Assist Reprod Genet, 35*(2), 265–271. doi:10.1007/s10815-017-1069-1

Roberts, L. (2001). The human genome: Controversial from the start. *Science (New York, N.Y.), 291*(5507), 1182–1188. doi:10.1126/science.291.5507.1182a

Warren, J. T., Jr., Peacock, M. L., Rodriguez, L. C., & Fink, J. K. (1993). An MspI polymorphism in the hyman serotonin receptor gene (HTR2): Detection by DGGE and RFLP analysis. *Hum Mol Genet, 2*(3), 338. doi:10.1093/hmg/2.3.338

Zarrei, M., MacDonald, J. R., Merico, D., & Scherer, S. W. (2015). A copy number variation map of the human genome. *Nat Rev Genet, 16*(3), 172–183. doi:10.1038/nrg3871

6 Neurogenetics

Take a moment to think about cells. Which type of cell is your favorite? If you were to ask biologists, you would likely get a wide variety of responses. Some might have a soft spot in their hearts for red blood cells, or liver cells, or maybe even single-celled organisms like bacteria. However, if you were to ask psychologists which cells they prefer, you would likely learn that most of them favor neurons. Because it is with *neural* mechanisms that animals access, process, and act on information. Neural activity underlies all behavior, and therefore neurons occupy a privileged position in psychology.

This chapter introduces neurons as a type of cell that is specialized for communication, and it addresses the role of genetic variation in neural structure and function. This chapter also focuses on the connections between neurons and the role that genetic variation plays in them. Some of the different methods used to examine neural activity are presented along with evidence for how neural activity is impacted by genetic variation. Finally, the chapter examines how drugs affect neural activity and how genetic variation affects the impact of drugs on neural function.

6.1 Neurons Are Cells Specialized for Communication

Neurons are the most consequential cells in mammalian nervous systems. To understand pathways from genes to behaviors it is important to consider the impact of genetic variation on the structure and function of neurons.

6.1.1 Neurons Carry Out Basic Cellular Functions

Although the primary reason that psychologists find neurons fascinating is that they have a unique role in information processing, it is important to first consider what neurons have in common with other animal cells. In neurons and other cells, basic functions are mediated by proteins and are therefore dependent on genetic mechanisms. Genetic variation affecting the structure or function of proteins involved in basic biological processes is likely to play a vital role in individual differences in behavior or in differential risk for the development of psychiatric disorders.

Cells have membranes to separate intracellular space from extracellular space (see Figure 6.1(a)). Typically, cellular membranes consist of a phospholipid bilayer that contains embedded proteins to achieve selective permeability by allowing some substances to cross, but not others. The capacity to regulate the contents of its intracellular space is especially important for neural function.

The intracellular space of neurons is filled with cytoplasm, which includes gel-like cytosol, organelles, and other components involved in cellular function, such as nutrients. Organelles are

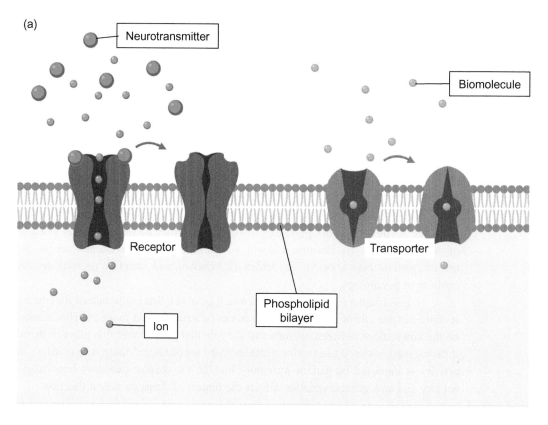

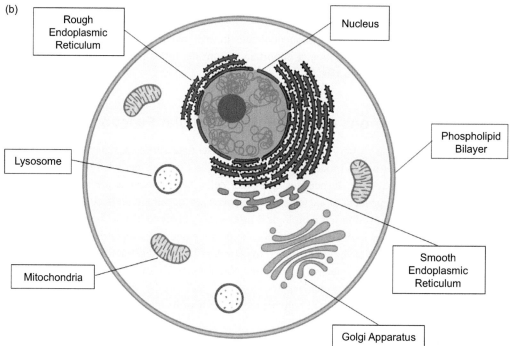

Figure 6.1. **Cell membrane and organelles.** (a) Semipermeable cellular membranes are made up of a phospholipid bilayer that contains embedded proteins such as ion channels and transporters. (b) Cells contain organelles to carry out specific metabolic functions. Source: Created with Biorender.com.

structures that carry out specific functions such as the production, storage, and transport of proteins, the production of energy, and the removal of wastes (see Figure 6.1(b)).

The nucleus is an organelle that contains most of the cell's genome (except for mitochondrial DNA, see below) and is where DNA is transcribed into mRNA, which was covered in Chapter 4. The nucleus is surrounded by a membrane that contains pores through which mRNA is transported for translation into protein, and which prevents the free movement of large molecules into or out of the nucleus.

Translation of mRNA into proteins, most of which will be used within the neuron, takes place in the rough endoplasmic reticulum (RER), which is located near the nuclear membrane. Neurons also contain smooth endoplasmic reticulum (SER) in which vesicles are made for transporting proteins made in the rough endoplasmic reticulum. The Golgi apparatus (GA) is the organelle that packages proteins into vesicles for transport to the locations within the neuron where they are used. Dysfunctions in protein processing that occurs in these organelles play a role in the development of many diseases including neurodegenerative diseases such as Alzheimer disease and Huntington's disease (Lindholm, Korhonen, Eriksson, & Koks, 2017). When protein folding systems fail, a condition known as ER Stress, the unfolded protein response (UPR) genes are activated to remove misfolded proteins and aid in the proper folding of subsequently translated proteins (Takayanagi, Fukuda, Takeuchi, Tsukada, & Yoshida, 2013). It is possible that genetic variation in UPR genes plays a role in risk for certain neurodegenerative disorders.

Mitochondria are organelles that generate adenosine triphosphate (ATP), which provides energy to drive many metabolic processes via oxidative phosphorylation. Mitochondria are unique in that they contain DNA that is separate from the chromosomes in the cell's nucleus. There are thirty-seven genes found in mitochondrial DNA, most of which code for enzymes involved in oxidative phosphorylation, and some that code for transfer RNA and ribosomal RNA involved in translating mRNA into proteins. Mitochondrial DNA was long thought to be inherited solely maternally in humans, although recent evidence suggests that in rare cases it is possible for fathers to pass on some of their mitochondrial DNA (Luo et al., 2018). Diseases caused by mutations in genes involved in mitochondrial function can produce a wide range of symptoms that are due to a reduction in the capacity for mitochondria to produce energy.

The cytosol of neurons also includes lysosomes, which are membrane-bound organelles that degrade cellular waste. Lysosomes contain enzymes that are synthesized in the rough endoplasmic reticulum. Genetic variants that impact the function of lysosomal enzymes or other aspects of lysosome function can have substantial health consequences by causing lysosomal storage diseases. The most common lysosomal storage disease is Gaucher disease, which can include neurological complications such as mental deterioration or difficulty controlling voluntary movements and is due to mutations in the gene that codes for the enzyme beta-glucocerebrosidase.

The main point of this section is that neurons are cells that carry out basic cellular processes. Genetic variations that adversely affect cellular processes can cause diseases that are inherited in Mendelian fashion and produce cognitive or behavioral symptoms. In general, when considering heredity–behavior relations it may be useful to think about how genetic differences that impact the expression, structure, or function of proteins might affect cellular functions.

6.1.2 Neurons Receive and Transmit Information

In addition to their basic cellular functions, neurons communicate. Neurons receive information from cells (or the environment in the case of sensory neurons) and then send information to

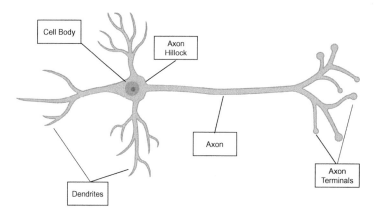

Figure 6.2. **Basic structure of a neuron.** Neurons have structures that receive (dendrites), process (axon hillock of cell body), conduct (axon), and transmit (axon terminals) information. Source: Created with Biorender.com.

other cells. Neurons can be classified into three main categories: (1) sensory neurons, which receive information from external stimuli, (2) interneurons, which receive information from and send information to other neurons, and (3) motor neurons, which send signals to the muscles. Neurons across the animal kingdom, from roundworms to blue whales, share structural and functional similarities.

For illustrative purposes, let us consider the basic structure of an interneuron (see Figure 6.2). The cell body of a neuron, or perikaryon, contains the nucleus and many other organelles. Structures emanating from the cell body are called dendrites. A structure that carries information away from the cell body to the target is called the axon. The end of the axon makes connections to other neurons and is called the axon terminal. These four main structures carry out the primary communication functions of neurons: (1) dendrites *receive* input from other cells, (2) the input is then *processed* in the cell body at the axon hillock, (3) the processed signal is then *conducted* down the axon to the terminal, and finally (4) a signal is *transmitted* from the axon terminal to the target cell in the synapse.

Information received by interneurons is generally in the form of small molecules or peptides called neurotransmitters, which bind to proteins called receptors. When the appropriate molecule binds to a receptor an action is initiated. The type of action depends on the type of receptor. Ionotropic receptors change their conformation to allow ions to flow into the neuron when activated. Most neurotransmitter receptors are metabotropic receptors, which initiate metabolic processes when activated. The specific metabolic process depends on which proteins are associated with the receptor. Metabotropic receptors are also called G-protein coupled receptors, and these G-proteins are associated with different second messenger systems that play roles in a variety of metabolic processes. Ligands bind to the metabotropic receptors on the extracellular side of the membrane, and on the intracellular side the receptor activates a guanine nucleotide-binding (G) protein. Diversity in metabotropic receptor systems means that one neurotransmitter can have multiple biological effects depending on which receptor is being activated.

Ions are electrically charged molecules. They are the currency of neural communication. Neurons spend energy to maintain an intracellular resting state that has a negative electrical charge relative to the extracellular environment. Much of that energy is used to power a sodium potassium pump, which is an integral membrane protein that ejects three sodium ions (Na^+) and takes in two potassium ions (K^+) each time it operates. As you can see, if you replace three positive ions with two, you decrease the intracellular electrical charge by one each time the pump operates. In addition, the intracellular concentration of Na^+ is reduced while K^+ is increased. The maintenance of a difference in electrical charge and molecular concentration between the intracellular space and the extracellular space creates the potential for work. The resting potential of a typical neuron is about -60 mV.

Negative ions are attracted to positive charges and repelled by negative charges. Therefore, when the intracellular space has fewer negative ions than the extracellular space the resulting electrostatic pressure causes negative ions to rush into the intracellular space when there is an opportunity (i.e., when the proper ion channels are open). In addition, when molecules are concentrated in one area, they tend to move to an area of lower concentration until they are evenly distributed throughout the space. This is a process known as diffusion. Together electrostatic pressure and diffusion are potent forces for moving ions across membranes when channels are open.

Information received at the dendrites opens ion channels, which allows ions (e.g., Na^+) to rush into the neuron. If enough of these positively charged ions enter the neuron so that the intracellular electrical charge at the axon hillock surpasses a threshold around -40mV an action potential will be produced (i.e., the neuron will "fire"). The information processing that occurs in the cell body consists of summing the inputs and determining whether the intracellular electrical charge surpasses its firing threshold. Input from cells can be depolarizing (i.e., positive charges that reduce the electrical charge difference between the inside and the outside of the cell), or hyperpolarizing (i.e., negative charges that make the interior more negative compared to the outside of the cell). The firing "decision" represents a determination of whether the intracellular electrical charge exceeds a threshold. If it does, an action potential is produced. If it does not, no action potential is produced. The decision is binary.

In an action potential, the depolarization of the cell body triggers the rapid and sequential opening of voltage-gated sodium channels along the axon. This allows Na^+ to rush into the axon which further propagates the depolarization toward the axon terminal. The action potential is an all-or-none phenomenon: once initiated it carries on to completion. There is no such thing as half an action potential. The action potential travels in one direction, from axon hillock to axon terminal because of a refractory period during which sodium channels are inactive after opening, inhibiting back propagation of the signal.

When the action potential reaches the axon terminal, voltage-gated calcium (Ca^{++}) channels open allowing Ca^{++} ions to rush in (see Figure 6.3). This influx of Ca^{++} ions causes neurotransmitter filled vesicles to move toward the synapse and spill their contents into it. The neurotransmitters in the synapse bind to receptors on the postsynaptic neuron initiating communication with it. When neurotransmitters are no longer receptor bound, they may be removed from the synapse via reuptake by transporters located on the presynaptic neuron or on glial cells. When neurotransmitters are transported into presynaptic cells, they may be either repackaged for re-release, or degraded by enzymes.

Interneurons receive neurochemical information (i.e., neurotransmitters) from other neurons, transduce it into electrochemical information (i.e., action potentials), and then transduce it into neurochemical information to communicate with other neurons. The fine details of the process are beyond the scope of this text. However, we will focus attention on biological components of the process and the role that genetic variation may play in differential neural function.

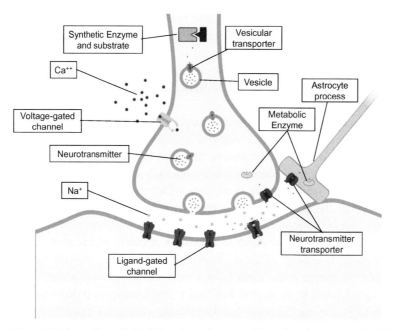

Figure 6.3. **Synaptic activity.** When the action potential reaches the axon terminal of the presynaptic neuron, neurotransmitters are released into the synapse for receptor binding. Reuptake into presynaptic cell or glial cell removes neurotransmitters from the synapse. Variation in genes that code for components of neural communication is common and impacts neurotransmission. Source: Created with Biorender.com.

Check-up

- Describe the basic cellular functions that are carried out by neurons.
- Compare and contrast resting potential and action potential.
- Describe the "life" of a neurotransmitter molecule from the time it is synthesized to the time that it is degraded.

6.2 Genetic Variation for Neural Components Is Common

As described in the previous section, many different proteins play important roles in the function of neurotransmitter systems (see Box 6.1). Such proteins are the products of genes that harbor sequence variations in protein coding and regulatory regions. Such variation is common in populations and likely contributes to individual differences in neurotransmission. To illustrate the scope of genetic variation in neurotransmitter system components, let us focus our attention on the serotonin system.

Box 6.1 Critical Concept: Neurotransmitter Systems

Neurons typically release one neurotransmitter into synapses, although there is growing evidence that some neurons are capable of releasing more than one neurotransmitter into synapses. The capacity to release more than one neurotransmitter substantially increases the versatility of neural communication. However, to simplify our discussion, we will refer to neurons by the primary neurotransmitter that they release. For example, serotonergic neurons are those that release serotonin; dopaminergic neurons are those that release dopamine, and so on. But it is important to keep in mind that by simplifying our thinking about neural function, we run the risk of misunderstanding and mischaracterizing pathways from genes to behavior.

Neurotransmitter systems can be defined to include the neurons that release the neurotransmitter of interest and their target cells. A description of a neurotransmitter system would include the brain area(s) in which the neuronal cell bodies are located and the brain areas to which those neurons project their axons. For example, the approximately 200,000 neurons that release serotonin have their cell bodies in either the midbrain or brainstem raphe nuclei (see Figure 6.4). Those originating in the midbrain raphe project to many forebrain areas including cerebral cortex, amygdala, hippocampus, hypothalamus, ventral tegmental area, and others. The serotonergic neurons originating in the brainstem raphe nucleus project to the peripheral nervous system via the spinal cord.

Components involved in synthesis, transport, release, reuptake, pre- and postsynaptic signaling (e.g., receptors), and degradation should also be considered as parts of a neurotransmitter system. As you can see, there are many components involved in a neurotransmitter system that can vary genetically thereby affecting its function.

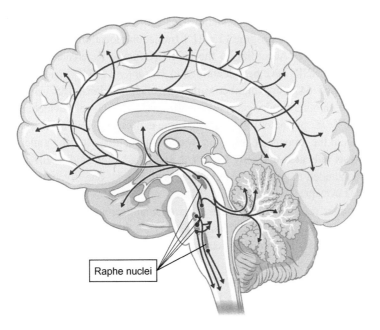

Raphe nuclei

Figure 6.4. **Serotonergic pathway in the brain.** Neurons that release serotonin have their cell bodies in raphe nuclei, which are located along the midline of the midbrain and the brainstem and project their axons to many brain areas and to the peripheral nervous system. Source: Created with Biorender.com.

Serotonin is a monoamine produced in and released by neurons that have cell bodies in brainstem raphe nuclei with axons that project to most areas of the CNS. These neurons synthesize

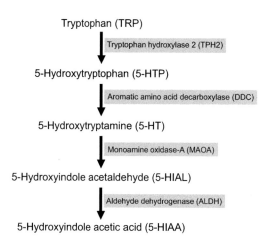

Tryptophan (TRP)

⬇ Tryptophan hydroxylase 2 (TPH2)

5-Hydroxytryptophan (5-HTP)

⬇ Aromatic amino acid decarboxylase (DDC)

5-Hydroxytryptamine (5-HT)

⬇ Monoamine oxidase-A (MAOA)

5-Hydroxyindole acetaldehyde (5-HIAL)

⬇ Aldehyde dehydrogenase (ALDH)

5-Hydroxyindole acetic acid (5-HIAA)

Figure 6.5. **Pathway of serotonin synthesis and metabolism.** Tryptophan hydroxylase 2 converts dietary tryptophan to 5-hydroxytryptophan, which is then converted by aromatic amino acid decarboxylase to 5-hydroxytryptamine (serotonin [5-HT]). Monoamine oxidase-A converts serotonin to 5-hydroxyindole acetaldehyde, which is then converted by aldehyde dehydrogenase to 5-hydroxyindole acetic acid and eliminated. Source: Created with Biorender.com.

serotonin from the dietary amino acid tryptophan via two enzymatic reactions catalyzed by tryptophan hydroxylase (TPH2) and aromatic amino acid decarboxylase (DDC; see Figure 6.5). Monoamine oxidase-A (MAOA) and aldehyde dehydrogenase (ALDH) catalyze the reactions in the breakdown of serotonin. Variation in the genes that code for these enzymes is common in human populations and may impact their catalytic activity. For example, the gene that encodes the TPH2 enzyme (gene name: *TPH2*, note that abbreviations for genes are italicized, but abbreviations for proteins are not) is located on chromosome 12.q.21.1 (molecular location: base pairs 71,938,846 to 72,032,441) and has 13 exons. According to the NCBI (Genome Reference Consortium Human genome build 38), 25,643 SNPs have been identified in *H. sapiens TPH2*. In addition to the SNPs, there have been identified 647 copy number variations, 491 deletions, 165 insertions, 38 short tandem repeats along with other sundry genetic variations in *TPH2*. There is evidence that particular genetic variants in the *TPH2* promoter region impact gene expression *in vitro*, which could produce individual differences in the amount of serotonin available in neurons (Chen, Vallender, & Miller, 2008). A meta-analysis indicated that only 69 *TPH2* SNPs had been studied for association with mental illness and concluded that seven are associated with at least one psychopathological condition (Ottenhof, Sild, Levesque, Ruhe, & Booij, 2018).

Neurotransmitter receptors are another class of neural proteins that vary genetically and may therefore play important roles in individual differences in behavior. Let us consider serotonin receptors as an example to illustrate the rich genetic diversity that exists in neurotransmitter system components.

There is only one serotonin receptor that is ionotropic, and it is called the 5-hydroxytryptamine receptor 3 (5-HT3). The 5-HT3 receptor, like other ligand-gated ion channels, is made up of five subunits (i.e., is pentameric) arranged around a pore through which positively charged ions (i.e., Na$^+$, K$^+$, or Ca^{++}) flow. The genes that code for subunits A and B (i.e., gene names: *HTR3* and *HTR3B*) lie near each other on chromosome 11q23.2. The genes that code for the other three subunits (C, D, and E; gene names: *HTR3C, HTR3D, HTR3E*) are located on chromosome 3q27.1. Each of these genes contains substantial genetic variation (see Table 6.1). Functional pentamers for 5-HT3 receptors contain a mix of A and other subunits (i.e., heteromeric). Homomeric receptors (i.e., made of only one type of subunit) are only functional when that subunit is the A subunit, which shows diminished function relative to heteromeric receptors.

Table 6.1 Serotonin receptor genetics

Receptor class	Serotonin receptor	Gene	Chromosomal location	Molecular location[a]	Exons	SNPs[b]	Missense[b]
Ionotropic	3A	HTR3A	11q23.2	113,975,075 to 113,990,313	9	4,418	412
	3B	HTR3B	11q23.2	113,898,923 to 113,949,119	11	12,953	322
	3C	HTR3C	3q27.1	184,053,047 to 184,060,673	9	2,200	317
	3D	HTR3D	3q27.1	184,031,544 to 184,039,369	10	2,199	345
	3E	HTR3E	3q27.1	184,097,064 to 184,106,995	9	2,775	387
Metabotropic	1A	HTR1A	5q12.3	63,960,048 to 63,962,292[c]	1	780	305
	1B	HTR1B	6q14.1	77,460,848 to 77,464,022[c]	1	1,000	233
	1D	HTR1D	1p36.12	23,191,895 to 23,194,729[c]	1	878	261
	1E	HTR1E	6q14.3	86,936,919 to 87,020,068	2	19,212	202
	1F	HTR1F	3p11.2-p11.1	87,792,767 to 87,994,856	6	49,880	214
	2A	HTR2A	13q14.2	46,831,542 to 46,897,076[c]	4	15,082	265
	2B	HTR2B	2q37.1	231,108,230 to 231,126,172[c]	4	4,156	356
	2C	HTR2C	Xq23	114,584,078 to 114,910,061	7	58,095	229
	4	HTR4	5q32	148,451,032 to 148,654,527[c]	12	51,890	494
	5A	HTR5A	7q36.2	155,070,324 to 155,087,392	2	4,948	282
	5BP[d]	HTR5BP	2q14.1	117,859,427 to 117,903,680	-	12,132	-
	6	HTR6	1p36.13	19,665,287 to 19,680,966	3	4,154	343
	7	HTR7	10q23.31	90,738,693 to 90,857,914[c]	5	28,403	268

Note: [a]Source: Genome Reference Consortium Human Build 38 Organism: *Homo sapiens*, from NCBI. [b]Source: NCBI variation viewer. SNPs indicates the number of single nucleotide polymorphisms identified in the human genome, and Missense identifies the number of SNPs that produce an amino acid substitution (i.e., non-synonymous). Other types of genetic variation are not shown here. [c]Complementary strand. [d]5BP is a pseudogene (i.e., resembles a gene but does not code for proteins).

There are thirteen metabotropic serotonin receptors in *H. sapiens*. Such receptors are characterized by seven transmembrane domains and association with G-proteins on the intracellular side that interact with second messenger systems to initiate downstream biological processes. Serotonin receptors utilize diverse second messenger systems, which can result in a variety of outcomes such as opening/closing ion channels or stimulating/inhibiting enzymes in biochemical pathways (e.g., adenylyl cyclase). Each metabotropic serotonin receptor is coded for by a single gene, and each of those genes harbor substantial genetic variability. Each serotonin receptor has its own specific tissue distribution and can be found in multiple brain areas. Some serotonin receptors, such as the 5-HT1A receptor, can function as either postsynaptic receptors or presynaptic auto-receptors, depending on the brain area in question. The variety of receptors and the outcomes of their activation enable a single neurotransmitter to produce a rich diversity of signals. The variation found in genes that code for components of the serotonin system is potentially an important contributor to individual differences in behavioral and psychological traits affected by serotonin neurotransmission.

Check-up

- Describe the pathways of serotonin releasing neurons in the human brain.
- How is serotonin produced in the brain?
- Compare and contrast ionotropic and metabotropic receptors in the serotonin system.

6.3 Formation and Maintenance of Synapses and Circuits Depends on Genes

In this section, let us consider aspects of brain development that are impacted by genetic variation. During embryonic (i.e., up to ten weeks after fertilization) and fetal development, cells in the neural tube along the cerebral ventricles divide and produce multipotent neural stem cells that will become neurons and glial cells. This process is called neurogenesis. The cells then migrate along radial glia to their destination before they differentiate into their final cell type. Cellular differentiation depends on differential gene expression, whereby one type of neuron expresses a different set of genes than does another type of neuron. As you may recall, such regulation of gene expression is called epigenetics (see Chapter 4).

Next, neurons extend their dendrites and axons to make connections with other neurons in a process called synaptogenesis. Chemical communication between cells is critical in directing cells to migrate to the proper location, in determining which type of cell to become, and in making connections between cells. During brain development many more neurons and connections are made than are needed, so the process of fine-tuning brain circuits includes the programmed death of neurons called apoptosis.

6.3.1 Genetic Variation Affects Synaptic Integrity

Defects in any of these developmental processes, whether of genetic or environmental origin, can have serious consequences for mental processes and risk for intellectual disability, psychiatric disorder, or health problems such as the development of certain types of cancer (Guarnieri, de Chevigny, Falace, & Cardoso, 2018). Let us consider genetic variants that impact the development

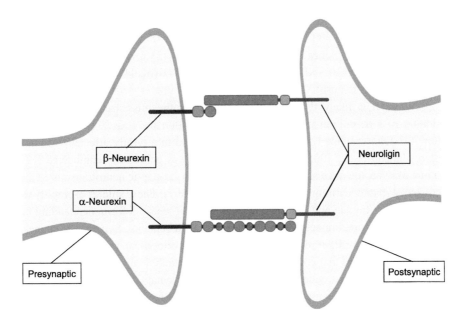

Figure 6.6. **Neurexins and neuroligins.** Neurexins and neuroligins are transmembrane proteins that connect presynaptic and postsynaptic neurons in the synapse. Neurexins are localized on presynaptic neurons, and neuroligins are localized on postsynaptic neurons. These cell adhesion molecules play roles in the development, maintenance, and function of synapses. Source: Created with Biorender.com. After Reichelt & Dachtler (2015).

and maintenance of synapses and appear to be associated with risk for autism spectrum disorder (Guang et al., 2018). Our purpose in this section is to present an example of how genetic variation may impact synapse formation and maintenance to illustrate potential biological mechanisms of synaptopathology – diseases caused by synaptic dysfunction.

Synaptic cell adhesion molecules are proteins that connect the presynaptic neuron to the postsynaptic neuron to establish and maintain synaptic integrity (i.e., proper synaptic physical conformation to facilitate neurotransmission), and to play a role in cell signaling. There are many different synaptic cell adhesion molecules expressed in the mammalian CNS. For illustrative purposes, let us focus on neurexins and neuroligins, which are among the best studied synaptic cell adhesion molecules and may play a role in traits relevant to autism spectrum disorders such as deficits in sociability (Baig, Yanagawa, & Tabuchi, 2017).

Neurexins are a family of transmembrane proteins that have a short intracellular domain, a larger extracellular domain, and are located on the presynaptic neuron (see Figure 6.6). Neurexins are coded by three large genes: *NRXN1* (chromosomal location: 2p16.3; 33 exons), *NRXN2* (11q13.1; 27 exons), *NRXN3* (14q24.3-q31.1; 32 exons). Neurexins have two main conformational types, where the β-form is a truncated version of the longer α-form. For a given neurexin gene, the α- and β-forms share much of their DNA sequence, but not all. Each form has its own promoter, and there is an exon that is specific to the β-form. Additionally, each NRXN gene carries several alternative splice sites, which creates the potential for thousands of neurexin isoforms. Substantial genetic variation exists in human NRXN genes: *NRXN1* (321,001 SNPs; 1,226 missense); *NRXN2* (29,206 SNPs; 1,381 missense); *NRXN3* (460,394 SNPs; 1,428 missense).

Neuroligins are a family of transmembrane proteins localized on the postsynaptic neuron (see Figure 6.6). Like neurexins, neuroligins have a short intracellular domain and a larger extracellular domain. Five genes in the human genome code for neuroligins: *NLGN1* (chromosomal location: 3q26.31; 16 exons), *NLGN2* (17p13.1; 8 exons), *NLGN3* (Xq13.1; 11 exons), *NLGN4X* (Xp22.32-p22.31; 13 exons), and *NLGN4Y* (Yq11.221; 18 exons). Substantial genetic variation exists in human NLGN genes: *NLGN1* (215,758 SNPs; 458 missense), *NLGN2* (4,250 SNPs; 596 missense), *NLGN3* (5,410 SNPs; 276 missense), *NLGN4X* (62,041 SNPs; 355 missense), *NLGN4Y* (8,830 SNPs; 175 missense).

While it is likely that even though most of the missense mutations do not affect the functioning of a neuroligin protein, a missense mutation in *NLGN3* that replaces an arginine at position 451 with cysteine (i.e., R451C) was identified in a family affected with autism spectrum disorders (Jamain et al., 2003). When this mutation was genetically engineered (i.e., knocked-in) into a line of mice, the mice showed increased inhibitory synaptic neurotransmission, social deficits, and enhanced spatial learning ability (Tabuchi et al., 2007). These studies exemplify the necessity of interplay between human and non-human animal model research for understanding mechanisms by which genetic variation impacts individual differences in behavior. Synaptic cell adhesion molecules like neurexin and neuroligin play critical roles in the development, maintenance, and functioning of synapses, and the genes that code for them contain substantial variation. It seems like a safe bet that as research on genes that code for proteins critical for synaptic integrity continues, more variants will be demonstrated to be associated with a variety of behaviors.

6.3.2 Synapses Are Where the Action Is

When an action potential reaches the axon terminal, voltage-gated Ca^{++} channels open and allow calcium ions to rush in. This causes neurotransmitter filled vesicles to mobilize toward the synapse and fuse with the membrane to spill their contents into the synapse in a process known as exocytosis. Neurotransmitters float around in the extracellular fluid in the synaptic cleft where they may then bind to specific sites on receptors.

Let us consider the 5-HT1B receptor as an example of how genetic variation can affect the binding of neurotransmitters to receptors. As you recall, the 5-HT1B receptor is a G-protein coupled serotonin receptor. In the CNS it is localized on presynaptic terminals and functions to regulate neurotransmitter release. It is one of the few serotonin receptors that has had its structure determined at high-resolution by X-ray crystallography (Wang et al., 2013). The general structure of G-protein coupled receptors includes seven transmembrane α-helical domains (TM1–7), and an intramembrane helix (H8), which are connected by three intracellular loops (IL) and three extracellular loops (EL; see Figure 6.7).

The 5-HT1B receptor comprises 390 amino acids. The binding site for ligands is located where TM3, TM5, TM6, TM7, and E2 form a pocket on the extracellular side of the receptor. This pocket confers selectivity for ligands. Induced mutations at several locations that result in amino acid replacement at critical locations in the binding pocket impact binding affinity of some ligands, but not others (Wang et al., 2013). Binding affinity can be thought of as an index of attraction of the receptor to the ligand. Higher affinity can lead to greater receptor occupancy, and therefore a greater degree of activation. Investigating the role of genetic differences in the binding of ligands to receptors is an active area of research that should result in advances in understanding heredity–behavior relations.

After binding to receptors, neurotransmitters are removed from the synapse via a process known as reuptake by integral membrane proteins called transporters. The gene that codes for the serotonin transporter (*SLC6A4*) is located on chromosome 17q11.2 and has 15 exons. There is

(a)

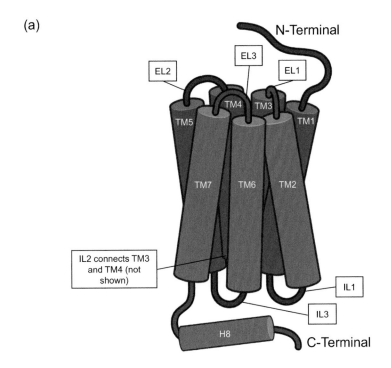

(b)

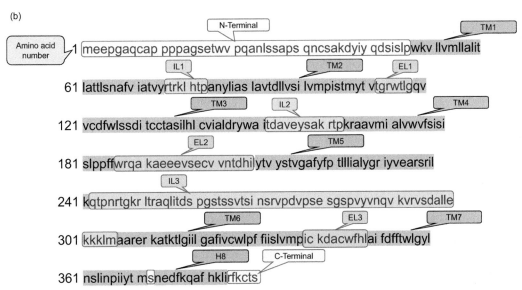

Figure 6.7. **Structure of the 5-HT1B receptor.** (a) Seven transmembrane domains connected by three intracellular loops, three extracellular loops, and an intramembrane helix make up the structure of the 5-HT1B receptor. This structure is characteristic of G-protein coupled receptors. (b) The amino acid sequence of 5-HT1B using the single letter code for amino acids. Different domains are labeled and indicated by differently shaded boxes. Source: (a) Created with Biorender.com.

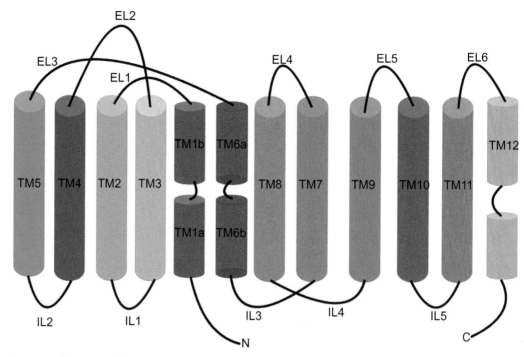

Figure 6.8. **Structure of the serotonin transporter.** As with other monoamine transporters, the serotonin transporter consists of an N-terminal domain, 12 transmembrane domains, 5 intracellular loops, 6 extracellular loops, and a C-terminal domain. Source: Created with Biorender.com. After Grouleff, Ladefoged, Koldsø, & Schiøtt (2015).

substantial variation in *SLC6A4*, with 9,953 SNPs (346 missense), and other typical variant types (i.e., copy number variations). The serotonin reuptake transporter (SERT) is one member of a family that includes transporters for other neurotransmitters such as dopamine, norepinephrine, glycine, and GABA. Its structure consists of 12 transmembrane domains with a central binding site (see Figure 6.8). The transporters work by changing their physical conformation from one state to another. In one conformational state, the binding site is accessible from the extracellular side. In the other state, the extracellular side closes, and the intracellular side opens, thereby moving the neurotransmitter molecule to the intracellular space of the presynaptic neuron or glial cell. The process is driven by the Na^+ gradient across the membrane, and requires chloride (Cl^-) and potassium (K^+) ions.

Once a neurotransmitter has re-entered the presynaptic cell it is either repackaged into a vesicle for re-release, or it is metabolized and eliminated from the system. Repackaging into a vesicle is accomplished by another transporter, an example of which is the vesicular monoamine transporter (VMAT2). The gene that codes for VMAT2 is known as *SLC18A2* and is located on chromosome 10q25.3 with 16 exons (SNPs: 9,299; missense: 317). If not transported into a vesicle, a neurotransmitter molecule is metabolized. Serotonin and other monoamines are metabolized by monoamine oxidase. The gene that codes for it is called *MAOA*, located on Xp11.3 with 16 exons (SNPs: 16,349; missense: 173).

Genetic variation of these neurotransmitter system components includes not only variants in protein coding regions, but also non-coding variants that may affect the regulation of gene expression, alternative splicing, or other aspects of processing. A comprehensive understanding of the biological mechanisms by which genetic variation causes individual differences in behavior is a challenging and perhaps elusive goal due to the large number of components, genetic variants, and the potential for interactions among them.

6.3.3 Neurons Adapt to Conditions

Healthy animals can maintain relatively stable neural function across time. Such stability includes the capacity to rapidly respond to changing internal and external environments and challenges, and then to return to a baseline level of functioning. For biological systems, this phenomenon of actively maintaining internal conditions to facilitate biological processes is known as homeostasis.

To achieve a combination of dynamic change and stability, neurons must be able to alter their functioning by managing the production of system components through gene expression. Such neuroadaptation is exemplified in the short term by learning and memory processes mediated by the deployment of glutamate receptors to strengthen a synaptic connection. In this case, the response can be relatively quick because the latent receptors are stored in the postsynaptic dendritic spines ready to be deployed. In other cases, changing conditions may trigger gene expression in the neuron's nucleus and the production of proteins, which will then be transported down the axon to the terminal before deployment in the synapse. Such a response may take hours, days, or even weeks to be implemented. Specific instances of neuroadaptation will be covered in more detail in Chapters 8, 9, and 11 in the context of response to mechanisms of learning and memory, antidepressant treatment, and addiction, respectively. It is mentioned here to emphasize the dynamic nature of gene expression in the function of neurotransmitter systems, and to suggest that genetic differences in such response systems may play an important role in individual differences in aspects of cognitive function and risk for behavioral disorders.

Check-up

- What are neurexins and neuroligins and what are their functions in a synapse?
- Describe the structure of the serotonin 1B receptor.
- Compare and contrast the structure and function of a metabotropic receptor (e.g., 5-HT1B) and a transporter (SERT).

6.4 Genetic Variation Affects Neural Activation Patterns

So, how does genetic variation at neurotransmitter system components affect neurotransmission? Can neurons compensate when they contain genetically dysfunctional components? Answers to these questions are important for understanding the role of genetic variation in heredity–behavior relations. It may be that in most cases, neurons can adjust certain aspects of their function to overcome a component that does not function within the usual parameters because of either gain-of-function, or loss-of-function genetic variants.

6.4.1 Neurotransmission Impacted by Genetic Differences

One way to investigate the role of genetic variation in neurotransmitter system function is to genetically engineer mutations in genes that code for neurotransmitter system components and test whether aspects of neurotransmission are affected. Many lines of mice have been engineered to study the impact of genetic variation on neurotransmission. Because of the substantial evidence for the involvement of serotonergic neurotransmission in common psychiatric disorders such as major depressive disorder, let us consider some evidence from lines of mice in which components of the serotonin system have been genetically engineered.

Neurotransmitter system function can be measured in a variety of ways, such as extracellular neurotransmitter availability and neural firing rate. For illustrative purposes, let us focus on a key component of the serotonergic system to show how these aspects of neurotransmission are affected by knocking it out. Effective neurotransmission requires that the neurotransmitter be removed from the synapse. The serotonin transporter (SERT) removes serotonin from the synapse via reuptake. Lines of SERT knockout mice have been generated and studied since the late 1990s (for review, see Murphy & Lesch, 2008). As one would expect, when the gene that codes for the component responsible for removing serotonin from the synapse is inactivated, levels of extracellular serotonin are elevated. Extracellular levels of serotonin are highest in mice homozygous for the SERT knockout (i.e., -/-), lowest for wild-type mice (i.e., +/+), and intermediate for mice heterozygote for the SERT KO (i.e., +/-). The firing rate for the presynaptic cell is also affected in a dose dependent manner by the SERT KO such that the firing rate is lowest for knockout homozygotes, highest for wild-type mice, and intermediate for knockout heterozygotes. The reduction in the firing rate of serotonergic neurons in mice carrying one or two copies of the SERT KO reflects neuroadaptation of those neurons to high levels of serotonin in the synapse.

Of course, completely inactivating a gene for the entire life of an animal is not the same as examining a genetic variant that partially reduces expression of the gene or impacts its function. However, the knockout heterozygotes or knockouts that can be induced later in life or only in specific tissues may be more realistic models of naturally occurring genetic variants. Genetic engineering technologies have been developing at a rapid rate and offer more precise ways to investigate heredity–behavior relations in non-human animal models.

6.4.2 The Role of Genetic Differences in Brain Structure and Neural Activation Patterns

In humans, it is not currently feasible to record the activity of single neurons, or to obtain measures of extracellular serotonin level. Nor is it permissible to genetically engineer human beings for research. Neuroimaging, however, provides an approach to investigate statistical associations between naturally occurring genetic variation in humans and brain structure and function (see Box 6.2). Studies in this area typically have been candidate gene association studies with relatively small sample sizes, due to the expense involved in neuroimaging. It is important to keep in mind the limitations of candidate gene association studies (discussed in Chapter 5) when considering their results. There has been a movement toward the establishment of consortia where multiple research-ers share data to achieve sample sizes large enough to conduct genome-wide association studies with neuroimaging data (e.g., Thompson et al., 2014). The basic question here is whether naturally occurring genetic variation between individuals is associated with individual differences in aspects of brain structure or neural function.

Box 6.2 Critical Concept: Neuroimaging Genetics

The last three decades have produced dramatic technological advances enabling investigations into the brain activity of living human beings. The capacity to observe changes in neural activity that are associated with aspects of cognition is an astounding leap forward in the quest to understand the role of biology in behavior. The technological development in neural imaging has paralleled that of the development in molecular genetic technology during that time. These areas have come of age together. Brain activity patterns represent a kind of phenotype that is in between genes and behavior and promises to play a crucial role in understanding mechanisms by which genetic variation contributes to individual differences in behavior. We briefly describe three types of neuroimaging.

Positron emission tomography (PET) uses radioactive chemicals (e.g., ligands or glucose) injected into the bloodstream to assess availability of neurotransmitter binding sites (e.g., receptors) or energy use by neurons. Genetic variation in receptor gene regulatory regions may affect how many of that receptor are present on neurons. Genetic variation may also affect activity patterns of neurons. Neurons that are more active use more glucose than neurons that are less active.

Magnetic resonance imaging (MRI) is a commonly used technique in neuroimaging genetics. It uses powerful magnets to manipulate protons into emitting radio waves, which are detected by the scanner and analyzed to provide information about tissue density. High-resolution MRI images can reveal subtle structural differences, such as the size of brain areas like amygdala.

Functional magnetic resonance imaging (fMRI) is a commonly used technique that enables investigators to visualize brain activity by using rapidly oscillating magnetic fields to detect changes in oxygen use and blood flow associated with neural activation. In fMRI, images taken during a task are compared to those taken when the individual is resting, and the difference is considered to be an index of neural activation resulting from engaging in the task.

Neuroimaging techniques are conducted in large scanners that have become rather common in hospitals and biomedical research facilities and are generally non-invasive (see Figure 6.9). Neuroimaging scans generate tremendous amounts of data that are analyzed by researchers who have had extensive statistical training.

In neuroimaging genetic studies, phenotypes (e.g., structure or function) are tested for statistical association with genetic variants. Such work has been subject to all the issues that confront other candidate gene association studies and GWAS including small genetic effect sizes and failure to replicate.

Neuroimaging genetics is an exciting research area that has and will continue to contribute to our understanding of heredity–behavior relations, especially when considered along with convergent evidence from other approaches.

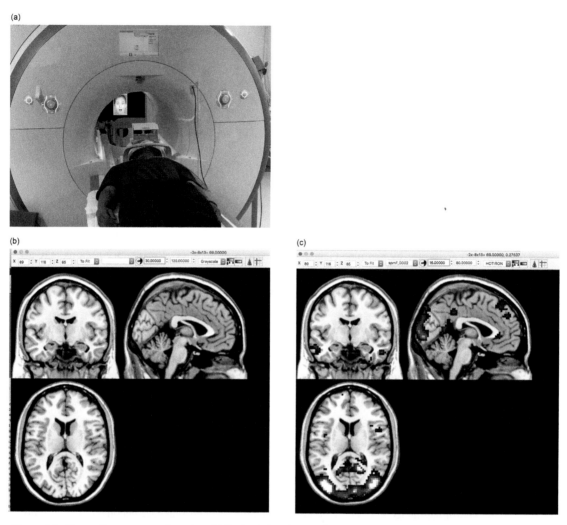

Figure 6.9. **Magnetic resonance imaging.** (a) For brain imaging, participants lie in the scanner and are asked to remain as still as possible. For fMRI, participants may be shown images and asked to make decisions. Note: face stimulus from Samuelsson et al. (2012). (b) Structural MRI provides detailed images of brain structure. (c) Functional MRI is used to index neural activity, often in response to tasks. Higher activity compared to a baseline is often indicated by warmer colors and lower activity by cooler colors. Source: Photos courtesy Dr. Maital Neta.

Radioactive chemicals that selectively bind to specific receptors have been a useful tool to investigate the availability of neurotransmitter receptors and transporters in living animals, including human beings. For example, a drug that has a strong binding affinity to 5-HTR1A receptors called Way-100635 can be labeled with the radio isotope carbon-11, injected into the bloodstream of research participants, and detected by PET scan. The radioactivity of such molecules decays quickly and is not considered to be harmful. A common SNP in the promoter region of *HT1A* (rs6295, aka C (-1019)G) affects a binding site for transcription repressors such that the less common G allele disables the binding site. There is some evidence that rs6295 G allele homozygotes have greater availability of 5-HTR1A receptors in the raphe nucleus, although the sample sizes of these studies are rather small, and some studies have only examined patients with depression. Therefore, firm conclusions about the role of genetic variation in *HT1A* on receptor availability are not possible, but this example illustrates how studies using PET scans can be a useful tool to address the question.

There are individual differences in the size of brain regions that may reflect differential behavioral capacity or risk for psychiatric disorder. Structural MRI is a useful tool to determine the sizes of subcortical brain structures. A logical candidate gene to test for association with the size of brain areas would be the one that codes for brain-derived neurotrophic factor (*BDNF*). The gene that codes for *BDNF* is located on chromosome 11p14.1 with 12 exons (SNPs: 15,322; missense: 180). The BDNF protein is expressed in the brain and plays an important role in the survival, growth, and differentiation of new neurons and synapses. BDNF is expressed in the hippocampus and is involved in learning and memory. A meta-analysis of candidate gene association studies testing the potential association of a common *BDNF* SNP (rs6265; aka Val66Met) and hippocampal volume in nearly 5,300 participants did not find a significant association (Harrisberger et al., 2014). A much larger GWAS that examined volume in several brain regions (nucleus accumbens, caudate, putamen, pallidum, amygdala, hippocampus, and thalamus) in nearly 31,000 participants found two SNPs significantly associated with hippocampal volume: rs77956314 (12q24) and rs61921502 (12q14.3). Much more work is needed to understand the role of genetic variation in brain structure.

To study neural activation patterns, participants in a scanner may be asked to complete cognitive tasks, or to just let their thoughts wander. Researchers might focus on patterns of whole-brain activation, on brain regions of interest, or on patterns of connectivity between regions. A candidate gene that has been widely studied for its potential impact on neural activity and cognition is the gene that codes for catechol-O-methyltransferase (COMT). COMT is an enzyme involved in the degradation of catecholamine neurotransmitters such as dopamine, epinephrine, and norepinephrine. The gene that codes for the enzyme (*COMT*) is located on chromosome 22q11.21 with 8 exons (SNPs: 8,033; missense: 458). The most investigated *COMT* polymorphism is a common missense SNP (rs4680, aka Val158Met). The activity of the COMT enzyme is reduced three- to four-fold in those who carry one or two copies of the Met allele compared to Val allele homozygotes. Such a decrease in the activity of an enzyme that is responsible for the breakdown of dopamine may produce a relatively higher level of dopamine availability and an impact on behaviors that are dependent on dopamine neurotransmission. There is meta-analytic evidence that rs4680 genotype is associated with level of neural activation in the prefrontal cortex (Mier, Kirsch, & Meyer-Lindenberg, 2010), but not for working memory (Nickl-Jockschat, Janouschek, Eickhoff, & Eickhoff, 2015).

Candidate genes such as *COMT* have been widely studied because they carry common variants that substantially impact the function of the resulting protein and neurotransmission. However, it is likely that homeostatic mechanisms in neural systems can adapt to even dramatically reduced function of their components. It may be that system dysfunctions arise when faced with multiple dysfunctional components and environmental challenges.

Check-up

- Define SERT KO and describe its effects.
- Which type of neuroimaging should be used to study the impact of genetic differences on the size of brain structures, and why?

6.5 Genetic Variation Can Moderate the Impact of Drugs on Neural Activity

Neurotransmitters are molecules produced in the body (i.e., endogenously). However, some molecules that originate outside of the body (i.e., exogenously) can affect neurotransmission or other biological functions. Let us refer to such exogenous molecules as drugs. Drugs can be medications such as antidepressants that are prescribed to treat a condition, or substances taken for recreation such as alcohol, or both such as benzodiazepines. Drugs have biological impact because their molecular structure has enough similarity with an endogenous molecule to enable them to interact with biological components such as receptors, transporters, or enzymes.

Pharmacology is the field of biomedicine that studies how drugs produce their effects and how to use drugs to treat disease. Psychopharmacology is the subfield of pharmacology in which the focus is on drugs used to treat mental illness. The next section discusses some of the ways in which drugs affect their targets (i.e., pharmacodynamics), how drugs move into and out of the body (i.e., pharmacokinetics), and how genetic variation can moderate those effects (i.e., pharmacogenetics).

6.5.1 Drugs Impact Neural Function

Of course, not all drugs affect neural function, but we will focus our attention on those that do. The molecular structure of some drugs facilitates their binding to neurotransmitter receptors. When a drug binds to a receptor and has a similar biological effect as the endogenous ligand, it is classified as an agonist with respect to that ligand (see Figure 6.10). The agonism may be full, partial, or inverse. In the first case, the drug could have an effect that is essentially identical to the endogenous ligand, and would therefore be described as a full agonist. Alternatively, the drug could activate the biological effect, but to a lesser degree than the endogenous ligand. In which case it would be classified as a partial agonist. Lastly, if the drug produces a biological effect that is opposite of the endogenous ligand, the drug would be classified as an inverse agonist. For example, if the effect of the endogenous ligand on the postsynaptic neuron is to increase its firing rate, but the effect of the drug decreases the firing rate to below the neuron's baseline rate, the drug would be classified as an inverse agonist. If a drug binds to a receptor and does not activate it, the drug is known as an antagonist, with respect to the endogenous ligand. It is important to note that a drug could be an agonist with respect to one neurotransmitter and an antagonist to another. The classification of agonist or antagonist is specific to the effects that the drug has on a given system.

To understand the pharmacodynamics of a drug it is important to identify the sites in the brain where the drug acts. Such studies can be conducted using brain tissue samples, radioactively labeled versions of the drug and X-ray film (i.e., autoradiography), or in living brains with neuroimaging (e.g., PET scans). Studies using these techniques enable the estimation of several pharmacodynamic parameters including the number of receptors in an area that bind the drug (i.e., receptor availability) and the strength of the attraction of the drug to the receptor (i.e., binding affinity).

Drugs can also impact other aspects of neural function by interacting with neurotransmitter system components other than receptors. The synthesis or degradation of neurotransmitters can be

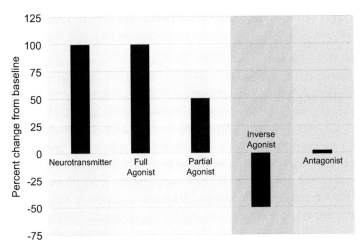

Figure 6.10. **Potential impact of drugs on neural activation.** Consider a postsynaptic neuron that increases its firing rate to 100% above baseline when the neurotransmitter binds to its receptors. A drug that is a full agonist also increases the firing rate to 100% above baseline when it is bound to receptors. A drug that is a partial agonist increases the firing rate, but not as much as a full agonist (e.g., 50% above baseline). An inverse agonist decreases the firing rate so that it is below the baseline (e.g., 50% below baseline). An antagonist does not alter baseline firing rate.

affected by drugs that interact with members of those pathways. For example, drugs known as monoamine oxidase inhibitors (MAOIs) hinder the catalytic activity of monoamine oxidase A and B, which results in an increased synaptic availability of serotonin and other neurotransmitters. MAOIs have antidepressant and/or anxiolytic effects and were widely prescribed for those purposes starting in the 1950s. Because of side-effects and potentially hazardous interactions with other drugs and foods, MAOIs are not widely prescribed today.

An important class of drugs called selective serotonin reuptake inhibitors (SSRIs) block the reuptake of serotonin into the presynaptic neuron, which results in increased synaptic availability of serotonin. SSRIs are a class of medications that have been widely prescribed around the world for depression and anxiety disorders since the late 1980s. Common examples of SSRIs include fluoxetine (brand name: Prozac), sertraline (Zoloft), paroxetine (Paxil), fluvoxamine (Luvox), citalopram (Celexa), and escitalopram (Lexapro). Each of these drugs has a unique chemical structure, but all selectively bind to serotonin transporters to temporarily disable them.

The movement of a drug into, through, and out of the body is known as pharmacokinetics. It is important to understand how much of the drug is available to act at its targets (i.e., bioavailability), as well as how the body distributes, stores, metabolizes, and eliminates the drug. Understanding the pharmacokinetics of a drug is critical in determining the dosage that is the most effective and has the least side-effects.

Enzymes are critically involved in drug metabolism, and therefore play an important role in drug bioavailability. Cytochrome P450 enzymes account for the majority of drug metabolism. They are found primarily in the liver but can also be found in endoplasmic reticulum of other cells.

In the next section we discuss the role of variation in genes that can affect drug pharmacodynamics and pharmacokinetics. Such genetic variants may play important roles in response to pharmaceutical treatment for psychiatric disorders and in risk for the development of substance use disorders.

6.5.2 Pharmacogenetics Investigates the Impact of Genetic Variation on Drug Effects

It is of great interest to understand how genetic differences between people produce individual differences in drug response. Such differences are likely important in the effectiveness of medications and in the ways in which people respond to drugs of abuse, which can affect risk for addiction. The study of the impact of genetic differences on pharmacodynamics and pharmacokinetics is called pharmacogenetics or pharmacogenomics depending on the number of variants considered.

Variants in gene regulatory regions can affect the expression of genes for receptors and other neurotransmitter components. Such genetic variants can directly affect the number of targets available for drug binding. For example, 5-HTTLPR is a common variant in the regulatory region of the structural gene for the serotonin transporter (*SLC6A4*). 5-HTTLPR has been widely studied because of its potential impact on serotonin transporter availability and SSRI response. In the name 5-HTTLPR, "5-HT" is the abbreviation of the chemical name for serotonin (5-hydroxytryptamine), "T" stands for transporter, and "LPR" stands for linked polymorphic region. So, the name is descriptive, indicating that it identifies a genetic variant that is not in the coding region for the serotonin transporter gene, but in a nearby region that regulates its expression.

Over 2,000 scientific papers addressing 5-HTTLPR have been published since its discovery in 1995 (Heils et al., 1995). The polymorphic region is located on chromosome 17q11.1–q12 in the promoter region of *SLC6A4* and consists of 14 to 22 copies of repeat elements that are each 20–23 bp long (see Figure 6.11). The most common alleles of 5-HTTLPR contain 14-repeats (Short) or 16-repeats (Long). A total of 14 allelic variants of 5-HTTLPR have been identified, although most of the research literature has investigated the two most common variants that are identified as S (Short) and L (Long).

There is evidence that the L allele is associated with higher levels of expression of the *SLC6A4* gene than the S allele, which results in higher SERT availability in the brain. The effect appears to act in a dominant fashion such that L/L is greater than L/S, which appears to be equivalent to S/S. Therefore, having a single copy of the S allele of 5-HTTLPR appears to reduce transcriptional efficiency of *SCL6A4*.

This expression difference also appears to depend on SNPs located in the 5-HTTLPR repetitive region called rs25531 and rs25532. For rs25531 the less frequent allele (G) appears to attenuate gene expression when combined with an L allele. In fact, when a G allele of rs25531 is paired with an L, it appears to reduce expression to the level of an S allele. So, when you consider expression levels of genotypes 5-HTTLPR and rs25531 together, L_A/L_A is the highest, and all other genotypes appear to have lower *SLC6A4* expression. The less frequent allele of rs25532 (A) also appears to reduce expression of the *SLC6A4* gene, but more research needs to be done to confirm its effect.

If 5-HTTLPR determines SERT availability, then it is logical to assume that the effective dose of SSRI for depression treatment may also depend on 5-HTTLPR and rs25531 genotype. One might hypothesize that individuals with more serotonin transporters (i.e., L_A/L_A genotype) may require higher doses of SSRI to effectively blockade serotonin reuptake. Alternatively, one might hypothesize more generally that if there is not a good match between genetically determined SERT availability and SSRI dose that (a) treatment response might be affected, or (b) that more side-effects might be experienced. Meta-analyses suggest that those with the L/L genotype may have a slightly higher probability of successful SSRI treatment for depression (Porcelli, Fabbri, & Serretti, 2012), and that those who carry one or more S alleles may have a higher risk of experiencing negative

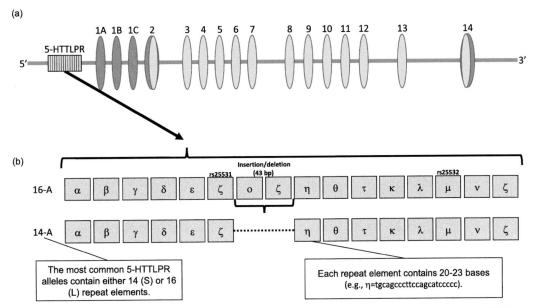

Figure 6.11. **The 5-HTTLPR polymorphism of the serotonin transporter gene.** (a) The structure of the *SLC6A4* gene includes an insertion/deletion polymorphism called 5-HTTLPR that is upstream of the coding region. *SLC6A4* contains 14 exons, of which, 1A, 1B, 1C and 14 can be alternatively spliced (indicated by dark ovals). (b) The two most common 5-HTTLPR alleles contain 16 (L) and 14 (S) copies of an imperfect repeat sequence of 20–23 bp. Greek letters are used to identify unique repeat elements. Repeat elements have nucleic acid sequences that are similar to that shown for η. Two SNPs that modulate the impact of 5-HTTLPR on gene expression are indicated above the repeat element in which they reside (rs25531 and rs25532). Sources: (a) After Murphy et al. (2008). (b) After Nakamura, Ueno, Sano, & Tanabe (2000); Wendland et al. (2008).

side-effects such as gastrointestinal adverse events (Zhu, Klein-Fedyshin, & Stevenson, 2017). However, there is still no firm consensus about whether 5-HTTLPR genotype plays a role in SSRI treatment response for depression. It should be noted that psychiatric disorder treatment studies are very challenging to conduct and can be difficult to compare. Such studies often have relatively small sample sizes and do not routinely control for factors that could affect the outcome such as comorbidity, symptom profile, or previous treatment history. It should also be noted that rs25531 genotype was not tested in many of the 5-HTTLPR studies, so it is difficult to draw firm conclusions at this time. Suffice it to say, that pharmacogenetics and pharmacogenomics are important and active areas of investigation.

Genetic variants in exons can affect the amino acid sequence of the resulting protein, which could impact a target's binding of a drug. Of course, not all variants in a gene have a direct effect on the structure and function of a resulting protein. A common variant in the gene that codes for the 5-HTR2C receptor (*HTR2C*, Xq23) results in the substitution of a serine for a cysteine at amino acid position 23 of the protein (Cys23Ser, rs6318). Although the high-resolution structure of 5-HTR2C has not yet been determined, the amino acid replacement occurs in the extracellular N-terminus of the G-protein coupled receptor and may affect the structure or stability of the receptor. There is some evidence that rs6318 genotype is associated with response to antipsychotic drugs in patients with schizophrenia, although the effect may be limited to males (Li, Hashimoto, & Meltzer, 2019).

There are fifty-seven genes that encode cytochrome P450 enzymes and each contains substantial genetic variability. Some genetic variants affect the rate at which the resultant enzyme metabolizes drugs. For some medications, getting the correct dose is critical. Too high a dose could mean adverse side-effects, and too low a dose could mean that the treatment is ineffective. Enzymes that break down a drug slowly mean that the patient is getting a higher than intended dose, whereas enzymes that break down a drug quickly mean that the patient is getting too low a dose. This topic is covered in more detail in Chapter 14 as part of a discussion of precision medicine.

Pharmacogenetics and pharmacogenomics are active areas of research that may have important applications in twenty-first-century medicine. It is likely that genotyping for genetic variants that impact pharmacodynamics and/or pharmacokinetics will be routine someday in a doctor's office near you.

Check-up

- Define pharmacodynamics and explain how it can be affected by genetic variation.
- Describe the impact of the following on the activity of a neuron: (a) full agonist, (b) partial agonist, (c) antagonist, and (d) inverse agonist.
- Describe the effects of the 5-HTTLPR polymorphism on *SLC6A4* expression.

6.6 SUMMARY

- Neurons are cells that carry out all basic cellular functions. Genetic variation that affects these cellular functions may cause diseases that produce behavioral symptoms.
- Neurons are specialized for communication and have many protein components that are coded for by genes. Variation in those genes is common and may play an important role in psychological traits, behaviors and risk for psychiatric disorder.
- The integrity of synapses depends on proteins expressed on the pre- and postsynaptic surfaces. Genetic variants that weaken synaptic connections may play a role in increased risk for autism spectrum disorders.
- Synaptic neurotransmission depends on components such as reuptake transporters, vesicular transporters, receptors, and synthetic and degradative enzymes. Neurons can adapt to changing conditions by up- and downregulating the expression of genes for such components.
- Neuroimaging describes a set of techniques that enable investigators to measure neural activity in living participants. Neuroimaging genetics is a relatively recent area where investigators examine the role of genetic variation in neural activity.
- Pharmacodynamics focuses on the actions of drugs at their targets in the body. Pharmacokinetics focuses on the movement of drugs into, throughout, and out of the body. Pharmacogenetics and genomics investigate the role of genetic variation on pharmacodynamics and pharmacokinetics and are important components of precision medicine.

RECOMMENDED READING

- Bogdan, R., Salmeron, B. J., Carey, C. E., Agrawal, A., Calhoun, V. D., Garavan, H., . . . Goldman, D. (2017). Imaging genetics and genomics in psychiatry: A critical review of progress and potential. *Biol Psychiatry, 82*(3), 165–175.

- Murphy, D. L., Fox, M. A., Timpano, K. R., Moya, P. R., Ren-Patterson, R., Andrews, A. M., ... Wendland, J. R. (2008). How the serotonin story is being rewritten by new gene-based discoveries principally related to SLC6A4, the serotonin transporter gene, which functions to influence all cellular serotonin systems. *Neuropharmacology, 55*(6), 932–960.
- Südhof, T. C. (2008). Neuroligins and neurexins link synaptic function to cognitive disease. *Nature, 455*(7215), 903–911.

REFERENCES

Baig, D. N., Yanagawa, T., & Tabuchi, K. (2017). Distortion of the normal function of synaptic cell adhesion molecules by genetic variants as a risk for autism spectrum disorders. *Brain Res Bull*, 129, 82–90. doi:10.1016/j.brainresbull.2016.10.006

Chen, G. L., Vallender, E. J., & Miller, G. M. (2008). Functional characterization of the human TPH2 5′ regulatory region: Untranslated region and polymorphisms modulate gene expression in vitro. *Hum Genet, 122*(6), 645–657. doi:10.1007/s00439-007-0443-y

Grouleff, J., Ladefoged, L. K., Koldsø, H., & Schiøtt, B. (2015). Monoamine transporters: Insights from molecular dynamics simulations. *Front Pharmacol, 6*(235). doi:10.3389/fphar.2015.00235

Guang, S., Pang, N., Deng, X., Yang, L., He, F., Wu, L., ... Peng, J. (2018). Synaptopathology involved in autism spectrum disorder. *Front Cell Neurosci, 12*, 470. doi:10.3389/fncel.2018.00470

Guarnieri, F. C., de Chevigny, A., Falace, A., & Cardoso, C. (2018). Disorders of neurogenesis and cortical development. *Dialogues Clin Neurosci, 20*(4), 255–266.

Harrisberger, F., Spalek, K., Smieskova, R., Schmidt, A., Coynel, D., Milnik, A., ... Borgwardt, S. (2014). The association of the BDNF Val66Met polymorphism and the hippocampal volumes in healthy humans: A joint meta-analysis of published and new data. *Neurosci Biobehav Rev, 42*, 267–278. doi:10.1016/j.neubiorev.2014.03.011

Heils, A., Teufel, A., Petri, S., Seemann, M., Bengel, D., Balling, U., ... Lesch, K. P. (1995). Functional promoter and polyadenylation site mapping of the human serotonin (5-HT) transporter gene. *J Neural Transm Gen Sect, 102*(3), 247–254.

Jamain, S., Quach, H., Betancur, C., Rastam, M., Colineaux, C., Gillberg, I. C., ... Bourgeron, T. (2003). Mutations of the X-linked genes encoding neuroligins NLGN3 and NLGN4 are associated with autism. *Nat Genet, 34*(1), 27–29. doi:10.1038/ng1136

Li, J., Hashimoto, H., & Meltzer, H. Y. (2019). Association of serotonin2c receptor polymorphisms with antipsychotic drug response in schizophrenia. *Front Psychiatry, 10*, 58. doi:10.3389/fpsyt.2019.00058

Lindholm, D., Korhonen, L., Eriksson, O., & Koks, S. (2017). Recent insights into the role of unfolded protein response in ER stress in health and disease. *Front Cell Dev Biol, 5*, 48. doi:10.3389/fcell.2017.00048

Luo, S., Valencia, C. A., Zhang, J., Lee, N. C., Slone, J., Gui, B., ... Huang, T. (2018). Biparental inheritance of mitochondrial DNA in humans. *Proc Natl Acad Sci USA, 115*(51), 13039–13044. doi:10.1073/pnas.1810946115

Mier, D., Kirsch, P., & Meyer-Lindenberg, A. (2010). Neural substrates of pleiotropic action of genetic variation in COMT: A meta-analysis. *Mol Psychiatry, 15*(9), 918–927. doi:10.1038/mp.2009.36

Murphy, D. L., & Lesch, K. P. (2008). Targeting the murine serotonin transporter: Insights into human neurobiology. *Nat Rev Neurosci, 9*(2), 85–96. doi:10.1038/nrn2284

Nakamura, M., Ueno, S., Sano, A., & Tanabe, H. (2000). The human serotonin transporter gene linked polymorphism (5-HTTLPR) shows ten novel allelic variants. *Mol Psychiatry, 5*(1), 32–38.

Nickl-Jockschat, T., Janouschek, H., Eickhoff, S. B., & Eickhoff, C. R. (2015). Lack of meta-analytic evidence for an impact of COMT Val158Met genotype on brain activation during working memory tasks. *Biol Psychiatry, 78*(11), e43–e46. doi:10.1016/j.biopsych.2015.02.030

Ottenhof, K. W., Sild, M., Levesque, M. L., Ruhe, H. G., & Booij, L. (2018). TPH2 polymorphisms across the spectrum of psychiatric morbidity: A systematic review and meta-analysis. *Neurosci Biobehav Rev, 92*, 29–42. doi:10.1016/j.neubiorev.2018.05.018

Porcelli, S., Fabbri, C., & Serretti, A. (2012). Meta-analysis of serotonin transporter gene promoter polymorphism (5-HTTLPR) association with antidepressant efficacy. *Eur Neuropsychopharmacol, 22*(4), 239–258. doi:10.1016/j.euroneuro.2011.10.003

Reichelt, A., & Dachtler, J. (2015). The role of neurexins and neuroligins in autism. In S. Fatemi (Ed.), *The Molecular Basis of Autism: Contemporary Clinical Neuroscience* (pp. 361–382). New York: Springer.

Tabuchi, K., Blundell, J., Etherton, M. R., Hammer, R. E., Liu, X., Powell, C. M., & Sudhof, T. C. (2007). A neuroligin-3 mutation implicated in autism increases inhibitory synaptic transmission in mice. *Science, 318*(5847), 71–76. doi:10.1126/science.1146221

Takayanagi, S., Fukuda, R., Takeuchi, Y., Tsukada, S., & Yoshida, K. (2013). Gene regulatory network of unfolded protein response genes in endoplasmic reticulum stress. *Cell Stress Chaperones, 18*(1), 11–23. doi:10.1007/s12192-012-0351-5

Thompson, P. M., Stein, J. L., Medland, S. E., Hibar, D. P., Vasquez, A. A., Renteria, M. E., . . . Drevets, W. (2014). The ENIGMA Consortium: Large-scale collaborative analyses of neuroimaging and genetic data. *Brain Imaging Behav, 8*(2), 153–182. doi:10.1007/s11682-013-9269-5

Wang, C., Jiang, Y., Ma, J., Wu, H., Wacker, D., Katritch, V., . . . Xu, H. E. (2013). Structural basis for molecular recognition at serotonin receptors. *Science, 340*(6132), 610–614. doi:10.1126/science.1232807

Wendland, J. R., Moya, P. R., Kruse, M. R., Ren-Patterson, R. F., Jensen, C. L., Timpano, K. R., & Murphy, D. L. (2008). A novel, putative gain-of-function haplotype at SLC6A4 associates with obsessive-compulsive disorder. *Hum Mol Genet, 17*(5), 717–723. doi:10.1093/hmg/ddm343

Zhu, J., Klein-Fedyshin, M., & Stevenson, J. M. (2017). Serotonin transporter gene polymorphisms and selective serotonin reuptake inhibitor tolerability: Review of pharmacogenetic evidence. *Pharmacotherapy, 37*(9), 1089–1104. doi:10.1002/phar.1978

Part III Behaviors and Behavioral Disorders

7 Serious Mental Illness

The first six chapters of this book introduced you to behavior genetics as a field, refreshed your memory about Mendelian and molecular genetics, introduced the research methods of behavior genetics, and discussed how genetic variation can affect the brain structure and function. In the remaining chapters, we explore some of the most important areas of behavior genetic research, consider the future of behavior genetics, and examine ethical questions at the forefront of behavior genetics.

One of the important motivating factors in behavior genetic research is to understand the biology underlying psychiatric disorders to inform prevention and treatment efforts. Identifying genetic variants that increase risk for the development of a psychiatric disorder may increase the precision of diagnosis and improve treatment decisions. It may also aid in the development of pharmacological treatments that are faster acting and have fewer side-effects than those that are currently being prescribed.

In this chapter, we introduce the concept of mental illness, how it is diagnosed, and examine its impact on people's lives. We then consider whether mental illnesses represent qualitative or quantitative traits and how this affects behavior genetic research. Finally, we focus attention on a severe mental illness that substantially impairs function: schizophrenia. Other mental illnesses will be discussed in Chapters 8–13.

7.1 Mental Illness and Its Impact

When people experience patterns of thinking, emotion, or behavior (or a combination of these) that interfere with their social relationships, their occupations or other important areas of life, and those patterns persist for an extended time and cause substantial problems and/or distress they may be suffering from a mental illness. Some mental illnesses tend to occur in childhood or adolescence, such as attention deficit/hyperactivity disorder (ADHD) or autism, while others are more likely to occur later in life, such as depression or substance use disorders. It is possible for an individual to have more than one mental illness, which is termed comorbidity.

Mental illnesses are not rare. In 2017 it was estimated that between 10 percent and 15 percent of people worldwide experienced one or more mental illness (see Figure 7.1). This represents nearly 1 billion people. Regardless of the exact number, these estimates dramatically show the widespread prevalence of mental illness. And the map in Figure 7.1 indicates that although the prevalence in countries across the world varies between 7.5 percent and 20 percent, no country is spared.

Mental illness can have substantial negative impact on the length and quality of a person's life. One way to quantify the burden of a disease or disorder in a population is to estimate the number of years lost to illness, disability, or premature death termed Disability-Adjusted Life Years (DALYs).

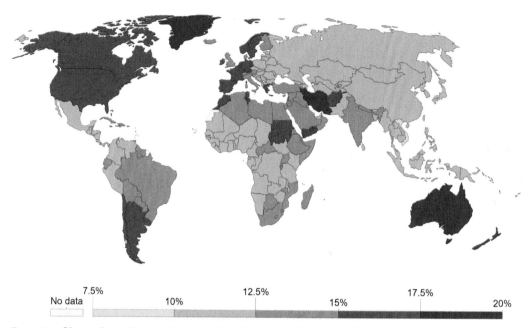

Figure 7.1. **Share of population with mental health and substance use disorders, 2017.** Share of population with any mental health or substance use disorder; this includes depression, anxiety, bipolar, eating disorders, alcohol or drug use disorders, and schizophrenia. Due to widespread under-diagnosis, these estimates use a combination of sources, including medical and national records, epidemiological data, survey data, and meta-regression models. Source: Hannah Ritchie and Max Roser (2020) "Mental Health." Published online at OurWorldInData.org. Retrieved from: https://ourworldindata.org/mental-health

To estimate DALYs for a given condition, the number of years of life lost because of the condition is added to the number of years lived with disability because of the condition. Mental illnesses account for approximately 7 percent of DALYs worldwide (see Figure 7.2), and account for approximately 19 percent of all years lived with a disability (Rehm & Shield, 2019). The take-home message here is that mental illnesses are relatively common and can substantially impact a person's life.

In addition to affecting potential lifespan and years lived with a disability, mental illness can have negative impacts on relationships, career trajectory, aspects of physical health and other areas of life that contribute to life satisfaction. It appears that it is not necessary to qualify for a diagnosis of a mental illness for negative impacts to manifest. Those with self-reported poor mental health, regardless of whether they have a diagnosis, also report lower levels of life satisfaction than those who report better mental health (Lombardo, Jones, Wang, Shen, & Goldner, 2018).

Even though mental illness can have dramatic impacts on people's lives, it is estimated that fewer than half of those who have a mental illness receive mental health services (SAMHSA, 2018). For those who do seek treatment, mental health services may be provided by primary care physicians, trained counselors, clinical psychologists, psychiatrists, and social workers depending on the availability of trained personnel, health insurance coverage, and other factors including patient need and preference. Treatment may consist of talk therapies, like cognitive behavioral therapy, medications, like antidepressants, and social services, like connecting clients to resources. Depending on the diagnosis, treatment may take place in a residential facility or in the context of outpatient visits. At this point in time, the use of genetic information to inform diagnostic and treatment decisions in psychiatry (i.e., precision medicine) has not been widespread or successful (see Chapter 14). Many researchers and clinicians remain optimistic that genetic information will be

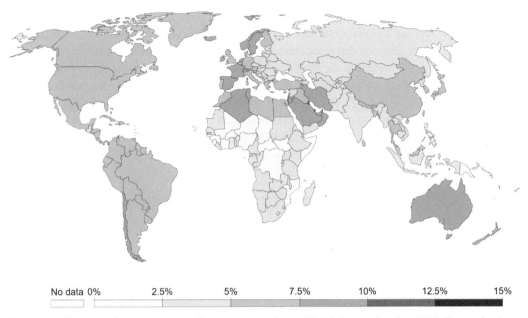

No data 0%   2.5%   5%   7.5%   10%   12.5%   15%

Figure 7.2. **Mental and substance use disorders as a share of total disease burden, 2017.** Disease burden is measured in DALYs (Disability-Adjusted Life Years). DALYs measure total burden of disease, both from years of life lost and years lived with a disability. One DALY equals one lost year of healthy life. Source: Hannah Ritchie and Max Roser (2020) "Mental Health." Published online at OurWorldInData.org. Retrieved from: https://ourworldindata.org/mental-health

useful for diagnosis and treatment, but they recognize that currently it is not (Gandal, Leppa, Won, Parikshak, & Geschwind, 2016).

Check-up

- What is mental illness and how is it treated?
- Discuss DALYs and how they index the burden of a disorder.

7.2 Risk for Developing Mental Illness

Although it is reasonable to assume that everyone is at some level of risk for developing mental illness at some point in their lives, the level of risk is not likely to be distributed evenly among individuals. If certain genetic variants increase risk for developing a mental illness, alternative alleles are likely to decrease risk. By convention, alleles associated with an increased risk are known as risk alleles and those that decrease risk are known as protective alleles. We can assume that a person's overall genetic risk for developing a condition is a function of the combination of risk and protective alleles that they carry.

Of course, a person's overall risk for developing one or more mental illnesses is not merely a function of their genetic risk but can also include all other non-genetic (i.e., environmental) risk and/or protective factors to which they are exposed. Environmental risk factors can include early life experiences such as childhood trauma, exposure to substances like cannabis, or social factors such as insecure parental attachment, or discrimination (WHO, 2012). Environmental protective factors can include social support, positive life events, and secure parental attachment.

One way that researchers have conceptualized a person's risk for developing mental illness across the lifespan is the diathesis-stress model (Monroe & Simons, 1991), which focuses on risk factors. In it, an individual's vulnerability to develop a mental illness is a function of their genetic risk (i.e., diathesis) and exposure to adverse life events (i.e., stress). In this model, exposure to the same level of environmental risk factors may lead to the development of a mental illness in a vulnerable person but would not be likely to in a resilient one (see Figure 7.3(a)). The difference between vulnerability and resilience is hypothesized to be genetic whereby the vulnerable person carries more risk alleles than does the resilient person.

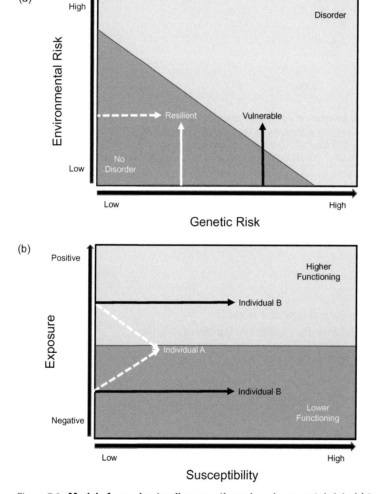

Figure 7.3. **Models for understanding genetic and environmental risk.** (a) In the diathesis-stress model risk for developing a disorder is a function of a person's genetic and environmental risk. If two individuals have been exposed to similar levels of environmental risk (i.e., stress), their level of genetic risk may differentiate who develops a disorder (i.e., is vulnerable) from who does not (i.e., is resilient). (b) In the Differential Sensitivity model genetic variation confers sensitivity to both negative and positive environmental exposure. Some individuals are hypothesized to be relatively insensitive to the environment, and their functioning is primarily dependent on their genotype (e.g., individual A). Alternatively, some individuals are hypothesized to carry genotypes that confer high sensitivity to environmental exposure such that exposure to negative environments produces lower levels of functioning, and exposure to positive environments produce higher levels of functioning (e.g., individual B).

A more recent theoretical model of the relation between genetic risk and environmental exposure considers exposure to both negative and positive environments and the potential for positive outcomes other than just not developing a disorder (see Figure 7.3(b)). It is called the differential sensitivity hypothesis and it posits that people carrying certain genotypes are more sensitive to both negative and positive environmental exposure than are those carrying other genotypes (Belsky & Pluess, 2009). It proposes to explain the conundrum that many alleles considered to confer risk for psychiatric disorders are at intermediate frequency in human populations. If the alleles conferred only vulnerability, they might be expected to have low frequencies in populations because they should be selected against by evolution. By hypothesizing sensitivity alleles, whereby particular alleles are more sensitive to both negative and positive exposures, they might be neutral with respect to selection overall and therefore found to have intermediate frequencies.

Hopefully, these models remind you of the genotype × environment interactions that we discussed in Chapter 3. Such interaction models posit that behavioral outcomes may not be a simple additive function of a person's genotype and the environments to which they have been exposed.

Check-up

- Explain the role of risk and protective alleles in the conceptualization of genetic risk for a disorder.
- Compare and contrast the diathesis stress model with the differential susceptibility hypothesis.

7.3 How Should Behavior Genetics Researchers Think About Mental Illness?

When investigating the role of genetic variation in individual differences in a trait, it is important to know whether the trait is best described as qualitative or quantitative. As we saw in Chapters 2 and 3, such a distinction may be the result of the number of genetic variants that influence the trait. Qualitative traits are likely determined by few genetic variants, whereas quantitative traits are likely determined by many genetic variants in combination with environmental influence.

To begin to consider whether mental illnesses represent qualitative or quantitative traits, we first need to discuss how psychiatric diagnoses are made. In the US, the primary framework for categorizing and diagnosing mental illness is the Diagnostic and Statistical Manual of Mental Disorders, Fifth Edition (DSM-5; APA, 2013), whereas in much of the rest of the world it is the International Classification of Diseases 11th Revision (ICD-11; WHO, 2020). Both provide a set of diagnostic criteria to assess whether a patient is experiencing symptoms that are characteristic of the disorder in question and whether the severity and duration of those symptoms represents clinically significant impairment or produces sufficient distress in the patient to qualify for a particular diagnosis. In this text, we will refer to ICD-11 diagnoses and diagnostic criteria.

Typically, in a clinical situation, information regarding a patient's symptoms is collected by a clinician or a trained mental health professional in the context of a structured diagnostic interview, in which the patient is asked about specific symptoms. Alternatively, in the context of research, psychiatric symptoms are often assessed by self-report questionnaire.

In Chapter 2 we discussed traits that are inherited in Mendelian patterns and you will recall that such traits are best classified as qualitative. The pea colors studied by Mendel were different colors, yellow and green, not shades of green. The fruit fly traits studied by Morgan and his students represented a mutant type, like a vestigial wing, compared to the typically developed wing, called wild-type. Such qualitative traits were found to have relatively straightforward inheritance patterns and were later determined to be caused by mutations in single genes.

From one perspective, mental illnesses can be considered qualitative traits. You either meet criteria for a psychiatric diagnosis or not. In this view, a dichotomy exists where people are either healthy, or ill. If the underlying genetics of mental illnesses corresponded to such a dichotomy, then mental illnesses could represent a class of single-gene disorders. One would expect to see Mendelian inheritance patterns in families (e.g., autosomal or X-linked, dominant or recessive) for mental illnesses.

Viewing mental illnesses as qualitative traits may serve an important purpose by providing a common framework by which people can be properly diagnosed and treated for behavioral problems. However, such a diagnostic system may not necessarily reflect the underlying causal structures of mental illnesses, which are likely more complex and may vary somewhat between individuals (i.e., show heterogeneity).

It also runs the risk of reification, whereby we take an abstract idea, like a diagnostic category, and start to think of it as a real biological entity. The diagnostic category may be clinically useful in identifying people who need help and in determining what type of help to provide, but it may not represent actual biological differences. By reifying diagnoses, we might waste time and resources on trying to understand the genetic basis of something that does not actually exist as a natural phenomenon. It is critical that we use our limited resources for investigating heredity–behavior relations on phenotypes that are real and not just artifacts of a system developed for use in the clinic.

There are many levels of analysis between genetic variation and mental illness (see Figure 7.4). Higher levels of analysis are built by, or comprised of, components from lower levels.

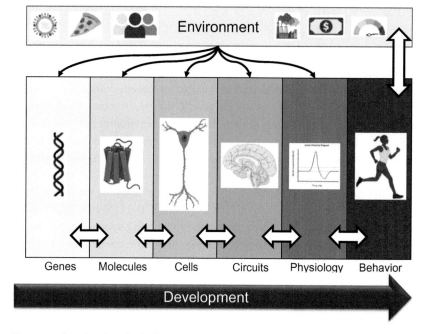

Figure 7.4. **Levels of analysis.** Pathways from genes to behavior traverse across levels of analysis that represent hierarchical steps across biology. Each level of analysis can be influenced by the environment and may change across development. Behavior can change environmental factors in ways that can impact biology across levels of analysis.

For example, a protein would be considered a higher level of analysis than a gene or an amino acid. The DNA sequence of the gene determines the amino acid sequence of the protein. Similarly, a protein (i.e., a molecule), like a neurotransmitter receptor, would be considered a lower level of analysis than a neuron (i.e., a cell). Because of this layered pathway from gene to behavior, genes cannot directly cause behaviors. Any association between genetic variation and individual differences in behavior must be indirect. In other words, the influence of genetic differences on behavior must be mediated by some level of analysis above the gene. Each level of analysis is complex in its own right, and changes at one level do not necessarily produce changes at another. A full understanding of pathways from genes to behavior will require the characterization of changes at each level. However, it may not be necessary to have a complete understanding of such pathways to make use of information from various levels of analysis to predict or even alter behavioral outcomes.

Of course, higher levels, such as social interactions and culture can also influence behavior. Additionally, the level of involvement and impact of each of these levels can change across development. It is important to keep in mind that to have an influence on behavior, genetic variation must act by affecting the structure or function of some biological component(s) at one or more levels of analysis. Genes cannot directly cause behavior. To cause individual differences in behavior, genetic variants must affect biology at some level of analysis. As we discussed in Chapters 5 and 6, genetic variants can alter expression of the gene or the function of the resultant protein, which may affect the function of molecules, such as receptors, that can have further impacts across levels of analysis.

One approach to better understand pathways from genes to mental illnesses has been to focus on traits that are "closer" to the genes than are the disorders. The National Institute of Mental Health (NIMH) has adopted this approach by focusing on so-called Research Domain Criteria (RDoC) (see Box 7.1). The RDoC approach may be considered one way to formalize the concept of endophenotypes (Gottesman & Gould, 2003). The general idea is that there are internal (i.e., not immediately visible) phenotypes that may be considered risk factors for developing the disorder, and that these endophenotypes are influenced by fewer genes than the disorder, and therefore may be simpler for genetic analysis (see Table 7.1).

This approach does not assume that the genetics underlying an endophenotype are simple, although it does suggest that its genetics are simpler than that of a mental illness. This assumption in part recognizes that the endophenotype may represent one of many risk indicators for the disorder (see Figure 7.5). It also recognizes that there is significant symptom heterogeneity with disorders because diagnostic systems allow diagnoses to reflect different symptom profiles. In other words, it

---

Table 7.1 Endophenotype criteria

To qualify as an endophenotype for a disorder, a trait must be:
1. associated with the disorder in the population
2. heritable
3. primarily state-independent (manifests in an individual whether or not the disorder is active)
4. co-segregating with the disorder within families
5. found in non-affected family members of a proband at a higher rate than in the general population

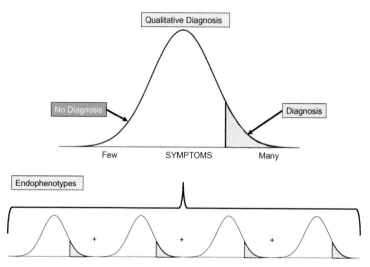

Figure 7.5. **Qualitative diagnoses as a function of endophenotypes.** From one perspective, a qualitative mental illness diagnosis could result from an underlying quantitative distribution of symptoms with a diagnostic threshold. In this case, most people do not qualify for a diagnosis of a mental illness, although they may display symptoms. Some number of symptoms is considered a diagnostic threshold such that those who exceed that number of symptoms qualify for a diagnosis. The overall symptom count can be considered a sum of risk across multiple endophenotypes. Within a diagnosis, the number of symptoms endorsed can distinguish between mild, moderate, and severe cases.

is possible for two people with completely different symptoms to meet criteria for the same diagnosis. Therefore, focusing on traits that are some number of levels of analysis "closer" to the genes, rather than on the diagnosis, may be a more fruitful approach to genetic analysis.

Endophenotypes may also represent actual steps on the causal pathway from gene to behavior. In this case, they mediate risk for the disorder rather than merely indicating risk (Kendler & Neale, 2010). Determining whether the endophenotype is a risk factor (i.e., is causal) or a risk indicator (i.e., is correlated with) may require an empirical approach which may be difficult or impossible with human populations. The term intermediate phenotype is sometimes used as a loose synonym for endophenotype, although because of its imprecision, it should probably be avoided (Lenzenweger, 2013).

Box 7.1 Critical Concept: Research Diagnostic Criteria (RDoC)

The National Institute of Mental Health (NIMH), in 2009, started to discuss a plan to develop an experimental system that could be used to classify mental illnesses with a goal of aiding progress in the use of precision medicine in psychiatry (Cuthbert, 2015). The NIMH is the largest funder of biomedical research on mental illnesses in the US and it recognized that psychiatric diagnoses based on signs and symptoms have limitations for use in identifying and understanding biological causal pathways. Although diagnostic categories may be useful in the clinic for making therapeutic decisions, they do not appear to represent unique biological entities. In other words, clinicians may find such diagnoses useful to help people, but diagnoses do not appear to be good phenotypes for genetic analyses. Therefore, the NIMH proposed RDoC as a classification system to be used in research with a goal of clarifying pathways from genes to behavior that could be refined as new findings appeared. These pathways focused on basic psychological constructs and their underlying biological components and circuits. RDoC is an explicit research framework to focus on potential endophenotypes rather than on diagnoses. Although the RDoC constructs may not meet all the criteria for endophenotypes, the RDoC approach is conceptually consistent with the notion of endophenotypes.

Constructs included in the RDoC are quantitative by definition and comprise six domains of function: (1) negative valence systems, (2) positive valence systems, (3) cognitive systems, (4) systems for social processes, (5) arousal/regulatory systems, and (6) sensorimotor systems. Each of the domains contains several constructs that represent different aspect of function, and each of the constructs can be assessed by different methods (i.e., units of analysis) across levels of analysis (see Figure 7.6).

The main idea behind RDoC is that because current diagnostic categories do not well reflect underlying biology, a system to better characterize relations between variability in biological systems and behavioral traits is more likely to lead to advances in understanding causes of mental illness. For example, research focused on identifying genetic variants associated with individual differences in attention, a construct in the cognitive systems domain, may be more likely to lead to an understanding of genetic risk for schizophrenia than would a study that used the categorical diagnosis of schizophrenia as the primary phenotype. In fact, understanding how genetic variation is associated with individual differences in attention may contribute to understanding genetic risk for any mental illness that has deficits in attention as a symptom.

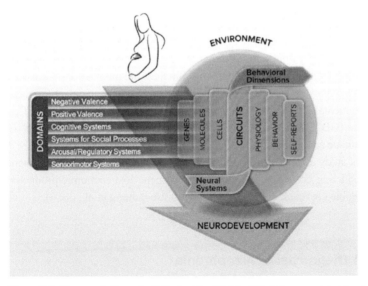

Figure 7.6. **Research Domain Criteria.** The NIMH's RDoC framework is intended to direct research away from categorical diagnoses of mental illness and toward six domains of function, each with corresponding psychological constructs. Research into the causes of individual differences in the constructs across levels of analysis from genes to physiology that can be assessed along different behavioral dimensions across development and considering environmental influences may be a more useful approach than a focus on categorical diagnoses. Source: www.nimh.nih.gov/research/research-funded-by-nimh/rdoc/about-rdoc.shtml. Image in the public domain.

Constructs within the RDoC domains of function are hypothesized to vary quantitatively in a population. In addition, it is thought that the extreme tails of those distributions may indicate aspects of mental illness. This assumption may be supported for disorders that involve certain constructs like anxiety in the negative valence domain, which is an important symptom of anxiety disorders; but may not be as well supported for constructs such as delusional beliefs, which is a symptom of schizophrenia (Ross & Margolis, 2019). Such criticisms suggest that some mental illnesses might represent extremes of normal function, whereas others represent qualitatively different functioning. In other words, there appears to be no definitive answer to the question of whether mental illnesses are qualitative or quantitative traits.

Check-up

- Describe how diagnoses are made in the US and in the rest of the world.
- Explain reification and why it may be problematic in behavior genetics.
- What is the relationship between endophenotypes and RDoC?

7.4 Schizophrenia Signs, Symptoms, and Diagnostic Criteria

About 7 individuals in 1,000 (i.e., just under 1 percent) will meet criteria for a schizophrenia diagnosis (see Box 7.2) at some point in their lives (McGrath, Saha, Chant, & Welham, 2008). Onset of schizophrenia is typically in late adolescence or early adulthood; although some cases do appear in early adolescence or in midlife. There is evidence that the age of schizophrenia onset for males is, on average, about a year or two earlier than for females (Eranti, MacCabe, Bundy, & Murray, 2013).

There is currently no cure for schizophrenia, but there are medications that can often be used to successfully treat its symptoms (Tandon, Nasrallah, & Keshavan, 2010). Schizophrenia is considered to be a chronic, severe mental illness that is estimated to be the twelfth highest cause of years lived with disability worldwide (GBD, 2016). Schizophrenia can make it difficult to manage social or family relationships or to pursue education or hold a job. The burdens on the individual, family, and society are substantial. A recent study estimated the cost to the US economy to be between $94 and $102 billion annually when considering costs related to medical treatment, lost economic productivity, premature mortality, and intangible costs associated with quality of life (Chong et al., 2016).

Box 7.2 ICD-11 Diagnosis: Schizophrenia

Schizophrenia is characterised by disturbances in multiple mental modalities, including thinking (e.g., delusions, disorganisation in the form of thought), perception (e.g., hallucinations), self-experience (e.g., the experience that one's feelings, impulses, thoughts, or behaviour are under the control of an external force), cognition (e.g., impaired attention, verbal memory, and social cognition), volition (e.g., loss of motivation), affect (e.g., blunted emotional expression), and behaviour (e.g., behaviour that appears bizarre or purposeless, unpredictable or inappropriate emotional responses that interfere with the organisation of behaviour). Psychomotor disturbances, including catatonia, may be present. Persistent delusions, persistent hallucinations, thought disorder, and experiences of influence, passivity, or control are considered core symptoms. Symptoms must have persisted for at least one month in order for a diagnosis of schizophrenia to be assigned. The symptoms are not a manifestation of another health condition (e.g., a brain tumour) and are not due to the effect of a substance or medication on the central nervous system (e.g., corticosteroids), including withdrawal (e.g., alcohol withdrawal).

Source: http://id.who.int/icd/entity/1683919430 (accessed February 22, 2021), World Health Organization (Copyright © 2020).

It is important to note that a distinction between positive symptoms and negative symptoms is often made. These are not value judgments (i.e., good versus bad) but reflect how the symptoms compare to "typical" experience. Positive symptoms loosely represent something that is over and above typical experience. For example, auditory hallucinations like hearing voices are not part of typical experience but represent an addition to it. Negative symptoms, on the other hand, indicate that something is less than typical experience. For example, avolition is a lack of motivation.

When trying to understand the genetic risk of developing a mental illness, such as schizophrenia diagnosed with either ICD-11 or DSM-5 criteria, it must be recognized that two individuals with the same diagnosis (i.e., schizophrenia) can have completely different symptom profiles. One may experience hallucinations and disorganized speech, while the other experiences delusions and avolition, or some other combination. This symptom heterogeneity in schizophrenia has long been recognized, and previously was used to distinguish clinical subtypes: disorganized (hebephrenic), catatonic, paranoid, and undifferentiated. These clinical subtypes have been eliminated in modern diagnostic schemes because they have not proven to be stable, useful in the clinic, or to aid in the understanding of the underlying biology of schizophrenia (Tandon et al., 2013).

Check-up

- What are the symptoms of schizophrenia?
- Compare and contrast positive and negative symptoms for schizophrenia.
- What is symptom heterogeneity and what does it mean for behavior genetic research?

7.5 Neurobiology of Schizophrenia

Given the broad array of symptoms that characterize schizophrenia, one should not expect the underlying neurobiology to be simple. Several lines of lines of evidence have been pursued in the investigation of the etiology of schizophrenia (Pesold, Roberts, & Kirkpatrick, 2004). The fluid filled spaces in the brain (cerebral ventricles) tend to be significantly larger in patients with schizophrenia, when compared with controls. The enlarged ventricles appear to be, at least partially, due to thinning of the cerebral cortex (see Figure 7.7). In addition, there is evidence of a reduction in hippocampal volume in patients, when compared with controls.

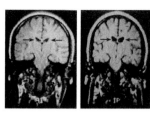

Figure 7.7. **Enlarged ventricles associated with schizophrenia diagnosis.** Enlarged ventricles are shown on the right (indicated by arrows) for an individual with schizophrenia. The left panel shows the individual's MZ twin, who does not have schizophrenia. Source: Banich & Compton (2018). Cambridge University Press. Used by Permission.

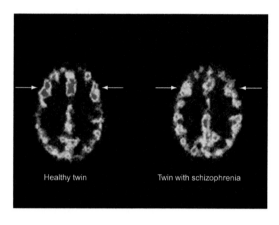

Healthy twin   Twin with schizophrenia

Figure 7.8. **Hypofrontality associated with schizophrenia diagnosis.** The white arrows indicate frontal lobe areas that show reduced activity in individuals with schizophrenia compared to individuals without schizophrenia. Source: Banich & Compton (2018). Cambridge University Press. Used by Permission.

In terms of functional brain differences, there is substantial evidence that when compared to controls, individuals with schizophrenia have decreased activity in the dorsolateral prefrontal cortex during working memory and attention tasks, which is termed hypofrontality (see Figure 7.8). Other brain areas, such as the hippocampus, thalamus, basal ganglia, and anterior cingulate cortex have also shown functional differences between patients with schizophrenia and controls.

In addition to brain volume and activity, there has been substantial research on potential neurotransmitter system dysfunction in schizophrenia (Pesold et al., 2004). Medications that relieve psychotic symptoms (i.e., antipsychotics) tend to block dopamine receptors. This observation led to the development of the dopamine hypothesis of schizophrenia, which proposed that excessive dopamine activity played a role in the disorder's etiology. This hypothesis was also consistent with the evidence that excessive amphetamine use can produce psychotic symptoms because amphetamines block reuptake of dopamine, which produces an excess of synaptic dopamine.

Others noted that the drug known as angel dust (aka phencyclidine, or PCP), which blocks a type of glutamate receptor, produced psychotic symptoms, and proposed that dysfunction in the glutamate system was associated with schizophrenia etiology. Activity in the GABA neurotransmitter system also differs between patients with schizophrenia and controls, which implicates it in schizophrenia etiology.

In addition, it is well documented that those with schizophrenia are more likely to smoke cigarettes than those without schizophrenia. Such a pattern of behavior suggests that the patients may be using tobacco to self-medicate schizophrenia symptoms, which led to investigations of the role of nicotinic acetylcholine receptors in schizophrenia. It is important to note that dysfunction in a single neurotransmitter system cannot explain the heterogeneity of symptoms that comprise a schizophrenia diagnosis, but that such evidence adds to our understanding of the disorder and can inform the development of medications to treat it.

Check-up

- Explain the cause of enlarged ventricles in patients with schizophrenia.
- How is hypofrontality related to observable schizophrenia symptoms?
- Discuss the role of drugs in the development of hypotheses for schizophrenia etiology.

7.6 Schizophrenia Genetics: Heritability

It has long been noted that schizophrenia tends to run in families, which suggests that genetic variation is associated with individual differences in risk, but family studies cannot rule out the influence of shared environment as a cause (Ritsner & Gottesman, 2011). Epidemiological studies that examined the rates of schizophrenia or related psychotic disorders in relatives of probands have generally found that the risk of diagnosis increases along with the degree of genetic relatedness (see Figure 7.9). As you may recall, first-degree relatives include those who share 50 percent of their genetic material, second-degree relatives include those who share 25 percent, and third-degree relatives share 12.5 percent. When risk for a disorder increases along with genetic relatedness, it can be considered supportive evidence of a genetic cause. Of course, it is not definitive evidence because typically environmental sharing also increases with genetic relatedness.

Since the 1940s twin studies have been conducted to estimate the heritability of schizophrenia, and a meta-analysis of twelve such studies estimated the heritability to be 0.81 (95 percent confidence interval 0.73–0.90), and the shared environment effect to be 0.11 (95 percent CI = 0.03–0.19) (Sullivan, Kendler, & Neale, 2003). Such evidence is consistent with the notion that the more genetic material shared by two people the greater the similarity between them for schizophrenia diagnosis. In other words, the more genes that two people share, the more likely they are to share a diagnosis. The shared environment contribution to twin similarity for schizophrenia is consistent

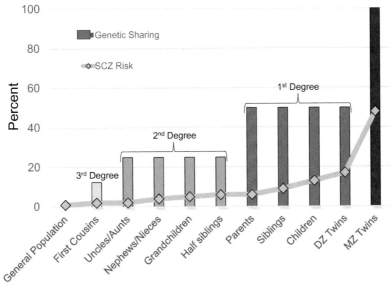

Figure 7.9. **Risk for developing schizophrenia-related psychoses.** An individual's risk for developing a psychotic illness varies as a function of whether they have a relative who has schizophrenia and the degree to which they are related. Those who share more genes are at higher risk. After Gottesman (2001).

with the notion that there are some environmental factors that tend to make twins similar for schizophrenia diagnosis status. This is consistent with evidence for environmental risk factors for schizophrenia (see Box 7.3).

Box 7.3 Environmental Risk Factors for Schizophrenia

As you may recall from Chapter 3, estimating the heritability of a trait does not require the measurement of specific aspects of the environment. Rather, researchers examine trait similarity in people with known genetic relatedness without necessarily measuring any environmental variables. Because the genetic part of the equation is known, whatever amount of trait variance that is left over after estimating the contribution of genetic variance is considered to be due to environmental variance.

Epidemiological studies, however, have identified several environmental risk factors for schizophrenia (Brown, 2011). Prenatal infection by rubella, influenza, *Toxoplasma gondii*, herpes simplex, or other agents increases risk for schizophrenia, although the neural mechanisms have not been fully characterized. Presumably, the infection itself or the immune system's response to it interferes with neurodevelopment in some way. Prenatal dietary insufficiency as seen in famine, poverty, or other maternal dietary exposure, including obesity also increases risk for schizophrenia. *In utero* exposure to toxins, such as lead, also appear to be a risk factor. Obstetric complications, either during pregnancy or delivery, and general maternal stress also increase risk for schizophrenia.

Advanced paternal age has long been identified as a risk factor for schizophrenia (Brown, 2011). It may be that *de novo* mutations are more likely to occur in older fathers. *De novo* mutations appear to be an important factor in schizophrenia genetics (see section below on molecular genetics). It also may be that regulation of epigenetic marks in sperm produced by older fathers may not function as well as in younger fathers. Although it is clear that advanced paternal age is a schizophrenia risk factor for offspring, the exact mechanisms are not fully understood.

There is also evidence for environmental factors occurring after the perinatal period that increase risk for schizophrenia (Brown, 2011). Adolescent cannabis use is one such risk factor. Several studies have found that early onset (e.g., before age 15) of heavy cannabis use increases risk for the development of schizophrenia, especially in those who are already at risk for psychotic illness. Evidence for the impact of socioeconomic status, exposure to childhood trauma, and other infections on schizophrenia risk exists but remains inconclusive.

When children who are at high risk for developing schizophrenia, usually because their mothers have schizophrenia, are adopted into families (or institutions) where schizophrenia is not present, they have a somewhat elevated rate of developing schizophrenia when compared to children who are not at high risk (Ingraham & Kety, 2000). Such studies are not common, and the sample sizes are typically quite small, so numeric estimates of the risk may not be reliable. However, the pattern is consistent with genetic or perinatal influence on schizophrenia risk. Similarly, when adopted children subsequently develop schizophrenia and investigators then examine both the adoptive and the biological families for schizophrenia, they typically find that rates of schizophrenia are higher in the biological families than in the adoptive families. Again, this is a pattern consistent with genetic factors increasing schizophrenia risk.

More recently, investigators have been estimating heritability of schizophrenia endophenotypes, such as those in the cognitive domain (Blokland et al., 2017). This approach enables the use of data from twin studies that were not specifically focused on schizophrenia but were aimed at better understanding genetic contribution to normal variation in traits that are considered to be risk factors for schizophrenia. Such findings suggest that in both clinical and non-clinical populations genetic variance explains a significant amount of variance in cognitive traits that are implicated in schizophrenia. In other words, cognitive endophenotypes for schizophrenia have significant (i.e., non-zero) heritability estimates (Blokland et al., 2017). These findings support the RDoC approach in the behavior genetics of mental illness.

Check-up

- Describe how familial relatedness is associated with risk for schizophrenia.
- What environmental factors increase risk for schizophrenia?
- Describe the evidence for non-zero heritability estimates for schizophrenia.

7.7 Schizophrenia Genetics: Molecular Genetics

In line with high estimates of heritability, there is substantial evidence that genetic variation between individuals is associated with differential risk for developing schizophrenia from studies that use molecular genetic approaches (Kotlar, Mercer, Zwick, & Mulle, 2015). As with nearly all behaviors and psychiatric disorders, it has become clear that many genetic loci contribute to risk for schizophrenia, in other words, schizophrenia is a polygenic trait. It is sobering to see that nearly every chromosome contains multiple loci that have been associated with schizophrenia risk. In fact, the Human Genome Navigator identifies over 1,800 genes that have been reported with schizophrenia as of 2018. We are far from having a complete understanding of the role of genetic variation in risk for schizophrenia, but we do know that there is no single gene that *causes* schizophrenia, and that many genes across the genome contribute to overall risk.

Copy number variants (CNVs, i.e., gains or losses of at least 1,000 bp [1 kb]), which can impact the expression level of a gene or the structure of the resulting protein have emerged as important contributors to schizophrenia risk. One CNV in particular, the 3q29 microdeletion, is associated with a forty-fold increase in risk for schizophrenia (Kotlar et al., 2015). This deletion usually arises *de novo*, that is, it is not present in either parent, but arises in either the formation of the egg or sperm, or during early embryogenesis. The 3q29 microdeletion produces a loss of 1.6 million base pairs (1.6 Mb) on the long arm of chromosome 3 containing 22 protein coding genes. In addition to increasing risk for schizophrenia, 3q29 microdeletion syndrome can produce intellectual disability, delayed speech and language development, certain facial features, and microcephaly although there is substantial variability in the expression of the syndrome (see Figure 7.10). 3q29 microdeletion syndrome is rare, with as few as seventy-five cases reported in the medical literature, but the strong association between the deletion and schizophrenia suggests that at least one of those deleted genes is involved in schizophrenia risk. Many other rare variants have been associated with schizophrenia risk and have thus contributed to the understanding of the biology underlying the disorder, but it is beyond the scope of this book to exhaustively review them.

Other risk variants that are more common have been identified in Genome Wide Association Studies (GWAS) and studied in candidate gene association studies. One of the problems with identifying common genetic variants (i.e., minor allele frequency ≥ 0.01) that impact risk for

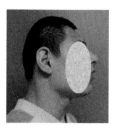

Figure 7.10. **Microcephaly in 3q29 microdeletion.** Decreased size of cranium, or microcephaly is one of the potential signs of 3q29 microdeletion syndrome. Source: Condition, gene, or chromosome summary: National Library of Medicine (US). Genetics Home Reference [Internet]. Bethesda (MD): The Library; February 11, 2020. 3q29 microdeletion syndrome; [reviewed 2019 May; cited 2020 February 21], https://ghr.nlm.nih.gov/condition/3q29-microdeletion-syndrome. Image in the public domain.

any mental illness or behavior is that the effect sizes for such variants are typically very small. Mental illnesses or behaviors are complex traits, where genetic differences between people are responsible for some, but not all, of the differences in risk. That is, there is no single gene that is primarily associated with risk for the disorder, but rather, many genes each contribute a small amount to the overall risk. In addition, there are non-genetic factors, such as exposure to a virus, or early life trauma, that also contribute to risk, and may do so in an interactive fashion. Most of the traits that are of interest to those in behavior genetics are polygenic, and small effect sizes are expected for each variant. That is, the difference in risk that is accounted for by having one allele of a SNP compared to having the other allele is very small.

The small effect size polygenes in traits and disorders, along with the plummeting cost and relative ease of genotyping has led to the GWAS era in behavior genetics, as we discussed in Chapter 5. In a simple statistical sense, one way to overcome the problem of small effect sizes is to conduct studies with very large sample sizes (Wray et al., 2014). For example, in a case-control study, to have sufficient statistical power (i.e., $\geq 80\%$) to detect the impact of a single variant with a minor allele frequency <0.20 or so requires at least 6,000 cases (i.e., individuals with a diagnosis of schizophrenia) and 6,000 controls (i.e., unrelated individuals without a diagnosis of schizophrenia). It is challenging and costly for researchers to conduct studies involving tens of thousands, or even hundreds of thousands of participants.

Obtaining suitably large numbers of participants for such studies typically requires the collaboration of many researchers, and has catalyzed the formation of research consortia, such as the Psychiatric Genomics Consortium (PGC) (Sullivan, 2010; Sullivan et al., 2018). A stated goal of the PGC is to obtain GWAS data on 100,000 cases for each of nine psychiatric disorders. As of 2018 they reported having data on nearly 61,000 cases with schizophrenia, and 155 independent genetic associations that have reached genome-wide significance (Sullivan et al., 2018). They note, however, that there may be as many as 1,000 genes that have an impact on risk for schizophrenia, so much work remains. It is also clear that the PGC is the largest and most ambitious coordinated effort to understand the biology underlying risk for developing psychiatric disorders. This "big science" approach in behavior genetics represents an exciting time, but one must recognize that it also consumes much of the available resources in behavior genetics and is at the mercy of the methodological problems inherent in GWAS (e.g., difficulty in accounting for epistatic interactions).

Several schizophrenia endophenotypes have been investigated using a candidate gene association study approach. The Consortium on the Genetics of Schizophrenia has tested associations between over 20 endophenotypes and 1,385 SNPs within 94 neurobiologically relevant candidate genes in 534 individuals from 130 families (proband, at least one unaffected sibling, and both parents) (Greenwood et al., 2016; Greenwood, Light, Swerdlow, Radant, & Braff, 2012). The endophenotypes were measures derived from neurophysiological and neuropsychological test batteries.

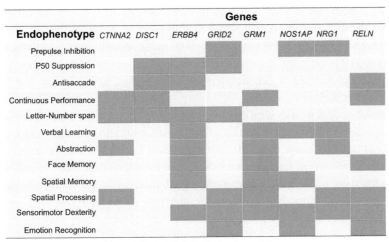

NOTE: Dark shaded (green) boxes indicate statistically significant association.

Figure 7.11. **Schizophrenia endophenotypes.** Endophenotypes associated with SNPs in 46 candidate genes. The dark shaded boxes indicate significant associations between SNPs and endophenotypes. Only those eight genes that had SNPs associated with four or more endophenotypes are shown. These results demonstrate pleiotropy, where a single gene is associated with more than one trait, and the polygenic nature of endophenotypes. After Greenwood et al. (2012).

The genotyping was done with a specific SNP genotyping microarray that was developed for the project, which included SNPs that had shown some association with schizophrenia or related endophenotypes. The 94 candidate genes tested were determined to be in five known biological pathways. Four of the pathways involve neurotransmitter systems that are known, from a variety of types of evidence, to play a role in schizophrenia.

SNPs in 46 of the 94 genes tested were associated with at least one endophenotype. SNPs in eight of the genes tested showed evidence of significant association with four or more endophenotypes (see Figure 7.11) (Greenwood et al., 2012). In other words, there was significant evidence of pleiotropy (i.e., one genetic variant being associated with multiple traits) in 8.5 percent of the genes tested. Many of the pleiotropic genes code for proteins that are involved in neurotransmission. So, it might not be too surprising that the gene that codes for a glutamate receptor (e.g., *GRM1*), for example, is associated with multiple neurophysiological or neuropsychological measures, since glutamate is the brain's most common excitatory neurotransmitter.

An important goal of research to identify genetic variants that increase risk for the development of schizophrenia is the construction of a polygenic risk score that can serve as an index of genetic risk. In the clinic, such an index may be combined with other information (e.g., family history, substance use history, life stresses) to help in diagnosis and treatment decisions. Such a polygenic risk score could be constructed using GWAS data from large international consortia to include loci that were found to be significant at the genome-wide level, and combined in a score for each individual that is based on their specific genotype weighted by the effect size that was observed in the GWAS (Bogdan, Baranger, & Agrawal, 2018; Schizophrenia Working Group of the Psychiatric Genomics Consortium, 2014). Such an approach allows the pooling of the effects of genetic variants that have small additive effects. Such polygenic risk scores have proven to be useful in the research lab to better characterize the genetic architecture of schizophrenia and relevant endophenotypes and may someday prove useful in the clinic.

One problem that is seen across biomedical research including behavior genetics is that most studies are conducted in populations with European or Asian ancestries. Findings in such populations may not generalize well to other populations. In addition, such populations contain only a subset of potential genetic variation that is seen in populations of African ancestry, which limits our understanding of the role of genetic variation in individual differences in risk for psychiatric disorders like schizophrenia.

A recent study sought to identify genetic variants associated with schizophrenia in 909 cases and 917 controls from the Xhosa population of South Africa matched on age, gender, education, and region of recruitment (Gulsuner et al., 2020). One of their findings is that the cases harbored more private damaging mutations than did controls. Private mutations were those found only in a single individual, so that these are likely *de novo* mutations that have arisen in one person. Damaging mutations were those that caused a frameshift, nonsense, or other type of mutation that were predicted to have negative impacts on the function of a gene. Furthermore, they found that the private damaging mutations in cases were more likely to be found in genes highly expressed in the brain (see Figure 7.12). These mutations were also more likely to be upregulated in schizophrenia or autism and downregulated

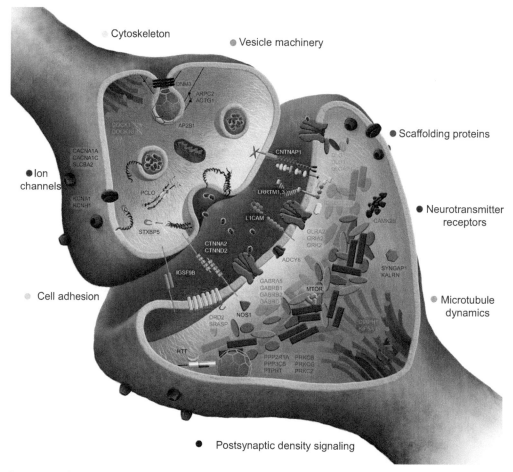

Figure 7.12. **Synaptic plasticity and neural circuitry genes harboring private damaging mutations.** Each of the proteins shown and labeled were found to harbor a private damaging mutation in cases with schizophrenia but not in healthy controls in Xhosa populations from South Africa. Each category in which a gene was identified with a private damaging mutation is noted by the terms surrounding the figure. Source: Gulsuner et al. (2020). Reprinted with permission from AAAS.

in bipolar disorder. And in a Swedish replication sample a similar pattern of private damaging mutations was observed.

If private damaging mutations are an important risk factor in causing schizophrenia, then it becomes easier to see why its genetic basis has been difficult to characterize. There may be no specific set of genetic variants that causes schizophrenia that is generally shared across patients. It may be that disruptions to various brain systems that can occur as a result of a small number of private mutations in some unknown number of genes can account for the high heritability of schizophrenia as well as its genetic and symptom heterogeneity.

This study also highlights the importance of studying populations with diverse ancestries. It should no longer be scientifically or ethically acceptable to study primarily racially homogeneous Western populations.

Check-up

- Discuss 3q29 microdeletion syndrome and its role in understanding the genetics of schizophrenia risk.
- What is the Psychiatric Genomics Consortium and what does it mean for behavior genetics as a "big science"?
- Discuss evidence for pleiotropy in schizophrenia.
- Explain the role of private damaging mutations in schizophrenia.

7.8 Schizophrenia Genetics: Non-Human Animal Models

Schizophrenia seems like a disorder that would be difficult, if not impossible, to model in non-human animals. At least two of the cardinal symptoms (i.e., delusions and disorganized speech) appear especially difficult to study in animals. It is notoriously challenging to assess higher level cognitive processes in rodents, for example. Although non-human animal models of schizophrenia might not perfectly parallel the human experience of the disorder, those models that express core behavioral signs and symptoms (i.e., have face validity), have similar neurochemical and structural deficits (i.e., have construct validity), or can be used to uncover new information about schizophrenia (i.e., have predictive validity) can contribute to its understanding in important ways.

Desirable characteristics in an animal model of schizophrenia would include: (1) post pubertal onset, (2) loss of function and connectivity between hippocampus and cortex, (3) dopamine dysregulation in limbic system, (4) glutamate hypofunction in cortex, (5) vulnerability to stress, (6) reward system dysfunction, (7) social withdrawal, and (8) cognitive impairment (Jones, Watson, & Fone, 2011). It is unlikely that any single animal model will have all these characteristics. But there are at least twenty animal models that are used to investigate the genetics of schizophrenia that have one or more of them. The models fall into four classes: developmental (e.g., maternal stress, or viral infection), drug induced (e.g., amphetamine, PCP), lesion (e.g., ventral hippocampus), and genetic (e.g., *NRG1* knockout).

Of course, for our purposes, it is the genetic non-human animal models that are of greatest interest. The most common approach to studying the role of genes in the development of psychiatric disorders is to first manipulate a gene in a line of mice, and then to test for neurobiological and behavioral differences between mice from the engineered line and mice that are genetically identical except for the engineered change. Different approaches include (1) production of transgenic mice that carry variations in the human sequence of a target gene, (2) engineered promoter(s) that can produce overexpression of the gene, and (3) targeted mutations in mouse gene to alter the resultant protein or eliminate it entirely.

The gene disrupted-in-schizophrenia 1 (*DISC1*) was first discovered in 1970 and has been the focus of hundreds of studies. In humans, *DISC1* is located on chromosome 1 (1q42.2; 231,626,815–232,041,272 bp). In mice, it is located on chromosome 8 (125,054,195–125,261,858 bp). *DISC1* codes for a scaffold protein that is involved in many cellular processes including neurotransmission. There is evidence that in mice with *DISC1* disrupted, some cognitive impairment occurs, and brain changes such as reduced cortical volume and enlarged ventricles have been observed (Jones et al., 2011). Furthermore, there is strong convergent evidence that DISC1 plays a role in the regulation of dopaminergic neurotransmission, and therefore consistent with what is known about the neurobiology of schizophrenia (Dahoun, Trossbach, Brandon, Korth, & Howes, 2017).

The neuregulin-1 (*NRG1*) gene codes for the growth factor neuregulin-1, which is involved in development and function of the nervous system (Jones et al., 2011). In humans, *NRG1* is located on chromosome 8 (8p12; 31,639,245–32,774,046 bp). The mouse ortholog, *Nrg1*, is coincidentally also located on chromosome 8 (31,807,452–32,891,609 bp). Alternative splicing of the human *NRG1* transcript results in thirty-one different isoforms, and these proteins are involved in neurotransmission, neuronal migration, synapse formation, myelination, and glial cell formation (Mostaid et al., 2016). Homozygosity for a *Nrg1* knockout is lethal, whereas heterozygosity for the knockout produces behaviors that appear to be consistent with various schizophrenia endophenotypes. Some of these effects are reversible with clozapine, an atypical antipsychotic medication, which strengthens the interpretation that neuregulin-1 plays a role in the etiology of schizophrenia.

The dystrobrevin-binding protein (*DTNBP1*) gene encodes a protein known as dysbindin, which plays an important role in basic synaptic functions for excitatory neurotransmission such as making vesicles and trafficking receptors. In humans, *DTNBP1* is located on chromosome 6 (6p22.3; 15,522,801–15,663,058 bp). The mouse ortholog, *Dtnbp1*, is located on chromosome 13 (44,922,075–45,002,147 bp). Mice with a naturally occurring mutation in this gene, as well as those carrying engineered knockouts show neurobiological abnormalities similar to those associated with schizophrenia in humans, as well as cognitive and social impairments that are consistent with schizophrenia.

The reelin (*RELN*) gene encodes a large protein thought to play a role in neural migration during brain development, and in synaptic plasticity. There is evidence that patients with schizophrenia show lowered levels of the reelin protein in certain brain areas (Jones et al., 2011). In humans, *RELN* is located on chromosome 7 (7q22.1; 103,471,784–103,989,658 bp). The mouse ortholog, *Reln*, is located on chromosome 5 (21,884,454–22,344,705 bp). A line of mice ("reeler") was identified in the 1950s that showed severe ataxia and was subsequently found to have abnormal brain development, especially in cortex, hippocampus, and cerebellum, which was decades later attributed to a mutation in the Reln gene (D'Arcangelo, 2005). Humans carrying homozygous loss of function mutations in RELN have severe lissencephaly (meaning "smooth brain") due to defective neural migration. These individuals also show severe ataxia, cognitive deficits, and other symptoms. Mice that are heterozygous for the reeler mutation display many, but not all schizophrenia-related endophenotypes to varying degrees (Jones et al., 2011).

The genes mentioned here do not represent an exhaustive list but are those that have been well studied. In GWAS studies, variants in these candidate genes are not typically significantly associated with the disorder or its endophenotypes. However, one should not totally discount all the other convergent evidence that supports the role of variants in these genes playing a role in the disorder. One approach does not nullify the data from all others. Genetic and symptom heterogeneity in schizophrenia is likely to accommodate genetic variants that are causal in some cases, but not in others.

Check-up

- What characteristics are desirable for a non-human animal model of schizophrenia?
- Name the four main genes that have been used to study schizophrenia in non-human animal models.

7.9 SUMMARY

- Patterns of thinking, emotion, and behavior that interfere with functioning are common around the world. Such mental illnesses account for a substantial proportion of years lost to disability and premature death. Mental illnesses are treatable with talk therapies and medication.
- A person's risk for mental illness is a function of the risk and protective alleles that they carry and their exposure to environmental risk factors. The diathesis-stress model and the differential susceptibility hypothesis are two theoretical approaches to understanding individual differences in risk.
- Psychiatric diagnoses are made by assessing signs and symptoms of mental illness according to a diagnostic scheme. Such an approach views mental illness as a qualitative trait. Other approaches focus on quantitative traits, such as endophenotypes, to advance understanding of the causes of mental illness.
- Schizophrenia is characterized by symptoms that represent changes from healthy psychological function classified into positive (e.g., delusions) and negative (e.g., avolition) categories. Two people with schizophrenia can have completely different symptom profiles (i.e., genetic heterogeneity), which complicates genetic research.
- Enlarged ventricles in the brain, which are likely due to cortical thinning, decreased activity in the dorsolateral prefrontal cortex, and neurotransmitter system dysfunction are thought to play a role in schizophrenia.
- Genetic similarity is correlated with risk for schizophrenia, and heritability estimates are high. Exposure to infection, toxins, stress, and other adverse environments also play a role in schizophrenia risk.
- Schizophrenia is polygenic with over 1,800 genes showing some association. Large consortia of researchers are using GWAS and large sample sizes to identify risk and protective alleles. Under-studied populations have shown that private damaging mutations in brain systems are important genetic causes of schizophrenia.
- Non-human animal models can focus attention on traits associated with schizophrenia and take advantage of genetic engineering to identify causal variants. Several genes have been well characterized in animal models as risk factors for schizophrenia.

RECOMMENDED READING

- Assary, E., Vincent, J. P., Keers, R., & Pluess, M. (2018). Gene–environment interaction and psychiatric disorders: Review and future directions. *Semin Cell Dev Biol*, *77*, 133–143. doi: 10.1016/j.semcdb.2017.10.016

- Gottesman, I. I., & Gould, T. D. (2003). The endophenotype concept in psychiatry: Etymology and strategic intentions. Am J Psychiatry, *160*(4), 636–645. doi:10.1176/appi.ajp.160.4.636
- Jones, C. A., Watson, D. J., & Fone, K. C. (2011). Animal models of schizophrenia. *Br J Pharmacol, 164*(4), 1162–1194. doi:10.1111/j.1476-5381.2011.01386.x
- Torrey, E. F. (2006). *Surviving Schizophrenia* (5th ed.). New York: HarperCollins.

REFERENCES

APA (2013). *Diagnostic and Statistical Manual of Mental Disorders: DSM-5* (pp. 0-1). Washington, DC: American Psychiatric Association.

Banich, M. T., & Compton, R. J. (2018). *Cognitive Neuroscience* (4th ed.). Cambridge: Cambridge University Press.

Belsky, J., & Pluess, M. (2009). Beyond diathesis stress: Differential susceptibility to environmental influences. *Psychol Bull, 135*(6), 885–908. doi:10.1037/a0017376

Blokland, G. A. M., Mesholam-Gately, R. I., Toulopoulou, T., Del Re, E. C., Lam, M., DeLisi, L. E., ... Petryshen, T. L. (2017). Heritability of neuropsychological measures in schizophrenia and nonpsychiatric populations: A systematic review and meta-analysis. *Schizophr Bull, 43*(4), 788–800. doi:10.1093/schbul/sbw146

Bogdan, R., Baranger, D. A. A., & Agrawal, A. (2018). Polygenic risk scores in clinical psychology: Bridging genomic risk to individual differences. *Annu Rev Clin Psychol, 14*, 119–157. doi:10.1146/annurev-clinpsy-050817-084847

Brown, A. S. (2011). The environment and susceptibility to schizophrenia. *Prog Neurobiol, 93*(1), 23–58. doi:10.1016/j.pneurobio.2010.09.003

Chong, H. Y., Teoh, S. L., Wu, D. B., Kotirum, S., Chiou, C. F., & Chaiyakunapruk, N. (2016). Global economic burden of schizophrenia: A systematic review. *Neuropsychiatr Dis Treat, 12*, 357–373. doi:10.2147/ndt.s96649

Cuthbert, B. N. (2015). Research domain criteria: Toward future psychiatric nosologies. *Dialogues Clin Neurosci, 17*(1), 89–97.

D'Arcangelo, G. (2005). The reeler mouse: Anatomy of a mutant. *Int Rev Neurobiol, 71*, 383–417. doi:10.1016/s0074-7742(05)71016-3

Dahoun, T., Trossbach, S. V., Brandon, N. J., Korth, C., & Howes, O. D. (2017). The impact of Disrupted-in-Schizophrenia 1 (DISC1) on the dopaminergic system: A systematic review. *Transl Psychiatry, 7*(1), e1015–e1015. doi:10.1038/tp.2016.282

Eranti, S. V., MacCabe, J. H., Bundy, H., & Murray, R. M. (2013). Gender difference in age at onset of schizophrenia: A meta-analysis. *Psychol Med, 43*(1), 155–167. doi:10.1017/S003329171200089X

Gandal, M. J., Leppa, V., Won, H., Parikshak, N. N., & Geschwind, D. H. (2016). The road to precision psychiatry: Translating genetics into disease mechanisms. *Nat Neurosci, 19*(11), 1397–1407. doi:10.1038/nn.4409

GBD (2016). Global, regional, and national incidence, prevalence, and years lived with disability for 310 diseases and injuries, 1990–2015: A systematic analysis for the Global Burden of Disease Study 2015. *Lancet, 388*(10053), 1545–1602. doi:10.1016/s0140-6736(16)31678-6

Gottesman, I. I. (2001). Psychopathology through a life span-genetic prism. *Am Psychol, 56*(11), 867–878. doi:10.1037/0003-066x.56.11.867

Gottesman, I. I., & Gould, T. D. (2003). The endophenotype concept in psychiatry: Etymology and strategic intentions. *Am J Psychiatry, 160*(4), 636–645. doi:10.1176/appi.ajp.160.4.636

Greenwood, T. A., Lazzeroni, L. C., Calkins, M. E., Freedman, R., Green, M. F., Gur, R. E., . . . Braff, D. L. (2016). Genetic assessment of additional endophenotypes from the Consortium on the Genetics of Schizophrenia Family Study. *Schizophr Res, 170*(1), 30–40. doi:10.1016/j.schres.2015.11.008

Greenwood, T. A., Light, G. A., Swerdlow, N. R., Radant, A. D., & Braff, D. L. (2012). Association analysis of 94 candidate genes and schizophrenia-related endophenotypes. *PLoS One, 7*(1), e29630. doi:10.1371/journal.pone.0029630

Gulsuner, S., Stein, D. J., Susser, E. S., Sibeko, G., Pretorius, A., Walsh, T., . . . McClellan, J. M. (2020). Genetics of schizophrenia in the South African Xhosa. *Science (New York, N.Y.), 367*(6477), 569–573. doi:10.1126/science.aay8833

Ingraham, L. J., & Kety, S. S. (2000). Adoption studies of schizophrenia. *Am J Med Genet, 97*(1), 18–22. doi:10.1002/(sici)1096-8628(200021)97:1<18::aid-ajmg4>3.0.co;2-l

Jones, C. A., Watson, D. J., & Fone, K. C. (2011). Animal models of schizophrenia. *Br J Pharmacol, 164*(4), 1162–1194. doi:10.1111/j.1476-5381.2011.01386.x

Kendler, K. S., & Neale, M. C. (2010). Endophenotype: A conceptual analysis. *Mol Psychiatry, 15*(8), 789–797. doi:10.1038/mp.2010.8

Kotlar, A. V., Mercer, K. B., Zwick, M. E., & Mulle, J. G. (2015). New discoveries in schizophrenia genetics reveal neurobiological pathways: A review of recent findings. *Eur J Med Genet, 58*(12), 704–714. doi:10.1016/j.ejmg.2015.10.008

Lenzenweger, M. F. (2013). Thinking clearly about the endophenotype-intermediate phenotype-biomarker distinctions in developmental psychopathology research. *Dev Psychopathol, 25*(4 Pt 2), 1347–1357. doi:10.1017/S0954579413000655

Lombardo, P., Jones, W., Wang, L., Shen, X., & Goldner, E. M. (2018). The fundamental association between mental health and life satisfaction: Results from successive waves of a Canadian national survey. *BMC Public Health, 18*(1), 342. doi:10.1186/s12889-018-5235-x

McGrath, J., Saha, S., Chant, D., & Welham, J. (2008). Schizophrenia: A concise overview of incidence, prevalence, and mortality. *Epidemiol Rev, 30*(1), 67–76. doi:10.1093/epirev/mxn001

Monroe, S. M., & Simons, A. D. (1991). Diathesis-stress theories in the context of life stress research: Implications for the depressive disorders. *Psychol Bull, 110*(3), 406–425. doi:10.1037/0033-2909.110.3.406

Mostaid, M. S., Lloyd, D., Liberg, B., Sundram, S., Pereira, A., Pantelis, C., . . . Bousman, C. A. (2016). Neuregulin-1 and schizophrenia in the genome-wide association study era. *Neurosci Biobehav Rev, 68*, 387–409. doi:10.1016/j.neubiorev.2016.06.001

Pesold, C., Roberts, R. C., & Kirkpatrick, B. (2004). Neuroscience of schizophrenia. In J. Panksepp (Ed.), *Textbook of Biological Psychiatry* (pp. 267–297). New York: Wiley.

Rehm, J., & Shield, K. D. (2019). Global burden of disease and the impact of mental and addictive disorders. *Curr Psychiatry Rep, 21*(2), 10. doi:10.1007/s11920-019-0997-0

Ritsner, M. S., & Gottesman, I. (2011). The schizophrenia construct after 100 years of challenges. In M. S. Ritsner (Ed.), *Handbook of Schizophrenia Spectrum Disorders* (Vol. 1). Berlin: Springer Science+Business Media.

Ross, C. A., & Margolis, R. L. (2019). Research domain criteria: Strengths, weaknesses, and potential alternatives for future psychiatric research. *Mol Neuropsychiatry, 5*(4), 218–236. doi:10.1159/000501797

SAMHSA (2018). *Key substance use and mental health indicators in the United States: Results from the 2017 National Survey on Drug Use and Health* (HHS Publication No. SMA 18-5068, NSDUH Series H-53). Rockville, MD.

Schizophrenia Working Group of the Psychiatric Genomics Consortium (2014). Biological insights from 108 schizophrenia-associated genetic loci. *Nature, 511*(7510), 421–427. doi:10.1038/nature13595

Sullivan, P. F. (2010). The psychiatric GWAS consortium: Big science comes to psychiatry. *Neuron, 68*(2), 182–186. doi:10.1016/j.neuron.2010.10.003

Sullivan, P. F., Agrawal, A., Bulik, C. M., Andreassen, O. A., Borglum, A. D., Breen, G., . . . O'Donovan, M. C. (2018). Psychiatric genomics: An update and an agenda. *Am J Psychiatry, 175*(1), 15–27. doi:10.1176/appi.ajp.2017.17030283

Sullivan, P. F., Kendler, K. S., & Neale, M. C. (2003). Schizophrenia as a complex trait: Evidence from a meta-analysis of twin studies. *Arch Gen Psychiatry, 60*(12), 1187–1192. doi:10.1001/archpsyc.60.12.1187

Tandon, R., Gaebel, W., Barch, D. M., Bustillo, J., Gur, R. E., Heckers, S., . . . Carpenter, W. (2013). Definition and description of schizophrenia in the DSM-5. *Schizophr Res, 150*(1), 3–10. doi:10.1016/j.schres.2013.05.028

Tandon, R., Nasrallah, H. A., & Keshavan, M. S. (2010). Schizophrenia, "just the facts" 5. Treatment and prevention. Past, present, and future. *Schizophr Res, 122*(1–3), 1–23. doi:10.1016/j.schres.2010.05.025

World Health Organization (2012). *Risks to Mental Health: An Overview of Vulnerabilities and Risk Factors.*

World Health Organization (2020). 6A20 Schizophrenia. ICD-11 for Mortality and Morbidity Statistics. http://id.who.int/icd/entity/1683919430

Wray, N. R., Lee, S. H., Mehta, D., Vinkhuyzen, A. A., Dudbridge, F., & Middeldorp, C. M. (2014). Research review: Polygenic methods and their application to psychiatric traits. *J Child Psychol Psychiatry, 55*(10), 1068–1087. doi:10.1111/jcpp.12295

8 Learning and Memory

You probably learned a lot more about individual differences in grade school than you realize. Grade school was the first place where many of us regularly interacted with a relatively large number of human beings. You were able to observe a rich diversity of individual differences, although you probably were not thinking about it in such terms, at the time. Children of the same age can differ in physical traits, such as height, weight, eye color, hair color, and skin color. They can also differ in behavior traits such as coordination, running speed, strength, and stamina. Children can also differ on psychological traits such as anxiety, aggression, extraversion, and impulsivity. Of course, you also probably noticed that grade school students can differ on their success in the classroom.

Obviously, there are many factors that influence a child's success in school. In this chapter, we discuss the construct of intelligence and the notion of normality. We discuss intellectual disabilities and learning disorders, as well as memory, which is a cognitive construct that contributes to intelligence. Finally, we examine some of the evidence for genetic influence on risk for Alzheimer disease.

8.1 Intelligence Is Indexed by IQ Tests

To properly investigate learning and memory, we must address the important, and often contentious issue of intelligence, sometimes referred to as general cognitive ability. Intelligence has been defined as "ability to learn from experience and to adapt to, shape, and select environments" (Sternberg, 2012). From that definition, it is apparent that the construct of intelligence consists of multiple components and depends on context. It has a strong focus on learning, but it also involves aspects of responding to (i.e., adapt) and manipulating (i.e., shape and select) environments. Of course, psychologists have been operationalizing challenging constructs such as this for more than a century, but it is important to consider how well our operational measures reflect the construct of interest.

Tests of intelligence have been and continue to be widely used, since the early twentieth century (Boake, 2002). Scores on intelligence tests are associated with many important life outcomes, such as education, career success, and health (Plomin & von Stumm, 2018). A full treatment of the history of intelligence testing is beyond the scope of this book, but it is important to note that intelligence has been, and continues to be, a phenotype of interest in behavior genetics (Plomin & Deary, 2015; Plucker & Shelton, 2015).

You may have taken an intelligence test at some point in your life. But even if you have not, you have undoubtedly encountered the term **intelligence quotient (IQ)**. An IQ score is based on the score of a test, and generally consists of a ratio of a person's score to the average score for their age group. This quotient is then multiplied by 100, which makes the number easier for people to use. So, if on a particular IQ test, you scored 175, and the average for your age group is 170, the ratio of your

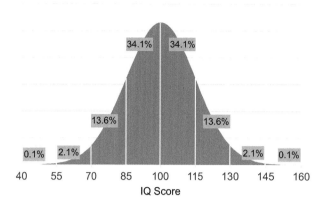

Figure 8.1. **Standardized IQ score distribution**. Scores on IQ tests are typically standardized so that the mean score is 100 and the distribution standard deviation is 15. Therefore, about 68% of people will have scores between 85 and 115, with just over 2% scoring 70 or below.

score to the average would be 175/170 = 1.029. Multiply that by 100 to get an IQ score of 102.9 (103 if you round up). IQ scores are standardized so that the mean is 100 and the standard deviation is 15. So, for standardized IQ scores, most people (68 percent) fall within 1 SD of the population mean (between 85 and 115; see Figure 8.1).

8.1.1 The Definition of Normal Can Vary

When thinking about IQ scores, or any behavioral measures, we tend to want to know what is considered a "normal" score. The word normal gets used a lot, as does its antonym, abnormal. These two categories have sometimes been used to classify psychological traits or behaviors. I suspect that you have wondered, at some point in your life, whether you are "normal."

One way to define normal has to do with frequency. Whatever is most common would then be considered normal, and anything that occurs uncommonly is considered abnormal. If we think about IQ scores as an example (or any trait that is normally distributed in a population), most people fall within one standard deviation of the mean. For IQ, scores between 85 and 115 would then be considered normal, and those outside of that range, both above and below, would be considered abnormal.

Of course, what occurs frequently in one culture, or group, might not occur frequently in another. For example, having tattoos is more common among young people than it is for older people (Heywood et al., 2012). The cultural norms have changed, so that now having a tattoo has positive connotations, whereas in the past, it had negative connotations. So, the point here is just that what is "normal" is not fixed but depends on context.

Sometimes, people define normal as what is "natural." So, for example, because sexual intercourse between a male and a female has the potential to produce offspring, heterosexual behavior is considered normal. Because homosexual behavior does not fulfill a natural reproductive purpose, it is considered, by some, to be abnormal. However, there are many examples, in nature, of homosexual behavior, such as in bonobos, *Pan paniscus* (de Waal, 1995). So, the behavior is natural, in the sense that it occurs in multiple species in nature. And while it may not have a reproductive purpose, it is thought to have important social functions (de Waal, 1995). It is interesting to note that views on the acceptability (i.e., normality) of homosexual behavior are also changing. In 1978 only 43 percent of adults agreed that homosexual behavior should be legal, whereas 72 percent agreed in 2017 (Gallup, 2018).

Again, what we see here is that what is considered normal is not set in stone. We can also see that the term abnormal can have a negative connotation, and even legal ramifications. Use of the terms normal and abnormal can carry the weight of value judgments: normal is good, abnormal is bad. One should use extreme caution when labeling behaviors as normal or abnormal.

For the remainder of this chapter, we examine disorders of cognition and individual differences in aspects of cognition, including evidence of genetic contributions. When we speak of disorders, we will not be making value judgments, but we will focus on conditions that are associated with significant distress or disability in social, occupational, or other important activities (APA, 2013). It should also be noted that although there is good evidence that IQ scores are good predictors of important life outcomes, we will not discuss investigations into the genetics of IQ scores or their proxies, such as academic achievement, because of concerns about their suitability as phenotypes for genetic analysis (Nisbett et al., 2012).

Check-up

- What is intelligence?
- Explain how IQ scores are standardized.
- Discuss different ways to think about what is normal.

8.2 Intellectual Disability Is a Developmental Disorder with Multiple Causes

Disorders of intellectual development (see Box 8.1) are a class of neurodevelopmental disorders with onset prior to adulthood (i.e., before age 18). Diagnoses of such disorders typically rely on both clinical assessment and intelligence testing. Essentially, a diagnosis of intellectual disability (the DSM-5 terminology) means that there are sufficient cognitive deficits that an individual is not keeping up with expected developmental milestones, which hampers appropriate functioning to the extent that ongoing support is required.

Box 8.1 ICD-11 Diagnosis: Disorders of Intellectual Development

Disorders of intellectual development are a group of etiologically diverse conditions originating during the developmental period characterised by significantly below average intellectual functioning and adaptive behaviour that are approximately two or more standard deviations below the mean (approximately less than the 2.3rd percentile), based on appropriately normed, individually administered standardised tests. Where appropriately normed and standardised tests are not available, diagnosis of disorders of intellectual development requires greater reliance on clinical judgment based on appropriate assessment of comparable behavioural indicators.

Source: http://id.who.int/icd/entity/605267007 (accessed February 23, 2021), World Health Organization (Copyright © 2020a).

The term intellectual disability replaced the term mental retardation. In 2010 the US Congress passed "Rosa's Law" (Public Law 111-256) to formalize the change in terminology for the government. The underlying condition, however, has not changed. It is interesting (or disheartening) to know that although we have changed the labels and refined the measures, our basic conception of intellectual disability has not changed much in the last century. In 1927, H. H. Goddard wrote an article entitled "Who is a moron?" that defined feeblemindedness as "defective mentality ... existing from birth or an early age ... whereby he is incapable of competing in the struggle for existence or of managing his own affairs with ordinary prudence" (Goddard, 1927). As you can see, the definition does not differ much from the current diagnosis of intellectual disability, despite the change in terminology.

The prevalence of disorders of intellectual development worldwide has been estimated to be 10.37 per 1,000 people, or about 1 percent (Maulik, Mascarenhas, Mathers, Dua, & Saxena, 2011). Therefore, in the US, with a total population of around 327 million, over 3 million people are likely to meet criteria for a diagnosis of intellectual disability. This appears to be a conservative estimate. Some estimates place the prevalence of disorders of intellectual development as high as 3 percent (National Academies of Sciences Engineering and Medicine, 2015), which would triple the number affected to more than 9 million.

8.2.1 Intellectual Disability Has Environmental and Genetic Causes

There are many potential causes of disorders of intellectual development. Problems during pregnancy that impact the fetus, such as fetal alcohol syndrome, where a developing fetus is exposed to large amounts of alcohol during developmentally critical periods is a relatively common cause of intellectual disability. Problems during (e.g., hypoxia) or shortly after birth (e.g., viral infection) can also cause intellectual disability. Growing up in poverty can also create conditions that increase risk of intellectual disability, such as malnutrition or lead exposure. In specific cases, the cause of disorders of intellectual development may not be known. In addition to environmental causes, there are known genetic causes of intellectual disability, of which we discuss two of the most common.

The most common cause of inherited intellectual disability is called Fragile X syndrome (Mila, Alvarez-Mora, Madrigal, & Rodriguez-Revenga, 2018). Fragile X syndrome occurs in approximately 1 in 4,000 live male births and 1 in 8,000 live female births. Mild to moderate intellectual disability and delayed speech and language development are characteristic of Fragile X syndrome, with most affected males and about one-third of affected females showing these symptoms. Those affected by Fragile X syndrome have an increased risk of being diagnosed with ADHD and/or autism spectrum disorder compared to unaffected individuals. In addition, it is common for those with Fragile X syndrome to have a long, narrow face and large ears, and forehead, unusually flexible hands, and in males after puberty, large testicles.

The name Fragile X is a descriptor of what appears during a cytological examination of a karyotype of an individual with the disorder. A region at the terminal end of the long arm of the X-chromosome (Xq27.3) shows a visible abnormality, which tends to break off during a particular assay. Research identified a gene in that region, called Fragile X Mental Retardation-1 (*FMR1*) that is mutated in nearly all cases of Fragile X syndrome.

Fragile X syndrome is an X-linked dominant disorder, such that having a single mutated copy is sufficient to develop the disorder, and inheritance goes from mother to either child, or from father to daughter. However, the inheritance pattern also shows sex-linked incomplete penetrance, where males show 80 percent penetrance and females show 30–50 percent penetrance (Mila et al., 2018). Penetrance

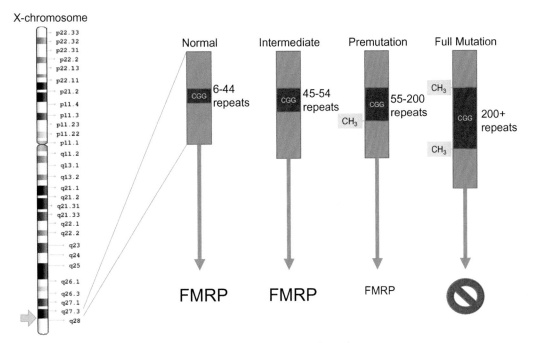

Figure 8.2. **FMR1.** The gene for Fragile X Mental Retardation Protein (FMR1) is located on the X-chromosome: Cytogenetic Location Xq27.3, and Molecular Location base pairs 147,911,919 to 147,951,127. The number of CGG repeats determines FMRP expression genotypes with higher numbers of repeats resulting in methylation and reduced or eliminated expression.

is a term that reflects the probability of showing the trait if you carry the risky genotype. Therefore, 80 percent penetrance indicates that 80 percent of males carrying an X-chromosome with the *FMR1* mutation are diagnosed with the disorder and 20 percent who carry it are not. The concept of penetrance recognizes that other factors play a role in the expression of traits, even when the traits are strongly influenced by genetic variation.

The *FMR1* gene contains a trinucleotide repeat, where the three-base sequence of CGG is repeated some number of times (i.e., CGG_n). When the number of repeats that a person carries in *FMR1* is fewer than 200, the gene is transcribed as usual and produces a protein called Fragile X Mental Retardation Protein (FMRP), which is found in many body tissues, including neurons (Mila et al., 2018). Individuals who have from 6 to 44 copies of CGG in *FMR1* have normal expression of the FMRP protein (see Figure 8.2). Those who have between 45 and 54 copies of CGG also have normal protein expression, but are considered to have an intermediate allele, which could expand when passed on to offspring and cause Fragile X syndrome. Those who have 55 to 200 CGG repeats are considered to have a premutation. They may have either normal or somewhat reduced FMRP protein levels. Those with the premuation are also at risk of passing on an allele that could further expand and cause Fragile X syndrome in their offspring. When the number of CGG repeats is greater than 200, it is considered to be a full mutation and the expression of the FMRP protein is epigenetically blocked by methylation.

People with typical levels of FMRP protein levels in the brain do not have Fragile X syndrome. Only those who have significantly reduced or absent levels of FMRP show the intellectual disability and other traits associated with Fragile X syndrome. However, parents who have an intermediate allele or a premutation are at risk for passing their X-chromosome to their offspring. During the process of gamete formation, the CGG repeat can expand (i.e., add more CGG copies), so that even if a parent did not have Fragile X they may pass an X-chromosome that has a larger number of CGG repeats on to their child, who may then develop Fragile X syndrome. Several other diseases are due to triplet repeat expansions in other genes such as Huntington's disease and Friedreich's ataxia.

Transcription takes place in a cell's nucleus and produces mRNA, which then needs to be transported out of the nucleus and into the cytoplasm for translation into protein. The FRMP is an RNA-binding and carrier-protein that is involved with mRNA processing in axons (Pfeiffer & Huber, 2009). It is involved with transporting mRNA into the cytoplasm, and also transporting the resulting proteins to dendritic spines where they are used in synaptic structure and function. FMRP transports many target mRNAs, and therefore represents an important regulator of synaptic structure and function, including synaptic plasticity, which is critical for learning and memory processes. The absence of FMRP, which occurs with a full mutation of *FMR1*, may impact the processing of 4–8 percent of all brain mRNAs, as well as affecting the balance of glutamate and GABA, the brain's most common excitatory and inhibitory neurotransmitters (Lozano, Hare, & Hagerman, 2015). The widespread impact of FMRP on mRNA processing and synaptic function also may help to explain the rather high rates of comorbidity of Fragile X syndrome with autism, ADHD, and anxiety disorders.

Another common genetic cause of intellectual disability has to do with a chromosomal abnormality called Trisomy 21, or Down syndrome. Trisomy 21 typically results from a failure of chromosomes to separate properly during meiosis (i.e., nondisjunction) producing a gamete with an extra copy of chromosome 21. As you may recall from Chapter 4, gametogenesis is a process for forming either eggs or sperm that involves DNA replication followed by two rounds of cell division resulting in gametes that contain half of a diploid (i.e., haploid) genome. For sexual reproduction, where genetic material is contributed by mothers and fathers, these reduction divisions are critically important to assure that the resulting offspring have the number of chromosomes typical for the species. In the case of humans, that is twenty-three chromosome pairs. So, when this process works as usual, each gamete contains twenty-two autosomes and either an X- or a Y-chromosome. Upon fertilization of egg by sperm, the two haploid (n) genomes are combined to form a diploid (2n) genome. In the case of Trisomy 21, chromosomes 1–20, 22 and the sex chromosome are present in the usual number (i.e., two), whereas three copies of chromosome 21 are present (see Figure 8.3). The term "aneuploidy" is a more general term that refers to any situation where the chromosome number is not typical for the species (i.e., euploidy).

Chromosomal abnormalities are not rare. In humans, approximately 50 percent of all spontaneously aborted (i.e., miscarried) fetuses have major chromosomal abnormalities (Gelehrter, Collins, & Ginsburg, 1998). Approximately 15 percent of all recognized pregnancies end in miscarriage, which means that around 7.5 percent of conceptions have major chromosomal abnormalities. Having too many or too few chromosomes typically has a negative impact on viability. However, aneuploidy for sex chromosomes does not cause miscarriages. We discuss specific instances of sex chromosome abnormalities (i.e., XYY and XO) in Chapter 13.

Trisomy 21 is a relatively common chromosomal abnormality that has significant, but variable, impact on intellectual disability (see Box 8.2). Trisomy 21 occurs in approximately 13 out of 10,000 live births, and there are an estimated 250,000 people in the US with the condition (Caban-Holt, Head, & Schmitt, 2015). Trisomy 21 not only affects cognition, but it is also associated with morphological traits impacting the face, ears, fingers, tongue, eyes, stature, and head size, among others. It also increases risk for several adverse health conditions including

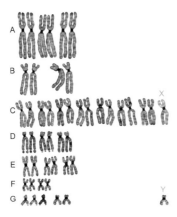

Figure 8.3. **Trisomy 21 karyotype.** Karyotype showing three copies of the 21st chromosome (row G) for a male. Source: BSIP / Contributor / Universal Images Group / Getty Images.

a congenital heart defect, gastrointestinal problems, hypothyroidism, childhood leukemia, attentional problems, obsessive-compulsive behavior, autism, and dementia with onset after age 50. Average life expectancy for those with Trisomy 21 is approximately 60 years and has been rising steadily in the recent decades. Risk for Trisomy 21 is strongly associated with maternal age, and increases dramatically for mothers over age 35 (Morris, Mutton, & Alberman, 2002).

The risk for dementia in those with Trisomy 21 appears to be related to the increased expression of a gene, amyloid-beta precursor protein (*APP*), located on chromosome 21 that is associated with risk for Alzheimer disease. Overexpression of *APP* is associated with accumulation of amyloid-β plaques and neurofibrillary tangles, which are hallmarks of Alzheimer disease, which we discuss in more detail later in this chapter.

Chromosome 21 is the smallest human chromosome, containing 46,709,983 base pairs and representing just under 2 percent of the human genome. That said, there are still over 200 protein coding genes located on chromosome 21, as well as over 400 genes that do not code for proteins but may have other critical functions. Several genes on chromosome 21 are thought to be involved in learning and memory pathways (e.g., estrogen and glucocorticoid signaling, MAP kinase and calcineurin signaling, and adult neurogenesis) (Gardiner & Costa, 2006).

Box 8.2 Mouse Models of Trisomy 21

Several mouse models of human Trisomy 21 have been developed (Xing et al., 2016). Because we share an evolutionary history with mice (i.e., have a shared ancestor), we also share the ordering of genes on certain chromosomes, known as synteny. For example, the sequential order of genes on much of human chromosome 21 (Hsa21) is found in mice, but the genes are distributed across three chromosomes: mouse chromosome 10 (Mmu10), Mmu16, and Mmu17 (see Figure 8.4). Most of the syntenic loci are found on Mmu16, and a line of mice was engineered to have three copies of that chromosome. However, having three entire copies of Mmu16 proved to be lethal in the embryonic stage, so it is not a good model for studying all aspects of Trisomy 21 (Xing et al., 2016). Although another strain has been developed, called Ts65Dn, that contains about two-thirds of the relevant genes on Mmu16, in which animals survive to adulthood and show many of the features of human Trisomy 21.

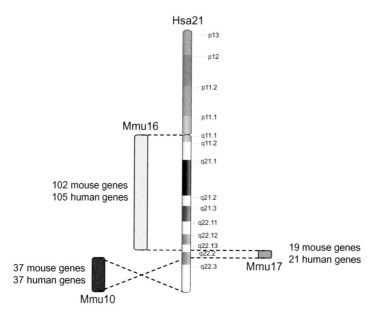

Figure 8.4. **Synteny of human chromosome 21 and three mouse chromosomes.** Most of the genes found on the long arm of human chromosome 21 are found on three mouse chromosomes, Mmu10, Mmu16, and Mmu17. The mouse orthologs contain nearly all the genes found in the regions shared with Hsa21. Chromosomes Mmu17 and Mmu17 have genes in the same linear order as on Hsa21, whereas the linear order on chromosome Mmu10 is reversed compared to Hsa21.

Another approach to using mice to study Trisomy 21 has been the development of lines of mice that contain some or all Hsa21. Such mice have been engineered to carry the same DNA sequence found on human chromosome 21. These mice also live to adulthood and show many phenotypes of Trisomy 21 and can therefore be used to study the underlying biology and development of the disorder. Such genetically engineered strains of mice are termed transchromosomal or transgenic and can be purchased from the Jackson Laboratory.

Using yet another genetic engineering approach that involves inducing chromosomal rearrangements, researchers have selectively triplicated large chromosomal regions and then deleted smaller sections to try to identify regions that are necessary and sufficient to cause specific Trisomy 21 phenotypes.

The evidence suggests that certain genes appear to be dosage sensitive, such that having three copies (as in Trisomy 21) produces deleterious outcomes. In addition, the evidence suggests that triplication of specific genes is associated with specific Trisomy 21 phenotypes (Lana-Elola, Watson-Scales, Fisher, & Tybulewicz, 2011). By better understanding the role of dosage sensitive genes in Trisomy 21 it may be possible to develop treatments to reduce or eliminate their effects.

Check-up

- Describe how IQ tests are used in the diagnosis of intellectual disability.
- What are the most common genetic causes of intellectual disability?
- Explain triplet repeat expansion and how it causes Fragile X syndrome.
- What causes Down syndrome?
- Discuss the role of human/mouse synteny in investigating Trisomy 21.

8.3 Learning Disorders Are Not Considered Intellectual Disabilities

When you think back to your grade school classroom, you may be able to recall that some of your fellow students may have had some trouble reading, spelling, or doing math, but did not have an intellectual disability, like those we have just discussed. They were typical kids in most other respects, but had trouble doing things that are important for academic success (see Box 8.3). Perhaps you were one of those students. Recent estimates suggest that 8 percent of children between the ages of 3 and 17 have a learning disorder (10 percent of boys and 6 percent of girls) (Bloom, Jones, & Freeman, 2013).

Box 8.3 ICD-11 Diagnosis: Developmental Learning Disorder

Developmental learning disorder is characterised by significant and persistent difficulties in learning academic skills, which may include reading, writing, or arithmetic. The individual's performance in the affected academic skill(s) is markedly below what would be expected for chronological age and general level of intellectual functioning, and results in significant impairment in the individual's academic or occupational functioning. Developmental learning disorder first manifests when academic skills are taught during the early school years. Developmental learning disorder is not due to a disorder of intellectual development, sensory impairment (vision or hearing), neurological or motor disorder, lack of availability of education, lack of proficiency in the language of academic instruction, or psychosocial adversity.

Source: http://id.who.int/icd/entity/2099676649 (accessed February 23, 2021), World Health Organization (Copyright © 2020b).

The DSM-5 diagnosis for developmental learning disorder is called specific learning disorder (APA, 2013). As part of the diagnosis, the clinician can further specify if the impairment is in reading, writing, or mathematics. Earlier terminology for these specifications included diagnoses of dyslexia, dysgraphia, or dyscalculia, respectively. So, for example, what used to be diagnosed as dyslexia would now be diagnosed as a specific learning disorder with an impairment of reading.

Specific learning disorders, by definition, make it difficult to learn information in school. Such difficulties can lead to lower grades, decreased motivation, and a less positive school experience overall. A thirty-year longitudinal study found that individuals with a reading disorder at age 7 achieved lower education levels and income in midlife, compared to those without a reading disorder even after controlling for other sociodemographic factors (McLaughlin, Speirs, & Shenassa, 2012).

Learning disorders are typically diagnosed by using a combination of reports from the individual regarding their personal and educational history, as well as some type of assessment to evaluate the suspected deficits. It is important to note that assessments should be developmentally appropriate. That is, skill in reading, writing, and mathematics is expected to change substantially across development, and it would be inappropriate to use an assessment that is targeted for a 14-year-old to evaluate a 5-year-old. There are many assessments that can be used to evaluate the nature of a specific learning disorder that have been developed to evaluate individuals in specific age groups. These assessments are typically conducted in a one-on-one setting, where an evaluator presents tasks to the individual to complete, such as a timed reading comprehension exercise. Comprehensive assessments evaluate individuals for reading, writing, and mathematical performance, and explicitly examine the potential for comorbidity across these and other diagnoses.

8.3.1 Genes Involved in Neuronal Migration Are Dyslexia Candidates

To discuss the evidence for genetic variants associated with risk for developing a learning disorder, we focus our attention on impairment in reading (aka dyslexia) because it is the condition for which there is the most evidence. Much of the early evidence of particular genetic loci came from linkage studies, some of which has been supported by candidate gene association studies, and there is also some recent evidence from genome-wide association studies (Newbury, Monaco, & Paracchini, 2014; Paracchini, Diaz, & Stein, 2016). A recent search using Phenopedia from the HuGe Navigator identified seventy-four candidate genes for which some evidence of association with dyslexia has been reported. Many of these genes are involved in neuronal migration, axonal growth, and dendritic connections (Paracchini et al., 2016).

The candidate gene that has been most studied is *KIAA0319*, which encodes a transmembrane protein that is involved in neuronal migration and cell adhesion. The *KIAA0319* gene contains a variant (rs4504469, also known as 931 C>T) for which the C allele results in an alanine at amino acid position 931, and the T allele leads to a substitution of a threonine at that position. There is fairly good evidence, supported by replication and meta-analysis, that the T allele is associated with higher risk for developing dyslexia (Zou et al., 2012), although not in all populations studied (Deng, Zhao, & Zuo, 2019).

Another interesting SNP in *KIAA0319* (rs9461045) appears to modulate expression of the gene by affecting the binding site of a transcription silencer. When the major allele, C, is present, there is no binding site, but when the minor allele, T, is present, a binding site for the OCT-1 transcription silencer is produced (Dennis et al., 2009). Interestingly, there is also evidence that the association between the T allele of rs9461045 may differ by ancestry, such that in populations of European ancestry it is a risk allele, but in those of Asian ancestry it is a protective allele (Shao et al., 2016). This finding is yet another example of the complexity of relations between DNA sequence variation and human behaviors and may stem from interactions between this locus and other genetic loci or with environmental factors that vary among populations.

Obviously, one cannot use animal models to study reading impairment. However, one can study the development and function of relevant brain areas in non-human animals. For example, one of the deficits in dyslexia has to do with ability to discriminate between different basic units of sounds that have meaning in language (i.e., phoneme). English has forty-four phonemes, each representing a different sound. For example, when you say "dad," the letter "d" phoneme sounds like "duh." When such basic speech sounds are presented to rats, neurons in their auditory cortex respond. When expression of *Kiaa0319* (the rat homolog of *KIAA0319*) is reduced (i.e., knocked down) by using a technique that interferes with messenger RNA (i.e., RNAi) *in utero*, the response of neurons in the auditory cortex to the speech sounds is diminished (see Figure 8.5) (Centanni et al., 2014). One can hypothesize that a similar change in neural activity could reflect a reduction in capacity to distinguish different phonemes as seen in humans with dyslexia. This and other animal models of dyslexia-related phenotypes may help to uncover their basic biology, which could eventually lead to interventions to reduce or eliminate the impact of specific learning disorders.

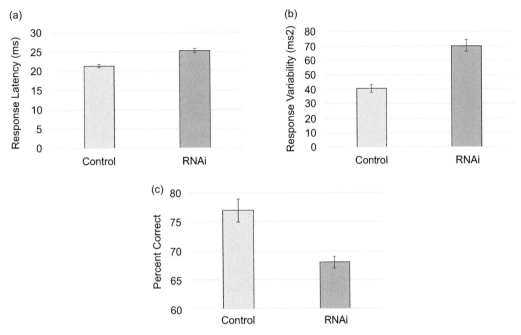

Figure 8.5. *In utero* **RNAi affects response of auditory cortex neurons to speech sounds in rats.** RNA interference of *Kiaa0319* mRNA in rats *in utero* affected responses to speech sounds when tested as adults. Those with less *Kiaa0319* gene expression (i.e., RNAi) showed (a) slower firing of neurons in the auditory cortex in response to speech sounds, (b) increased variability in onset of neural firing in response to speech sounds, and (c) reduced accuracy in responding to different consonants. Source: Centanni et al. (2014).

Check-up

- Compare and contrast intellectual disability with specific learning disorders.
- Discuss the most likely neural mechanism for dyslexia.
- Describe an animal model used to study dyslexia and the candidate gene *Kiaa0319*.

8.4 Memory Is a Crucial Aspect of Cognitive Ability

Most of us can easily think back to a particular moment in life and recall specific details, like who you were with at the senior high school dance, or that time when you crashed your bike and broke your arm. Maybe you can recall an incident connected to a particular smell, like that time you brought the turkey to a Thanksgiving dinner. Such recollections are known as episodic memories because they are about specific episodes in your life. This type of memory can be contrasted with memories of specific facts, such as your home address, or the name of the current President of the United States. Such memories are known as semantic memories. Both types of memory are known as declarative memories because they comprise information that you can share by speaking. The processes for acquiring, encoding, storing, and retrieving declarative memories are mediated by specific brain circuits, and display individual differences. Memory dysfunction can be acquired through chronic drug use, disease processes, or brain injury. Of course, for our purposes, we are interested in understanding the role of genetic variation in individual differences in memory processes.

Another type of memory included in the NIMH's Research Domain Criteria is called working memory, which is what you are using to hold information in mind for use. Working memory involves the active maintenance of information that is relevant to the current goal or task. It has a limited capacity. When you first meet someone, they say their name, and for a few seconds, you have it in your working memory. As the conversation moves along, you may notice that you no longer can recall their name. Because you did not rehearse it, or somehow connect it with other information in your memory, the name was not encoded into long-term storage. So, working memory can be thought of like a desktop where relevant items are kept and actively manipulated for a particular task. The desktop can only hold so many items, so that new ones may crowd others off. Individual differences in working memory capacity exist and are related to capacity for higher level thought, like the way that more random-access memory (RAM) in your computer enables you to run more applications at the same time.

8.4.1 Memory Dysfunction Can Cause Substantial Impairment and Distress

We have all experienced declarative memory failure. Those times when you were taking an exam and just could not recall information that you were certain that you had learned. Running into someone whose name you just cannot recall. Examples of everyday memory failure are too numerous to mention and so common that we all have experienced it many times, maybe even today! Occasional lapses in declarative memory are normal and no cause for concern.

One of the most important health-care issues in the twenty-first century, Alzheimer disease, is characterized by a progressive dementia of which memory loss is a cardinal feature. As the disease progresses, patients experience a profound memory loss, that fundamentally robs them of their identity. We discuss Alzheimer disease in the next section, but it is important to note here that there is a known genetic component to risk for Alzheimer disease and that by better understanding it, we may be more likely to develop effective strategies for combating the disease.

Another type of memory problem is when there are memories that people would like to forget but cannot. Traumatic experiences often produce very strong memories that are resistant to forgetting, and can sometimes be recurrent, intrusive, and cause clinically significant stress or impairment. Such memories are a core symptom of post-traumatic stress disorder (PTSD) and reflect a dysfunction of episodic memory. We will examine the role of genetic variation in risk for PTSD in Chapter 10, but it is important to mention here that advances in understanding the basic biological mechanism of declarative memory may have widespread clinical applications.

A commonly used method to assess episodic declarative memory is to first present participants with a list of words, either in writing or verbally, and then after some delay, ask participants to recall as many of the words as they can. Typically, the word list is presented on a computer screen with one word presented at a time, and only for a short period of time, say one second. Often, recall is tested immediately after the completion of the list, and then again after a delay of twenty-five minutes or so. Another method to test episodic memory is to ask the participant to either read or listen to a story, and then ask them to repeat as many details of the story as they can recall.

8.4.2 A Gene Associated with Dendritic Growth May Be Important for Memory Formation

There is considerable evidence that a single nucleotide polymorphism (SNP) in the gene for the kidney and brain expressed protein called KIBRA (gene name: *WWC1*; rs17070145) is associated with individual differences in episodic memory (Papassotiropoulos et al., 2006; Schwab, Luo, Clarke, & Nathan, 2014). There is also evidence that this same SNP is associated with risk for Alzheimer disease (Ling, Huang, Zhang, Wei, & Cheng, 2018). It appears that homozygosity for the C allele of rs17070145 is associated with weaker episodic memory and higher risk for Alzheimer disease compared with those who carry one or more T alleles. A meta-analysis that included data from 8,909 participants for episodic memory tasks and 4,696 participants for working memory tasks indicated that rs17070145 explained a statistically significant but exceedingly small percentage (0.5 percent and 0.1 percent) of the variance in memory performance (Milnik et al., 2012). Although explaining less than 1 percent of the variance in a behavior seems like a tiny amount (and it is), the number of factors that influence memory performance is likely very large and probably includes hundreds of genetic variants.

The exciting part about the KIBRA-memory story is the strength of the convergent evidence, across species, across memory tasks, and across study designs and populations. The bulk of the evidence suggests that the KIBRA protein plays a role in memory formation, and it seems to be one of the stronger findings in the behavior genetics of cognition. There is strong evidence that was obtained using mice that implicates the KIBRA protein directly in synaptic plasticity and long-term potentiation in hippocampal neurons (Heitz et al., 2016), which is exactly where and how they would be expected to have a profound impact on memory. When expression of KIBRA is knocked down, the hippocampal neurons have less arborization (i.e., dendritic branching) than control hippocampal neurons (see Figure 8.6). And when KIBRA expression is increased, the hippocampal neurons show increased arborization (Heitz et al., 2016). So, there is a dose–response relationship between the expression of the KIBRA protein and the dendritic growth in the neurons responsible for making new connections during the formation of

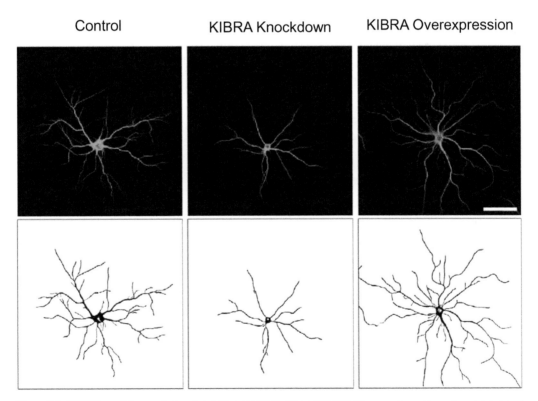

Figure 8.6. **KIBRA protein regulates dendritic growth in hippocampus.** The use of genetic engineering to knock down and overexpress KIBRA protein in rats has dramatic effects on growth and arborization of neurons in the hippocampus. Source: Reprinted from Heitz et al. (2016) with permission from Elsevier.

memories in the hippocampus. The growth of dendritic spines on hippocampal neurons is a key mechanism that mediates the acquisition of short- and long-term memories (Frankfurt & Luine, 2015). The KIBRA protein may have a role in increasing the availability of certain glutamatergic AMPA receptors that are critical components of LTP and memory formation (Heitz et al., 2016).

The KIBRA protein, encoded by the *WWC1* gene is a good example of how a specific gene and its variants can impact an aspect of cognition, such as episodic memory. There are likely to be thousands of genetic variants that are associated with individual differences in episodic memory. We have focused on this one because it shows how a GWAS could be used to identify a particular SNP of interest (i.e., rs17070145), and how other types of evidence are brought to bear in the effort to understand the basic biology underlying episodic memory.

Box 8.4 Species Spotlight: Dissecting Learning and Memory in Fruit Flies

For more than four decades, *Drosophila melanogaster* have been used to identify and characterize genes that affect memory formation (Margulies, Tully, & Dubnau, 2005; Quinn, Harris, & Benzer, 1974; Tully & Quinn, 1985). As we have discussed previously, *D. melanogaster* are outstanding subjects for genetic research, and they can certainly learn information and form memories.

In the acquisition phase of this classical conditioning task, a group of flies is given an electric shock (Unconditioned stimulus, US) when one odor is present (Conditioned stimulus, CS+), but not when another odor is present (CS-). There can be one or many acquisition sessions, depending on the design of the study.

After the acquisition phase, there is the testing phase where the flies are presented the two odors in a T-maze. Avoiding the odor that was paired with shock is interpreted as evidence of the formation of a memory (see Figure 8.7). A series of 10 sessions with 15 minutes of rest between each session is capable of producing memories that last up to 10 days in wild-type flies (Margulies et al., 2005).

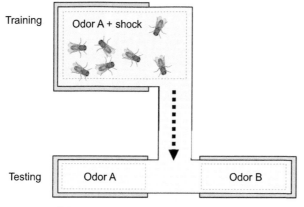

Figure 8.7. **Olfactory conditioning in fruit flies.** A schematic of the apparatus used to test learning and memory in *D. melanogaster* that exposes a group of flies to an electrical shock when they are simultaneously exposed to a distinct odorant (i.e., odor A) during the training phase. After a brief rest, the group of flies is moved to the T-maze choice point. One arm of the T-maze exposes flies to odor A, and the other arm exposes flies to an odor that is novel and has not been previously paired with shock (i.e., odor B). Flies that avoid the odor that had been paired with shock (odor A) and move toward odor B are considered to have learned to avoid odor A. Source: Created with Biorender.com. After Waddel & Quinn (2001).

This assay has been useful in the identification of mutations that impact learning and memory at different stages in the process. We discuss specific mutations that impact memory formation in *D. melanogaster* below.

8.4.3 Dissection of Learning and Memory in Fruit Flies

For the remainder of this section, let us turn our attention to the fruit fly to discuss screening for learning and memory mutants (see Box 8.4). Finding and/or generating mutants in *D. melanogaster* has been a staple of genetics for over a century, since T. H. Morgan reported finding a white-eyed male and mapped the mutation to the X-chromosome (Morgan, 1910). Thousands of *D. melanogaster* mutations have been generated with X-rays, chemicals (e.g., ethyl methanesulphonate [EMS]), or with the tools of molecular biology (St Johnston, 2002). Fortunately, there are repositories that maintain pure breeding lines of many mutant strains, such as the Bloomington Drosophila Stock Center in Indiana, which houses over 40,000 genetically unique lines. An investigator who wishes to test whether certain mutations affect behavioral performance can request flies from a plethora of mutant lines to test in their behavioral assay.

The general procedure for the olfactory classical condition assay is to run hundreds of flies (about 150 for each session) from a mutant line of flies (i.e., a line of flies carrying a single genetic mutation), and to compare their performance to that of the wild-type line of flies from which the mutant line was derived. By comparing the mutant line performance to that of wild-type flies who are genetically similar, one is better able to characterize the impact of the single gene mutation. It is important to note that there are also marked differences in the performance of different wild-type strains in this assay (Tully & Quinn, 1985).

Let us focus our attention on one of the first mutations identified that impacts olfactory learning and memory in *D. melanogaster, dunce*. Here again we see that genes in *D. melanogaster* are often named for the trait that enabled their identification. So, as with the white-eyed mutant identified by Morgan in 1910, which is called *white* (*w*), the mutant *dunce* (*dnc*) was named because of its poor performance in an olfactory shock avoidance test (Dudai, Jan, Byers, Quinn, & Benzer, 1976). The *dunce* line was founded via EMS mutagenesis of flies from the Canton-S wild-type strain. The dunce line was the only one out of approximately 500 mutagenized lines that performed poorly in the olfactory shock avoidance test and did not show some significant sensory or motor defect. The dunce mutation is located in a gene that codes for a cAMP phosphodiesterase, which is a key enzyme in the deactivation of the second messenger cyclic AMP (Byers, Davis, & Kiger Jr., 1981), thereby regulating the excitability of neurons involved in learning and memory (Lee, 2015). It is worth noting that the *rutabaga* mutation, which also affects memory, codes for adenylate cyclase, an enzyme that converts AMP to cAMP. So, two mutations that affect memory in fruit flies impact the cAMP, via its synthesis (i.e., *rutabaga*) or its breakdown (*dunce*). At least nineteen mutations have been identified that impact olfactory learning and memory (see Figure 8.8). And although there has been substantial progress in understanding the impact of genetic variation on individual differences in learning in *D. melanogaster*, it is likely that other genetic influences remain to be identified, especially as new techniques are developed (Walkinshaw et al., 2015).

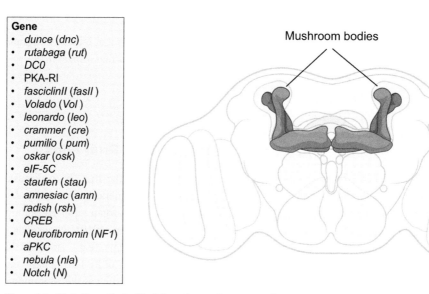

Gene
- *dunce (dnc)*
- *rutabaga (rut)*
- *DC0*
- *PKA-RI*
- *fasciclinII (fasII)*
- *Volado (Vol)*
- *leonardo (leo)*
- *crammer (cre)*
- *pumilio (pum)*
- *oskar (osk)*
- *eIF-5C*
- *staufen (stau)*
- *amnesiac (amn)*
- *radish (rsh)*
- *CREB*
- *Neurofibromin (NF1)*
- *aPKC*
- *nebula (nla)*
- *Notch (N)*

Mushroom bodies

Figure 8.8. **Mutations that affect learning and memory.** Genes that affect olfactory conditioning in *D. melanogaster* impact the function of neurons in brain structures called the mushroom bodies. Source: Created with Biorender.com.

Check-up

- Discuss the different types of memory of interest in behavior genetics.
- What is the KIBRA protein and how is it involved in learning and memory?
- Describe how fruit flies are used to investigate the genetics of learning and memory.

8.5 Alzheimer Disease Is a Common Cause of Neurocognitive Disorder

When a person experiences a decline in cognitive functions (e.g., attention, memory, executive function), they may have a neurocognitive disorder. For this to be the case, it means that they had already developed a level of cognitive function that enabled them to function independently in social and occupational contexts, and then experienced decline. Unfortunately, many of us have seen this happen to someone in our lives. You may have had a grandparent who had a full and productive life, but at some point in their later years they became unable to manage on their own because of cognitive decline.

Both the ICD-11 (WHO, 2020c) and the DSM-5 (APA, 2013) list several separate diagnoses under the broad Neurocognitive Disorders umbrella (see Box 8.5). We focus on Alzheimer disease because it is the most common cause of neurocognitive disorder (previously known as dementia) (van der Flier & Scheltens, 2005).

Alzheimer disease is the most common cause of neurocognitive disorder for those aged 65 and older, and it is projected to increase in prevalence as the US population ages. Currently, approximately 5.5 million people in the US are estimated to have Alzheimer disease, and that number is expected to increase to 13.8 million by the middle of the century (AA, 2017). This increase is likely to do with the aging of the large Baby Boomer generation. There is currently no cure for Alzheimer disease and few treatments to slow the progression of symptoms. Most cases of Alzheimer disease have symptom onset after age 65, although around 5 percent have symptom onset in their forties or fifties. Alzheimer disease is the sixth leading cause of death in the US, and it is on the rise. It is estimated that Alzheimer disease and other neurocognitive disorders cost the US$259 billion, which is estimated to rise by the middle of the century to $1.1 trillion. It is difficult to overstate the importance of Alzheimer disease.

8.5.1 Genetic Information Can Be Used to Diagnose Alzheimer Disease

Some degree of age-related cognitive decline is considered typical; however, the process is variable and dynamic. People may experience age-related decline in some cognitive domains (complex attention, executive function, learning and memory, language, perceptual-motor, or social cognition), but not all, or may even experience improvement in some domains (Institute of Medicine, 2015). To meet the criterion for a major neurocognitive disorder diagnosis, the decline has to interfere with independence in everyday activities, and not be better explained by other disorders or conditions (APA, 2013).

Box 8.5 ICD-11 Diagnosis: Dementia Due to Alzheimer Disease

Dementia due to Alzheimer disease is the most common form of dementia. Onset is insidious with memory impairment typically reported as the initial presenting complaint. The characteristic course is a slow but steady decline from a previous level of cognitive functioning with impairment in additional cognitive domains (such as executive functions, attention, language, social cognition and judgment, psychomotor speed, visuoperceptual or visuospatial abilities) emerging with disease progression. Dementia due to Alzheimer disease is often accompanied by mental and behavioural symptoms such as depressed mood and apathy in the initial stages of the disease and may be accompanied by psychotic symptoms, irritability, aggression, confusion, abnormalities of gait and mobility, and seizures at later stages. Positive genetic testing, family history and gradual cognitive decline are highly suggestive of Dementia due to Alzheimer disease.

Source: http://id.who.int/icd/entity/795022044 (accessed February 24, 2021), World Health Organization (Copyright © 2020c).

In addition to the symptoms of cognitive decline, there are specific neuropathological signs that are characteristic of Alzheimer disease: brain shrinkage, accumulation of amyloid plaques, and neurofibrillary tangles (see Figure 8.9). The behavioral signs of Alzheimer disease are much easier to detect and document than are the neuropathological signs, in a living person. However, promising techniques have been developed that can be used with neuroimaging to detect the presence of amyloid plaques. But the buildup of amyloid plaques alone is not definitive because some people have amyloid plaque deposits, but do not show any cognitive decline. Structural brain imaging can detect brain shrinkage, but there are no clear diagnostic thresholds. Therefore, a careful behavioral assessment, with a focus on assessing cognitive decline over time, is still the standard procedure for diagnosing Alzheimer disease.

Amyloid plaques consist of aggregations of β-amyloid (Aβ), which is a 38 or 43 amino acid peptide that is produced when amyloid precursor protein (APP) is sequentially cleaved by β- and γ-secretases (Chow, Mattson, Wong, & Gleichmann, 2010). Normal (i.e., non-amyloidogenic) APP processing occurs when the APP is first cleaved by α-secretase and then by γ-secretase (see Figure 8.10). The products of this cleavage (sAPPα) and P3 are thought to play a role in healthy neural function.

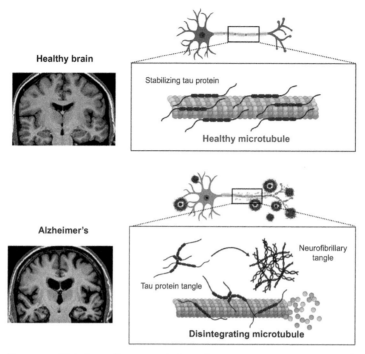

Figure 8.9. **Alzheimer disease pathology.** Brain shrinkage, amyloid plaques (not shown), and neurofibrillary tangles comprising the components of disintegrating microtubules characterize part of the neuropathology of Alzheimer disease. Source: Created with Biorender.com.

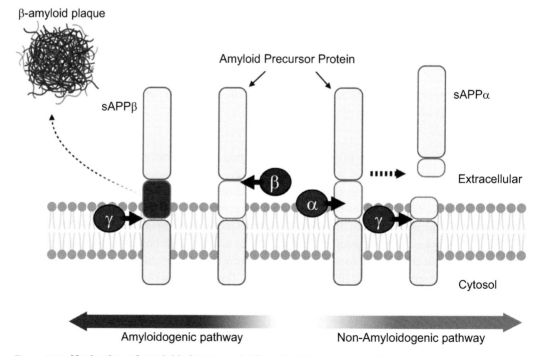

Figure 8.10. **Mechanism of amyloid plaque production.** Amyloid precursor protein is cleaved by α-secretase and then by γ-secretase in the non-amyloidogenic pathway (right side of figure). However, in Alzheimer disease, APP is first cleaved by β-secretase and then γ-secretase producing β-amyloid, which can then form clumps called amyloid plaques. Source: Created with Biorender.com. After Chow et al. (2010).

However, when the first cleavage is made by β-secretase and then by γ-secretase, the resultant fragment Aβ clump together to form amyloid plaques. It is thought that the accumulation of Aβ plaques is critical in the initiation of Alzheimer disease.

It is important to note here that the gene for APP is located on chromosome 21 (21q21.3), and that nearly all individuals with Trisomy 21 have significant accumulation of amyloid plaques, and approximately 50 percent of those with Trisomy 21 will develop Alzheimer disease. This and many other sources of convergent evidence implicates APP in the neuropathogenesis of Alzheimer disease.

8.5.2 Early and Late Onset Alzheimer Disease Have Different Genetic Causes

As we mentioned earlier, most people who develop Alzheimer disease start to experience their cognitive decline after age 65 (i.e., late onset), whereas 5 percent start to experience their symptoms during their forties and fifties (i.e., early onset). Although the symptom profiles and underlying neuropathology appear to be the same, the underlying genetics is not (Karch, Cruchaga, & Goate, 2014; Naj & Schellenberg, 2017).

Early onset Alzheimer disease (EOAD) follows a Mendelian dominance inheritance pattern, which enabled the identification of four genes: *APP*, *PSEN1*, *PSEN2*, and *ADAM10*. The *APP* gene, which we have previously discussed, codes for the amyloid precursor protein, which is a ubiquitously expressed transmembrane protein that is critical in the formation of amyloid plaques. Approximately 14 percent of EOAD cases are due to mutations in *APP*. At least thirty dominant *APP* mutations have been identified, as well as two that are recessive (Karch et al., 2014).

PSEN1 (14q.24.3) and *PSEN2* (1q31–q42) code for structurally similar transmembrane proteins that are part of the γ-secretase complex, which is involved in pathogenic APP processing. The abbreviation *PSEN* stands for presenillen, which indicates their role in senility, a formerly commonly used term to describe age-related cognitive decline. Approximately 80 percent of EOAD cases are due to dominant mutations in *PSEN1*. At least 185 such mutations have been identified. Approximately 5 percent of EOAD cases are due to dominant mutations in *PSEN2*. At least thirteen such mutations have been identified (Karch et al., 2014). *ADAM10* codes for the α-secretase enzyme, and two rare mutations have been found to be linked to EOAD in a few families to date.

Although EOAD only accounts for 5 percent of Alzheimer disease cases, all the implicated genes code for proteins involved in APP processing, and thus identify it and the resulting accumulation of amyloid plaques as a critical feature in the development of Alzheimer disease (Figure 8.11). As a result, APP processing is an important target in the search for treatments and cures for Alzheimer disease (Kulshreshtha & Piplani, 2016).

The majority of cases of Alzheimer disease are (1) late onset (i.e., LOAD), (2) not caused by mutations in the four EOAD genes, (3) sporadic (i.e., not familial), and (4) influenced by midlife lifestyle factors (e.g., blood pressure, obesity, diabetes) (Guerreiro, Gustafson, & Hardy, 2012). Variants in the gene that codes for the apolipoprotein E (*APOE*) are associated with increased risk for LOAD. Apolipoprotein E combines with lipids (i.e., fats) to form a molecule that is involved with the transportation of cholesterol and other lipids in the bloodstream.

Apolipoprotein E occurs in three isoforms (functionally similar proteins that differ in amino acid sequence) that differ genetically at two locations (i.e., amino acid 112 [rs429358] and 158 [rs7412]). The *APOEε2* allele has cysteine (T/T genotype) at both locations; *APOEε3* has a cysteine at 112 and an arginine at 158 (T/C genotype); *APOEε4* has arginine (C/C genotype) at both

(a)　　　　　　　　　　　　　　　　(b)

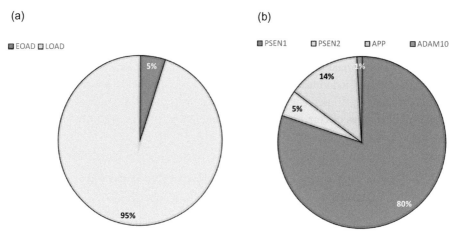

Figure 8.11. **Genes associated with early onset Alzheimer disease.** (a) Most cases of Alzheimer disease are late onset (LOAD). (b) Of those cases that are early onset (EOAD), most are due to mutations in *PSEN1*.

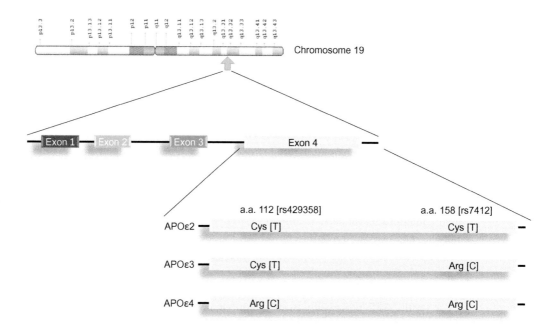

Figure 8.12. **APOE genotypes.** The gene for APOE is located on chromosome 19 and consists of four exons. Two SNPs located in the fourth exon are considered together to determine APOE genotypes.

locations (see Figure 8.12). *APOEε4* is a risk allele for LOAD, such that when compared to those who do not carry an *APOEε4* allele, heterozygous carriers are at three times higher risk, and homozygotes are at eight to ten times higher risk for developing LOAD (Raber, Huang, & Ashford, 2004). The least common allele (i.e., *APOEε2*) appears to decrease risk for LOAD and delay age of onset when it does occur. APOE binds to Aβ and has a role in its clearing thereby influencing the rate of Aβ accumulation differentially by isoform.

Genome-wide association studies and other studies that have employed whole-exome and whole-genome sequencing approaches have identified another twenty genes that impact risk for

Alzheimer disease (Karch et al., 2014; Naj & Schellenberg, 2017). The known genetic variants explain about 28 percent of the heritability of Alzheimer disease, with 23 percent explained by APOE ε4 genotype alone (Cuyvers & Sleegers, 2016). The search continues for genetic variants that increase risk for one of the most important disorders that will impact many of us in the coming years.

8.5.3 Several Non-Human Animal Models of Alzheimer Disease Have Been Developed

Several non-human animal models are being used to understand the role of genes in the development and progression of Alzheimer disease (LaFerla & Green, 2012). There are animal models that focus on APP processing, as well as those that focus on the other primary neuropathology, neurofibrillary tangles (NFT), which are largely composed of the microtubule-associated protein, tau. Microtubules in neurons play a role in intracellular transport, axon stabilization, and neurite growth. The gene that codes for tau is called *MAPT*, for microtubule-associated protein, and is found on chromosome 17 (17q21.31). The gene contains fifteen exons and produces six isoforms of tau by alternative splicing. At least ten different mouse models have been developed to investigate the role of genetic variation on the neuropathologies and behaviors that characterize Alzheimer disease (Webster, Bachstetter, Nelson, Schmitt, & Van Eldik, 2014).

The 3xTg-AD mouse model, for example, was genetically engineered to carry human mutations of the *APP*, *PSEN1*, and *MAPT* genes (Oddo, Caccamo, Kitazawa, Tseng, & LaFerla, 2003). The mice display age-related increases in both amyloid plaques and neurofibrillary tangles and show age-related cognitive dysfunction. Such mouse models can advance the understanding of the progressive nature of Alzheimer disease neuropathologies and cognitive deficits and will likely play a large role in prevention and treatment efforts.

Check-up

- Describe the information needed to make a diagnosis of Alzheimer disease.
- Describe the neuropathological signs of Alzheimer disease.
- What is early onset Alzheimer disease and what genes are associated with it?
- What is late onset Alzheimer disease and what genes are associated with it?

8.6 SUMMARY

- Intelligence is indexed by IQ tests, which can be used in the diagnosis of intellectual disability. There are multiple ways to define normal, and its use can be interpreted as a value judgment.
- Intellectual disabilities are characterized by cognitive deficits that interfere with social, occupational and other functioning. Fragile X syndrome and Trisomy 21 are the most common genetic causes of intellectual disability.
- Specific learning disorders are common and not due to intellectual disability. Dyslexia is a specific learning disorder of reading that may be due to defects in neural migration and synaptic development. Animal models of dyslexia focus on responses to hearing speech sounds, which is one area that is often affected in those with the disorder.

- Memory is a critical cognitive function and is therefore a potentially important endophenotype for neurocognitive disorders. KIBRA protein is involved in dendritic growth and aborization in the hippocampus and is a good candidate to be involved with memory based on convergent evidence in humans and non-human animal models. Fruit flies have been important in the genetic dissection of learning and memory.
- Alzheimer disease is a common age-related neurocognitive disorder that is increasing in prevalence as the population ages. Early onset Alzheimer disease makes up 5 percent of cases and is inherited in Mendelian fashion in families. Late onset Alzheimer disease is the most common form and appears to be polygenic with APOE ε4 as a common risk allele.

RECOMMENDED READING

- Caban-Holt, A., Head, E., & Schmitt, F. (2015). Down Syndrome. In R. N. Rosenberg & J. M. Pascual (Eds.), *Rosenberg's Molecular and Genetic Basis of Neurological and Psychiatric Disease* (5th ed.) (pp. 163–170). Boston: Academic Press.
- Goddard, H. H. (1927). Who is a moron? *Scientific Monthly, 24*, 41–46.
- Karch, C. M., Cruchaga, C., & Goate, A. M. (2014). Alzheimer disease genetics: From the bench to the clinic. *Neuron, 83*(1), 11–26. doi:10.1016/j.neuron.2014.05.041
- Lozano, R., Hare, E. B., & Hagerman, R. J. (2015). Fragile X-associated disorders. In R. N. Rosenberg & J. M. Pascual (Eds.), *Rosenberg's Molecular and Genetic Basis of Neurological and Psychiatric Disease* (5th ed.) (pp. 183–195). Boston: Academic Press.
- Nisbett, R. E., Aronson, J., Blair, C., Dickens, W., Flynn, J., Halpern, D. F., & Turkheimer, E. (2012). Intelligence: New findings and theoretical developments. *Am Psychol, 67*(2), 130–159. doi:10.1037/a0026699

REFERENCES

AA (2017). 2017 Alzheimer disease facts and figures. *Alzheimer's Dement, 13*(4), 325–373. https://doi.org/10.1016/j.jalz.2017.02.001

APA (2013). *Diagnostic and Statistical Manual of Mental Disorders: DSM-5* (pp. 0-1). Washington, DC: American Psychiatric Association.

Bloom, B., Jones, L. I., & Freeman, G. (2013). Summary health statistics for U.S. children: National Health Interview Survey, 2012. *Vital Health Stat 10*(258), 1–81.

Boake, C. (2002). From the Binet-Simon to the Wechsler-Bellevue: Tracing the history of intelligence testing. *J Clin Exp Neuropsychol, 24*(3), 383–405. doi:10.1076/jcen.24.3.383.981

Byers, D., Davis, R. L., & Kiger Jr., J. A. (1981). Defect in cyclic AMP phosphodiesterase due to the dunce mutation of learning in Drosophila melanogaster. *Nature, 289*, 79. doi:10.1038/289079a0

Caban-Holt, A., Head, E., & Schmitt, F. (2015). Down Syndrome. In R. N. Rosenberg & J. M. Pascual (Eds.), *Rosenberg's Molecular and Genetic Basis of Neurological and Psychiatric Disease* (5th ed.) (pp. 163–170). Boston: Academic Press.

Centanni, T. M., Booker, A. B., Sloan, A. M., Chen, F., Maher, B. J., Carraway, R. S., … Kilgard, M. P. (2014). Knockdown of the dyslexia-associated gene Kiaa0319 impairs temporal responses to speech stimuli in rat primary auditory cortex. *Cereb Cortex, 24*(7), 1753–1766. doi:10.1093/cercor/bht028

Chow, V. W., Mattson, M. P., Wong, P. C., & Gleichmann, M. (2010). An overview of APP processing enzymes and products. *Neuromolecular Med, 12*(1), 1–12. doi:10.1007/s12017-009-8104-z

Cuyvers, E., & Sleegers, K. (2016). Genetic variations underlying Alzheimer disease: Evidence from genome-wide association studies and beyond. *Lancet Neurol, 15*(8), 857–868. doi:10.1016/s1474-4422(16)00127-7

de Waal, F. B. (1995). Bonobo sex and society. *Sci Am, 272*(3), 82–88.

Deng, K. G., Zhao, H., & Zuo, P. X. (2019). Association between KIAA0319 SNPs and risk of dyslexia: A meta-analysis. *J Genet, 98*(2), 62. doi:10.1007/s12041-019-1103-4

Dennis, M. Y., Paracchini, S., Scerri, T. S., Prokunina-Olsson, L., Knight, J. C., Wade-Martins, R., . . . Monaco, A. P. (2009). A common variant associated with dyslexia reduces expression of the KIAA0319 gene. *PLoS Genet, 5*(3), e1000436. doi:10.1371/journal.pgen.1000436

Dudai, Y., Jan, Y. N., Byers, D., Quinn, W. G., & Benzer, S. (1976). Dunce, a mutant of Drosophila deficient in learning. *Proc Natl Acad Sci USA, 73*(5), 1684.

Frankfurt, M., & Luine, V. (2015). The evolving role of dendritic spines and memory: Interaction(s) with estradiol. *Horm Behav, 74*, 28–36. doi:10.1016/j.yhbeh.2015.05.004

Gallup (2018). Gay and Lesbian Rights. Retrieved from: http://news.gallup.com/poll/1651/gay-lesbian-rights.aspx

Gardiner, K., & Costa, A. C. S. (2006). The proteins of human chromosome 21. *Am J Med Genet C Semin Med Genet, 142C*(3), 196–205.

Gelehrter, T. D., Collins, F. S., & Ginsburg, D. (1998). *Principles of Medical Genetics* (2nd ed.). Baltimore, MD: Williams & Wilkins.

Goddard, H. H. (1927). Who is a moron? *Scientific Monthly, 24*, 41–46.

Guerreiro, R. J., Gustafson, D. R., & Hardy, J. (2012). The genetic architecture of Alzheimer disease: Beyond APP, PSENs and APOE. *Neurobiol Aging, 33*(3), 437–456. doi:10.1016/j.neurobiolaging.2010.03.025

Heitz, F. D., Farinelli, M., Mohanna, S., Kahn, M., Duning, K., Frey, M. C., . . . Mansuy, I. M. (2016). The memory gene KIBRA is a bidirectional regulator of synaptic and structural plasticity in the adult brain. *Neurobiol Learn Mem, 135*, 100–114. doi:10.1016/j.nlm.2016.07.028

Heywood, W., Patrick, K., Smith, A. M. A., Simpson, J. M., Pitts, M. K., Richters, J., & Shelley, J. M. (2012). Who gets tattoos? Demographic and behavioral correlates of ever being tattooed in a representative sample of men and women. *Ann Epidemiol, 22*(1), 51–56. doi:10.1016/j.annepidem.2011.10.005

Institute of Medicine (2015). *Cognitive Aging: Progress in Understanding and Opportunities for Action.* Washington, DC: The National Academies Press.

Karch, C. M., Cruchaga, C., & Goate, A. M. (2014). Alzheimer disease genetics: From the bench to the clinic. *Neuron, 83*(1), 11–26. doi:10.1016/j.neuron.2014.05.041

Kulshreshtha, A., & Piplani, P. (2016). Current pharmacotherapy and putative disease-modifying therapy for Alzheimer disease. *Neurol Sci, 37*(9), 1403–1435. doi:10.1007/s10072-016-2625-7

LaFerla, F. M., & Green, K. N. (2012). Animal models of Alzheimer disease. *Cold Spring Harb Perspect Med, 2*(11). doi:10.1101/cshperspect.a006320

Lana-Elola, E., Watson-Scales, S. D., Fisher, E. M., & Tybulewicz, V. L. (2011). Down syndrome: Searching for the genetic culprits. *Dis Model Mech, 4*(5), 586–595. doi:10.1242/dmm.008078

Lee, D. (2015). Global and local missions of cAMP signaling in neural plasticity, learning, and memory. *Front Pharmacol, 6*, 161. doi:10.3389/fphar.2015.00161

Ling, J., Huang, Y., Zhang, L., Wei, D., & Cheng, W. (2018). Association of KIBRA polymorphism with risk of Alzheimer disease: Evidence based on 20 case-control studies. *Neurosci Lett, 662*, 77–83. doi:10.1016/j.neulet.2017.08.057

Lozano, R., Hare, E. B., & Hagerman, R. J. (2015). Fragile X-associated disorders. In R. N. Rosenberg & J. M. Pascual (Eds.), *Rosenberg's Molecular and Genetic Basis of Neurological and Psychiatric Disease* (5th ed.) (pp. 183–195). Boston: Academic Press.

Margulies, C., Tully, T., & Dubnau, J. (2005). Deconstructing memory in Drosophila. *Curr Biol, 15*(17), R700–R713. doi:10.1016/j.cub.2005.08.024

Maulik, P. K., Mascarenhas, M. N., Mathers, C. D., Dua, T., & Saxena, S. (2011). Prevalence of intellectual disability: A meta-analysis of population-based studies. *Res Dev Disabil, 32*(2), 419–436. doi:10.1016/j.ridd.2010.12.018

McLaughlin, M. J., Speirs, K. E., & Shenassa, E. D. (2012). Reading disability and adult attained education and income: Evidence from a 30-year longitudinal study of a population-based sample. *J Learn Disabil, 47*(4), 374–386. doi:10.1177/0022219412458323

Mila, M., Alvarez-Mora, M. I., Madrigal, I., & Rodriguez-Revenga, L. (2018). Fragile X syndrome: An overview and update of the FMR1 gene. *Clin Genet, 93*(2), 197–205. doi:10.1111/cge.13075

Milnik, A., Heck, A., Vogler, C., Heinze, H. J., de Quervain, D. J., & Papassotiropoulos, A. (2012). Association of KIBRA with episodic and working memory: A meta-analysis. *Am J Med Genet B Neuropsychiatr Genet, 159b*(8), 958–969. doi:10.1002/ajmg.b.32101

Morgan, T. H. (1910). Sex limited inheritance in drosophila. *Science, 32*(812), 120–122. doi:10.1126/science.32.812.120

Morris, J. K., Mutton, D. E., & Alberman, E. (2002). Revised estimates of the maternal age specific live birth prevalence of Down's syndrome. *J Med Screen, 9*(1), 2–6. doi:10.1136/jms.9.1.2

Naj, A. C., & Schellenberg, G. D. (2017). Genomic variants, genes, and pathways of Alzheimer disease: An overview. *Am J Med Genet B Neuropsychiatr Genet, 174*(1), 5–26. doi:10.1002/ajmg.b.32499

National Academies of Sciences Engineering and Medicine (2015). *Mental Disorders and Disabilities Among Low-Income Children*. Washington, DC: National Academies Press.

Newbury, D. F., Monaco, A. P., & Paracchini, S. (2014). Reading and language disorders: The importance of both quantity and quality. *Genes (Basel), 5*(2), 285–309. doi:10.3390/genes5020285

Nisbett, R. E., Aronson, J., Blair, C., Dickens, W., Flynn, J., Halpern, D. F., & Turkheimer, E. (2012). Intelligence: New findings and theoretical developments. *Am Psychol, 67*(2), 130–159. doi:10.1037/a0026699

Oddo, S., Caccamo, A., Kitazawa, M., Tseng, B. P., & LaFerla, F. M. (2003). Amyloid deposition precedes tangle formation in a triple transgenic model of Alzheimer disease. *Neurobiol Aging, 24*(8), 1063–1070.

Papassotiropoulos, A., Stephan, D. A., Huentelman, M. J., Hoerndli, F. J., Craig, D. W., Pearson, J. V., . . . de Quervain, D. J. F. (2006). Common Kibra alleles are associated with human memory performance. *Science, 314*(5798), 475–478.

Paracchini, S., Diaz, R., & Stein, J. (2016). Advances in dyslexia genetics: New insights into the role of brain asymmetries. *Adv Genet, 96*, 53–97. doi:10.1016/bs.adgen.2016.08.003

Pfeiffer, B. E., & Huber, K. M. (2009). The state of synapses in fragile X syndrome. *The Neuroscientist, 15*(5), 549–567. doi:10.1177/1073858409333075

Plomin, R., & Deary, I. J. (2015). Genetics and intelligence differences: Five special findings. *Mol Psychiatry, 20*(1), 98–108. doi:10.1038/mp.2014.105

Plomin, R., & von Stumm, S. (2018). The new genetics of intelligence. *Nat Rev Genet, 19*(3), 148–159. doi:10.1038/nrg.2017.104

Plucker, J. A., & Shelton, A. L. (2015). General intelligence (g): Overview of a complex construct and its implications for genetics research. *Hastings Cent Rep, 45*(5 Suppl), S21–S24. doi:10.1002/hast.494

Quinn, W. G., Harris, W. A., & Benzer, S. (1974). Conditioned behavior in Drosophila melanogaster. *Proc Natl Acad Sci USA, 71*(3), 708–712.

Raber, J., Huang, Y., & Ashford, J. W. (2004). ApoE genotype accounts for the vast majority of AD risk and AD pathology. *Neurobiol Aging, 25*(5), 641–650. doi:10.1016/j.neurobiolaging.2003.12.023

Schwab, L. C., Luo, V., Clarke, C. L., & Nathan, P. J. (2014). Effects of the KIBRA single nucleotide polymorphism on synaptic plasticity and memory: A review of the literature. *Curr Neuropharmacol, 12*(3), 281–288. doi:10.2174/1570159x11666140104001553

Shao, S., Niu, Y., Zhang, X., Kong, R., Wang, J., Liu, L., . . . Song, R. (2016). Opposite associations between individual KIAA0319 polymorphisms and developmental dyslexia risk across populations: A stratified meta-analysis by the study population. *Sci Rep, 6*, 30454. doi:10.1038/srep30454

St Johnston, D. (2002). The art and design of genetic screens: Drosophila melanogaster. *Nat Rev Genet, 3*(3), 176–188. doi:10.1038/nrg751

Sternberg, R. J. (2012). Intelligence. *Dialogues Clin Neurosci, 14*(1), 19–27.

Tully, T., & Quinn, W. G. (1985). Classical conditioning and retention in normal and mutant Drosophila melanogaster. *J Comp Physiol A, 157*(2), 263–277.

van der Flier, W. M., & Scheltens, P. (2005). Epidemiology and risk factors of dementia. *J Neurol Neurosurg Psychiatry, 76*(Suppl 5), v2–v7.

Waddell, S., & Quinn, W. G. (2001). Flies, genes, and learning. *Annu Rev Neurosci, 24*, 1283–1309. doi:10.1146/annurev.neuro.24.1.1283

Walkinshaw, E., Gai, Y., Farkas, C., Richter, D., Nicholas, E., Keleman, K., & Davis, R. L. (2015). Identification of genes that promote or inhibit olfactory memory formation in Drosophila. *Genetics, 199*(4), 1173–1182.

Webster, S. J., Bachstetter, A. D., Nelson, P. T., Schmitt, F. A., & Van Eldik, L. J. (2014). Using mice to model Alzheimer dementia: An overview of the clinical disease and the preclinical behavioral changes in 10 mouse models. *Front Genet, 5*, 88. doi:10.3389/fgene.2014.00088

World Health Organization (2020a). 6A00 Disorders of intellectual development. ICD-11 for Mortality and Morbidity Statistics. http://id.who.int/icd/entity/605267007

World Health Organization (2020b). 6A03 Developmental learning disorder. ICD-11 for Mortality and Morbidity Statistics. http://id.who.int/icd/entity/2099676649

World Health Organization (2020c). 6D80 Dementia due to Alzheimer disease. ICD-11 for Mortality and Morbidity Statistics. http://id.who.int/icd/entity/795022044

Xing, Z., Li, Y., Pao, A., Bennett, A. S., Tycko, B., Mobley, W. C., & Yu, Y. E. (2016). Mouse-based genetic modeling and analysis of Down syndrome. *Br Med Bull, 120*(1), 111–122. doi:10.1093/bmb/ldw040

Zou, L., Chen, W., Shao, S., Sun, Z., Zhong, R., Shi, J., . . . Song, R. (2012). Genetic variant in KIAA0319, but not in DYX1C1, is associated with risk of dyslexia: An integrated meta-analysis. *Am J Med Genet B Neuropsychiatr Genet, 159b*(8), 970–976. doi:10.1002/ajmg.b.32102

9 Emotion and Depressive Disorders

Have you experienced any emotions today? Of course, you have. Perhaps you were irritated when your alarm woke you from a peaceful slumber thereby reminding you to go to class this morning. Maybe your roommate had already made the coffee, which cheered you up slightly. Such feelings are an integral part of human experience. When your emotions are functioning appropriately, they can help you navigate life by giving you a way to assess how the current situation aligns with your goals and to help prepare you to face new challenges. When your emotions are not functioning properly, you may find it difficult to deal with stressful situations, which may lead to social or occupational problems over time.

In this chapter, we define emotions, discuss how they are measured and their potential as phenotypes for genetic analysis, and discuss the importance of their regulation. We then present the diagnostic criteria for depressive disorders and examine their prevalence and burden. Next, we discuss evidence for genetic variation explaining variance in risk for depressive disorders, as well as potential candidate genetic mechanisms for their development and treatment. We then examine non-human animal models for depressive disorders. Finally, we discuss bipolar disorder and evidence that genetic variation is associated with individual differences in its risk.

9.1 Emotions Prepare for Action and Communicate

If you were asked to name a few emotions, you could probably do it rather quickly. Such a list is likely to include happiness, sadness, fear, and anger. Other emotions such as disgust, affection, surprise, or expectation might also find their way on the list. It is easy to name a few emotions, but you might run into some difficulty if you tried to name all emotions that humans experience. Part of the difficulty would be that there is no real consensus on how many emotions people experience. In addition, there are cultural and language differences that would affect the contents of your list. For example, unless you speak German, you might not have a word to describe that feeling of happiness that you may feel when you see someone else, especially your enemies, suffer. In German, the word schadenfreude describes such a feeling. Therefore, even though it is possible that all humans have the capacity to feel all the same emotions, cultural and language differences might affect people's capacity to accurately report their emotional experience (Shiota & Kalat, 2017).

Sometimes people use the term feelings to define emotions. Researchers use the more precise term, interoception, to denote one's perception of their own physiological state. Emotions are more than just feelings however, because they also involve a cognitive component. The same pattern of physiological arousal can be experienced as excitement or anxiety depending on one's cognitive appraisal of the situation. Sympathetic nervous system activation produces an increase in

(a)

(b)

(c)

Figure 9.1. **Emotion in dogs and cats.** These images show different inferred emotional states of animals and were used by Darwin to make the point of the continuity of emotional communication across species. Sources: (a) and (b) Universal Images Group / Contributor / Getty Images. (c) Photo 12 / Contributor / Universal Images Group / Getty Images.

heart rate and sweaty palms, but it is your knowledge of the situation, whether it is right before a birthday party or an exam, that enables you to correctly label the emotion.

Emotions help to prepare you for action. Your body can prepare for an active response (e.g., fight or flight), and your appraisal of the situation enables you to choose the right behavioral responses. Emotions help you determine which type of response is appropriate and how intense the response should be.

The capacity to communicate emotional information has been favored by natural selection (see Figure 9.1). Charles Darwin considered the expression of emotion to be important enough to write a book about it, in which he compared emotional responses across species to illustrate their continuity (Darwin, 1872). Communicating one's emotions can be done by facial expression, body postures, and vocalizations. Displays of anger can warn others of the potential for physical violence. Displays of sadness can elicit comforting responses. Displays of fear can warn others of potential danger. And so on. Emotions help us to understand our current situation and provide information to others about that assessment, which can then be used to determine appropriate behavioral responses.

Check-up

- Explain how culture and language might impact the number of emotions that we can list.
- How does our appraisal of the context determine which emotion we feel?
- What can we conclude about emotion by looking at other species?

9.2 There Are Many Ways to Measure Emotion

Researchers measure human emotion in many ways. Each of these broad categories of assessments has strengths and limitations. Conducting research always entails some tradeoffs because resources are limited. Many studies use self-report questionnaires to collect data about a person's subjective experience of emotion. Self-report questionnaires are simple to use and inexpensive. Many have been well validated and shown to be reliable (Mauss & Robinson, 2009). Study participants can be well-meaning and strive to respond truthfully, but sometimes people respond in ways that are not accurate. They can have poor insight into their emotions (i.e., alexithymia), have poor memories, may not want to portray themselves negatively (i.e., social desirability), or even may have an unconscious bias to respond in ways that they think the researcher desires (i.e., demand characteristics). Current emotional state can be more reliably reported than emotions experienced in the past, or even predictions about future emotional responses.

Personality traits are commonly assessed by self-report questionnaire and represent a person's response tendencies across situations. The personality trait neuroticism is the Big Five personality trait that indexes a person's tendencies to experience negative emotions such as depression, anxiety, and anger. A meta-analysis of over 29,000 twin pairs estimated the heritability of neuroticism to be 0.48 (van den Berg et al., 2014). Candidate gene association studies and GWAS on human personality traits indicate that individual genetic variants have a very small effect and that personality traits are polygenic (Sanchez-Roige, Gray, MacKillop, Chen, & Palmer, 2018).

Physiological measures can be used to directly assess the biological component of emotional experience. Heart rate, blood pressure, and skin conductance response (e.g., sweat glands) are examples of physiological measure that index activation of the autonomic nervous system (i.e., sympathetic and parasympathetic). It should be noted that autonomic nervous system activity is not solely dedicated to emotional responding, so that observed changes may result from the system responding to other bodily demands. In other words, these physiological measures are not specific to emotions, and it may be reasonable to consider them as assessments of arousal level rather than emotions (Mauss & Robinson, 2009). Very little research has addressed the role of genetic variation in individual differences in physiological responses to emotion.

Measures of brain activity can also be used to investigate biological emotional state. Electroencephalograms (EEGs) passively record neural activity (e.g., "brain waves") through the scalp. Other neuroimaging approaches such as functional magnetic resonance imaging (fMRI) can be used to identify the patterns of brain activity during the experiencing of emotions or while viewing facial expressions of people representing different emotions. EEGs have better time resolution than fMRI and are less expensive, whereas fMRI has better spatial resolution than EEG (Mauss & Robinson, 2009). Because these types of assays are relatively expensive and involve access to specialized equipment, genetic studies using such phenotypes typically have sample sizes that are considered rather small for genetic research. Therefore, studies that test associations with candidate genes and brain activity responses have explored aspects of emotional response (see Box 9.1), but their findings should be interpreted with caution (Avinun, Nevo, Knodt, Elliott, & Hariri, 2018).

Box 9.1 Genetic Differences in Amygdala Activation in Response to Facial Expressions of Threat

Human beings have a remarkable capacity to recognize many different facial expressions that are key to social communication. Facial expressions are of critical importance in communicating emotional states. Investigations of the neural mechanisms of the face-response system using fMRI have been ongoing for more than two decades (Haxby, Hoffman, & Gobbini, 2002).

The amygdala is part of the limbic system and therefore a key player in the processing of emotional information. It is particularly sensitive to facial expressions of fear or potential threat (e.g., anger; see Figure 9.2). In addition, its activity is increased when a viewed face is making eye contact, and when the face is unfamiliar. Threat-related amygdala activity is associated with risk for psychopathology such as depression and anxiety disorders and is a potential mechanism through which genetic variation may impact individual differences in risk for those conditions (Avinun et al., 2018). Well over 100 research papers reporting results of investigations into the association of candidate gene variants and threat-related amygdala reactivity have been published.

A typical threat-related amygdala reactivity task involves presenting participants images of people making facial expressions of different emotions (often fearful, angry [i.e., threat-related], surprised, or neutral) and engaging in a task. For example, three faces could be presented with one in the top row and two in the bottom row, and the participant is asked to identify which of the two bottom row faces is expressing the emotion that matches the top row face. Typically, amygdala activation is stronger when the viewed faces are expressing fear and anger, than when they are expressing other emotions.

The question addressed by candidate gene association studies is whether the pattern of robust activation of the amygdala in response to viewing threat-related facial expressions differs by genotype. In a replication study that tested thirty-seven reported associations between genetic variants and threat-related amygdala activation with a large sample (N = 1,117), only three showed significant effects in the same direction as the original report (Avinun et al., 2018). Fifteen SNPs were found to have significant associations in the opposite direction (i.e., the allele originally associated with higher activation was found to be associated with lower activation). Although, when significance levels were adjusted to account for the thirty-seven statistical tests that were

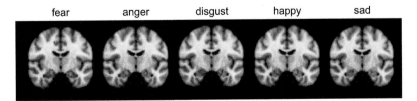

Figure 9.2. **Amygdala activation in response to facial expressions of threat.** Amygdala response to viewing faces showing different emotions in comparison with responses to viewing buildings. The average amygdala response is highest to faces showing anger and fear. Source: Mattavelli et al. (2014). Adapted and reproduced by permission of Oxford University Press.

conducted, none of the findings remained statistically significant. In other words, when the risk of finding false positives was adjusted to account for multiple comparisons, none of the findings were replicated.

Replication studies such as this make it clear that effect sizes of genetic variants in polygenic traits tend to be small and therefore large sample sizes are needed to detect them reliably. Findings such as this are a sobering reminder of the importance of strong study design (including sufficient sample size) and replication efforts in behavior genetics. The Enhancing NeuroImaging Genetics through Meta-Analysis (ENIGMA) Consortium (Thompson et al., 2014) is an effort by hundreds of researchers around the world to combine data from brain imaging, clinical assessments, other phenotyping methods and genomics to collaboratively investigate genotype–phenotype relationships with sample sizes large enough to detect small effects (e.g., tens of thousands).

Behavioral studies have also been used to investigate emotions. Measures such as vocal characteristics (e.g., pitch), facial expressions, facial electromyography (electrical activity of facial muscles), and body posture have been used to index emotion. In these studies, people may be exposed to stimuli, such as images that have been previously identified to elicit specific emotions, and then their behavioral responses are observed or recorded. Facial expressions may be the most sensitive of these behavioral indices, although factors such as gender or culture may moderate their impact (Mauss & Robinson, 2009).

In behavior genetic studies, the types of measure used are sometimes dictated by the genetic aspects of the study design. For example, if you planned a GWAS with 100,000 participants, it may be impractical to collect data about emotions using a neuroimaging measure. So, in that case, you might opt to collect data about emotions using an online self-report questionnaire. While it might be preferable to have both questionnaire and neuroimaging data, the cost of collecting neuroimaging data can be well over $500 per participant, which might make the study impossible to conduct. Virtually no single study can afford to spend $50 million on the collection of behavioral data alone. This is one of the reasons that large-scale research consortia that can pool their resources have arisen in the last decade. These consortia continue the internationally collaborative model pioneered by the Human Genome Project. This Big Science approach promises to reveal much about heredity–behavior relations that would otherwise remain hidden.

Many measures of emotion used in research are quantitative, which is an advantage for the genetic analysis of such likely polygenic traits. It is logical to assume that individual differences in emotional traits are due to variation in many genes with small effects, as well as being subject to environmental influence. It is easy to recognize, in oneself and in others, gradations of emotional traits and their dependence on context. Some emotional traits may be endophenotypes for mental illness. Sadness, for example, is represented by the NIMH Research Domain Criterion construct of "Loss." We will see in an upcoming section that depressed mood, which is synonymous with sadness, is one of the cardinal symptoms of Major Depressive Disorder.

Genome-wide association studies have enabled researchers to estimate SNP heritability (h^2_{SNP}), which represents the proportion of variation in a trait that is accounted for by the additive contribution of all observed single nucleotide polymorphisms. The SNP heritability estimate, in other words, is an index of the observed additive polygenic effects on a trait, excluding any non-additive effects (i.e., gene × gene interactions, gene × environment interactions, and dominance effects). SNP heritability estimates have generally been substantially smaller than heritability estimates derived from twin studies. The difference between the estimates has been termed "missing heritability" and is thought to be mostly due to the effects of genetic variants that are rare, or that have very small effects, and to non-additive genetic effects (Lopez-Cortegano & Caballero, 2019).

The SNP heritability of depression-relevant traits like neuroticism has recently been estimated to be around 10 percent (Sallis, Davey Smith, & Munafo, 2018). In other words, approximately 10 percent of individual differences in neuroticism are accounted for by differences in SNP genotypes between people. The heritability of neuroticism when estimated using twin pair resemblance is around 48 percent, which leaves quite a bit missing (i.e., not explained by SNP genotypes). In addition to non-additive genetic effects and the impact of rare genetic variants, it is also possible that traditional estimates of heritability that rely on familial resemblance are inaccurate. It is useful to interpret both SNP and traditional heritability estimates with caution. For the most part, precise heritability estimates are not important. Heritability estimates that are significantly different from zero indicate that genetic differences play a role in individual differences in a trait and therefore seeking to identify genetic variants associated with differences is sensible. We can be confident that genetic differences between people play a role in individual differences in depression-relevant traits like neuroticism. Recent large GWAS have found evidence for a few SNPs associated with depression-relevant traits and suggest that hundreds or thousands of variants are likely to play a role in individual differences in such traits (Okbay et al., 2016; Sanchez-Roige et al., 2018).

Check-up

- Compare and contrast methods for measuring emotion.
- Discuss the tradeoffs that researchers face when deciding which measure of emotion to use in a behavior genetic study.
- Explain missing heritability using neuroticism as an example.

9.3 Emotion Regulation Difficulties May Lead to Psychopathology

As you can see, emotions are an important part of life and researchers in behavior genetics are interested in understanding the role of genetic variation in individual differences in emotion. One aspect of emotion that plays a critical role in a person's life and in their risk for emotional problems and mental illness is the capacity for emotion regulation (Sheppes, Suri, & Gross, 2015).

It is healthy to be able to experience sadness in response to the loss of a loved one, for example, because sadness can help cope with a loss by facilitating the recruitment of social support. For most of us, the experience of emotions, such as sadness, is typically of appropriate intensity and limited duration. At some point, the intensity of sadness in response to a loss diminishes, although it may never completely disappear, as in the loss of a child, for example.

Emotional problems can arise when a person experiences an emotion with inappropriate intensity or duration. The tendency to generate emotions with intensities that are out of proportion to the situation, or to experience emotions that are unusually persistent, can begin to cause social or occupational difficulties or distress. Persistent and intense sadness that is out of proportion to the loss experienced could very well add stress to relationships and negatively impact performance at work or in school. If such emotional problems persist or worsen, they may contribute to the development of a mental illness.

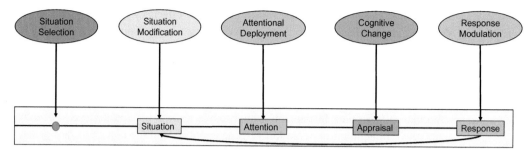

Figure 9.3. **The process model of emotion regulation.** Different strategies can be used to regulate emotions at different stages of emotional experience. Source: Republished with permission of The Guilford Press from Gross & Thompson (2007). Permission conveyed through Copyright Clearance Center, Inc.

We all employ strategies to regulate our emotions, and some of us are better at it than others. Such individual differences in emotion regulation become apparent early in development, where some infants appear to have great capacity to calm their emotional responses to situations, while others appear to have less. There is strong evidence that emotion regulation capacity in childhood and adolescence is associated with risk for both internalizing (i.e., keeps problems to themselves, such as depression) and externalizing (i.e., directs behavior outward, such as conduct disorder) disorders (Compas et al., 2017).

A theoretical model that has been a useful framework for investigating emotional regulation is called the process model (Gross & Jazaieri, 2014). Emotion regulation encompasses implicit or explicit efforts to alter emotional experience through different strategies over time (Sheppes et al., 2015). Individuals are hypothesized to vary in the capacity to engage in different emotion regulation strategies and in the awareness of the need to use them.

According to the process model, strategies for emotion regulation can be employed at different stages in the experience of an emotion (see Figure 9.3). Individuals may select to avoid a situation that may trigger an emotional experience, thereby preventing it (i.e., situation selection). Once an emotional response has occurred, an individual could modify the situation in some way to regulate the emotion (i.e., situation modification). An individual may choose to pay attention to something else in the situation to regulate the emotional experience (i.e., attentional deployment). An individual could change the way that they think about a situation to regulate their emotional response to it (i.e., cognitive change). Finally, a person could attempt to alter their response to a situation, for example, hiding one's facial expression, to regulate their emotions.

More sophisticated models have been developed to incorporate iterative changes across time and the addition of valuation systems to help select emotion regulation strategies (Sheppes et al., 2015), but these models are beyond the scope of this text. For our purposes it is important to note that there are individual differences in the tendencies to select different strategies and the capacity to employ them. Very little research has been done to investigate the role of genetic variation in such tendencies and capacities, but it is an interesting potential avenue that should be pursued.

Heritability estimates of emotion regulation traits are around 0.40 (Hawn, Overstreet, Stewart, & Amstadter, 2015). Nearly all of the molecular genetic studies to identify genetic variants associated with individual differences in emotion regulation have been candidate gene association studies (Barzman, Geise, & Lin, 2015; Hawn et al., 2015). Most of those have tested only a few commonly tested genetic variants such as 5-HTTLPR, with sample sizes of less than 1,000, which raises concerns regarding replicability.

At this time, few GWAS have investigated emotion regulation. A recent GWAS analysis of the UK Biobank sample of N = 363,705 identified forty-six genetic loci across the genome that were associated with emotional instability with a SNP heritability of 0.09 (Ward et al., 2020). Many of the genetic variants identified are expressed in the brain and are involved in neuron development and differentiation. Additional studies will be necessary to confirm these findings and to investigate the biological pathways that were identified.

Check-up

- What is emotion regulation and why is it important?
- Discuss the process model of emotion regulation.

9.4 Mood Disorders Are Common, and Symptomatically Heterogeneous

So far in this chapter, we have discussed emotions and their regulation, but have not addressed how emotional problems can be a part of mental illness. Several psychiatric disorders have symptoms that involve some type of emotional dysfunction. For example, in Chapter 7 we discussed anhedonia, reduced capacity to experience emotion, as one of schizophrenia's negative symptoms. Emotional symptoms of other psychiatric disorders are mentioned in other chapters when appropriate. In this chapter, we focus on two main psychiatric diagnoses that have depressed mood as a primary feature, (1) bipolar disorder and (2) depressive disorders (see Box 9.2).

Box 9.2 ICD-11 Diagnosis: Mood Disorders

Mood Disorders refers to a superordinate grouping of Bipolar and Depressive Disorders. Mood disorders are defined according to particular types of mood episodes and their pattern over time. The primary types of mood episodes are Depressive episode, Manic episode, Mixed episode, and Hypomanic episode. Mood episodes are not independently diagnosable entities, and therefore do not have their own diagnostic codes. Rather, mood episodes make up the primary components of most of the Depressive and Bipolar Disorders.

Bipolar or Related Disorders
Bipolar and related disorders are episodic mood disorders defined by the occurrence of Manic, Mixed or Hypomanic episodes or symptoms. These episodes typically alternate over the course of these disorders with Depressive episodes or periods of depressive symptoms.

Depressive Disorders
Depressive disorders are characterised by depressive mood (e.g., sad, irritable, empty) or loss of pleasure accompanied by other cognitive, behavioural, or neurovegetative symptoms that significantly affect the individual's ability to function. A depressive disorder should not be diagnosed in individuals who have ever experienced a manic, mixed or hypomanic episode, which would indicate the presence of a bipolar disorder.

Source: http://id.who.int/icd/entity/ 76398729 (accessed February 24, 2021), World Health Organization (Copyright © 2020a).

9.4.1 Genetic Risk for Bipolar Disorder Is Polygenic and Shared with Other Psychopathologies

The lifetime prevalence of bipolar I disorder (see Box 9.3) is approximately 2 percent (Clemente et al., 2015). Family studies show that bipolar disorder runs in families. People who have first-degree relatives who are affected with either are at ten times higher risk for developing the disorder compared to those with unaffected relatives (Smoller & Finn, 2003). Heritability of bipolar disorder has been estimated, primarily via twin studies, at 0.80–0.85 (Barnett & Smoller, 2009). Several candidate genes have been investigated for their role in the etiology of bipolar disorder, often in the context of genotype × environment interactions with early life stress (Misiak et al., 2018). But given the well-known issues with replication of such studies, we will reserve judgment on them at this time.

Substantial efforts have been made by large consortia to identify genetic variants that are associated with risk for developing bipolar disorder. For example, the Psychiatric Genomics Consortium reported a GWAS using a discovery sample with 20,352 cases and 31,358 controls, with a replication sample of 9,412 cases and 137,760 controls (Stahl et al., 2019). Thirty genetic variants were found to be associated with bipolar disorder, many of which were located in genes whose proteins are involved in neurotransmission.

Recently, efforts have also focused on genetic associations between disorders that may represent general risk factors for developing mental illness, rather than disorder-specific genetic risk. A good example of such efforts is from the Cross-Disorder Group of the Psychiatric Genomics

Box 9.3 ICD-11 Diagnosis: Bipolar Type I Disorder, Current Episode Manic, without Psychotic Symptoms

Bipolar type I disorder, current episode manic, without psychotic symptoms is diagnosed when the definitional requirements for Bipolar type I disorder are met, the current episode is manic, and there are no delusions or hallucinations present during the episode. A manic episode is an extreme mood state lasting at least one week unless shortened by a treatment intervention characterised by euphoria, irritability, or expansiveness, and by increased activity or a subjective experience of increased energy, accompanied by other characteristic symptoms such as rapid or pressured speech, flight of ideas, increased self-esteem or grandiosity, decreased need for sleep, distractibility, impulsive or reckless behaviour, and rapid changes among different mood states (i.e., mood lability).

Source: http://id.who.int/icd/entity/ 374726152 (accessed April 12, 2021), World Health Organization (Copyright © 2020b).

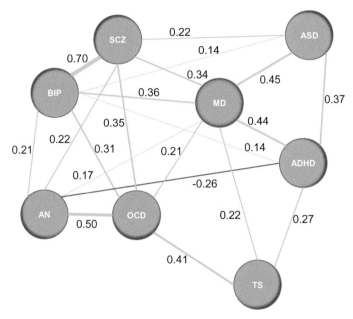

Figure 9.4. **Genetic correlations across psychiatric disorders.** SNP-based genetic correlations where each node represents a psychiatric disorder and the lines connecting them represent pair-wise correlations. Correlation coefficients for each pair-wise correlation are given. The take-home message is that some genetic variants impact risk for more than one psychiatric disorder. Source: Adapted from Cross-Disorder Group of the Psychiatric Genomics Consortium (Smoller, 2019). Copyright (© 2019), with permission from Elsevier.

Consortium (Smoller, 2019). In this study, the researchers conducted a meta-analysis of GWAS with 232,964 cases and 494,162 controls across eight psychiatric disorders (anorexia nervosa, ADHD, autism spectrum disorder, bipolar disorder, major depression, obsessive-compulsive disorder, schizophrenia, and Tourette syndrome). Their findings indicated substantial pleiotropy across these eight disorders, with 109 loci being associated with at least two disorders, and 23 loci that were associated with 4 or more disorders. If an allele of a SNP is associated with increased risk for more than one disorder, those disorders are considered genetically correlated. An overall genetic correlation coefficient indexes the strength of the genetic correlation between disorders accounting on a genome-wide basis. The pattern of genetic correlations for the eight psychiatric disorders tested suggests that genetic risk for mental illness does not conform with current diagnostic categories (see Figure 9.4). Variation in certain genes, perhaps those that have a critical role in the development and function of neurons, may affect risk for developing more than one psychiatric disorder. Based on genomic sharing, bipolar disorder, major depressive disorder, and schizophrenia can be grouped together (Smoller, 2019).

New findings in the genomics of psychiatric disorders, including depressive disorders are being made at a rapid rate. No doubt remains that genetic variation plays a role in individual differences in risk for developing depressive disorders. However, much work remains to be done in identifying relevant genetic variants and understanding the biological pathways involved in depressive disorders. Most importantly, much work remains to be done in making use of genetic findings in prevention and treatment efforts. So far, attempts to use polygenic risk scores derived from GWAS studies to predict depression phenotypes and outcomes have not yielded much fruit (Mistry, Harrison, Smith, Escott-Price, & Zammit, 2018).

Check-up

- Compare and contrast bipolar depressive disorders.
- What does it mean that bipolar disorder, schizophrenia, and major depressive disorder are genetically correlated?

9.5 Prevalence and Symptoms of Depressive Disorders

It is estimated that around 322 million people worldwide meet diagnostic criteria for a depressive disorder (GBD, 2016). According to the World Health Organization, the prevalence of depressive disorder ranges from 9 percent in the African Region to 27 percent in the South-East Asia Region (see Figure 9.5). Females have a higher prevalence of depressive disorder than males in every WHO region and in every age group. In the US over 20 million Americans experienced an episode of depressive disorder in 2018 (SAMHSA, 2019). Such demographic differences are due to some combination of biological and environmental sources.

In 2016, depressive disorders were in the top 20 causes of cause-specific disability-adjusted life years (DALYs) worldwide (see Figure 9.6 and Box 9.4). A DALY can be thought of as one lost year of living a "healthy" life. In other words, if someone was either disabled for a year, or they died one year sooner than they would have if they did not have a disorder, it would count as one DALY. Therefore, DALYs are one way to index how much burden a disease or disorder represents. Ischemic heart disease (aka coronary artery disease) accounts for the most DALYs of all causes worldwide at 7.6 percent of all DALYs. Depressive disorders account for the most DALYs of all psychiatric disorders

Box 9.4 ICD-11 Depressive Disorders

Depressive disorders are characterised by depressive mood (e.g., sad, irritable, empty) or loss of pleasure accompanied by other cognitive, behavioural, or neurovegetative symptoms that significantly affect the individual's ability to function. A depressive disorder should not be diagnosed in individuals who have ever experienced a manic, mixed or hypomanic episode, which would indicate the presence of a bipolar disorder.

Source: http://id.who.int/icd/entity/1563440232 (accessed February 24, 2021), World Health Organization (Copyright © 2020c).

As we discussed in Chapter 7 in the context of schizophrenia, there is also substantial symptom heterogeneity in depressive disorder diagnoses. To be clear, any diagnostic system where it is possible to meet criteria for diagnosis by endorsing only a subset of possible symptoms will produce symptom heterogeneity. Depressive disorder, however, seems to represent an extreme case where patients who meet criteria for diagnosis may have unique symptom profiles.

A study to examine the extent to which people who qualify for a diagnosis of depressive disorder share symptoms revealed surprising variety in symptom profiles (Fried & Nesse, 2015). In the study, the symptom patterns of 3,703 patients who sought treatment for depressive disorder were examined. One thousand and thirty (1,030) unique combinations of symptoms were identified. Most of the symptom profiles (83.9 percent) were found in five or fewer patients, and nearly half of the

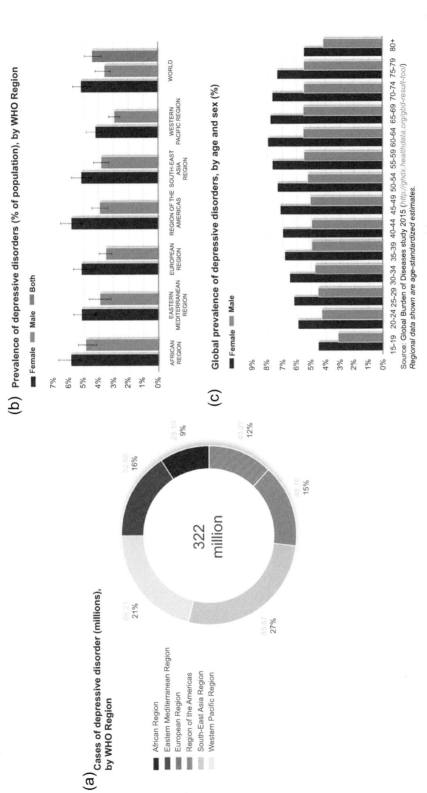

Figure 9.5. **Prevalence of an episode of depressive disorder around the world as well as sex and age differences.** (a) An estimated 322 million people have depressive disorder worldwide. Prevalence rates vary across World Health Organization regions. (b) Females have a higher prevalence rate of depressive disorder in each of the WHO regions. (c) Females have higher prevalence rate of depressive disorder than males in each age category. Source: Hannah Ritchie and Max Roser (2018) "Mental Health." Published online at OurWorldInData.org. Retrieved from: https://ourworldindata.org/mental-health [Online Resource].

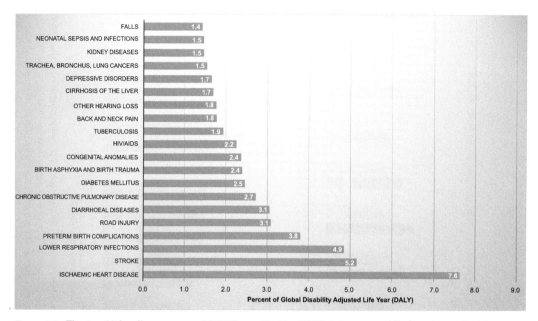

Figure 9.6. **The top 20 leading causes of DALYs worldwide.** DALYs index years of life lost due to disability or death. The percentage of DALYs accounted for by the top 20 specific causes are shown. Source: Global Health Estimates 2016: Disease burden by cause, age, sex, by country and by region, 2000–2016. Geneva: World Health Organization, 2018.

symptom profiles (48.6 percent) were found in only one patient. Yet all patients met criteria for the same diagnosis of depressive disorder. The most common symptom profile was only observed in 1.8 percent of patients.

In the context of behavior genetics, it is important to consider whether the diagnosis for depressive disorder represents an adequate phenotype. It may be that different biological systems are associated with different system profiles and that lumping them all together into a single group (i.e., those with a diagnosis of depressive disorder) introduces too much noise. The NIMH's Research Domain Criteria were developed to provide phenotypes with potentially simpler biological pathways.

Check-up

- Describe the prevalence and burden of depressive disorders.
- Discuss the importance of depressive mood and loss of pleasure in the diagnosis of major depressive disorder.
- What is symptom heterogeneity and why is it important in behavior genetics?

9.6 The Genetic Epidemiology of Depressive Disorders

One of the first types of evidence that we seek for understanding the role of heredity in a human phenotype is whether it runs in families. One way to assess such familiality is to assess whether first-degree relatives (i.e., those that share 50 percent of their genetic material) of those with depressive

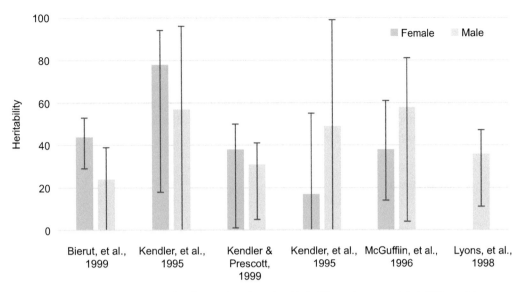

Figure 9.7. **Heritability estimates for depressive disorder.** Heritability estimates and their 95% confidence intervals for men and women. It is important to note that the 95% confidence intervals of the heritability estimates are quite large but indicate that heritability estimates are significantly greater than zero for 7 of the 11 estimates shown. Sex differences in heritability estimates are not consistent across studies. After Sullivan et al. (2000).

disorders are at increased risk to develop it compared to unrelated individuals. The evidence indicates that first-degree relatives of probands with depression are 2.84 times (95% CI = 2.31–3.49) more likely to have depression than is someone who does not have a first-degree relative with depression (Sullivan, Neale, & Kendler, 2000). Of course, such studies do not enable us to determine whether the increased risk is due to shared genes or to shared environment (or a combination of the two), because people in families share both. Evidence from other types of studies is needed to strengthen the position that genetic variation plays a role in individual differences in depression risk.

Twin (or adoption) studies are often a next step in gathering evidence for the influence of heredity on human behavioral variation. As you recall, twins can either share all (i.e., monozygote) or half (i.e., dizygote) of their genetic material. The logic is that people who share more genetic material will be more like each other on a given behavior if genetic variation plays a significant role in individual differences in behavior. In the cases of categorical diagnoses, like depression, the concordance rate (i.e., the probability that one twin has depression if the other does) for monozygote twin pairs is compared to that of dizygote twin pairs. If genes play a role in risk for depression, the concordance rates of monozygote twin pairs should be higher than that of dizygotic twin pairs. Heritability estimates can be derived from such data (see Figure 9.7). Heritability estimates vary somewhat across studies with an overall estimate of 0.37 (95% CI = 0.33–0.42; [Sullivan et al., 2000]).

Of course, the large confidence intervals and the relative lack of data from adoption studies on this question do not inspire confidence in the precision of the heritability estimates of depression (Sullivan et al., 2000). A more recent study examined twin correlations from 2,748 twin studies published between 1958 and 2012 investigating 17,804 traits including self-reported experience of a depressive episode (Polderman et al., 2015). It reports data from over 2 million twins from 39 countries. The correlation for MZ twin pairs on experiencing a depressive episode was rMZ = 0.454. For DZ pairs it was rDZ = 0.253. As you recall, heritability can be estimated by the formula

2(rMZ-rDZ). So, in this case 2(0.454–0.253) = 0.402. This estimate of 0.402 is consistent with the estimate of 0.37 that we previously mentioned.

Evidence from both family and twin studies indicate that individual differences in depression risk depend, in part, on genetic differences between people. Such results also can be interpreted to mean that genes alone do not determine risk for depression. Family and twin studies can provide some confidence in regard to efforts to identify genetic variants that affect risk for depression, but they cannot indicate how many genetic variants may play a role in depression risk or help to identify which variants may be involved.

Check-up

- Summarize the evidence that depression runs in families.
- What do twin studies tell us about depression?

9.7 Efforts to Characterize Genetic Mechanisms of Depressive Disorders Are Ongoing

Studies designed to find genetic variants that either increase or decrease risk for developing major depressive disorder in humans began in the 1990s. Three decades later, our thinking about the role of genetic variants in depression risk has become more sophisticated, but there is still much to learn, and many more depression risk variants to find.

Early efforts assumed that a relatively small number of genes played a role in depression risk. Between 1998 and 2010 at least twelve linkage studies were conducted to identify chromosomal regions that co-segregated with depression diagnosis in large family pedigrees (McIntosh, Sullivan, & Lewis, 2019). Linkage studies were instrumental in identifying genes for diseases such as cystic fibrosis and Huntington's disease where mutations in a single gene are a sufficient cause (Gelehrter, Collins, & Ginsburg, 1998). By investigating major depressive disorder with a linkage study, one assumes that the disorder is caused by a small number of genes with large effects. None of the linkage studies of depression produced findings that replicated in other linkage studies or that overlap with findings in GWAS (McIntosh et al., 2019). The safest way to interpret this pattern of results is that depressive disorders are not caused by a small number of genes with large effects.

Candidate gene association study designs also assume that the effect sizes of at least some genetic variants on depression are moderate to large, and that a hypothesis-driven approach for selecting variants to test based on the biology of depression may increase the chances of detecting significant associations. We discussed the limitations of candidate gene association studies in Chapter 5. For the most part, candidate gene association studies have used sample sizes that are too small to reliably detect the small effect sizes that appear to be common in polygenic traits. And it is generally accepted that depressive disorder and other depression-related phenotypes are polygenic.

Over 1,200 candidate gene association studies were conducted between 1991 and 2016, and most tested variants in 18 candidate genes, that are sometimes called the "usual suspects" (Border et al., 2019). By far, the most studied candidate gene for depression between 1991 and 2016 was the gene that codes for the serotonin transporter, *SLC6A4* (see Figure 9.8), and the most studied variant was 5-HTTLPR, which we discussed in Chapter 6. The serotonin transporter gene is a logical candidate because its protein product is the target site for selective serotonin reuptake inhibitors (SSRIs), which are commonly prescribed antidepressants.

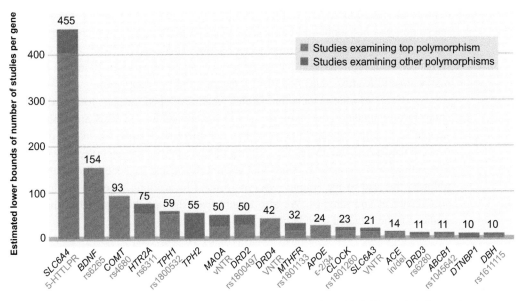

Figure 9.8. **Candidate gene association studies for depression 1991–2016.** The x-axis indicates the gene and the most common variant studied for the 18 candidate genes that were investigated in at least 10 studies. Source: Border et al. (2019). Reprinted with permission from the American Journal of Psychiatry (Copyright © 2019). American Psychiatric Association. All rights reserved.

Failures to replicate, biases in the scientific literature that favor the publication of statistically significant novel findings over non-significant replication attempts, and small effect sizes of variants identified in GWAS have called candidate gene association study findings into question. Large meta-analyses with ample statistical power to detect small effects have not generally replicated findings from candidate gene association studies on depression (Border et al., 2019).

The 5-HTTLPR polymorphism of *SLC6A4* was the focus of additional attention as a potential moderator of depression risk for those exposed to childhood trauma or other life stress. A study published in 2003 received a lot of media attention and inspired many replication attempts because it appeared to show evidence that individuals who carried one or more S alleles of 5-HTTLPR and who were exposed to stressful life events while growing up were at increased risk for developing depression in adulthood (Caspi et al., 2003). This study has been cited in thousands of research papers and was covered widely in the popular press. It seemed to show evidence that a person's genotype at a single variant moderated the impact of exposure to stressful life events, like childhood maltreatment, on risk for experiencing a depressive episode later in life. It appeared to be a classic case of a genotype × environment (G×E) interaction.

Hundreds of studies and several meta-analyses have been conducted to determine whether 5-HTTLPR genotype moderates the impact of life stress on risk for depression, with mixed results. A recent pre-registered, collaborative study attempted to address the question with new analyses of 31 data sets with 38,802 subjects of European ancestry (Culverhouse et al., 2018). They analyzed two different types of stressors (childhood maltreatment and general life stress) and two measures of depression (current and lifetime), while statistically controlling for the effects of age and sex. The results showed a strong significant effect of stressors on depression risk regardless of how either was defined. Experiencing maltreatment or life stress doubles the risk for depression (odds ratio = 2.16; 95% CI = 1.65, 2.82). Carrying an S allele of 5-HTTLPR was not associated with increased depression risk (odds ratio = 1.0; 95% CI = 0.95–1.05). And finally, the hypothesis of a G×E interaction was not supported because carrying an S allele did not increase risk for depression for those who experienced maltreatment or life stress (odds ratio = 0.95; 95% CI = 0.91–1.21). The weight of evidence indicates that carrying an S allele of 5-HTTLPR on its own or coupled with maltreatment/life stress does not affect a person's risk for depression.

Genome-wide association studies were developed, in part, to remedy some of the shortcomings of candidate gene association and linkage studies. GWAS are typically conducted with sample sizes large enough to detect the small effect sizes expected of polygenic risk alleles, and because they assess genotypes for millions of SNPs across the genome, they could potentially find associations with variants in genes that are not the "usual suspects." In addition, researchers have followed the lead of the Human Genome Project by working together in global collaborations to pool resources and samples. We also benefit from the fact that researchers have been doing these studies for more than a decade now.

A review that examined the results of 18 large (N>10,000) GWAS published between 2011 and 2019 indicated that 227 loci have been associated with depression phenotypes, including clinical diagnoses, self-reported diagnoses, and self-reported symptoms or traits (Schwabe et al., 2019). Because of some overlap in samples across studies due to data sharing, it is difficult to know exactly how many individual subjects contributed data to these studies, but it is safe to say that the overall sample was in the millions.

One of the studies reviewed was a meta-analysis of the three largest GWAS on depression to date with data from 246,363 cases and 561,190 controls (Howard et al., 2019). They tested 8,098,588 genetic variants and found evidence for association with a broad depression phenotype for 102 independent variants in 269 genes. In an independent sample of 414,055 cases and 892,299 controls, 87 of the 102 variants replicated their association with depression. The total sample size in this study is a staggering 2,113,907. The SNP heritability was estimated to be 0.089.

Many of the associated variants are expressed in pathways involved in synaptic structure and neurotransmission, especially in the prefrontal cortex. Interestingly, genetic variants in the dopamine neurotransmitter system, notably the gene for the D2 dopamine receptor (DRD2), were associated with depression, but those in the serotonin neurotransmitter system were not. GWAS findings will be critical in understanding the biological pathways involved in depression and its treatment.

It appears that in depression, as in other polygenic traits, the contribution of any single genetic variant to a person's risk is vanishingly small. So, one way to use data from GWAS is to create a polygenic risk score (Wray et al., 2014). Fisher's model of quantitative traits serves as the basis of polygenic risk scores (see Chapter 5). We assume that a trait has some large number of genetic variants, each with an increasing and a decreasing allele, that contribute to trait variability in the population. To calculate polygenic risk scores using GWAS data, one first must identify which allele at a locus is associated with increased risk for the trait or disorder. For example, if a C allele at a SNP is associated with depression, and the T allele not, then the C is designated as the risk allele. Each person is genotyped for that SNP and those with C/C genotype are given a score of 2, those with C/T genotype are given a score of 1, and those with the T/T genotype are given a score of 0. These scores represent the number of risk alleles at this locus that a person carries.

If we extend this approach to all the SNPs that have been found to be associated with depression, we can then sum them for each person's polygenic risk score. This simple polygenic risk score assumes that all loci contribute equally to risk. However, one can weight each score by various methods (e.g., effect size) to account for differential contributions. Determination of which genetic variants to use in the construction of a polygenic risk score can be based on allele frequency, effect size, p-value threshold, correlations between loci, or other factors (Wray et al., 2014). It is considered best practice to construct the polygenic risk score in a discovery sample and then to test it in an independent target sample.

One of the ultimate goals of behavior genetic research into psychiatric disorders is to be able to use a patient's genetic information to improve response to treatment. This area of research is called pharmacogenetics or pharmacogenomics, based on the amount of genetic information used. We cover it in detail in Chapter 14. But for now, let us consider its use in understanding response to treatment for major depressive disorder with antidepressant medication.

In the 1950s and 1960s biomedical researchers were making systematic observations about the role of neurotransmitter systems and psychopathology (Hirschfeld, 2000). Such observations led to the development of the monoamine hypothesis of depression, which proposed that the availability of certain neurotransmitters, like serotonin, played a causal role in depression. Drugs that decreased serotonin availability in the brain appeared to be capable of initiating depressive episodes, and drugs that increased serotonin availability appeared to be capable of ending them. A class of drugs called tricyclic antidepressants reduced reuptake of norepinephrine and serotonin by blocking reuptake via the norepinephrine and serotonin transporters, respectively. Another class of drugs, selective serotonin reuptake inhibitors (SSRIs), primarily inhibited the reuptake of serotonin by blocking serotonin transporters (see Figure 9.9). Blocking the reuptake of neurotransmitters back into the presynaptic cell increases their concentration in the synapse, thereby enhancing neurotransmission.

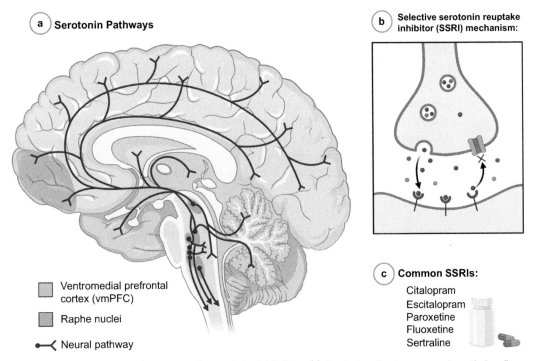

Figure 9.9. **Action of selective serotonin reuptake inhibitors.** (a) Serotonin releasing neurons have their cell bodies in the dorsal raphe and project to many brain areas including the ventromedial prefrontal cortex. (b) SSRIs block the reuptake of serotonin into the presynaptic neuron via serotonin transporters thereby producing an increase in serotonin synaptic availability. (c) Several commonly prescribed antidepressant medications are SSRIs. Source: Created with Biorender.com.

Decades of research have made it clear that depression is not merely due to a serotonin deficit (Jesulola, Micalos, & Baguley, 2018). However, mental health is dependent on neurotransmitter system function, which is influenced by variation in genes that code for protein components such as receptors, enzymes, and transporters. Because SSRIs bind to serotonin transporters and thereby reduce serotonin reuptake, it is logical to hypothesize that variants in the serotonin transporter gene (*SLC6A4*) such as 5-HTTLPR may contribute to individual differences in response to SSRI treatment for depression. There is evidence that carriers of the L allele of 5-HTTLPR may respond better to treatment for depression with SSRIs, and that the effect may differ by demographic factors such as race/ethnicity, gender, and age, and possibly by depression severity (Porcelli, Fabbri, & Serretti, 2012). Such differential success in SSRI treatment for depression may be due to increased rates of adverse effects experienced by patients who carry an S allele of 5-HTTLPR (Zhu, Klein-Fedyshin, & Stevenson, 2017). Adverse effects such as antidepressant-induced mania and gastrointestinal problems could lead patients to stop taking the medication.

Check-up

- Explain the rationale for considering *SLC6A4* a candidate gene for depression.
- Discuss 5-HTTLPR and its potential role in moderating risk for depression.
- Compare and contrast discovery and target samples in GWAS.
- What is the monoamine hypothesis of depression and what is its current status?

9.8 Genetic Evidence from Non-Human Animal Models

Lines of rodents identified or selectively bred for behavioral or other depression-like traits (e.g., response to certain medications [see Box 9.5]) have long been used to investigate the genetics and biology of depression, and to identify drugs with antidepressant effects (Overstreet, 2012). Comparing lines of animals that are different genetically but raised and tested in conditions that are as similar as possible, differences between the lines are the result of the genetic differences. Let us consider some lines of rats that have been used to investigate depression-like traits. As you will see, each line displays some depression-like traits, but not all. No single animal model is a complete model of human depression.

Box 9.5 Non-Human Animal Models for Investigating Depression-Like Behaviors

Behavior genetic investigations of depression in non-human animal models examine depression-like behaviors using the myriad tools available, such as genetic engineering. Because of shared ancestry and biology, findings in non-human animal models are of great interest in efforts to understand depression in humans.

Of course, self-report of depression symptoms and subsequent diagnosis with major depressive disorder is not possible in non-human animals. But experimental approaches have been developed to produce depression-like behavior that is consistent with human depression symptoms

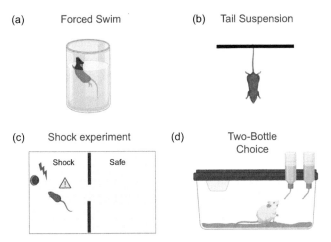

Figure 9.10. **Depression-like behavior paradigms.** In (a) the forced swim test, the (b) tail suspension test, and the (c) shock avoidance test immobility is considered a depression-like behavior. Decreased preference for sweetened water is considered to be an index of anhedonia, a common symptom of depression, and can be assessed in a two-bottle choice test (d). Source: Created with Biorender.com.

(Czeh, Fuchs, Wiborg, & Simon, 2016; Wang, Timberlake, Prall, & Dwivedi, 2017). Of course, certain symptoms like suicidal ideation, or feelings of worthlessness or guilt, are not possible to model in non-human animals. Here we focus on a few of the more commonly used depression-like behavior paradigms.

The fear conditioning paradigm pairs a loud noise or a foot-shock (unconditioned stimulus [UCS]) with a previously neutral stimulus like a light or a quiet tone (conditioned stimulus [CS]; see Figure 9.10). The unconditioned stimulus produces unconditioned responses (UCR) such as increased blood pressure and freezing behavior. After pairing the UCS with the CS, successful fear conditioning is indicated when the animal (typically a rodent) shows blood pressure increases and anticipatory freezing behavior (i.e., conditioned responses [CR]) when only the CS is presented. Anticipatory freezing may model motivational and cognitive symptoms of depression and anxiety, and it is worth noting that patients with depressive disorders often have anxiety.

The forced swim test and the tail suspension test may model behavioral despair. In the forced swim test, rodents are typically placed in a beaker of water and their activity is monitored. Rodents will initially attempt to escape the situation by vigorously swimming and trying to climb the walls of the beaker. At some point during the timed test, the rodents will become immobile. The time spent immobile is the objective definition of behavioral despair. Similarly, in the tail suspension test, rodents are suspended by taping their tail to a hook or a rod across the top of a small chamber. The time that the animal spends immobile is the index of behavioral despair. Both tests are used to screen drugs for antidepressant efficacy because drugs that are effective antidepressants in humans reduce the time that rodents remain immobile.

Rodents can also be tested for shock avoidance. First, the animals are placed in a compartment that contains an electrical grid on the floor. During the training phase, the animals are exposed to inescapable shocks at random intervals. During the testing phase, twenty-four hours later, they are placed in a chamber with two sections called a shuttle-box, one has an electrifiable grid and the other does not. They are then exposed to a few shocks that they can escape if they move into the area without the grid. The time it takes for the animal to move from the grid section to the safe section is recorded. Depression-like behavior is defined as slower than normal times to avoid the shock.

The symptom of anhedonia (reduction in capacity to feel pleasure) can be assessed in non-human animal models by simply measuring consumption of water containing sucrose in a two-bottle choice test. One bottle containing only water and one bottle containing a sucrose and water solution is presented to the animals for a time. Depression-like behavior would be indicated when a rodent shows a decreased interest in the sweetened water. A more complicated measure of anhedonia requires the implantation of stimulating electrodes in the reward pathway of an animal. In this intracranial self-stimulation paradigm, an apparatus can provide electrical stimulation as a function of lever presses. Depression-like behavior in this case would be indicated when a rodent displays a lower-than-normal lever pressing behavior.

Using objective behavioral measures in non-human animal models, such as these, that respond to antidepressant medication enables researchers to experimentally investigate biological pathways that may be involved in human depression.

The Flinders sensitive line (FSL) rat was established by selectively breeding for sensitivity to a drug that targets the acetylcholine neurotransmitter system. People with depression are sensitive to this class of drugs. Rats from the FSL display reduced appetite and psychomotor functions and altered circadian rhythms. They also show alterations in serotonergic, cholinergic, dopaminergic, and neuro-peptide Y (NPY) systems, and have been used to test drugs for antidepressant effects (Czeh et al., 2016).

The Wistar-Kyoto (WKY) line of rats was selectively bred for use as the normal control for a line of rats identified with high blood pressure. The WKY line shows several depressive-like traits in hormone systems, physiology, and behavior. They are hyper-reactive to stress and show dysre-gulation of the HPA axis (Czeh et al., 2016).

The Fawn Hooded (FH) rat strain was found to be highly immobile in the forced swim test and to voluntarily consume large amounts of ethanol and has therefore been considered as a model for comorbid depression and alcoholism (Overstreet, 2012). Antidepressant treatment reduces immobility in the FST but does not affect the alcohol consumption of FH rats.

The Learned Helplessness (LH) line of rats was selectively bred for over fifty generations based on performance in the Learned Helplessness paradigm, which is like the shock avoidance paradigm (see Box 9.5). Rats from the LH line freeze when presented with shock, rather than trying to avoid it. They also have a lower sucrose preference than other rats, which suggests the depression-like behavior anhedonia. Antidepressant drugs have been tested in LH rats (Overstreet, 2012).

Because it is possible to develop and maintain lines of rats that display depression-like behaviors, the biological basis of those traits is demonstrated. Such lines have been and continue to be used to test existing and identify novel antidepressant medications.

Depression-like behaviors can be induced in rodents in a variety of ways, many of which involve exposure to stressors. Such an approach has face validity because, in humans, an episode of depression can be triggered by exposure to life stresses and trauma, as we discussed previously. Stressors such as maternal deprivation, social isolation, social defeat, chronic foot-shock, and chronic restraint have all been shown to increase immobility times in the forced swim test, for example (Bogdanova, Kanekar, D'Anci, & Renshaw, 2013). It is possible then to examine potential differences in depression-like stress responses in animals from different inbred or selected strains.

A substantial amount of research has also been conducted using mice that have been genetically modified to either silence or enhance the expression of candidate genes (Cryan & Mombereau, 2004). Much of the work has focused on candidate genes that impact the function of neurotransmitter systems (e.g., serotonin transporter), the HPA axis (e.g., corticotropin releasing factor), and intracellular signaling and transcription factors (e.g., brain-derived neurotrophic factor).

Lines of mice with the serotonin transporter gene (*Slc6a4*) knocked out have been generated on different background strains (Barkus, 2013). As you recall, lines of mice are inbred and individuals within a given strain are considered genetically identical, whereas individuals from different strains are considered genetically different. Interestingly, the pattern of depression-like and anxiety-like behaviors for *Slc6a4* knockouts varied by background strain, which indicates that the effect of the gene is context dependent and that epistatic interactions play a role in individual differences in these traits. This pattern of results seems to be consistent with the genetic effects on depression found in human studies being of small effect size and moderated by a variety of demographic factors.

Because exposure to stress is a potent risk factor in depression, it is logical to hypothesize that a dysfunctional stress response may be involved in the development of depression. There are many components of the HPA axis that vary genetically in humans and could therefore play a role in individual differences in risk for depression (see Figure 9.11). The HPA axis and the sympathetic nervous system are activated in response to stressors, each playing roles to increase readiness to respond. Ideally, HPA axis activation should be initiated quickly in response to needs and then terminated. Dysfunctions in the HPA axis could include activation in response to inappropriate stimuli, over- or under-activation of the system, or response termination that is slow or incomplete.

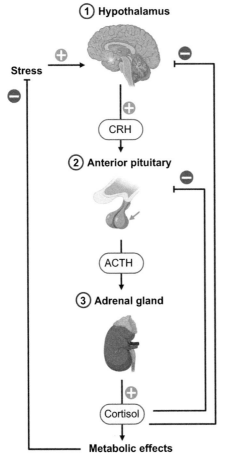

Figure 9.11. **Hypothalamic-Pituitary-Adrenal Axis.** The HPA axis involves the hypothalamus, the anterior pituitary, and the adrenal glands in a negative feedback system that is involved in the response to stress and the regulation of several metabolic processes. Source: Created with Biorender.com.

An important signaling molecule in the HPA axis is corticotropin releasing hormone (CRH), also known as corticotropin releasing factor (CRF). CRF is a 41-amino acid peptide that is released by neuroendocrine cells in the paraventricular nucleus of the hypothalamus and binds to CRF type 1 receptors (CRF1) expressed by cells in the anterior pituitary. The anterior pituitary cells then release adrenocorticotropic hormone (ACTH), which subsequently triggers the release of glucocorticoids from the adrenal cortex (cortisol in humans, corticosterone in rodents [Dedic, Chen, & Deussing, 2018]). CRF type 2 (CRF2) receptors share 70 percent of their amino acid sequence with CRF1 receptors and are involved in the stress response but have a different distribution in brain and peripheral tissues. Both are G-protein coupled receptors. CRF2 may be primarily involved in the regulation of HPA axis activation via negative feedback.

Lines of mice have been developed to target CRF signaling in a variety of ways. First, mice that have been engineered to overexpress CRF have reduced immobility in the forced swim test and reduced attention. However, these effects appear to be conditional on whether the overexpression is ubiquitous and occurs only in specific brain areas or in specific developmental stages (Dedic et al., 2018). Next, lines of mice have been engineered that have the gene that codes for CRF knocked out. Although these mice had reduced expression of glucocorticoids, which indicates that HPA axis function was compromised, they did not show alterations in depressive-like behavior. Third, knocking out the gene that codes for the CRF1 receptor appears to affect anxiety-like behavior, but not depression-like behavior. Finally, knocking out the gene that codes for the CRF2 receptor has not yet been shown to dramatically affect depression-like behavior.

Brain-derived neurotrophic factor (BDNF) promotes the maturation, development, and plasticity of neurons. Its structural gene harbors many variants, and one in particular, Val66Met (rs6265), has been widely studied because it produces an amino acid substitution that impacts protein function (Notaras, Hill, & van den Buuse, 2015). The rs6265 SNP has been considered a candidate gene for psychiatric disorders and other psychological traits, including depression, and aspects of brain morphology and function. A line of mice that carry the human Met allele of rs6265 (i.e., $BDNF_{Met}$ knock-in mouse) has been generated and used to investigate depression-like, and other relevant traits. This mouse model appears to have good face validity for a specific type of depression because the mice show elevated depression-like behaviors after seven days of restraint stress that are "rescued" by treatment with tricyclic antidepressant medications, but not selective serotonin reuptake inhibitors (Yu et al., 2012). Such non-human animal models of depression are critical tools in the quest to understand the genetic basis of depression and in the search for effective treatments.

Check-up

- Compare and contrast the forced swim test and the shock avoidance paradigm.
- Discuss the use of rat lines in testing potential antidepressant drugs.
- How might genetic differences impact HPA axis function?

9.9 SUMMARY

- Human beings have the capacity to feel many emotions and their capacity to report them is affected by culture and language. Emotions comprise physiological feelings and cognitive appraisals, and they prepare you for action. Darwin studied the expression of emotions in humans and in animals and observed similarities resulting from shared evolutionary history.

- Emotions are routinely measured in research using self-report questionnaires, physiological measures, brain activity measures, and behaviors. Each measure has advantages and disadvantages. Heritability estimates for behaviors that are depression-like have been estimated in twin studies at 0.48 and in GWAS at 0.10. The difference is termed missing heritability.
- Difficulties in regulating emotions may lead to emotional problems, which may become symptoms of mental illness. The process model of emotion regulation describes different stages of emotional experience where a person can intervene to attempt to alter the outcome. There is evidence that genetic differences between people play a role in individual differences in emotion regulation.
- Depressive disorders are relatively common and are a substantial burden worldwide. A diagnosis of major depressive disorder requires endorsement of depressed mood and/or diminished pleasure, as well as other symptoms that impact weight loss, sleep, movement, energy, feelings of guilt, attention and suicidal ideation or attempts. Substantial symptom heterogeneity means that many people with depression have different symptoms.
- Family studies, as well as twin studies have strongly demonstrated that genetic differences account for a significant amount of differential risk for depression. Heritability estimates for major depressive disorder are around 0.40.
- Candidate gene studies have focused on neurotransmitter system variants, but because of suboptimal study designs, it is difficult to draw conclusions from them. 5-HTTLPR is a variant in the serotonin transporter gene that has been widely studied for its potential moderation of stressful life experiences on depression risk. Replication studies and meta-analyses suggest that 5-HTTLPR genotype, when considered alone or in the context of life stress, does not affect risk for depression. GWAS has identified many loci with small effects to be associated with risk for depression. Polygenic risk scores may prove to be useful in predicting depression risk or treatment response.
- Many non-human animal models have been used to study the genetics of depression-like traits. Lines of rats have been identified or selected, and lines of mice have been engineered to study depression-like traits. Many of these models implicate components of the HPA axis and certain neurotransmitter systems in depression-like traits. Such lines are useful for testing potential antidepressant drugs.
- Manic episodes involve elevated moods, decreased need for sleep, talkativeness, racing thoughts, decreased attention, increased activity, and risky behaviors. Manic episodes can also involve psychotic symptoms. Bipolar disorder is less common than major depressive disorder, and has a heritability estimate of about 0.80. GWAS have identified genetic correlations among psychiatric disorders, which indicates that some genetic risk for mental illness may be general, rather than specific to a particular disorder.

RECOMMENDED READING

- Barrett, L. F. (2017). *How Emotions Are Made*. Boston: Houghton Mifflin Harcourt.
- Fried, E. I., & Nesse, R. M. (2015). Depression sum-scores don't add up: Why analyzing specific depression symptoms is essential. *BMC Med, 13*, 72. doi:10.1186/s12916-015-0325-4
- Jesulola, E., Micalos, P., & Baguley, I. J. (2018). Understanding the pathophysiology of depression: From monoamines to the neurogenesis hypothesis model – are we there yet? *Behav Brain Res, 341*, 79–90. doi:10.1016/j.bbr.2017.12.025
- Sanchez-Roige, S., & Palmer, A. A. (2020). Emerging phenotyping strategies will advance our understanding of psychiatric genetics. *Nat Neurosci, 23*, 475–480.

REFERENCES

APA (2013). *Diagnostic and Statistical Manual of Mental Disorders: DSM-5* (pp. 0-1). Washington, DC: American Psychiatric Association.

Avinun, R., Nevo, A., Knodt, A. R., Elliott, M. L., & Hariri, A. R. (2018). Replication in imaging genetics: The case of threat-related amygdala reactivity. *Biol Psychiatry*, *84*(2), 148–159. doi:10.1016/j.biopsych.2017.11.010

Barkus, C. (2013). Genetic mouse models of depression. *Curr Top Behav Neurosci*, *14*, 55–78. doi:10.1007/7854_2012_224

Barnett, J. H., & Smoller, J. W. (2009). The genetics of bipolar disorder. *Neuroscience*, *164*(1), 331–343. doi:10.1016/j.neuroscience.2009.03.080

Barzman, D., Geise, C., & Lin, P. I. (2015). Review of the genetic basis of emotion dysregulation in children and adolescents. *World J Psychiatry*, *5*(1), 112–117. doi:10.5498/wjp.v5.i1.112

Bogdanova, O. V., Kanekar, S., D'Anci, K. E., & Renshaw, P. F. (2013). Factors influencing behavior in the forced swim test. *Physiol Behav*, *118*, 227–239. doi:10.1016/j.physbeh.2013.05.012

Border, R., Johnson, E. C., Evans, L. M., Smolen, A., Berley, N., Sullivan, P. F., & Keller, M. C. (2019). No support for historical candidate gene or candidate gene-by-interaction hypotheses for major depression across multiple large samples. *Am J Psychiatry*, *176*(5), 376–387. doi:10.1176/appi.ajp.2018.18070881

Caspi, A., Sugden, K., Moffitt, T. E., Taylor, A., Craig, I. W., Harrington, H., . . . Poulton, R. (2003). Influence of life stress on depression: Moderation by a polymorphism in the 5-HTT gene. *Science*, *301*(5631), 386–389. doi:10.1126/science.1083968

Clemente, A. S., Diniz, B. S., Nicolato, R., Kapczinski, F. P., Soares, J. C., Firmo, J. O., & Castro-Costa, E. (2015). Bipolar disorder prevalence: A systematic review and meta-analysis of the literature. *Braz J Psychiatry*, *37*(2), 155–161. doi:10.1590/1516-4446-2012-1693

Compas, B. E., Jaser, S. S., Bettis, A. H., Watson, K. H., Gruhn, M. A., Dunbar, J. P., . . . Thigpen, J. C. (2017). Coping, emotion regulation, and psychopathology in childhood and adolescence: A meta-analysis and narrative review. *Psychol Bull*, *143*(9), 939–991. doi:10.1037/bul0000110

Cryan, J. F., & Mombereau, C. (2004). In search of a depressed mouse: Utility of models for studying depression-related behavior in genetically modified mice. *Mol Psychiatry*, *9*(4), 326–357. doi:10.1038/sj.mp.4001457

Culverhouse, R. C., Saccone, N. L., Horton, A. C., Ma, Y., Anstey, K. J., Banaschewski, T., . . . Bierut, L. J. (2018). Collaborative meta-analysis finds no evidence of a strong interaction between stress and 5-HTTLPR genotype contributing to the development of depression. *Mol Psychiatry*, *23*(1), 133–142. doi:10.1038/mp.2017.44

Czeh, B., Fuchs, E., Wiborg, O., & Simon, M. (2016). Animal models of major depression and their clinical implications. *Prog Neuropsychopharmacol Biol Psychiatry*, *64*, 293–310. doi:10.1016/j.pnpbp.2015.04.004

Darwin, C. (1872). *The Expression of Emotions in Man and Animals*. London: J. Murray.

Dedic, N., Chen, A., & Deussing, J. M. (2018). The CRF family of neuropeptides and their receptors: Mediators of the central stress response. *Curr Mol Pharmacol*, *11*(1), 4–31. doi:10.2174/1874467210666170302104053

Fried, E. I., & Nesse, R. M. (2015). Depression sum-scores don't add up: Why analyzing specific depression symptoms is essential. *BMC Med*, *13*, 72. doi:10.1186/s12916-015-0325-4

GBD (2016). Global, regional, and national incidence, prevalence, and years lived with disability for 310 diseases and injuries, 1990–2015: A systematic analysis for the Global Burden of Disease Study 2015. *Lancet*, *388*(10053), 1545–1602. doi:10.1016/s0140-6736(16)31678-6

Gelehrter, T. D., Collins, F. S., & Ginsburg, D. (1998). *Principles of Medical Genetics* (2nd ed.). Baltimore, MD: Williams & Wilkins.

Gross, J. J., & Jazaieri, H. (2014). Emotion, emotion regulation, and psychopathology: An affective science perspective. *Clin Psychol Sci, 2*(4), 387–401. doi:10.1177/2167702614536164

Gross, J. J., & Thompson, R. A. (2007). Emotion regulation: Conceptual foundations. In J. J. Gross (Ed.), *Handbook of Emotion Regulation* (pp. 3–24). New York: Guilford Press.

Hawn, S. E., Overstreet, C., Stewart, K. E., & Amstadter, A. B. (2015). Recent advances in the genetics of emotion regulation: A review. *Curr Opin Psychol, 3*, 108–116. doi:10.1016/j.copsyc.2014.12.014

Haxby, J. V., Hoffman, E. A., & Gobbini, M. I. (2002). Human neural systems for face recognition and social communication. *Biol Psychiatry, 51*(1), 59–67. doi:10.1016/s0006-3223(01)01330-0

Hirschfeld, R. M. (2000). History and evolution of the monoamine hypothesis of depression. *J Clin Psychiatry, 61*(Suppl 6), 4–6.

Howard, D. M., Adams, M. J., Clarke, T. K., Hafferty, J. D., Gibson, J., Shirali, M., . . . McIntosh, A. M. (2019). Genome-wide meta-analysis of depression identifies 102 independent variants and highlights the importance of the prefrontal brain regions. *Nat Neurosci, 22*(3), 343–352. doi:10.1038/s41593-018-0326-7

Jesulola, E., Micalos, P., & Baguley, I. J. (2018). Understanding the pathophysiology of depression: From monoamines to the neurogenesis hypothesis model – are we there yet? *Behav Brain Res, 341*, 79–90. doi:10.1016/j.bbr.2017.12.025

Lopez-Cortegano, E., & Caballero, A. (2019). Inferring the nature of missing heritability in human traits using data from the GWAS catalog. *Genetics, 212*(3), 891–904. doi:10.1534/genetics.119.302077

Mattavelli, G., Sormaz, M., Flack, T., Asghar, A. U. R., Fan, S., Frey, J., . . . Andrews, T. J. (2014). Neural responses to facial expressions support the role of the amygdala in processing threat. *Soc Cogn Affect Neurosci, 9*(11), 1684–1689. doi:10.1093/scan/nst162

Mauss, I. B., & Robinson, M. D. (2009). Measures of emotion: A review. *Cogn Emot, 23*(2), 209–237. doi:10.1080/02699930802204677

McIntosh, A. M., Sullivan, P. F., & Lewis, C. M. (2019). Uncovering the genetic architecture of major depression. *Neuron, 102*(1), 91–103. doi:10.1016/j.neuron.2019.03.022

Misiak, B., Stramecki, F., Gaweda, L., Prochwicz, K., Sasiadek, M. M., Moustafa, A. A., & Frydecka, D. (2018). Interactions between variation in candidate genes and environmental factors in the etiology of schizophrenia and bipolar disorder: A systematic review. *Mol Neurobiol, 55*(6), 5075–5100. doi:10.1007/s12035-017-0708-y

Mistry, S., Harrison, J. R., Smith, D. J., Escott-Price, V., & Zammit, S. (2018). The use of polygenic risk scores to identify phenotypes associated with genetic risk of bipolar disorder and depression: A systematic review. *J Affect Disord, 234*, 148–155. doi:10.1016/j.jad.2018.02.005

Notaras, M., Hill, R., & van den Buuse, M. (2015). The BDNF gene Val66Met polymorphism as a modifier of psychiatric disorder susceptibility: Progress and controversy. *Mol Psychiatry, 20*(8), 916–930. doi:10.1038/mp.2015.27

Okbay, A., Baselmans, B. M., De Neve, J. E., Turley, P., Nivard, M. G., Fontana, M. A., . . . Cesarini, D. (2016). Genetic variants associated with subjective well-being, depressive symptoms, and neuroticism identified through genome-wide analyses. *Nat Genet, 48*(6), 624–633. doi:10.1038/ng.3552

Overstreet, D. H. (2012). Modeling depression in animal models. *Methods Mol Biol, 829*, 125–144. doi:10.1007/978-1-61779-458-2_7

Polderman, T. J., Benyamin, B., de Leeuw, C. A., Sullivan, P. F., van Bochoven, A., Visscher, P. M., & Posthuma, D. (2015). Meta-analysis of the heritability of human traits based on fifty years of twin studies. *Nat Genet, 47*(7), 702–709. doi:10.1038/ng.3285

Porcelli, S., Fabbri, C., & Serretti, A. (2012). Meta-analysis of serotonin transporter gene promoter polymorphism (5-HTTLPR) association with antidepressant efficacy. *Eur Neuropsychopharmacol, 22*(4), 239–258. doi:10.1016/j.euroneuro.2011.10.003

Sallis, H., Davey Smith, G., & Munafo, M. R. (2018). Genetics of biologically based psychological differences. *Philos Trans R Soc Lond B Biol Sci, 373*(1744). doi:10.1098/rstb.2017.0162

SAMHSA (2019). *Key substance use and mental health indicators in the United States: Results from the 2018 National Survey on Drug Use and Health (HHS Publication No. PEP19–5068, NSDUH Series H-54)*. Rockville, MD.

Sanchez-Roige, S., Gray, J. C., MacKillop, J., Chen, C. H., & Palmer, A. A. (2018). The genetics of human personality. *Genes Brain Behav, 17*(3), e12439. doi:10.1111/gbb.12439

Schwabe, I., Milaneschi, Y., Gerring, Z., Sullivan, P. F., Schulte, E., Suppli, N. P., . . . Middeldorp, C. M. (2019). Unraveling the genetic architecture of major depressive disorder: Merits and pitfalls of the approaches used in genome-wide association studies. *Psychol Med, 49*(16), 2646–2656. doi:10.1017/s0033291719002502

Sheppes, G., Suri, G., & Gross, J. J. (2015). Emotion regulation and psychopathology. *Annu Rev Clin Psychol, 11*, 379–405. doi:10.1146/annurev-clinpsy-032814-112739

Shiota, M., & Kalat, J. (2017). *Emotion* (3rd ed.). Oxford: Oxford University Press.

Smoller, J. W. (2019). Genomic relationships, novel loci, and pleiotropic mechanisms across eight psychiatric disorders. *Cell, 179*(7), 1469–1482. doi:10.1016/j.cell.2019.11.020

Smoller, J. W., & Finn, C. T. (2003). Family, twin, and adoption studies of bipolar disorder. *Am J Med Genet C Semin Med Genet, 123c*(1), 48–58. doi:10.1002/ajmg.c.20013

Stahl, E. A., Breen, G., Forstner, A. J., McQuillin, A., Ripke, S., Trubetskoy, V., . . . Sklar, P. (2019). Genome-wide association study identifies 30 loci associated with bipolar disorder. *Nat Genet, 51*(5), 793–803. doi:10.1038/s41588-019-0397-8

Sullivan, P. F., Neale, M. C., & Kendler, K. S. (2000). Genetic epidemiology of major depression: Review and meta-analysis. *Am J Psychiatry, 157*(10), 1552–1562. doi:10.1176/appi.ajp.157.10.1552

Thompson, P. M., Stein, J. L., Medland, S. E., Hibar, D. P., Vasquez, A. A., Renteria, M. E., . . . Drevets, W. (2014). The ENIGMA Consortium: Large-scale collaborative analyses of neuroimaging and genetic data. *Brain Imaging Behav, 8*(2), 153–182. doi:10.1007/s11682-013-9269-5

van den Berg, S. M., de Moor, M. H., McGue, M., Pettersson, E., Terracciano, A., Verweij, K. J., . . . Boomsma, D. I. (2014). Harmonization of neuroticism and extraversion phenotypes across inventories and cohorts in the Genetics of Personality Consortium: An application of Item Response Theory. *Behav Genet, 44*(4), 295–313. doi:10.1007/s10519-014-9654-x

Wang, Q., Timberlake, M. A., Prall, K., & Dwivedi, Y. (2017). The recent progress in animal models of depression. *Prog Neuropsychopharmacol Biol Psychiatry, 77*, 99–109. doi:10.1016/j.pnpbp.2017.04.008

Ward, J., Tunbridge, E. M., Sandor, C., Lyall, L. M., Ferguson, A., Strawbridge, R. J., . . . Smith, D. J. (2020). The genomic basis of mood instability: Identification of 46 loci in 363,705 UK Biobank participants, genetic correlation with psychiatric disorders, and association with gene expression and function. *Mol Psychiatry, 25*(11), 3091–3099. doi:10.1038/s41380-019-0439-8

World Health Organization (2020a). Mood Disorders. ICD-11 for Mortality and Morbidity Statistics. http://id.who.int/icd/entity/76398729

World Health Organization (2020b). Bipolar type I disorder, current episode manic, without psychotic symptoms. ICD-11 for Mortality and Morbidity Statistics. http://id.who.int/icd/entity/374726152

World Health Organization (2020c). Depressive Disorders. ICD-11 for Mortality and Morbidity Statistics. http://id.who.int/icd/entity/1563440232

Wray, N. R., Lee, S. H., Mehta, D., Vinkhuyzen, A. A., Dudbridge, F., & Middeldorp, C. M. (2014). Research review: Polygenic methods and their application to psychiatric traits. *J Child Psychol Psychiatry, 55*(10), 1068–1087. doi:10.1111/jcpp.12295

Yu, H., Wang, D. D., Wang, Y., Liu, T., Lee, F. S., & Chen, Z. Y. (2012). Variant brain-derived neurotrophic factor Val66Met polymorphism alters vulnerability to stress and response to antidepressants. *J Neurosci, 32*(12), 4092–4101. doi:10.1523/jneurosci.5048-11.2012

Zhu, J., Klein-Fedyshin, M., & Stevenson, J. M. (2017). Serotonin transporter gene polymorphisms and selective serotonin reuptake inhibitor tolerability: Review of pharmacogenetic evidence. *Pharmacotherapy, 37*(9), 1089–1104. doi:10.1002/phar.1978

10 Fear and Anxiety

Imagine that you are about to give a presentation in front of an auditorium full of people. As you walk to the podium, what physical sensations do you feel? Is your heart pounding? Are your palms sweaty? Do you feel a bit nauseous? What are you thinking about? Are you concerned that you might forget what you are planning to say, or that people will evaluate you negatively? Although it is very common to have such feelings and thoughts at the prospect of speaking in public, there are individual differences such that some people experience few if any negative feelings and thoughts, while others may experience so many that they find it difficult to speak even to a few people. Most of us are somewhere in between (Figure 10.1).

In this chapter, we begin by defining the subjective experience of fear and anxiety, and discussing the biological systems that produce them. Next, we focus attention on the mouse model that has been instrumental in characterizing the relevant biological circuits. Then we discuss personality traits as potential phenotypes for genetic analysis, with a special focus on one that involves fear and anxiety, neuroticism. Finally, we present the current evidence for the role of genetic variation in risk for anxiety disorders, obsessive-compulsive disorder, and post-traumatic stress disorder (PTSD).

10.1 Fear and Anxiety Are Defensive Responses to Threats

Fear and anxiety are basic emotions that can enhance survival by facilitating the detection of and response to potential harm. Fear and anxiety are subjective mental states that are a product of physical feelings, behaviors, and thoughts (LeDoux & Pine, 2016). All animals face the potential for

Figure 10.1. **Public-speaking anxiety.** Most people experience anxiety about the prospect of speaking in front of a group. Source: uschools / E+ / Getty Images.

harm, and natural selection favors biological systems that can rapidly detect and effectively respond to threats. When the source of potential harm (i.e., the threat) is *nearby* or *imminent*, we typically use the term fear to describe the experienced subjective mental state. In contrast, when the threat is *distant*, in either space or time, or *uncertain*, we typically use the term anxiety to describe the experienced subjective mental state. With some exceptions, the subjective mental states of fear and anxiety are produced by the same biological systems, which can be referred to as defensive circuits, defensive behaviors, or defensive physiological adjustments (LeDoux & Pine, 2016).

10.1.1 Defensive Circuits Provide Information About Potential Threats

The defensive circuits involve sensory systems that project to the amygdala either directly (i.e., olfaction) or via the thalamus, and provide information about potential threats. The amygdala includes several anatomically distinct nuclei that receive inputs from and send outputs to various brain areas. The amygdala is a critical defensive circuit hub for getting information about threats and sending signals to generate defensive reactions (e.g., freezing or flight) and actions (e.g., escape or avoidance).

The hypothalamus gets input from the amygdala and plays an important role in initiating defensive physiological adjustments via the autonomic nervous system and the HPA axis. The autonomic nervous system enervates organs to govern the balance of sympathetic and parasympathetic activation. Sympathetic nervous system activation prepares the body for dealing with perceived threats by increasing heart rate, inhibiting digestion, increasing sweating, and so on (i.e., fight or flight). Parasympathetic nervous system activation conserves energy and enables the body to recuperate (i.e., rest and digest).

The hypothalamus also plays a critical role in controlling the body's endocrine system. In Chapter 9 we discussed the HPA axis and its role in responding to stress. If the immediate response to the threat has been effective, physiological adjustments involving the HPA axis may not be initiated. If the initial threat response did not eliminate the threat, the HPA axis may be activated to further mobilize bodily resources to enhance the response. The threat, whether actual or perceived, may be considered a stressor and the HPA axis can be considered part of the stress response system. Therefore, when an organism is experiencing stress, their defensive physiological adjustments have been initiated. Defensive physiological adjustments are terminated by activation of the parasympathetic nervous system and by inhibition of the HPA axis by negative feedback. Ideally, threat responses are occasional and brief. Repeated or chronic stress has deleterious effects on multiple physiological systems and is a risk factor for the development of cardiovascular and other diseases. When significant stressors are encountered early in life there is an increased risk for developing mental illness in adulthood, which is associated with HPA axis dysregulation (Hassell, Nguyen, Gates, & Lowry, 2019). From the perspective of behavior genetics, fear and anxiety represent important research targets. There are individual differences in many aspects of the defense response systems that underlie subjective feelings of fear and anxiety. Many biological systems are involved in threat response and each comprises multiple cellular and molecular components that vary genetically.

10.1.2 Certain Behaviors Are Associated with Fear and Anxiety

Fear and anxiety may produce different defensive behaviors. Defensive reactions associated with fear are likely to produce movement away from a specific life-threatening situation. The subjective mental state of fear is brief and phasic. Whereas defensive actions associated with anxiety may represent an approach–avoidance conflict and therefore may produce movement toward the threat, which may be uncertain or not well defined. The subjective mental state of anxiety may be long lasting. Such behavioral differences have been leveraged into the development of a variety of behavioral paradigms for investigating the underlying systems.

Investigators have used many different paradigms in humans and in non-human animal models to study fear and anxiety. Defensive reactions may be reflexive responses to an imminent threat and have been operationally defined in many ways such as a startle response to a strong, sudden stimulus (e.g., loud noise) or freezing in the presence of a predator (e.g., rats exposed to cats). You have probably noticed that there are individual differences in the magnitude of people's startle response. Some people respond to unexpected loud noises by visibly jumping whereas other people may not even flinch. Such differences can be assessed with the startle-blink and are likely due, at least in part, to genetic differences in components of the biological circuits involved in fear responses (Vaidyanathan, Malone, Miller, McGue, & Iacono, 2014).

Anxiety-like behavior is often assessed in mice by assaying exploratory behaviors, where time spent exploring is an inverse index of anxiety. In other words, more exploration is defined as less anxiety. Elevated mazes of various shapes with "open" and "closed" areas are commonly used to assess anxiety. The amount of time an individual spends in the open areas is considered exploratory and is therefore defined as less anxiety (see Figure 10.2). The light-dark box is a compartment with two sides, one side is illuminated and the other is not. An open door connects the two sides, and the mouse is free to spend its time in either compartment. More time spent in the lighted compartment and/or a higher number of transitions between the two compartments is considered exploratory and is defined as less anxiety. Several other assays have been developed to assess anxiety-like behavior in rodents (Campos, Fogaça, Aguiar, & Guimarães, 2013). One way that these paradigms have been tested for validity is by the administration of anxiolytic drugs, which decrease anxiety-like behavior in a dose dependent fashion.

Self-report questionnaires are commonly used to index fear and anxiety in humans. Self-report data can be collected in person or online, depending on the instrument. Details about a

(a) Elevated Zero Maze   (b) Light-Dark Box

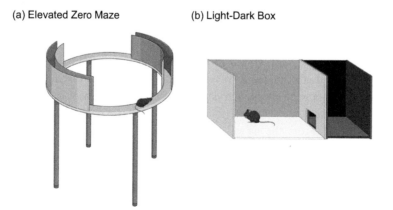

Figure 10.2. **Rodent assays for fear- and anxiety-like behavior.** Exploratory behavior in rodents is considered to reflect the inverse of anxiety-like behavior. Therefore, more exploration is equivalent to low levels of anxiety. (a) The elevated zero maze has sections where the circular track has walls (i.e., closed) and sections where it does not (i.e., open). Time spent in the open sections is an inverse index of anxiety. (b) The light-dark box has two connected compartments, one that is illuminated (i.e., light) and one that is not (i.e., dark). Time spent in the light side and/or the number of times the animal goes from the dark into the light side are indexes of anxiety (e.g., more time in the light side is interpreted as less anxiety). Source: Created with Biorender.com.

person's recent history of feeling fear and anxiety can be an important part of making a psychiatric diagnosis, or for phenotyping in a genetic study. In later sections of this chapter, we will discuss personality traits that are characterized by negative emotions such as fear and anxiety, as well as anxiety disorders and their symptoms.

Experimental methods can also be used to assess behaviors and physiology associated with fear and anxiety (Grillon, Robinson, Cornwell, & Ernst, 2019). Cognitive psychologists sometimes use methods that measure the time it takes to complete simple tasks (e.g., button press) after showing images on a computer screen that differ in their emotional content. If average reaction times are faster after the presentation of a threatening image (e.g., picture of a person with a gun) compared to a non-threatening image (e.g., puppy), the interpretation is that the person has an attention bias toward threat. Such a bias could facilitate the early identification of a threat and response to it, but could also be associated with increased levels of anxiety.

Anxiety can be generated in laboratory tasks when participants are instructed to anticipate the presentation of an aversive stimulus (e.g., electrical shock). Such an approach can be used to examine individual differences in self-reported anxiety or in physiological measures that index sympathetic nervous system activation such as heart rate, or electrodermal response (i.e., sweaty palms). It is beyond the scope of this chapter to review all the methods that have been used to investigate fear and anxiety; however, certain approaches will be described in more detail in later sections where appropriate.

Check-up

- Compare and contrast fear and anxiety.
- Describe the role of defensive circuits.
- What is the HPA axis and what is its role in response to stressors?
- Give examples of behavioral measures of (a) fear, and (b) anxiety.

10.2 The Genetics of Fear and Anxiety in Mice

Comparing the behavior of different inbred lines of mice is a common way to investigate the role of genetic differences in individual differences in behavior. Inbred strains of mice are considered genetically the same within strain, but genetically different between strains. When raised and tested in the same environmental conditions, consistent behavioral differences between the strains are attributed to the genetic differences between them. These strategies have been used extensively to investigate the genetics of fear and anxiety in mice.

10.2.1 Two Common Laboratory Mouse Strains Differ on Measures of Fear and Anxiety

The C57BL/6J line is one of the most used inbred laboratory strains in biomedical research and was derived from a line founded in 1921 (see Figure 10.3). It is well known to be a good breeder and was the first strain to have its genome sequence published. The BALB/cByJ line is another common laboratory strain that is derived from one established in 1913. A consistent finding is that mice from the C57BL/6J line show more exploratory behavior in most assays than do BALB/cByJ mice.

(a)

Figure 10.3. **Two mouse strains that differ on anxiety-like behaviors.** Strain comparisons on performance in the open field, the elevated plus maze, the light-dark box have consistently shown (a) BALB/cByJ mice to show more anxiety-like behaviors on average than (b) C57BL/6J mice. Source: Images copyright of The Jackson Laboratory 2020, used with permission.

(b)

In addition, whereas the anxiolytic drug diazepam increases exploratory behavior in mice from both strains, it does so at lower doses in the C57BL/6J mice (Lepicard, Joubert, Hagneau, Perez-Diaz, & Chapouthier, 2000). These findings provide evidence that genetic differences are associated with differences in anxiety-like behavior and suggests that genetic variation in the target of the drug diazepam may play a role.

10.2.2 Neurotransmitter Systems and the HPA Axis Are Involved in Fear and Anxiety Circuits

Diazepam is one of the many members of the synthetic anxiolytic drug class known as benzodiazepines (see Figure 10.4(a)). Benzodiazepines bind to $GABA_A$ receptors thereby potentiating inhibitory GABA neurotransmission by increasing the amount of time the channel is open to chloride ions (Cl^-). $GABA_A$ receptors comprise five subunits. In humans, there are 19 genes that code for different $GABA_A$ receptor subunits (α_{1-6}, β_{1-3}, γ_{1-3}, δ, ε, θ, π, and ρ_{1-3}) with coding genes located on chromosomes 4, 5, 15, and X (Sigel & Steinmann, 2012). Mature subunits are approximately 450 amino acids in length. The combination of subunits most found in mammalian $GABA_A$ receptors includes two α_1-subunits, two β_2-subunits, and one γ_2-subunit to form an integral membrane protein with intra- and extracellular domains.

Investigators have tested the impact of knocking out the structural genes for some of the $GABA_A$ receptor subunits on anxiety-like behaviors in mice (Scherma, Giunti, Fratta, & Fadda, 2019). Mice homozygous for a γ_2 knockout (i.e., γ_2 $GABA_A$ -/-) are non-viable, but those heterozygous for the knockout (i.e., +/-) show higher levels of anxiety-like behavior in the elevated plus maze and the light-dark box when compared to wild-type (i.e., +/+). In addition, the heterozygote knockout mice are insensitive to the anxiolytic effects of diazepam. Knocking out the gene for the α_1-subunit is not homozygous lethal, so comparisons of -/- and +/+ mice are possible. It appears that α_1 $GABA_A$ knockouts do not differ from wild-type on anxiety-like behavior or in sensitivity to

(a) diazepam

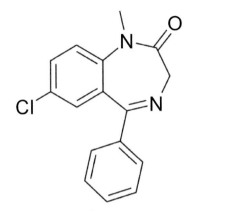

(b) GABA$_A$ receptor

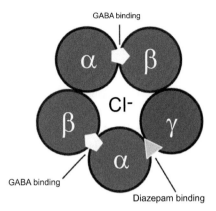

Figure 10.4. **Diazepam modulates GABA$_A$ receptors.** (a) Chemical structure of diazepam. (b) GABA$_A$ receptors comprise five subunits that form a chloride ion (Cl$^-$) pore. This view from above shows the most common structure in mammals includes two α-subunits, two β-subunits, and one γ-subunit. Note that the chemical structure of diazepam is not shown to scale with the receptor diagram. Source: National Center for Biotechnology Information. PubChem Database. Diazepam, CID=3016, https://pubchem.ncbi.nlm.nih.gov/compound/Diazepam (accessed May 11, 2020).

diazepam. However, α$_2$ GABA$_A$ knockouts show more anxiety-like behavior and are insensitive to the anxiolytic effects of diazepam. These and other studies show that genetic variation in genes that code for certain GABA A receptor subunits may contribute to individual differences in anxiety and in sensitivity to anxiolytic drugs.

Because selective serotonin reuptake inhibitors (SSRIs) can successfully treat anxiety disorders in humans, genes that code for serotonin system components are candidates for contributing to individual differences in anxiety-like phenotypes. Investigators have knocked out some serotonin system genes in mice and tested them for anxiety-like behavior. Specifically, mice that have had either the gene for the serotonin transporter (*Slc6a4*) or the 1A receptor (*Htr1a*) knocked out show increased anxiety-like behavior in multiple behavioral testing paradigms (Scherma et al., 2019). There is also evidence that increasing the expression of the *Htr1a* gene (i.e., producing more receptors) and the *Slc6a4* gene (i.e., producing more transporters) reduces anxiety-like behavior (Mohammad et al., 2016). The serotonin transporter protein mediates serotonin reuptake into the presynaptic neuron. It is the site of action of SSRIs. The serotonin 1A receptor plays an important role as an autoreceptor by regulating serotonin release. These and other studies indicate that the serotonin transporter and the Htr1a receptor play roles in anxiety-like behavior in the mouse.

Genes that code for components in the HPA axis have been knocked out to test their impact on anxiety-like behaviors in mice (Scherma et al., 2019). Three that have been investigated include the gene that codes for corticotropin releasing hormone (*Crh*), and two genes that code for its receptors (corticotropin releasing hormone receptors 1 and 2 [*Crhr1*, *Crhr2*]). Knocking out *Crh* does not appear to impact anxiety-like behavior in mice. However, mice with *Crhr1* knocked out appear to have *reduced* anxiety, compared to controls, in the elevated plus maze and in the light-dark box in addition to blunted HPA axis activation. Interestingly, mice with *Crhr2* knocked out appear to have *increased* anxiety-like behaviors, but no change in HPA axis activation. These and other results implicate components of the HPA axis in anxiety-like phenotypes in mice and appear to provide convergent evidence that the stress response system mediated by the HPA axis contains genetic variation that may play a role in naturally occurring individual differences in anxiety. Of course, such results do not exclude the involvement of other neural circuits and/or physiological systems in anxiety, but they do provide a starting point for further investigation (see also Box 10.1).

Check-up

- Describe the ways in which mice from the C57BL/6J line differ on measures of fear and anxiety from mice from the BALB/cByJ line.
- What is the evidence that the GABA neurotransmitter system plays a role in fear and anxiety?
- What is the evidence that the serotonin neurotransmitter system plays a role in fear and anxiety?
- What is *Crh* and what is the result when it is knocked out?

Box 10.1 Selection for Tameness in Silver Foxes

In 1959 Dmitry Belyaev started an experiment to selectively breed silver foxes (*Vulpes vulpes*) for tameness (Wang et al., 2018). The experiment continues at an experimental farm near the Institute of Cytology and Genetics in Novosibirsk, Russia, currently led by Lyudmila Trut. The foxes were farm-bred and initially selected for low levels of fear and aggression toward humans and later for contact-seeking behavior. In 1970 a separate line selected for aggression was established (see Figure 10.5(a)). Substantial response to selection was observed in both lines.

Of course, there are practical reasons for breeding animals raised for fur to be tame, but this study was designed to investigate domestication. Traits such as pigmentation changes (e.g., white spots), reduced facial skeleton (e.g., shortened snout), reduced tooth size, floppy ears, and other changes were identified by Charles Darwin as being associated with domestication (Wilkins, Wrangham, & Fitch, 2014). Belyaev was interested in whether selection for tameness would produce the suite of traits known as domestication syndrome. Within six generations of selection for tameness, some animals began to wag their tails when humans approached, licked their hands, and whined when they left (Dugatkin, 2018). In the tenth generation of selection for tameness, the first pup was born with floppy ears (Figure 10.5(b)).

Continued selection for tameness produced foxes with traits associated with domestication syndrome including floppy ears, curly tails, shorter and rounder facial features, and thicker limbs. Selection for tameness also produced foxes with higher serotonin levels, lower stress hormone (glucocorticoid) levels, and smaller adrenal glands than unselected foxes. Comparing patterns of gene expression in the brains of foxes from the tame selected line to those of foxes from the aggression selection line identified 146 genes in the prefrontal cortex and 33 genes in the basal forebrain that differed in their expression (Wang et al., 2018). Many of the differences were in the serotonin and glutamate neurotransmitter systems.

Selective breeding for behavior related to fear and anxiety produced foxes with domesticated genes, brains, and behaviors. This remarkable study supports the notion that modern, domesticated dogs are a product of selective breeding against fear and anxiety. Of course, such selection was unsystematic, but even weak selection pressure can produce changes in populations if it is practiced over many generations.

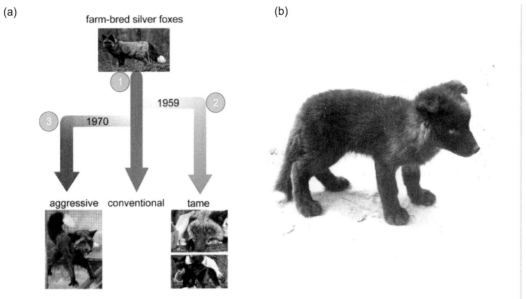

Figure 10.5. **Silver fox domestication study.** (a) The basic design of the study, producing three lines of silver foxes, (1) unselected and lines selected for (2) tameness and (3) aggression. (b) Mechta "Dream," born in 1969, was the first pup to be born with floppy ears. Source: Modified from Wang et al. (2018).

10.3 Anxiety-Related Personality Traits as Phenotypes for Genetic Analysis

One way that investigators have studied the role of genetic differences in individual differences in anxiety is to focus on the human personality trait of neuroticism. Personality traits are patterns of behavior (including thoughts and feelings) that are stable for a person over time and across situations. If you think about the people you know, you can probably easily think of someone who seems to worry a lot, and someone else who seems never to worry. Most people are somewhere in between those extremes.

10.3.1 Heritability Estimates for Anxiety-Related Personality Traits

Neuroticism is one of the personality traits in the so-called "Big Five": Openness to experience, Conscientiousness, Extraversion, Agreeableness, and Neuroticism (i.e., OCEAN). The scope of this book does not permit a review of personality theories and their history, but the interested reader is likely to find many comprehensive sources (e.g., Corr & Matthews, 2009). It should be noted that there are a variety of viable theories regarding the structure of human personality, but we focus on the Five Factor Model to keep things simple.

Neuroticism is the dimension of the Five Factor Model that captures a person's tendency to experience negative emotions such as anger, depression, and anxiety. For the most part, personality traits are assessed via self-report questionnaire (see Figure 10.6). Higher scores on a scale indicate higher levels of the construct. So, higher neuroticism scores indicate a greater tendency to experience negative emotions.

I see myself as someone who...					
	Strongly Disagree (1)	Disagree (2)	Neither disagree nor agree (3)	Agree (4)	Strongly Agree (5)
Is depressed, blue	O	O	O	O	O
Is relaxed, handles stress well*	O	O	O	O	O
Can be tense	O	O	O	O	O
Worries a lot	O	O	O	O	O
Is emotionally stable, not easily upset*	O	O	O	O	O
Can be moody	O	O	O	O	O
Remains calm in tense situations*	O	O	O	O	O
Gets nervous easily	O	O	O	O	O

Figure 10.6. **Self-report items from the Big Five Inventory.** A publicly available instrument to assess dimensions of the Five Factor Model is the Big Five Inventory (John & Srivastava, 1999), which can be found on the NIH funded website www.phenxtoolkit.org/. A person's neuroticism score is calculated by summing across their responses to nine items. Note: * identifies items that are reverse scored.

If you tend to be a worrier, you might have noticed that others in your family are anxious as well. Researchers in behavior genetics have long been interested in the role of heredity in individual differences in personality. Francis Galton (Galton, 1884) made it clear that "character, which shapes our conduct is a definite and durable 'something', and therefore it is reasonable to attempt to measure it." Galton also claimed to have evidence that character ran in families and was similar in twins.

More recently, a meta-analysis included sixty-two independent effect size estimates from studies investigating the heritability of personality traits (Vukasović & Bratko, 2015). The average effect sizes of personality traits that index anxiety were estimated to be 0.39 (95% CI = 0.34–0.43) for Eysenck's Neuroticism; 0.47 (0.43–0.51) for Tellegen's Negative emotionality, and 0.37 (0.28–0.47) for the Five Factor Model's neuroticism. So, there is consistency across estimates for three main personality measures providing evidence of genetic variation explaining about 40 percent of individual differences in anxiety-like personality traits.

10.3.2 Candidate Gene Association Studies and GWAS on Neuroticism

Based on findings from non-human animal models and other research, hundreds of candidate gene association studies have been conducted on personality traits, including neuroticism, since the late 1990s. As with other candidate gene association studies, those on personality should be considered with caution. It is clear now that personality traits, including neuroticism, are polygenic and that genetic variants contributing to differences in these traits each have a small effect. Many of the candidate gene association studies focused on commonly studied variants such as the 5-HTTLPR variant in the promoter region of the serotonin transporter gene (*SLC6A4*). Findings from large studies and meta-analyses appears to indicate that 5-HTTLPR genotype does not have a reliably strong effect on self-reported neuroticism scores and that the questionnaire used to measure it may make a difference (Munafò et al., 2009). It remains to be determined whether genetic variation in the serotonin transporter gene contributes to anxiety-related traits in humans, although it is clear that none of the common genetic variants in the serotonin system have large effects on anxiety as observed in *Htr1a* and *Slc6a4* knockouts in mice.

Several GWAS have sought to identify genetic variants associated with neuroticism. A meta-analysis with a combined sample size of N = 449,484 identified 136 variants that were significantly associated with neuroticism explaining 10 percent (h^2_{SNP}) of variance in the trait (Nagel et al., 2018). The associated genetic variants are expressed in several brain regions and in different cell types including serotonergic neurons, dopaminergic neuroblasts, and medium spiny neurons. In addition, two variants in the gene that codes for the corticotrophin hormone receptor (*CRHR1*) were found to be associated with neuroticism. GWAS studies such as this make it clear that individual differences in traits such as anxiety are clearly impacted by genetic differences between people, and that some of the specific candidate genes studied previously may have provided some convergent evidence of the involvement of their biological system.

Overall, there is strong evidence that heredity plays a role in individual differences in neuroticism. Candidate gene association studies and GWAS have supported the findings from mouse knockout studies that genetic variants in the serotonin system and the HPA axis stress response system likely play a role in individual differences in neuroticism. However, the search for genetic variants is not complete and it appears that neuroticism is a classic polygenic trait where hundreds of variants (or more) each contribute a small effect. Using quantitative traits like neuroticism rather than categorical psychiatric disorder diagnoses is consistent with the NIMH's Research Domain Criteria and with the concept of endophenotypes, which we have previously discussed.

Check-up

- What does it mean that heritability estimates for neuroticism are significantly non-zero?
- Summarize what is known about specific genetic variants playing a role in individual differences in neuroticism.

10.4 Anxiety Disorders Are Common

When a person experiences anxiety that is persistent or reaches levels that interfere with social interactions, school, work, or other responsibilities they may meet diagnostic criteria for an anxiety disorder. Epidemiological studies estimate that about 33 percent of people will experience an anxiety disorder at some time in their lives (Bandelow & Michaelis, 2015).

10.4.1 Anxiety Disorder Prevalence

Both the ICD-11 (WHO, 2020a) and the DSM-5 (APA, 2013) recognize seven main types of anxiety disorders: (1) generalized anxiety disorder, (2) panic disorder, (3) agoraphobia, (4) specific phobia, (5) social anxiety disorder, (6) separation anxiety disorder, and (7) selective mutism. See Box 10.2 for ICD-11 descriptions of anxiety or fear-related disorders, and generalized anxiety disorder, for example. It should be noted that studies will sometimes report a combined category

Box 10.2 ICD-11 Diagnosis: Anxiety or Fear-Related Disorders

Anxiety and fear-related disorders are characterised by excessive fear and anxiety and related behavioural disturbances, with symptoms that are severe enough to result in significant distress or significant impairment in personal, family, social, educational, occupational, or other important areas of functioning. Fear and anxiety are closely related phenomena; fear represents a reaction to perceived imminent threat in the present, whereas anxiety is more future-oriented, referring to perceived anticipated threat. A key differentiating feature among the Anxiety and fear-related disorders are disorder-specific foci of apprehension, that is, the stimulus or situation that triggers the fear or anxiety. The clinical presentation of Anxiety and fear-related disorders typically includes specific associated cognitions that can assist in differentiating among the disorders by clarifying the focus of apprehension.

Generalised Anxiety Disorder

Generalised anxiety disorder is characterised by marked symptoms of anxiety that persist for at least several months, for more days than not, manifested by either general apprehension (i.e., 'free-floating anxiety') or excessive worry focused on multiple everyday events, most often concerning family, health, finances, and school or work, together with additional symptoms such as muscular tension or motor restlessness, sympathetic autonomic overactivity, subjective experience of nervousness, difficulty maintaining concentration, irritability, or sleep disturbance. The symptoms result in significant distress or significant impairment in personal, family, social, educational, occupational, or other important areas of functioning. The symptoms are not a manifestation of another health condition and are not due to the effects of a substance or medication on the central nervous system.

Source: http://id.who.int/icd/entity/1336943699,   and   http://id.who.int/icd/entity/1712535455 (accessed February 26, 2021), World Health Organization (Copyright © 2020a).

called "anxiety disorders" that includes data from anyone who met diagnosis for any anxiety disorder. Such a "lumping" strategy could have implications for understanding the role of genetic variation in individual differences in risk for anxiety disorders.

It is estimated that around 264 million people worldwide meet diagnostic criteria for an anxiety disorder (GBD, 2016). According to the World Health Organization, the prevalence of anxiety disorders ranges from 10 percent in the African Region to 23 percent in the South-East Asia Region (see Figure 10.7). Females have a higher prevalence of anxiety disorders than males in every WHO region and in every age group. Such demographic differences are due to some combination of biological and environmental sources.

Check-up

- Describe the prevalence of anxiety disorders.
- What is "free-floating anxiety" and what role might it play in the diagnosis of generalized anxiety disorder?

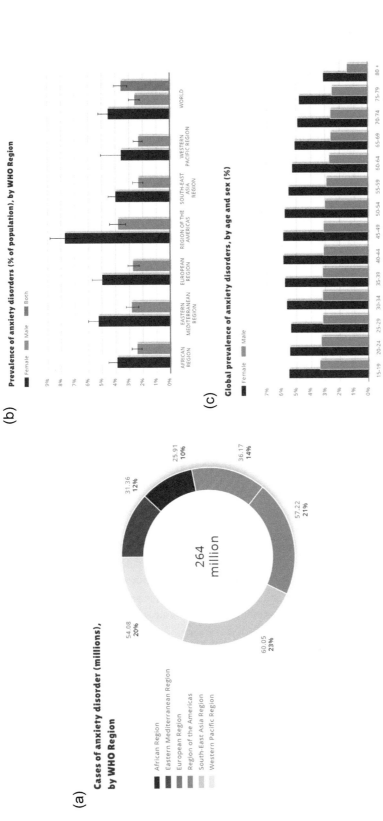

Figure 10.7. **Prevalence of anxiety disorders around the world as well as sex and age differences.** (a) An estimated 264 million people have an anxiety disorder worldwide. Prevalence rates vary across World Health Organization regions. (b) Females have a higher prevalence rate of anxiety disorders in each of the WHO regions. (c) Females have higher prevalence rate of anxiety disorders than males in each age category. Source: Hannah Ritchie and Max Roser (2018) "Mental Health." Published online at OurWorldInData.org. Retrieved from: https://ourworldindata.org/mental-health [Online Resource].

(a)

Cases of anxiety disorder (millions), by WHO Region

54.08
20%

31.36
12%

25.91
10%

36.17
14%

264 million

57.22
21%

60.05
23%

- African Region
- Eastern Mediterranean Region
- European Region
- Region of the Americas
- South-East Asia Region
- Western Pacific Region

(b)

Prevalence of anxiety disorders (% of population), by WHO Region

■ Female ■ Male ■ Both

9%
8%
7%
6%
5%
4%
3%
2%
1%
0%

AFRICAN REGION   EASTERN MEDITERRANEAN REGION   EUROPEAN REGION   REGION OF THE AMERICAS   SOUTH-EAST ASIA REGION   WESTERN PACIFIC REGION   WORLD

(c)

Global prevalence of anxiety disorders, by age and sex (%)

■ Female ■ Male

7%
6%
5%
4%
3%
2%
1%
0%

15-19 20-24 25-29 30-34 35-39 40-44 45-49 50-54 55-59 60-64 65-69 70-74 75-79 80 +

Source: Global Burden of Disease Study 2015 (http://ghdx.healthdata.org/gbd-results-tool)
Regional data shown are age-standardized estimates.

10.5 Anxiety Disorders Run in Families and Are Polygenic

Anxiety disorders run in families. Having a first-degree relative (i.e., one that shares 50 percent of genes) with an anxiety disorder increases a proband's risk for developing that same anxiety disorder about 4–6 times compared to someone without an affected first-degree relative (Hettema, Neale, & Kendler, 2001). For example, having a first-degree relative with panic disorder increases the risk of developing panic disorder for a proband by a factor of 5 (i.e., odds ratio = 5.0, 95% CI = 3.0 8.2). A similar pattern of familial aggregation is also seen for other anxiety disorders. Furthermore, having family members who has *any* anxiety disorder increases the risk for the development of any anxiety disorder in probands compared to those without an affected relative. Such a pattern of familiality is consistent with the notion that diagnostic categories may not represent distinct biological entities.

10.5.1 Anxiety Disorder Heritability Estimates

Heritability estimates of anxiety disorders are typically around 0.30–0.50. For generalized anxiety disorder, a meta-analysis that included two large twin studies and a somewhat smaller one estimated heritability to be 0.316 (95% CI = 0.24–0.39; [Hettema et al., 2001]). Additionally, in the same meta-analysis the heritability of panic disorder was estimated to be 0.48 (95% CI = 0.41–0.54). These estimates are in the same ballpark as seen for specific phobias for animals (0.45) and blood-injury-injection (0.33; [Van Houtem et al., 2013]). Taken together, there is good evidence that genetic similarity is associated with phenotypic similarity for anxiety disorder diagnosis. In other words, genetic variation explains a significant amount of population variation in risk for anxiety disorders. These data also support the notion that there is no single gene that causes anxiety disorders and that non-genetic factors (i.e., environment) also play a significant role in anxiety disorder risk.

10.5.2 Candidate Gene Association Studies of Anxiety Disorders

Non-human animal models and our understanding of the biological systems involved in anxiety have provided researchers with some obvious candidate genes to test for association with anxiety disorders. As with all candidate gene association test study results, these findings need to be considered in the context of the general limitations of such studies. However, it is unlikely that all candidate association study results are wrong. Although it is not clear which may be correct, those that are convergent with findings from other study designs should be understood as contributing to existing evidence. In the case of anxiety disorders, it makes sense to examine the findings for genes involved in GABAergic and serotonergic neurotransmission and those involved in HPA axis activation.

Relatively few candidate gene association studies for specific anxiety disorders have been reported that test variants in the GABA neurotransmitter system (Lacerda-Pinheiro et al., 2014). Although it is clear that anxiolytic drugs bind to $GABA_A$ receptors and that knocking out some $GABA_A$ receptor subunit genes affects anxiety-like behavior in mice, genetic variation in those receptors may not substantially increase risk for the development of anxiety disorders in humans.

There have been some candidate gene association studies for anxiety disorders to report significant associations with variants in the serotonin transporter gene (*SLC6A4*), the serotonin 1A receptor (*HTR1A*), and monoamine oxidase A (*MAOA*) (Gottschalk & Domschke, 2017). Other studies have examined potential moderators of some of these associations that include other genes (e.g., *BDNF*) or experiences (e.g., childhood trauma).

Genes that code for components of the HPA axis are obvious candidate genes for anxiety disorders. There is some evidence that genetic variation in the corticotrophin releasing hormone receptor (*CRHR1*) is associated with risk for the development of panic disorder (Weber et al., 2016). In addition, the gene that codes for a protein that is critical in the regulation of the HPA axis response, *FKBP5*, plays a role in anxiety-like behaviors in mice, and may be associated with risk for anxiety and mood disorders when coupled with early-life stress in humans (Jabbi & Nemeroff, 2019).

It is important to note that evidence that converges across species and measurement paradigms should carry more weight than findings that do not. It is also important that findings be replicated, and candidate gene association study findings for anxiety disorders, such as panic disorder, have not been (Howe et al., 2016).

10.5.3 GWAS of Anxiety Disorders

Genome-wide association studies have identified several loci to be associated with anxiety disorder phenotypes that converge on data from other sources. One study tested associations with two anxiety disorder-related phenotypes and over 700,000 SNPs in more than 200,000 participants (Levey et al., 2020). The participants are part of the Million Veteran Program (MVP), which has been ongoing since 2011, and is focused on understanding how genes, lifestyle, and military exposures affect health and illness for US military veterans.

Such large sample sizes make it possible to detect relatively small genetic effects. However, they also pose phenotyping challenges. In the MVP study, two self-report anxiety disorder-related phenotypes were tested: quantitative score on a two-item questionnaire that assessed frequency in last two weeks of (1) feeling nervous anxious or on edge and (2) inability to control worrying. Both items were rated on a 4-point Likert scale where 0 is "not at all" and 3 is "nearly every day." Each participant's responses to the two items were summed together for a score that could range from 0 to 6 that indexed recent anxiety levels. In addition, participants were asked whether they had been diagnosed with an anxiety disorder to create a categorical variable (i.e., yes [cases] or no [controls]). Although scale scores based on two items are not necessarily the best way to assess anxiety, and self-report of a diagnosis is not as good as an actual diagnostic interview, the investigators made efforts to collect both quantitative and qualitative measures relevant to anxiety disorders. Such a tradeoff between sample size and careful phenotyping can be one of the limitations of the current GWAS era in behavior genetics.

It is important to note that quantitative scores do not always approximate normal distributions. Positively skewed distributions are often seen for items that reflect symptom counts. In such cases, most people experience few or no symptoms. Statisticians have provided tools that should be used to analyze data with distributions that depart from normality (e.g., data transformations). In addition, statistical analyses typically attempt to control for variability that may be associated with the outcome of interest but is not the focus of the current analysis. Demographic variables such as age, sex, and race/ethnicity are often statistically controlled in behavior genetic analyses to better identify differences that are due to genetic variants. Figure 10.8 shows that the distribution of scores on the two-item anxiety assessment has a positive skew, and the distributions of scores for European Americans and African Americans are similar, but not the same. Although such considerations are beyond the scope of this book, anyone who analyzes data should use the analyses best suited to the data.

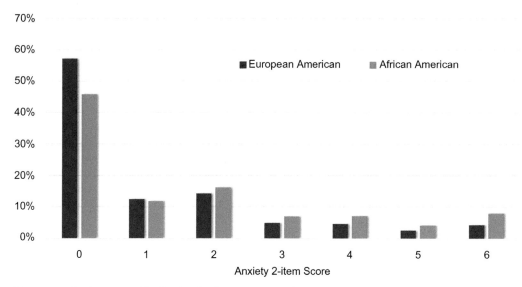

Figure 10.8. **Anxiety score distribution for European American and African American veterans.** Scores comprised responses to two items assessing levels of worry and anxiety in the last two weeks for European Americans (n = 175,163) and African Americans (n = 24,448) in the MVP study. Source: Levey et al. (2020).

Six loci were associated with the two-item anxiety score after controlling for multiple comparisons, one in the African American sample and five in the European American sample. Three of the significant associations in European Americans are with genetic variants in or near genes that impact pathways that are known to play a role in anxiety. The first is a SNP located near *SATB1*, which is a gene that codes for a transcription factor known to regulate expression of the gene that codes for corticotropin releasing hormone (CRH). The second significant association is in an intron of the estrogen receptor *ESR1*. Knocking out the mouse ortholog of this gene produces anxiety-like behavior. In addition, genetic differences in a receptor for a sex hormone may help to explain the sex differences in the prevalence of anxiety disorders. The third significant association is located near *MAD1L1*, which is a gene that had been implicated in earlier studies of bipolar disorder and schizophrenia, and again suggests that diagnoses do not reflect underlying biology.

Overall, individual differences in anxiety and in risk for anxiety disorders are at least in part due to genetic differences between people. Non-human animal models have been instrumental in characterizing the biological circuits involved in fear and anxiety and continue to play a role because of their advantages as experimental models including the tools for genetic engineering. Anxiety disorders run in families and have moderate heritability estimates. Candidate gene association studies have, in some cases, supported findings from non-human animal models. GWAS are in the early stages but have begun to identify genetic variants associated with anxiety and risk for anxiety disorders.

Check-up

- What is the evidence that anxiety disorders run in families?
- Which genes have been studied as candidates for anxiety disorders?
- Describe the Million Veteran Program and what it has contributed to the understanding of the genetics of anxiety disorders.

10.6 Obsessive-Compulsive and Related Disorders

Another category of disorders that has a connection with anxiety is the obsessive-compulsive or related disorders. These disorders are conceptually connected by the performance of compulsive behaviors that may be done to prevent or reduce anxiety. They include (1) obsessive-compulsive disorder, (2) body dysmorphic disorder, (3) olfactory reference disorder, (4) hypochondriasis, (5) hording disorder, (6) body-focused repetitive behavior disorders (WHO, 2020b; see Box 10.3).

Box 10.3 ICD-11 Diagnosis: Obsessive-Compulsive or Related Disorders

Obsessive-compulsive and related disorders is a group of disorders characterised by repetitive thoughts and behaviours that are believed to share similarities in aetiology and key diagnostic validators. Cognitive phenomena such as obsessions, intrusive thoughts and preoccupations are central to a subset of these conditions (i.e., obsessive-compulsive disorder, body dysmorphic disorder, hypochondriasis, and olfactory reference disorder) and are accompanied by related repetitive behaviours. Hoarding disorder is not associated with intrusive unwanted thoughts but rather is characterised by a compulsive need to accumulate possessions and distress related to discarding them. Also included in the grouping are body-focused repetitive behaviour disorders, which are primarily characterised by recurrent and habitual actions directed at the integument (e.g., hair-pulling, skin-picking) and lack a prominent cognitive aspect. The symptoms result in significant distress or significant impairment in personal, family, social, educational, occupational, or other important areas of functioning.

Obsessive-Compulsive Disorder

Obsessive-Compulsive Disorder is characterised by the presence of persistent obsessions or compulsions, or most commonly both. Obsessions are repetitive and persistent thoughts, images, or impulses/urges that are intrusive, unwanted, and are commonly associated with anxiety. The individual attempts to ignore or suppress obsessions or to neutralize them by performing compulsions. Compulsions are repetitive behaviours including repetitive mental acts that the individual feels driven to perform in response to an obsession, according to rigid rules, or to achieve a sense of 'completeness'. In order for obsessive-compulsive disorder to be diagnosed, obsessions and compulsions must be time consuming (e.g., taking more than an hour per day) or result in significant distress or significant impairment in personal, family, social, educational, occupational or other important areas of functioning.

Source: http://id.who.int/icd/entity/1321276661, and http://id.who.int/icd/entity/1582741816 (accessed February 26, 2021), World Health Organization (Copyright © 2020b).

10.6.1 OCD in Families

There is strong evidence that OCD runs in families (Pauls, Abramovitch, Rauch, & Geller, 2014). Relatives of people who are diagnosed with OCD have a substantially greater risk of developing OCD than do relatives of people who do not have an OCD diagnosis (see Figure 10.9). These data are consistent with the hypothesis that genetic variation is associated with individual differences in

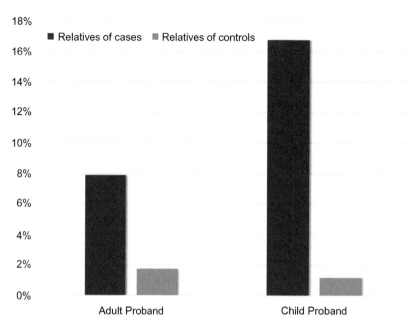

Figure 10.9. **Obsessive-compulsive disorder runs in families.** Relatives of people who have been diagnosed with OCD (i.e., probands) are at greater risk for being diagnosed with OCD than relatives of controls (i.e., those without OCD). Findings from six studies with probands diagnosed as adults show that 8% of their relatives are affected. Findings from three studies with probands diagnosed as children show that 17% of their relatives are affected. Therefore, OCD runs in families and the effect is stronger in those families with earlier age of onset. Source: Data from Pauls et al. (2014).

OCD risk. In addition, when the results of family studies are split into those that have probands that were diagnosed as adults and those that have probands that were diagnosed as children an important pattern emerges. Families in which the onset of OCD in the proband is in childhood have a higher frequency of OCD when compared to families in which the onset of OCD in the proband is in adulthood. This pattern suggests that childhood onset OCD may be an indicator of higher genetic risk. In other words, families with early onset OCD may carry more OCD risk alleles than families with later onset. A similar pattern is seen in other disorders, such as Alzheimer disease where the early onset form is inherited in a Mendelian pattern and caused by single gene mutations, and the late onset form does not run in families and is thought to be polygenic. In general, it seems that early onset forms of disorders may represent stronger genetic influence than later onset disorders.

Many twin studies have been conducted to estimate the heritability of OCD. A meta-analysis of the data from 37 samples of twins from 14 different studies estimated the heritability of OCD to be 0.41 (99% CI: 0.35–0.46; [Taylor, 2011]). The bottom line is that findings from twin studies are consistent with the findings from family studies that heredity is likely to play an important role in the development of OCD.

10.6.2 OCD Candidate Genes and GWAS

Hundreds of candidate gene association studies have been conducted on OCD. As with most candidate gene association studies in behavior genetics, the focus has mostly been on genetic variants in neurotransmitter systems. Meta-analyses of these studies have identified a small number of genetic variants that appear to confer risk for OCD (Taylor, 2013). Two variants in serotonin system genes (*SLC6A4* [5-HTTLPR+rs25531] and *HTR2A* [rs6311 or rs6313]) were associated with

OCD. Two other variants only showed association with OCD in males (*COMT* [rs4680] and *MAO* [rs1337070]). Another meta-analysis further investigated the sex specificity of the COMT rs4680 finding, and replicated that the A allele, which substitutes a methionine for a valine at amino acid position 158 is associated with increased risk for OCD in males only (Kumar & Rai, 2020).

Combining the data from several studies in a meta-analysis can produce large sample sizes, which can help to identify genetic effects that are too weak to detect in small studies. Although it is important not to over interpret these findings, we can have more confidence in them if they converge with studies using other designs. It is fair to say that genetic variation in neurotransmitter systems such as serotonin and dopamine remains of interest to researchers seeking to understand the role of genetic differences in individual differences in risk for OCD.

Although GWAS efforts are underway to identify loci associated with risk for developing OCD, none have reported finding significant associations that survive correction for multiple comparisons when using the diagnosis (Arnold, 2018) or a quantitative self-report of compulsive symptoms (Smit et al., 2020). Undoubtedly, consortia will continue to collaborate and produce GWAS with even larger sample sizes. The convergence of evidence is clear that while heredity is involved in risk for developing OCD, no single genes have been identified that confer large effects. In addition, some of the genes that impact OCD risk may be dependent on context, such as sex, certain environments (i.e., G×E interaction), or the presence of other alleles (i.e., G×G interaction, aka epistasis).

10.6.3 Knockout Mice to Model OCD

Mouse models of OCD are likely to provide researchers with the tools to understand at least some aspects of the biology underlying the disorder (Ahmari, 2016). Of course, we cannot ask mice to self-report on whether they experience obsessions, so compulsive behaviors are the targets of non-human animal studies. Mice will spontaneously engage in behaviors such as repetitive hair biting or pulling, repetitive licking, and pacing around cages that appear to model compulsions. These stereotyped behaviors appear purposeless and can sometimes perseverate to the point of injury. Researchers have also identified other behaviors such as shredding of nest material, digging, chewing on screens, and burying marbles that may serve as models of compulsive behavior.

To date, three lines of knockout mice have been developed that display some compulsive-like behaviors (Ahmari, 2016). Homeobox b8 (*Hoxb8*) is a gene that encodes a transcription factor. In mice it is located on chromosome 11, and in humans its ortholog is located on chromosome 17. When *Hoxb8* is knocked out in mice they harm themselves by grooming excessively, and continue to do so even after significant injury.

This pattern of self-injurious behavior is also seen when the gene *Sapap3* is knocked out in mice (see Figure 10.10). This gene encodes a protein thought to play a role in communication in excitatory postsynaptic neurons (Welch et al., 2007). *Sapap3* is located on chromosome 4 in mice, and its ortholog is located on chromosome 1 in humans. When it is knocked out in mice, they exhibit excessive grooming and show high levels of anxiety in the elevated zero maze, compared to wild-type mice. Both behaviors are alleviated by treatment with a selective serotonin reuptake inhibitor.

When the gene *Slitrk5* is knocked out in mice, they exhibit excessive grooming as seen in the other mouse models, as well as increased anxiety-like behaviors. The protein encoded by Slitrk5 appears to play a role in neurogenesis and synapse formation. Its structural gene is located on chromosome 14 in mice, and its ortholog is located on chromosome 13 in humans.

Mouse models, such as these, will continue to play an important role in investigating the neurobiology of OCD. Dogs provide another non-human animal model to study the neurobiology of

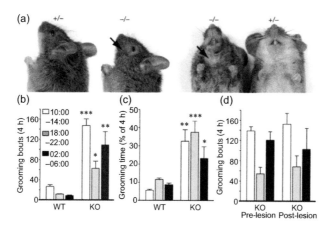

Figure 10.10. **Self-destructive grooming behavior of *Sapap3* knockouts.** (a) Mice heterozygous (+/-) and homozygous (-/-) for the *Sapap3* knockout are shown. Facial injuries (see arrow) are the result of repetitive self-grooming in the -/- mice. (b) Knockout homozygotes (KO) spend more time grooming at each observation time than wild-type mice (WT) and even continue grooming after the appearance of facial lesions. Source: Welch et al. (2007). Reprinted by permission from Springer Nature, Nature.

fear and anxiety (Zapata, Serpell, & Alvarez, 2016). Although some of the experimental methods available in mice, such as genetic engineering, are not available in dogs, the canine genome has been mapped and they can provide more evidence that may converge on genes of interest.

Check-up

- What are the diagnostic features of OCD?
- What do family and twin studies tell us about the role of genetic variation in individual differences in OCD risk?
- Discuss the evidence from candidate gene association studies and GWAS for specific genetic variants associated with OCD.
- What is self-destructive grooming behavior and how does it reflect OCD symptoms?

10.7 Trauma- and Stressor-Related Disorders

Another category of disorders that has a connection with anxiety is Disorders Specifically Associated with Stress (see Box 10.4). These disorders are conceptually connected in that they all develop after exposure to neglect, deprivation, exposure to real or threatened traumatic events, or some other stressor.

Box 10.4 ICD-11 Diagnosis: Disorders Specifically Associated with Stress

Disorders specifically associated with stress are directly related to exposure to a stressful or traumatic event, or a series of such events or adverse experiences. For each of the disorders in this grouping, an identifiable stressor is a necessary, though not sufficient, causal factor. Although not all individuals exposed to an identified stressor will develop a disorder, the disorders in this grouping would not have occurred without experiencing the stressor. Stressful events for some disorders in this grouping are within the normal range of life experiences (e.g., divorce, socio-economic problems, bereavement). Other disorders require the experience of a stressor of an extremely threatening or horrific nature (i.e., potentially traumatic events). With all disorders in this grouping, it is the nature, pattern, and duration of the symptoms that arise in response to the stressful events – together with associated functional impairment – that distinguishes the disorders.

Post Traumatic Stress Disorder

Post-traumatic stress disorder may develop following exposure to an extremely threatening or horrific event or series of events. It is characterised by all of the following: 1) re-experiencing the traumatic event or events in the present in the form of vivid intrusive memories, flashbacks, or nightmares. Re-experiencing may occur via one or multiple sensory modalities and is typically accompanied by strong or overwhelming emotions, particularly fear or horror, and strong physical sensations; 2) avoidance of thoughts and memories of the event or events, or avoidance of activities, situations, or people reminiscent of the event(s); and 3) persistent perceptions of heightened current threat, for example as indicated by hypervigilance or an enhanced startle reaction to stimuli such as unexpected noises. The symptoms persist for at least several weeks and cause significant impairment in personal, family, social, educational, occupational or other important areas of functioning.

Source: http://id.who.int/icd/entity/991786158, and http://id.who.int/icd/entity/2070699808 (accessed February 26, 2021), World Health Organization (Copyright © 2020c).

10.7.1 Prevalence and DSM-5 Diagnosis of PTSD

Post-traumatic stress disorder is the most common and most studied of these disorders, so we will focus on it. The lifetime prevalence of PTSD is approximately 7 percent of trauma-exposed adults. Many people experience traumatic events in their lives, but only some develop PTSD (see Figure 10.11). In a very real sense, the search for genetic variants that increase risk for PTSD will also reveal genetic variants that protect against its development. The alleles associated with protection from PTSD (i.e., resilience) will be the alternative alleles to the PTSD risk alleles.

10.7.2 Family and Twin Studies of PTSD

Because the development of PTSD requires exposure to trauma, it is challenging to determine whether it runs in families. Family members of a proband with PTSD may not be exposed to a trauma, so it is not possible to determine their risk. However, in the few family studies that have tested whether PTSD is hereditary, there is some evidence that relatives of a proband have a somewhat higher risk of a PTSD diagnosis compared to relatives of a control person without PTSD (Smoller, 2016).

Twin studies compare the risk of PTSD in co-twins of an affected proband across monozygotic (MZ) and dizygotic (DZ) twin pairs. Because MZ twins share 100 percent of their genetic material and DZ twins share only 50 percent of their genetic material, on average, greater

Figure 10.11. **Witnessing trauma**. First responders indirectly experience trauma on a regular basis and are at elevated risk for developing PTSD. Source: vm / E+ / Getty Images.

phenotypic similarity in MZ compared to DZ twin pairs is assumed to be due to their greater genetic similarity. Four large twin studies of PTSD have been conducted with heritability estimates ranging from 0.24 to 0.71 with an average of 0.45 (Duncan, Cooper, & Shen, 2018). There is a trend in those studies for higher heritability estimates to be correlated with the percentage of females in the study samples. Although it is not obvious how to interpret such a sex moderation effect, the overall evidence is strong that genetic differences between people play a role in their different risk for developing PTSD.

10.7.3 PTSD Candidate Gene Association Studies and GWAS

Candidate gene association studies for PTSD have focused primarily on genetic variants involved in neurotransmission and stress response (Almli, Fani, Smith, & Ressler, 2014). Given the limitations of candidate gene association studies that we have previously discussed, one should interpret any of these findings with caution. Serotonin system genes with some support include the serotonin transporter (*SLC6A4*) and the 2A receptor (*HT2A*). Dopamine system genes with some support for association with PTSD include the dopamine transporter (*SLC6A3*), the D2 receptor (*DRD2*), dopamine-β-hydroxylase (*DBH*), and catecholamine-o-methyltransferase (*COMT*). Genes in the HPA axis system that have some evidence for association with PTSD include the glucocorticoid receptor (*NR3C1*), the FK506-binding protein 51 (*FKBP5*), and an adenylate cyclase activating polypeptide receptor (*ADCYAP1R1*). Once again, such findings may or may not survive replication, and should be considered along with other evidence for the involvement of those systems and genetic polymorphisms.

A GWAS of over 20,000 participants combined from 11 different studies identified no variants that achieved genome-wide significance (Duncan, Ratanatharathorn, et al., 2018). Even though no single SNP was significantly associated with PTSD the h^2_{SNP} estimate for females was 0.29 and for males it was 0.07 when the combined contribution of all of SNPs was considered. This heritability pattern fits that seen in the twin studies where estimates in heritability tend to be higher in females than in males. Another, even larger GWAS (over 30,000 PTSD cases and 170,000 controls) found h^2_{SNP} estimates with the same pattern. Overall, the female h^2_{SNP} estimate was 0.10 and the male estimate was much lower at 0.01 and not significantly different from zero (Nievergelt et al., 2019).

The large sample sizes of GWAS enable researchers to test whether SNP associations are specific to groups. For example, associations can be tested separately by ancestry or sex to determine whether those demographic characteristics moderate genetic associations. In one large study, no genome-wide associations were identified when the entire sample was analyzed together (Nievergelt et al., 2019). However, when analyses were done only for those with European ancestry, two genome-wide SNPs (rs34517852, rs9364611) were significantly associated with PTSD, and for those with African ancestry, one SNP (rs115539978) was significant. When those ancestry groups were further subdivided by sex, two additional loci were identified only in men with European ancestry (rs571848662, rs148757321) and another in men with African ancestry (rs142174523). Such findings are likely the tip of the iceberg of genetic effects that are moderated by other factors in PTSD, but also in other phenotypes of interest.

10.7.4 Non-Human Animal Models of PTSD

As with other human phenotypes, modeling certain symptoms of PTSD in non-human animals is impossible. One cannot assess whether mice are having intrusive memories or bad dreams. However, aspects of elevated arousal and behavioral aspects of anxiety (e.g., avoidance) can be assessed in animals. Exposure to some stressor is typically a feature of non-human animal models of PTSD. The type of stressor used in such studies could include exposure to predators, electric foot shock, physical restraint, being held under water, social defeat, social isolation, maternal separation, tail suspension, chronic exposure to noise, heat, vibration or food/water deprivation, or other stressful experience (Schöner, Heinz, Endres, Gertz, & Kronenberg, 2017). The typical study design involves the comparison of the behavior, neurobiology, or physiology of genetically different strains after exposure to a stressor. The development of non-human animal models that are specific to PTSD is ongoing, but so far, there is little to report regarding genetic findings.

Check-up

- What is PTSD and how is it diagnosed?
- If PTSD requires a trauma, how can it run in families?
- How would you characterize the evidence for specific genetic variants being associated with PTSD risk?

10.8 SUMMARY

- Fear and anxiety are basic emotions that aid us in detecting and responding to threats. Defensive circuits include the amygdala and HPA axis.
- Non-human animal models of fear and anxiety typically use behavioral measures to assess these emotions, such as the elevated plus maze or the light-dark box.

- Strain differences for fear and anxiety can be seen in some mouse strains, such as C57BL/6J and BALB/cByJ.
- The GABA and serotonin neurotransmitter systems play a role in fear and anxiety, as does the HPA axis.
- Neuroticism is a personality trait that reflects aspects of fear and anxiety. Neuroticism runs in families and has significant non-zero heritability estimates. No genetic variants have been identified with a large effect on neuroticism.
- Approximately 33 percent of people will experience an anxiety disorder at some time in their life. Excessive anxiety or worry is a key feature of generalized anxiety disorder. Anxiety disorders run in families and are polygenic, with evidence of variants in GABA and serotonin neurotransmitter genes being associated with increased risk. GWAS evidence identifies a variant in a transcription factor that regulates expression of a protein critical in the HPA axis.
- Obsessive-compulsive disorder is characterized by urges to behave in ways to reduce anxiety. OCD runs in families and has non-zero heritability estimates. Genes in serotonin and dopamine neurotransmitter systems have been associated with OCD risk. Knockout mice have been used to study the genetics of self-destructive grooming behavior.
- Post-traumatic stress disorder can be diagnosed in those who have experienced or witnessed trauma. Significant non-zero heritability estimates have been made for PTSD. The evidence for specific genetic variants increasing risk for PTSD is scant.

RECOMMENDED READING

- Corr, P. J., & Matthews, G. (Eds.) (2009). *The Cambridge Handbook of Personality Psychology.* New York: Cambridge University Press.
- Dugatkin, L. A. (2018). The silver fox domestication experiment. *Evolution: Education and Outreach, 11*(1), 16. doi:10.1186/s12052-018-0090-x

REFERENCES

Ahmari, S. E. (2016). Using mice to model obsessive compulsive disorder: From genes to circuits. *Neuroscience, 321*, 121–137. doi:10.1016/j.neuroscience.2015.11.009

Almli, L. M., Fani, N., Smith, A. K., & Ressler, K. J. (2014). Genetic approaches to understanding post-traumatic stress disorder. *Int J Neuropsychopharmacol, 17*(2), 355–370. doi:10.1017/s1461145713001090

APA (2013). *Diagnostic and Statistical Manual of Mental Disorders: DSM-5* (pp. 0-1). Washington, DC: American Psychiatric Association.

Arnold, P. (2018). Revealing the complex genetic architecture of obsessive-compulsive disorder using meta-analysis. *Mol Psychiatry, 23*(5), 1181–1188. doi:10.1038/mp.2017.154

Bandelow, B., & Michaelis, S. (2015). Epidemiology of anxiety disorders in the 21st century. *Dialogues Clin Neurosci, 17*(3), 327–335.

Campos, A. C., Fogaça, M. V., Aguiar, D. C., & Guimarães, F. S. (2013). Animal models of anxiety disorders and stress. *Braz J Psychiatry, 35*(Suppl 2), S101–S111. doi:10.1590/1516-4446-2013-1139

Corr, P. J., & Matthews, G. (Eds.) (2009). *The Cambridge Handbook of Personality Psychology.* New York: Cambridge University Press.

Dugatkin, L. A. (2018). The silver fox domestication experiment. *Evolution: Education and Outreach, 11*(1), 16. doi:10.1186/s12052-018-0090-x

Duncan, L. E., Cooper, B. N., & Shen, H. (2018). Robust findings from 25 years of PTSD genetics research. *Curr Psychiatry Rep, 20*(12), 115. doi:10.1007/s11920-018-0980-1

Duncan, L. E., Ratanatharathorn, A., Aiello, A. E., Almli, L. M., Amstadter, A. B., Ashley-Koch, A. E., . . . Koenen, K. C. (2018). Largest GWAS of PTSD (N=20 070) yields genetic overlap with schizophrenia and sex differences in heritability. *Mol Psychiatry, 23*(3), 666–673. doi:10.1038/mp.2017.77

Galton, F. (1884). Measurement of character. *Fortnightly Review, 36*, 179–185.

GBD (2016). Global, regional, and national incidence, prevalence, and years lived with disability for 310 diseases and injuries, 1990–2015: A systematic analysis for the Global Burden of Disease Study 2015. *Lancet, 388*(10053), 1545–1602. doi:10.1016/s0140-6736(16)31678-6

Gottschalk, M. G., & Domschke, K. (2017). Genetics of generalized anxiety disorder and related traits. *Dialogues Clin Neurosci, 19*(2), 159–168.

Grillon, C., Robinson, O. J., Cornwell, B., & Ernst, M. (2019). Modeling anxiety in healthy humans: A key intermediate bridge between basic and clinical sciences. *Neuropsychopharmacology, 44*(12), 1999–2010. doi:10.1038/s41386-019-0445-1

Hassell, J. E., Jr., Nguyen, K. T., Gates, C. A., & Lowry, C. A. (2019). The impact of stressor exposure and glucocorticoids on anxiety and fear. *Curr Top Behav Neurosci, 43*, 271–321. doi:10.1007/7854_2018_63

Hettema, J. M., Neale, M. C., & Kendler, K. S. (2001). A review and meta-analysis of the genetic epidemiology of anxiety disorders. *Am J Psychiatry, 158*(10), 1568–1578. doi:10.1176/appi.ajp.158.10.1568

Howe, A. S., Buttenschøn, H. N., Bani-Fatemi, A., Maron, E., Otowa, T., Erhardt, A., . . . De Luca, V. (2016). Candidate genes in panic disorder: Meta-analyses of 23 common variants in major anxiogenic pathways. *Mol Psychiatry, 21*(5), 665–679. doi:10.1038/mp.2015.138

Jabbi, M., & Nemeroff, C. B. (2019). Convergent neurobiological predictors of mood and anxiety symptoms and treatment response. *Expert Rev Neurother, 19*(6), 587–597. doi:10.1080/14737175.2019.1620604

John, O. P., & Srivastava, S. (1999). The Big Five Trait taxonomy: History, measurement, and theoretical perspectives. In L. A. Pervin & O. P. John (Eds.), *Handbook of Personality: Theory and Research* (2nd ed.) (pp. 102–138). New York: Guilford Press.

Kumar, P., & Rai, V. (2020). Catechol-O-methyltransferase gene Val158Met polymorphism and obsessive compulsive disorder susceptibility: A meta-analysis. *Metab Brain Dis, 35*(2), 241–251. doi:10.1007/s11011-019-00495-0

Lacerda-Pinheiro, S. F., Pinheiro Junior, R. F., Pereira de Lima, M. A., Lima da Silva, C. G., Vieira dos Santos Mdo, S., Teixeira Júnior, A. G., . . . Bianco, B. A. (2014). Are there depression and anxiety genetic markers and mutations? A systematic review. *J Affect Disord, 168*, 387–398. doi:10.1016/j.jad.2014.07.016

LeDoux, J. E., & Pine, D. S. (2016). Using neuroscience to help understand fear and anxiety: A two-system framework. *Am J Psychiatry, 173*(11), 1083–1093. doi:10.1176/appi.ajp.2016.16030353

Lepicard, E. M., Joubert, C., Hagneau, I., Perez-Diaz, F., & Chapouthier, G. (2000). Differences in anxiety-related behavior and response to diazepam in BALB/cByJ and C57BL/6J strains of mice. *Pharmacol Biochem Behav, 67*(4), 739–748. doi:10.1016/s0091-3057(00)00419-6

Levey, D. F., Gelernter, J., Polimanti, R., Zhou, H., Cheng, Z., Aslan, M., . . . Stein, M. B. (2020). Reproducible genetic risk loci for anxiety: Results from ∼200,000 participants in the Million Veteran Program. *Am J Psychiatry, 177*(3), 223–232. doi:10.1176/appi.ajp.2019.19030256

Mohammad, F., Ho, J., Woo, J. H., Lim, C. L., Poon, D. J. J., Lamba, B., & Claridge-Chang, A. (2016). Concordance and incongruence in preclinical anxiety models: Systematic review and meta-analyses. *Neurosci Biobehav Rev, 68*, 504–529. doi:10.1016/j.neubiorev.2016.04.011

Munafò, M. R., Freimer, N. B., Ng, W., Ophoff, R., Veijola, J., Miettunen, J., . . . Flint, J. (2009). 5-HTTLPR genotype and anxiety-related personality traits: A meta-analysis and new data. *Am J Med Genet B Neuropsychiatr Genet, 150b*(2), 271–281. doi:10.1002/ajmg.b.30808

Nagel, M., Jansen, P. R., Stringer, S., Watanabe, K., de Leeuw, C. A., Bryois, J., ... Posthuma, D. (2018). Meta-analysis of genome-wide association studies for neuroticism in 449,484 individuals identifies novel genetic loci and pathways. *Nat Genet, 50*(7), 920–927. doi:10.1038/s41588-018-0151-7

Nievergelt, C. M., Maihofer, A. X., Klengel, T., Atkinson, E. G., Chen, C. Y., Choi, K. W., ... Koenen, K. C. (2019). International meta-analysis of PTSD genome-wide association studies identifies sex- and ancestry-specific genetic risk loci. *Nat Commun, 10*(1), 4558. doi:10.1038/s41467-019-12576-w

Pauls, D. L., Abramovitch, A., Rauch, S. L., & Geller, D. A. (2014). Obsessive-compulsive disorder: An integrative genetic and neurobiological perspective. *Nat Rev Neurosci, 15*(6), 410–424. doi:10.1038/nrn3746

Scherma, M., Giunti, E., Fratta, W., & Fadda, P. (2019). Gene knockout animal models of depression, anxiety and obsessive compulsive disorders. *Psychiatr Genet, 29*(5), 191–199. doi:10.1097/ypg.0000000000000238

Schöner, J., Heinz, A., Endres, M., Gertz, K., & Kronenberg, G. (2017). Post-traumatic stress disorder and beyond: An overview of rodent stress models. *J Cell Mol Med, 21*(10), 2248–2256. doi:10.1111/jcmm.13161

Sigel, E., & Steinmann, M. E. (2012). Structure, function, and modulation of GABA(A) receptors. *J Biol Chem, 287*(48), 40224–40231. doi:10.1074/jbc.R112.386664

Smit, D. J. A., Cath, D., Zilhão, N. R., Ip, H. F., Denys, D., den Braber, A., ... Boomsma, D. I. (2020). Genetic meta-analysis of obsessive-compulsive disorder and self-report compulsive symptoms. *Am J Med Genet B Neuropsychiatr Genet, 183*(4), 208–216. doi:10.1002/ajmg.b.32777

Smoller, J. W. (2016). The genetics of stress-related disorders: PTSD, depression, and anxiety disorders. *Neuropsychopharmacology, 41*(1), 297–319. doi:10.1038/npp.2015.266

Taylor, S. (2011). Etiology of obsessions and compulsions: A meta-analysis and narrative review of twin studies. *Clin Psychol Rev, 31*(8), 1361–1372. doi:10.1016/j.cpr.2011.09.008

Taylor, S. (2013). Molecular genetics of obsessive-compulsive disorder: A comprehensive meta-analysis of genetic association studies. *Mol Psychiatry, 18*(7), 799–805. doi:10.1038/mp.2012.76

Vaidyanathan, U., Malone, S. M., Miller, M. B., McGue, M., & Iacono, W. G. (2014). Heritability and molecular genetic basis of acoustic startle eye blink and affectively modulated startle response: A genome-wide association study. *Psychophysiology, 51*(12), 1285–1299. doi:10.1111/psyp.12348

Van Houtem, C. M., Laine, M. L., Boomsma, D. I., Ligthart, L., van Wijk, A. J., & De Jongh, A. (2013). A review and meta-analysis of the heritability of specific phobia subtypes and corresponding fears. *J Anxiety Disord, 27*(4), 379–388. doi:10.1016/j.janxdis.2013.04.007

Vukasović, T., & Bratko, D. (2015). Heritability of personality: A meta-analysis of behavior genetic studies. *Psychol Bull, 141*(4), 769–785. doi:10.1037/bul0000017

Wang, X., Pipes, L., Trut, L. N., Herbeck, Y., Vladimirova, A. V., Gulevich, R. G., ... Clark, A. G. (2018). Genomic responses to selection for tame/aggressive behaviors in the silver fox (Vulpes vulpes). *Proc Natl Acad Sci USA, 115*(41), 10398–10403. doi:10.1073/pnas.1800889115

Weber, H., Richter, J., Straube, B., Lueken, U., Domschke, K., Schartner, C., ... Reif, A. (2016). Allelic variation in CRHR1 predisposes to panic disorder: Evidence for biased fear processing. *Mol Psychiatry, 21*(6), 813–822. doi:10.1038/mp.2015.125

Welch, J. M., Lu, J., Rodriguiz, R. M., Trotta, N. C., Peca, J., Ding, J. D., ... Feng, G. (2007). Cortico-striatal synaptic defects and OCD-like behaviours in Sapap3-mutant mice. *Nature, 448*(7156), 894–900. doi:10.1038/nature06104

Wilkins, A. S., Wrangham, R. W., & Fitch, W. T. (2014). The "domestication syndrome" in mammals: A unified explanation based on neural crest cell behavior and genetics. *Genetics, 197*(3), 795–808. doi:10.1534/genetics.114.165423

World Health Organization (2020a). Anxiety or Fear-Related Disorders. ICD-11 for Mortality and Morbidity Statistics. http://id.who.int/icd/entity/1336943699

World Health Organization (2020b). Obsessive-Compulsive or Related Disorders. ICD-11 for Mortality and Morbidity Statistics. http://id.who.int/icd/entity/1321276661

World Health Organization (2020c). Disorders Specifically Associated with Stress. ICD-11 for Mortality and Morbidity Statistics. http://id.who.int/icd/entity/991786158

Zapata, I., Serpell, J. A., & Alvarez, C. E. (2016). Genetic mapping of canine fear and aggression. *BMC Genomics*, *17*, 572. doi:10.1186/s12864-016-2936-3

11 Addiction

Have you ever drunk more alcohol than you intended? Or smoked a cigarette after telling yourself that you were quitting smoking? Have you ever gotten a headache because you did not drink your morning coffee? By the time we are adults, nearly all of us have used substances such as alcohol, tobacco, or caffeine. Most of us can control our use of substances, but a sizeable minority develop one or more disorders due to substance use at some point in their lives. You probably know someone who has problems that are a result of substance use.

In this chapter, we first discuss substance use and the behavioral symptoms used to diagnose substance use disorders. We then discuss a model of addiction neurobiology. For the remainder of the chapter, we focus primarily on alcohol use disorder because of its prevalence and the large amount of research that has been done to investigate the role of genetic differences in individual differences related to alcohol use. We first examine non-human animal models for their contribution to understanding alcohol use disorder. Next, we discuss evidence for the role of heredity in alcohol use disorder from family studies as well as twin and adoption studies. We then present an important example of the role of genetic variation in alcohol metabolism on risk for alcohol use disorder. Finally, we examine evidence from candidate gene association studies and GWAS to identify genetic variants that increase risk for developing a disorder due to alcohol use.

11.1 Addiction Is Characterized by Impaired Control Over Substance Use, Tolerance, and Withdrawal

The term addiction is widely used by the public to describe difficulty controlling one's behavior with respect to a specific target. If I say that I am addicted to potato chips, people generally understand it to mean that I have a strong desire to eat potato chips and that I have trouble stopping once I start eating them. Such uncontrolled behavior is understood to have potentially negative consequences. As you will see when we discuss the ICD-11 symptoms for disorders due to substance use, this lay understanding of addiction captures important features, but does not fully characterize the nature of such disorders. We will limit our coverage to disorders due to psychoactive substances, although we recognize that it is possible to develop addictive-like patterns of behavior to other targets like gambling, sex, or cell phone use. Psychoactive substances act in the brain and can affect perception, thinking, motivation, emotion, and behavior. Hereafter, we refer to them as substances.

11.1.1 Substance Use Is Common

Most adults use substances. Caffeine is the most widely used substance with approximately 85 percent of adults in the US consuming at least one caffeinated beverage each day (Mitchell, Knight, Hockenberry, Teplansky, & Hartman, 2014). The World Health Organization estimated that

Past Month Substance Use among People Aged 12 or Older in the U.S.: 2019

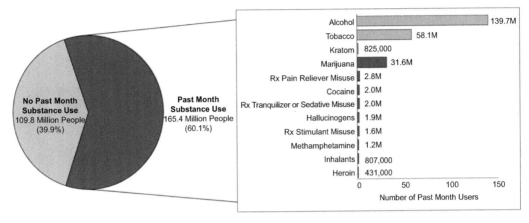

Rx = prescription.

Note: Substance Use includes any illicit drug, kratom, alcohol, and tobacco use.

Note: The estimated numbers of current users of different substances are not mutually exclusive because people could have used more than one type of substance in the past month.

Figure 11.1. **Past month substance use in the US.** The 2019 National Survey on Drug Use and Health indicated that alcohol, tobacco, and marijuana are the three most used substances by Americans aged 12 and older. Source: www.samhsa.gov/data/release/2018-national-survey-drug-use-and-health-nsduh-releases. Image in the public domain.

271 million people aged 15–64 had used substances, not including caffeine, alcohol, or tobacco in the past year (World Health Organization, 2019). In the US, the 2019 National Survey on Drug Use and Health (NSDUH) estimated that 60.1 percent of Americans, aged 12 and over, used a substance (not including caffeine) in the past month (see Figure 11.1; SAMHSA, 2020). Every year since 1971 in the US, the NSDUH reports data from a nationally representative sample with a sample size of approximately 70,000. The NSDUH provides important data for researchers and policy makers to identify and understand trends in drug use.

Substance use is not uniform across the globe. Although substances are used in every country, the percentage of the population that use them varies. Furthermore, men are more likely to use substances than are women. For example, alcohol use varies from less than 10 percent to over 90 percent of the population in certain countries; and in every country a higher percentage of men drank alcohol in the past year than did women (see Figure 11.2).

Of course, not everyone who uses a substance develops a substance use disorder; however, a significant percentage do. Estimates in the US from the National Epidemiologic Survey on Alcohol and Related Conditions III indicate that lifetime prevalence rates are approximately 29.1 percent for alcohol use disorder (Grant et al., 2015), 27.9 percent for tobacco use disorder (Chou et al., 2016), and 9.9 percent for any other drug use disorder (Grant et al., 2016). There is substantial comorbidity for these diagnoses, such that if a person meets criteria for one, they are at increased risk for being diagnosed with another, when compared to someone with none of these diagnoses. It is important to note here that lifetime prevalence means that at some point in a person's life they meet criteria for a disorder. It does not mean that they meet criteria for their entire lives. It is not unusual for someone to meet criteria at one point in their life (e.g., during college), but not to do so later in life. For example, a person could have an alcohol use disorder for a couple of years in their twenties, but "mature out" into a healthier drinking pattern in their thirties. A person showing such a pattern would be considered a "case" by an epidemiologist in the context of lifetime prevalence.

(a)

Share of adults who drank alcohol in last year, 2010
Share of adults (aged 15+) who drank any form of alcohol within the previous 12 months. This is measured across both sexes.

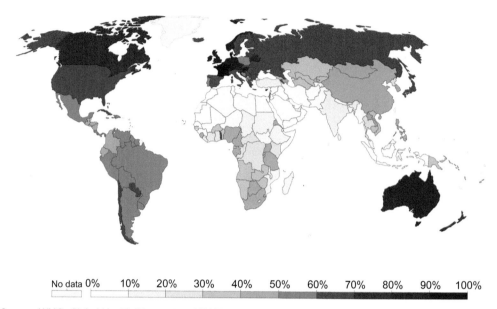

Figure 11.2. **Alcohol use.** (a) Percentage of the population of each country that reported drinking alcohol in the past year. (b) For each country, the percentage of men that reported drinking alcohol in the past year is presented on the y-axis, and the percentage of women that reported drinking alcohol in the past year is presented on the x-axis. When the data point for a country is above the diagonal line it means that a higher percentage of men than women reported drinking alcohol. Source Hannah Ritchie (2018) "Alcohol Consumption." Published online at OurWorldInData.org. Retrieved from: https://ourworldindata.org/alcohol-consumption [Online Resource].

Point prevalence, on the other hand, refers to the percentage of the population that meets criteria for a disorder at a given point in time (i.e., a specific date). Estimates of the point prevalence for a disorder will necessarily be lower than the estimates of the lifetime prevalence for a disorder, because on a given date, the population will contain people who have previously been diagnosed with the disorder, but have recovered, and therefore currently do not meet diagnostic criteria.

11.1.2 Diagnosing Disorders Due to Substance Use

The ICD-11 describes disorders due to the use of seventeen psychoactive substances, namely (1) alcohol, (2) cannabis, (3) synthetic cannabinoids, (4) opioids, (5) sedatives, hypnotics, or anxiolytics, (6) cocaine, (7) stimulants including amphetamine, methamphetamine, and methcathinone, (8) synthetic cathinones, (9) caffeine, (10) hallucinogens, (11) nicotine, (12) volatile inhalants, (13) MDMA (3,4-Methylenedioxymethamphetamine, commonly known as ecstasy) or related drugs, (14) dissociative drugs, including ketamine and phencyclidine (PCP), (15) other specified psychoactive substances, including medications, (16) multiple specified psychoactive substances, including medications, (17) unknown or unspecified psychoactive substances (World Health Organization,

(b)

Share of men vs. share of women who drank alcohol in last year, 2010
Includes men and women aged 15 years or older.

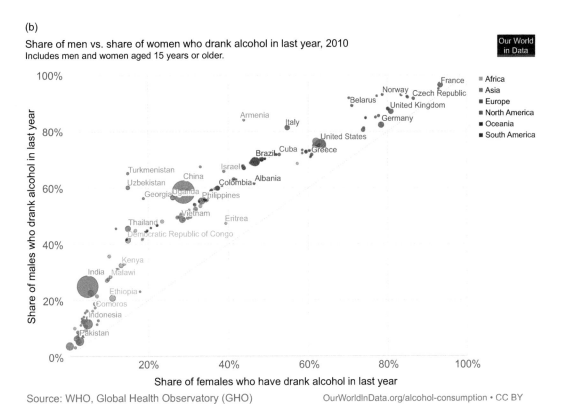

Source: WHO, Global Health Observatory (GHO)   OurWorldInData.org/alcohol-consumption • CC BY

Figure 11.2. (*cont.*)

2020). In 2016, over 2 percent of the world's population was estimated to have an alcohol or drug use disorder, with men being more likely than women to meet diagnostic criteria (see Figure 11.3).

As with all psychiatric disorders, the diagnosis of substance use disorder is typically made during a clinical interview. Space does not permit the description of diagnostic criteria for all substance disorders, therefore we present criteria for alcohol dependence as an example (see Box 11.1). However, it should be noted that the criteria are nearly identical across substances.

One important exception is that although each disorder has withdrawal as one of the potential diagnostic criteria (i.e., symptom), each class of substances has a specific withdrawal syndrome. It is important to note that many symptoms of withdrawal syndromes can be considered the opposite of the primary effect of the drug. For alcohol, the primary effect is the depression of neural activity. Many alcohol withdrawal symptoms have to do with neural overactivation, such as increased heart rate, hand tremor, insomnia, hallucinations, anxiety, and seizures. To be considered withdrawal symptoms they should occur sometime after cessation of heavy or prolonged alcohol use. The symptoms appear to represent homeostatic changes to neural function due to chronic alcohol use, such that when alcohol's depressant effect is no longer acting on the system, hyperactivity results.

Several substance use disorder symptoms reflect *impaired control over use* of the drug, *increased life impact* of the drug on important aspects of living, *increased risk* for negative life or

(a)

Share of the population with alcohol or drug use disorders, 2016
Alcohol or drug use dependence is defined by the International Classification of Diseases as the presence of three
or more indicators of dependence for at least a month within the previous year.

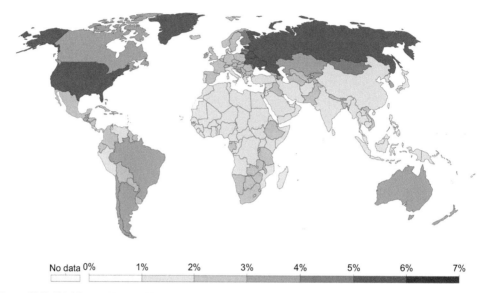

No data 0%   1%   2%   3%   4%   5%   6%   7%

Source: IHME, Global Burden of Disease (GBD)   OurWorldInData.org/substance-use • CC BY
Note: Tobacco smoking is not included. Due to the widespread under-diagnosis, these estimates use a combination of sources, including
medical and national records, epidemiological data, survey data, and meta-regression models.

Figure 11.3. **Alcohol or drug use disorders.** (a) Estimates for the point prevalence of alcohol or drug use disorder
vary across the globe from a low of 1–2% to a high of 6–7% in 2016. (b) In virtually every country around the world, men
were more likely than women to have an alcohol or drug use disorder. Overall, men are about twice as likely as women to
have an alcohol or drug use disorder. Source: Hannah Ritchie (2018) "Alcohol Consumption." Published online at
OurWorldInData.org. Retrieved from: https://ourworldindata.org/alcohol-consumption [Online Resource].

health outcomes, and potential *psychobiological changes*. As you can see, these symptoms do not
include drinking alone, or some threshold of drinking frequency, or volume of alcohol consumed.
Rather, the symptoms reflect changes in behavioral control, motivation, decision-making, and brain
function because of alcohol use. People take psychoactive substances because they are psychoactive,
and in turn, may develop a substance use disorder because chronic use of psychoactive substances
produces psychological changes via neuroadaptations (Koob & Volkow, 2016).

Check-up

• Which are the most commonly used substances?
• Discuss the key diagnostic criteria for disorders of substance use.
• What is withdrawal and what role does it play in the diagnosis of substance abuse disorder?

(b)

Share with alcohol or drug use disorders, men vs. women, 2016
Alcohol or drug use dependence is defined by the International Classification of Diseases as the presence of three
or more indicators of dependence for at least a month within the previous year. Tobacco smoking is not included.

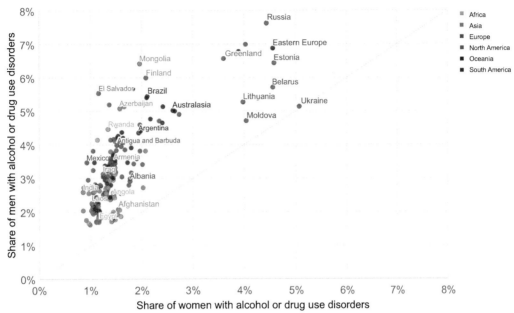

Source: IHME, Global Burden of Disease (GBD)   CCBY

Figure 11.3. (*cont.*)

Box 11.1 ICD-11 Diagnosis: Alcohol Dependence

Alcohol dependence is a disorder of regulation of alcohol use arising from repeated or continuous use of alcohol. The characteristic feature is a strong internal drive to use alcohol, which is manifested by impaired ability to control use, increasing priority given to use over other activities and persistence of use despite harm or negative consequences. These experiences are often accompanied by a subjective sensation of urge or craving to use alcohol. Physiological features of dependence may also be present, including tolerance to the effects of alcohol, withdrawal symptoms following cessation or reduction in use of alcohol, or repeated use of alcohol or pharmacologically similar substances to prevent or alleviate withdrawal symptoms. The features of dependence are usually evident over a period of at least 12 months but the diagnosis may be made if alcohol use is continuous (daily or almost daily) for at least 1 month.

Source: http://id.who.int/icd/entity/1580466198 (accessed March 1, 2021), World Health Organization (Copyright © 2020).

11.2 The Neurobiology of Addiction

Why do so many people use potentially addictive substances? There are important social, cultural, and developmental factors that influence substance use, but they are beyond the scope of this text. We focus on basic psychological constructs and their neurobiology because it is where genetic variation can have identifiable, functional effects.

According to an influential conceptual framework (Koob & Volkow, 2010, 2016), addiction is a chronic relapsing disorder comprising three stages with different psychological and neurobiological features. The answer to the question of why people continue to use potentially addictive substances depends on which stage of addiction they are at. In the binge/intoxication stage, substances activate brain reward systems resulting in a pleasurable feeling that is positively reinforcing. In the withdrawal/negative affect stage, substance use relieves the aversive withdrawal state and/or the negative feelings resulting from neuroadaptations to chronic use. Therefore, in this stage, substance use is considered negatively reinforcing. In the preoccupation/anticipation stage, deficits in executive function caused by substance use drive craving and disrupt motivational and behavioral control circuits. Substance use in this stage is considered compulsive. Each of these three stages is described in more detail below.

11.2.1 Binge/Intoxication Stage

Psychoactive substances have molecular structures that facilitate interaction with components of neurotransmitter systems, thereby increasing or decreasing neurotransmission, depending on the substance and the neurotransmitter system. Some of these effects are positively reinforcing (i.e., rewarding), in that they increase the probability that the substance will be taken again. In other words, because it feels good to take psychoactive substances, we are more likely to take them again in the future. Such positively reinforcing properties of substances appears to be due to their activation of the brain reward system, primarily mediated by the release of dopamine and opioid peptides. This reward system is involved in classical conditioning whereby previously neutral stimuli acquire new significance as predictors of substance availability. Stimuli that are repeatedly paired with intoxicating levels of substance use, like a bottle opener, can themselves become powerful activators of the reward system and thereby facilitate habit learning. Such learning sets the stage for cue-induced compulsive drug seeking that can hamper efforts to quit or reduce substance use. The reinforcing properties of psychoactive drugs are often greater than those of typical unconditioned stimuli like food or social contact.

Chronic overactivation of the reward system during the binge/intoxication stage can lead to homeostatic neuroadaptation whereby dopamine and opioid function are reduced. Such a reduction can be accomplished by downregulating the production of the neurotransmitters, removing receptors from the synapses of target neurons, or otherwise decreasing dopaminergic and opioid neurotransmission. Of course, this downregulation of reward system responsiveness means that when the substance is not present in the system to overactivate it, the capacity to deliver rewards for other stimuli is reduced. In that case, things like having a conversation with a friend, eating good food, or having sex may not feel as enjoyable as they used to. The inability to feel pleasure is called anhedonia, and it is often discussed as a risk factor in recovery when someone is trying to abstain from substance use. Such a state is a particular risk for relapse to substance use because the addicted person knows that the substance can produce positive feelings.

In addition, such a reduction in reward system responsiveness is a likely mechanism in the development of tolerance to the psychoactive substance. As the reward system becomes less

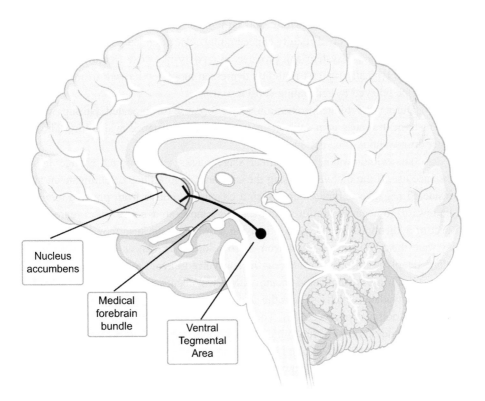

Figure 11.4. **Reward pathway.** Neurons originating in the ventral tegmental area (VTA) project to the nucleus accumbens, where they release dopamine. The axons of dopaminergic neurons in the reward pathway are collectively known as the medial forebrain bundle. Source: Created with Biorender.com.

responsive, it becomes necessary to use larger amounts of the substance to achieve desired levels of reward.

An important brain area in the reward pathway is the nucleus accumbens, which receives input from dopaminergic neurons that originate in the ventral tegmental area (see Figure 11.4). The nucleus accumbens is activated when people receive reward, and after learning, can be activated when merely anticipating reward. The nucleus accumbens has connections to the basal ganglia, which is involved in motor control. Therefore, this circuit is critical to motivated, reward-seeking behavior (Banich & Compton, 2018). The neurotransmitter and neuromodulators involved in this circuit include dopamine, opioid peptides, GABA, glutamate, serotonin, acetylcholine, and the endocannabinoid system (Koob & Volkow, 2016).

In summary, an important motivation for substance use in the binge/intoxication stage of addiction is to activate the brain reward system. Repeated episodes of intoxication produce neural adaptations that counteract the reward systems overactivation leading to the next stage in addiction.

11.2.2 Withdrawal/Negative Affect Stage

The withdrawal/negative affect stage of addiction is a result of the neuroadaptations to the reward system caused by psychoactive substance exposure in the binge/intoxication stage. The substance's withdrawal syndrome occurs when use of the substance is reduced or stopped. As mentioned previously, typical symptoms of withdrawal syndrome are opposite of the effects of the substance. Withdrawal symptoms for depressants, such as alcohol, reflect neural hyperactivity (e.g., increased heart rate, insomnia), whereas withdrawal symptoms for stimulants, such as caffeine, reflect neural hypoactivity (e.g., fatigue, difficulty concentrating). An extended period of withdrawal activates the body's stress response system and produce an anxiety-like state (Koob & Volkow, 2016). In this stage, people typically report irritability, depressed mood, and a lack of motivation. Such aversive states can be relieved by reinstating substance use.

During the binge/intoxication stage, because of repeated pairing with the substance, previously neutral cues gain salience as predictors of substance availability. Those cues may then trigger drug wanting (i.e., craving).

The withdrawal/negative affect stage marks an important change in the motives for substance use. If the motive for using the substance is to reduce or eliminate an aversive state it is considered negative reinforcement. Such a change in motive from positive reinforcement (i.e., to gain reward) to negative reinforcement (i.e., to remove an aversive state) represents a fundamental aspect of addiction. Now the person is using a drug, not because they like its effects, but because they want them (Berridge & Robinson, 2016). So, rather than using a substance to obtain a good feeling, people in this stage are taking the substance to avoid or relieve a bad feeling.

Brain areas implicated in the withdrawal/negative affect stage of addiction include the extended amygdala (which includes the shell of the nucleus accumbens and other structures) and the habenula (Koob & Volkow, 2016). The neurotransmitters and neuromodulators involved in these circuits include serotonin, dopamine, corticotropin releasing factor, norepinephrine, dynorphin, acetylcholine, neuropeptide Y, and endocannabinoids.

In summary, the withdrawal/negative affect stage is characterized by a reward deficit/stress excess, and the motivation for substance use is to relieve that aversive state. Neuroadaptations in the brain reward system and the stress response system produce unpleasant feelings in the absence of the substance. Natural rewards are insufficient to activate the reward system or to relieve the stress response but use of the drug can provide relief. However, increasing doses of the substance are required for relief, which sets the stage for additional neuroadaptive responses and further dysfunction.

11.2.3 Preoccupation/Anticipation Stage

The preoccupation/anticipation stage can be characterized as the craving stage of addiction. This stage is a culmination of the neuroadaptations that have occurred in the earlier stages and that produce an increased sensitivity to cues that predict drug availability, and deficits in executive function (e.g., behavioral control, decision-making; Koob & Volkow, 2016). Cues in the environment that have become potent predictors of drug availability can initiate intense craving that powerfully motivates drug-seeking behavior. In addition, executive function has been compromised, which can increase impulsive behavior and impair decision-making capacity. Attempts to abstain can be derailed by exposure to cues that trigger craving and initiate compulsive drug-seeking behavior that can override a person's longer-term goals.

The brain areas involved in the preoccupation/anticipation stage of addiction include structures in the prefrontal cortex and the insula. Neurotransmitter systems and neuromodulators include dopamine, serotonin, GABA, glutamate, norepinephrine, and corticotropin releasing factor.

In summary, the preoccupation/anticipation stage of addiction combines the aversive state generated in earlier stages with weakened executive function such that decision-making devalues future goals in favor of immediate ones. Powerful craving triggered by learned associations and combined with an aversive state sets the stage for compulsive drug use for relief even with the knowledge that such behavior may jeopardize long-term goals. Such a pattern of feeling, thinking, and behaving characterizes addiction and is the result of prolonged substance use and the resulting adaptations of brain circuits.

It should be noted that the neural circuits involved in addiction did not evolve so that human beings could enjoy taking psychoactive substances, but rather to help us identify aspects of the environment that are good for us so that we can remember them and be motivated to interact with them again. These systems are for learning, motivation, emotion, and decision-making in general. Psychoactive drugs happen to powerfully activate these systems because of their molecular structure and addictions are the result of the neuroadaptations deployed to counteract them. Variants in genes that code for components of the relevant brain systems involved in each stage of addiction may produce individual differences in responses to substances, and in aspects of substance-induced neuroadaptation, and ultimately for risk for addiction.

Check-up

- Compare and contrast positive reinforcement and negative reinforcement in the context of motives for substance use.
- What is homeostatic neuroadaptation and how does it contribute to addiction?
- Explain the role of anhedonia in addiction.
- Explain the role of craving in addiction.

11.3 Non-Human Animal Models of Alcohol Use Disorder Genetics

Rodents have been used to investigate the role of genetic variation on individual differences in alcohol-related traits for nearly a century (Crabbe, 2014). Of course, as with all non-human animal models of human disorders, it is important to keep in mind that they only model aspects of the disorder. Rodents do not develop alcohol use disorders, and risk factors for humans such as peer pressure or cultural influence cannot be adequately modeled. There are alcohol-related behaviors, such as voluntary consumption or sensitivity to alcohol's intoxicating effects that may share enough biology to be useful models.

11.3.1 Strain Comparisons for Alcohol Preference

Early work on rodents focused on voluntary alcohol consumption in rats by testing their "preference" for drinking ethanol in the so-called two-bottle choice test. In this test, an individual rodent in its cage is provided two bottles from which it can drink over a 24-hour period. One bottle contains an alcohol solution, while the other contains plain tap water. Preference ratios can be calculated (volume alcohol solution/total volume of fluid consumed). Preference ratios higher than 50 percent indicate a preference for the alcohol solution. Rats seem to prefer alcohol solutions when the concentration of ethanol is around 4 percent by volume (ABV), which is similar to the alcohol concentration in beer. Initial studies found individual differences in the volume of alcohol consumed, both within and between inbred lines of rats and mice. When environmental differences between the tested animals are minimized, between line differences are evidence of genetic influence because inbred lines differ genetically. Individual differences within inbred lines can be interpreted

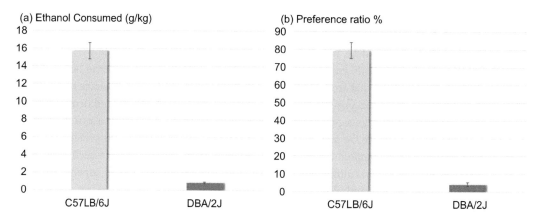

Figure 11.5. **Alcohol preference in two inbred lines of mice.** One of the most replicated and stable alcohol-related traits in inbred lines of mice is that C57BL/6J mice show a very strong preference for alcohol and DBA/2J mice are alcohol averse. (a) C57BL/6J mice will, on average, drink about 15 times more alcohol per day than DBA/2J mice. (b) The preference ratio for C57BL/6J mice is about 20 times higher, on average, than for DBA/2J mice. Source: Wahlsten et al. (2006).

as the result of a lack of (a) genetic or environmental homogeneity, (b) random developmental processes, or (c) measurement error.

Inbred lines of mice have been intensively studied for alcohol-related traits, including alcohol preference, since the middle of the twentieth century. One of the most consistent findings of the two-bottle choice test with a 10 percent alcohol solution is that C57BL/6J mice show a strong preference, and DBA/2J mice show a strong aversion (Crabbe, 2014). The C57BL/6J mice, on average, drink about fifteen times more of a 10 percent alcohol solution per day than do DBA/2J mice (see Figure 11.5). This stark difference in alcohol drinking behavior is consistent across labs and has been stable for decades (Wahlsten, Bachmanov, Finn, & Crabbe, 2006). In an era of replication failures, the difference in drinking behavior between these two genetically distinct lines is noteworthy.

Selective breeding for alcohol preference also clearly demonstrates the influence of heredity on this alcohol-related trait. Several lines of rats have been divergently selected for alcohol-related behavior. One of the best known is the preferring (P) and non-preferring (NP) lines that were established from an outbred, albino, laboratory stock (i.e., Wistar). At each generation of selection, those that voluntarily consumed an intoxicating amount of ethanol were bred in the P line and those that did not were bred in the NP line. Substantial changes in alcohol-related behavior, neurobiology, and neurochemistry were achieved by selective breeding. In fact, the P line of rats are one of the only non-human animal models of alcoholism that will voluntarily consume enough alcohol to become intoxicated. The fact that alcohol-related traits responded to selective breeding indicates that genetic variation plays a role in individual differences in those traits.

The P line rats have substantial validity as non-human models for alcohol-related traits because they (1) voluntarily consume alcohol, (2) drink enough alcohol to be pharmacologically relevant, (3) will work for alcohol (i.e., it is positively reinforcing), (4) are consuming alcohol for its psychoactive effects (e.g., not for its taste or calories). And after chronic alcohol consumption they (5) develop tolerance to its effects, (6) experience withdrawal symptoms when it is terminated, and (7) show relapse-like behavior after abstinence (Bell, Rodd, Lumeng, Murphy, & McBride, 2006).

Alcohol naïve P rats, when compared to alcohol naïve NP rats, have lower levels of brain (1) serotonin and its metabolites, (2) dopamine and its metabolites, and (3) corticotropin releasing factor. They also have higher levels of (4) GABAergic terminals, and (5) mu-opioid receptors (Bell et al., 2006). Such differences are the result of selective breeding and show the involvement of these neurotransmitter systems in the alcohol-related behavioral differences between the selected lines. It is important to note that such differences cannot be the direct result of alcohol exposure because they are observed in the animals prior to exposure to alcohol.

Lines of mice selected for divergent alcohol drinking behaviors have also been developed, but just as in rats, most lines of mice do not voluntarily consume intoxicating amounts of alcohol. In humans, many alcohol-related problems stem from binge drinking, which is consuming an intoxicating amount of alcohol in a relatively short period of time. Binge drinking produces blood alcohol concentrations (BAC) of 0.08 percent or higher and is associated with increased risk for motor vehicle accident, victimization, memory blackouts, and, when done repeatedly, the development of an alcohol use disorder. It is of great interest to have mouse models of binge drinking behavior for the study of the etiology of alcohol use disorder in humans.

The "drinking in the dark" (DID) assay takes advantage of the fact that mice tend to do most of their eating and drinking near the start of the dark period of the daily light–dark cycle (Crabbe, 2014). In this procedure, the mice are provided a single bottle of a 20 percent ethanol solution for the first two hours when the lights go out. C57BL/6J mice will drink enough to reach intoxicating BAC levels, and to show behavioral evidence of intoxication (e.g., reduction of motor coordination) with this procedure. Different strains respond to the DID assay by drinking at levels that correlate with their two-bottle choice performance. It is important to note that some of the rodent lines that do not voluntarily drink alcohol may be avoiding it because they find the smell or taste to be aversive. A detailed critique of rodent alcohol drinking paradigms is beyond the scope of this text, but we need to carefully consider and test alternative hypotheses when investigating biological causes of behavior.

Clearly, the evidence from strain comparisons and selection studies supports the position that heredity plays a role in alcohol-related traits. The selection study results make it clear that such traits were not due to variation at a single genetic locus. If one, or a small number, of loci were responsible for alcohol-related traits, selective breeding would fix each line for alternative alleles after a few generations. Instead, alcohol-related traits, like alcohol preference, responded to divergent selection, but substantial progress required many generations. This pattern of significant but gradual selection response is expected when the selected trait is polygenic.

11.3.2 Quantitative Trait Loci Mapping

To identify genomic regions containing genetic variants that cause differences in alcohol-related traits, researchers used a QTL mapping approach with recombinant inbred lines (see Box 11.2). In 1971, twenty-six recombinant inbred lines called BXD lines were developed from C57BL/6J (i.e., B) and DBA/2J (i.e., D) parental lines. The original BXD lines maintained by brother–sister mating, and additional BXD lines that have been developed by mating those two parental strains are still available for use from commercial suppliers such as The Jackson Laboratories.

Box 11.2 Recombinant Inbred Lines

Researchers working to identify genetic variants that cause individual differences in behavior have developed many tools, including recombinant inbred lines of mice. Generating standard recombinant inbred lines requires two inbred parental lines that differ on some phenotype of interest, like alcohol drinking, to start. Animals from these parental lines are intermated to produce heterozygous F_1 generation individuals, which are then intermated to produce F_2 generation offspring.

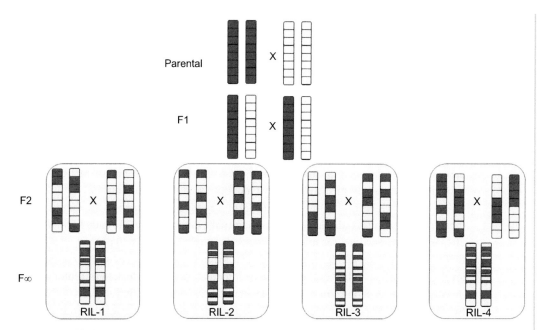

Figure 11.6. **Mating scheme to develop recombinant inbred lines.** In this simplified mating scheme to produce four recombinant inbred lines (RIL-1 through RIL-4) the parents are drawn from two different isogenic lines. Their F_1 offspring are mated to produce many F_2 generation offspring. Mated pairs of F_2 generation offspring establish lines that will be inbred generation after generation to produce recombinant inbred lines that are homozygously fixed (i.e., isogenic) for different combinations of genetic material from the parental lines.

Next, each recombinant inbred line is established by mating an F_2 generation male to an F_2 generation female. Their subsequent offspring are inbred within that line by brother–sister mating each generation (see Figure 11.6).

The recombination events that occur during gamete production in the F_1 generation produce F_2 generation individuals that carry unique combinations of genetic material from the parental lines. In other words, the resulting recombinant inbred lines are *genetically different between lines*. The subsequent inbreeding within each new recombinant inbred line produces lines that are *genetically identical within line*.

For recombinant inbred lines to be useful for mapping QTL the locations of genetic markers across chromosomes for each of the parental strains must be known. Genetic markers are merely polymorphisms of known location. They are not candidate genes because they are not suspected of causing individual differences in the trait. They are markers because they "mark" a known position on a chromosome.

Work with recombinant inbred strains in the late twentieth century relied on a relatively sparse map of genetic markers on each chromosome. Currently, high-density SNP arrays can be used to dramatically increase the mapping precision (Ashbrook et al., 2019). The B and D parental strains have had their genomes sequenced, so it is possible to determine which one contributed a DNA sequence in a recombinant inbred line. Prior to the availability of genome sequence data, any genetic variant with known genomic location and that differed between the strains could serve as a genetic marker in QTL analyses.

When tested across multiple recombinant inbred lines, correlations between markers on a stretch of a chromosome and the phenotype of interest suggest that the region contains a gene of interest. Such a finding indicates that finer genetic mapping of the region may uncover the causal variant. The size of the genomic region in question depends upon the number of markers in the region that vary between the lines.

BXD recombinant lines have been widely studied for alcohol-related traits. QTL analyses with them have identified regions on mouse chromosomes 1, 2, 3, 4, 9, 11, and 19 associated with alcohol preference and/or withdrawal. Some of these are convergent with syntenic regions of human chromosomes linked to alcohol-related phenotypes (Ehlers, Walter, Dick, Buck, & Crabbe, 2010).

For the most part, mapping approaches using recombinant inbred lines to identify genetic causes of individual differences in alcohol-related traits have given way to studies of genetically modified mice. Many alcohol-related phenotypes have been investigated using lines of mice that have had the function of a gene knocked out (globally, or conditionally), or overexpressed, or replaced by a human version of the gene (Bilbao, 2013). Some of the traits studied concern aspects of the early stages of addiction, such as sensitivity to alcohol's intoxicating effects, or sensitivity to reinforcing effects. Other studied traits model behaviors representing later stages in addiction that include aspects of chronic alcohol intake, craving, relapse, or withdrawal.

11.3.3 Genetically Engineering Mice

By far, most studies to examine the impact of genetic modification on alcohol-related behaviors have focused on the reinforcing effects of voluntary alcohol consumption modeled in two-bottle preference tests, with over 137 genes tested (Mayfield, Arends, Harris, & Blednov, 2016). Modifying genes in the following systems has been shown to impact voluntary alcohol consumption in mice: (1) neurotransmitters (GABA, glutamate, dopamine, serotonin, adenosine), (2) cannabinoids and opioids, (3) immune-related genes, (4) ion channels, (5) protein kinases, (6) enzymes, (7) neuropeptides/hormones, and (9) other gene targets (Mayfield et al., 2016). Many genes in these systems were considered candidate genes because of the roles of their products in circuits known to be involved in addiction-related processes. Some of the genetic effects identified are dependent on sex, alcohol concentration, time of access to alcohol, genetic background of line studied, or drinking test employed. These findings are consistent with work in humans in that many genes appear to be involved in individual differences in alcohol-related phenotypes and that the effects of the genetic variants are sometimes contingent on other factors.

Without a doubt, research into alcohol-related phenotypes with mice has shown that genetic differences play a role in individual differences, and there is no single gene that causes alcohol drinking or alcohol-related outcomes. Alcohol-related traits are polygenic and genetic effects are mediated by multiple, diverse biological circuits.

11.3.4 Using Fruit Flies to Investigate Alcohol-Related Traits

Fruit flies have also been used to investigate the impact of heredity on alcohol-related behaviors. Although fruit flies are more distant ancestors to humans than are rodents, we share enough biology for studies into basic aspects of the physiological and behavioral effects of alcohol to yield useful information. *Drosophila melanogaster* encounter alcohol in their natural environments in decaying fruits, and they can use it as a food source (Devineni & Heberlein, 2013). Many assays have been developed to test the effects of alcohol on fruit flies. The inebriometer is a good example that consists of a chamber into which alcohol vapor is introduced, and the time that it takes a fly to lose postural control and fall out of the chamber is operationalized as an index of alcohol sensitivity. Flies that are more sensitive to alcohol's intoxicating effects fall out of the inebriometer more quickly than do flies that are less sensitive. The assay has been a valuable screen to identify mutations that impact alcohol sensitivity.

Several other assays have been developed to test alcohol preference, tolerance, withdrawal, and of other alcohol-related traits in fruit flies. With such assays, the power of *D. melanogaster* genetic techniques and the newly developed tools available in "Big Data," fruit flies are well positioned to make important contributions to our understanding of the role of heredity on individual differences in alcohol-related behaviors (Engel, Taber, Vinton, & Crocker, 2019).

As in mice, alcohol-related behaviors and outcomes in fruit flies are polygenic. Voluntary alcohol consumption in *D. melanogaster* appears to be influenced by variation in nearly 300 genes (Fochler et al., 2017). In addition, there is evidence that genetic effects on alcohol consumption in fruit flies are sex-specific, and that genetic factors impacting the development and function of neural systems are crucial in alcohol-related behaviors. Such convergent evidence across non-human animal models should inform investigations into the role of heredity in individual differences in human alcohol-related behaviors.

Check-up

- Explain how to conduct a selective breeding study for alcohol preference with rodents.
- What are recombinant inbred lines and how are they used to investigate the genetics of alcohol-related traits?
- What is an inebriometer and how is it used?

11.4 Alcohol-Related Traits and Alcohol Use Disorder Run in Families

Long before there were systematic studies about the familial nature of alcohol problems, people recognized that they were more common in some families than in others. Systematic studies to determine whether alcoholism was hereditary began in earnest in the middle of the twentieth century (Cotton, 1979). The main finding is that a person who has family members with alcohol problems is more likely to develop alcohol problems than is someone who has no family members with alcohol problems. Of course, as we have pointed out in previous chapters, people in families typically share both genetic material and environments, so family studies alone cannot prove that genetic factors cause disorders like alcoholism. In fact, psychoactive substances are themselves environmental factors. They are found in the environment and without exposure to psychoactive substances, developing an addiction to them is impossible.

11.4.1 Measures of Family History

In general, family history should be considered an important indicator of risk for many health-related conditions. For example, age of onset of cardiovascular disease in parents is predictive of age of onset of cardiovascular disease in their offspring (Allport, Kikah, Abu Saif, Ekokobe, & Atem, 2016). Therefore, if one of your parents died of a heart attack at age 40, you should consider yourself to also be at high risk for early onset cardiovascular disease and should consider making lifestyle choices to maintain a healthy heart. So, what is the evidence that family history of alcoholism can predict risk for developing problems with alcohol?

Approximately twenty different methods of indexing family history of alcoholism have been developed and tested (Stoltenberg, Mudd, Blow, & Hill, 1998). Several measures dichotomously classify individuals as either being family history positive (FH+) or negative (FH-) based on the diagnosis of an alcohol use disorder, or the presence of alcohol problems, for someone in the family. For example, a proband may be considered FH+ if their father had been diagnosed with an alcohol use disorder, but FH- if not. Other measures produce quantitative indices to estimate the magnitude of familial risk. No single measure has emerged to be the dominant method of assessing alcoholism familiality, although the quantitative measures are better predictors of alcohol-related outcomes than dichotomous ones (Pandey et al., 2020).

Family history measures may seem quaint in the era of genome-wide data, but they can provide information about a person's combined genetic and environmental risk for alcoholism in a cost-effective way. For example, recent studies have found family history density of alcoholism to be associated with differences in the size of brain structures involved in addiction, specifically the nucleus accumbens (Cservenka, Gillespie, Michael, & Nagel, 2015), the hippocampus, and amygdala (Maksimovskiy et al., 2019). On a personal level, if you know that you have a family history of alcoholism, you may choose to reduce your risk of developing an alcohol use disorder by reducing your alcohol intake, or by abstaining entirely.

11.4.2 Longitudinal Studies to Investigate Alcoholism Risk

Most studies to understand the role of heredity and other risk factors in the development of substance use disorders are cross-sectional studies, in which adults are asked to provide retrospective, self-report data. Participants in such studies might donate blood or saliva for genotyping and complete self-report surveys about their current and past behavior. Their involvement is typically a one-shot affair.

Longitudinal studies, on the other hand, follow individual participants over time. In this way, the limitations of retrospective reports are avoided. In addition, when the focus of the study is the identification of biological and environmental risk factors for a substance use disorder, prospective longitudinal studies have the potential to gather data about individuals prior to their first use of a substance. Of course, such studies may begin in childhood and may continue for several years, or even decades, which requires long-term funding and dedication.

The Michigan Longitudinal Study (MLS) is an example of a prospective, longitudinal study of children from families with different levels of risk for developing alcoholism (Zucker, 2014). The MLS was established in the mid-1980s and continues to characterize differences in biology, behavior, and mental health outcomes of children at different levels of risk for alcoholism as defined by father's alcoholism status (Trucco, Villafuerte, Hussong, Burmeister, & Zucker, 2018). The bottom line with the MLS is that there are dramatic differences in risk for developing substance use disorders, including alcohol use disorder, based on father's alcoholism status, which strongly supports the evidence from cross-sectional family studies. In addition, the MLS provides strong evidence that substantial biological and behavioral differences between children from different risk groups are apparent *before* onset of their substance use and are therefore not caused by it.

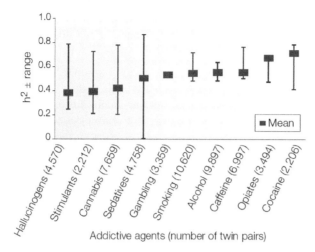

Figure 11.7. **Heritability estimates for addictive disorders.** Heritability estimates from twin studies, of substance use disorders for nine psychoactive substances and for gambling disorder. Source: Goldman, Oroszi, & Ducci (2005). Reprinted by permission from Springer Nature, Nature Reviews Genetics.

11.4.3 Alcohol Use and Alcohol Use Disorder Heritability Estimation

Twin and adoption studies have been widely used to estimate heritability of substance use disorders (see Figure 11.7). A meta-analysis that included thirteen twin studies and five adoption studies estimated the heritability of alcohol use disorder to be 0.49 (95% CI = 0.47–0.54; Verhulst, Neale, & Kendler, 2015). Such findings are consistent with the hypothesis that genetic differences between people play an important role in individual differences in risk for the development of substance use disorders, and that environmental factors also play an important role. Although heritability estimates do not indicate how many genes or which genes contain relevant variants, their findings when combined with those from family studies, rule out a single causal gene. Findings from family, twin, and adoption studies converge with evidence from non-human animal models that risk for developing substance use disorders is likely to be a combination of polygenic effects (i.e., many genes, with small effects) and environmental exposure (e.g., alcohol availability).

Data collected from twin studies has been used to characterize relations among substance use disorders, other psychiatric disorders, and personality traits (McGue, Irons, & Iacono, 2014). These efforts using sophisticated statistical modeling have provided evidence that at least some of the risk for the development of substance use disorders arises via a general risk for externalizing psychopathology. In other words, a compromised capacity for controlling one's own behavior (i.e., impulsivity) increases risk for adolescent alcohol use, drug use, and delinquency. Such behaviors can carry over into adulthood potentially resulting in alcohol use disorder, drug use disorder, or antisocial personality disorder. These findings indicate that subsequent work to identify genetic variants associated with substance use disorders should consider genes involved in behavioral control pathways, which is consistent with the conceptual model of addiction presented earlier in the chapter.

Check-up

- What does it mean to say that someone has a family history of alcoholism?
- Compare and contrast cross-sectional studies and longitudinal studies.
- What do the heritability estimates of substance use disorders tell us?

11.5 Alcohol Metabolism Genes Affect Risk for Alcohol Use Disorder

Psychoactive drugs, like alcohol (i.e., ethanol), are molecules that enter a person's body, act on biological targets, and then are removed by metabolic processes. Ethanol typically is ingested and therefore enters the bloodstream via the gastrointestinal tract and travels to the liver and eventually to the brain, where it interacts with its biological targets thereby producing its psychoactive effects. As blood continues to circulate carrying ethanol, it passes through the liver where metabolic enzymes break down some of the ethanol. For an average healthy person, the liver can metabolize the alcohol contained in one standard drink (approximately 7 g) in about an hour. Two families of liver enzymes, alcohol dehydrogenases (ADHs) and aldehyde dehydrogenases (ALDHs), catalyze ethanol metabolism (see Figure 11.8).

11.5.1 The Alcohol Flushing Response Reduces Alcoholism Risk

Genetic differences between people may affect the movement of a drug through their bodies (i.e., pharmacokinetics) and/or the actions of a drug at its target (i.e., pharmacodynamics), as we discussed in Chapter 6. For ethanol pharmacokinetics, each of the primary metabolic steps can be catalyzed by multiple enzymes that are each coded for by a different gene, although most alcohol is metabolized by ADH1B and ALDH2 (Edenberg & McClintick, 2018).

Typically, the two steps in ethanol metabolism occur at approximately the same rate. In which case, levels of acetaldehyde in the bloodstream remain low. When the reaction catalyzed by ADH is relatively faster than the reaction catalyzed by ALDH, a buildup of acetaldehyde occurs, which produces

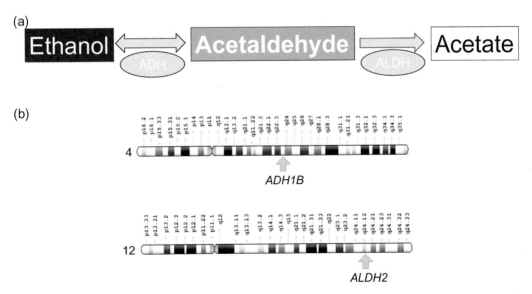

Figure 11.8. **Ethanol metabolism.** (a) Ethanol metabolism in the liver occurs when ethanol is converted by alcohol dehydrogenase (ADH) to acetaldehyde, which is then converted by acetaldehyde dehydrogenase (ALDH) to acetate. (b) Seven genes that code for ADH enzymes, and 19 genes that code for ALDH enzymes have been identified in the human genome. The bulk of ethanol metabolism is accomplished by ADH1B (located on chromosome 4) and ALDH2 (located on chromosome 12). Other enzymes involved in ethanol metabolism, but playing lesser roles include ADH1C, ADH4, ADH7, ALDH1B1, and ALDH1A1.

unpleasant effects called the alcohol flushing response that can include facial flushing (i.e., increased skin temperature), nausea, and tachycardia (i.e., increased heart rate) (see Box 11.3).

Box 11.3 Alcohol Dehydrogenase (ADH)

Seven genes that code for different alcohol dehydrogenase (ADH) enzymes are located in a cluster on chromosome 4q. ADH1B plays an important role in alcohol metabolism in the liver and its DNA sequence harbors three relatively common variants (see Table 11.1). The most common variant is *ADH1B*1*, which codes for an enzyme that metabolizes ethanol at the slowest rate of the three variants. *ADH1B*2* and *ADH1B*3* each differ from *ADH1B*1* in DNA sequence by a single SNP. The rates at which the resulting enzymes metabolize ethanol *in vitro*, however, are quite different, with *ADH1B*2* and *ADH1B*3* representing gain of function mutations over *ADH1B*1* (Edenberg & McClintick, 2018).

ADH1C contains two SNPs that produce amino acid substitutions that are in linkage disequilibrium (i.e., usually inherited together) (Table 11.2). The difference in the activity of the enzyme appears to be due to the arginine at amino acid position 272 (Edenberg & McClintick, 2018).

Gain of function mutations that increase the rate at which ADH converts ethanol to acetaldehyde in the liver should be associated with decreased alcohol drinking and risk for alcohol use disorders. Such a protective effect is supported *for ADH1B*2, ADH1B*3*, and *ADH1C*1* with odds ratios for each between 0.20 and 0.80, which would mean that carriers of these alleles would have a lower risk for developing alcoholism than someone with alternative alleles. For example, if a person homozygous for *ADH1B*1* had a 10 percent risk of having an alcohol use disorder, a person with one copy of *ADH1B*2* might have 20 percent of 10 percent, or 2 percent risk of having an alcohol use disorder.

Table 11.1 *ADH1B* single nucleotide polymorphisms and relative reaction rates of three genotypes

ADH1B	a.a. 48 (rs1229984)	a.a. 370 (rs2066702)	Relative rate
*ADH1B*1*	Arginine (G)	Arginine (G)	×
*ADH1B*2*	Histidine (T)	Arginine (G)	11×
*ADH1B*3*	Arginine (G)	Cysteine (A)	3×

Note: *ADH1B* genotypes are a combination of SNP genotypes at rs1229984 and rs2066702, each of which are missense mutations. Compared to the reaction rate of *ADH1B*1*, the other two mutations result in enzymes that catalyze ethanol to acetaldehyde faster.

Table 11.2 *ADH1C* single nucleotide polymorphisms and relative reaction rates of two genotypes

ADH1C	a.a. 272 (rs1693482)	a.a. 350 (rs698)	Relative rate
*ADH1C*1*	Arginine (C)	Isoleucine (T)	1.5 to 2×
*ADH1C*2*	Glutamine (A)	Valine (C)	×

Note: *ADH1C* genotypes are a combination of SNP genotypes at rs1693482 and rs698, each of which are missense mutations. Compared to the reaction rate of *ADH1C*2*, the other two mutations result in enzymes that catalyze ethanol to acetaldehyde faster.

A single nucleotide polymorphism in the gene that codes for ALDH2 (rs671, A:G) substitutes a lysine for a glutamate at amino acid 504, which renders the enzyme inactive (Edenberg & McClintick, 2018). The more common allele (A) is known as 504glu (previously referred to as ALDH2*1), and the less common allele (G) is known as 504lys (previously referred to as ALDH2*2). People who drink alcohol and carry either one or two copies of 504lys can have blood acetaldehyde levels that are six to nineteen times higher than those who are homozygous for 504glu, respectively (Li, Zhao, & Gelernter, 2012) (Figure 11.9).

As one might expect, people who experience a severe flushing response when drinking alcohol because they carry one or more copies of 504lys are more likely to be abstainers than those who do not experience the flushing response (i.e., 504glu homozygotes). Even when they do drink alcohol, those who experience the flushing response tend to drink less than those who do not. People who are homozygous for the 504lys allele are almost completely protected from developing alcoholism because they cannot tolerate drinking alcohol (Li et al., 2012).

To be clear, what we are describing here is a single nucleotide polymorphism that almost completely determines one's risk for developing an alcohol use disorder. The 504lys allele at rs671 is a direct protective factor because it effectively abolishes a person's capacity to metabolize alcohol, which impacts their alcohol consumption pattern and risk for addiction. Reducing alcohol metabolism via ALDH inhibition has long been known to reduce alcohol consumption, and it is the mechanism by which the alcoholism treatment medication Antabuse (disulfiram) works.

11.5.2 High and Low Drinking Rat Lines

Convergent evidence that variation in genes coding for ALDH2 impacts both enzyme activity and alcohol drinking behavior was obtained in lines of rats selected for voluntary alcohol consumption. In 1950, a selective breeding study for voluntary alcohol drinking established the high drinking UChB and the low drinking UChA lines (Quintanilla, Israel, Sapag, & Tampier, 2006). For over seventy generations of selection, animals were given access to 10 percent ethanol solution along with tap water in a two-bottle choice design.

Following up findings that the UChA line had lower rates of acetaldehyde metabolism than the UChB line, genetic variants were identified in *Aldh2* (see Figure 11.10(a)). The wild-type allele observed in the original Wistar rats was identified as $Aldh2^1$. At amino acid position 67, a variant was identified that substituted an arginine (Arg^{67}) for the wild-type glutamine (Gln^{67}). Another substitution mutation was found at amino acid position 479 where a lysine (Lys^{479}) was substituted for the wild-type glutamic acid (Glu^{479}). The genotypes at these two loci were strongly associated with indices of Aldh2 activity and the amount of alcohol voluntarily consumed (Quintanilla et al., 2006). The rats that had inactive Aldh2 enzymes (i.e., $Aldh2^2$ homozygotes) essentially abstained from voluntary alcohol drinking (see Figure 11.10(b)), which is the same pattern observed in humans. This pattern of behavior is also seen when the gene for Aldh2 is knocked out in lines of mice that typically consume alcohol voluntarily (i.e., C57BL/6). Compared to those with the gene intact (i.e., +/+) the *Aldh2* knockouts (-/-) with a C57BL/6 background avoid drinking alcohol (Isse et al., 2002). Without a doubt, variation in genes that code for the aldehyde dehydrogenase causes at least some individual differences in alcohol drinking behavior.

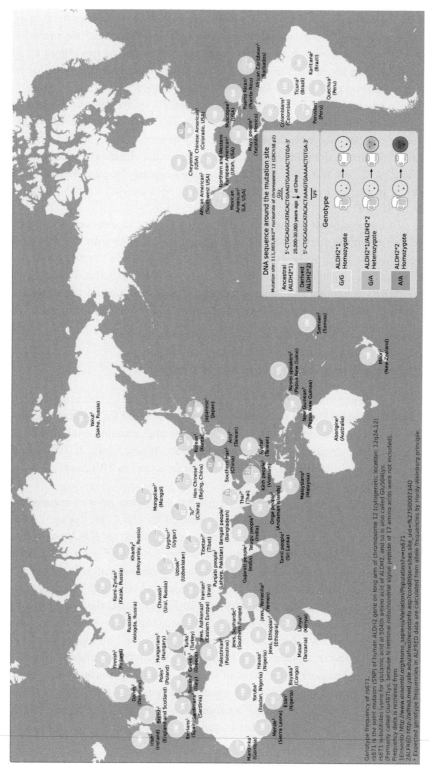

Figure 11.9. **Genotype frequency of rs671.** The approximate overall frequency of the A allele (504lys) at rs671 in the gene that codes for ALDH2 worldwide is approximately 0.14%. However, for those descended from Asian populations the frequency of the A allele is around 0.23% (Li et al., 2012). In many populations, the 504lys (A) allele is not found. Source: https://commons.wikimedia.org/wiki/File:ALDH2_rs671_genotype_frequency.png

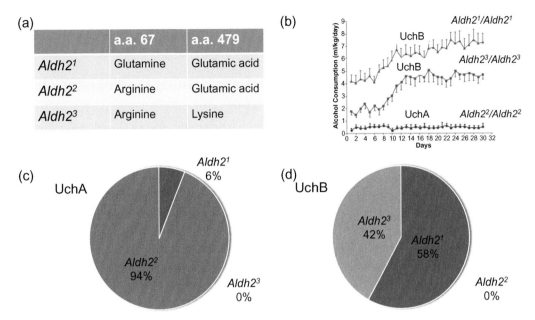

Figure 11.10. **Voluntary alcohol consumption in rats with different *Aldh2* genotypes.** (a) Three *Aldh2* alleles were identified in the selected lines that represented amino acid substitutions at positions 67 and 479. (b) The line of rats that abstain from voluntary alcohol drinking (i.e., UChA) are typically homozygous for *Aldh2²*, which codes for a low activity version of the enzyme. Rats from the UChB line voluntarily consume relatively large volumes of alcohol, with those homozygous for *Aldh2¹* drinking more on average than those homozygous for *Aldh2³*. Frequencies of the three *Aldh2* alleles are shown for (c) UchA and (d) UchB. Panel (b) Source: Quintanilla et al. (2006). © 2006 The Authors. Journal compilation © 2006 Society for the Study of Addiction, used by permission.

Check-up

- Explain how ethanol metabolism impacts alcoholism risk.
- What causes the flushing response and who is likely to get it?
- How does genetic variation at *Aldh2* impact the alcohol preference of rats?

11.6 There Are Many Genes That Contribute to Risk for Alcohol Use Disorder

In addition to the genes that code for alcohol metabolizing enzymes, there have been many candidate genes tested for association with alcohol-related behaviors and alcohol use disorder. A recent search on the Human Genome Epidemiology (HuGE) Navigator, a publicly searchable database of published genetic association and human genome epidemiological studies (Yu, Gwinn, Clyne, Yesupriya, & Khoury, 2008), identified 845 genes that have been associated with alcoholism. Of course, it is important to keep in mind the limitations of candidate gene association studies when interpreting their findings. In general, substance-related behaviors and substance use disorders are polygenic, with potentially hundreds of genes with variants that contribute to individual differences along with many environmental risk factors. Candidate gene association studies have typically been statistically underpowered (i.e., too small sample size) to detect small genetic effects. That is not to say that genetic variation in candidate genes plays no role in individual differences in these traits, but that the methods used to test such associations in human populations have not been optimal.

11.6.1 Candidate Gene Association Study Findings for Alcohol-Related Traits

This book is not the right venue for a critical review of candidate gene findings, but we discuss some of the important alcoholism candidate gene findings to provide a sense of the work that has been done. When the phenotypes in question are alcohol-related behaviors, the typical approaches include self-report questionnaires, or behavioral tasks depending on the trait in question.

As a reminder, dichotomous traits, such as diagnosis of alcohol use disorder, are typically studied using a case-control approach that compares allele frequencies. A significantly higher frequency of an allele in the cases (i.e., those with the disorder) is evidence for that allele to be considered a risk allele. For quantitative phenotypes, the basic conceptual approach is to test whether mean scores on the measure differ for groups defined by their genotype.

Eighteen of the 845 genes reported to be associated with alcoholism on the HuGE Navigator (Yu et al., 2008) have been cited in at least twenty published reports (see Figure 11.11). The products of these eighteen genes are involved in alcohol metabolism or neurotransmission. Sixty-eight percent (576/845) of the genes identified by the HuGE Navigator to be associated with alcoholism were cited only once.

The most-studied candidate genes for alcoholism involved in dopamine neurotransmission include dopamine receptors (*DRD2*, *DRD4*, *DRD3*), the dopamine transporter (*SLC6A3*), and monoamine oxidase A (*MAOA*). The dopamine system is an important candidate system because of the role of dopamine neurotransmission in the brain's reward pathway. DRD2 receptor isoforms can be either expressed presynaptically or postsynaptically, depending on the circuit. The most studied variant in *DRD2*, rs1800497, is located ~10 kb downstream of the *DRD2* gene in ankyrin repeat and kinase domain containing 1 (*ANKK1*) gene. There is some evidence that the T allele of rs1800497 is associated with a reduction in DRD2 receptor availability in the brain compared to the

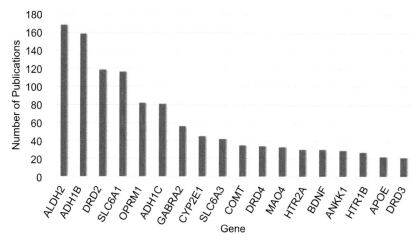

Figure 11.11. **Genes most studied for association with alcoholism.** Of the 845 genes identified by the HuGE Navigator (Yu et al., 2008) to be associated with alcoholism, the top 18 have been cited by at least 20 published reports. Products of these genes are involved in alcohol metabolism or neurotransmission.

C allele (Pohjalainen et al., 1998). A meta-analysis of sixty-two studies suggests that although the T allele may be statistically associated with alcohol use disorder (OR = 1.23), the association is primarily due to low frequencies of that allele in controls, which reduces statistical power (Jung, Montel, Shen, Mash, & Goldman, 2019). Furthermore, they suggest that there are likely other polymorphisms in *DRD2* that may account for the observed associations.

Three genes associated with serotonergic neurotransmission were cited in at least twenty published reports. They include the serotonin transporter (*SLC6A4*) and two serotonin receptors (*HTR2A, HTR1B*). The serotonin system modulates many other neurotransmitter systems including, but not limited to, dopamine and GABA. The HTR1B receptor is an autoreceptor located on the presynaptic neuron that regulates the release of serotonin. A variant in the *HTR1B* gene (rs6296) received early attention for its potential linkage with a type of alcoholism distinguished by early age of onset and comorbidity with antisocial personality disorder, called antisocial alcoholism (Lappalainen et al., 1998). The finding was convergent with earlier work showing increased aggression and alcohol consumption in *Htr1b* knockout mice (Crabbe et al., 1996). Subsequent studies have not supported these associations in humans (Dick & Foroud, 2003).

The opioid system is involved with the brain reward system, and much of its effect is mediated by the μ-opioid receptor. A variant in the gene that codes for the μ-opioid receptor (*OPRM1*, rs1799971, A118G) has been widely studied because it produces an amino acid substitution (Asn40Asp), which appears to have functional effects. The variant does appear to be associated with alcohol use disorder (Kong et al., 2017), although it may play a role in response to alcoholism treatment with the opioid receptor antagonist naltrexone, but if so, the effect is small (Hartwell et al., 2020).

Genes that code for GABA receptor subunits have been a focus of candidate gene association studies because GABA receptors mediate alcohol's sedative effects. GABA is the brain's primary inhibitory neurotransmitter with two primary receptor types $GABA_A$ and $GABA_B$. Without going into too much detail, eleven genes code for GABA receptor subunits whose products combine to make receptors. A SNP in the *GABRA2* gene (rs279858) may be weakly associated with alcohol dependence (Olfson & Bierut, 2012) via a lower subjective response to alcohol's effects (Uhart et al., 2013).

11.6.2 Genome-Wide Association Studies Findings for Alcohol-Related Traits

Genome-wide association studies have consistently supported the association of variants in ADH genes in a cluster on chromosome 4 with alcohol use disorders (see Figure 11.12). The strong convergence of evidence for alcohol metabolism genes across organisms and methods leaves little doubt of their role in alcohol-related traits and risk for alcohol use disorder. Similarly, evidence of genetic variation in *DRD2* playing a role in alcoholism is compelling.

One of the most promising developments in the GWAS era is that investigators are joining international consortia and sharing data. In this way, very large sample sizes can be brought to bear, and meta-analyses can combine data across studies making large sample sizes even larger. A review identified ten genes in which SNPs were significantly associated with either alcohol consumption or alcohol use disorder across two or more GWAS (Sanchez-Roige, Palmer, & Clarke, 2020). In addition to the *ADH* gene cluster on chromosome 4, the meta-analysis found strong associations with rs1260326 in the glucokinase receptor (*GCKR*) gene, and with rs35538052 in the alpha-ketoglutarate dependent dioxygenase (*FTO*) gene. It is interesting to note that *GCKR* plays a role in glucose metabolism and *FTO* is associated with obesity, which suggests new biological pathways to consider when investigating alcohol use disorders.

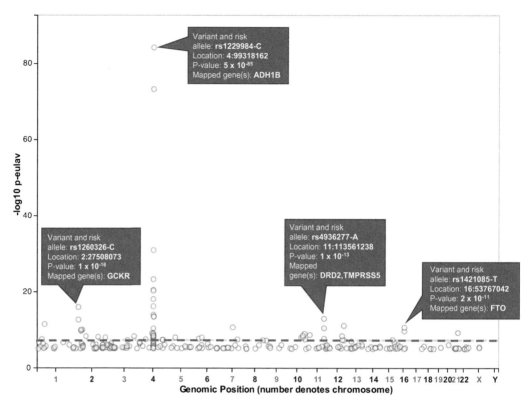

Figure 11.12. **Manhattan plot of GWAS findings for alcohol dependence.** A Manhattan plot shows the significance level of associations for SNPs in GWAS with the location across chromosomes on the x-axis. Each dot represents a SNP and those that are above the dashed line are considered to have reached genome-wide significance after controlling for multiple comparisons. Note that variants in *ADH1B*, *DRD2*, *GCKR*, and *FTO* genes are significantly associated with alcohol dependence across GWAS. Source: Plot generated June 12, 2020 using the GWAS Catalog (www.ebi.ac.uk/gwas/efotraits/EFO_0003829).

We have just scratched the surface on the fast-moving world of GWAS for alcohol use disorders. The tremendous amounts of genetic and behavioral data that are being analyzed together with bioinformatics to understand gene expression and molecular pathways will dramatically increase our understanding of pathways from genes to addiction.

We know with certainty that substance use disorders, including alcoholism, run in families and are polygenic. We also know that alcohol metabolism genes play an important role in voluntary alcohol consumption and risk for alcohol use disorders. More addiction risk variants are being identified every year. Hopefully, such information will lead to improvements in addiction prevention and treatment efforts.

Check-up

- Discuss the important findings from candidate gene association studies on alcohol-related traits.
- Discuss the important findings from GWAS on alcohol-related traits.
- Compare and contrast the findings of candidate gene association studies and GWAS on alcohol-related traits.

11.7 SUMMARY

- Most people use substances like caffeine, alcohol, tobacco, or marijuana. Substance use disorders represent a pattern of substance use that can cause problems in a person's life. Impaired control over use, the development of tolerance, and experiencing withdrawal are symptoms of a substance use disorder.
- Neuroadaptations to restore function to normal following intoxicating levels of substance use likely produce the symptoms of addiction. Three stages of addiction: binge/intoxication, withdrawal/negative affect, and preoccupation/anticipation involve different brain areas and neurotransmitter systems.
- Non-human animal models, especially rodents, have been crucial in investigating the role of genetic variation in individual differences in substance use behaviors. Strain comparisons, divergent selection, genetic mapping, and mutagenesis have provided convergent evidence of the role of heredity in substance use.
- Risk for addiction runs in families and has significant non-zero heritability estimates.
- Variation in genes that code for alcohol metabolizing enzymes play a role in alcoholism risk.
- Alcohol use disorders have polygenic influence. Candidate gene association studies and GWAS have provided evidence of polygenes on alcoholism risk.

RECOMMENDED READING

- Koob, G. F., & Volkow, N. D. (2016). Neurobiology of addiction: A neurocircuitry analysis. *Lancet Psychiatry*, *3*(8), 760–773. doi:10.1016/s2215-0366(16)00104-8
- Stoltenberg, S. F. (Ed.) (2014). *Genes and the Motivation to Use Substances*. Nebraska Symposium on Motivation 61. New York: Springer.

REFERENCES

Allport, S. A., Kikah, N., Abu Saif, N., Ekokobe, F., & Atem, F. D. (2016). Parental age of onset of cardiovascular disease as a predictor for offspring age of onset of cardiovascular disease. *PLoS One*, *11*(12), e0163334. doi:10.1371/journal.pone.0163334

Ashbrook, D. G., Arends, D., Prins, P., Mulligan, M. K., Roy, S., Williams, E. G., . . . Williams, R. W. (2019). The expanded BXD family of mice: A cohort for experimental systems genetics and precision medicine. *bioRxiv*, 672097. doi:10.1101/672097

Banich, M. T., & Compton, R. J. (2018). *Cognitive Neuroscience* (4th ed.). Cambridge: Cambridge University Press.

Bell, R. L., Rodd, Z. A., Lumeng, L., Murphy, J. M., & McBride, W. J. (2006). The alcohol-preferring P rat and animal models of excessive alcohol drinking. *Addict Biol*, *11*(3–4), 270–288. doi:10.1111/j.1369-1600.2005.00029.x

Berridge, K. C., & Robinson, T. E. (2016). Liking, wanting, and the incentive-sensitization theory of addiction. *Am Psychol*, *71*(8), 670–679. doi:10.1037/amp0000059

Bilbao, A. (2013). Advanced transgenic approaches to understand alcohol-related phenotypes in animals. *Curr Top Behav Neurosci*, *13*, 271–311. doi:10.1007/7854_2012_204

Chou, S. P., Goldstein, R. B., Smith, S. M., Huang, B., Ruan, W. J., Zhang, H., ... Grant, B. F. (2016). The epidemiology of DSM-5 nicotine use disorder: Results from the National Epidemiologic Survey on Alcohol and Related Conditions-III. *J Clin Psychiatry, 77*(10), 1404–1412. doi:10.4088/JCP.15m10114

Cotton, N. S. (1979). The familial incidence of alcoholism: A review. *J Stud Alcohol, 40*(1), 89–116. doi:10.15288/jsa.1979.40.89

Crabbe, J. C. (2014). Use of animal models of alcohol-related behavior. *Handb Clin Neurol, 125*, 71–86. doi:10.1016/b978-0-444-62619-6.00005-7

Crabbe, J. C., Phillips, T. J., Feller, D. J., Hen, R., Wenger, C. D., Lessov, C. N., & Schafer, G. L. (1996). Elevated alcohol consumption in null mutant mice lacking 5-HT1B serotonin receptors. *Nat Genet, 14*(1), 98–101. doi:10.1038/ng0996-98

Cservenka, A., Gillespie, A. J., Michael, P. G., & Nagel, B. J. (2015). Family history density of alcoholism relates to left nucleus accumbens volume in adolescent girls. *J Stud Alcohol Drugs, 76*(1), 47–56.

Devineni, A. V., & Heberlein, U. (2013). The evolution of Drosophila melanogaster as a model for alcohol research. *Annu Rev Neurosci, 36*, 121–138. doi:10.1146/annurev-neuro-062012-170256

Dick, D. M., & Foroud, T. (2003). Candidate genes for alcohol dependence: A review of genetic evidence from human studies. *Alcohol Clin Exp Res, 27*(5), 868–879. doi:10.1097/01.alc.0000065436.24221.63

Edenberg, H. J., & McClintick, J. N. (2018). Alcohol dehydrogenases, aldehyde dehydrogenases, and alcohol use disorders: A critical review. *Alcohol Clin Exp Res, 42*(12), 2281–2297. doi:10.1111/acer.13904

Ehlers, C. L., Walter, N. A., Dick, D. M., Buck, K. J., & Crabbe, J. C. (2010). A comparison of selected quantitative trait loci associated with alcohol use phenotypes in humans and mouse models. *Addict Biol, 15*(2), 185–199. doi:10.1111/j.1369-1600.2009.00195.x

Engel, G. L., Taber, K., Vinton, E., & Crocker, A. J. (2019). Studying alcohol use disorder using Drosophila melanogaster in the era of "Big Data." *Behav Brain Funct, 15*(1), 7. doi:10.1186/s12993-019-0159-x

Fochler, S., Morozova, T. V., Davis, M. R., Gearhart, A. W., Huang, W., Mackay, T. F. C., & Anholt, R. R. H. (2017). Genetics of alcohol consumption in Drosophila melanogaster. *Genes Brain Behav, 16*(7), 675–685. doi:10.1111/gbb.12399

Goldman, D., Oroszi, G., & Ducci, F. (2005). The genetics of addictions: Uncovering the genes. *Nat Rev Genet, 6*(7), 521–532. doi:10.1038/nrg1635

Grant, B. F., Goldstein, R. B., Saha, T. D., Chou, S. P., Jung, J., Zhang, H., ... Hasin, D. S. (2015). Epidemiology of DSM-5 alcohol use disorder: Results from the National Epidemiologic Survey on Alcohol and Related Conditions III. *JAMA Psychiatry, 72*(8), 757–766. doi:10.1001/jamapsychiatry.2015.0584

Grant, B. F., Saha, T. D., Ruan, W. J., Goldstein, R. B., Chou, S. P., Jung, J., ... Hasin, D. S. (2016). Epidemiology of DSM-5 drug use disorder: Results from the National Epidemiologic Survey on Alcohol and Related Conditions-III. *JAMA Psychiatry, 73*(1), 39–47. doi:10.1001/jamapsychiatry.2015.2132

Hartwell, E. E., Feinn, R., Morris, P. E., Gelernter, J., Krystal, J., Arias, A. J., ... Kranzler, H. R. (2020). Systematic review and meta-analysis of the moderating effect of rs1799971 in OPRM1, the mu-opioid receptor gene, on response to naltrexone treatment of alcohol use disorder. *Addiction, 115*(8), 1426–1437. doi:10.1111/add.14975

Isse, T., Oyama, T., Kitagawa, K., Matsuno, K., Matsumoto, A., Yoshida, A., ... Kawamoto, T. (2002). Diminished alcohol preference in transgenic mice lacking aldehyde dehydrogenase activity. *Pharmacogenetics, 12*(8), 621–626. doi:10.1097/00008571-200211000-00006

Jung, Y., Montel, R. A., Shen, P. H., Mash, D. C., & Goldman, D. (2019). Assessment of the association of D2 dopamine receptor gene and reported allele frequencies with alcohol use disorders: A systematic review and meta-analysis. *JAMA Netw Open, 2*(11), e1914940. doi:10.1001/jamanetworkopen.2019.14940

Kong, X., Deng, H., Gong, S., Alston, T., Kong, Y., & Wang, J. (2017). Lack of associations of the opioid receptor mu 1 (OPRM1) A118G polymorphism (rs1799971) with alcohol dependence: Review and meta-analysis of retrospective controlled studies. *BMC Med Genet, 18*(1), 120. doi:10.1186/s12881-017-0478-4

Koob, G. F., & Volkow, N. D. (2010). Neurocircuitry of addiction. *Neuropsychopharmacology, 35*(1), 217–238. doi:10.1038/npp.2009.110

Koob, G. F., & Volkow, N. D. (2016). Neurobiology of addiction: A neurocircuitry analysis. *Lancet Psychiatry, 3*(8), 760–773. doi:10.1016/s2215-0366(16)00104-8

Lappalainen, J., Long, J. C., Eggert, M., Ozaki, N., Robin, R. W., Brown, G. L., . . . Goldman, D. (1998). Linkage of antisocial alcoholism to the serotonin 5-HT1B receptor gene in 2 populations. *Arch Gen Psychiatry, 55*(11), 989–994. doi:10.1001/archpsyc.55.11.989

Li, D., Zhao, H., & Gelernter, J. (2012). Strong protective effect of the aldehyde dehydrogenase gene (ALDH2) 504lys (*2) allele against alcoholism and alcohol-induced medical diseases in Asians. *Hum Genet, 131*(5), 725–737. doi:10.1007/s00439-011-1116-4

Maksimovskiy, A. L., Oot, E. N., Seraikas, A. M., Rieselbach, M., Caine, C., Sneider, J. T., . . . Silveri, M. M. (2019). Morphometric biomarkers of adolescents with familial risk for alcohol use disorder. *Alcohol Clin Exp Res, 43*(11), 2354–2366. doi:10.1111/acer.14201

Mayfield, J., Arends, M. A., Harris, R. A., & Blednov, Y. A. (2016). Genes and alcohol consumption: Studies with mutant mice. *Int Rev Neurobiol, 126*, 293–355. doi:10.1016/bs.irn.2016.02.014

McGue, M., Irons, D., & Iacono, W. G. (2014). The adolescent origins of substance use disorders: A behavioral genetic perspective. *Nebr Symp Motiv, 61*, 31–50. doi:10.1007/978-1-4939-0653-6_3

Mitchell, D. C., Knight, C. A., Hockenberry, J., Teplansky, R., & Hartman, T. J. (2014). Beverage caffeine intakes in the U.S. *Food Chem Toxicol, 63*, 136–142. doi:10.1016/j.fct.2013.10.042

Olfson, E., & Bierut, L. J. (2012). Convergence of genome-wide association and candidate gene studies for alcoholism. *Alcohol Clin Exp Res, 36*(12), 2086–2094. doi:10.1111/j.1530-0277.2012.01843.x

Pandey, G., Seay, M. J., Meyers, J. L., Chorlian, D. B., Pandey, A. K., Kamarajan, C., . . . Porjesz, B. (2020). Density and dichotomous family history measures of alcohol use disorder as predictors of behavioral and neural phenotypes: A comparative study across gender and race/ethnicity. *Alcohol Clin Exp Res, 44*(3), 697–710. doi:10.1111/acer.14280

Pohjalainen, T., Rinne, J. O., Någren, K., Lehikoinen, P., Anttila, K., Syvälahti, E. K., & Hietala, J. (1998). The A1 allele of the human D2 dopamine receptor gene predicts low D2 receptor availability in healthy volunteers. *Mol Psychiatry, 3*(3), 256–260. doi:10.1038/sj.mp.4000350

Quintanilla, M. E., Israel, Y., Sapag, A., & Tampier, L. (2006). The UChA and UChB rat lines: Metabolic and genetic differences influencing ethanol intake. *Addict Biol, 11*(3–4), 310–323. doi:10.1111/j.1369-1600.2006.00030.x

Ritchie, H. (2018). Alcohol consumption. Retrieved from: https://ourworldindata.org/alcohol-consumption

SAMHSA (2020). *Key substance use and mental health indicators in the United States: Results from the 2019 National Survey on Drug Use and Health* (HHS Publication No. PEP20–07-01-001, NSDUH Series H-55). Rockville, MD. Retrieved from: www.samhsa.gov/data/

Sanchez-Roige, S., Palmer, A. A., & Clarke, T. K. (2020). Recent efforts to dissect the genetic basis of alcohol use and abuse. *Biol Psychiatry, 87*(7), 609–618. doi:10.1016/j.biopsych.2019.09.011

Stoltenberg, S. F., Mudd, S. A., Blow, F. C., & Hill, E. M. (1998). Evaluating measures of family history of alcoholism: Density versus dichotomy. *Addiction, 93*(10), 1511–1520. doi:10.1046/j.1360-0443.1998.931015117.x

Trucco, E. M., Villafuerte, S., Hussong, A., Burmeister, M., & Zucker, R. A. (2018). Biological underpinnings of an internalizing pathway to alcohol, cigarette, and marijuana use. *J Abnorm Psychol, 127*(1), 79–91. doi:10.1037/abn0000310

Uhart, M., Weerts, E. M., McCaul, M. E., Guo, X., Yan, X., Kranzler, H. R., . . . Wand, G. S. (2013). GABRA2 markers moderate the subjective effects of alcohol. *Addict Biol, 18*(2), 357–369. doi:10.1111/j.1369-1600.2012.00457.x

Verhulst, B., Neale, M. C., & Kendler, K. S. (2015). The heritability of alcohol use disorders: A meta-analysis of twin and adoption studies. *Psychol Med, 45*(5), 1061–1072. doi:10.1017/s0033291714002165

Wahlsten, D., Bachmanov, A., Finn, D. A., & Crabbe, J. C. (2006). Stability of inbred mouse strain differences in behavior and brain size between laboratories and across decades. *Proc Natl Acad Sci USA, 103*(44), 16364–16369. doi:10.1073/pnas.0605342103

World Health Organization (2019). *World Drug Report* (Vol. Sales No. E.19.XI.8), United Nations.

World Health Organization (2020). Alcohol Dependence. ICD-11 for Mortality and Morbidity Statistics. http://id.who.int/icd/entity/1580466198

Yu, W., Gwinn, M., Clyne, M., Yesupriya, A., & Khoury, M. J. (2008). A navigator for human genome epidemiology. *Nat Genet, 40*(2), 124–125. doi:10.1038/ng0208-124

Zucker, R. A. (2014). Genes, brain, behavior, and context: The developmental matrix of addictive behavior. *Nebr Symp Motiv, 61*, 51–69. doi:10.1007/978-1-4939-0653-6_4

Part IV Health, Social Behavior, and Implications

12 Eating and Exercising

Have you ever tried to lose weight? Many of us would like to weigh less than we do. On the other hand, some people struggle to gain weight. The topic of weight control is a stark reminder of the complex interplay between biology, psychology, and environment that has major implications for well-being. We may intend to change our weight by altering our behavior, but someone brings donuts, and we feel too tired to exercise after a long day of sitting at a desk. For many of us, it is all too easy to gain weight, and as we age it becomes increasingly difficult to lose it.

In this chapter, we first discuss aspects of modern life that have impacted our energy balance and produced a public health problem. We also outline a biological circuit involved in managing our energy intake and output. Next, we discuss obesity and the evidence that genetic factors play a role in individual differences in obesity risk. Then, we introduce eating disorders and discuss evidence of individual differences in risk being due to genetic variation. Finally, we discuss individual differences in voluntary exercise and evidence that genetic differences between individuals play a role.

12.1 Eating and Exercising in Context

For most of the world, the twenty-first century is a time of food availability that is unprecedented in human history (see Figure 12.1). Certainly, there are still parts of the world where people experience shortages of food and where access to sufficient food varies as a function of socioeconomic factors. But for many of us, food is abundantly available and food costs make up a relatively small fraction of our income.

12.1.1 The Nutrition Transition and Thrifty Genotypes

Throughout most of human history food has not been as widely available as it is today. One way to think about the historical changes in food availability is the so-called nutrition transition (Popkin, 2006). In this model, there are five stages through which human populations move over time (see Figure 12.2). Transitions from one stage to the next are driven by increases in modernization, urbanization, economic development, and increased wealth.

Obesity is a condition in which excess body fat increases risk for health problems. Prior to modernization, when a tremendous amount of physical activity is necessary for survival and when access to energy-dense food is limited, rates of obesity are low. The modern environment, where low levels of physical activity are coupled with virtually unlimited access to energy-dense food, is sometimes termed obesogenic because it facilitates the development of obesity.

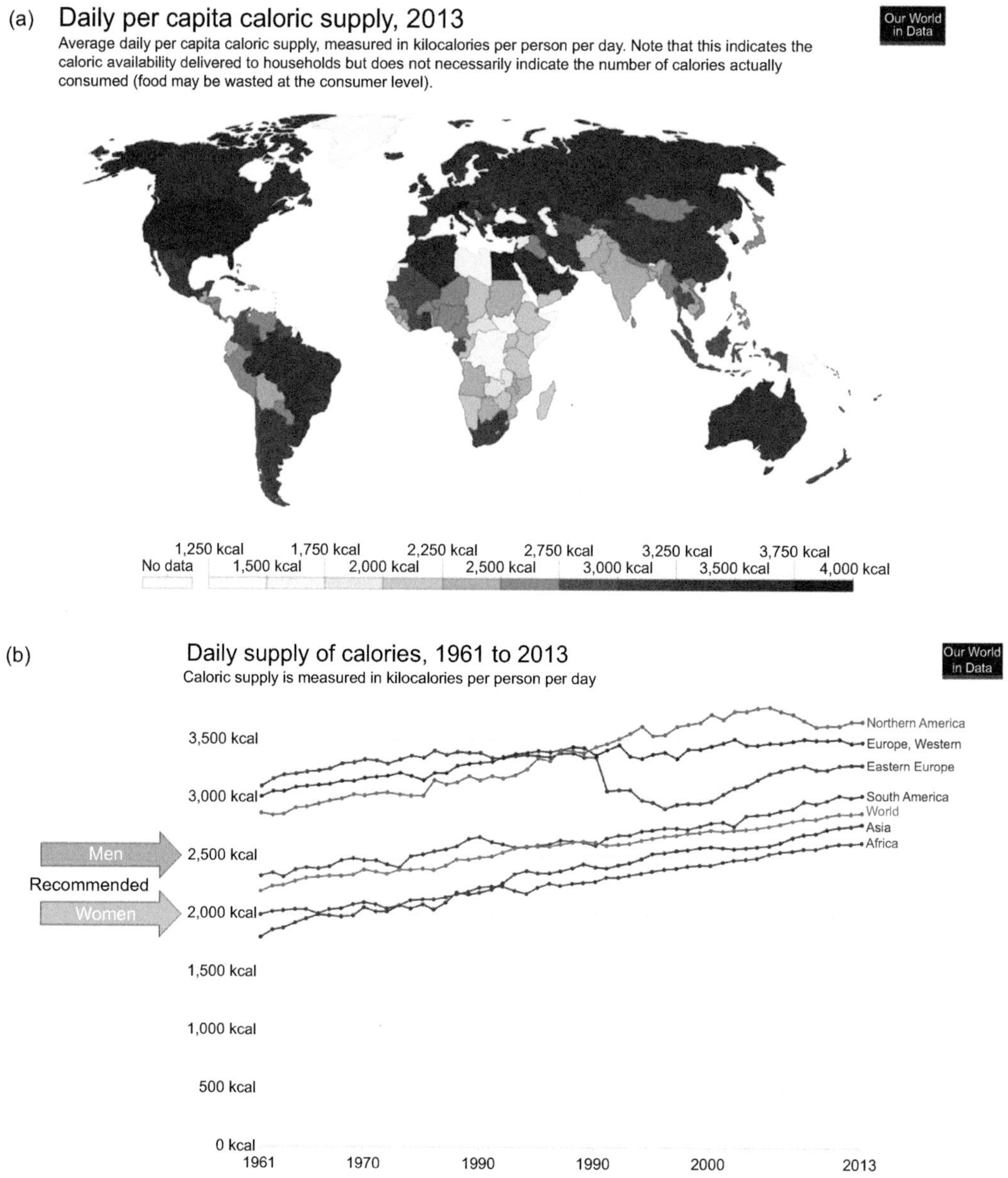
(a) Daily per capita caloric supply, 2013
Average daily per capita caloric supply, measured in kilocalories per person per day. Note that this indicates the caloric availability delivered to households but does not necessarily indicate the number of calories actually consumed (food may be wasted at the consumer level).
Our World in Data
No data
1,250 kcal
1,500 kcal
1,750 kcal
2,000 kcal
2,250 kcal
2,500 kcal
2,750 kcal
3,000 kcal
3,250 kcal
3,500 kcal
3,750 kcal
4,000 kcal
(b)
Daily supply of calories, 1961 to 2013
Caloric supply is measured in kilocalories per person per day
Our World in Data
3,500 kcal
3,000 kcal
2,500 kcal
2,000 kcal
1,500 kcal
1,000 kcal
500 kcal
0 kcal
1961
1970
1990
1990
2000
2013
Men
Recommended
Women
Northern America
Europe, Western
Eastern Europe
South America
World
Asia
Africa

Figure 12.1. **Food availability worldwide.** (a) Nearly all countries around the world are estimated to have at least 2,000 kcal of food available per person. Most countries have significantly more food available per capita. (b) When examined over time, food availability on all continents has risen dramatically since the middle of the twentieth century. Arrows indicate the number of kcal for men and women recommended by the World Health Organization. Source: Max Roser and Hannah Ritchie (2013) "Food Supply." Published online at OurWorldInData.org. Retrieved from: https://ourworldindata.org/food-supply

Obviously, there are many factors that can account for population level changes in rates of eating and exercising. We will focus our attention on the ways in which genetic differences between people can help to explain individual differences in those behaviors and in their outcomes.

An early attempt at understanding the impact of genetic differences on individual differences in obesity was the **thrifty genotype hypothesis** that posits combinations of genetic variants that were once favored by natural selection are now deleterious (Neel, 1962). Combinations of

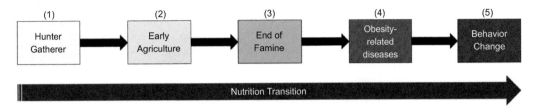

Figure 12.2. **Nutrition transition.** (1) Human populations originated as hunter-gatherers, where lifestyles were very active and diets consisted mainly of plants and lean meat. (2) Next, as early agriculture developed, lifestyles were active, and famines were relatively common. (3) As agricultural practices improve, lifestyles were still relatively active, but famines occurred less frequently. (4) As modernization, industrialization, and mechanized transport increases, lifestyles become more sedentary, and access to high-calorie, high-fat foods increases. Obesity and obesity-related diseases, such as heart disease, increase. (5) Finally, people change their diet and lifestyles to reduce obesity.

genetic variants that enhanced survival in times of feast-or-famine by efficiently storing energy as fat and by reducing energy expenditures now cause disease when energy-dense food is widely available and sedentary lifestyles are the norm. This hypothesis defines a specific G×E interaction such that a genotype, or set of genotypes, produces a distinct outcome (i.e., health benefit) in one environment, and another outcome (i.e., health risk) in an alternative environment. Other hypotheses have extended the thrifty genotype hypothesis to explain the origins of obesity by considering development, genetic drift, and epigenetics (Qasim et al., 2018). On the other hand, famines may not have been a potent selective force in human evolutionary history (Speakman, 2006). Although we may not fully understand the ways in which evolutionary forces have produced human beings susceptible to obesity, we have made advances in understanding the biological mechanism involved.

Organisms need to take in energy to fuel biological processes. The energy content of food is measured in calories, where 1 calorie (cal) is the amount of energy needed to raise the temperature of 1 gram of water by $1\,^{\circ}C$. Therefore, a kilocalorie (kcal) is equal to 1,000 calories, which is sometimes written as Calorie (Cal, note, upper case C). However, by convention, the term calorie is often used to represent a kilocalorie when discussing food. So, for example, when it says 200 calories per serving on a food label, it means 200 kcal.

Biological processes, including behavior, consume calories. Nutritionists recommend that each day men consume 2,000–3,000 kcal, and women consume 1,600–2,400 kcal, depending on age and activity level. These recommendations provide sufficient energy to fuel an average person's basal metabolism, which is the energy required for life-sustaining functions such as respiration, circulation, and cellular activities. Total energy expenditure includes basal metabolism, the energy required to digest food, and calories expended through physical activity. When more calories are consumed than are expended, the excess are stored for later use. One way to store calories is to convert them to fat (i.e., adipose tissue).

12.1.2 Mice That Have Defective Leptin Signaling Are Obese

In 1949, a spontaneous mutation arose in a line of mice that produced noticeably fat mice (Ingalls, Dickie & Snell, 1950). One of them weighed 90g and another 75g at 10 months old, when an average control mouse weighed 29g (see Figure 12.3). The spontaneous recessive mutation was dubbed *obese* (*ob*). Homozygous mice (*ob/ob*) were obese, ate more than control mice (i.e., hyperphagia), and developed diabetes. The mutated gene was identified in 1994 and its product was hypothesized to be a signaling molecule that provided information about fat stores, which was later identified and called leptin (Zhang et al., 1994).

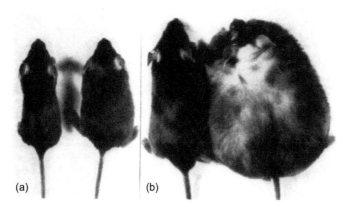

Figure 12.3. **Obese mice.** A spontaneous mutation in mice dubbed obese (ob) causes an increase in eating and a decrease in physical activity. A wild-type (left, +/+) and an obese (right, ob/ob) mouse are shown at (a) 21 days and (b) 10 months of age. Source: Ingalls et al. (1950), by permission of Oxford University Press.

Adipose cells produce the hormone leptin, which is part of the body's appetite control circuit. Leptin provides information about the body's current fat stores. Higher levels of leptin indicate higher levels of fat and therefore signal that the body has sufficient energy reserves. Leptin is a satiety signal (i.e., stop eating). Lower levels of leptin indicate lower fat levels and signal hunger (i.e., start eating).

A line of mice that developed diabetes and were overweight was identified in 1966 (Hummel, Dickie, & Coleman, 1966). These phenotypes were caused by a recessive mutation called *diabetes* (*db*). To determine whether the *ob* and *db* mutations were alternative alleles of the same gene or mutations of different genes, a complementation test was conducted. To begin a complementation test, parents that are heterozygous for the two mutations in question are mated together (i.e., +/*ob* mice are mated to +/*db* mice). If the two mutations represent different alleles of the same gene, some of the hybrid offspring should show the affected phenotype (i.e., obesity). For example, if the mutation is recessive and fully penetrant, one would expect 25 percent of the offspring to carry the "homozygous" genotype and display the trait. In other words, the results would be similar to what is expected for the F_2 generation of a monohybrid cross. However, if the mutations are in different genes, the wild-type alleles contributed by the parents would "complement" the mutant alleles so that the offspring would be "heterozygous" at both loci and therefore would not display the affected trait. In other words, the results would be similar to what is expected in the F_1 generation of a dihybrid cross. In the case of *ob* and *db*, all twenty-one offspring produced had the wild-type (i.e., non-obese) phenotype, thereby showing that the mutations complemented each other and were therefore in different genes (Hummel et al., 1966).

Subsequent work showed that the *db* gene coded for the leptin receptor. Therefore, a mutation in the gene that codes for the signaling molecule (*ob*) and a mutation in the gene that codes for its receptor (*db*) produces animals that have faulty signaling about their fat stores and therefore continue to eat as if they were starving.

Appetite control circuits provide signals that motivate eating (appetite) or inhibit it (satiety). Leptin plays a role in one of those circuits by providing information about energy reserves in the form of fat. Other signaling circuits provide information about blood glucose levels and presence of food in the gut (see Box 12.1). A detailed description of such circuits is beyond the scope of this text; however, it is important to note that each circuit relies on hormone or neurotransmitter systems all of which require many components that are gene products, such as receptors. Any genetic variation that impacts the structure or function of such circuits potentially contributes to individual differences in eating behavior. In addition, eating also activates the brain's reward system, and relies on executive functions, and often occurs in a social and cultural context. So, although the basic circuitry of appetite control is known, the regulation of eating behavior involves multiple circuits and crosses levels of analysis. Eating behavior is neither simply explained nor easily controlled.

Check-up

- What is the nutrition transition and how does it relate to the current availability of food in the world?
- Explain the thrifty genotype hypothesis.
- What is a complementation test and what did it tell us about the *ob* and *db* mutations?

Box 12.1 Appetite Control Circuits

Hormones secreted by fat (leptin), the stomach (ghrelin), the pancreas (insulin), and the intestines (PYY$_{3-36}$) provide information to neurons in the arcuate nucleus of the hypothalamus about the current state of energy stores (see Figure 12.4). Leptin signals long-term energy stores (i.e., fat levels). High levels of leptin stimulate neurons that project to the lateral hypothalamus to release POMC, which binds to postsynaptic MC4R receptors. Those neurons relay satiety signals to the nucleus of the solitary tract thereby reducing appetite and eating behavior. High leptin levels inhibit neurons that project from the arcuate nucleus to the paraventricular nucleus and release neuropeptide Y (NPY).

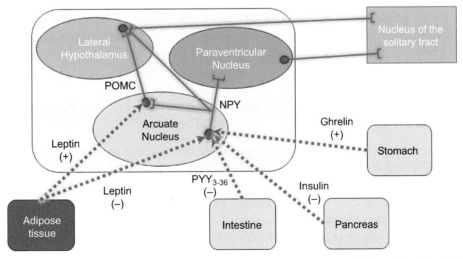

Figure 12.4. **Appetite control circuits.** Hormones produced in the body provide information to hypothalamic nuclei regarding availability of food, fat, and nutrients. Hypothalamic nuclei trigger hunger-associated feelings and food-seeking behavior.

Levels of ghrelin, insulin, and PYY_{3-36} signal the hypothalamus about the shorter-term energy stores. Ghrelin levels build during fasting and drop after eating. Levels of PYY_{3-36} increase after food is eaten. Levels of insulin increase around mealtimes. High levels of insulin and PYY_{3-36} inhibit NPY releasing neurons, whereas high levels of ghrelin activate them. Activation of NPY neurons can be considered a hunger signal that stimulates appetite and eating behavior.

Other biological circuits (e.g., reward pathway) are also involved in regulating appetite as are non-biological cues such as time of day, the sight or smell of food, the sight of others eating, and so on. Genes for each component in the appetite control circuits have variants that could contribute to individual differences in appetite.

12.2 Genetic Variation Partially Explains Risk for Obesity

Excessive accumulation of body fat can lead to health problems. An indirect measure of the accumulation of body fat is the body mass index (BMI), which has become standard in assessing body composition. Its advantage over using weight alone is that it accounts for height. A person's BMI is calculated by dividing their weight in kilograms (kg) by the square of their height in meters (m^2). Online calculators or charts are handy ways to estimate BMI (see Figure 12.5). Guidelines for interpreting BMI define four basic categories: Underweight (BMI <18.5), Normal weight (BMI = 18.5–24.9), Overweight (BMI = 25–29.9), and Obese (BMI ≥ 30).

BMI is not a perfect tool for assessing body composition. Athletes, for example, may have higher than average muscle mass and lower than average fat mass, which results in a BMI that may indicate obesity, when they are clearly not obese. Other measures such as waist circumference, waist-to-hip ratio, skin fold thickness, magnetic resonance imaging, bioelectric impedance, or densitometry may be more accurate than BMI in measuring body composition, but each has its limitations. Many of these measures require special equipment, or a visit to a health-care professional, which adds to the logistical difficulties and expense of studies. For many human genetic studies, measurements like BMI are used because directly measuring height and weight or obtaining it by participant self-report is easily done. And for most people, BMI serves its function as a screen for obesity.

12.2.1 Prevalence and Impact of Obesity

Rates of obesity around the world are on the rise (see Figure 12.6). Every world region has experienced dramatic increases in obesity over the last four decades. In the US, for example, since 1975 the rate of obesity has tripled from about 12 percent to about 36 percent in 2016. The WHO estimates that in 2016 1.6 billion adults (age 18 and above) around the world were overweight or obese, with over 650 million of those being obese.

Obesity in children and adolescents is also a substantial and growing problem in many parts of the world (NCD-RisC, 2017). Rates of obesity in girls rose from 0.7 percent in 1975 to 5.6 percent in 2016. For boys, rates of obesity rose from 0.9 percent in 1975 to 7.8 percent in 2016. The obesity rates in high-income countries appears to have leveled off but they are accelerating in parts of Asia. In the US, for example, the rate of obesity for those aged 2–18 is estimated at 18.5 percent.

Weight lbs	100	105	110	115	120	125	130	135	140	145	150	155	160	165	170	175	180	185	190	195	200	205	210	215	220	225	230	235	240	245	250
kgs	45.4	47.6	49.9	52.2	54.4	56.7	59.0	61.2	63.5	65.8	68.0	70.3	72.6	74.8	77.1	79.4	81.6	83.9	86.2	88.4	90.7	93.0	95.2	97.5	99.8	102.0	104.3	106.6	108.8	111.1	113.4

Height in/cms																															
54 137.2	24.1	25.3	26.5	27.7	28.9	30.1	31.3	32.5	33.7	35.0	36.2	37.4	38.6	39.8	41.0	42.2	43.4	44.6	45.8	47.0	48.2	49.4	50.6	51.8	53.0	54.2	55.4	56.7	57.9	59.1	60.3
55 139.7	23.2	24.4	25.6	26.7	27.9	29.0	30.2	31.4	32.5	33.7	34.9	36.0	37.2	38.3	39.5	40.7	41.8	43.0	44.2	45.3	46.5	47.6	48.8	50.0	51.1	52.3	53.4	54.6	55.8	56.9	58.1
56 142.2	22.4	23.5	24.7	25.8	26.9	28.0	29.1	30.3	31.4	32.5	33.6	34.7	35.9	37.0	38.1	39.2	40.3	41.5	42.6	43.7	44.8	46.0	47.1	48.2	49.3	50.4	51.6	52.7	53.8	54.9	56.0
57 144.8	21.6	22.7	23.8	24.9	26.0	27.0	28.1	29.2	30.3	31.4	32.5	33.5	34.6	35.7	36.8	37.9	38.9	40.0	41.1	42.2	43.3	44.4	45.4	46.5	47.6	48.7	49.8	50.8	51.9	53.0	54.1
58 147.3	20.9	21.9	23.0	24.0	25.1	26.1	27.2	28.2	29.3	30.3	31.3	32.4	33.4	34.5	35.5	36.6	37.6	38.7	39.7	40.7	41.8	42.8	43.9	44.9	46.0	47.0	48.1	49.1	50.2	51.2	52.2
59 149.9	20.2	21.2	22.2	23.2	24.2	25.2	26.3	27.3	28.3	29.3	30.3	31.3	32.3	33.3	34.3	35.3	36.3	37.3	38.4	39.4	40.4	41.4	42.4	43.4	44.4	45.4	46.4	47.5	48.5	49.5	50.5
60 152.4	19.5	20.5	21.5	22.5	23.4	24.4	25.4	26.4	27.3	28.3	29.3	30.3	31.2	32.2	33.2	34.2	35.2	36.1	37.1	38.1	39.1	40.1	41.0	42.0	43.0	44.0	44.9	45.9	46.9	47.8	48.8
61 154.9	18.9	19.8	20.8	21.7	22.7	23.6	24.6	25.5	26.4	27.4	28.3	29.3	30.2	31.2	32.1	33.1	34.0	34.9	35.9	36.8	37.8	38.7	39.7	40.6	41.6	42.5	43.5	44.4	45.3	46.3	47.2
62 157.5	18.3	19.2	20.1	21.0	21.9	22.9	23.8	24.7	25.6	26.5	27.4	28.3	29.3	30.2	31.1	32.0	32.9	33.8	34.7	35.7	36.6	37.5	38.4	39.3	40.2	41.1	42.1	43.0	43.9	44.8	45.7
63 160.0	17.7	18.6	19.5	20.4	21.3	22.1	23.0	23.9	24.8	25.7	26.6	27.5	28.3	29.2	30.1	31.0	31.9	32.8	33.7	34.5	35.4	36.3	37.2	38.1	39.0	39.8	40.7	41.6	42.5	43.4	44.3
64 162.6	17.2	18.0	18.9	19.7	20.6	21.5	22.3	23.2	24.0	24.9	25.7	26.6	27.5	28.3	29.2	30.0	30.9	31.7	32.6	33.5	34.3	35.2	36.0	36.9	37.8	38.6	39.5	40.3	41.2	42.0	42.9
65 165.1	16.6	17.5	18.3	19.1	20.0	20.8	21.6	22.5	23.3	24.1	25.0	25.8	26.6	27.5	28.3	29.1	29.9	30.8	31.6	32.4	33.3	34.1	34.9	35.8	36.6	37.4	38.3	39.1	39.9	40.8	41.6
66 167.6	16.1	16.9	17.8	18.6	19.4	20.2	21.0	21.8	22.6	23.4	24.2	25.0	25.8	26.6	27.4	28.2	29.0	29.9	30.7	31.5	32.3	33.1	33.9	34.7	35.5	36.3	37.1	37.9	38.7	39.5	40.3
67 170.2	15.7	16.4	17.2	18.0	18.8	19.6	20.4	21.1	21.9	22.7	23.5	24.3	25.1	25.8	26.6	27.4	28.2	29.0	29.8	30.5	31.3	32.1	32.9	33.7	34.5	35.2	36.0	36.8	37.6	38.4	39.1
68 172.7	15.2	16.0	16.7	17.5	18.2	19.0	19.8	20.5	21.3	22.0	22.8	23.6	24.3	25.1	25.8	26.6	27.4	28.1	28.9	29.6	30.4	31.2	31.9	32.7	33.4	34.2	35.0	35.7	36.5	37.2	38.0
69 175.3	14.8	15.5	16.2	17.0	17.7	18.5	19.2	19.9	20.7	21.4	22.1	22.9	23.6	24.4	25.1	25.8	26.6	27.3	28.1	28.8	29.5	30.3	31.0	31.7	32.5	33.2	34.0	34.7	35.4	36.2	36.9
70 177.8	14.3	15.1	15.8	16.5	17.2	17.9	18.6	19.4	20.1	20.8	21.5	22.2	23.0	23.7	24.4	25.1	25.8	26.5	27.3	28.0	28.7	29.4	30.1	30.8	31.6	32.3	33.0	33.7	34.4	35.1	35.9
71 180.3	13.9	14.6	15.3	16.0	16.7	17.4	18.1	18.8	19.5	20.2	20.9	21.6	22.3	23.0	23.7	24.4	25.1	25.8	26.5	27.2	27.9	28.6	29.3	30.0	30.7	31.4	32.1	32.8	33.5	34.2	34.9
72 182.9	13.6	14.2	14.9	15.6	16.3	16.9	17.6	18.3	19.0	19.7	20.3	21.0	21.7	22.4	23.1	23.7	24.4	25.1	25.8	26.4	27.1	27.8	28.5	29.2	29.8	30.5	31.2	31.9	32.5	33.2	33.9
73 185.4	13.2	13.9	14.5	15.2	15.8	16.5	17.1	17.8	18.5	19.1	19.8	20.4	21.1	21.8	22.4	23.1	23.7	24.4	25.0	25.7	26.4	27.0	27.7	28.4	29.0	29.7	30.3	31.0	31.7	32.3	33.0
74 188.0	12.8	13.5	14.1	14.8	15.4	16.0	16.7	17.3	18.0	18.6	19.3	19.9	20.5	21.2	21.8	22.5	23.1	23.7	24.4	25.0	25.7	26.3	27.0	27.6	28.2	28.9	29.5	30.2	30.8	31.5	32.1
75 190.5	12.5	13.1	13.7	14.4	15.0	15.6	16.2	16.9	17.5	18.1	18.7	19.4	20.0	20.6	21.2	21.9	22.5	23.1	23.7	24.4	25.0	25.6	26.2	26.9	27.5	28.1	28.7	29.4	30.0	30.6	31.2
76 193.0	12.2	12.8	13.4	14.0	14.6	15.2	15.8	16.4	17.0	17.6	18.3	18.9	19.5	20.1	20.7	21.3	21.9	22.5	23.1	23.7	24.3	24.9	25.6	26.2	26.8	27.4	28.0	28.6	29.2	29.8	30.4
77 195.6	11.9	12.4	13.0	13.6	14.2	14.8	15.4	16.0	16.6	17.2	17.8	18.4	19.0	19.6	20.2	20.7	21.3	21.9	22.5	23.1	23.7	24.3	24.9	25.5	26.1	26.7	27.3	27.9	28.5	29.0	29.6
78 198.1	11.6	12.1	12.7	13.3	13.9	14.4	15.0	15.6	16.2	16.8	17.3	17.9	18.5	19.1	19.6	20.2	20.8	21.4	22.0	22.5	23.1	23.7	24.3	24.8	25.4	26.0	26.6	27.2	27.7	28.3	28.9
79 200.7	11.3	11.8	12.4	13.0	13.5	14.1	14.6	15.2	15.8	16.3	16.9	17.5	18.0	18.6	19.1	19.7	20.3	20.8	21.4	22.0	22.5	23.1	23.7	24.2	24.8	25.3	25.9	26.5	27.0	27.6	28.2
80 203.2	11.0	11.5	12.1	12.6	13.2	13.7	14.3	14.8	15.4	15.9	16.5	17.0	17.6	18.1	18.7	19.2	19.8	20.3	20.9	21.4	22.0	22.5	23.1	23.6	24.2	24.7	25.3	25.8	26.4	26.9	27.5

Figure 12.5. **Body mass index chart.** The number at the intersection of your height in inches (or cm) and your weight in pounds (or kg) estimates your BMI. Regions of different shading (starting from lower left) indicate underweight, normal weight, overweight, and obese categories.

(a)

Share of adults that are obese, 1975

Obesity is defined as having a body-mass index (BMI) equal to or greater than 30. BMI is a person's weight in kilograms divided by his or her height in metres squared.

No data 0%   5%   10%   15%   20%   25%   30%   35%   >40%

(b)

Share of adults that are obese, 2016

Obesity is defined as having a body-mass index (BMI) equal to or greater than 30. BMI is a person's weight in kilograms divided by his or her height in metres squared.

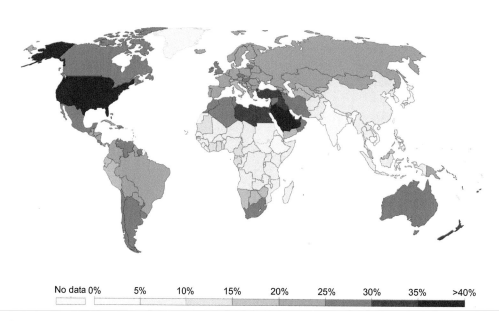

No data 0%   5%   10%   15%   20%   25%   30%   35%   >40%

Figure 12.6. **Worldwide obesity rates.** The percentage of obese adults in most countries around the world increased from (a) 1975 to (b) 2016. Source: Hannah Ritchie (2017) "Obesity." Published online at OurWorldInData.org. Retrieved from: https://ourworldindata.org/obesity [Online Resource].

The reason that there is great concern about rates of obesity is because of its impact on public health and the economy. Being overweight or obese increases the risk for cardiovascular disease, diabetes, osteoarthritis, and various cancers (i.e., endometrial, breast, ovarian, prostate, liver, gallbladder, kidney, and colon). The risks for such diseases are positively correlated with BMI.

Annual medical spending on obesity in the US in 2014 was estimated to be $149.4 billion, which is equivalent to each obese person spending $1,901 more, on average, than a non-obese person for medical expenses (Kim & Basu, 2016). Worldwide in 2015, high BMI (i.e., excess weight) was estimated to have accounted for 4 million deaths and 120 million DALYs (Disability-Adjusted Life Years; the sum of years of potential life lost due to premature mortality and the years of productive life lost due to disability), most being due to cardiovascular disease (Afshin et al., 2017).

The rapid changes seen in rates of overweight and obesity worldwide clearly demonstrate the important role of environment. Increasing availability of high-calorie, high-fat foods, and decreasing physical activity that is part of the nutrition transition are the main drivers of the increasing waistlines. However, genetic differences between people may determine whether a person gains weight in an obesogenic environment and if so, how much.

12.2.2 Obesity Can Be Familial or Syndromic

Family and twin studies have convincingly demonstrated that obesity runs in families. Estimates of heritability differ somewhat depending on study design and population, but they range from 0.24 to 0.81 in family studies and from 0.47 to 0.90 in twin studies (Elks et al., 2012). The basic take-home message is that people who share genetic material are likely to have more similar BMIs than do people who share no genetic material. In other words, individual differences in BMI are at least partially due to genetic differences between people.

As we saw with intellectual disability in Chapter 8, one type of evidence that genetic differences are responsible, at least partially, for trait variation in obesity risk is that some single-gene disorders produce syndromic obesity (Butler, 2016). Prader-Willi syndrome (PWS) is one of these, affecting 1 in 10,000–30,000 worldwide. Most cases are produced by a paternally derived deletion on chromosome 15 (15q11–q13), but some are due to maternal disomy 15 (i.e., carrying two copies of the maternally derived chromosome), or more rarely, imprinting defects. Several physical features of Prader-Willi syndrome are apparent, including, but not limited to, narrow forehead, almond shaped eyes, short stature, and small hands and feet. Behaviorally, some of the symptoms include mild learning impairment, stubbornness, high pain tolerance, and insatiable appetite that can lead to hyperphagia (i.e., overeating).

Leptin levels in people with PWS are elevated, as is also seen in obese individuals without PWS (Khan, Gerasimidis, Edwards, & Shaikh, 2018). So, although genetic variation in leptin signaling may play a role in obesity for those with PWS, it does not appear to differentiate the syndromic obesity from that seen in the general population.

Ghrelin, a hormone that stimulates appetite, may play an important role in PWS-related obesity (Khan et al., 2018). Ghrelin is a 28-peptide hormone that is produced in the stomach and acts in the arcuate nucleus of the hypothalamus. Typically, ghrelin levels in the blood increase as a result of fasting and decrease after eating. Ghrelin stimulates appetite. Levels of plasma ghrelin are chronically slightly elevated in obese people and appear to be even higher in obese people with PWS (Makris et al., 2017). The mechanisms driving obesity in people with PWS have not been fully characterized, but there does seem to be evidence that appetite control circuits that include hormones acting in the hypothalamus are dysfunctional producing a combination of chronic overeating and reduced physical activity levels. The evidence that obesity is an outcome of a genetic syndrome supports the overall hypothesis that genetic variation is at least partially responsible for individual differences in risk for obesity.

12.2.3 Candidate Genes Associated with Obesity

The genes that code for leptin (*LEP*, 7q32.1), the leptin receptor (*LEPR*, 1p31.3), ghrelin (*GHRL*, 3p25.3) or its receptor (*GHSR*, 3q26.31) are not located on human chromosome 15q11–q13, which is deleted in most cases of PWS. So, a direct impact of the deletion cannot explain the potential involvement of these signaling molecules and PWS. However, it may be that there are products of genes on 15q11–q13 that regulate the expression of those genes or otherwise act in the appetite control circuitry.

Five genes located in the PWS deletion region on chromosome 15q11–q13 (*MAGEL2*, *NDN*, *PWLS*, *SNORD116*, and *SNRPN*) are of special interest with respect to obesity (Butler, McGuire, & Manzardo, 2015). The proteins coded for by melanoma antigen genes *MAGEL2* and *NDN* appear to function together to regulate the abundance and activity of leptin receptors, which could impact leptin signaling (Wijesuriya et al., 2017). In a mouse model, investigators blocked expression of the *Snord116* locus (cluster of non-coding RNAs) in the hypothalamus, which produced hyperphagia and growth retardation, which are commonly seen in PWS (Polex-Wolf et al., 2018). Some, but not all, of the mice developed obesity as well. It appears that the leptin signaling pathway was not affected in the *Snord116*-deficient mice. Ghrelin signaling was not tested. The *SNRPN* gene codes for RNA-binding SmN protein and a polygenic risk score based on four of its SNPs has been associated with severe, early onset obesity in a recent, relatively small sample size candidate gene association study (Albuquerque et al., 2017). As with all such studies, it will be necessary to replicate their findings before we can have confidence in their results. However, it is clear that variations in genes that code for components of hypothalamic appetite control circuits remain potential important contributors to individual risk for obesity.

An important candidate gene for obesity is the melanocortin receptor 4 (*MC4R*, 18q21.32), which encodes a G-protein coupled receptor expressed in the hypothalamus. It is important because of the convergent evidence that supports its role in obesity: (1) the receptor is part of the hypothalamic appetite circuit, (2) knocking out the gene in mice causes obesity (Huszar et al., 1997), (3) at least one nearby SNP (i.e., rs17782313) is associated with obesity, eating behavior, and brain structure in humans (Horstmann et al., 2013; Loos et al., 2008).

One of the most consistent findings in obesity GWAS is that genetic variants in a gene called *FTO* (fat mass and obesity associated gene; 16q12.2) are associated with obesity (Loos & Yeo, 2014). The causal variant(s) has not been identified, but it is likely located in the gene's first intron. Based on its sequence, the gene codes for protein in the alpha-ketoglutarate dependent dioxygenase family, but the physiological function of the FTO protein has not been characterized. One potential function of the FTO protein is to modify (i.e., demethylate) RNA in ways that may impact its translation and/or degradation (Salem, Vonberg, Borra, Gill, & Nakamura, 2019). Knocking out *Fto* in mice leads to lean animals, and overexpressing it produces obesity (Church et al., 2010). This gene is a good example of the use of GWAS to identify new candidate genes that may not have been identified by testing the "usual suspects" that are components of well-known biological pathways (see Figure 12.7).

In summary, even though rates of obesity worldwide are rising because of the increased availability of high-calorie and high-fat foods, genetic factors play an important role in individual

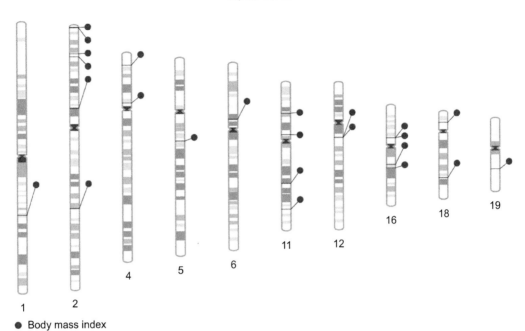

Top 25 Genes Associated with BMI

● Body mass index

Figure 12.7. **Twenty-five genes associated with BMI.** This phenogram shows the chromosomal locations of 25 genes that have SNPs in or nearby that have been associated with BMI. The SNPs are those that were most strongly associated with BMI in 179 studies in the GWAS Catalog (7/1/2020). Source: Phenogram was constructed at http://visualization.ritchielab.org/phenograms

differences in obesity risk. Components of appetite control circuits can harbor genetic variants that impact their expression, structure, or function, such as MC4R. Genetic variants, such as those in FTO, have been identified via GWAS and represent new potential targets for the development of obesity treatments.

Check-up

- Provide an overview of worldwide obesity trends.
- What is syndromic obesity?
- Explain how genetic variation in hypothalamic appetite circuits impacts obesity risk.

12.3 Genetic Variation Partially Explains Risk for Eating Disorders

Although obesity is the most prevalent dysfunctional pattern of eating and exercise, it is not the only one. The ICD-11 (Box 12.2) recognizes eight feeding and eating disorders: (1) anorexia nervosa, (2) bulimia nervosa, (3) binge eating disorder, (4) avoidant-restrictive food intake disorder, (5) pica, (6) rumination-regurgitation disorder, (7) other specified feeding or eating disorder, and (8) feeding or eating disorders, unspecified (World Health Organization, 2020a).

Box 12.2 ICD-11 Diagnosis: Feeding and Eating Disorders

Feeding and Eating Disorders involve abnormal eating or feeding behaviours that are not explained by another health condition and are not developmentally appropriate or culturally sanctioned. Feeding disorders involve behavioural disturbances that are not related to body weight and shape concerns, such as eating of non-edible substances or voluntary regurgitation of foods. Eating disorders involve abnormal eating behaviour and preoccupation with food as well as prominent body weight and shape concerns.

Source: http://id.who.int/icd/entity/1412387537 (accessed March 3, 2021), World Health Organization (Copyright © 2020a).

12.3.1 Eating Disorders Are Common

Worldwide, the point prevalence of anorexia nervosa and bulimia nervosa combined was estimated to be 0.21 percent in 2017 (see Figure 12.8(a)). This represents an increase from 0.18 percent in 1990.

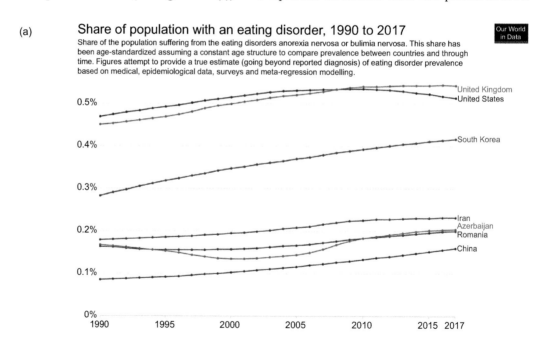

(a) **Share of population with an eating disorder, 1990 to 2017**

Share of the population suffering from the eating disorders anorexia nervosa or bulimia nervosa. This share has been age-standardized assuming a constant age structure to compare prevalence between countries and through time. Figures attempt to provide a true estimate (going beyond reported diagnosis) of eating disorder prevalence based on medical, epidemiological data, surveys and meta-regression modelling.

Figure 12.8 **Number of females and males with anorexia nervosa or bulimia nervosa from 1990 to 2017.**
(a) The estimated share of the population that met criteria for anorexia nervosa or bulimia nervosa has increased across the globe from 1990 to 2017. Rates of eating disorders are not the same for all countries. (b) In 2017, it is estimated that 3.7 times more people met criteria for a diagnosis of bulimia nervosa than anorexia nervosa worldwide. (c) More females than males meet criteria for anorexia nervosa or bulimia nervosa, and the numbers of people with either have increased substantially over the last 27 years. Source: Global Burden of Disease Collaborative Network. Global Burden of Disease Study 2017 (GBD, 2016) Results. Seattle: Institute for Health Metrics and Evaluation (IHME), 2018.

(b)
Number of people with an eating disorder, World, 1990 to 2017
Total number of people with the eating disorders anorexia or bulimia nervosa, differentiated by sex. This is measured across all ages. Figures attempt to provide a true estimate (going beyond reported diagnosis) of the number of people with anorexia or bulimia based on medical, epidemiological data, surveys and meta-regression modelling.

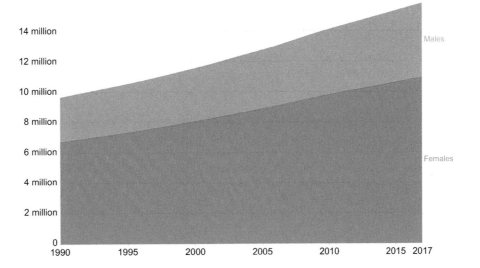

(c)
Number with anorexia and bulimia nervosa, World, 1990 to 2017
Total number of people with anorexia and bulimia nervosa. This is measured across both sexes and all ages.

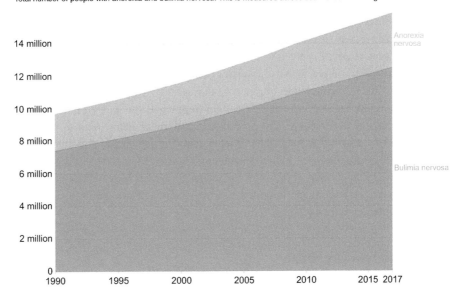

Figure 12.8 (*cont.*)

In terms of percentages, that does not seem like a lot, but it is out of 7.511 billion people. It is estimated that 3.36 million people met diagnostic criterion for anorexia nervosa worldwide in 2017 (see Figure 12.8(b)). This represents an increase from 2.27 million in 1990. It is estimated that 12.51 million people met diagnostic criteria for bulimia nervosa worldwide in 2017. This represents an increase from

7.44 million in 1990. Eating disorders are typically thought to occur more often in females. It is estimated that 10.93 million females and 4.88 million males met criteria for a diagnosis of anorexia nervosa or bulimia nervosa in 2017, and that this represents a substantial increase since 1990 (see Figure 12.8(c)).

Although anorexia nervosa is not the most common psychiatric disorder, it is particularly troubling. For about 25 percent of those who develop anorexia nervosa it is a chronic, relapsing disorder, and it has the highest mortality rate of all psychiatric disorders (Smink, van Hoeken, & Hoek, 2012).

12.3.2 Diagnosing Feeding or Eating Disorders

As with all psychiatric disorders, the diagnosis of a feeding or eating disorder is typically made during a clinical interview. We first present the ICD-11 diagnostic criteria for anorexia nervosa, then bulimia nervosa (see Box 12.3).

Box 12.3 ICD-11 Diagnosis: Anorexia Nervosa and Bulimia Nervosa

Anorexia Nervosa

Anorexia Nervosa is characterised by significantly low body weight for the individual's height, age and developmental stage that is not due to another health condition or to the unavailability of food. A commonly used threshold is body mass index (BMI) less than 18.5 kg/m2 in adults and BMI-for-age under 5th percentile in children and adolescents. Rapid weight loss (e.g., more than 20% of total body weight within 6 months) may replace the low body weight guideline as long as other diagnostic requirements are met. Children and adolescents may exhibit failure to gain weight as expected based on the individual developmental trajectory rather than weight loss. Low body weight is accompanied by a persistent pattern of behaviours to prevent restoration of normal weight, which may include behaviours aimed at reducing energy intake (restricted eating), purging behaviours (e.g., self-induced vomiting, misuse of laxatives), and behaviours aimed at increasing energy expenditure (e.g., excessive exercise), typically associated with a fear of weight gain. Low body weight or shape is central to the person's self-evaluation or is inaccurately perceived to be normal or even excessive.

Bulimia Nervosa

Bulimia Nervosa is characterised by frequent, recurrent episodes of binge eating (e.g., once a week or more over a period of at least one month). A binge eating episode is a distinct period of time during which the individual experiences a subjective loss of control over eating, eating notably more or differently than usual, and feels unable to stop eating or limit the type or amount of food eaten. Binge eating is accompanied by repeated inappropriate compensatory behaviours aimed at preventing weight gain (e.g., self-induced vomiting, misuse of laxatives or enemas, strenuous exercise). The individual is preoccupied with body shape or weight, which strongly influences self-evaluation. There is marked distress about the pattern of binge eating and inappropriate compensatory behaviour or significant impairment in personal, family, social, educational, occupational or other important areas of functioning. The individual does not meet the diagnostic requirements of Anorexia Nervosa.

Source: http://id.who.int/icd/entity/263852475 and http://id.who.int/icd/entity/509381842 (accessed March 3, 2021), World Health Organization (Copyright © 2020b and 2020c).

12.3.3 Eating Disorders Run in Families

Data from family, twin, and adoption studies provide evidence that shared genetic material contributes to phenotypic similarity for eating disorders (see Box 12.4). Having a family member with either anorexia nervosa or bulimia nervosa increases the risk of having a diagnosis of an eating disorder, especially in female family members (Strober, Freeman, Lampert, Diamond, & Kaye, 2000). Heritability estimates are between 0.48 and 0.74 for anorexia nervosa and between 0.28 and 0.83 for bulimia nervosa depending on how they are defined (Baker, Schaumberg, & Munn-Chernoff, 2017; Trace, Baker, Peñas-Lledó, & Bulik, 2013). As usual, it is good to keep in mind that the precision of heritability estimates is not critically important because they are dependent on the variation that exists in the sample population at the time of the study. Any changes in genetic variation or environmental variation may affect the heritability estimate. The most important information gained from heritability estimates is whether they are significantly different from zero. Because the heritability estimates for anorexia nervosa and bulimia nervosa are reliably greater than zero, we can have confidence that genetic variation is at least a partial cause of individual differences in risk for eating disorders.

Box 12.4 The Role of Puberty in Disordered Eating

Rates of eating disorders do not differ for males and females before the onset of puberty. But after puberty, females are much more likely than males to be diagnosed with an eating disorder (Ma, Mikhail, Fowler, Culbert, & Klump, 2019).

Furthermore, eating disorder symptoms are consistently correlated with pubertal development in females, but such a pattern is not consistently seen in males. Such symptom counts are dimensional and enable the inclusion of people who do not meet formal criteria for a diagnosis, but nonetheless, exhibit eating-related problems. In addition, because there is substantial symptom overlap among eating disorders, as well as comorbidity, the use of global eating disorder symptoms represents a transdiagnostic approach that reflects general eating disorder risk.

Twin studies have shown that the heritability estimates for eating disorder symptoms in females increased from 0.06 at age 11 to 0.45 at age 14. Of course, a person's DNA sequence does not change at the onset of puberty, but gene expression does. The coordinated physical and hormonal changes that drive sexual maturation are the result of epigenetic changes in gene expression (Rzeczkowska, Hou, Wilson, & Palmert, 2014). Therefore, changes in heritability estimates may be indexing the increased expression of genes involved in pubertal maturation. Such changes could also reflect changes in environmental variance.

In females, an increase in estrogen levels occurs during puberty. Estrogen plays an important role in the development and maintenance of female reproductive organs and secondary sexual characteristics, and the ovulatory cycle. Estrogen also regulates the expression of genes including those that code for components of the brain's reward system, the serotonin neurotransmitter system, and brain-derived neurotrophic factor that are involved in mood, appetite, and body weight regulation (Ma et al., 2019). Although there is still much to learn about the role of estrogen in eating disorder risk, it may be an important contributor to the sex difference in rates of eating disorders observed after puberty.

12.3.4 Candidate Genes Associated with Feeding or Eating Disorders

As with every other psychiatric disorder, candidate gene association studies for anorexia nervosa and bulimia nervosa have primarily focused on the "usual suspects" of well-studied variants in neurotransmitter systems (Trace et al., 2013). Serotonin system function impacts mood, appetite, body weight regulation, impulsivity, and other aspects of behavior and cognition. Dopamine system function impacts feeding, motor activity, reinforcement motivation, and other aspects of cognition. Therefore, genetic variation in components of these two systems represent reasonable candidates for feeding or eating disorders. Other reasonable candidate gene systems that have been studied include opioid, endocannabinoid, and those implicated in appetite or feeding behavior, such as ghrelin, or MC4R. Hundreds of candidate gene association studies examining phenotypes related to eating disorders, including diagnoses, and sub-diagnostic threshold eating behavior problems have been conducted. The bottom line appears to be that candidate gene studies for eating disorders have been beset by all the typical candidate gene association study limitations, mainly related to failures to replicate. At this time, one must consider these studies to be largely inconclusive.

12.3.5 Feeding or Eating Disorder GWAS

Early GWAS for feeding or eating disorders were statistically underpowered and did not find reliable evidence for associations. The first reported GWAS of anorexia nervosa tested highly polymorphic microsatellite markers in 320 cases and 341 controls and reported that markers in two genomic regions (i.e., 1q41 and 11q22) were associated with the diagnosis (Nakabayashi et al., 2009). The strongest association was with a variant near the gene that codes for a spermatogenesis-associated protein *SPATA17*. It is not clear how such a protein may be involved in risk for an eating disorder, and it does not appear that this finding has been replicated.

A meta-analysis with 16,992 cases and 55,525 controls from 33 data sets of European ancestry from 17 countries identified 8 loci that were significantly associated with anorexia nervosa (Watson et al., 2019). This change in sample size that has occurred in GWAS over a decade is astounding and appears to be typical, and is only possible in the context of research consortia and international collaboration. Eight loci were significantly associated with anorexia nervosa at the genome-wide level (see Figure 12.9). The gene(s) nearest each were identified; in order of their strength of association they are: (1) *NCKIPSD* [*NCK interacting protein with SH3 domain*], (2) *CADM1* [*Cell adhesion molecule 1*], (3) *ASB3* [*Ankyrin repeat and SOCS box protein 3*], *ERLEC1* [*Endoplasmic reticulum lectin 1*], (4) *MGMT* [*Methylated-DNA-protein-cysteine methyltransferase*], (5) *FOXP1* [*Forkhead box protein P1*], (6) *PTBP2* [*Polypyrimidine tract-binding protein 2*], (7)

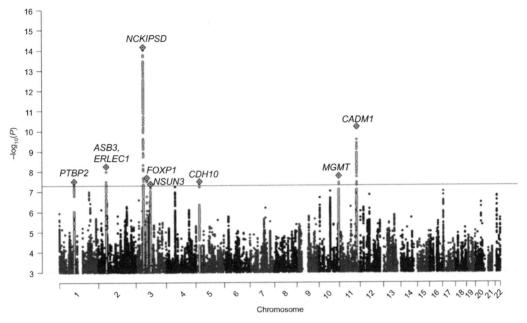

Figure 12.9. **Manhattan plot of anorexia nervosa GWAS.** Variants in eight genes were significantly associated with anorexia nervosa diagnosis in a recent, large, meta-analysis. Source: Watson et al. (2019). Reprinted by permission from Springer Nature, Nature Genetics.

CDH10 [Cadherin-10], and (8) *NSUN3 [tRNA (cytosine(34)-C(5))-methyltransferase*, mitochondrial]. You may have noticed that none of these are the "usual suspects" that are typically tested in candidate gene association tests. One of the real benefits of GWAS is the identification of genes that have not been previously considered. The h^2_{SNP} for anorexia was estimated to be 0.11–0.17 (Watson et al., 2019).

An important focus in GWAS is on identifying genetic variants that are shared across psychiatric disorders. In many GWAS databases, participants provide a large amount of data including, but not limited to, diagnoses for other psychiatric or medical conditions, aspects of socioeconomic status, psychological or cognitive assessments, and body measurements. Assessing correlations between the SNPs associated with anorexia nervosa and such measurements can provide some insight into shared **genetic architecture**. In this case, significant correlations were identified for obsessive-compulsive disorder, major depressive disorder, schizophrenia, anxiety, and depression symptoms. Such correlations are consistent with the notion that diagnoses may not reflect underlying biology and that endophenotypes such as anxiety may capture an underlying risk for a variety of mental health outcomes.

As we have mentioned previously, one important issue to consider in behavior genetic studies is whether dimensional phenotypes (i.e., endophenotypes) will prove more useful than the categorical phenotypes (i.e., diagnoses). The NIMH's RDoC provide a framework by which investigators can identify dimensionally measured traits that may reflect aspects of a behavioral disorder. For example, measures of negative valence systems (e.g., anxiety), positive valence systems (e.g., low reward sensitivity), cognitive control systems (e.g., poor cognitive flexibility), and social processing systems (e.g., body dysmorphia) may characterize aspects of anorexia nervosa and may turn out to be more fruitful targets of behavior genetic studies (Dunlop, Woodside, & Downar, 2016).

It is important to keep in mind that appetite control, eating behavior, and weight control are the products of multiple biological circuits, made up of many components, and modified by a variety of factors including development, sex, society, and food availability. One should not expect such phenotypes to be determined by a small number of genes with large effects. However, there is no doubt that genetic variation between people contributes to individual differences in eating and eating-related phenotypes. It is important for behavior genetic students and investigators to temper their expectations. By now it is clear that feeding or eating disorders are not caused by mutations in a single gene. We see that these disorders run in families, but that the effect of any single genetic variant is small. Our "usual suspects" have not been reliably associated with risk for eating disorders. Dimensional measures may prove more useful than categorical diagnoses. When GWAS use very large sample sizes they have the potential to identify novel candidate genes, which then can be rigorously tested in both human and non-human animal models. There is still much work to be done to understand the role of heredity in feeding or eating disorders.

Check-up

- Describe the worldwide trends in the prevalence of feeding or eating disorders.
- Compare and contrast anorexia nervosa and bulimia nervosa.
- Summarize what is known about genetic variants that increase risk for developing feeding or eating disorders.

12.4 Exercise Motivation and Benefits Show Genetic Influence

Hypotheses to explain the increase in obesity across human history, such as the thrifty genotype hypothesis, suggested that individual differences in preference for high-fat and high-calorie foods, the capacity to eat large meals, and efficiency in storing excess calories as fat were partially due to genetic differences. These theories also posited that individual differences in aspects of energy expenditure were also partially due to genetic differences. When coupled with eating behaviors that promoted fat accumulation, behavioral tendencies to reduce physical activity would further enhance survival in times of famine. This combination of traits would also lead to obesity when energy-rich food was widely available and when technological development decreased the need for physical activity.

12.4.1 Voluntary Physical Activity

So far, in this chapter much of our discussion has been about the calorie intake part of the energy balance equation. For the remainder of the chapter, we focus on the role of genetic variation in individual differences in aspects of physical activity.

Physical activity involves movement produced by skeletal muscles and requires the expenditure of energy. It includes a broad range of movements from fidgeting while you sit at your desk to running an ultra-marathon. Exercise is a special type of physical activity that is goal-oriented, structured, and can include repetitive elements that are designed to maintain or improve some aspect of physical fitness.

Engaging in regular physical activity has many health benefits including a reduction in all-cause mortality. It can reduce the risk of developing at least twenty-five chronic medical conditions such as cardiovascular disease, type 2 diabetes, and some cancers (Warburton & Bredin, 2017). It can also reduce risk factors for diseases including high blood pressure, high blood cholesterol levels, and obesity. Regular physical activity strengthens bones and muscles and can increase aerobic capacity. There is evidence that regular physical activity can improve overall brain health, and reduce symptoms associated with anxiety disorders, depression, and Alzheimer disease.

The World Health Organization and the Centers for Disease Control and Prevention (CDC) have published recommendations to encourage people to engage in healthy levels of physical activity (HHS, 2018; World Health Organization, 2010). The main recommendation for adults is to engage in 150 minutes of moderate-intensity (e.g., walking) or 75 minutes of vigorous-intensity (e.g., jogging) physical activity each week. It should be noted that this recommendation is not based on empirical research and that such a threshold may actually discourage people from engaging in physical activity because they might not be able to meet it when even a small increase in activity would be beneficial (Warburton & Bredin, 2017).

A study found that 27.5 percent of adults worldwide did not meet the recommended amount of physical activity (Guthold, Stevens, Riley, & Bull, 2020). The rate of insufficient physical activity was higher for women than men (31.5 percent vs. 25.5 percent, respectively). The rates of insufficient physical activity are not evenly distributed across the globe, with the highest levels found in Latin America, the Caribbean, and in high-income Western and Asian countries (see Figure 12.10). Differences in physical activity levels across the globe are primarily due to variation in cultural practices, availability and use of mechanized transportation, and prevalence of sedentary occupations (e.g., office worker). In 2017, 49.7 percent of adults in the US were estimated to have insufficient physical activity by the CDC. The highest rate of insufficient physical activity was in Texas with 58.1 percent, and the lowest was in Vermont with 40.3 percent.

Of course, there are many people who engage in physical activity or exercise regularly. For our purposes, the primary question is whether some of the variability observed in physical activity/exercise rate is due to genetic differences between people.

12.4.2 Physical Activity Runs in Families

Most studies use self-report questionnaires to assess how often participants engage in different types and intensities of physical activity. Some studies use accelerometers to collect data on actual movement. To date, eight family studies have been conducted with the aim of estimating the heritability of physical activity using parent–offspring correlations, seven used self-report questionnaires and one used accelerometers (Zhang & Speakman, 2019). Heritability estimates of physical activity from the questionnaire studies ranged from 0.09 to 0.32, with a mean of 0.24. The study that used accelerometers estimated heritability to be 0.56. While these estimates are quite different, the main takeaway is that all the estimates are significantly greater than zero, so we can have some confidence that people who share genes are likely to resemble each other in terms of physical activity. Having a precise heritability estimate is not necessarily important.

There have been twenty twin studies that have estimated the heritability of physical activity. Fifteen used self-report questionnaires and five used accelerometers. The weighted means of the heritability estimates from the studies that provided overall heritability estimates were 0.40 for questionnaires and 0.51 for accelerometers (Zhang & Speakman, 2019). Therefore, the results of

Men

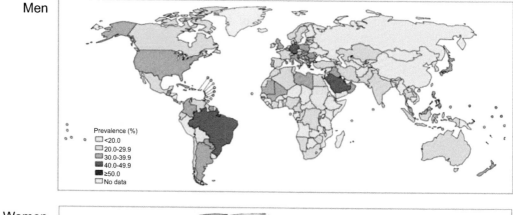

Women

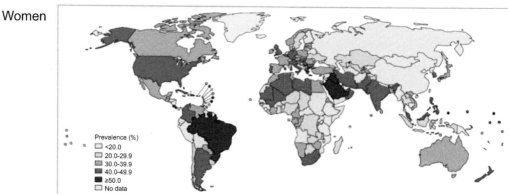

Figure 12.10. **Rates of insufficient physical activity across the globe for men and women.** The highest rates of insufficient physical activity (i.e., less than 150 minutes of moderate-intensity activity per week) are found in Latin America, the Caribbean, and in high-income Western and Asian countries. Source: Guthold et al. (2020).

both the family and twin studies provide evidence that genetic variation between people is associated with individual differences in physical activity.

12.4.3 Candidate Genes Associated with Individual Differences in Physical Activity

At least eighteen candidate gene association studies have been conducted on physical activity, most (15 of 18) using questionnaires (Zhang & Speakman, 2019). The mean sample size for the questionnaire-based studies was 2,029 ranging from 97 to 12,929. Only four of the studies had sample sizes that were greater than 1,000, which has become a somewhat arbitrary benchmark for candidate gene association studies. Some of the most interesting results were from studies testing variants in the leptin receptor gene (*LEPR*) and the gene for the melanocortin receptor 4 (*MC4R*). Each gene was found to have a variant that was statistically associated with physical activity. A variant in *LEPR* (rs1137101; Gln223Arg) was associated with physical activity scores on a questionnaire as well as with indices of physical activity as measured in a respiratory chamber. Different variants in *MC4R* were found to be associated with physical activity as measured by questionnaire (rs7242169) and by accelerometer (SNP 1704). However, variants in the *FTO* gene, which is associated with BMI, are not associated with physical activity. This finding suggests that *FTO* variants may be associated with the input (i.e., eating) side of the energy balance equation, but not with the output side.

12.4.4 Physical Activity GWAS

Several GWAS have been conducted to identify loci associated with physical activity. A search on the GWAS Catalog identified 22 studies and 276 associations. The top 25 genes that harbor variants associated with physical activity are shown in Figure 12.11. These associations are the ones in the database that had the strongest statistical association with physical activity. None of them are in the typically studied candidate genes, which seems to be a usual trend for GWAS. It may be that while relatively rare variants in typical candidate genes (e.g., MC4R) have significant effects on physical activity, common genetic variants as tested in GWAS may not. However, it is likely that some of the variants identified in GWAS play important roles in circuits that regulate behavior that had been previously ignored or underappreciated.

   An interesting trend in GWAS is to focus on particular behaviors in a kind of endophenotype approach. One GWAS focused on different types of sedentary behaviors using the UK Biobank database, which is a population-based cohort of 503,325 participants aged 40–69 years (van de Vegte, Said, Rienstra, van der Harst, & Verweij, 2020). Participants were asked to estimate the number of hours that they spent in a typical day on three leisure-time activities: watching television, using the computer (not for work), and driving. They found 169 loci that were significantly associated with sedentary behaviors, 145 were associated with television watching, 36 were associated with computer use and 4 were associated with driving. Again, as in many other GWAS, no variants were associated with sedentary behaviors in the typically studied candidate genes for physical activity. Fifteen loci were associated with both television watching and computer use, and

Top 25 Genes Associated with Physical Activity

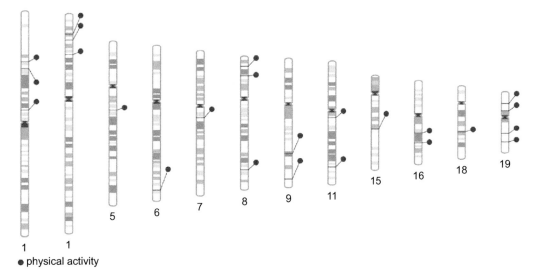

● physical activity

Figure 12.11. **Twenty-five genes associated with physical activity.** This phenogram shows the chromosomal locations of 25 genes that have SNPs in or nearby that have been associated with physical activity. The SNPs are those that were most strongly associated with physical activity in 22 studies in the GWAS Catalog (7/1/2020). Source: Phenogram was constructed at http://visualization.ritchielab.org/phenograms

one was associated with both television watching and driving. Shared genetic loci could be due to pleiotropy (i.e., genetic correlation) or to aspects of the traits that are not independent (i.e., phenotype correlation).

12.4.5 Voluntary Physical Activity in Rodents

Voluntary physical activity has also been studied by measuring wheel running in rodents. For example, mice that are deficient in leptin (i.e., ob/ob) become obese because they eat more food and are less active than wild-type mice. When leptin-deficient mice are given chronic doses of leptin, they eat less, increase their voluntary wheel running, and lose weight. The leptin replacement increases both ambulatory behavior (i.e., physical activity) and voluntary wheel running (i.e., exercise; Morton et al., 2011).

If you have ever owned a pet gerbil, hamster, mouse, or rat, you know that they will spontaneously engage in wheel running. Wheel running has been measured in laboratory rodents for nearly a century. It is a good behavioral measure because it varies between individuals, it is inexpensive to assess, and recording it can be automated. There are differences between strains on average wheel running behavior, and it responds to divergent selection with a realized heritability of 0.19 (Swallow, Carter, & Garland, 1998). Several QTLs spread across the mouse genome have been associated with differences in voluntary wheel running (Kostrzewa & Kas, 2014). Thus, there is strong evidence that genetic variants are associated with individual differences in voluntary exercise as indexed by wheel running in rodents.

One of the reasons that animals, including humans, engage in vigorous exercise is that it has reinforcing properties. After episodes of intense aerobic exercise, such as long-distance running, some people report that they experience feelings of euphoria, relief from anxiety, and reduced ability to feel pain. This experience is often called the runner's high and was first thought to be due to increased plasma levels of β-endorphin, an opioid. However, because β-endorphin cannot pass the blood–brain barrier, it is unlikely to mediate the runner's high.

The next likely mechanism for this pleasant feeling is activation of the endocannabinoid system. The endocannabinoid system primarily comprises two neurotransmitters (anandamide [AEA], 2-arachidonoylglycerol [2-AG]) that are found in both the peripheral and central nervous systems and that bind to two receptors (CB_1, CB_2). Both AEA and 2-AG are retrograde neurotransmitters that are released by postsynaptic neurons and bind to presynaptic receptors to alter the neurotransmitter release of the presynaptic neuron (see Figure 12.12). CB_1 receptors are widely distributed in the brain, and CB_2 receptors are mainly found in immune cells outside the brain.

Mice that have had CB_1 receptors knocked out on GABA releasing neurons in the ventral tegmental area, which is part of the brain's reward system, show decreased voluntary wheel running compared to wild-type mice (Dubreucq et al., 2013). So, it is clear that mice are running less when their CB_1 receptors in the reward system are deactivated. But is it because they no longer feel the high? To address this, a study gave one group of mice access to a running wheel and compared them to a control group that did not have access to a running wheel (Fuss et al., 2015). Mice with access to the running wheel had increased level of endocannabinoids, decreased anxiety, and decreased pain sensitivity compared to control mice. They further showed that the anxiolytic effects of running were mediated by the CB_1 receptors on GABA releasing neurons in the brain, and the pain reduction was mediated by CB_1 and CB_2 receptors outside the brain. There is also evidence that divergent selective breeding for wheel running impacts the endocannabinoid system such that AEA levels were relatively low in mice selected for high levels of wheel running (Thompson, Argueta, Garland, Jr., & DiPatrizio, 2017). At this time, no candidate gene association study or GWAS has been conducted on the runner's high.

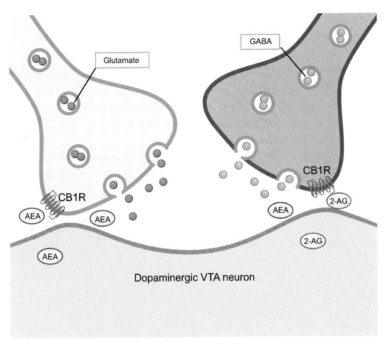

Figure 12.12. **Endocannabinoid system.** The retrograde release of endocannabinoids (i.e., AEA and 2-AG) by postsynaptic neurons inhibits the release of neurotransmitters from presynaptic neurons via CB1R activation.

There is no doubt that individual differences in physical activity or tendency to engage in exercise are, at least in part, due to genetic differences between people. Identifying genetic variants that are associated with differences in predispositions to exercise or in the outcomes of exercise may help in the development of treatments for obesity, or for the compulsive exercise behavior that is symptomatic of some feeding or eating disorders.

Check-up

- Explain the role of physical activity in obesity risk.
- Summarize the evidence from studies with human participants on the role of genetic variation in individual differences in physical activity.
- What is the runner's high, and how does the endocannabinoid system contribute to it?

12.5 SUMMARY

- The availability of food in most countries around the world has increased. The nutrition transition has ended famine in most parts of the world and has resulted in the increase of obesity-related disease. The thrifty genotype hypothesis posits that genetic variants that were once advantageous during times of periodic famine are now deleterious in a time of abundant food and sedentary lifestyles. Mutations in leptin signaling produce mice that are obese.

- Body mass index is an indirect gauge of body fat. A BMI of 30 or more is one way to define obesity. More than 1.6 billion adults worldwide are overweight or obese as defined by BMI, and the numbers are on the rise. Obesity runs in families and can also be a result of certain genetic diseases. Genetic variants in hypothalamic appetite control circuits are associated with obesity risk, as are variants in other genes.
- Eating disorders are common and can be deadly, and prevalence rates of anorexia nervosa and bulimia nervosa are on the rise. Eating disorders run in families. Some genetic variants associated with eating disorder risk have been identified.
- Physical activity constitutes an important part of the energy balance equation. A substantial minority of adults worldwide do not meet recommended amounts of physical activity. Physical activity, including voluntary exercise, runs in families. Some genetic variants have been identified to be associated with individual differences in physical activity. Voluntary wheel running is easily studied in rodents. Genetic variants in components of the endocannabinoid system may partially explain individual differences in experiencing the runner's high.

RECOMMENDED READING

- Qasim, A., Turcotte, M., de Souza, R. J., Samaan, M. C., Champredon, D., Dushoff, J., . . . Meyre, D. (2018). On the origin of obesity: Identifying the biological, environmental and cultural drivers of genetic risk among human populations. *Obes Rev, 19*(2), 121–149. doi:10.1111/obr.12625

REFERENCES

Afshin, A., Forouzanfar, M. H., Reitsma, M. B., Sur, P., Estep, K., Lee, A., . . . Murray, C. J. L. (2017). Health effects of overweight and obesity in 195 countries over 25 years. *N Engl J Med, 377*(1), 13–27. doi:10.1056/NEJMoa1614362

Albuquerque, D., Manco, L., González, L. M., Gervasini, G., Benito, G. M., González, J. R., & Rodríguez-López, R. (2017). Polymorphisms in the SNRPN gene are associated with obesity susceptibility in a Spanish population. *J Gene Med, 19*(5). doi:10.1002/jgm.2956

Baker, J. H., Schaumberg, K., & Munn-Chernoff, M. A. (2017). Genetics of anorexia nervosa. *Curr Psychiatry Rep, 19*(11), 84. doi:10.1007/s11920-017-0842-2

Butler, M. G. (2016). Single gene and syndromic causes of obesity: Illustrative examples. *Prog Mol Biol Transl Sci, 140*, 1–45. doi:10.1016/bs.pmbts.2015.12.003

Butler, M. G., McGuire, A., & Manzardo, A. M. (2015). Clinically relevant known and candidate genes for obesity and their overlap with human infertility and reproduction. *J Assist Reprod Genet, 32*(4), 495–508. doi:10.1007/s10815-014-0411-0

Church, C., Moir, L., McMurray, F., Girard, C., Banks, G. T., Teboul, L., . . . Cox, R. D. (2010). Overexpression of Fto leads to increased food intake and results in obesity. *Nat Genet, 42*(12), 1086–1092. doi:10.1038/ng.713

Dubreucq, S., Durand, A., Matias, I., Bénard, G., Richard, E., Soria-Gomez, E., . . . Chaouloff, F. (2013). Ventral tegmental area cannabinoid type-1 receptors control voluntary exercise performance. *Biol Psychiatry, 73*(9), 895–903. doi:10.1016/j.biopsych.2012.10.025

Dunlop, K. A., Woodside, B., & Downar, J. (2016). Targeting neural endophenotypes of eating disorders with non-invasive brain stimulation. *Front Neurosci, 10*, 30. doi:10.3389/fnins.2016.00030

Elks, C. E., den Hoed, M., Zhao, J. H., Sharp, S. J., Wareham, N. J., Loos, R. J., & Ong, K. K. (2012). Variability in the heritability of body mass index: A systematic review and meta-regression. *Front Endocrinol (Lausanne)*, *3*, 29. doi:10.3389/fendo.2012.00029

Fuss, J., Steinle, J., Bindila, L., Auer, M. K., Kirchherr, H., Lutz, B., & Gass, P. (2015). A runner's high depends on cannabinoid receptors in mice. *Proc Natl Acad Sci USA*, *112*(42), 13105–13108. doi:10.1073/pnas.1514996112

GBD (2016). Global, regional, and national incidence, prevalence, and years lived with disability for 310 diseases and injuries, 1990–2015: A systematic analysis for the Global Burden of Disease Study 2015. *Lancet*, *388*(10053), 1545–1602. doi:10.1016/s0140-6736(16)31678-6

Guthold, R., Stevens, G. A., Riley, L. M., & Bull, F. C. (2020). Global trends in insufficient physical activity among adolescents: A pooled analysis of 298 population-based surveys with 1.6 million participants. *Lancet Child Adolesc Health*, *4*(1), 23–35. doi:10.1016/s2352-4642(19)30323-2

HHS (2018). *Physical Activity Guidelines for Americans*. Washington, DC: Department of Health and Human Services.

Horstmann, A., Kovacs, P., Kabisch, S., Boettcher, Y., Schloegl, H., Tönjes, A., . . . Villringer, A. (2013). Common genetic variation near MC4R has a sex-specific impact on human brain structure and eating behavior. *PLoS One, 8*(9), e74362. doi:10.1371/journal.pone.0074362

Hummel, K. P., Dickie, M. M., & Coleman, D. L. (1966). Diabetes, a new mutation in the mouse. *Science*, *153*(3740), 1127–1128. doi:10.1126/science.153.3740.1127

Huszar, D., Lynch, C. A., Fairchild-Huntress, V., Dunmore, J. H., Fang, Q., Berkemeier, L. R., . . . Lee, F. (1997). Targeted disruption of the melanocortin-4 receptor results in obesity in mice. *Cell*, *88*(1), 131–141. doi:10.1016/s0092-8674(00)81865-6

Ingalls, A. M., Dickie, M. M., & Snell, G. D. (1950). Obese, a new mutation in the house mouse. *J Hered*, *41*(12), 317–318. doi:10.1093/oxfordjournals.jhered.a106073

Khan, M. J., Gerasimidis, K., Edwards, C. A., & Shaikh, M. G. (2018). Mechanisms of obesity in Prader-Willi syndrome. *Pediatr Obes*, *13*(1), 3–13. doi:10.1111/ijpo.12177

Kim, D. D., & Basu, A. (2016). Estimating the medical care costs of obesity in the United States: Systematic review, meta-analysis, and empirical analysis. *Value Health*, *19*(5), 602–613. doi:10.1016/j.jval.2016.02.008

Kostrzewa, E., & Kas, M. J. (2014). The use of mouse models to unravel genetic architecture of physical activity: A review. *Genes Brain Behav*, *13*(1), 87–103. doi:10.1111/gbb.12091

Loos, R. J., Lindgren, C. M., Li, S., Wheeler, E., Zhao, J. H., Prokopenko, I., . . . Mohlke, K. L. (2008). Common variants near MC4R are associated with fat mass, weight and risk of obesity. *Nat Genet*, *40*(6), 768–775. doi:10.1038/ng.140

Loos, R. J., & Yeo, G. S. (2014). The bigger picture of FTO: The first GWAS-identified obesity gene. *Nat Rev Endocrinol*, *10*(1), 51–61. doi:10.1038/nrendo.2013.227

Ma, R., Mikhail, M. E., Fowler, N., Culbert, K. M., & Klump, K. L. (2019). The role of puberty and ovarian hormones in the genetic diathesis of eating disorders in females. *Child Adolesc Psychiatr Clin N Am*, *28*(4), 617–628. doi:10.1016/j.chc.2019.05.008

Makris, M. C., Alexandrou, A., Papatsoutsos, E. G., Malietzis, G., Tsilimigras, D. I., Guerron, A. D., & Moris, D. (2017). Ghrelin and obesity: Identifying gaps and dispelling myths. A reappraisal. *In Vivo*, *31*(6), 1047–1050. doi:10.21873/invivo.11168

Morton, G. J., Kaiyala, K. J., Fisher, J. D., Ogimoto, K., Schwartz, M. W., & Wisse, B. E. (2011). Identification of a physiological role for leptin in the regulation of ambulatory activity and wheel running in mice. *Am J Physiol Endocrinol Metab*, *300*(2), E392–E401. doi:10.1152/ajpendo.00546.2010

Nakabayashi, K., Komaki, G., Tajima, A., Ando, T., Ishikawa, M., Nomoto, J., . . . Shirasawa, S. (2009). Identification of novel candidate loci for anorexia nervosa at 1q41 and 11q22 in Japanese by a genome-wide association analysis with microsatellite markers. *J Hum Genet, 54*(9), 531–537. doi:10.1038/jhg.2009.74

NCD-RisC (2017). Worldwide trends in body-mass index, underweight, overweight, and obesity from 1975 to 2016: A pooled analysis of 2416 population-based measurement studies in 128.9 million children, adolescents, and adults. *Lancet, 390*(10113), 2627–2642. doi:10.1016/s0140-6736(17)32129-3

Neel, J. V. (1962). Diabetes mellitus: A "thrifty" genotype rendered detrimental by "progress"? *Am J Hum Genet, 14*(4), 353–362.

Polex-Wolf, J., Lam, B. Y., Larder, R., Tadross, J., Rimmington, D., Bosch, F., . . . Yeo, G. S. (2018). Hypothalamic loss of Snord116 recapitulates the hyperphagia of Prader-Willi syndrome. *J Clin Invest, 128*(3), 960–969. doi:10.1172/jci97007

Popkin, B. M. (2006). Global nutrition dynamics: The world is shifting rapidly toward a diet linked with noncommunicable diseases. *Am J Clin Nutr, 84*(2), 289–298. doi:10.1093/ajcn/84.1.289

Qasim, A., Turcotte, M., de Souza, R. J., Samaan, M. C., Champredon, D., Dushoff, J., . . . Meyre, D. (2018). On the origin of obesity: Identifying the biological, environmental and cultural drivers of genetic risk among human populations. *Obes Rev, 19*(2), 121–149. doi:10.1111/obr.12625

Rzeczkowska, P. A., Hou, H., Wilson, M. D., & Palmert, M. R. (2014). Epigenetics: A new player in the regulation of mammalian puberty. *Neuroendocrinology, 99*(3–4), 139–155. doi:10.1159/000362559

Salem, E. S. B., Vonberg, A. D., Borra, V. J., Gill, R. K., & Nakamura, T. (2019). RNAs and RNA-binding proteins in immuno-metabolic homeostasis and diseases. *Front Cardiovasc Med, 6*, 106. doi:10.3389/fcvm.2019.00106

Smink, F. R., van Hoeken, D., & Hoek, H. W. (2012). Epidemiology of eating disorders: Incidence, prevalence and mortality rates. *Curr Psychiatry Rep, 14*(4), 406–414. doi:10.1007/s11920-012-0282-y

Speakman, J. R. (2006). Thrifty genes for obesity and the metabolic syndrome: Time to call off the search? *Diab Vasc Dis Res, 3*(1), 7–11. https://doi.org/10.3132/dvdr.2006.010

Strober, M., Freeman, R., Lampert, C., Diamond, J., & Kaye, W. (2000). Controlled family study of anorexia nervosa and bulimia nervosa: Evidence of shared liability and transmission of partial syndromes. *Am J Psychiatry, 157*(3), 393–401. doi:10.1176/appi.ajp.157.3.393

Swallow, J. G., Carter, P. A., & Garland, T., Jr. (1998). Artificial selection for increased wheel-running behavior in house mice. *Behav Genet, 28*(3), 227–237. doi:10.1023/a:1021479331779

Thompson, Z., Argueta, D., Garland, T., Jr., & DiPatrizio, N. (2017). Circulating levels of endocannabinoids respond acutely to voluntary exercise, are altered in mice selectively bred for high voluntary wheel running, and differ between the sexes. *Physiol Behav, 170*, 141–150. doi:10.1016/j.physbeh.2016.11.041

Trace, S. E., Baker, J. H., Peñas-Lledó, E., & Bulik, C. M. (2013). The genetics of eating disorders. *Annu Rev Clin Psychol, 9*, 589–620. doi:10.1146/annurev-clinpsy-050212-185546

van de Vegte, Y. J., Said, M. A., Rienstra, M., van der Harst, P., & Verweij, N. (2020). Genome-wide association studies and Mendelian randomization analyses for leisure sedentary behaviours. *Nat Commun, 11*(1), 1770. doi:10.1038/s41467-020-15553-w

Warburton, D. E. R., & Bredin, S. S. D. (2017). Health benefits of physical activity: A systematic review of current systematic reviews. *Curr Opin Cardiol, 32*(5), 541–556. doi:10.1097/hco.0000000000000437

Watson, H. J., Yilmaz, Z., Thornton, L. M., Hübel, C., Coleman, J. R. I., Gaspar, H. A., . . . Bulik, C. M. (2019). Genome-wide association study identifies eight risk loci and implicates metabo-psychiatric origins for anorexia nervosa. *Nat Genet, 51*(8), 1207–1214. doi:10.1038/s41588-019-0439-2

Wijesuriya, T. M., De Ceuninck, L., Masschaele, D., Sanderson, M. R., Carias, K. V., Tavernier, J., & Wevrick, R. (2017). The Prader-Willi syndrome proteins MAGEL2 and necdin regulate leptin receptor cell surface abundance through ubiquitination pathways. *Hum Mol Genet, 26*(21), 4215–4230. doi:10.1093/hmg/ddx311

World Health Organization (2010). *Global Recommendations on Physical Activity for Health*. Geneva: WHO.

World Health Organization (2020a). Feeding or eating disorders. ICD-11 for Mortality and Morbidity Statistics. http://id.who.int/icd/entity/1412387537

World Health Organization (2020b). Anorexia nervosa. ICD-11 for Mortality and Morbidity Statistics. http://id.who.int/icd/entity/263852475

World Health Organization (2020c). Bulimia nervosa. ICD-11 for Mortality and Morbidity Statistics. http://id.who.int/icd/entity/509381842

Zhang, X., & Speakman, J. R. (2019). Genetic factors associated with human physical activity: Are your genes too tight to prevent you exercising? *Endocrinology, 160*(4), 840–852. doi:10.1210/en.2018-00873

Zhang, Y., Proenca, R., Maffei, M., Barone, M., Leopold, L., & Friedman, J. M. (1994). Positional cloning of the mouse obese gene and its human homologue. *Nature, 372*(6505), 425–432. doi:10.1038/372425a0

13 Social Behavior

Have you interacted with anyone today? For nearly everyone, the answer to that question is "yes." We tend to live with or around other people, and our lives are greatly impacted by their behaviors. Our behaviors impact their lives too. Broadly speaking, animals act in ways that enhance their survival and reproduction. When those behaviors involve others of the same species, we define them as social behaviors. Social psychology is the subdiscipline of psychology that studies how people impact the thoughts, feelings, and behaviors of others. Of course, humans are not the only animals affected by the behaviors of others. Social behavior can be studied in many species and is sometimes even studied between species such as humans and dogs.

Understanding the relations among genetic variants, gene expression, brain activity, and social behavior is a daunting challenge. Social animals inhabit a complex environment in which the behavior of others can trigger gene expression and physiological activation of systems in their own bodies that can produce thoughts, feelings, and behaviors, which can then initiate biological processes and behaviors in others (see Figure 13.1). A smile or a wink from your significant other can activate a cascade of events that is different from the one that is triggered when they cry. And your responses would likely be different if those cues were produced by someone else. Genetic variation undoubtedly plays a role in individual differences in responses to social cues but characterizing and understanding its impact may be one of the most difficult challenges facing behavior genetics.

In this chapter, we focus most of our discussion on the role of genetic variation in individual differences in social behavior. However, we also discuss examples where social behavior influences the expression of genes in the brain, which then impacts behavior. First, we discuss some of the social behaviors that are targets of behavior genetic research and their importance in psychology. Next, we examine the key biological systems that are known to impact social behaviors. Then we discuss the role of sex chromosome number in social cognition. Finally, we discuss evidence that genetic variation impacts individual differences in three categories of social behavior: affiliation, sexual behavior, and aggression.

13.1 Individual Differences in Social Behavior Are an Important Part of Life

The earliest, and perhaps the most important social relationships that an individual has is with caregivers, typically their parents. For many animal species, including humans, newborns are not capable of living without the assistance of caregivers. Newborns may not be able to feed, care for, or protect themselves from harm in any meaningful way, therefore some type of care is necessary for survival. The care can be provided by the mother (i.e., maternal care), the father (i.e., paternal care), another conspecific (i.e., alloparental care), or by some combination of these.

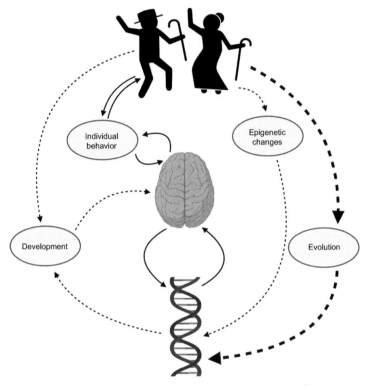

Figure 13.1. **Relations among genes, brains, and social behavior.** Social interactions can reciprocally impact brain function and gene expression on different timescales: physiological (solid line), developmental (dotted line), and evolutionary (dashed line). After Robinson, Fernald, & Clayton (2008).

13.1.1 Reproductive Strategies

Of course, parental investment in offspring depends on the reproductive "strategy" of the species. In species that are relatively short-lived and that live in unstable environments, it is advantageous to produce many offspring and to invest in them minimally. In the context of non-human animal models in behavior genetics, *Drosophila melanogaster* are an example of such a species, where a fertilized female can lay approximately 500 fertilized eggs and neither parent engages in parental care.

Species that are relatively long-lived and that live in stable environments often produce few offspring that are slow to mature. Such offspring require substantial parental care. In the context of non-human animal models in behavior genetics, the mouse (*Mus musculus*) is an example of such a species, where litter size varies from about three to eight, depending on the strain. Maternal care for mice (and rats) includes, but is not limited to, pup retrieval, nursing, licking, nest building, and defense (Kuroda, Tachikawa, Yoshida, Tsuneoka, & Numan, 2011). Of course, this is also the reproductive strategy of human beings.

13.1.2 Child Development

Parental care is not always optimal for offspring developmental outcomes. Childhood maltreatment is a well-established risk factor for negative outcomes including, but not limited to, depressive disorders, drug use, suicide attempts, sexually transmitted diseases, and risky sexual behavior (Norman et al., 2012). The term maltreatment is somewhat broad. It includes physical abuse, sexual abuse, emotional/psychological abuse, and neglect. Approximately 10–15 percent of children worldwide experience childhood maltreatment. There is growing evidence that the experience of childhood maltreatment triggers epigenetic mechanisms, such as DNA methylation, that can influence long-term patterns of gene expression (Lutz & Turecki, 2014).

Early and repeated interactions between parents and offspring can determine the strength of the emotional bonds between them. Three primary attachment styles characterize a child's connection to their caregiver and to others as (1) secure (i.e., seeks close contact and intimacy, and able to regulate emotions), (2) avoidant (i.e., actively avoids intimacy and suppresses emotions), and (3) anxious-ambivalent (i.e., seeks contact, but has difficulty controlling emotions). Attachment theory was primarily developed by Bowlby and Ainsworth in the middle of the twentieth century (Bretherton, 1992) and continues to provide a framework for understanding social connections between people and their role in important life outcomes such as neurodevelopmental disorders (Antonucci, Taurisano, Coppola, & Cassibba, 2018).

Another important aspect of childhood and adolescence is the development of social cognition. Social cognition involves thinking about and communicating with others and includes an understanding that other individuals have their own minds. To interact with others appropriately it is important to understand that they communicate via facial expressions and have their own mental states and perspectives. In addition, children develop feelings for the plight of others (e.g., empathy) and preferences for outcomes of social interactions (e.g., fairness or cooperation). Individual differences in aspects of social cognition are apparent in healthy (i.e., non-clinical) populations; and many psychiatric, neurological, or developmental condition are characterized by deficits in social cognition (Cotter et al., 2018).

13.1.3 Courtship, Agonistic Behaviors, and Social Dominance

It is obvious that sexual reproduction is a social act. Mate choice is a critical feature of evolutionary theory. At the bare minimum, it is important to interact with an opposite sex individual from the same species for successful reproduction. Courtship behavior in *Drosophila* species, for example, includes species-specific components that can be rather elaborate and are influenced by genetic variation. Courtship involves a complex interplay of multisensory communication between individuals. Preference for certain traits drives sexual selection when individual differences in those traits are at least partially due to genetic differences between them.

Agonistic behaviors are those that are related to fighting. Typically, agonistic behaviors involve social behaviors between conspecifics for access to limited resources, such as mates, food, or territory. Because physical fights can cause serious injury, many species engage in threat displays that often make them appear ready to fight (e.g., baring teeth) and serve to intimidate their opponent (see Figure 13.2).

Dominance hierarchies are social structures in which individuals each have a rank that determines their access to resources. Higher rank may entail more access to food and mates but maintaining rank may require enhanced vigilance and can involve risk of injury when the social order is challenged by subordinates. Agonistic and aggressive behaviors are widely studied in non-human animal models, such as mice and zebra fish.

In this section we provided a brief overview of topics in social psychology that are of great interest in behavior genetics. By their nature, social behaviors are a dynamic interplay between individuals, which adds to the already daunting empirical challenges in behavior genetics. Before

Figure 13.2. **Agonistic behavior.** One black-backed jackal (*Canis mesomelas*) confronting another, with a spotted hyena in the background. Masai Mara National Reserve, Kenya, East Africa. The jackal on the left is exhibiting submissive behaviors (e.g., crouching posture, ears lowered) and the jackal on the right is exhibiting dominant behaviors (e.g., erect posture and ears). Such agonistic displays reduce the frequency of actual fighting, thereby reducing risk of injury. Source: Auscape / Contributor / Universal Images Group / Getty Images.

discussing the evidence that individual differences in social behaviors are due to genetic differences, we will outline the current understanding of their neurobiology.

Check-up

- How might the reproductive strategies of different species impact interactions between parents and offspring?
- Compare and contrast attachment styles.
- What are agonistic behaviors and what purpose do they serve?

13.2 The Neurobiology of Social Behavior

The biology of social behavior has been studied for decades in humans and in many non-human animal models, such as fruit flies, zebra fish, and rodents. Of course, work with mice is especially instructive because of the existence of several reliable behavioral assays for key social behaviors such as mating, parenting, and aggressive behaviors, in addition to the well-established techniques to investigate genetics and brain circuits.

13.2.1 Social Interactions Are Dynamic

To illustrate a step-by-step approach to analyzing social behavior let us consider interactions between two individuals (see Figure 13.3). You can think of social interactions occurring in a dynamically reciprocal fashion with three basic stages: (1) sensory, (2) decision, and (3) execution (Chen & Hong, 2018). It is important to note that each stage references internal states, such as memory or motivation, to inform the process as well as to update its status. So, at the initiation of social contact, an individual gathers sensory information about the other. Depending on the species, different sensory information may take precedence. For example, humans may rely more on visual than olfactory information, whereas rodents may do the opposite. The sensory information can be analyzed to identify the individual and determine if they are known and whether previous interactions are represented in memory. The current state of arousal and aspects of motivation can be checked, and so on. These assessments can take place rapidly so that within an instant a behavioral

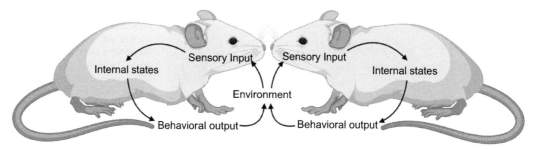

Figure 13.3. **Social interaction dynamics.** Sensory information from the environment and the other individual alters internal states of social interaction participants, which leads to behavioral output that can impact the environment and available sensory information in a dynamic fashion. Source: Created with Biorender.com. After Chen & Hong (2018).

decision can be made, and the behavior can be executed. If the other individual is of the appropriate sex, and communicates receptivity either through visual, olfactory, or other means, the decision to pursue courtship behaviors rather than aggressive behaviors may be selected and executed.

The social interaction is dynamically reciprocal because the other individual is also behaving, and therefore sensory inputs change. It may be that although the individual appears to be a sexually receptive partner, their behaviors are rejecting, and therefore a decision to cease courtship behavior may be selected and executed. The relative strength of different internal states can change over time or in different contexts. The decision to continue or stop courtship behavior may depend on initial attraction based on sensory information or on internal states such as memory of rejection or on presence of a competitor, which may affect motivation.

The main point of this social interaction model is that social interaction engages multiple physiological and psychological mechanisms in a dynamic fashion that depends on reciprocal interactions with another. Further, these mechanisms depend on multiple neural circuits, which means that they also depend on many gene products and suggests that genetic variation is likely to impact circuit function.

13.2.2 Social Brain Circuits

The brain circuits involved with social behavior in mice have been mapped (Chen & Hong, 2018). The circuits include brain areas that are involved in processing sensory input, such as olfactory (i.e., the main olfactory bulb) or pheromonal (i.e., the accessory olfactory bulb) cues (see Figure 13.4). Various nuclei in the amygdala that are involved in processing those sensory inputs and integrating it with information from memory and emotions are critical in social behavior circuits. Signals from the amygdala are either processed by the bed nucleus of the stria terminalis (BNST), which then sends information to various hypothalamic nuclei, or sent directly to the hypothalamus. Depending on the type of behavior in question, different hypothalamic nuclei may be involved. For example, the medial preoptic area (MPOA) of the hypothalamus is involved in parenting behaviors, but not in aggression. Finally, various nuclei in the midbrain, such as the periaqueductal gray are critical in behavioral decision-making.

This model of the social behavior pathway is a product of decades of research involving lesioning brain areas and observing potential behavioral effects. From the perspective of behavior genetics, any component of the circuit that is a gene product, such as a receptor on a neuron, has the potential to impact the function of the circuit, which then means that any genetic variation affecting its expression, structure, or function is a potential candidate to test. Genes encoding key proteins and their regulatory regions become targets for genetic manipulation in non-human animal models. In the sections that follow, we discuss different classes of social behaviors and examine some of the evidence for the role of genetic variation in individual differences.

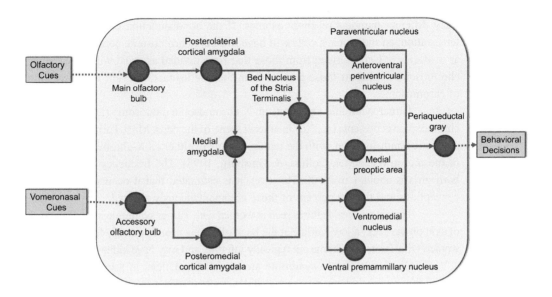

Figure 13.4. **Brain circuits for social behavior in mice.** Social cues from olfaction and vomeronasal (i.e., pheromones) systems are processed in social circuits leading to the amygdala, the bed nucleus of the stria terminalis, several hypothalamic nuclei, and then to the periaqueductal gray. After Chen & Hong (2018).

Check-up

- Discuss the reciprocal nature of social interactions.
- Discuss the brain circuits involved in social interactions.

13.3 Individual Differences in Social Cognition and Sociability

Social cognition refers to the role of cognitive processes in interactions among individuals. Individuals can learn by observing others (i.e., social learning), and they can learn about the minds of others by interacting with them, which can inform future interactions (Frith & Frith, 2012). Sociability refers to the drive to interact with others. Understanding others can involve meta-cognition where we think about our own thoughts and thought processes, in addition to thinking about the thoughts and thought processes of others. One type of evidence that genetic variation influences individual differences in social phenotypes is that several genetic conditions impact aspects of social cognition and sociability. In this section we discuss a few such examples.

13.3.1 Turner Syndrome and Social Competence

As we mentioned in Chapter 5, one of the ways that individuals can differ genetically is on the number of chromosomes that they have. Typically, humans have twenty-two pairs of autosomes and either two X-chromosomes (i.e., female), or one X- and one Y-chromosome (i.e., male). Atypical assortment of chromosomes because of nondisjunction during meiosis can produce gametes that carry different numbers of chromosomes. If the nondisjunction occurs during mitosis soon after fertilization, an individual's cells will have different chromosome complements, a condition known as mosaicism. Cells derived from those that have divided as usual will have the typical number of chromosomes, whereas those derived from the nondisjunction event will have an atypical number of chromosomes.

Turner syndrome represents an X-chromosome monosomy (i.e., 45, X), where a single sex chromosome is present (i.e., X0) in at least some of the cells. Most Turner syndrome cases are due to a meiotic nondisjunction, with the remainder due to either an X-chromosome structural abnormality or mosaicism (Gelehrter, Collins, & Ginsburg, 1998). The frequency of Turner syndrome in live-born girls is about 1 in 2,500. However, it is estimated that it occurs in as many as 4 percent of conceptions and that 99 percent of those are spontaneously aborted.

Typical physical features seen in women with Turner syndrome include short stature, extra folds of skin on the neck, a low hairline at the back of the neck, and some skeletal abnormalities. In addition, women with Turner syndrome are typically infertile, and may have kidney and/or heart problems.

Girls with Turner syndrome are at risk for deficits in several domains of neuropsychological function including visuospatial skills, mathematics, processing speed, and executive function (Hutaff-Lee, Bennett, Howell, & Tartaglia, 2019). In addition, they are at increased risk for developing ADHD and symptoms of anxiety.

Turner syndrome also impacts aspects of social function. Those with Turner syndrome often have fewer friends than those without it and may be considered less socially competent than their typically developing peers (Hutaff-Lee et al., 2019). They may also be shy, have low self-esteem, and be less emotionally mature than their peers. These social outcomes may be due to deficits in the capacity to recognize faces, emotional facial expressions, and to interpret social cues. There seems to be reliable evidence that women with Turner syndrome are significantly worse at identifying faces expressing fear or anger than their typically developing peers (Morel et al., 2018).

Sex chromosome trisomies are genetic conditions that also arise from nondisjunctions involving the X- or Y-chromosome occurring in an estimated 1 in 650 to 1 in 1,000 live births (Urbanus, van Rijn, & Swaab, 2020). Examples of sex chromosome trisomies include Klinefelter syndrome (i.e., 47, XXY) and XYY syndrome (i.e., 47, XYY) in males, and trisomy X (i.e., 47, XXX) in females. Although the physical and psychological features of these conditions are rather subtle, it seems that one shared feature is difficulties in recognizing emotional facial expressions.

Although the mechanisms by which alterations in sex chromosome number impact aspects of social cognition like facial emotion recognition are unknown, it is striking to see such a consistent pattern across different genetic conditions. Based on these findings, genetic variants on the X-chromosome become interesting candidates for playing a role in individual differences in emotion recognition.

13.3.2 Williams Syndrome and Sociability

Strong evidence for the impact of genetic variation on individual differences in traits is when deletions and duplications of a DNA sequence have opposite effects on a phenotype. A good example of that is the impact of deletions and duplications on a region of chromosome 7 (7q11.23) on social phenotypes (Crespi & Procyshyn, 2017). Deletion of twenty-eight genes in that region (aka Williams syndrome critical region) causes Williams syndrome, which is characterized by hyper-sociability, including decreased social anxiety (see Figure 13.5). And, although there is less

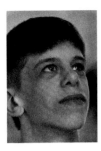

Figure 13.5. **Williams syndrome critical region on chromosome 7.** Characteristic facial features of Williams syndrome include, but are not limited to, broad forehead, short nose, wide mouth, large earlobes. Source: Star Tribune via Getty Images / Contributor / Star Tribune / Getty Images.

evidence about the impact of duplications in this region, it appears that they are associated with high levels of separation anxiety and may also be associated with increased risk for autism in children and for schizophrenia in adults. The deletions and duplications in this region are due to non-allelic homologous recombination (see Box 13.1).

Box 13.1 Non-Allelic Homologous Recombination

As you recall from earlier chapters, homologous recombination, or crossing over, occurs during meiosis and is responsible for generating genetic variation by exchanging matching DNA sequences from one parental chromosome to the other. When this mechanism works well, the same DNA sequence is exchanged between homologous chromosomes. In that case, the two homologous chromosomes exchange material between recombination breakpoints. This specificity is determined by aligning the DNA sequences of the two homologous chromosomes.

There are many regions in the genome, however, where such homologous alignment is difficult because they contain copy number variants where a DNA sequence is repeated some number of times (see Figure 13.6). In such a repeat-rich region, several repeats on one chromosome may be paired with repeats on the homologous chromosome, but in such a way that the two chromosomes are misaligned. In this case, when recombination exchanges material from the two chromosomes, one ends up shorter and the other ends up longer. In other words, DNA sequence is functionally "deleted" from one chromosome and "duplicated" onto the other.

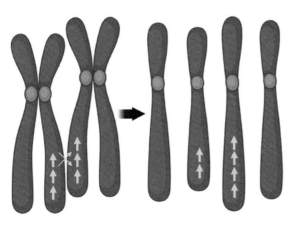

Figure 13.6 **Non-allelic homologous recombination.** In chromosomal regions where the presence of copy number variants facilitates misalignment of homologous chromosomes during crossing over in meiosis, resulting sister chromatids may carry unequal numbers of the repeats. Chromosomal material within and around the repeats is effectively deleted in one chromatid and inserted into the other.

Williams syndrome was first identified and described based on clinical presentation in the early 1960s, and its deletion was mapped in the late 1990s. The first cases of 7q11.23 duplication were identified in 2005, although they were suspected to exist because the deletion was thought to be due to non-allelic homologous recombination (Morris et al., 2015).

Williams syndrome affects approximately 1 in 7,500 to 1 in 10,000 people and impacts multiple phenotypes. People with Williams syndrome are at increased risk for cardiovascular disease, connective tissue abnormalities, low growth rate and short stature, endocrine dysfunction such as hypothyroidism, and characteristic facial features. Those with Williams syndrome may have mild to severe intellectual disability, with strong verbal short-term memory language abilities, as well as weak visuospatial construction ability (i.e., replicating a pattern of objects after viewing them).

One of the most striking characteristics of people with Williams syndrome is that they are hyper-social. They are very outgoing and interested in others and have low levels of social anxiety. In contrast, people with duplication of 7q11.23 appear to have elevated levels of social anxiety. In one study that used parental report, 22 of 46 (47.8 percent) children with duplication of 7q11.23 meet criteria for social phobia; and in another study of 7 adults with the duplication, 5 (71.4 percent) met criteria for social phobia (Morris et al., 2015). These findings are suggestive evidence that one or more of the 28 genes in 7q11.23 play a role in social anxiety.

Two of the genes that are typically deleted in Williams syndrome, and have gained attention for their impact on social phenotypes, are general transcription factor Iii (*GTF2I*) and GTF2I repeat domain containing protein 1 (*GTF2IRD1*) (Kopp et al., 2020). As indicated in the names, both genes code for proteins that serve as transcription factors, and therefore genetic variants in them have the potential to impact the expression of other genes. In fact, the transcription factors encoded by *GTF2I* and *GTF2IRD1* have been shown to regulate genes that encode synaptic proteins. Thus far, the evidence suggests that knocking out either gene impacts balance and anxiety phenotypes in mice, but neither knockout shows the complete array of behaviors observed in Williams syndrome.

Interestingly, there is evidence that variants in *GTF2I* and *GTF2IRD1* are associated with human-directed sociability in domesticated dogs (vonHoldt et al., 2017). Such convergent evidence across species increases confidence that transcription factors encoded by *GTF2I* and *GTF2IRD1* play an important role in brain circuits that are crucial for individual differences in social behavior.

Check-up

- What is Turner syndrome and what can it tell us about the role of genes in social behavior?
- Explain non-allelic homologous recombination.
- What are the typical social features of Williams syndrome?

13.4 Affiliation and Attachment

Affiliation and attachment comprise one of the RDoC constructs in the domain of social processes. Affiliation has to do with engaging in positive social interactions with others, and attachment occurs when affiliation with a specific individual produces a social bond. In this section we will focus attention on the role of the well-studied peptide oxytocin on affiliation and attachment.

13.4.1 Oxytocin's Role in Social Interaction

Oxytocin is a neuropeptide that is released by neuroendocrine cells that project from hypothalamic nuclei to capillaries in the posterior pituitary. Hundreds of studies have established that oxytocin plays important roles in social behavior (Bartz, 2016). For our purposes, we will focus on evidence for the role of variation in genes coding for oxytocin (OXT) and its receptor (OXTR) in individual differences in affiliation and attachment.

In humans, the *OXT* gene consists of three exons and is located on chromosome 20p13. The biosynthesis of oxytocin involves the synthesis of an inactive precursor protein that undergoes a series of enzymatic cleavages to produce the nine-peptide oxytocin neuropeptide. The oxytocin receptor is encoded by the oxytocin receptor gene (*OXTR*), which is located on chromosome 3p25.3 (see Figure 13.7). The gene consists of four exons, which encode a 389 amino acid G-coupled protein receptor. The oxytocin receptor is found in many brain areas including, but not limited to, olfactory nuclei, the amygdala, the hippocampus, hypothalamic nuclei, and brainstem areas. Because of the wide distribution of oxytocin receptors, it is clear that oxytocin is positioned to have a broad impact across behavioral domains.

Oxytocin is involved with aspects of reproduction such as uterine contractions during childbirth. It also triggers the milk-letdown reflex, which is the contraction of mammary glands to produce milk during breast feeding. Sexual stimulation and orgasm cause an increase of oxytocin in plasma. Oxytocin plays a crucial role in reproductive functions. It is also involved in many other psychological domains such as addiction, fear and anxiety, and depression.

Our focus is on evidence for the role of genetic variation in *OXT* and *OXTR* in individual differences in social behaviors. Rather than review the entire research literature relevant to the question, let us consider the evidence from gene knockouts in mice and then genetic associations in humans.

Social animals interact with certain individuals on a recurring basis so that the capacity to recognize individuals and have a memory of interactions with them facilitates ongoing social

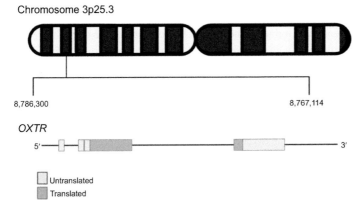

Figure 13.7. **Oxytocin receptor.** The structural gene for the oxytocin receptor is located on chromosome 3p25.3 (genomic location: 8,786,300–8,767,114). It comprises four exons and contains many SNPs. Source: Feldman, Monakhov, Pratt, & Ebstein (2016).

relationships. It is safe to say that social recognition memory is fundamental to social interaction because without it every interaction is with a stranger. In mice, social recognition memory relies on the vomeronasal system, which detects pheromone signals from conspecifics. Signals from the vomeronasal organ are sent to the accessory olfactory bulb and to the amygdala for processing. Typically, social recognition memory in mice is tested with the five-trial habituation-dishabituation test where the amount of time that the subject investigates the target is measured. Intact social recognition memory is shown when the subject spends decreasing amounts of time investigating the target individual on subsequent trials. A normal, healthy mouse spends more time investigating novel objects and unfamiliar conspecifics than familiar objects and known conspecifics.

13.4.2 Oxytocin System Knockout Mice

Capacity for social recognition memory is impaired in mice that have either the *Oxt* gene or the *Oxtr* gene knocked out (Caldwell, Aulino, Freeman, Miller, & Witchey, 2017). Knocking out these genes does not affect olfaction or basic social behaviors, like social approach, but appears to specifically impair social recognition memory. Blocking oxytocin receptors pharmacologically with an antagonist also disrupts social recognition memory. Injecting oxytocin into the medial amygdala of *Oxt* knockout mice restores social recognition memory. Wild-type female mice (i.e., *Oxt* +/+) abort their pregnancy when they are exposed to the scent of an unfamiliar male (i.e., Bruce effect). Females with *Oxt* knocked out (*Oxt* -/-) show the Bruce effect when a familiar male that has been removed for twenty-four hours is re-introduced. All in all, the evidence shows that the oxytocin system is critical in social recognition memory and that the products of *Oxt* and *Oxtr* play important roles.

Female mice with either *Oxt* or *Oxtr* knocked out have normal fertility, pregnancy, and parturition (i.e., giving birth). However, they are unable to eject milk from their milk glands and are therefore unable to nurse their young (Caldwell et al., 2017). There is also evidence that pup retrieval is somewhat impaired in both knockouts. Overall, the evidence for the impact of these knockouts on maternal behavior is rather mixed. It is reasonable to interpret these findings as a recognition that the systems governing maternal behavior may be more varied and complex than social recognition memory, and that inactivating these single genes alone does not abolish maternal behavior.

Interestingly, adult *Oxt* -/- males whose dam (i.e., mother) was also *Oxt* -/- show higher rates of intermale aggression than do *Oxt* -/- males whose dam was *Oxt* +/- (Caldwell et al., 2017). This increase in aggression remains when the males are cross-fostered to wild-type females, which suggests that the difference is not due to maternal behavior but may be due to developmental effects of a maternal oxytocin deficit on aggression-related brain circuits in their offspring.

A similar pattern on adult aggression is seen in *Oxtr* knockouts, where the male *Oxtr* -/- is more aggressive if born to an *Oxtr* -/- female. It should also be noted that *Oxtr* -/- male mice do not show heightened levels of aggression to males of different strains. Typically, male mice show higher levels of aggression to male mice from other strains (i.e., interstrain) than to males from their own strain (i.e., intrastrain). Perhaps this is due to decreased social recognition memory capacity affecting the ability to distinguish between strains.

13.4.3 Oxytocin System Genetic Variants as Candidate Genes

With respect to the oxytocin system, the genes most tested for associations with human social behaviors are *OXT*, *OXTR*, and *CD38*. The structural gene for CD38 is located on chromosome

4p15.32 and encodes a transmembrane protein involved in oxytocin release. Hundreds of studies have been conducted to test variants in *OXT*, *OXTR*, and *CD38* for associations with individual differences in social behaviors including parental attachment, romantic/couple relationships, friendship, empathy, theory of mind, management of stress via social relationships, depression, schizophrenia, and autism spectrum disorders (Feldman et al., 2016).

It is important to remember that many of these candidate gene association studies have relatively small sample sizes and are likely statistically underpowered to detect small genetic effects. Because there has been such interest in characterizing the potential impact of genetic variation in *OXTR* on social behavior phenotypes there exist several meta-analyses that combine the data from smaller studies to take advantage of the resulting larger sample size. Let us focus on meta-analyses of associations between *OXTR* variants and social behavior phenotypes.

Although there appears to be good evidence that the administration of oxytocin intranasally impacts a person's feelings of attachment in experimental settings, a meta-analysis did not find significant associations between commonly studied *OXTR* variants rs53576 and rs2254298 and aspects of social attachment (Gong et al., 2020). The rs53576 variant, however, appears to be associated with general sociality, which is a loose term that includes social phenotypes such as empathy, loneliness, prosocial behavior, and other measures that refer to the general tendency to interact with others (Li et al., 2015). In this study, the G allele of rs53576 was associated with higher levels of general sociability. This is consistent with another meta-analysis that focused on the same variant (rs53576) and empathy that found an association with the G allele and higher levels of empathy (Gong et al., 2017). Another meta-analysis of six studies found that another *OXTR* variant (rs237887) may be associated with antisocial behavior, although they note that their finding should be interpreted with caution because of concerns about the studies (Poore & Waldman, 2020). Overall, when one considers the convergent evidence from non-human animal models, experimental approaches using intranasal oxytocin administration in humans, and the meta-analyses of candidate gene association studies, there is reason to have some confidence that genetic variation in the oxytocin system plays a role in individual differences in certain social behaviors.

13.4.4 Autism Spectrum Disorder

What is the evidence that genetic variation is associated with risk for disorders that are characterized by atypical social phenotypes such as autism spectrum disorder? The prevalence of autism spectrum disorder worldwide is 1–2 percent, with about four to five times more boys being diagnosed with it than girls (see Figure 13.8 and Box 13.2). The heritability of autism spectrum disorder is estimated to be 0.56–0.90 (Colvert et al., 2015).

One meta-analysis found that a haplotype block that contained five *OXTR* SNPs (rs237897–rs13316193–rs237889–rs2254298–rs2268494) was transmitted to autism spectrum disorder probands from parents more often than would be expected by chance (Kranz et al., 2016). Specifically, the A allele of rs237889 was transmitted to affected offspring more often than the G allele. Evidence that a certain variant is transmitted more often from parents to offspring with a disorder suggests that the variants play a role in causing the disorder. Conversely, SNP alleles that are not associated with the disorder are equally likely to be transmitted from parents to proband offspring. Their finding was consistent with another meta-analysis that found four SNPs in *OXTR* (rs7632287, rs237887, rs2268491, and rs2254298) to be associated with autism spectrum disorder diagnosis (LoParo & Waldman, 2015). For our purposes, these two meta-analyses are supportive of an association between genetic variation in *OXTR* and autism spectrum disorder diagnosis.

(a)

Prevalence of autistic spectrum disorder, 2017

Share of the total population with autistic spectrum disorder, which is inclusive of autism and Asperger Syndrome. This prevalence is age-standardized to compare between countries and with time.

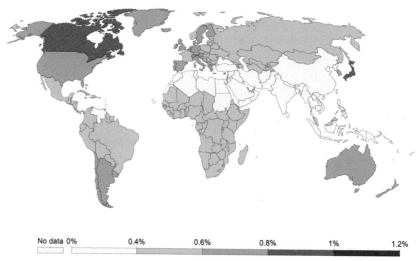

(b)

Share of males vs. females with autistic spectrum disorder, 2017

Share of males versus females with autistic spectrum disorder, which is inclusive of autism and Asperger Syndrome. This prevalence is age-standardized to compare between countries and with time.

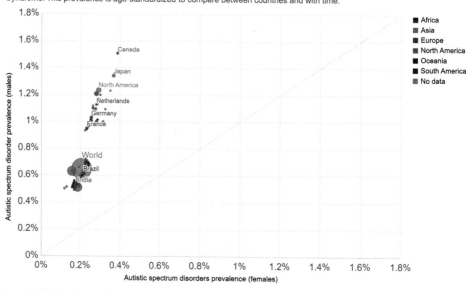

Figure 13.8. **Autism spectrum disorder.** (a) Prevalence of autism spectrum disorder around the world. (b) Boys are more likely than girls to be diagnosed with autism spectrum disorder. Source: Hannah Ritchie and Max Roser (2020) "Mental Health." Published online at OurWorldInData.org. Retrieved from: https://ourworldindata.org/mental-health

Box 13.2 ICD-11 Diagnosis: Autism Spectrum Disorder

Autism spectrum disorder is characterised by persistent deficits in the ability to initiate and to sustain reciprocal social interaction and social communication, and by a range of restricted, repetitive, and inflexible patterns of behaviour, interests or activities that are clearly atypical or excessive for the individual's age and sociocultural context. The onset of the disorder occurs during the developmental period, typically in early childhood, but symptoms may not become fully manifest until later, when social demands exceed limited capacities. Deficits are sufficiently severe to cause impairment in personal, family, social, educational, occupational or other important areas of functioning and are usually a pervasive feature of the individual's functioning observable in all settings, although they may vary according to social, educational, or other context. Individuals along the spectrum exhibit a full range of intellectual functioning and language abilities.

Source: http://id.who.int/icd/entity/437815624 (accessed April 3, 2021), World Health Organization (Copyright © 2020).

The details about which SNP is the one driving the association matters less than the general support these findings lend to the notion that genetic variation in *OXTR* contributes to autism spectrum disorder risk (see Figure 13.9).

A large GWAS of autism spectrum disorder, with 18,381 cases and 27,969 controls, identified five loci that reached genome-wide significance level (Grove et al., 2019). Undoubtedly more loci that contribute to the polygenic risk for autism spectrum disorders will be identified as sample sizes increase and enable even larger meta-analyses across studies.

Other types of genetic variation are also known to contribute to risk for autism spectrum disorders, such as *de novo* mutations. In fact, it is estimated that *de novo* mutations contribute to autism spectrum disorder risk in 25 percent of cases in boys and in 45 percent of cases in girls (Iakoucheva, Muotri, & Sebat, 2019). Evidence suggests that *de novo* mutations occurring in at least twenty-four genes increase risk for autism spectrum disorder (Ruzzo et al., 2019). Genetic influences on autism spectrum disorder appear to be due to different types of genetic variation including common variants in the oxytocin system and newly arising mutations (see Figure 13.9).

There is strong evidence that genetic variation plays a role in individual differences in a wide variety of social behaviors. A substantial amount of work remains, however, to identify and fully characterize the genes and the pathways involved.

Check-up

- Summarize the evidence that genetic variation in *OXTR* is associated with individual differences in social phenotypes.
- What are the defining features of an autism spectrum disorder diagnosis?
- What are the strengths and limitations of the evidence that genetic variation in the oxytocin system is associated with autism spectrum disorder risk?

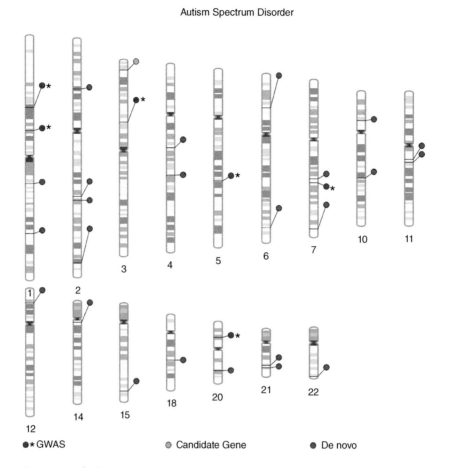

Figure 13.9. **Autism spectrum disorder risk genes.** The locations of genetic variants that have been associated with risk for autism spectrum disorders by GWAS (*), candidate gene association studies (light gray), and *de novo* mutations (dark gray). Source: Phenogram was constructed at http://visualization.ritchielab.org/phenograms

13.5 Sexual Behavior Circuits

In sexually reproducing species, reproductive success typically requires the identification of a potential opposite sex partner of the same species, engaging in appropriate behavior to attract the potential partner, consummating the sexual act, and may also involve post-copulatory behaviors such as parental care. In this section we discuss the role of genetic variation in individual differences in behaviors related to sexual reproduction. Rather than reviewing the entire literature, we focus on courtship behavior in fruit flies, sexual orientation in humans, and pair bonding in voles.

13.5.1 Sexual Selection

The entire edifice of evolutionary theory is built on differential reproductive success. Reproductive success is a dimensional outcome that considers the number and quality (e.g., health) of descendants produced by an individual. Only those who reproduce contribute genes directly to subsequent generations. Individual differences in reproductive success are a primary driver of evolution.

Figure 13.10. **Female Satin Bowerbird inspects bower.** Satin Bowerbird (*Ptilonorhynchus violaceus*) female visiting bower while the male who constructed it moves a blue bottle cap. Lamington National Park, Queensland Australia, September. Source: Photo by Education Images/Universal Images Group via Getty Images.

Individual differences in behavior are an important determinant of differential reproductive success. Such behaviors are social because they involve the interaction between (at least) two individuals, and they play a role in the identification of an appropriate mating partner and in the selection of a favorable one. Typically, in sexually reproducing species, one sex is more selective when it comes to choosing mating partners. The more selective mating partner is usually the one that makes the largest investment in reproduction. For example, in species where females produce relatively few eggs and males produce relatively many sperm, females are typically more choosy than males.

Sexual selection occurs when one sex prefers to mate with individuals that display a particular trait over those who do not. The trait may be considered an advertisement of genetic value. The trait could be morphological, like the classic example of a peacock's tail, or behavioral as seen in the elaborate building skills of the male bowerbird (see Figure 13.10). When the choosy sex tends to favor partners with certain genetically determined traits over those without, the favored traits will increase in frequency in subsequent generations.

Sexual selection has shaped the courtship repertoires of many species, including *D. melanogaster*. Male courtship behavior in the genus *Drosophila* is species specific, thereby enabling courted females to identify suitable mating partners. As you may have guessed, the *Drosophila* species with the most studied male courtship behavior is *D. melanogaster*. The male's courtship "dance" contains five basic steps that are carried out in stereotypical fashion: (a) orienting, (b) tapping, (c) singing, (d) licking, and (e) copulation (see Figure 13.11).

Orienting occurs when the male appears to begin to pay attention to the female using visual and olfactory cues. The male then moves behind the female and taps his foreleg onto her abdomen. Flies can "taste" pheromones using sensory apparatus on their legs. The male then moves to the side of or in front of the female, extends a single wing (the one nearest her head) and begins to "sing" by flapping the wing rapidly. The song is characterized by two distinct phases. One is called the pulse song because it contains bursts of high frequencies interspersed with brief periods of silence. The pulse songs of different species are characterized by different inter-pulse intervals. The other phase of the courtship song is called the sine song because it resembles the regular oscillation of a sine wave when viewed on an oscilloscope. After a bout of singing, the male may extend his proboscis to "lick" the female's genitalia. The male may then attempt to copulate with the female by mounting her back and attempting intromission. If the female is receptive, she will spread her wings and allow the male to copulate. If not, she will keep her wings together and attempt to escape by either flying

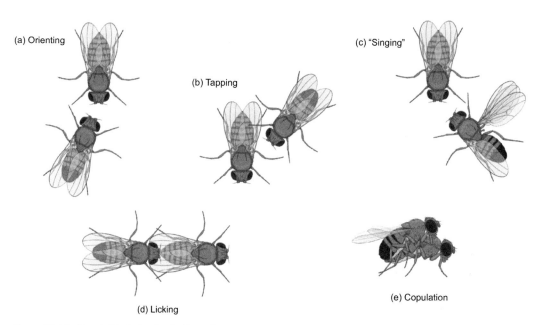

(a) Orienting

(b) Tapping

(c) "Singing"

(d) Licking

(e) Copulation

Figure 13.11. **Courtship behavior in *D. melanogaster*.** Courtship behavior in fruit flies contains a sequence where (a) the male orients his head toward the female, (b) the male taps the female's body with his forelegs, (c) the male "sings" a species-specific courtship song by vibrating his wing, (d) the male licks the female's genitals with his proboscis, (e) the male mounts the female for successful copulation. Source: Created with Biorender.com.

or running away. The male will often continue to pursue a non-receptive female for some time, repeating the courtship cycle of behaviors until successful or until he loses interest.

Courtship behavior in *D. melanogaster* is a prototypical social behavior that involves the dynamic interplay between individuals and utilizes multiple sensory systems, and psychological constructs (e.g., motivation, decision-making). There is strong evidence that genetic variation plays a role in individual differences in courtship behavior including that around twenty genes have been identified in which mutations impact aspects of courtship behavior; and that divergent selection on mating speed has been successful (Mackay et al., 2005). Given what we know about genes and their impacts on complex behaviors, we should expect that many genes with small effects impact courtship behavior in fruit flies.

One gene has garnered a lot of attention for its impact on *D. melanogaster* courtship behavior, mainly because when it is mutated (1) males court females less often or not at all, (2) they are unlikely to copulate with females, and (3) they court other males (Yamamoto & Koganezawa, 2013). Females that carry a mutation in the gene do not appear to be affected by it. The gene is named *fruitless* (*fru*) and it encodes a transcription factor that plays a critical role in the sex determination pathway. Of the approximately 100,000 neurons in the *D. melanogaster* nervous system, about 2,000 express *fru*. The wild-type version of the gene has a sex-specific splicing pattern that produces a slightly longer protein in males than in females. Certain mutations of *fru* alter the sex-specific splicing such that the male-specific protein is not produced. Typical male courtship of females depends on expression of the male-specific *fru* protein in specific sensory, central, and motor system neurons. Although a human version of the *D. melanogaster fru* gene does not exist, the notion of genetic variation in developmental processes resulting in sex-specific neural circuits that influence sexual behavior is worth considering.

In humans, sex determination occurs early in embryonic development. When a Y-chromosome is present with the SRY gene, a male will develop, whereas a female develops in its absence. The developmental cascade that follows for each eventually produces adults that differ in morphology, physiology, and behavior. Many of these effects can be traced to differences in the expression levels of gonadal hormones such as testosterone.

13.5.2 Sexual Orientation in Humans

As one would expect in a sexually reproducing species, most adult humans prefer sex partners of the opposite sex (i.e., heterosexual orientation), although 3–10 percent report preferring partners of the same sex (i.e., homosexual orientation; Balthazart, 2020). It may be that adult sexual orientation is at least partially determined by early developmental events and exposures (e.g., hormones) in the sex-determination process. The causes of sexual orientation have been contentiously debated for quite some time (Bailey et al., 2016). Our goal is not to settle the debate, but to discuss the evidence that genetic differences between people play a role in individual differences in sexual orientation.

When assessing such evidence, it is important to consider how the phenotype is measured. It is possible to ask people their sexual orientation in terms of attraction (e.g., "who are you sexually attracted to?"), in terms of behavior (e.g., "who have you had sex with?"), in terms of genital arousal (e.g., measured while viewing erotic stimuli), or in terms of identity (e.g., "do you consider yourself heterosexual") (Bailey et al., 2016). In addition to these measures, one can consider sexuality a dimensional, rather than a categorical trait. And it can also be thought of as one that is fluid (i.e., situation dependent).

Heritability estimates from twin studies vary substantially depending on the way that participants were recruited (Bailey et al., 2016). When participants are recruited explicitly for a study on sexual orientation, the median estimate of heritability is 0.70 (MZ concordance = 0.52, DZ concordance = 0.17). But when they are recruited from a general twin registry or from a representative population sample, the median heritability estimate of sexual orientation is 0.18 (MZ concordance = 0.24, DZ concordance = 0.15). Therefore, sampling bias appears to lead to overestimates of the heritability of sexual orientation when targeted sampling is used for participant recruitment. For our purposes, precise heritability estimates are not necessary. The important information obtained by these studies is that the heritability estimates are significantly greater than zero, which suggests that genetic variation plays a role in individual differences in sexual orientation.

A large-scale study (N = 477,522) from the UK Biobank sample in which 4.1 percent of males and 2.8 percent of females self-reported that they had ever had sex with someone of the same sex identified five loci to be associated with homosexual behavior (Ganna et al., 2019). When considering all the SNPs that were associated with same-sex sexual behavior (regardless of overall statistical significance) the h^2_{SNP} ranged between 0.08 and 0.25 depending on the analytic model. One of the SNPs associated with same-sex sexual behavior in males (rs34730029; 11q12.1) is located near some genes that code for olfactory receptors. Another (rs28371400; 15q21.3) is speculated to play a role in hormone regulation. From this study we can see that there is not a single gene that determines same-sex sexual behavior in humans. Sexual attraction, identity, and behavior are traits that illustrate some of the complexity of studying the behavior genetics of social behaviors in humans. The evidence is consistent with genetic variation playing some role in sexual orientation, but the precise details of the genetic contribution remain elusive.

- How can sexual selection explain the elaborate courtship dance of male *D. melanogaster*?
- Discuss the evidence that genetic variation is associated with individual differences in sexual orientation in humans.

13.6 Aggression: Harming Someone Else

Aggressive behaviors are those intended to physically or emotionally harm another. They can be categorized into reactive and proactive aggression. Reactive aggression is considered impulsive and in response to perceived threats or provocation, whereas proactive aggression is planned and involves some type of anticipated reward. Aggressive behaviors can be used to protect or acquire resources and aggressiveness is considered an important evolutionary trait that is under stabilizing selection (i.e., extremes are selected against; Anholt & Mackay, 2012). A wide variety of behaviors can be considered aggressive, from making a rude comment about someone to killing them. Some level of aggression is considered normative, but higher levels (depending on species and context) can be deleterious because it can significantly harm others, increase risk of injury, and damage social relationships. Bullying, child maltreatment, intimate partner violence, assault and battery, murder, terrorist attack, and war illustrate a range of aggressive behaviors of which humans are capable.

13.6.1 Genetic Variation and Individual Differences in Aggression

As we saw in Chapter 10, generations of selective breeding for tameness in silver foxes produced animals that were no longer aggressive to humans (Dugatkin, 2018). Other instances of selective breeding have produced lines of mice, rats, and fruit flies, for example, that are more and less aggressive. Moderate heritability estimates for aggression have been observed in human twin studies and in non-human animal studies in many species (Anholt & Mackay, 2012). Such results demonstrate that differences between individuals in aggressive behaviors are at least partially due to genetic differences between them. Of course, the measurement of aggressive behavior varies across species (see Box 13.3). In humans, individual aggressive behavior is measured in many ways, including self-reported behavior (e.g., fights) or traits (e.g., anger), third-party reports (e.g., parents reporting on their children), in-lab experimental paradigms, and criminal records.

In 1993, the first study was published that identified a genetic variant associated with "impulsive aggression" and intellectual deficiency in humans, now called Brunner syndrome (Brunner et al., 1993). The genetic variant was a rare mutation in the structural gene for monoamine oxidase A (*MAOA*), which codes for an enzyme that metabolizes monoamines such as serotonin and dopamine (see Chapter 6). The mutation identified in the large Dutch kindred produced inactive MAOA enzymes, which led to low levels of serotonin breakdown as shown by low levels of its metabolite 5-hydroxyindoleacetic acid (5-HIAA) in the cerebral spinal fluid of affected males. This and many other studies that implicated the serotonin system as being critical in aggressive behavior led to the genetic engineering of several lines of mice to have different serotonin system genes knocked out.

For example, when exons 2 and 3 of the 15-exon mouse *Maoa* gene were deleted, the catalytic activity of the enzyme was abolished, and several behavioral phenotypes became apparent (Cases et al., 1995). The pups appeared to startle very easily and tended to bite the people that

Box 13.3 Measuring Aggressive Behavior in Non-Human Animal Models

Male fruit flies (*Drosophila melanogaster*) display aggression when food deprived and then exposed to a small food resource, especially when in the presence of a potential mating partner (see Figure 13.12(a)). Behaviors such as wing threats, charges, head butts, chases, kicks, and boxing are typically recorded by video camera and quantified for analysis (Chen, Lee, Bowens, Huber, & Kravitz, 2002).

In honeybees (*Apis mellifera*), the aggression of the colony can be assessed by simulating an attack on the hive by hitting it and providing a target for the bees to sting (Nouvian, Reinhard, & Giurfa, 2016) (see Figure 13.12(b)). The target typically consists of several small patches of black suede on a string placed near the hive. Bees that fly to the patches after the hive is disturbed can be collected for genotyping or other analysis.

In zebra fish (*Danio rerio*) aggression is measured either by using a mirror, or by introducing a similar-sized same-sex zebra fish into the test tank (Zabegalov et al., 2019). When presented with a mirror, zebra fish aggressive behaviors include approaching the image, displays of fin erection, attempted bites, and chasing (see Figure 13.12(c)). When presented with a conspecific, similar aggressive behaviors can be observed with the potential for actual biting and chasing.

In mice (*Mus musculus*), aggression is often measured using the resident-intruder paradigm, in which an "intruder" male is placed in the same cage as a "resident" male that has been housed there for some time (see Figure 13.12(d)). The primary measurements typically reported are latency to attack and attack frequency.

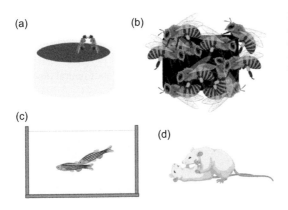

(a)   (b)

(c)

(d)

Figure 13.12. **Aggression in other non-human animal models**. (a) Male fruit flies display aggressive behavior. (b) Bees attack a target (black cloth) by stinging. (c) A male zebra fish bites another. (d) A resident mouse attacks an intruder. Source: Created with Biorender.com.

handled them. As adults, the mice from this knockout line tended to have short attack latencies in the resident-intruder paradigm and showed evidence of fighting (i.e., wounds) when housed in groups. The levels of serotonin, dopamine, and norepinephrine were elevated in the brains of the pups, but not in adults. This suggests developmental neuroadaptation such that other enzymes in the brain (e.g., Maob) were breaking down the monoamine neurotransmitters in the absence of Maoa, or a downregulation of monoamine production. These results demonstrate that while a genetic difference can cause long-lasting behavioral effects, biological systems can compensate for dysfunctional system components.

Since those early reports, studies using genetic engineering (e.g., knockouts), pharmacology, and neurophysiology across species have provided strong evidence that genetic variation in neurotransmitter systems such as serotonin and dopamine, and in hormone signaling systems such as the HPA axis, play an important role in individual differences in aggressive behavior. Many candidate gene association studies have been done to test variants in these genes for association with violence and aggression in humans, although it appears that none of the associations were statistically significant in a large meta-analysis (Vassos, Collier, & Fazel, 2014). This is another stark reminder that *Homo sapiens* is not the ideal species for studying heredity–behavior relations, especially when considering complex social behaviors.

A meta-analysis of 17 GWAS identified 10 loci that were significantly associated with aggression, along with 817 variants that were "suggestive" (Odintsova et al., 2019). Modern bioinformatic approaches that combine data from a wide variety of sources to understand biological networks have recently been applied to understand the biology of aggression. Data from human aggression GWAS can be combined with data from mouse aggression studies using gene expression, and knockouts to identify common biological pathways. In one such study, several common pathways were identified that were enriched with genetic variants that contribute to individual differences in aggression such as G-protein coupled receptor signaling pathways, and axon guidance (Zhang-James et al., 2019). In addition, they identified the forty top-ranked and highly interconnected genes associated with aggression that played roles in (1) nervous system development and function, (2) neurological disease and psychological disorders, and (3) cellular function and maintenance. It is important to note that this analysis found strong support for the role of genetic variants in *MAOA* playing a role in aggressive behavior. It seems to be one of the candidate gene association findings that has stood the test of time.

Overall, it appears that aggression is like most of the behaviors of interest in behavior genetics. It is present across species and it varies within populations. At least some of the differences in aggression between individuals is due to genetic differences between them. Most of the genetic differences between individuals in aggression appear to be polygenic. And the biological pathways involved with genetic differences in aggression include neurotransmitter systems and aspects of neural development.

Check-up

- Give some examples of (a) reactive aggression, and (b) proactive aggression.
- What is Brunner syndrome and what can it tell us about the role of genetic variation in individual differences in aggression?
- How is aggressive behavior measured?

13.7 SUMMARY

- Social behavior involves interaction among individuals and can impact relations between genome, brain, and behavior across physiological, developmental, and evolutionary timescales.
- Parent–offspring interactions are early and important. Interaction between potential mates and between rivals for resources can also have important implications.

- Social interactions are dynamic interplays where sensory input affects internal states, which produce behavioral output that can impact the environment. Such reciprocal interactions involve many brain areas.
- Genetic conditions, such as Turner syndrome and Williams syndrome impact social behavior.
- Oxytocin is a widely studied molecule involved in social circuits. Genetic variants in the oxytocin receptor gene (*OXTR*) have been associated with individual differences in many social phenotypes, including autism spectrum disorder.
- Sexual selection drives sexual dimorphism in morphology and behavior. Individual differences in sexual orientation in humans are likely at least partially associated with genetic differences; however, the details are largely yet unknown.
- Aggressive behaviors are common in animal species. Non-human animal models of aggressive behavior are widely studied. Brunner syndrome is characterized by impulsive aggression and is associated with a rare variant of monoamine oxidase. Aggression is likely polygenic and highly dependent upon environment and genetic variants of small effect.

RECOMMENDED READING

- Balthazart, J. (2020). Sexual partner preference in animals and humans. *Neurosci Biobehav Rev, 115*, 34–47. doi:10.1016/j.neubiorev.2020.03.024
- Chen, P., & Hong, W. (2018). Neural circuit mechanisms of social behavior. *Neuron, 98*(1), 16–30. doi:10.1016/j.neuron.2018.02.026
- Iakoucheva, L. M., Muotri, A. R., & Sebat, J. (2019). Getting to the cores of autism. *Cell, 178*(6), 1287–1298. doi:10.1016/j.cell.2019.07.037
- Robinson, G. E., Fernald, R. D., & Clayton, D. F. (2008). Genes and social behavior. *Science, 322*(5903), 896–900. doi:10.1126/science.1159277

REFERENCES

Anholt, R. R., & Mackay, T. F. (2012). Genetics of aggression. *Annu Rev Genet, 46*, 145–164. doi:10.1146/annurev-genet-110711-155514

Antonucci, L. A., Taurisano, P., Coppola, G., & Cassibba, R. (2018). Attachment style: The neurobiological substrate, interaction with genetics and role in neurodevelopmental disorders risk pathways. *Neurosci Biobehav Rev, 95*, 515–527. doi:10.1016/j.neubiorev.2018.11.002

Bailey, J. M., Vasey, P. L., Diamond, L. M., Breedlove, S. M., Vilain, E., & Epprecht, M. (2016). Sexual orientation, controversy, and science. *Psychol Sci Public Interest, 17*(2), 45–101. doi:10.1177/1529100616637616

Balthazart, J. (2020). Sexual partner preference in animals and humans. *Neurosci Biobehav Rev, 115*, 34–47. doi:10.1016/j.neubiorev.2020.03.024

Bartz, J. A. (2016). Oxytocin and the pharmacological dissection of affiliation. *Curr Dir Psychol Sci, 25*(2), 104–110. doi:10.1177/0963721415626678

Bretherton, I. (1992). The origins of attachment theory: John Bowlby and Mary Ainsworth. *Dev Psychol, 28*(5), 759–775. doi:10.1037/0012-1649.28.5.759

Brunner, H. G., Nelen, M. R., van Zandvoort, P., Abeling, N. G., van Gennip, A. H., Wolters, E. C., . . . van Oost, B. A. (1993). X-linked borderline mental retardation with prominent behavioral disturbance:

Phenotype, genetic localization, and evidence for disturbed monoamine metabolism. *Am J Hum Genet*, *52*(6), 1032–1039.

Caldwell, H. K., Aulino, E. A., Freeman, A. R., Miller, T. V., & Witchey, S. K. (2017). Oxytocin and behavior: Lessons from knockout mice. *Dev Neurobiol*, *77*(2), 190–201. doi:10.1002/dneu.22431

Cases, O., Seif, I., Grimsby, J., Gaspar, P., Chen, K., Pournin, S., . . . De Maeyer, E. (1995). Aggressive behavior and altered amounts of brain serotonin and norepinephrine in mice lacking MAOA. *Science*, *268*(5218), 1763–1766. doi:10.1126/science.7792602

Chen, P., & Hong, W. (2018). Neural circuit mechanisms of social behavior. *Neuron*, *98*(1), 16–30. doi:10.1016/j.neuron.2018.02.026

Colvert, E., Tick, B., McEwen, F., Stewart, C., Curran, S. R., Woodhouse, E., . . . Bolton, P. (2015). Heritability of autism spectrum disorder in a UK population-based twin sample. *JAMA Psychiatry*, *72*(5), 415–423. doi:10.1001/jamapsychiatry.2014.3028

Cotter, J., Granger, K., Backx, R., Hobbs, M., Looi, C. Y., & Barnett, J. H. (2018). Social cognitive dysfunction as a clinical marker: A systematic review of meta-analyses across 30 clinical conditions. *Neurosci Biobehav Rev*, *84*, 92–99. doi:10.1016/j.neubiorev.2017.11.014

Crespi, B. J., & Procyshyn, T. L. (2017). Williams syndrome deletions and duplications: Genetic windows to understanding anxiety, sociality, autism, and schizophrenia. *Neurosci Biobehav Rev*, *79*, 14–26. doi:10.1016/j.neubiorev.2017.05.004

Dugatkin, L. A. (2018). The silver fox domestication experiment. *Evolution: Education and Outreach*, *11*(1), 16. doi:10.1186/s12052-018-0090-x

Feldman, R., Monakhov, M., Pratt, M., & Ebstein, R. P. (2016). Oxytocin pathway genes: Evolutionary ancient system impacting on human affiliation, sociality, and psychopathology. *Biol Psychiatry*, *79*(3), 174–184. doi:10.1016/j.biopsych.2015.08.008

Frith, C. D., & Frith, U. (2012). Mechanisms of social cognition. *Annu Rev Psychol*, *63*, 287–313. doi:10.1146/annurev-psych-120710-100449

Ganna, A., Verweij, K. J. H., Nivard, M. G., Maier, R., Wedow, R., Busch, A. S., . . . Zietsch, B. P. (2019). Large-scale GWAS reveals insights into the genetic architecture of same-sex sexual behavior. *Science*, *365*(6456). doi:10.1126/science.aat7693

Gelehrter, T. D., Collins, F. S., & Ginsburg, D. (1998). *Principles of Medical Genetics* (2nd ed.). Baltimore, MD: Williams & Wilkins.

Gong, P., Fan, H., Liu, J., Yang, X., Zhang, K., & Zhou, X. (2017). Revisiting the impact of OXTR rs53576 on empathy: A population-based study and a meta-analysis. *Psychoneuroendocrinology*, *80*, 131–136. doi:10.1016/j.psyneuen.2017.03.005

Gong, P., Wang, Q., Liu, J., Xi, S., Yang, X., Fang, P., . . . Zhang, M. (2020). The OXTR polymorphisms are not associated with attachment dimensions: A three-approach study. *Psychoneuroendocrinology*, *120*, 104780. doi:10.1016/j.psyneuen.2020.104780

Grove, J., Ripke, S., Als, T. D., Mattheisen, M., Walters, R. K., Won, H., . . . Børglum, A. D. (2019). Identification of common genetic risk variants for autism spectrum disorder. *Nat Genet*, *51*(3), 431–444. doi:10.1038/s41588-019-0344-8

Hutaff-Lee, C., Bennett, E., Howell, S., & Tartaglia, N. (2019). Clinical developmental, neuropsychological, and social-emotional features of Turner syndrome. *Am J Med Genet C Semin Med Genet*, *181*(1), 126–134. doi:10.1002/ajmg.c.31687

Iakoucheva, L. M., Muotri, A. R., & Sebat, J. (2019). Getting to the cores of autism. *Cell*, *178*(6), 1287–1298. doi:10.1016/j.cell.2019.07.037

Kopp, N. D., Nygaard, K. R., Liu, Y., McCullough, K. B., Maloney, S. E., Gabel, H. W., & Dougherty, J. D. (2020). Functions of Gtf2i and Gtf2ird1 in the developing brain: Transcription, DNA binding and long-term behavioral consequences. *Hum Mol Genet, 29*(9), 1498–1519. doi:10.1093/hmg/ddaa070

Kranz, T. M., Kopp, M., Waltes, R., Sachse, M., Duketis, E., Jarczok, T. A., . . . Chiocchetti, A. G. (2016). Meta-analysis and association of two common polymorphisms of the human oxytocin receptor gene in autism spectrum disorder. *Autism Res, 9*(10), 1036–1045. doi:10.1002/aur.1597

Kuroda, K. O., Tachikawa, K., Yoshida, S., Tsuneoka, Y., & Numan, M. (2011). Neuromolecular basis of parental behavior in laboratory mice and rats: With special emphasis on technical issues of using mouse genetics. *Prog Neuropsychopharmacol Biol Psychiatry, 35*(5), 1205–1231. doi:10.1016/j.pnpbp.2011.02.008

Li, J., Zhao, Y., Li, R., Broster, L. S., Zhou, C., & Yang, S. (2015). Association of oxytocin receptor gene (OXTR) rs53576 polymorphism with sociality: A meta-analysis. *PLoS One, 10*(6), e0131820. doi:10.1371/journal.pone.0131820

LoParo, D., & Waldman, I. D. (2015). The oxytocin receptor gene (OXTR) is associated with autism spectrum disorder: A meta-analysis. *Mol Psychiatry, 20*(5), 640–646. doi:10.1038/mp.2014.77

Lutz, P. E., & Turecki, G. (2014). DNA methylation and childhood maltreatment: From animal models to human studies. *Neuroscience, 264*, 142–156. doi:10.1016/j.neuroscience.2013.07.069

Mackay, T. F., Heinsohn, S. L., Lyman, R. F., Moehring, A. J., Morgan, T. J., & Rollmann, S. M. (2005). Genetics and genomics of Drosophila mating behavior. *Proc Natl Acad Sci USA, 102*(Suppl 1), 6622–6629. doi:10.1073/pnas.0501986102

Morel, A., Peyroux, E., Leleu, A., Favre, E., Franck, N., & Demily, C. (2018). Overview of social cognitive dysfunctions in rare developmental syndromes with psychiatric phenotype. *Front Pediatr, 6*, 102. doi:10.3389/fped.2018.00102

Morris, C. A., Mervis, C. B., Paciorkowski, A. P., Abdul-Rahman, O., Dugan, S. L., Rope, A. F., . . . Osborne, L. R. (2015). 7q11.23 Duplication syndrome: Physical characteristics and natural history. *Am J Med Genet A, 167a*(12), 2916–2935. doi:10.1002/ajmg.a.37340

Norman, R. E., Byambaa, M., De, R., Butchart, A., Scott, J., & Vos, T. (2012). The long-term health consequences of child physical abuse, emotional abuse, and neglect: A systematic review and meta-analysis. *PLoS Med, 9*(11), e1001349. doi:10.1371/journal.pmed.1001349

Nouvian, M., Reinhard, J., & Giurfa, M. (2016). The defensive response of the honeybee Apis mellifera. *J Exp Biol, 219*(Pt 22), 3505–3517. doi:10.1242/jeb.143016

Odintsova, V. V., Roetman, P. J., Ip, H. F., Pool, R., Van der Laan, C. M., Tona, K. D., . . . Boomsma, D. I. (2019). Genomics of human aggression: Current state of genome-wide studies and an automated systematic review tool. *Psychiatr Genet, 29*(5), 170–190. doi:10.1097/ypg.0000000000000239

Poore, H. E., & Waldman, I. D. (2020). The association of oxytocin receptor gene (OXTR) polymorphisms with antisocial behavior: A meta-analysis. *Behav Genet, 50*(3), 161–173. doi:10.1007/s10519-020-09996-6

Robinson, G. E., Fernald, R. D., & Clayton, D. F. (2008). Genes and social behavior. *Science, 322*(5903), 896–900. doi:10.1126/science.1159277

Ruzzo, E. K., Pérez-Cano, L., Jung, J. Y., Wang, L. K., Kashef-Haghighi, D., Hartl, C., . . . Wall, D. P. (2019). Inherited and de novo genetic risk for autism impacts shared networks. *Cell, 178*(4), 850–866.e826. doi:10.1016/j.cell.2019.07.015

Urbanus, E., van Rijn, S., & Swaab, H. (2020). A review of neurocognitive functioning of children with sex chromosome trisomies: Identifying targets for early intervention. *Clin Genet, 97*(1), 156–167. doi:10.1111/cge.13586

Vassos, E., Collier, D. A., & Fazel, S. (2014). Systematic meta-analyses and field synopsis of genetic association studies of violence and aggression. *Mol Psychiatry, 19*(4), 471–477. doi:10.1038/mp.2013.31

vonHoldt, B. M., Shuldiner, E., Koch, I. J., Kartzinel, R. Y., Hogan, A., Brubaker, L., . . . Udell, M. A. R. (2017). Structural variants in genes associated with human Williams-Beuren syndrome underlie stereotypical hypersociability in domestic dogs. *Sci Adv, 3*(7), e1700398. doi:10.1126/sciadv.1700398

World Health Organization (2020). Autism spectrum disorder. ICD-11 for Mortality and Morbidity Statistics. http://id.who.int/icd/entity/437815624

Yamamoto, D., & Koganezawa, M. (2013). Genes and circuits of courtship behaviour in Drosophila males. *Nat Rev Neurosci, 14*(10), 681–692. doi:10.1038/nrn3567

Zabegalov, K. N., Kolesnikova, T. O., Khatsko, S. L., Volgin, A. D., Yakovlev, O. A., Amstislavskaya, T. G., . . . Kalueff, A. V. (2019). Understanding zebrafish aggressive behavior. *Behav Processes, 158*, 200–210. doi:10.1016/j.beproc.2018.11.010

Zhang-James, Y., Fernàndez-Castillo, N., Hess, J. L., Malki, K., Glatt, S. J., Cormand, B., & Faraone, S. V. (2019). An integrated analysis of genes and functional pathways for aggression in human and rodent models. *Mol Psychiatry, 24*(11), 1655–1667. doi:10.1038/s41380-018-0068-7

14 Behavior Genetics in Real Life

If you have read the preceding chapters of this book, you know more about the field of behavior genetics than the average person on the street. But you may be wondering if the body of behavior genetic knowledge has any applications in real life. To be sure, most research in behavior genetics is basic research. In other words, the research is focused on better describing, predicting, and explaining heredity–behavior relations. It is not typically applied research where the focus is on solving practical problems, such as changing behavior.

In this chapter, we begin by considering one of the types of behavior genetic data that is becoming more and more available, namely direct-to-consumer genetic testing. Next, we examine whether knowing genetic information about a person with mental illness aids in their diagnosis or improves their treatment. We then explore how behavior genetic information is used in the justice system. Next, we examine human genetic engineering. Finally, we consider whether behavior genetics is of any use.

14.1 Direct-to-Consumer Genetic Testing

For a relatively small amount of money ($100–$200) you can learn something about your genome (Majumder, Guerrini, & McGuire, 2021). Several companies offer direct-to-consumer genetic testing without the involvement of a health-care provider. Sample collection kits can be purchased online or in stores. Collecting a sample typically involves spitting saliva into a tube, registering the sample online, and mailing the tube to the company (Figure 14.1). After a few weeks, the genotyping results and reports are usually available online for viewing and downloading. Depending on the company and the reports you select, you can learn something about specific health risks, general wellness, traits of interest, and your ancestry. More than 26 million people worldwide have used such direct-to-consumer genetic tests (Regalado, 2019). Direct-to-consumer genetic tests are even available for your pet dog.

14.1.1 Carrier Screening

When your saliva sample arrives at the laboratory, the DNA is extracted, and genotyping is completed. Typically, genotyping is done by using SNP arrays that genotype hundreds of thousands of variants spread across the genome. Many of the tested SNPs have been associated with diseases, health-related traits, other traits of interest, or are informative for genetic ancestry. The type of reports that you can receive vary by company but can include the results of tests for (a) carrier screening, (b) genetic health risk, (c) pharmacogenetics, (d) cancer predisposition, (e) low-risk general wellness, (f) traits of interest, and (g) ancestry. Some of these tests are regulated by the Food and Drug Administration (www.fda.gov/medical-devices/vitro-diagnostics/direct-consumer-tests). Reputable companies will base their reports on the available scientific data and will provide information that can help you to interpret it (see Box 14.1).

Figure 14.1. **Direct-to-consumer genetic testing kit.** 23andMe is one of the largest direct-to-consumer genetic testing companies. The testing kit includes a vial into which a person spits to provide a saliva sample for DNA testing. Source: ERIC BARADAT / Contributor / AFP / Getty Images.

Box 14.1 ClinVar

Direct-to-consumer genetic testing companies rely on research conducted by academic investigators or genetic testing laboratories to support assertions of association between genetic variants and traits. It is reasonable to be leery of claims made by companies, and it is important for claims of associations between genetic variants and traits to be based on the best available scientific evidence.

The National Center for Biotechnology Information (NCBI) maintains ClinVar, which is a freely accessible public database of associations between genetic variants and traits. It is intended to serve as the repository for expert interpretations and evidence of associations between genomic variation and aspects of human health. Reputable companies benefit by the availability of such expert support that is unaffiliated with the companies.

ClinVar was established in 2013 and contains over 600,000 submitted interpretations representing 430,000 unique variants (Landrum & Kattman, 2018). ClinVar rates the status of the evidence for each variant-trait association using a "star" system. Associations rated as "one star review status" are those that have been submitted with some supporting documentation (e.g., a scientific publication) and an assertion that the variant is either pathogenic, benign, or of uncertain significance. So, associations rated at one star have some evidence in their support but should not be considered fully established. Associations rated at "three star review status" refer to those that have more evidence in support and have been subjected to review by an "expert panel." Associations rated at "four star review status" are those that have met an even higher bar of evidence and are considered "practice guideline" assertions. In other words, these are well established by evidence and are considered to be of use in health-care.

ClinVar is not a complete compendium of associations of all genomic variants and traits. It focuses on traits that are medically relevant and on associations supported by evidence. On 23andMe, there are links to ClinVar for the cancer predisposition reports, but not for the reports on traits like baldness or ear wax.

Carrier screening tests can determine whether you carry a genetic variant associated with a recessive genetic disease. One of the largest companies that provides direct-to-consumer genetic testing, 23andMe, offers over forty carrier screening tests. Although recessive genetic disorders are relatively rare, knowing one's carrier status may be important in reproductive decision-making. Examples of recessive genetic disorders for which carrier status is typically determined are cystic fibrosis, sickle cell anemia, and Tay-Sachs disease.

14.1.2 Health Risk Reports

Genetic health risk tests can provide insight into one's risk for developing certain disorders. 23andMe provides reports on fourteen different health risks such as late onset Alzheimer disease, Parkinson disease, and age-related macular degeneration. For late onset Alzheimer disease risk, the number of *APOE* ε4 alleles that you carry is reported. As we discussed in Chapter 8, when compared to people who carry no *APOE* ε4 alleles, people who carry one ε4 allele are at three times higher risk, and people carrying two ε4 alleles are at eight to ten times higher risk for developing late onset Alzheimer disease (Raber, Huang, & Ashford, 2004). Customers of 23andMe can opt out of receiving certain reports, including the one for late onset Alzheimer disease, if they would rather not be burdened with this information.

It should be noted that the FDA barred 23andMe from providing health-risk information to its customers from 2013 to 2017 for tests that may have a medical impact. The FDA is the federal agency with the responsibility to determine whether medical devices, such as kits intended to diagnose diseases are safe and effective. Of course, it is safe to spit in a tube. But is it safe to receive information about whether you have an elevated risk for cancer? Is the test accurate? What if the test is wrong? How should risk information be interpreted? What does it mean if you carry a risk allele? How should you respond to such information? For a test to be approved by the FDA, it assesses (1) the accuracy and reliability of the test, (2) how well the test predicts a certain health state, and (3) what the company says about the test. In 2017, the FDA gave approval for 23andMe to provide health risk information for ten tests (Check Hayden, 2017). Since then, three more tests have been approved.

A full appreciation of these health risk reports requires the consumer to have a fairly sophisticated understanding of the role of genetic variants in health. Understanding the difference between strong (direct) and weak (indirect) causation helps make sense of such genetic reports. A simplistic interpretation that a particular allele causes a disorder will likely cause stress for those carrying it. The conditions tested in the health risk category are typically polygenic, and therefore whether a person develops the disorder will depend on their genotype at many risk alleles and on their environmental exposure. Knowing that you carry one of the risk alleles (out of many) may motivate lifestyle changes but should not be a cause for despair. Genetic counseling and information on interpreting genetic results are available for customers of reputable direct-to-consumer genetic testing companies.

14.1.3 Pharmacogenetics and Cancer Risk

Pharmacogenetic reports identify variants in genes that have been associated with individual differences in the movement of drugs through the body (i.e., pharmacokinetics) or the actions of drugs at their targets (i.e., pharmacodynamics). Many of the variants genotyped for pharmacogenetic relevance include enzymes in the liver that degrade medicines. Genetic variants in such enzymes can play an important role in the level of medicine available in the body. Genetic variants are known to impact catalytic rates of such metabolic enzymes, and for drugs that require a specific dosage, knowing whether a person carries a "slow metabolizer," or "fast metabolizer" variant could improve treatment decisions and outcomes.

Reports of cancer predisposition are regulated by the FDA and are provided by some direct-to-consumer genetic testing companies. Obviously, just as with Alzheimer disease, a report on a person's cancer predisposition can have dramatic implications. 23andMe provides a guide for interpreting the results of their tests for specific genetic variants in the *BRCA1* and *BRCA2* genes, which are associated with increased risk for developing certain kinds of cancer. The guide provides a discussion of how many genetic variants, in addition to these, play a role in the development of cancer, as does environmental exposure and lifestyle. The guide provides links to US government supported websites that explain genetics in general, and the role of genes in cancer risk. It also provides citations and links to the scientific articles on which their reports are based. That said, many customers may have difficulty understanding the scientific content, especially if they are carriers of the risk alleles and have just learned about their genetic risk for developing cancer. Recommendations to consult with health-care providers are typically included in such reports.

14.1.4 Wellness and Other Traits

Low-risk general wellness reports contain information about how a person's genome might contribute to the likelihood that they might experience an alcohol flushing response (i.e., alcohol metabolism variants), or that they might consume more or less caffeine than the average person, or that they might be overweight.

For example, my 23andMe report indicates that I carry 368 variants associated with higher weight and 364 variants associated with lower weight (see Figure 14.2). Average weight for a man my age and height is 201 pounds. 23andMe estimates that based on the genetic variants that I carry, that I am predisposed to weigh 6 percent above average (213 pounds). Thankfully, I am beating my genetic predisposition and weigh around 190 pounds (i.e., 5.5 percent less than average). To be honest, I exercise three to five times per week, carefully watch my portion sizes at meals, avoid fast food, and try to avoid snacking to maintain that weight. I think it would be very easy for me to achieve 213 pounds.

Other traits that might be reported include physical features, aspects of taste and smell, and miscellaneous traits. Physical features can include eye color, hair color, skin color, ear wax type, and whether you are likely to have a unibrow. Aspects of taste and smell can include whether you are likely to be able to smell an odor in urine after eating asparagus, whether you are likely to be able to taste bitter tastes (i.e., PTC), and whether you prefer sweet or salty foods. Some miscellaneous traits that can be reported on include whether you are likely to have a fear of heights or public speaking, and what time you are likely to wake up. For wakeup time 23andMe tested 450 SNPs and estimated that I would wake up at 7:30am on days off given my genotypes. I typically wake up at around 5:30am. Clearly, predictions based on population averages do not necessarily accurately predict the behavior of an individual.

14.1.5 Ancestry Reports

Ancestry reports are one of the most common reasons that people use direct-to-consumer genetic testing. To generate ancestry reports direct-to-consumer genetic testing companies access

How we determine your result

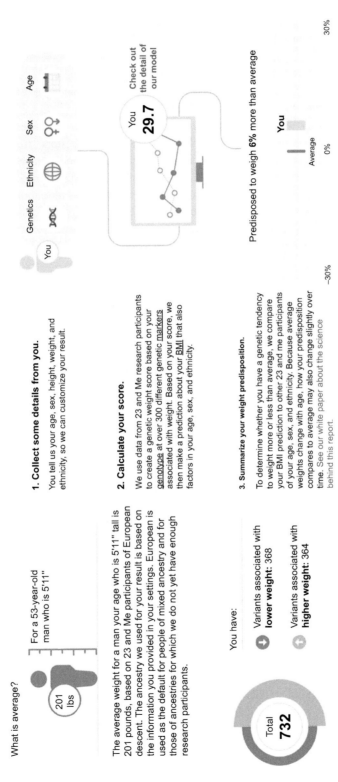

What is average?

For a 53-year-old man who is 5'11"

201 lbs

The average weight for a man your age who is 5'11" tall is 201 pounds, based on 23 and Me participants of European descent. The ancestry we used for your result is based on the information you provided in your settings. European is used as the default for people of mixed ancestry and for those of ancestries for which we do not yet have enough research participants.

Total 732

You have:

➡ Variants associated with **lower weight: 368**

⬅ Variants associated with **higher weight: 364**

Genetics Ethnicity Sex Age

You

You 29.7

Check out the detail of our model

1. Collect some details from you.

You tell us your age, sex, height, weight, and ethnicity, so we can customize your result.

2. Calculate your score.

We use data from 23 and Me research participants to create a genetic weight score based on your genotype at over 300 different genetic markers associated with weight. Based on your score, we then make a prediction about your BMI that also factors in your age, sex, and ethnicity.

3. Summarize your weight predisposition.

To determine whether you have a genetic tendency to weight more or less than average, we compare your BMI prediction to other 23 and me participants of your age, sex, and ethnicity. Because average weights change with age, how your predisposition compares to average may also change slightly over time. See our white paper about the science behind this report.

Predisposed to weigh **6%** more than average

You

Average

–30% 0% 30%

Figure 14.2. **23andMe genetic weight report.** The author's weight report from 23andMe. Out of 732 variants tested associated with weight, I carry 368 associated with lower weight and 364 associated with higher weight. Source: © 23andMe, Inc. 2021. All rights reserved and distributed pursuant to a limited license from 23andMe.

databases of genetic variants from ancestral reference populations that comprise thousands of people with known ancestry. People in these reference populations have lived in a location for generations and are considered to be genetically representative of people from that area. Regions of your genome that closely match with those found predominantly in a specific reference population are thought to indicate that you had an ancestor from that reference population. 23andMe currently uses data from 224 reference populations from around the world. Segments of your chromosomes are assigned to the closest matching reference population until your entire genome has been accounted for.

My ancestry composition, for example, is mostly northwestern European, which matches well with my known family history, with ancestors from Germany and the Netherlands. However, I also believe that I have ancestors from Denmark, based on information that I have obtained from my relatives, although the 23andMe report indicates Sweden as the most likely Scandinavian match. Of course, there was a lot of migration between northwestern European countries, and borders have changed over time. It is probably wise to consider both genealogy and DNA results when trying to understand your ancestry. It is entirely possible that I was mistaken in thinking that some of my ancestors came from Denmark. But it is also possible that the 23andMe ancestry report is incorrect for some unknown reason. It is even possible that both could be correct (or incorrect). Thankfully, nothing important is at stake on the absolute certainty of my ancestry.

14.1.6 Concerns About Direct-to-Consumer Genetic Testing

Are there privacy concerns with giving one's DNA to direct-to-consumer genetic testing companies? Some people do not appear to be concerned that their genetic information is produced (i.e., that they have been genotyped) and available. Others see potential danger in turning over their private genomes to corporations. Direct-to-consumer genetic testing companies typically have extensive privacy statements and empower the user to specify with whom data is shared. And in cases where third-party users are involved in research with the data, users must consent for their data to be included. In the US, federal law is in place to restrict the use of genetic information by health insurers and employers (The Genetic Information Nondiscrimination Act of 2008 [GINA]). However, GINA does not cover other types of insurance (e.g., life, disability, or long-term care) or employers with fewer employees (Majumder et al., 2021). To date, it appears that there have been no widespread breaches of privacy with respect to genetic data from participation in direct-to-consumer genetic testing, but the privacy of such personal information remains a potential issue of concern.

It is possible that individuals may uncover information by using these direct-to-consumer genetic tests that is surprising. Issues of non-paternity could certainly be discovered. It is also possible that people may discover that they have relatives that were previously unknown to them. A recent example is when a women discovered that she has 300–600 half-siblings because her father ran a fertility clinic and used his own sperm to inseminate many women (CBC, 2020).

Reading this textbook is good preparation for interpreting the reports provided by direct-to-consumer genetic test companies. It is more training than most physicians have received on the topic. For some, reading the reports may be life changing. It might motivate a meeting with a health-care provider, or a search for a previously unknown relative. For most of us, these reports are mostly entertainment and food for thought.

Check-up

- What is direct-to-consumer genetic testing?
- What type of reports are typically provided by direct-to-consumer genetic testing companies?
- What do you think consumers should know about heredity–behavior relations when they consider the reports provided by direct-to-consumer genetic testing companies?

14.2 Precision Medicine for Mental Illness

Have you ever given your health-care provider a DNA sample for genotyping? Most of us have not because the use of genetic information in making health-care decisions is not yet widely practiced. Many people are optimistic that the era of precision medicine is not too far off in the future. Precision medicine considers the genetic, environment, and lifestyle factors of the individual patient rather than defaulting to a standard treatment that was developed for the average patient. The hope is that such an approach will improve health outcomes by helping to identify the treatment that will be the most effective and have the fewest adverse side-effects.

14.2.1 The Precision Medicine Initiative

In 2015, President Obama announced that the US government was undertaking a Precision Medicine Initiative, which would support the development of diagnostic and treatment practices to account for a person's genetics, environment, and lifestyle (see Figure 14.3). A similar effort is also underway in the UK.

The "All of Us" research program at NIH is a result of the Precision Medicine Initiative (Denny et al., 2019). It plans to enroll a diverse sample of one million or more participants who will contribute their DNA and their health data over ten years. It began recruitment in 2018 from over 340 recruiting sites, and by mid-2019 they had enrolled over 175,000 core participants in the study. Clearly, the era of big health-related genomic science is in full swing. It is too early to know the impact of the All of Us study on precision medicine, but without efforts like this, precision medicine will remain a pipe dream.

One of the recurring themes in this book is that the effect of most genetic variants on behaviorally relevant traits is small and potentially influenced by environmental factors. In other words, polygenicity appears to be the rule rather than the exception. Can genomic information help

Figure 14.3. **Precision Medicine Initiative.**
President Obama announced the Precision Medicine Initiative in 2015. Source: ERIC MANDEL NGAN / Staff / AFP / Getty Images.

in predictions of complex traits like mental illness risk, or treatment response? A recent attempt to predict height from genetic information in the large UK Biobank study sample suggests that polygenic traits influenced by thousands of genetic variants can be predicted quite accurately (Lello et al., 2018). Although the genetic architecture of height is likely less complex than that of mental illnesses like depression, these results seem to be a step in the right direction.

14.2.2 Precision Psychiatry

Potentially, psychiatry has a lot to gain from precision medicine given our current lack of understanding of the fundamental mechanisms underlying individual differences in risk for developing mental illnesses and in treatment response (Rees & Owen, 2020). Precision psychiatry will benefit in the same four key areas as precision medicine.

The first is in the identification of individuals who are at high risk to develop one or more mental illnesses (see Figure 14.4). Risk indices could include some combination of polygenic risk scores, presence of rare variants, and information on other risk factors, such as early life trauma exposure, or family history. Individuals who are identified to be at high risk for developing mental illness could be monitored for symptoms and given the opportunity to access early intervention programs with the aim of preventing onset or reducing severity of the disorder.

It is well known that there is substantial variability in the pattern and course of symptoms experienced by patients who have been diagnosed with the same psychiatric disorder (i.e., symptom heterogeneity). Precision psychiatry aims to use patient information, such as genomic, biomarker, family history, environmental history, and endophenotype data to stratify patients into more homogeneous groups that might maximally benefit from more tailored treatment strategies.

Pharmacogenomic data should add precision to psychiatry by improving pharmacological treatment outcomes. Genetic variants that affect pharmacokinetic and/or pharmacodynamic profiles

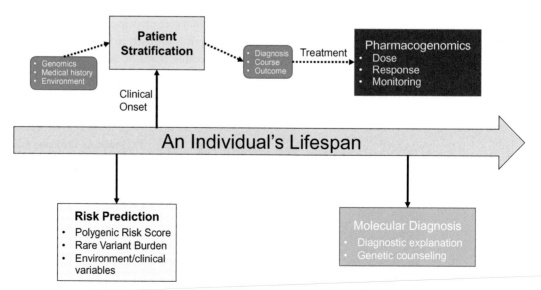

Figure 14.4. **Precision medicine in psychiatry.** Precision medicine in psychiatry will use information from genomics, medical history, and environment to aid in risk prediction, patient stratification, diagnosis, and treatment of mental illness. After Rees & Owen (2020).

of psychiatric medications may have a substantial impact on their tolerability, dosages, and effectiveness (see Box 14.2).

Box 14.2 5-HTTLPR Genotype and SSRI Treatment Response

The most prescribed medication to treat depression is a class of drugs known as selective serotonin reuptake inhibitors (SSRIs). SSRIs act on the serotonin transporter, which is an integral membrane protein of presynaptic neurons that removes the neurotransmitter from synapses where it can either be repackaged into vesicles for re-release or degraded by monoamine oxidase (see Figure 14.5). In Chapter 6 we discussed a common variant in the promoter region of the gene that codes for the serotonin transporter (*SLC6A4*) known as 5-HTTLPR.

The question of interest for precision psychiatry is whether patients with depression who carry different 5-HTTLPR genotypes respond differently to SSRI treatment. Because the serotonin transporter protein is the target of SSRIs, it is logical to test whether such genetic variation is associated with treatment response differences. Recall that 5-HTTLPR consists of an insertion/deletion polymorphism where the L allele contains sixteen repeat elements, and the S allele contains fourteen. This polymorphism is associated with differences in transcriptional efficiency, such that the L allele is associated with more serotonin transporters in synapses than the S allele.

A meta-analysis of forty-nine studies found that patients carrying one or two copies of the L allele (i.e., L/S and L/L) were more likely to respond to SSRI treatment for depression and experience remission than those homozygous for the S allele (Ren et al., 2020). However, this pattern of results was only seen in Caucasian patients, not in those of Asian descent. This is exactly the kind of information on which precision medicine will be based. If these results are replicated, it may be that in the future Caucasian homozygotes for the 5-HTTLPR S allele presenting for initial depression treatment may not be given SSRIs but will instead be treated with another medication.

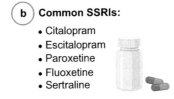

a Selective serotonin reuptake inhibitor (SSRI) mechanism:

b Common SSRIs:
- Citalopram
- Escitalopram
- Paroxetine
- Fluoxetine
- Sertraline

Figure 14.5. **Selective serotonin reuptake inhibitors.** (a) SSRIs block reuptake of serotonin from the synapse into the presynaptic neuron, which results in greater availability of serotonin in the synapse. (b) Five common SSRI medications. Source: Created with Biorender.com.

It is likely that response to antidepressant treatment is influenced by multiple genetic variants, as well as other factors such as race/ethnicity, treatment compliance, and comorbidities. Precision psychiatry seeks to identify such factors and account for them when developing treatment strategies. This work is still in its infancy.

Finally, genomic information may improve diagnoses for psychiatric disorders. In cases where symptom-based diagnoses are not clear cut, consideration of a patient's genomic profile and other relevant data may aid in differential diagnosis.

Precision psychiatry is a goal that has not yet been achieved. But it has the potential to substantially improve lives if realized.

Check-up

- Explain precision medicine and discuss its current status.
- Explain how precision medicine will impact psychiatry.

14.3 Behavior Genetics and the Justice System

Perhaps the most well-known application of genetics in the justice system is the use of so-called DNA fingerprinting to match DNA extracted from materials at crime scenes, such as blood, semen, or saliva to DNA samples of potential crime suspects. DNA fingerprinting uses genotypes from multiple hyper-variable loci to generate genetic profiles that are likely to be unique and can therefore be used to identify individuals. The loci are typically short tandem repeats that have multiple alleles. For example, D16S539 is the name of one such short tandem repeat that is one of the twenty core markers used by the US Federal Bureau of Investigation's CODIS (Combined DNA Index System) database. The D16S539 polymorphism has 21 alleles that have between 4 and 16 repeats of the four-base sequence GATA.

If the profile of a DNA sample from a crime scene matches that of a suspect at all twenty CODIS loci it is considered evidence that the suspect was the source of the DNA found at the scene. Because many hyper-variable loci are used in the profile, the probability that a random person has the exact same DNA profile is small, but not zero. If the DNA profile of the crime scene sample does not match that of the suspect, then they may be excluded from being a suspect. As of mid-2020 the National DNA Index (NDIS) contains over 14,287,909 offender DNA profiles and has assisted in more than 512,917 investigations (FBI, 2020). DNA profiles can also be used to determine paternity.

14.3.1 Genetic Genealogy

A more recent use of genetic information in the criminal justice system is called genetic genealogy (Greytak, Moore, & Armentrout, 2019). It takes advantage of the fact that millions of people have made use of direct-to-consumer genetic testing to help identify potential crime suspects, typically for cold cases. DNA samples from a crime scene are genotyped using a SNP array and uploaded to GEDmatch, a public database to which people who have direct-to-consumer genetic testing raw data can upload their genetic data file and find other users to whom they are related. Individuals who are related share stretches

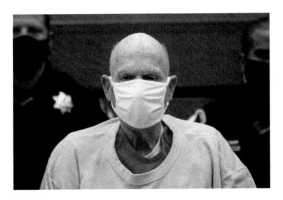

Figure 14.6. **Genetic genealogy**. Joseph James DeAngelo, Jr. was arrested with the aid of genetic genealogy. He subsequently pleaded guilty to thirteen counts of first-degree murder and admitted to many other crimes. He was sentenced to life in prison. Source: San Francisco Chronicle/Hearst Newspapers via Getty Images / Contributor / Hearst Newspapers / Getty Images.

of DNA that have survived recombination. The closer the relation, the more DNA is identical by descent (IBD). When individuals share many large segments of DNA (i.e., share identical SNP genotypes) the individuals are likely to be closely related. Genetic relationships can be estimated by assessing the total DNA shared in centimorgans (cM). First-degree relatives share, on average, 2,000–3,600 cM of DNA, second-degree relatives share 1,060 to 2,500 cM, and so on with diminishing sharing as one moves further away from the proband on the pedigree (Greytak et al., 2019).

When relatives of a suspect are identified in GEDmatch and their degree of relatedness estimated, genealogists construct potential pedigrees using standard genealogy tools. Then, based on additional information about the crime (e.g., dates, locations) potential suspects may be identified (Greytak et al., 2019). As of early 2021, approximately thirty cases have used genetic genealogy to identify a potential suspect. The first and most well known of these is the Golden State Killer (see Figure 14.6). Joseph James DeAngelo, Jr. was arrested in 2018 and sentenced to life in prison without the possibility of parole for crimes he admitted to committing in the 1970s and 1980s in central and southern California (Egel, 2018). He pleaded guilty to 13 counts of first-degree murder and admitted to committing more than 50 rapes and 120 burglaries while he was a police officer.

14.3.2 Forensic DNA Phenotyping

DNA fingerprinting and genetic genealogy are used to help match genotypes of potential suspects to genotypes of biological evidence at a crime scene. If no match is made, the DNA evidence typically ceases to be useful. However, there have been recent efforts to use research-based associations and computer models to generate probabilistic predictions about physical characteristics, biogeographic origins, and age of a suspect who left biological material at a crime scene. Such efforts are called forensic DNA phenotyping (Schneider, Prainsack, & Kayser, 2019). Kits are available commercially to genotype SNPs or other variants for creating the phenotype predictions. Predicted phenotypes can include facial features (Matheson, 2016), and at least one company, Parabon Nanolabs, offers a product called Snapshot™ DNA phenotyping that uses SNP array genotyping to make probabilistic predictions of physical features and ancestry (see, e.g., Parabon-Nanolabs, 2020). Will DNA as a "biological witness" play as big a role as eyewitnesses do in the justice system? It is too early to know if this approach will help to identify suspects and gain wide use and acceptance; however, it is clear that there is a potential for mistaken identifications, and for racial profiling by arresting people that "fit the description."

14.3.3 Genetic Information in the Courtroom

Genetic information has been used less widely in the courtroom than in the police station. The use of genetic and other neuroscience evidence, such as neuroimaging, in the courtroom is called neurolaw, and it is becoming more common. When it has been used, it has typically been presented as a mitigating factor to reduce the sentence of a person convicted of a crime (Sabatello & Appelbaum, 2017).

Judges have broad discretion in determining what evidence is admissible. It is possible to argue that a biological predisposition to a given criminal act (e.g., aggressive behavior leading to murder) lessens a person's responsibility for the act. Therefore, if the societal role of the courts is to punish those responsible for committing undesirable acts, a person who has diminished responsibility for the act should be punished less. Alternatively, if the societal role of the courts is to protect the rest of society from dangerous members, it would make sense to increase the sentences of those who are genetically predisposed to violent acts because they may be more likely than the non-predisposed to reoffend. Of course, these arguments only make sense when such a predisposition substantially reduces or eliminates a person's free will to act. However, as we have seen throughout this book, genetic variants do not directly cause behavior.

Behavior genetic evidence in court has typically been expert testimony regarding family history or heritability estimates of mental illness, such as substance-related and addictive disorders, and other mental illnesses (McSwiggan, Elger, & Appelbaum, 2017). Another type of behavior genetic evidence is based on candidate gene association studies, where particular genetic variants are considered to be associated with increased risk for undesirable behavior, such as violence or aggression. As you may recall, in Chapter 13 we discussed a Dutch kindred that was found to have a deletion in *MAOA* and a high rate of violent and criminal behavior, so-called Brunner syndrome (Brunner et al., 1993). Although the deletion causing Brunner syndrome has only been identified in one large family, there are many variants in the *MAOA* gene and one, in particular, has garnered substantial attention. A 30 bp variable number tandem repeat located upstream of the transcription initiation site is often called *MAOA* uVNTR (Sabol, Hu, & Hamer, 1998). The transcriptional efficiency and catalytic activity of the MAOA enzyme is associated with the number of repeats such that alleles with 2- and 3-repeats are considered low (L) activity, and those with 3.5-, 4-, 5-, and 6-repeats are considered high (H) activity (Huang et al., 2004).

Hundreds of candidate gene association studies have investigated the potential association of *MAOA* uVNTR alleles and behaviors that are associated with criminality, such as aggression and impulsivity. There is not space here to properly review the entire literature on *MAOA* uVNTR and behaviors of interest, but there seems to be some support for an association between the L allele and impulsive aggressive and antisocial behavior that appears to be specific to Caucasian males who have experienced severe childhood maltreatment (McSwiggan et al., 2017). However, all the caveats we have given to results of candidate gene association studies should also be considered.

Between 1995 and 2016 there were eleven criminal proceedings where *MAOA* uVNTR genotype was considered (McSwiggan et al., 2017). Nine of the cases were in the US, and two were in Italy. Out of those eleven cases, genotype evidence was introduced during the guilt determination phase in two cases. In one case, the genetic evidence was found to be inadmissible, but in the other case, it may have contributed to the suspect being convicted of a lesser offense. In the remaining cases, the genotype information was introduced either during the sentencing phase or on appeal. In three cases, sentences were reduced, in five cases there was no sentencing change, and in the remaining case the genetic evidence was not considered. The current use of molecular behavior genetic evidence in court suggests that judges and juries appear to be ambivalent about its value.

Check-up

- Describe DNA fingerprinting and its role in the justice system.
- Explain how genetic genealogy can identify crime suspects.
- What is forensic DNA phenotyping and what are its benefits and risks?
- How has genetic information been applied in determining guilt or innocence, or in sentencing?

14.4 Designer Babies

When people are asked whether they support human genetic engineering, a substantial majority approve of it for preventing or reducing risk for inherited disorders. Approximately two-thirds of those recently surveyed were in favor of using genetic engineering to prevent diseases such as Huntington's disease, cancer, or even conditions like blindness (see Figure 14.7). Only about 18 percent were opposed to editing human genes for those conditions.

When traits such as intelligence, athletic ability, or height were considered, however, only 10–12 percent were in favor of genetically engineering humans, with another 18–19 percent indicating that they were neither in favor nor opposed. Clearly, people are making a distinction between medical conditions and other traits. People want to have healthy babies and to reduce suffering and premature death caused by disease, and a substantial majority are willing to edit the human genome to that end. Approximately 30 percent of adults are in support of or have no firm opinion about using genetic engineering to make smarter and taller babies as well.

14.4.1 Sex Selection

It is already possible to screen for genetic diseases and to select the sex of a child using *in vitro* fertilization and pre-implantation genetic diagnoses offered by fertility clinics. Over 400 diseases

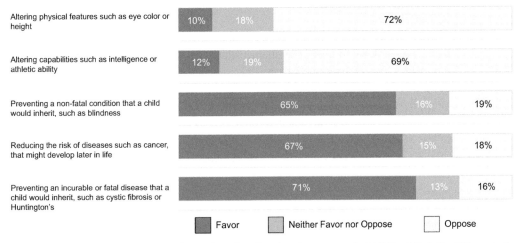

Figure 14.7. **Views on human genetic engineering.** Results of a recent poll of 1,067 adults in the US on whether they supported genetically engineering human embryos. Source: AP-NORC (2018).

caused by single genes can be detected by these methods. Sperm can be sorted by centrifugation because sperm carrying an X-chromosome are heavier than those carrying the smaller Y. Therefore, chances of having a female child are increased when sperm from the heavier layer of the centrifuged sample are used. Fertilized embryos develop for a few days and then a sample can be taken for karyotype analysis and microarray-based genetic analysis. Non-disease carrying embryos that carry the desired sex chromosomes can then be implanted in the mother for the remainder of the pregnancy. Currently, these practices are not regulated in the US, but are elsewhere in the world, such as the UK.

In the case of *in vitro* fertilization and pre-implantation genetic screening, the process involves increasing the probability of the desired sex and selecting embryos that do not carry known disease-causing genetic variants. Although these techniques were controversial when they were first developed, they no longer seem to be. We do, however, currently live in a post-human genome editing world, which raises many ethical questions about whether and how to make changes to the human genome.

14.4.2 Genetically Engineering Human Babies

Late in 2018, the first genetically engineered human babies were born in China (Regalado, 2018). A team of researchers at the Southern University of Science and Technology had recruited couples with an HIV infected father to participate in a trial where CRISPR/Cas9 would be used to disable the *CCR5* (C-C motif chemokine receptor 5; cytogenic location: 3p21.31) gene. The CCR5 protein is expressed in immune system cells (i.e., T cells and macrophages) and is the route through which HIV enters cells to infect them (see Figure 14.8). Homozygosity for mutated *CCR5* genes is thought to cause immunity to HIV.

A pair of twin girls was born, both carrying the CRISPR/Cas9 edited *CCR5* gene. A third child is also believed to have been born in 2019 carrying the edited gene. The dawn of the era of human genome editing caused significant dismay among scientists who called for a moratorium on human genome editing that can be inherited (Lander et al., 2019; NAS, 2020). Eventually, the lead scientist He Jiankui was sentenced to three years in prison for "illegal medical practice" and fined 3 million yuan (US$430,000). In addition, He and two of his colleagues were banned from conducting research in reproduction technology and from applying for government research funding (Cyranoski, 2020).

Gene edits that are made in gametes or any cells that give rise to gametes are capable of being passed down to later generations. When CRISPR/Cas9 is used to edit genes at early embryonic stages, the cell lines that later produce testes and ovaries will contain the edits. Therefore, those genetic changes can be called germline and are said to be heritable. Such changes alter the human gene pool and are of great concern to ethicists (NAS, 2020).

Gene edits that are made to somatic cells (i.e., body cells that do not produce gametes) are of less of an ethical concern because the edits cannot be passed down to future generations. Most of the cells in a human body are somatic cells. Genetic engineering of somatic cells for the treatment of cancer immunotherapy, viral infections, and inherited hematologic, metabolic, and eye disorders is already underway (Ernst et al., 2020).

Whereas diseases caused by mutations in single genes, such as sickle cell anemia, are good targets for somatic cell genetic engineering, the polygenic nature of mental illness and psychological traits probably makes them unsuitable targets for genetic engineering. The hundreds or thousands of genes involved, the influence of environmental factors, as well as potential interactions among them may make the outcomes of editing too unpredictable. The potential for unintended consequences of

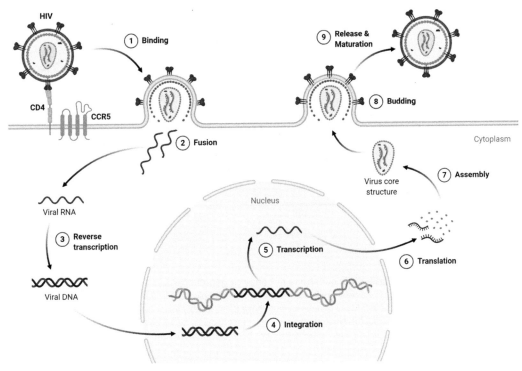

Figure 14.8. **CCR5 receptor and the HIV replication cycle.** HIV enters immune system cells by binding to the CCR5/CD4 complex. Once inside the cell it uses reverse transcription to integrate its genetic material into the cell's DNA. The cell then begins to produce HIV. It is thought that by editing the *CCR5* gene HIV immunity might be attained. Source: Created with Biorender.com.

widespread human genome editing for polygenic traits should give us pause. Experimenting with human lives should never be allowed, especially when those affected have no chance of providing informed consent.

Check-up

- Discuss the public's view on human genetic engineering.
- How was CRISPR/Cas9 used to engineer humans recently.
- Compare and contrast somatic and germline genetic engineering.

14.5 What Use Is Behavior Genetics?

Behavior genetic research has shown conclusively that (a) behavior traits tend to run in families, (b) individuals who share more genes by descent tend to resemble each other behaviorally, (c) atypical chromosome complements or arrangements can affect behavior, (d) DNA variants are statistically associated with behavioral differences in populations, (e) selective breeding in non-human animal models impacts behavior distribution in subsequent generations, and (f) genetic engineering in non-human animal models produces behavior change. So overall, there is unequivocal support for the position that genetic variation is associated with individual differences in behavior. The first question of behavior genetics that we mentioned in Chapter 1 has been convincingly answered in

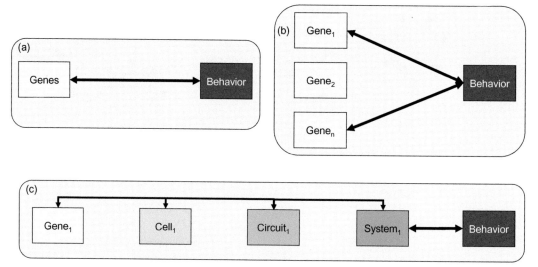

Figure 14.9. **Three main questions in behavior genetic research revisited.** (a) Is genetic similarity statistically associated with behavioral similarity? The answer is unequivocally "yes." (b) Which genetic variants are associated with behavioral similarity? Many genetic variants have been reliably associated with individual differences in behavior, but much work remains. (c) What are the molecular mechanisms by which genetic similarity produces behavioral similarity? Some pathways from genes to behavior have been characterized, but most have not.

the affirmative (see Figure 14.9(a)). Our friendly pet dogs are a wonderful reminder of the influence of genetic variation on individual differences in behavior because dog breeds are the result of selective breeding for behavior.

Many genetic variants have been shown to be associated with individual differences in behavior (see Figure 14.9(b)). For over two decades researchers in behavior genetics have been using a variety of techniques in both humans and in non-human animal models to identify genetic variants that play some role in behavioral variation. Such work has made it clear that while there are rare instances of single genetic variants having large effects on behavior, most of the genetic effects on behavior are relatively small. Little is known about the potential impact of epistatic (i.e., gene × gene) and gene × environment interactions on individual differences in behavior. Therefore, even if we were able to identify all of the genetic variants that contribute to individual differences in behavior, we may not be able to predict behavior with certainty because of potential interactions and developmental uncertainties inherent in the development of individuals (Turkheimer, 2015).

Behavior genetics is not a field unto itself. It stands firmly within psychology and biology. Genes represent one level of analysis in pathways that cross many. Identifying the biological pathways that contribute to individual differences in behavior has been and continues to be the purview of areas known as biological psychology, physiological psychology, and neuroscience. Behavior genetics adds its perspective, techniques, and data to that effort and there is no end in sight to this important and exciting work (see Figure 14.9(c)).

14.5.1 Strong versus Weak Genetic Explanation

It is important to distinguish between weak and strong genetic explanation when considering the potential for behavior genetic research (Turkheimer, 2016). Weak genetic explanation refers to the simple observation that genetic differences between people are statistically associated with

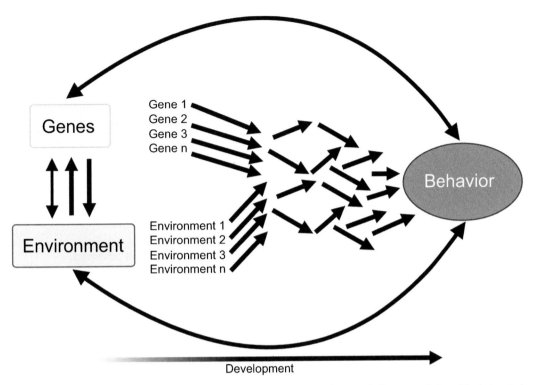

Figure 14.10. **Weak and strong genetic explanations.** Double-headed arrows indicate correlations. Single-headed arrows represent causal effects. Identifying correlations between genetic variants and behavior, or environmental factors and behavior is rather easy to do. Both represent weak causation because they do not identify causal mechanisms. Strong explanations require the identification of mechanisms. Pathways from genes and environment to behavior across development are likely complex and interactive, defying simple characterization. After Turkheimer (2000).

individual differences in behavior (see Figure 14.10). In our terminology, the first and second questions in behavior genetic research contribute to weak genetic explanation. They document correlations between genetic differences and individual differences in behavior. Strong genetic explanation, however, requires the identification and characterization of a specific genetic mechanism that accounts for the behavioral differences. Such an explanation necessarily involves biological components other than genes and can be considered causal. Our third question of behavior genetic research aims to deliver strong genetic explanation.

Will collecting more data and having better predictive models enable us to predict whether a person will develop a mental illness or have an outgoing personality? And by extension, if we can predict it, can we then genetically engineer a person to be free of mental illness or have a desired personality? It may be that the pathways from genes to behavior contain complexities that defy reliable prediction for most behaviors of interest.

We already have some ability to predict behavioral outcomes with varying levels of certainty. For example, if you carry two copies of the *APOE* ε4 allele you are at increased risk for developing Alzheimer disease after age 65 compared to the general population risk. If you are born into a family in which many members have developed substance use disorders, you are at higher risk than someone without a family history for developing one as well.

We soon may be able to predict a person's risk for developing mental illness with a polygenic risk score. These predictions will likely be probabilities, not certainties. Weather forecasts are much more accurate than they were in decades past. However, even with all the data available for use in computer modeling, we still sometimes carry an umbrella on days when it does not rain.

When such uncertainty is coupled with the inability to do controlled experiments in human beings, the prospect of genetically engineering human behaviors seems too risky. The potential for unintended consequences in living, breathing, reproducing human beings is too great. It seems likely, however, that we will eventually be able to use genetic information for a precision medicine approach to mental illness diagnosis and treatment, which will be an amazing achievement for medicine and for behavior genetics.

Check-up

- How have the three main questions of behavior genetics been answered?
- Compare and contrast weak and strong genetic explanation.
- What do you think is the use of behavior genetics?

14.6 SUMMARY

- Direct-to-consumer genetic testing is common and becoming more so. Customers are typically provided reports on wellness, health risks, certain traits, and ancestry. Such reports should primarily be considered entertainment at this time. Some risks to privacy and misinterpretation exist.
- Precision medicine seeks to use genomic information along with other information to improve medical care. The goal of precision psychiatry is to use the information to better predict who is at risk, to better classify patients, to improve diagnoses, and to develop more targeted treatments for mental illness.
- Genetic information helps to match suspects to biological samples left at a crime scene and to identify new suspects. Genetic genealogy seeks to use public genealogy databases to identify new suspects in cold cases. Forensic DNA phenotyping seeks to use genetic information from crime scenes to predict physical features of a suspect. Genetic information in court cases has sometimes been used to mitigate sentences and less frequently to help determine charges.
- The public is largely in favor of genetic engineering to prevent disease or inherited adverse health conditions. A minority are in favor of genetic engineering to improve traits such as cognitive ability. Sex selection is being used in assisted reproduction. CRISPR/Cas9 has been used to genetically engineer humans to have reduced risk of HIV infection. Most scientists have called for a moratorium on human germline genetic engineering.
- Genetic variation is associated with individual differences in behavior. Some genetic variants have been associated with individual differences in behavior. Few pathways from genes to behavior have been fully characterized. The lack of strong genetic explanations may limit our understanding of complex pathways from genes to behavior.

RECOMMENDED READING

- Doudna, J. A. & Sternberg, S. H. (2017). *A Crack in Creation: Gene Editing and the Unthinkable Power to Control Evolution*. Boston: Houghton Mifflin Harcourt.
- Majumder, M. A., Guerrini, C. J., & McGuire, A. L. (2021). Direct-to-consumer genetic testing: Value and risk. *Annu Rev Med*, *72*, 151–166. doi:10.1146/annurev-med-070119-114727
- Parens, E., Chapman, A. R., & Press, N. (Eds.) (2006). *Wrestling with Behavioral Genetics: Science, Ethics, and Public Conversation*. Baltimore, MD: Johns Hopkins University Press.

REFERENCES

AP-NORC (2018). *Human Genetic Engineering*. Retrieved from: https://apnorc.org/projects/human-genetic-engineering/

Brunner, H. G., Nelen, M. R., van Zandvoort, P., Abeling, N. G., van Gennip, A. H., Wolters, E. C., . . . van Oost, B. A. (1993). X-linked borderline mental retardation with prominent behavioral disturbance: Phenotype, genetic localization, and evidence for disturbed monoamine metabolism. *Am J Hum Genet*, *52*(6), 1032–1039.

CBC (2020). How a Toronto woman discovered she has up to 600 half-siblings. Retrieved from: www.cbc.ca/radio/docproject/how-a-toronto-woman-discovered-she-has-up-to-600-half-siblings-1.5727049

Check Hayden, E. (2017). The rise and fall and rise again of 23andMe. *Nature*, *550*(7675), 174–177. doi:10.1038/550174a

Cyranoski, D. (2020). What CRISPR-baby prison sentences mean for research. *Nature*, *577*(7789), 154–155. doi:10.1038/d41586-020-00001-y

Denny, J. C., Rutter, J. L., Goldstein, D. B., Philippakis, A., Smoller, J. W., Jenkins, G., & Dishman, E. (2019). The "All of Us" research program. *N Engl J Med*, *381*(7), 668–676. doi:10.1056/NEJMsr1809937

Egel, B. (2018). Here's the string of crimes tied to the East Area Rapist in years of California terror. Retrieved from: www.sacbee.com/news/local/crime/article209788654.html

Ernst, M. P. T., Broeders, M., Herrero-Hernandez, P., Oussoren, E., van der Ploeg, A. T., & Pijnappel, W. (2020). Ready for repair? Gene editing enters the clinic for the treatment of human disease. *Mol Ther Methods Clin Dev*, *18*, 532–557. doi:10.1016/j.omtm.2020.06.022

FBI (2020). CODIS – NDIS Statistics. Retrieved from: www.fbi.gov/services/laboratory/biometric-analysis/codis/ndis-statistics

Greytak, E. M., Moore, C., & Armentrout, S. L. (2019). Genetic genealogy for cold case and active investigations. *Forensic Sci Int*, *299*, 103–113. doi:10.1016/j.forsciint.2019.03.039

Huang, Y. Y., Cate, S. P., Battistuzzi, C., Oquendo, M. A., Brent, D., & Mann, J. J. (2004). An association between a functional polymorphism in the monoamine oxidase A gene promoter, impulsive traits and early abuse experiences. *Neuropsychopharmacology*, *29*(8), 1498–1505. doi:10.1038/sj.npp.1300455

Lander, E. S., Baylis, F., Zhang, F., Charpentier, E., Berg, P., Bourgain, C., . . . Winnacker, E. L. (2019). Adopt a moratorium on heritable genome editing. *Nature*, *567*(7747), 165–168. doi:10.1038/d41586-019-00726-5

Landrum, M. J., & Kattman, B. L. (2018). ClinVar at five years: Delivering on the promise. *Hum Mutat*, *39*(11), 1623–1630. doi:10.1002/humu.23641

Lello, L., Avery, S. G., Tellier, L., Vazquez, A. I., de Los Campos, G., & Hsu, S. D. H. (2018). Accurate genomic prediction of human height. *Genetics*, *210*(2), 477–497. doi:10.1534/genetics.118.301267

Majumder, M. A., Guerrini, C. J., & McGuire, A. L. (2021). Direct-to-consumer genetic testing: Value and risk. *Annu Rev Med*, *72*, 151–166. doi:10.1146/annurev-med-070119-114727

Matheson, S. (2016). DNA phenotyping: Snapshot of a criminal. *Cell*, *166*(5), 1061–1064. doi:10.1016/j.cell.2016.08.016

McSwiggan, S., Elger, B., & Appelbaum, P. S. (2017). The forensic use of behavioral genetics in criminal proceedings: Case of the MAOA-L genotype. *Int J Law Psychiatry, 50,* 17–23. doi:10.1016/j.ijlp.2016.09.005

NAS (2020). *Exploring the Current Landscape of Consumer Genomics: Proceedings of a Workshop.* Washington, DC: The National Academies Press. Retrieved from: https://doi.org/10.17226/25713

Parabon-Nanolabs (2020). Murder of Rhonda "Chantay" Blankinship Brown County Sheriff's Office, Brown County, TX. Retrieved from: https://snapshot.parabon-nanolabs.com/snapshot-case-summary–lake-brownwood-tx–chantay-blankinship-murder.html

Raber, J., Huang, Y., & Ashford, J. W. (2004). ApoE genotype accounts for the vast majority of AD risk and AD pathology. *Neurobiol Aging, 25*(5), 641–650. doi:10.1016/j.neurobiolaging.2003.12.023

Rees, E., & Owen, M. J. (2020). Translating insights from neuropsychiatric genetics and genomics for precision psychiatry. *Genome Med, 12*(1), 43. doi:10.1186/s13073-020-00734-5

Regalado, A. (2018). EXCLUSIVE: Chinese scientists are creating CRISPR babies. *MIT Technology Review.* Retrieved from: www.technologyreview.com/2018/11/25/138962/exclusive-chinese-scientists-are-creating-crispr-babies/

Regalado, A. (2019). More than 26 million people have taken an at home ancestry test. *MIT Technology Review.* Retrieved from: https://www.technologyreview.com/2019/02/11/103446/more-than-26-million-people-have-taken-an-at-home-ancestry-test/

Ren, F., Ma, Y., Zhu, X., Guo, R., Wang, J., & He, L. (2020). Pharmacogenetic association of bi- and triallelic polymorphisms of SLC6A4 with antidepressant response in major depressive disorder. *J Affect Disord, 273,* 254–264. doi:10.1016/j.jad.2020.04.058

Sabatello, M., & Appelbaum, P. S. (2017). Behavioral genetics in criminal and civil courts. *Harv Rev Psychiatry, 25*(6), 289–301. doi:10.1097/hrp.0000000000000141

Sabol, S. Z., Hu, S., & Hamer, D. (1998). A functional polymorphism in the monoamine oxidase A gene promoter. *Hum Genet, 103*(3), 273–279. doi:10.1007/s004390050816

Schneider, P. M., Prainsack, B., & Kayser, M. (2019). The use of forensic DNA phenotyping in predicting appearance and biogeographic ancestry. *Dtsch Arztebl Int, 51–52,* 873–880. doi:10.3238/arztebl.2019.0873

Turkheimer, E. (2000). Three laws of behavior genetics and what they mean. *Curr Dir Psychol Sci, 9*(5), 160–164. doi:10.1111/1467-8721.00084

Turkheimer, E. (2015). Genetic prediction. *Hastings Cent Rep, 45*(5 Suppl), S32–S38. doi:10.1002/hast.496

Turkheimer, E. (2016). Weak genetic explanation 20 years later: Reply to Plomin et al. (2016). *Perspect Psychol Sci, 11*(1), 24–28. doi:10.1177/1745691615617442

15 Eugenics

Behavior genetics addresses questions of fundamental importance to humanity. We seek to understand what makes us unique individuals, but also what we share with our families and with other species. We seek to explain why we tend to act in certain ways while others tend to act differently. We also strive to contribute to the development of treatments for behavioral problems. We ask these and many other questions with a limited set of tools in the human behavior genetic toolbox. Ethical and technological constraints on human behavior genetic research combined with the inherent complexity of pathways from genes to behavior mean that a firm grasp of causality may forever remain out of reach. Even in cases where causality can be known, moral and ethical constraints limit potential applications of human behavior genetic findings. Any such applications to human beings are fraught with concerns about human rights.

It is reasonable to want healthy babies and it makes sense to use science to help us improve our chances at good outcomes. But who decides which traits are desirable and which are not? How are a person's values reflected in such decisions? If you happen to carry a trait that is deemed undesirable, is your life worth living? Behavior genetics can seem like an exciting academic pursuit, but it has potential consequences that cannot be ignored. The human rights abuses that have been perpetrated on a foundation of behavior genetic research are sobering and serve as a cautionary tale that must be heeded. It is fair to say that behavior genetics has only been around as a field since about 1960, therefore modern behavior genetics cannot be blamed for eugenic abuses. On the other hand, eugenic policies and practices were based on early research that purported to show the inheritance of behavioral traits like feeblemindedness. The subject matter of behavior genetics resides within the eugenic framework.

This chapter examines the role of behavior genetics in eugenics. It first describes the intellectual underpinnings of eugenics. Next it discusses the implementation of eugenic policies in the US and Nazi Germany. Then it examines the role of race in behavior genetics. Finally, the chapter concludes with a discussion of current and future eugenic trends.

15.1 Social Darwinism

Any discussion of eugenics must begin with the recognition that racism lies at its heart. Racism consists of beliefs, actions, social norms, and laws that assert the superiority of one group over another. The definitions of the relevant groups in question (i.e., races) are not fixed, but historically have relied on physical attributes, such as skin color, or on country of origin. It was long believed that races were biologically different, but the preponderance of evidence supports the notion that race is a dynamic social construction that depends on characteristics of the target, characteristics of the perceiver, and the social/societal context (Richeson & Sommers, 2016). Perception of someone as being from a different race can lead to stereotyping, prejudice, and discrimination.

15.1.1   The Beginning of Scientific Racism

There is abundant evidence that Europeans in the eighteenth and nineteenth centuries considered people who had dark skin to be savages. White skin was considered, by those same Europeans, to be a trait that defined racial superiority. Not surprisingly, people tended to consider their own traits to be superior to those of others. Racism on its own led to many atrocities, but when it was coupled with science it led to eugenics. The apparent authority derived by support from leading thinkers of the day provided a framework and a justification to implement laws that limited support to the poor, reduced immigration from certain countries, and eventually led to involuntary sterilizations, and to the murder of millions of people. Scientific racism got its start in eighteenth-century England.

Three historical developments in England provided the context in which scientific racism developed (Chase, 1976). The first was the agricultural revolution in which the food production capacity of farmers increased dramatically. Beginning in the early 1700s new crops were introduced along with new methods such as crop rotation, and animal husbandry as exemplified by Bakewell's sheep breeding practices mentioned in Chapter 2. The second development was the industrial revolution, which included the transition from producing goods by hand to producing them by machine, the increased use of steam- and water-power, and the rise of factories. The third was the passage of the Enclosure Acts, which enabled large landowners to expel the small non-landowning farmers from their land. Such expulsions were made economically feasible by the advances of both the agricultural and industrial revolutions, which made large-scale farming possible with fewer workers. The wider availability of food and affordable products such as soap reduced death rates and led to net population increases, especially in poor families.

As early as medieval times (1349) there were laws in England that provided some type of "relief" to the poor. Such relief often took the form of food or clothing or housing (i.e., almshouses) and was subsidized by taxes. Workhouses were also established that housed and fed the poor in exchange for their manual labor. Not everyone supported such government intervention in what they considered to be the natural order of things.

15.1.2   The Malthusian Argument

Thomas Malthus (1798) (Figure 15.1) argued that it was a natural law that population growth rates are exponential and, if left unchecked, will eventually outpace the linear rate of food production. Malthus' claims about the dire course of humanity appeared to largely ignore or minimize the successes of the ongoing agricultural revolution and appear to have been motivated by his opposition to relief to the poor (Chase, 1976). He argued that providing relief to the poor blocked the ultimate natural check on population growth (i.e., the "want of food"), and that the poor had no right to the relief.

Charles Darwin noted in his autobiography (Darwin, 1950) that he read Malthus' book "for amusement" and was struck by the idea that when a population was undergoing a struggle for

Figure 15.1. **Thomas Malthus.** Malthus argued that the reproduction rate of human populations is exponential and that it will necessarily exceed the capacity to produce food. His book influenced many, including Charles Darwin. Source: Bettmann / Contributor / Bettmann / Getty Images.

existence brought on by a growing population that was outstripping its resources that "favourable variations would tend to be preserved, and unfavourable ones destroyed." Further, that this could lead to the formation of new species. Clearly, Malthus' view had an important impact on Darwin's development of his theory of evolution by natural selection. When Darwin finally tackled the thorny issue of evolution in human populations in *The Descent of Man and Selection in Relation to Sex* (Darwin, 1924) he thought that natural selection was no longer fully operating in humans because of charity and relief efforts for the poor. He noted, however, that the motivation to help others was itself a product of natural selection and that suppressing it by allowing the less fortunate to suffer and die would harm human nature (Paul, 2003). It seems that Darwin was sympathetic to the foundational ideas of eugenics, that natural selection pressures are reduced in societies that help the poor, and that the result of such relief may be that people who are considered "less gifted" may increase in population at the expense of those who are "more gifted." Moreover, he considered the problem to be a great one that could potentially lead to the downfall of nations. However, he did not propose interfering in human reproduction.

15.1.3 Survival of the Fittest

Others were also taking up the position that providing relief to the poor relaxed the laws of nature and was bound to lead to degeneracy. Herbert Spencer (Figure 15.2) introduced the term "survival of the fittest" (Spencer, 1898). Spencer saw Darwin's theory of evolution by natural selection to be a universal natural law, applying equally to biology, politics, and economics. He also considered evolution to be progressive, so that lower forms would necessarily lead to more highly evolved forms if given the opportunity. His argument was that providing social supports for the poor impeded the progression of evolution because with relief the unfit would survive and multiply, and without it they would not. He argued that it was only when these artificial supports are removed that natural selection could act to cull the unfit, which would lead to progress toward higher levels. Allowing the unfit to survive and multiply would diminish the overall fitness of the population and lead to its stagnation or degeneration. Such views came to be called Social Darwinism.

Check-up

- What were Malthus' views on population growth and how did they influence Darwin?
- What is Social Darwinism?

Figure 15.2. **Herbert Spencer.** Spencer coined the term "survival of the fittest" and argued that helping the poor survive was impeding the progress of evolution. His views came to be known as "Social Darwinism." Source: Rischgitz / Stringer / Hulton Archive / Getty Images.

15.2 Galton's Theory and Its Reception

Looking back, it seems that the 1860s must have been a heady time for those interested in heredity. Charles Darwin had just published *On the Origin of Species by Means of Natural Selection, or the Preservation of Favored Races in the Struggle for Life* (Darwin, 1936). His theory of evolution by natural selection provided a framework for thinking about continuity between species and changed biology forever, although his model of heredity (i.e., pangenesis) was incorrect. Seven years later, Gregor Mendel published *Versuche über Pflanzenhybriden* [Experiments on Plant Hybrids] (1866), which proposed laws of inheritance that we now know to be correct. They were simple and proved to be irresistible to those considering the inheritance of traits in human populations. Of course, as stated earlier, Mendel's work was largely ignored until its "rediscovery" in 1900.

15.2.1 Galton's Long-Term Interest in Eugenics

Francis Galton published *Hereditary Genius: An Inquiry into Its Laws and Consequences* (Galton, 2012) in 1869. Galton was well aware of and made explicit reference to the works of his half-cousin Charles Darwin. In fact, he used both the theory of evolution by natural selection and pangenesis to frame his thinking with respect to human populations.

In *Hereditary Genius* Galton's goal was to show that success in life was determined by a person's "natural abilities," which are inherited. In it he created pedigrees of influential families in England based on information about graduates of Oxford and Cambridge universities in published biographical dictionaries and other such sources. He noted that natural abilities tended to run in these leading families. Galton also proposed that because human populations are subject to the same laws that govern evolution in other species, several generations of selective breeding for desirable traits would be successful and would ultimately produce dramatic improvements to the human condition. He included tables of statistics and mathematical formulae, which gave the appearance of a rigorous science.

Encouraging the marriage of those with more desirable traits for the apparent betterment of society was one of Galton's primary and ongoing scientific interests. Fourteen years later Galton coined the term "eugenics" in his book *Inquiries into Human Faculty and Its Development* (1883):

> That is, with questions hearing on what is termed in Greek, eugenes, namely, good in stock, hereditarily endowed with noble qualities. This, and the allied words, eugeneia, etc., are equally applicable to men, brutes, and plants. We greatly want a brief word to express the science of improving stock, which is by no means confined to questions of judicious mating, but which, especially in the case of man, takes cognisance of all influences that tend in however remote a degree to give to the more suitable races or strains of blood a better chance of prevailing speedily over the less suitable than they otherwise would have had. The word eugenics would sufficiently express the idea; it is at least a neater word and a more generalised one than viriculture, which I once ventured to use.

Galton clearly seized on the notion that humans are subject to the same laws of heredity as non-human animals and plants. He reiterated his argument that selective breeding, which is well known to be effective for increasing or decreasing expression of target traits in livestock and crops, should be used in human populations to increase the frequency of traits found in a "higher race" over those found in a "low" one. He is mostly remembered for advocating what would later be called "positive" eugenics where people with desirable traits were encouraged to marry and reproduce.

However, he did not shy away from advocating the restriction of reproduction for those who did not carry traits deemed desirable. As he wrote in *Inquiries into Human Faculty*:

> Whenever a low race is preserved under conditions of life that exact a high level of efficiency, it must be subjected to rigorous selection. The few best specimens of that race can alone be allowed to become parents, and not many of their descendants can be allowed to live. On the other hand, if a higher race be substituted for the low one, all this terrible misery disappears. The most merciful form of what I ventured to call "eugenics" would consist in watching for the indications of superior strains or races, and in so favouring them that their progeny shall outnumber and gradually replace that of the old one.

The topic of eugenics seems to have always been on Galton's mind. Thirty-five years after publishing *Hereditary Genius* Galton had honed his thinking about the aims and scope of eugenics, which he laid out in a speech that was published in brief in *Nature* (1904). In it he espoused (1) support for education about heredity, (2) research into the differential contribution of social classes to the rise and fall of nations, (3) the initiation of record-keeping on traits in large, "thriving" families to study the factors that determine their success, (4) research to determine which types of social influences are effective at reducing the number of "unsuitable" marriages, (5) the notion that to be successful eugenics first needs to be an acceptable academic study, then it needs to be seen as effective, and finally it needs to be faithfully and uncritically practiced, like a religion.

15.2.2 Institutionalizing Eugenics in England

Ironically, Galton died childless in 1911. He left a significant portion of his estate to the University of London for the establishment of an endowed professorship to be named "The Galton Professorship of Eugenics" (Solanke, 2020). He had already funded the establishment of the Eugenics Records Office there, which later became the Francis Galton Laboratory for the Study of National Eugenics, both run by Karl Pearson. Pearson became the first Galton Professor of Eugenics in the world's first Department of Eugenics and held the chair for twenty-two years (see Figure 15.3). Ronald Aylmer Fisher was the second Galton Professor of Eugenics (1933–1943). If you have taken statistics, you probably recognize the names of Pearson and Fisher. The product-moment correlation coefficient bears Pearson's name (i.e., Pearson's r), and he made major contributions to regression analysis, the chi-square statistic, the p-value, and other well-known and important concepts in statistics. Fisher made similarly important contributions to statistics and essentially founded quantitative genetics. It is important to note that eugenics was not a movement on the fringes of academia, and some of its adherents were considered among the most important scientists of the day.

Figure 15.3. **Karl Pearson and Francis Galton.** Pearson and Galton were important early figures in the eugenics movement in England. Pearson was often called a disciple of Galton and was the first to hold the Galton Professorship of Eugenics (1911–1933). Lionel Penrose was named to the Galton Professorship in Eugenics in 1945, and gave its present name, the Galton Professorship in Human Genetics, in 1963. In early 2020 the University of London announced that it was renaming the Galton and Pearson lecture halls and the Pearson building. Source: adoc-photos / Contributor / Corbis Historical / Getty Images.

Check-up

- In what ways did Galton support eugenic efforts in England?
- What are some connections between Pearson and Fisher?
- What are your thoughts on the University of London renaming classrooms and buildings that were associated with eugenics?

15.3 The Eugenics Records Office in the United States

Eugenic ideas quickly made their way from England to the US, where they merged with the stark racial sociopolitical climate that followed the Civil War and Reconstruction into the dawning of the twentieth century (see Box 15.1). In addition to the racial strife existing between white and black Americans, recent decades had brought immigrants to the US from Central, Southern, and Eastern Europe. These new immigrants were not from Germany or other "Nordic" countries, and they were seen by many as a threat and a source of racial degeneration (Black, 2003). In Madison Grant's *The Passing of the Great Race* (Grant, 1970) he argued that blond, blue-eyed Nordics represented the racial ideal and that their descendants were America's founding fathers. Grant warned against race mixing and termed it race suicide. It is important to realize that the notion of a master race did not originate in Adolf Hitler's Nazi Germany, but in the US. Further, these ideas were promulgated by mainstream academics, respected industrialists, and politicians. As in England, eugenics in the US was not a fringe movement.

Box 15.1 The Kallikak Family

Henry H. Goddard opened a laboratory to study feeblemindedness in children at the Training School for Backward and Feebleminded Children at Vineland, New Jersey, in 1906. The resulting book *The Kallikak Family: A Study in the Heredity of Feeble-Mindedness* (Goddard, 1912) was a national best seller.

The name Kallikak is a pseudonym derived from the Greek words Kallos (beauty) and Kakos (bad) and refers to the "worthy" and "degenerate" family lines that issued from Martin Kallikak. Martin had been a soldier in the Revolutionary War and fathered an illegitimate child with a feebleminded bar maid. Their descendants were considered the "bad" family because of the high rates of feeblemindedness and other signs of degeneracy documented by the field worker. Martin later married and fathered children with a "normal" woman. Their descendants were considered the "good" family, with no documented cases of feeblemindedness and substantial evidence of their good character (see Figure 15.4).

The history of the Kallikak family neatly supports Goddard's eugenic ideas. He used it as a morality tale to encourage upstanding young people to avoid "sowing wild oats." He also used the story to advocate the segregation and sterilization of the feebleminded:

> When we conclude that had the nameless girl been segregated at an institution, this defective family would not have existed, we of course do not mean that one single act of precaution would have solved the problem, but we mean that all such cases, male and female, must be taken care of before their propagation will cease.

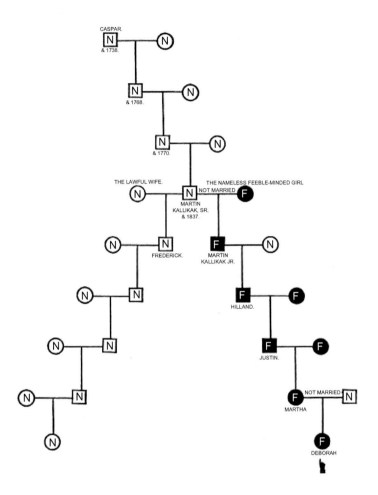

Figure 15.4. **Kallikak's pedigree**. Deborah was the proband interviewed at the Vineland school. A field worker traced her ancestors back several generations and found that Martin Kallikak had sired two family lines. Those indicated with an "F" were deemed by the field worker to be feebleminded. Those indicated with an "N" were deemed normal. This pedigree was consistent with the interpretation that feeblemindedness was inherited as a "unit character" in a dominant Mendelian fashion. Source: Goddard (1912). Image in the public domain.

This book influenced legislators and educators for decades (Chase, 1976). It provided scientific legitimacy to eugenic policies even though its "data" was collected by a single field worker with little training or experience in collecting family history data or making diagnoses.

15.3.1 Philanthropists Fund Eugenics

Andrew Carnegie helped to fund the incipient eugenic efforts in the US. He had made his fortune in the steel industry and then focused on supporting causes that were important to him. For example, he funded the construction of 2,509 libraries between 1883 and 1929 in thirteen countries, with most of them (67 percent) in the US. On a personal note, the library in the small town that I grew up in was a Carnegie Library (see Figure 15.5). Carnegie also funded science, and established the

Figure 15.5. **Carnegie Library, Luverne, MN.** One of over 2,500 libraries built by the Carnegie Foundation. This one, in the author's hometown, nurtured his love of books. Does such philanthropy balance Carnegie's support for eugenics? Source: Copyright © Minnesota Historical Society, used by permission.

Carnegie Institution in 1902 for the "improvement of mankind" (Black, 2003). With that aim in mind, the Carnegie Institution also funded the establishment of the Biological Experiment Station at Cold Spring Harbor with Charles Davenport as its director. You may have recognized the name Cold Spring Harbor. It was founded in 1890, and it currently employs over 600 scientists and technicians, holds well-known conferences, and teaches technical courses every year. The Cold Spring Harbor Laboratory has had eight Nobel Prize winners on its staff, including James Watson, who served as its director and president for thirty-five years.

Davenport earned a PhD in biology from Harvard in 1892 and eventually taught zoology both there and at the University of Chicago. He later got a job directing the Brooklyn Institute of Arts and Science's biological laboratory located at Cold Spring Harbor in Long Island, New York. Davenport became an immediate convert to eugenics after reading Galton's work, and began corresponding with him as early as 1897 (Black, 2003). In 1902 he visited Europe to drum up support for his eugenic program, including a meeting with Galton. In 1903 Davenport gave a talk at the annual meeting of the ABA and argued that they should add a Eugenics Committee to their organization. The Eugenics Committee was officially added in 1906 and was led by Luther Burbank. Its goal was to "emphasize the value of superior blood and the menace to society of inferior blood" (Black, 2003).

The Station for Experimental Evolution of the Carnegie Institution was established in 1904 with Davenport as its director. It established a strong foothold for the eugenics movement in US academic institutions and intellectual life. The initial focus was on constructing a building, doing genetic research on animals, and solidifying eugenics in the ABA (Black, 2003). Along with Alexander Graham Bell, Davenport devised a questionnaire focused on identifying defects such as feeblemindedness in American families with which he hoped to document Mendelian inheritance patterns of inferiority. Davenport established a Eugenics Records Office (ERO) at Cold Spring Harbor in 1910 to serve as the repository for the questionnaires, and he began collecting data with funding from Mary Harriman, the widow of the railroad and financial tycoon E. H. Harriman.

15.3.2 Extending the Reach of American Eugenics

Davenport hired Harry H. Laughlin as the superintendent of the ERO in 1910. Laughlin grew up in rural Missouri and became a school teacher there (Black, 2003). He was a dedicated eugenicist and had attended one of the summer courses at Cold Spring Harbor and was a member of the ABA. Under his leadership, the ERO recruited and trained field workers to visit prisons and insane asylums to collect data (see Figure 15.6). The field workers documented pedigrees of individuals

Cold Spring Harbor Laboratory. Noncommercial, educational use only.

Figure 15.6. **Field worker training at the ERO.** Field workers at the Eugenics Records Office were instructed on the collection of pedigree data from families. They focused on identifying "genetic defectives," such as those with feeblemindedness and tracing their family histories. In the first row, Davenport is third from right, and Laughlin is on the far right. Source: www.eugenicsarchive.org/html/eugenics/static/images/1660.html. Used by permission.

that were identified as, or suspected of being, feebleminded, or carrying any trait that was considered inferior, such as deafness, criminality, sexual perversion, or stuttering.

In 1911 the ABA created a new committee, chaired by Laughlin, to investigate the best approach to "cutting off the defective germ-plasm of the American population" (Black, 2003). The term germ-plasm refers to gametes. The establishment of such a committee comprising members who were influential in fields such as medicine, law, politics, and biology with a stated goal of applying eugenic principles signaled the start of a new phase that would lead to much human suffering in the form of involuntary sterilizations, immigration restrictions, and Nazi extermination camps.

Check-up

- Describe Davenport's role in institutionalizing eugenics in America.
- Who were the Kallikaks?
- How did Andrew Carnegie help to further eugenics in the US?

15.4 Involuntary Sterilization Laws and Immigration Policies

On their own, some physicians at the start of the twentieth century were advocating and practicing the sterilization of prisoners and insane asylum patients as a way to reduce the chances that their defects would be passed on to the next generation (Black, 2003). These procedures were conducted without consent of the prisoner or patient and were not legal – that is, until states started passing compulsory sterilization laws beginning in 1907 in Indiana.

15.4.1 Systematic Efforts to Make Involuntary Sterilization the Law of the Land

Harry Laughlin was a key figure in documenting and promoting compulsory sterilization laws. He published a book called *Eugenical Sterilization in the United States* (Laughlin, 1922) in which he analyzed each state law that proposed to sterilize the unfit. He included the text of each law and documented all litigation surrounding them. The book also included detailed family histories and pedigrees of people who had been sterilized as case studies. One of the chapters was entitled "The right of the state to limit human reproduction in the interests of race betterment." He provides protocols to follow when making "Eugenical diagnosis," in other words, identifying individuals who are "defective" in some way and should therefore not reproduce. The book included an extensive table of traits that had been shown to be inherited such as Jewish facial type, wanderlust, toothlessness, stuttering, and of course feeblemindedness. The book recommended sterilization procedures and provided step-by-step instructions for them including diagrams of where to make the incisions. The book concluded with chapters that provided detailed recommendations for planning and executing an attempt to pass a eugenic sterilization law, and a model law on which to base it. It even included example forms to use during the process of writing the law, potential litigation, and for documenting sterilizations once the law was adopted. The 502-page tour de force is a clear demonstration of the organizational skills and the determination of Laughlin and others to implement compulsory sterilization of those whom they considered to be unfit across the US.

However, the fundamental legality of compulsory sterilization had not been tested, and without the unambiguous support of the US Supreme Court, eugenic sterilization efforts were not progressing as rapidly as Laughlin and others had hoped. They reasoned that if the US Supreme Court were to uphold the constitutionality of involuntary sterilization by a state, other states would be certain to adopt eugenic sterilization laws and use them.

15.4.2 A Test Case

Laughlin sent a copy of his book to Dr. Albert Priddy, who had already been sterilizing inmates at the Virginia Colony for Epileptics and Feebleminded until a judge ordered him to stop in 1918. The Colony was one of many such institutions that segregated people who were considered to be defective, including women who were considered to be promiscuous. Virginia had not yet passed a eugenic sterilization law, but Priddy campaigned for it, and used Laughlin's book as a guide. The Virginia Sterilization Act of 1924 was the result.

Priddy wanted a solid case for sterilization that could make its way to the US Supreme Court and selected Carrie Buck to be the test case. Carrie's widowed mother had been an inmate in the Colony for several years after having been convicted of prostitution and carrying syphilis. Seventeen-year-old Carrie had been in a foster home since early childhood and had been an average student until sixth grade when she was taken out of school. Thereafter, she did housework for her foster family and others in the neighborhood. At age 16 she was raped. As a result, her foster parents wanted to have her committed to the Colony on the basis of her immoral behavior. She gave birth to a daughter whom she named Vivian and was admitted to the Colony days after the passage of the Virginia Sterilization Act of 1924 (Black, 2003). Carrie's daughter was taken in by the foster family for which she had worked.

Carrie was sentenced to be sterilized. To initiate the test case, she was appointed a representative, who happened to have eugenic views and was one of the founders of the Colony.

(a)   (b)

Figure 15.7. **Buck v. Bell.** (a) Carrie Buck and her mother. (b) Oliver Wendell Holmes, Jr. who famously wrote, "three generations of imbeciles are enough." Sources: (a): Arthur Estabrook Papers, Special Collections & Archives, University at Albany, SUNY. Used by permission. (b) MPI / Stringer / Archive Photos / Getty Images.

In other words, her representative was not acting as her advocate, but was helping to shepherd the case through the courts. As the case started to work its way through the legal system, Priddy died, and his assistant J. H. Bell was named in his place as defendant resulting in the well-known name for the case, *Buck v. Bell* (see Figure 15.7).

When Vivian was just months old, Priddy had had her examined and declared her to be feebleminded. It was important for the sterilization argument to demonstrate the hereditary nature of the defect by showing it was present in three generations, from Emma to Carrie to infant Vivian. Harry Laughlin examined documents in the case and provided his expert testimony that all three were feebleminded.

15.4.3 Three Generations of Imbeciles

The case *Buck v. Bell* was argued in the US Supreme Court on April 22, 1927 and decided on May 2, 1927 (Holmes, O. W. & Supreme Court of the United States, 1927). The court voted 8 to 1 that the Virginia Sterilization Act of 1924 did not violate the US Constitution. Therefore, state-sponsored compulsory sterilization was now the law of the land. Supreme Court Justice Oliver Wendell Holmes, Jr. wrote the opinion for the majority:

> We have seen more than once that the public welfare may call upon the best citizens for their lives. It would be strange if it could not call upon those who already sap the strength of the State for these lesser sacrifices, often not felt to be such by those concerned, in order to prevent our being swamped with incompetence. It is better for all the world if, instead of waiting to execute degenerate offspring for crime or to let them starve for their imbecility, society can prevent those who are manifestly unfit from continuing their kind. The principle that sustains compulsory vaccination is broad enough to cover cutting the Fallopian tubes. *Jacobson v. Massachusetts,* 197 U.S. 11. Three generations of imbeciles are enough.

Eventually, thirty-three states passed compulsory sterilization laws and more than 65,000 Americans were sterilized without their consent, and often without their knowledge. After World War II and the Nazi atrocities (see below) eugenic sterilization lost much of its appeal in the US. However, some states kept sterilizing people through the 1970s. Oregon practiced compulsory sterilization until 1981.

The Virginia Sterilization Act of 1924 was repealed in 1970 after over 7,000 people had been sterilized. The Virginia Colony for Epileptics and Feebleminded was later renamed the Central Virginia Training Center and continued to be a residential facility for the developmentally disabled until 2020 when it was closed. In 2015 the Virginia legislature passed the Victims of Eugenics Sterilization Compensation Program, which provided up to $25,000 to those claimants who could prove that they were involuntarily sterilized by the state.

15.4.4 Keeping Out the Unfit

Another important aim of American eugenic leaders was to restrict immigration from countries that were not considered Nordic. The Immigration Act of 1924 banned immigration from Asia and set a quota of 165,000 immigrants from countries outside the Western Hemisphere. Quotas were set for each country at 2 percent of the number from that country present in the US at the 1890 census. The decision to base the immigration quotas on the 1890 census rather than the most recent 1920 census was to restrict the flow of immigrants from countries like Italy, Poland, and Hungary, and to favor immigration from countries like England, Holland, and Germany. These decisions were made to appear to be based on the scientific assessment of intelligence.

During World War I, the US Army administered over 1.7 million IQ tests to recruits (Chase, 1976). IQ tests were relatively new, and this was certainly the largest IQ database at the time. In Chapter 8 we discussed IQ tests and their use in diagnosing intellectual disability and noted that they were also used in the early 1900s to diagnose feeblemindedness. The Army's goal was to use scores on the IQ test to aid in the assignment of soldiers to jobs that best fit their abilities (see Box 15.2). The data showed that performance on the IQ tests was related to a recruit's (1) years of education, (2) home state expenditures on education, (3) years of residence and education in the US, if foreign-born, and (4) native language (i.e., those who were native English speakers did best).

Box 15.2 Army Mental Tests

The US entered World War I in 1917, with over 4.7 million men and women serving in the regular armed forces during the conflict. Robert Yerkes, who chaired the American Psychological Association (APA) Committee on the Psychological Examination of Recruits, offered the Army a way to identify recruits of high and low intelligence to aid in job classification. The committee developed three tests, the Alpha, the Beta, and the Individual Examination.

The Alpha emphasized verbal skills and consisted of eight subtests. It was given in large groups. Example items include:

1. Why do inventors patent their inventions? Because (a) it gives them control of their inventions, (b) it creates greater demand, (c) it is the custom to get patents.
2. "Guns" is to "shoots" as "Knife" is to: (a) runs, (b) cuts, (c) hat, (d) bird.

The Beta was a non-verbal test given to recruits who were illiterate or were non-English speakers. Comprising seven tests, the Beta required recruits to complete mazes, to complete pictures with incomplete elements, and to solve puzzles (see Figure 15.8). It was also administered in groups.

The Individual Examination was administered to those who failed the Army Beta. The Individual Examination consisted of a Binet-Simon test, which was fifty-six tasks and questions that were

(a)

(b)

Figure 15.8. **Army mental tests.** (a) Component of the Army Beta test that required picture completion. (b) Administration of the Individual Examination. Sources: Image (a) in the public domain. (b) Bettmann / Contributor / Bettmann / Getty Images.

developed for use with children. Later, the Stanford-Binet Intelligence Scales were based on the original Binet-Simon test. Tasks could be as simple as naming items or stating their name and the date.

Henry Herbert Goddard was a eugenicist who sought to use IQ tests to identify mental defectives and to restrict them from immigrating to the US. Goddard translated and adapted Alfred Binet's tests and in 1913 administered them to immigrants at Ellis Island (Chase, 1976). His data showed that approximately 80 percent of Jewish, Hungarian, Italian, and Russian immigrants were feebleminded. Lewis M. Terman was a Stanford University professor who also revised Binet's tests into the Revised Stanford-Binet IQ test. He focused on the test scores of children and argued that the differences in scores that he observed were related to a child's family's social class, and that that class was hereditary. Both Goddard and Terman earned their PhDs under G. Stanley Hall, who was partial to the ideas of Galton and Spencer (Chase, 1976).

Harry Laughlin provided expert testimony at the hearings for the Immigration Act of 1924. He made it clear that, based on the Army mental tests, immigrants from certain countries were likely to have mental defects and that allowing them into the country would result in racial degeneration. The number of immigrants from Italy, Russia, Poland, and other countries in Central, Eastern, and Southern Europe, many of whom were Jewish, plummeted in the years after 1924. Laughlin and other like-minded eugenicists must have felt that 1924 was a real watershed year for American eugenics with the passage of eugenic sterilization laws and the Immigration Act.

Check-up

- Describe Harry Laughlin's efforts to increase compulsory sterilization.
- Who was Carrie Buck?
- In what ways did the field of psychology impact immigration laws in the US?

15.5 America Exports Eugenics to Nazi Germany

The US was one of the world's hotspots for eugenics in the 1920s. Eugenics courses were taught at many major universities. Several professional groups such as the American Eugenics Society aided in networking and organization. They had been successful in legitimizing compulsory sterilization of so-called defectives. And they were able to convince the US government to limit the immigration of people from undesirable (i.e., non-Nordic) countries. However, they were not content with these victories. Davenport, Laughlin, and other leading American eugenicists wanted to bring such measures to the rest of the world. In 1925 they established the International Federation of Eugenic Organizations to coordinate and lead such efforts (Black, 2003).

15.5.1 Hitler's Inspiration

The successes of the American eugenicists inspired their counterparts throughout the world, especially in Germany. While Adolf Hitler was in prison in 1924, he studied eugenic texts including Madison Grant's *The Passing of the Great Race* (Grant, 1970). Later, he wrote a letter to Grant saying that it was "his Bible" (Black, 2003). American eugenics inspired and provided the foundation for Hitler's efforts to rid the world of Jews and other so-called defectives, and to promote the Nordic "master race." Hitler was not the only German who was paying attention to American eugenic efforts, but he was the most influential. The manifesto he wrote while in prison, *Mein Kampf* (Hitler, 1943), espoused Social Darwinism and eugenics and his admiration for the eugenic policies practiced in the United States (Black, 2003).

To be fair, eugenics was already well established in Germany by the time Hitler put pen to paper. Brothers-in-law Ernst Rüdin and Alfred Ploetz, both physicians, founded the Society for Racial Hygiene in 1905 (Gottesman & Bertelsen, 1996). The group promoted the prophylactic sterilization of alcoholics and criminals with the goal of reducing the burden of such hereditary conditions on Germany's economy. It should be noted that Rüdin was an early investigator into the heredity of schizophrenia. Of course, as seen in the US and elsewhere, the leading thinkers in Germany thought that such traits were inherited in simple Mendelian fashion. At first, sterilizations were intended to be voluntary, requiring consent and authorization from a medical tribunal.

When Hitler took control of the German government in 1933, he began to institute eugenic policies. "The Law for the Prevention of Genetically Diseased Offspring" went into effect in early 1934 and legalized the sterilization of anyone with a hereditary defect including feeble-mindedness, deafness, blindness, epilepsy, and even severe alcoholism, as determined by a Genetic Health Court. By 1945 at least 400,000 people are believed to have been sterilized under this law. The law appears to have been based on US sterilization laws. American eugenicists were very supportive of German efforts and regularly communicated with their counterparts in Germany (Black, 2003).

Hitler's Nazi regime was not only focused on eliminating the reproduction of people with physical or mental defects. It was also committed to racial hygiene, which involved prohibitions on miscegenation (i.e., interbreeding of races), and laws that discriminated against Jews, Gypsies, and other non-Aryans, and eventually to concentration camps and euthanasia, a euphemism for state-sponsored murder. The Nazi euthanasia program started in 1939 and may have killed as many as 300,000 people.

The segregation of certain groups of people in camps began in 1933. The first prisoners of concentration camps were political, mostly communists, but the list of undesirables to be

(a)

Figure 15.9. **Nazi extermination camps**. One extermination camp was Auschwitz. (a) Personal items, such as eyeglasses were taken from victims before they were killed. (b) The bodies of extermination victims were cremated in ovens. Sources: (a) LAPI / Contributor / Roger Viollet / Getty Images. (b) Roger Viollet / Contributor / Roger Viollet / Getty Images.

(b)

incarcerated was soon expanded to include criminals, Gypsies, homosexuals, and other "asocials." Inmates in concentration camps were typically forced to work under brutal conditions and were poorly fed. Conditions were inhumane in concentration camps and approximately 1 million inmates died. Six extermination camps were constructed with the sole purpose of the mass murder of Jews (see Figure 15.9). More than 3 million people were killed in the extermination camps. These camps were a direct result of eugenic policies to rid Germany of hereditary defects and "lower" races of people that were considered to be vermin.

15.5.2 Breeding More Aryans

The most aggressive eugenic efforts by the Nazis were concerned with sterilization and murder of non-Aryans. However, they also had policies and practices that facilitated the reproduction of those that they considered to best represent the "Aryan race." In 1935 the Lebensborn Program was established to support SS (Schutzstaffel) members so that they could have large families. The SS were the Nazi elite. They were given rigorous physical examinations and their family histories were investigated, as were their wives, to assure Aryan purity. The program also supported unwed mothers who could prove the racial purity of their expected children (Thompson, 1971).

Figure 15.10. **Lebensborn Program.** The Lebensborn Program provided support for those who were able to certify "pure" German ancestry to produce large families, either in or out of wedlock. Source: Keystone-France / Contributor / Gamma-Keystone / Getty Images.

The Lebensborn Program was intended to repopulate Germany with the master race. As many as 20,000 children were born in Lebensborn homes (see Figure 15.10).

Nazi Germany represented an example of what ruthless government-sponsored eugenics policies and practices could do. Millions of people were murdered, and hundreds of thousands were sterilized against their will. The belief that traits such as feeblemindedness were inherited in Mendelian fashion coupled with virulent racism (i.e., scientific racism) enabled human rights abuses on a stunning scale.

Check-up

- How did laws in the US impact eugenic efforts in Nazi Germany?
- Explain the Lebensborn Program and how it contributed to Nazi eugenic efforts.

15.6 Race and Its Place in Behavior Genetics

It is obvious that eugenics is focused on race. The wobbly stool of eugenics rests on the legs of racial essentialism and an overly simplistic view of the inheritance of complex human traits. Racial essentialism involves the belief that certain physical trait differences between groups of people are true indicators of unobservable and immutable properties for which groups naturally vary in hierarchical fashion (Ho, Roberts, & Gelman, 2015). For example, the view that lighter colored skin is a marker for higher intelligence, and therefore whites are more intelligent than blacks, regardless of educational spending or opportunities. Such a view ignores differences within groups and the demonstrable impact of factors such as education and socioeconomic status on test performance.

15.6.1 Superiority and Inferiority

Racism developed into scientific racism when leading academics of the day, such as Francis Galton and Charles Davenport, asserted that traits like feeblemindedness followed Mendelian inheritance patterns in human families. The scientific establishment was explaining the heredity of complex human traits in simple Mendelian terms without carefully considering other potential factors that could influence the traits such as socioeconomic status or acculturation. In addition, little attention was paid to the validity of the trait definition.

The superiority of one group over others is a fundamental position of racism. Of course, it turns out that the traits that an individual views as superior are those observed in the group to which they belong. Racial differences in IQ scores of World War I recruits were considered to be hereditary, and low scores were thought to be signs of racial inferiority (Chase, 1976). It was not considered to be important that some recruits were not able to read or write or came from states where spending on education was low. The pattern of scores, where white recruits did better, on average, than black recruits fit the notions of Nordic racial supremacy.

Eugenicists are against miscegenation because of the belief that introducing genetic material of the inferior race into the gene pool of the superior one causes degeneration and race suicide. The Nuremberg Laws in Nazi Germany made it illegal for anyone of "German or related blood" to marry or to have sexual intercourse with anyone from another group, including Jews, Gypsies, blacks, or their offspring. Jews were defined by the number of Jewish great-grandparents that they had. Having only one Jewish great-grandparent out of eight (i.e., 1/8) still qualified a person as having German blood. Of course, to qualify as pure Aryan, all great-grandparents needed to be white Germans. Having two, three, or four Jewish great-grandparents resulted in a classification of mixed race, and therefore being considered only partly German, although such people qualified for citizenship in the Reich. Having five or more Jewish great-grandparents was defined as being Jewish and was disqualification from being a citizen of the Reich.

Black ancestry classification has a similar history whereby a person may be considered black when they have even a single black ancestor. This has been known as the "one drop rule" (Glasgow, Shulman, & Covarrubias, 2009). Nearly all US states (forty-one out of fifty) had laws against miscegenation at some point. For example, Virginia's Racial Integrity Act of 1924 prohibited interracial marriage and defined whites as having only white ancestors. Everyone else was defined as colored. State laws banning interracial marriage were declared unconstitutional by the US Supreme Court in 1967 (*Loving v. Virginia*, 388 U.S. 1 (1967)).

Eugenic views also tend to apply Mendelian inheritance to traits of interest, such as intelligence. As we have seen throughout this text, nearly all the traits that are of interest to behavior genetics are polygenic and therefore do not follow Mendelian patterns of inheritance. We have spent much of this text providing evidence for polygenic inheritance of psychological and behavioral traits and will not take the time to add to it here. Suffice it to say that polygenic inheritance, where hundreds or thousands of genes contribute to individual differences along with environmental factors, is a strong argument against racial essentialism.

Nazi Germany's applied eugenics program of marriage laws, forced sterilizations, concentration camps, and extermination camps rightly disgusted and horrified many people, including many academics. To some extent, human behavior genetic research was seen in a negative light for decades following World War II. This was exacerbated by some academics who seemed to be preoccupied with race differences in IQ scores.

15.6.2 Eugenics in Post-War America

William Shockley shared the 1956 Nobel Prize in Physics with colleagues for their invention of the transistor. He is considered a founding father of Silicon Valley. He was also a eugenicist concerned with human population growth and "genetic deterioration" (Tucker, 1994). He was clearly a Social Darwinist who thought that any kind of charity or relief from poverty, such as welfare and food stamps, was against nature and would permit increased reproduction by those with genetic defects. He was in favor of involuntary sterilization of the less fit. Shockley was outspoken in his view that whites were superior to blacks on a variety of measures and that heredity was the cause. The cachet

(a)   (b)

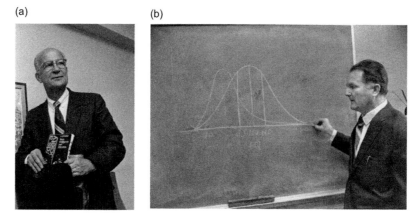

Figure 15.11. **Scientific racism in the 1960s.** (a) William Shockley and (b) Arthur Jensen provided a scientific veneer to eugenic arguments in the 1960s. Sources: (a) Bettmann / Contributor / Bettmann / Getty Images. (b) Michael Rougier / Contributor / The LIFE Picture Collection / Getty Images.

provided by his Nobel Prize and position at Stanford University was substantial and outweighed the fact that his training and degree was in physics, not in any area relevant to questions of genetics, cognitive ability, education, or poverty. He called for more research on the causes of such racial differences and the potential for racial deterioration and accused those who disagreed with him of trying to muzzle free speech and scientific freedom (Tucker, 1994).

Shockley was convinced that differences in cognitive ability between blacks and whites were due to genetic differences, and that this meant that environmental improvements would have no effect. It is, however, a logical fallacy to think that environmental interventions are incapable of affecting traits that are influenced by heredity. For example, when a genetic mutation causes phenylketonuria (PKU), the treatment is purely dietary. When left untreated, severe intellectual disability results. But when phenylalanine is omitted from the diet, most of the negative impact of the disease is avoided. In other words, a single gene disorder can be effectively treated with a purely environmental approach. Genetic does not mean inevitable or untreatable.

Shockley enlisted Arthur Jensen, an educational psychologist at the University of California, Berkeley, into the fight (see Figure 15.11). Jensen continued to stir the race controversy in 1969 with the publication of his article "How much can we boost IQ and scholastic achievement?" (Jensen, 1969). In it he argued that social programs, such as Lyndon Johnson's War on Poverty, would do little to improve cognitive abilities. He was especially concerned with the fact that "Negro" families in America were having more children than were white families, and that this coupled with the difference in cognitive abilities between the races would eventually prove to be problematic for the Negro families. He thought that social programs that focused on sterilization and contraception would be more beneficial than antipoverty programs (Tucker, 1994).

Jensen's overall message was eugenic (Tucker, 1994). It argued against social programs and for sterilization and contraception. It argued for basic level instruction for the disadvantaged (i.e., black) children to help them prepare for their future menial jobs. Jensen's article stirred controversy and was used to support racist political opinions. It added fuel to the fire during the civil rights movement in the US. The eugenic views of Shockley and Jensen provided a scientific basis for racist and eugenic views and policies, slowing the civil rights movement.

It should be noted that making reproductive decisions for others violates their human rights. If you choose not to have children, for whatever reasons, it is your choice. If someone else decides that you are unfit to be a parent and sterilizes you against your will, your human rights have been violated.

This section should not be considered a comprehensive review of the history of eugenics and the role of behavior genetics in scientific racism. It should, however, serve as a cautionary note that research cannot be completely divorced from its social context, and that research into heredity–behavior relations has played a key role in perpetuating eugenics and racism. Racism continues to be a significant problem and it is important for those in behavior genetics to be aware of the field's connections to eugenics.

Human behavior genetic studies are not designed to investigate differences between groups. Twin, adoption, and family studies can be used to estimate the proportion of phenotyping variation in a population that is due to genetic differences in that population. Thus, heritability is a within-population measure, not a between-population measure. A non-zero heritability estimate suggests that genetic differences between people explain at least some of the individual differences in behavior in that population. It does not provide any useful information regarding differences between populations. For the most part, behavior genetic data does not address differences between groups of people.

The use of heritability estimates to make social policy that is based on the superiority of one group over another is an echo of the eugenics of the early twentieth century. It represents an oversimplification of a scientific finding to promote a racist agenda. Such an approach assumes that concepts of race, heritability, and traits like intelligence are simple and provide useful information that can be directly applied to public policy. None of these assumptions withstand scrutiny. The concept of race is a social construct. Although genomic data can be used to approximate a person's ancestry, human populations show substantial genetic overlap and are therefore not genetically distinct (Jorde & Wooding, 2004). Heritability estimates for a trait can vary between groups because of environmental differences between them. Intelligence tests do not measure a trait that has a simple genetic causal structure, but rather many traits that are highly polygenic. Policies that pit one group against another are often popular, but popularity does not mean that the policies are based on sound science or that they respect human rights. Those educated in behavior genetics have a responsibility to oppose public policies that oversimplify heredity–behavior relations and that may lead to human rights abuses.

Check-up

- Explain racial essentialism and its connection to miscegenation laws.
- Who was William Shockley and what was his main argument?
- Why are racial differences not the focus of behavior genetics?

15.7 SUMMARY

- Arguments that human populations will necessarily exceed their capacity for food production, and that helping the poor survive impedes evolutionary progress set the stage for eugenics.

- Galton spent decades thinking and writing about eugenics. When he died, he helped to institutionalize eugenics by funding a professorship held by Pearson, Fisher, and others.
- The institutionalization of eugenics in the US started at Cold Spring Harbor and supported efforts in compulsory sterilization and immigration restrictions.
- Nazi Germany based some of its eugenic policies on US laws. The Nazi eugenic efforts surpassed those in the US by conducting mass murder and a breeding program.
- Eugenics is based on racism, which continues to be a problem. The field of behavior genetics cannot ignore its connections to eugenic thinking and has a responsibility to oppose racism and eugenics.

RECOMMENDED READING

- Black, E. (2003). *War Against the Weak: Eugenics and America's Campaign to Create a Master Race*. New York: Four Walls Eight Windows.
- Chase, A. (1976). *The Legacy of Malthus: The Social Costs of the New Scientific Racism*. New York: Knopf.
- Lifton, R. J. (2017). *The Nazi Doctors: Medical Killing and the Psychology of Genocide*. New York: Basic Books.
- Tucker, W. H. (1994). *The Science and Politics of Racial Research*. Urbana: University of Illinois Press.

REFERENCES

Black, E. (2003). *War Against the Weak: Eugenics and America's Campaign to Create a Master Race*. New York: Four Walls Eight Windows.

Chase, A. (1976). *The Legacy of Malthus: The Social Costs of the New Scientific Racism*. New York: Knopf.

Darwin, C. (1924). *The Descent of Man and Selection in Relation to Sex*. New York: D. Appleton.

Darwin, C. (1936). *The Origin of Species by Means of Natural Selection; or, The Preservation of Favored Races in the Struggle for Life and The Descent of Man and Selection in Relation to Sex*. New York: Modern Library.

Darwin, C. (1950). *Charles Darwin's Autobiography, with his notes and letters depicting the growth of the Origin of Species; edited by Sir Francis Darwin. And an introductory essay, The meaning of Darwin, by George Gaylord Simpson*. New York: Schuman.

Galton, F. (1883). *Inquiries into Human Faculty and Its Development*. London: Macmillan.

Galton, F. (2012). *Hereditary Genius: An Inquiry into Its Laws and Consequences*. New York: Barnes & Noble Digital Library.

Glasgow, J., Shulman, J., & Covarrubias, E. (2009). The ordinary conception of race in the United States and its relation to racial attitudes: A new approach. *Journal of Cognition and Culture*, 9(1–2), 15. doi:10.1163/156853709X414610

Goddard, H. H. (1912). *The Kallikak Family: A Study in the Heredity of Feeble-Mindedness*. New York: Macmillan.

Gottesman, I. I., & Bertelsen, A. (1996). Legacy of German psychiatric genetics. *Am J Med Genet (Neuropsychiatric Genetics)*, 67, 317–322.

Grant, M. (1970). *The Passing of the Great Race*. New York: Arno Press.

Hitler, A. (1943). *Mein Kampf*, trans. Ralph Manheim. Boston: Houghton Mifflin.

Ho, A. K., Roberts, S. O., & Gelman, S. A. (2015). Essentialism and racial bias jointly contribute to the categorization of multiracial individuals. *Psychol Sci*, *26*(10), 1639–1645. doi:10.1177/0956797615596436

Jensen, A. R. (1969). How much can we boost IQ and scholastic achievement? *Harvard Educational Review*, *39*(1), 1–123. doi:10.17763/haer.39.1.l3u15956627424k7

Jorde, L., & Wooding, S. (2004). Genetic variation, classification and 'race'. *Nat Genet*, *36*, S28–S33. doi:10.1038/ng1435

Laughlin, H. H. (1922). *Eugenical Sterilization in the United States by Harry Hamilton Laughlin, D.Sc., Assistant Director of the Eugenics Record Office, Carnegie Institution of Washington, Cold Spring Harbor, Long Island, New York, and Eugenics Associate of the Psychopathic Laboratory of the Municipal Court of Chicago*. Chicago: Psychopathic Laboratory of the Municipal Court of Chicago.

Malthus, T. (1798). *An Essay on the Principle of Population As It Affects the Future Improvement of Society, with Remarks on the Speculations of Mr. Goodwin, M. Condorcet and Other Writers*. London: J. Johnson in St Paul's Church-yard. Retrieved March 5, 2021 via Internet Archive.

Paul, D. B. (2003). Darwin, social Darwinism and eugenics. In G. Radick & J. Hodge (Eds.), *The Cambridge Companion to Darwin* (pp. 214–239). Cambridge: Cambridge University Press.

Richeson, J. A., & Sommers, S. R. (2016). Toward a social psychology of race and race relations for the twenty-first century. *Annu Rev Psychol*, *67*, 439–463. doi:10.1146/annurev-psych-010213-115115

Solanke, I. (2018). *Inquiry into the History of Eugenics at UCL – Final Report*. University College London. Retrieved from: www.ucl.ac.uk/provost/sites/provost/files/ucl_history_of_eugenics_inquiry_report.pdf

Spencer, H. (1898). *The Principles of Biology*. New York: D. Appleton and Company.

Thompson, L. V. (1971). Lebensborn and the eugenics policy of the Reichsführer-SS. *Central European History*, *4*(1), 54–77.

Tucker, W. H. (1994). *The Science and Politics of Racial Research*. Urbana: University of Illinois Press.

Glossary

abnormal Not normal. Abnormal is a term that has negative connotations and can have different meanings depending on how normal is defined. It is a term that should be avoided in behavior genetics.

activator proteins A class of transcription factors that bind to enhancer DNA sequences to facilitate gene expression.

active genotype–environment correlation An individual's genotype predisposes them to seek environments that are consistent with their preferences.

additive effects Genetic effects that are summed across polygenic loci. Such effects can be passed from parent to offspring and are independent of interaction effects.

adenosine triphosphate (ATP) Small biomolecule that is used as an energy source in many metabolic processes.

adoption studies A type of study primarily used to estimate heritability in human populations. It takes advantage of the dissociation of genes and environment when an unrelated child is raised in a family.

affiliation Characterized by engaging in positive social interactions with others.

aggressive behaviors Are those intended to physically or emotionally harm another. They can be categorized into reactive and proactive aggression.

agonist Exogenous receptor ligand that produces the same or similar biological impact as the receptor's endogenous ligand.

agonistic behavior Behavior related to fighting. Typically, agonistic behaviors involve social behaviors between conspecifics for access to limited resources, such as access to mates, food, or territory. Because physical fights can cause serious injury, many species engage in threat displays that often make them appear ready to fight (e.g., baring teeth) and serve to intimidate their opponent.

agricultural revolution Beginning in the early 1700s new crops were introduced along with new methods such as crop rotation, and animal husbandry, which increased food production capacity of farmers.

alcohol flushing response After drinking alcohol, some people experience increased skin temperature around face and neck, nausea, increased heart rate, and other unpleasant symptoms that are due to elevated levels of acetaldehyde in the bloodstream.

alexithymia Having a limited capacity to identify and describe emotions in oneself or others.

alleles Alternative versions of a genetic variant.

alloparental care Care for offspring provided by a conspecific other than parents.

all-or-none Characteristic of action potentials that they either occur fully or not at all.

alternative splicing For genes with multiple exons, different proteins can be produced from the same primary mRNA transcript by changing which exons are translated via selectively excising those to be omitted.

Alzheimer disease Neurodegenerative disorder characterized by cognitive dysfunction, especially memory loss, that typically has onset after age 65.

amino acids Organic compounds that each contain an amine (NH2), a carboxyl (COOH) group, and its own unique "side chain." Twenty amino acids serve as the building blocks of proteins.

amnion The innermost membrane surrounding embryos.

amyloid plaques Aggregations of β-amyloid (Aβ) in the brain that are thought to play a role in the initiation of Alzheimer disease.

ancestral reference populations Groups of people with known ancestry who have lived in a location for generations that provide a genetic baseline for ancestry reports from direct-to-consumer genetic testing companies.

aneuploidy Carrying an atypical number of chromosomes for the species resulting from non-disjunction during cell division.

anhedonia The inability to feel pleasure, often discussed as a risk factor in recovery when someone is trying to abstain from substance use. Such a state is particularly risky for relapse to substance use because the addicted person knows that the substance can produce positive feelings.

animalculists Those who believed that sperm cells contain preformed embryos and therefore that fathers were primarily responsible for producing offspring.

annealing In the context of polymerase chain reaction, the step in which primers bind to their complementary targets on the template DNA, which takes place at around 50°–65 °C.

antagonist Exogenous receptor ligand that does not produce a biological impact.

anticodon A site on transfer RNAs that binds to a complementary three-base nucleic acid sequence on messenger RNA.

antisocial alcoholism A type of alcoholism that is characterized by early onset (prior to age 21) and is comorbid with antisocial personality disorder.

anxiety Subjective mental state experienced when the source of potential harm is either distant or uncertain.

apoptosis Process of eliminating unwanted or damaged cells (e.g., pruning) that can occur after cellular proliferation or to fine tune circuits.

applied research Research focused on solving practical problems, like determining which therapy most effectively treats a disorder.

appraisal Cognitive evaluation of a situation that can impact how a physiological feeling is interpreted.

Aryans In Nazi Germany, a person having all eight great-grandparents who were white and German.

ataxia Loss of control of bodily movements, such as walking.

attachment Affiliation with a specific individual produces a social bond.

attachment styles Three primary attachment styles characterize a child's connection to their caregiver and to others as (1) secure (i.e., seeks close contact and intimacy, and able to regulate emotions), (2) avoidant (i.e., actively avoids intimacy and suppresses emotions), and (3) anxious-ambivalent (i.e., seeks contact, but has difficulty controlling emotions).

attention bias Heightened attention to some features in the environment over others.

autism spectrum disorder Characterized by persistent deficits in the ability to initiate and to sustain reciprocal social interaction and social communication, and by a range of restricted, repetitive, and inflexible patterns of behavior, interests or activities that are clearly atypical or excessive for the individual's age and sociocultural context.

autosomal dominant A pattern of inheritance in a pedigree in which the affected trait appears in each generation and without respect to sex.

autosomal recessive A pattern of inheritance in a pedigree in which the affected trait appears without respect to sex, but not in each generation.

autosomes All nuclear chromosomes that are not sex chromosomes (i.e., X and Y). In humans there are twenty-two pairs of autosomes.

axon The neurite that carries the action potential from the cell body to the axon terminal.

axon hillock Structure connecting cell body to axon where incoming information is processed, and the neuron's firing threshold is put into practice.

axon terminal Presynaptic neuron's structure that contains neurotransmitter for release into the synapse.

backcross When F_1 generation individuals are mated to individuals from one of the parental lines.

basal metabolism The energy required for life-sustaining functions such as respiration, circulation, and cellular activities.

basic research Research focused on understanding natural phenomena that may not solve practical problems, like heredity–behavior relations.

behavior genetics The scientific study of heredity–behavior relations.

behavioral studies Research methods in which emotions are assessed on the basis of bodily responses to emotions, such as facial expressions.

binding affinity Indexes the degree to which a ligand binds to a receptor.

binge drinking A drinking episode that produces blood alcohol concentrations (BAC) of 0.08 percent or higher. It is associated with increased risk for motor vehicle accident, victimization, memory blackouts, and, when done repeatedly, the development of an alcohol use disorder.

bioavailability The proportion of a drug in the body that can have an effect on its target.

Biometricians Academics in the early twentieth century who noted that traits do not always fall neatly into categories but can be distributed along a dimension in a population. They established the field of quantitative genetics.

blending inheritance When the expression of a categorical trait in the offspring is intermediate to that of the two parents. This theory of inheritance was disproven by Mendel's theory of inheritance.

blood alcohol concentrations An operational measure of alcohol intoxication that estimates the fraction of blood volume that is ethanol. A BAC of 0.10 percent means that a person's blood supply contains one part alcohol for every 1,000 parts blood.

body mass index (BMI) An indirect measure of body fat composition calculated by dividing a person's weight in kilograms (kg) by the square of their height in meters (m^2). Obesity is defined as a BMI ≥ 30.

brain reward system Brain areas involved in positive reinforcement. Dopamine releasing neurons projecting from the ventral tegmental area to the nucleus accumbens are considered crucial in the reinforcing effects of drugs of abuse.

bred true In hybridization studies it is important to start with a line that has proven to consistently produce offspring with the same trait across generations.

broad sense heritability (H^2) An index of the degree of phenotypic variation that is due to all sources of genetic variation, including additive and non-additive (i.e., dominance and epistasis) genetic effects.

Brunner syndrome A condition caused by a rare mutation in *MAOA* that produces impulsive aggression and intellectual deficiency.

calorie One calorie is the amount of energy needed to raise the temperature of 1 gram of water by 1 °C.

candidate gene association studies A study methodology in human populations that tests statistical associations between genetic variants and behaviors or traits of interest. Variants in candidate genes to be tested are selected on the basis of previous evidence or theoretical considerations. Such studies have been plagued by small sample sizes and failure to replicate.

candidate genes Genes hypothesized to harbor variants likely to be associated with disorders or behaviors of interest.

Canis lupus familiaris The domestic dog.

centimorgan (cM) A unit of measurement named to honor T. H. Morgan that indexes the recombination rate between two loci on a chromosome. One cM represents 1 percent recombination.

central nervous system The brain and the spinal cord.

centromere Region of a chromosome that connects sister chromatids during cell division. It also serves to divide the short and long arms of the chromosome.

childhood maltreatment Risk factor for negative outcomes. The experience of physical abuse, sexual abuse, emotional/psychological abuse, or neglect occurring during childhood.

chorion The outermost membrane surrounding embryos.

chromatids Two identical copies of a chromosome produced by DNA replication.

chromatin Chromosomal DNA together with proteins used to pack it tightly.

chromatin remodeling Processes by which tightly packed DNA changes shape to allow DNA-binding proteins to access for transcription.

chromosomes Structures typically found in a cell's nucleus comprised of DNA and packaging proteins.

codon A sequence of three nucleic acids that specifies one of the twenty amino acids used in translating mRNA sequence to a polypeptide chain. Codons also specify the sequence used to start or stop translation.

comorbidity The simultaneous presence of multiple disorders in a person.

complementary base pairing In DNA, adenine (A) always pairs with thymine (T) and guanine (G) always pairs with cytosine (C). In RNA, adenine

(A) always pairs with uracil (U) and guanine (G) always pairs with cytosine (C). In other words, purines always pair with pyrimidines.

complementation test A study design whereby parents that are heterozygous for the two mutations in question are mated together (i.e., +/ob mice are mated to +/db mice). If the two mutations represent different alleles of the same gene, some of the hybrid offspring should show the affected phenotype (e.g., obesity). However, if the mutations are in different genes, the wild-type alleles contributed by the parents would "complement" the mutant alleles so that the offspring would be "heterozygous" at both loci and therefore would not display the affected trait.

compulsions Repetitive behaviors that an individual feels driven to perform in response to an obsession, according to rigid rules, or to achieve a sense of "completeness."

compulsive Behavior driven by urges to satisfy short-term goals that can override motivation for longer-term goals. Single-minded drug-seeking behavior triggered by cravings or other conditioned stimuli can be considered compulsive.

concentration camps In Nazi Germany, camps where inmates were typically forced to work under brutal conditions and were poorly fed. Prisoners included communists, Gypsies, homosexuals, and other "asocials."

concordance The probability that a twin who has a trait of interest has a co-twin who shares the trait.

conditional knockout techniques Approaches using molecular biological tools to restrict the targeted mutation of a gene to certain tissues or developmental stages.

conservative Mutations that cause a change in an amino acid (i.e., missense), but because the new amino acid shares chemical or physical properties with the old, the substitution does not produce substantial change in the resulting protein.

conserved In biology, when different species share DNA sequences it is considered evidence that the species had a common ancestor.

convergent evidence Findings from research conducted with different methods or species that support the same conclusion.

copy number variant (CNV) A type of genetic variation in which a given DNA sequence is repeated.

courtship behavior Interactions between male and female of the same species that serve as a prelude to copulation.

CpG islands The "p" represents the phosphate of the DNA backbone, and C and G represent cytosine and guanine, respectively. CpG islands are typically found in a gene's regulatory region and are typically 1,000–4,000 bases (1–4 kilobases [kb]) in length. Cytosines in CpG islands are typical sites of methylation.

craving State of drug wanting that can manifest with obsessive desire for drug use and with physiological components such as salivation.

CRISPR-Cas9 A method of genome editing that takes advantage of a natural system used by bacteria to defend against viruses. The acronym stands for **c**lustered **r**egularly **i**nterspaced **s**hort **p**alindromic **r**epeats.

cross-fostering designs An experimental approach in which offspring are placed with parents other than their own to examine the impact of differential parenting on offspring traits.

crossing over The exchange of chromosomal material by sister chromatids during meiosis, and the process by which recombination takes place.

crossover interaction In the context of G×E interactions, it is when the lowest scoring genotype in one environment is the highest scoring in another.

cross-sectional studies Study design that collects data from participants at one point in time.

cytochrome P450 enzymes Class of liver enzymes that account for the majority of drug metabolism. Some cytochrome P450 enzymes carry genetic variants that impact their catalytic rate and should be considered when determining dosages of certain medications.

cytoplasm Substance that fills cells and includes cytosol, organelles, and other components involved in cellular function.

***de novo* mutation** A genetic change that arises anew after fertilization. It was not present in either parent.

declarative memories Memories that can be shared by speaking, including both semantic and episodic memories.

decreasing allele In Fisher's polygenic model where an individual's trait score is determined by summing their genetic score across many loci, a decreasing allele reduces the trait score and is typically denoted by a lowercase letter (e.g., a).

defensive circuits Involve sensory systems that project to the amygdala either directly (e.g., olfaction) or via the thalamus, and provide information about potential threats, as well as nervous and endocrine systems that generate defensive actions or escape behaviors.

degenerate A characteristic of the genetic code whereby multiple codons can specify a single amino acid.

demand characteristics Pattern of responding by participants that corresponds to the inferred wishes of the researcher.

denaturation In the context of polymerase chain reaction, the step in which the reaction mix is heated to around $90°–95°C$ to break apart the double-stranded DNA template to allow the DNA polymerase access to single-stranded DNA for copying.

denature To denature a protein or nucleic acid is to alter its structure and thereby disrupt its function, often by heating.

dendrites Neurites that receive information.

deoxyribonucleic acid (DNA) Deoxyribonucleic acid (DNA) consists of a double helix made of a sugar-phosphate backbone and nucleic acid bases: adenine, cytosine, guanine, and thymine. Each strand of the helix has a sequence of bases that pair in a complementary fashion with the bases on the other strand. The sequence of bases is the genetic information.

depolarizing Input that results in greater electrical charge difference between the inside and the outside of a neuron. Such input can be considered excitatory and may be the result of an excitatory postsynaptic potential (EPSP).

depression-like behavior In non-human animals, behaviors that appear to be valid models of depression. For example, the amount of time that rodents spend just floating (i.e., not swimming or trying to escape) in the forced swim test.

Diagnostic and Statistical Manual of Mental Disorders Handbook used primarily in the US as a guide for diagnosing mental illness.

diathesis-stress model A model of disease risk whereby an individual's vulnerability to develop a mental illness is a function of their genetic risk (i.e., diathesis) and exposure to adverse life events (i.e., stress).

diazepam A benzodiazepine that acts on $GABA_A$ receptors and has anxiolytic effects.

differential sensitivity hypothesis A model of disease risk in which people carrying certain genotypes are more sensitive to both negative and positive environmental exposure than are those carrying other genotypes.

differentiation A developmental process by which cells change from one cell type to another that is dependent on differential gene expression.

diffusion Physical process whereby solutes move from an area of high concentration to low concentration. One of the forces that moves ions across neural membranes.

dihybrid cross The design of a hybridization study in which the inheritance of two categorical traits are investigated.

diploid (2n) Having two copies of each chromosome, one paternally derived, the other maternally derived.

Disability-Adjusted Life Years (DALYs) A measure of disease burden that estimates the number of years lost to illness, disability, or premature death.

discovery sample In a two-stage study design to test the association of genetic variants to behaviors, risk alleles are first identified in a sample of participants (i.e., discovery sample), which is independent of another sample in which they are subsequently tested when combined into a polygenic risk score (i.e., the target sample).

dizygotic twin (DZ) Siblings resulting from the same pregnancy that was due to the fertilization of two separate eggs each by a separate sperm. Also called fraternal twins, they share an average of 50 percent of their genetic material.

DNA fingerprinting The most well-known application of genetics in the justice system, which is to match DNA from samples at a crime scene to that of suspects. It uses genotypes from multiple hyper-variable loci to generate genetic profiles that are likely to be unique and can therefore be used to identify individuals.

DNA polymerase An enzyme involved in replicating DNA. It binds to a single strand of DNA and adds new bases complementary to the template strand.

dNTPs Deoxynucleotide triphosphates are PCR components that are added one at a time to the newly copied DNA strand. The "N" stands for nucleotide and can be replaced by A, T, C, or G to represent a specific base, as in dATP for deoxyadenosine triphosphate.

dog breed A line of dogs that share similar physical and behavioral traits maintained by selective breeding.

domestication syndrome Traits that are associated with tame animals such as floppy ears, curly tails, shorter and rounder facial features, and thicker limbs. Selective breeding for tameness produced silver foxes with such traits, and that wagged their tails when humans approached, licked their hands, and whined when they left.

dominance hierarchies Social structures in which individuals each have a rank that determines their access to resources.

dominance variance (V_D) When partitioning trait variance in a population, dominance variance is that due to departures from additivity resulting from dominance/recessive relations at single loci.

dominant When having only one copy of the allele is sufficient to produce the phenotype.

dopamine hypothesis The hypothesis that excess dopaminergic neural activity played a role in the development of schizophrenia.

dosage compensation Strategies to equalize the contribution of sex chromosomes when one sex carries two X-chromosomes and the other carries only one. In some species, one copy of the X-chromosome is transcriptionally silenced in XX females (e.g., *Homo sapiens*). In others, the expression of the X is doubled in XY males (e.g., *Drosophila melanogaster*).

dosage sensitive Genes for which having an additional copy produces deleterious outcomes.

dose dependent In the context of drugs, effects correspond to the amount taken. In the context of knockouts, the outcomes are related to number of knockout alleles present.

double crossovers A second crossover event that essentially restores the original chromosome complement to each sister chromatid. In a dihybrid cross, resulting offspring are phenotypically of a parental type although two recombination events occurred, which contributes to an underestimation of the recombination rate.

Down syndrome Condition caused by carrying three copies of chromosome 21 (i.e., Trisomy 21) characterized by intellectual disability and a variety of physical and medical symptoms.

drinking in the dark A paradigm to study binge drinking behavior in mice that takes advantage of the fact that mice tend to do most of their eating and drinking near the start of the dark period of the daily light-dark cycle, by providing access to alcohol at the start of the dark cycle.

drugs Substances that have biological impact because their molecular structure has enough similarity with an endogenous molecule to enable them to interact with biological components such as receptors, transporters, or enzymes.

dyslexia Specific learning disorder characterized by reading impairment.

early onset When a disorder develops earlier in development than is typical. Early onset types of a disorder may have a stronger genetic basis than later onset types.

early onset Alzheimer disease (EOAD) Less common form that has onset prior to age 65 and follows a Mendelian dominance inheritance pattern, caused by mutations in four genes: *APP*, *PSEN1*, *PSEN2*, and *ADAM10*.

electrodermal response Sweaty palms caused by sympathetic nervous system activation can affect the electrical activity of the skin and be measured by using passive electrodes.

electrostatic pressure Physical process whereby like electrically charged molecules (i.e., ions) repel each other and differently electrically charged particles are attracted to each other. One of the forces that moves ions across neural membranes.

elevated mazes Used to assess anxiety-like behavior in rodents. Such mazes typically are held several feet off of the ground and have sections with walls (i.e., closed) and sections without walls (i.e., open). More time spent in closed areas than open areas is considered to reflect anxiety.

elongation In the context of polymerase chain reaction, the step in which DNA polymerase begins to add bases to copy the target DNA sequence when the temperature is raised to around 72 °C.

emotion regulation Encompasses implicit or explicit efforts to alter emotional experience through different strategies over time.

emotional problems When a person experiences an emotion with inappropriate intensity or duration.

Enclosure Acts Enabled large landowners to expel the small non-landowning farmers from their land, which forced impoverished workers to move to cities to find alternative employment.

endocannabinoid system Neurons that release anandamide [AEA], 2-arachidonoylglycerol [2-AG], and their target receptors (CB_1 and CB_2).

endophenotypes The general idea is that there are internal (i.e., not immediately visible) phenotypes that may be considered risk factors for developing the disorder, and that these so-called endophenotypes are influenced by fewer genes, and therefore may be simpler genetically than the disorder.

environmental effect When individuals of the same genotype that are raised in different environments have different mean trait scores.

environmental factors Non-genetic features in the environment that have the potential to cause behavioral differences.

environmental risk Non-genetic risk factors such as childhood trauma, exposure to substances like cannabis, or social factors such as insecure parental attachment, or discrimination.

environmental variance (V_E) When partitioning trait variance in a population, any variance not explained by genetic causes or measurement error is considered environmental variance.

epigenetic marks Histone modification and DNA methylation are often referred to as epigenetic marks because they are physical changes that can be observed with standard molecular biology techniques and they are considered to be signs of genetic regulation.

epigenetics An area of study that focuses on changes in gene expression that can survive cell division and that are not the result of changes in DNA sequence, such as histone modification and methylation.

episodic memories Memories of specific incidents in a person's life.

epistasis When the effect of one genotype on a trait depends on another genotype. Also known as gene×gene interaction.

equal environments assumption When estimating heritability in twin studies, it is assumed that monozygotic twin pairs and dizygotic twin pairs do not experience systematically different environments.

euchromatin Chromatin that has been unpacked to allow for transcription.

eugenics The term coined by Francis Galton to describe efforts to manage traits in human populations by restricting (i.e., negative) or promoting (i.e., positive) reproduction.

euploidy Carrying the typical chromosome number for a species.

evocative genotype–environment correlation When an individual's genotype predisposes them to behave in certain ways, which are observed by another person who provides access to environments that facilitate the behavior.

evolution Charles Darwin's theory of how populations change in response to natural selection across generations.

exercise A special type of physical activity that is goal-oriented, structured, and can include repetitive elements that are designed to maintain or improve some aspect of physical fitness.

exocytosis Process of releasing neurotransmitters into synapses.

exons Stretches of DNA (and subsequently mRNA) sequence that are used to specify amino acids.

extermination camps In Nazi Germany, camps constructed with the sole purpose of mass murdering Jews. More than 3 million people were killed in extermination camps.

externalizing Emotional problems that are focused outward, toward other people or objects (e.g., conduct disorder).

familial resemblance People in the same family are often similar in appearance and behavior, and the similarity is partially due to shared genetic variants.

fear Subjective mental state experienced when the source of potential harm is either nearby or imminent.

fear conditioning A research paradigm that has been widely used to investigate the biological basis of fear and anxiety. It relies on classical conditioning to pair previously neutral stimuli (e.g., a tone) with a loud noise or an electric shock.

feeblemindedness An old, disused term for intellectual disability.

first filial generation The F_1 generation consists of offspring of parental line crosses.

five-trial habituation-dishabituation test A standard test of social recognition memory in mice where the amount of time that the subject investigates the target is measured. Intact social recognition memory is shown when the subject spends decreasing amounts of time investigating the target individual on subsequent trials.

forced swim test A commonly used measure of depression-like behavior in rodents. When first placed in a beaker of water, rodents swim and try to escape, but eventually stop swimming and passively float. Administration of antidepressant drugs results in longer bouts of swimming.

forensic DNA phenotyping Using existing knowledge of genotype–phenotype relations to make probabilistic predictions about physical characteristics, biogeographic origins, and age of a suspect who left biological material at a crime scene.

Fragile X syndrome The most common cause of inherited mild to moderate intellectual disability. It is caused by an expanded triplet repeat on the X-chromosome.

frameshift mutation Insertions or deletions in DNA sequence may cause a shift in reading frame of a codon during translation if the number of nucleotides inserted or deleted is not divisible by three. Such a change can produce proteins with completely different amino acid sequences downstream of the mutation.

fraternal twins Siblings born at the same time and are the result of two sperm fertilizing two eggs (i.e., dizygotic). Such twins share 50 percent of their genomes, on average.

full agonist Exogenous ligand that produces same effect as endogenous ligand on binding.

full mutation When 200 or more CGG repeats are present in the *FMR1* gene causing Fragile X syndrome.

functional magnetic resonance imaging (fMRI) Neuroimaging technique that assesses indices of neural function to understand patterns of neural activation. Study design typically includes a resting (baseline) condition and an experimental (task) condition for comparison.

gametes Germ cells that carry a haploid genetic complement that can unite in fertilization (i.e., sperm and eggs).

gel electrophoresis Technique used to estimate the size of nucleic acid or protein samples. The sample is placed into a gel substrate through which an electrical charge is run. Smaller fragments move farther than larger ones.

gene In Mendelian genetics, a hypothetical unit of inheritance responsible for the phenotype of interest.

gene expression The process by which DNA sequence is transcribed into mRNA, which is then translated into protein.

general cognitive ability Another term for intelligence.

generalize When research findings in one population provide useful information about another population.

generation A broadly used concept in the early 1800s that combined aspects of reproduction, heredity, and development and was used to explain familial resemblance.

genetic architecture Complete accounting of all genetic variants and their interactions that contribute to individual differences in a trait.

genetic code The system by which mRNA sequence specifies the start of translation, the termination of translation, or particular amino acids. Codons representing sixty-four combinations of three RNA bases (i.e., A, U, G, and C) specify twenty amino acids, a start codon, and three stop codons.

genetic determinism The view that genetic variants cause individual differences in traits and that environmental factors play little to no role. It is a fundamental aspect of eugenics.

genetic effect When individuals with different genotypes have different mean trait scores.

genetic essentialism A cognitive bias in which people consider genetic causes to be more important than other factors, and that traits influenced by genetic causes are unchangeable, fundamental, shared by all, and natural.

genetic genealogy The use of genetic information that has been uploaded to public genealogy databases to identify potential suspects in cold cases where crime scene DNA samples have been collected.

genetic markers Genetic variants of a known chromosomal location used in studies that aim to identify regions of chromosomes that are co-inherited with a disease or behavioral trait.

genetic risk The sum of alleles that increase the probability of developing a disorder (i.e., risk alleles) and those that decrease the probability (i.e., protective alleles).

genetic variance (V_G) When partitioning trait variance in a population, any variance due to additive genetic factors, dominance/recessive relations among loci, or interactions between genetic variants and environments is considered genetic variance.

genetically correlated When genetic risk factors for one phenotype also impact risk for another phenotype. In other words, two phenotypes can share risk alleles.

genome The entire genetic complement of a species or individual, both coding and non-coding sequences.

genome-wide association study (GWAS) Tests associations of many markers (typically millions) across the genome with a disorder or behavior in human participants. Sample sizes often exceed hundreds of thousands, so GWAS are typically conducted by consortia of researchers.

genotype Genetic complement at a given locus. In Mendelian genetics, genotypes often comprise the two alleles inherited from one's parents (e.g., AA, Aa, or aa).

genotype–environment correlations (GE) Genotypes are not randomly distributed across environments. Some genotypes are found more often in certain environments than in others.

germ cells Cells that carry a haploid genetic complement that can unite in fertilization (i.e., sperm and eggs).

germline Gene edits that are made in germline cells (i.e., gametes or any cells that give rise to gametes) are capable of being passed down to later generations.

germ-plasm Refers to the reproductive capacity, or gametes, of undesirables.

ghrelin Hormone that stimulates appetite that is produced in the stomach and acts in the hypothalamus.

Golgi apparatus (GA) Organelle that packages proteins into vesicles for transport.

G×E interaction When the impact of a genotype on a phenotype depends on the environment in which it is found.

haploid (n) One copy of each chromosome, such as the genetic complement of gametes.

haplotype block A region of an organism's genome where there is little evidence of recombination such that a group of alleles are typically inherited together.

helicase An enzyme that "unzips" the DNA helix to allow access for transcriptional machinery.

hemizygous A genotype carried on one allele, such as seen in males for X-chromosome-linked genotypes.

heritable A potentially problematic term in behavior genetics because it labels a specific scientific term, with a word that implies something else in non-scientific circles. Scientifically, heritable can be used to describe a trait for which the heritability is non-zero. For non-scientists, heritable means something that can be passed down intact from one generation to the next.

heterochromatin Chromatin that is tightly packed and therefore transcriptionally inactive.

heteromeric Proteins, like neurotransmitter receptors, that are composed of a mix of subunit types.

heterozygosity At a single locus, heterozygosity indicates carrying more than one allele type (e.g., Aa). When used to describe a group of individuals (e.g., an outbred line of mice) it is an index of the amount of genetic variability in that group.

heterozygous A genotype carrying different alleles, such as Aa.

histones Small proteins around which DNA is wrapped for tight packaging.

homeostasis For biological systems, the phenomenon of actively maintaining internal conditions to facilitate biological processes.

homeostatic neuroadaptation The downregulation of dopamine and opioid systems following chronic overactivation of the reward system during the binge/intoxication stage of addiction.

homologous chromosomes For a given pair of homologous chromosomes in a diploid species, one copy is paternally derived and the other maternally derived. Homologs share size, banding pattern, and sequence of genes.

homologous pair For a given pair of homologous chromosomes in a diploid species, one copy is paternally derived and the other maternally derived. Homologs share size, banding pattern, and sequence of genes.

homologous recombination A technique that enables targeted insertion of an engineered gene into a specific genomic location.

homomeric Proteins, like neurotransmitter receptors, that are composed of a single subunit type.

homozygous A genotype carrying the same allele, such as AA or aa.

humanized mouse lines Lines of mice that have been genetically engineered to carry DNA sequences of human genes to take advantage of the experimental control available when using mouse models of human behaviors or conditions.

hybrid crosses An experimental approach to genetics used by Mendel that involves controlled matings starting with parents from lines that breed true for alternative phenotypes.

hyperphagia Excessive eating due to increased appetite.

hyperpolarizing Input that increases the electrical charge difference between the inside and outside of a neuron. Such input can be considered inhibitory and may be the result of an inhibitory postsynaptic potential (IPSP).

hypofrontality Decreased activity in the dorsolateral prefrontal cortex during working memory and attention tasks typically observed in those with schizophrenia when compared to healthy controls.

hypomanic A hypomanic episode is a period of time where mood and energy are somewhat elevated, but not to the level that would qualify for a diagnosis of manic episode.

identical twins Siblings born at the same time and are the result of one sperm fertilizing one egg (i.e., monozygotic). Such twins share 100 percent of their genomes at fertilization.

imprinted inactivation A method of dosage compensation whereby the paternally inherited X-chromosome is transcriptionally silenced.

inbred strains Closed breeding groups of animals that are bred with other members of the group to reduce genetic variability within the line.

increasing allele In Fisher's polygenic model where an individual's trait score is determined by summing their genetic score across many loci, an increasing allele raises the trait score and is typically denoted by an uppercase letter (e.g., A).

indel A common class of genetic variant. The term is shorthand for insertion/deletion. Indels typically consist of DNA sequences between 1 bp and 10,000 bp.

individual differences Trait variation among members of a population. Such variation is the raw material of evolution; understanding the role of genetic variants in producing it is the focus of behavior genetics.

industrial revolution The transition from producing goods by hand to producing them by machine, the increased use of steam- and water-power, and the rise of factories.

inebriometer A paradigm to study sensitivity to the intoxicating effects of alcohol on fruit flies. Flies are exposed to ethanol vapor in the inebriometer and those that lose postural control are collected at the bottom of the device. It has been used to identify mutations that impact alcohol sensitivity.

Institutional Animal Care and Use Committee Local groups that oversee research with vertebrate, non-human animals.

Institutional Review Boards Local groups that oversee research with human participants.

intellectual disability The presence of sufficient cognitive deficits so that an individual is not keeping up with expected developmental milestones, which hampers appropriate functioning to the extent that ongoing support is required. Formerly termed mental retardation or feeblemindedness.

intelligence A construct comprising multiple components that depends on context. It has a strong focus on learning, but it also involves aspects of responding to (i.e., adapt) and manipulating (i.e., shape and select) environments.

intelligence quotient (IQ) A score derived from tests of cognitive ability that is standardized by age.

interaction variance (V_I) When partitioning genetic variance, interaction variance is due to interactions among variants at more than one locus.

intergenerational When an epigenetic modification is passed from parent to offspring.

intermediate allele When 45–54 CGG repeats are present in the *FMR1* gene. Carriers of the intermediate allele are at risk of having children with Fragile X syndrome.

intermediate phenotype A term that is sometimes used as a synonym for endophenotypes, but because it is less precise, it should be avoided.

internalizing Emotional problems that are focused inward toward the self (e.g., depression).

International Classification of Diseases Handbook used worldwide as a guide for diagnosing mental illness.

interoception An individual's perception of their own physiological state.

introns Stretches of DNA sequence that are not subsequently encoded into the protein's amino acid sequence.

inverse agonist Ligand that produces an effect opposite of the typical endogenous ligand. For example, if the endogenous ligand depolarizes, an inverse agonist hyperpolarizes.

inversions When there are two breaks in a chromosome and the genomic material between them rotates and the breaks are repaired. Such an event does not alter the overall number of bases, but reorients genomic sequence, which may affect gene expression and recombination in the region.

ionotropic receptors A type of receptor for which ligand binding opens an ion channel directly.

ions Molecules that carry an electrical charge.

isoforms Proteins that vary in amino acid sequence that may have different structure and functional properties.

isogenic A typical descriptor of lines of inbred mice in which there is no substantial genetic variation. In other words, all individuals are homozygously fixed for the same genotype.

karyotype Photographs of chromosomes stained during cell division, taken through a microscope, and arranged neatly for inspection. Alterations of chromosomal number, such as trisomy, can be identified using karyotypes.

large deletions Mutations that result in the loss of thousands of genes.

late onset Alzheimer disease (LOAD) Typical form of Alzheimer disease with onset after age 65. It does not run in families, but risk is increased for those carrying one or more copies of *APOEε4*.

Law of Independent Assortment Mendel's second law that explained patterns of inheritance observed in dihybrid crosses. It states that alleles for each trait are distributed to gametes without respect to alleles for other traits.

Law of Segregation Mendel's first law that explained patterns of inheritance observed in monohybrid crosses. It states that traits are determined by two factors and that each individual receives one factor from their father and one from their mother. Each parent generates gametes that contain a single factor for that phenotype.

Lebensborn Program In Nazi Germany, a program established to support elite SS (Schutzstaffel) members so that they could have large Aryan families. It was intended to repopulate Germany with the master race.

leptin Adipose cells produce the hormone leptin, which is part of the body's appetite control circuit. Leptin provides information about the body's current fat stores. Higher levels of leptin indicate higher levels of fat and therefore signal that the body has sufficient energy reserves. Leptin is a satiety signal (i.e., stop eating). Lower levels of leptin indicate lower fat levels and signal hunger (i.e., start eating).

level of analysis Individual differences in behavior may be the result of variation at points along pathways from molecules to society that are conceptually and methodologically distinct, each comprising an independent domain of study.

levels of analysis Pathways from genes to behaviors involve molecules, cells, circuits, physiology, and are impacted by social and cultural factors. Each of these levels can be studied using techniques and methods suited for that level, which may not translate across levels. Such complexity presents serious challenges to understanding causal heredity–behavior relations.

lifetime prevalence From epidemiology, the percentage of people in a population that meet criteria for a disorder at least once in their lives.

light-dark box Used to assess anxiety-like behavior in rodents. It consists of a compartment with two sides, one illuminated and the other not. An open door connects the two sides, and the animal is free to spend its time in either compartment. Time spent in the lighted compartment and/or the number of transitions between the two compartments is considered exploratory and is defined as less anxiety.

linkage The concept that when alleles for two different traits are located on the same chromosome they are sometimes inherited together, thereby violating Mendel's Law of Independent Assortment.

linkage analysis Research methodology used to identify stretches of chromosomes that are co-inherited with a disorder. This approach requires genetic markers throughout the genome and large pedigrees with multiple affected members. It was used to identify the genes that cause many single-gene disorders, such as cystic fibrosis.

locus A location on a chromosome.

longitudinal studies Study design that collects data from participants at more than one point in time.

loss A construct in NIMH's Research Domain Criteria that represents a state of deprivation of a motivationally significant conspecific, object, or situation.

lysosomes Membrane-bound organelles that degrade cellular waste.

magnetic resonance imaging (MRI) Imaging technique that can produce detailed images of biological structures, like the brain.

major allele The most common allele at a locus.

manic episode A manic episode is a period of time where mood and energy are highly elevated to the extent that it causes problems in social, occupational, or other areas of life.

map distance An estimate of the distance between loci on a chromosome based on observed recombination rate derived from hybridization studies.

maternal care Parental care provided by the mother.

mean Arithmetic average.

meiosis The process of producing haploid gametes from diploid cells.

meiosis I The first cell division in meiosis where one diploid parent cell divides into two diploid daughter cells.

meiosis II The second cell division in meiosis where each diploid daughter cell produced in meiosis I is divided into two haploid gametes.

membranes Phospholipid bilayers that separate intracellular from extracellular space and often carry embedded protein channels that allow some substances to cross (e.g., ions), but not others.

Mendelians Academics in the early twentieth century who focused on applying Mendelian genetics to categorical traits.

mental health services Typically consist of talk therapies, medications, and social services, and may take place in a residential facility, or in the context of outpatient visits.

mental illness Patterns of thinking, emotion, or behavior (or a combination of these) that interfere with social relationships, occupations, or other important areas of life, and which persist for an extended time and cause substantial problems and/or distress.

mental retardation Term formerly used to indicate intellectual disability.

messenger RNA (mRNA) The product of DNA transcription that is typically translated into a polypeptide chain.

meta-analysis A study design that uses data from multiple studies to take advantage of the resulting large sample size.

metabotropic receptors A type of receptor for which ligand binding has biological effects that are mediated by G-coupled proteins and second messenger systems. The majority of neurotransmitter receptors are metabotropic.

mid-parent value An estimate of offspring trait scores that is a simple average of the scores from the fathers and mothers.

minor allele The least common allele at a locus.

miscegenation Interracial mating, which was prohibited in forty-one of fifty US states and in Nazi Germany.

missense mutation Changes in DNA sequence that result in a different amino acid being placed in a polypeptide chain.

missing heritability The difference between phenotypic variance in a population that is explained by observed genetic variants (i.e., SNP heritability in a GWAS) and that is explained by heritability estimates derived from twin studies.

mitochondria Organelles that generate adenosine triphosphate (i.e., ATP), which provides energy to drive many metabolic processes via oxidative phosphorylation. Mitochondria are unique in that they contain their own genome.

mitochondrial genome Mitochondria are organelles in cells that contain their own genome comprising 16,569 base pairs (bp) of DNA.

mitosis Cell division that takes place in eukaryotic non-germ cells for the purpose of increasing the number of cells, as in growth.

mobile element insertion (MEI) Copy number variant that is the result of the actions of transposable elements, which are repetitive DNA sequences that have moved from one position in the genome to another. Repetitive sequences due

to transposable elements make up about 45 percent of the human genome.

molecular mechanisms Variation in components of biological pathways that helps to understand the causes of individual differences in behavior.

monoamine Class of small molecule neurotransmitters (e.g., serotonin) containing a single amine group.

monoamine hypothesis That the availability of certain neurotransmitters, like serotonin, play a causal role in depression.

monoamine oxidase inhibitors (MAOIs) A class of drugs with antidepressant effects that inhibit catalytic activity of monoamine oxidase.

monohybrid cross The design of a hybridization study in which the inheritance of one categorical trait is investigated.

monosomy Having a single copy of a chromosome, such as in Turner syndrome, where individuals carry one X-chromosome with no other accompanying sex chromosome.

monozygotic twin (DZ) Siblings resulting from the same pregnancy that was due to the fertilization of a single egg by a single sperm with a zygote that splits and continues development as two. Also called identical twins. With the exception of *de novo* mutations, they share the same DNA sequence.

morphological The physical form or structure of a trait (e.g., fruit fly wing shape).

mosaicism When cells in the same individual have a different genetic makeup.

multiple comparisons As more statistical tests are conducted in an analysis, the probability that a false positive association will be identified increases. The risk for finding false positives can be reduced by adjusting significance levels to account for the number of comparisons tested.

mutagenesis The generation of new mutations, often accomplished by using X-rays, chemicals, or molecular biological techniques.

mutations DNA sequence changes.

narrow sense heritability (h^2) An index of the fraction of phenotypic variance that is due to additive genetic variance in a population.

natural The property of existing in nature. Not artificial. Some consider natural things to be normal.

natural selection The mechanism by which Darwin's theory of evolution operates. Variation of traits that impact reproductive success and vary in a population can drive changes in trait expression across generations when there is competition, and the traits are at least partially determined by heredity.

nature versus nurture A false dichotomy that has characterized efforts to understand the contributions of heredity and environment to individual differences in behavior.

negative symptoms In schizophrenia, those symptoms that represent a deficit from healthy function, such as avolition (a lack of motivation).

negatively reinforcing A behavior that relieves an aversive state, and is therefore likely to be repeated, is negatively reinforcing. For example, using a drug to relieve withdrawal symptoms.

neural activity patterns Data produced by neuroimaging that seeks to identify populations of neurons that change their firing rate during some task as compared to a resting state.

neurexins A family of transmembrane proteins that are located on the presynaptic neuron that play a role in neural development and synaptic integrity. Neurexins bind to neuroligins.

neuroadaptation Neural systems homeostatically alter their structure or function to dynamically respond to challenges.

neuroendocrine cells Neurons that secrete hormones into the bloodstream.

neurogenesis The formation of new neurons.

neurolaw The use of genetic and other neuroscience evidence, such as neuroimaging, in the courtroom.

neuroligins A family of transmembrane proteins that are located on the postsynaptic neuron that play a role in neural development and synaptic integrity. Neuroligins bind to neurexins.

neurons Cells specialized for communication. They are the basic functional units of nervous systems.

neuroticism A personality trait that indexes a person's tendency to experience negative emotions such as depression, anxiety, and anger.

neurotransmitters Small molecules or peptides that are the currency of neural communication.

Next generation sequencing DNA sequencing techniques that benefit from automation, small reaction volumes, and computer software for analysis.

niche specialization A process by which a species evolves traits via natural selection that are suited to a particular environment.

non-additive genetic variance Includes variance due to dominance/recessive relations, epistatic interactions, and genotype × environment interactions.

non-conservative Mutations that cause a change in an amino acid (i.e., missense), and because the new amino acid differs in important chemical or physical properties with the old, the substitution produces substantial change in the resulting protein.

non-human animal models Species used to address research questions that are relevant to human conditions or disorders, such as mice or fruit flies. Such species are widely used in behavior genetic research because of methodological advantages and shared biology.

nonsense mutation A change in DNA sequence that specifies a stop codon instead of an amino acid.

non-shared environmental factors Non-genetic factors that tend to make members of a twin pair less similar to each other.

non-sister chromatids During meiosis, DNA replication produces a copy of the paternally derived chromosome and the maternally derived chromosome. Non-sister chromatids represent chromosome copies derived from different parents and can produce genetic diversity via recombination with each other.

normal Term to describe behavior that is either common, natural, or healthy. Can be contrasted with abnormal, which can carry negative connotations.

normal distribution The classic bell curve distribution where most observations are near the population average and fewer observations are on the extremes.

norms In social groups, behaviors or traits considered acceptable.

nuclear genome The complement of genetic information in a cell's nucleus.

nucleus Organelle that contains most of the cell's genome (except for mitochondrial DNA) and is where DNA is transcribed into mRNA.

Nuremberg Laws Made it illegal for anyone of "German or related blood" to marry or to have sexual intercourse with anyone from another group, including Jews, Gypsies, blacks, or their offspring.

nutrition transition A theoretical model describing historical changes in food availability driven by increases in modernization, urbanization, economic development, and increased wealth.

obesity A condition in which excess body fat increases risk for health problems. Defined as a body mass index (BMI) $\geq$ 30.

obesogenic Environments that facilitate obesity, in which low levels of physical activity are coupled with virtually unlimited access to energy-dense food.

obsessions Repetitive and persistent thoughts, images, or impulses/urges that are intrusive, unwanted, and are commonly associated with anxiety.

oligonucleotides Relatively short (i.e., around 15–25 bp) synthetic nucleotide sequences that can be designed to bind to specific complementary DNA sequences. Oligonucleotides can be used as primers, which serve as the starting point for copying a DNA template.

one drop rule When a person may be considered black when they have even a single black ancestor.

operational definition In research methodology, a way to specify how a theoretical construct will actually be measured.

organelles Cellular structures that carry out specific functions such as protein production, storage and transport, the production of energy, and the removal of wastes.

outbred strains Groups of animals where the level of genetic variation is maintained at a level that is similar to naturally breeding groups of the same species.

ovists Those who believed that ova contain preformed embryos and therefore that mothers were primarily responsible for producing offspring.

oxytocin A peptide hormone that plays an important role in social behaviors.

pangenesis Darwin's disproven theory of the mechanism of heredity.

parasympathetic nervous system Component of the autonomic nervous system that conserves energy and enables the body to recuperate (i.e., rest and digest).

parental generation The first generation in hybrid crosses. Parental generation individuals are typically from lines that breed true for the trait of interest.

parental types Refers to phenotypes of offspring in hybrid crosses that are indistinguishable from the phenotypes of the parental lines.

partial agonist Exogenous ligand that produces same effect as endogenous ligand on binding, but to a lesser extent.

passive genotype–environment correlation Offspring genotypes are provided by parents, as are the environments in which they are found. Such associations are passive with respect to the offspring contribution.

paternal care Parental care provided by the father.

pedigree A diagram of a family that indicates relationships, sex, and affected status. They can be used to determine whether a trait is inherited in Mendelian fashion.

penetrance The probability of showing the trait if you carry the risk allele.

pentameric Protein, such as a neurotransmitter receptor, composed of five subunits.

perikaryon Cell body of a neuron.

pharmacodynamics The actions of drugs on their biological targets.

pharmacogenetics The role of genetic variation, on the scale of a few genotypes, in drug pharmacokinetics or pharmacodynamics.

pharmacogenomics The role of genetic variation, on the scale of many genotypes, in drug pharmacokinetics or pharmacodynamics.

pharmacokinetics The movement of drugs into, throughout, and out of the body.

pharmacology The field of biomedicine that studies how drugs produce their effects and how to use drugs to treat disease.

phenotype The observed trait of interest.

phenotypic variance (V_P) A statistical measure that indexes the amount of variation there is in a population on the trait in question.

phospholipid bilayer Structural element of membranes comprising two layers of a phosphate head and two fatty acid chains.

physical activity Movement produced by skeletal muscles and which requires the expenditure of energy. It includes a broad range of movements from fidgeting while you sit at your desk to running an ultra-marathon.

physiological measures Bodily measures such as heart rate or blood pressure can be used to assess emotional experience in research.

pleiotropy When one genetic variant is associated with more than on trait.

point mutations A change in DNA sequence that only affects a single nucleotide base.

point prevalence From epidemiology, the percentage of people in a population that meet criteria for a disorder at a given point in time (e.g., last year).

pollen Sperm containing gametes of male plants.

polygenes Fisher hypothesized that for quantitative traits there are many loci that each contribute a small amount to phenotypic variance in a population. It is these polygenes, acting in an additive fashion with some associated with an increase in the trait and others a decrease, that can be passed on from one generation to the next.

polygenic risk scores Sum scores that are meant to aggregate the impact of multiple genetic variants.

polymerase chain reaction (PCR) A technique to copy DNA that uses cycles of three temperatures to break apart the double helix of the DNA template (i.e., denaturation), enables oligonucleotide primers to bind to their complementary DNA target sequence (i.e., annealing), and enables the DNA polymerase to add complementary nucleotides to make copies of the template.

population stratification In a case-control study, when allele frequencies in the two groups differ for reasons other than their association with the condition in question.

population thinking The recognition that trait variation in a population is the raw material of evolution and therefore immensely valuable.

positive symptoms In schizophrenia, those symptoms that represent an addition to healthy function, such as hallucinations.

positively reinforcing A behavior that produces a pleasurable feeling, and is therefore likely to be repeated, is positively reinforcing. For example, using a drug because you like its euphoric effects.

positron emission tomography (PET) Neuroimaging method that uses radioactive chemicals (e.g., ligands, or glucose) injected into the bloodstream to assess availability of neurotransmitter binding sites (e.g., receptors) or energy use by neurons.

precision medicine An approach to treating a patient that takes into account their specific situation and their biology (e.g., genotypes) to tailor an individualized therapy, rather than to use an approach that works for most people, on average.

preference ratios In a two-bottle choice test, preference ratios (volume alcohol solution/total volume of fluid consumed) higher than 50 percent indicate a preference for the alcohol solution.

preformationist Theory that one parent contributes nearly everything necessary to produce offspring and that the other parent either serves only to initiate the reproductive process or to nourish and house the offspring.

premutation When 55–200 CGG repeats are present in the *FMR1* gene. Carriers of the premutation are at risk of having children with Fragile X syndrome.

primary investigators Researchers who lead projects. In behavior genetics, most primary investigators are employed by universities or research hospitals.

primary transcript The initial mRNA product of DNA transcription.

primers Oligonucleotide primers provide specificity to DNA copying because their sequence can be used to define a unique genomic sequence for binding. Most primers used in polymerase chain reactions are between eighteen and twenty-five bases in length.

private damaging mutations Mutations that are found in only one individual, likely the result of *de novo* mutation, that have a negative impact on the function of the gene.

proactive aggression Planned aggression that involves an anticipated reward.

proband The individual of interest in a pedigree. Also known as the index case.

probes Oligonucleotide probes have nucleic acid sequences that enable them to bind to complementary DNA sequence. Probes typically have a reporter construct attached to them so that investigators can determine which probe binds to the DNA to identify the underlying DNA sequence.

process model A theoretical model that describes strategies for emotion regulation that can be employed at different stages in the experience of an emotion.

protective alleles Genetic variants that are associated with decreased risk for a disorder.

proteins Large biomolecules composed of chains of amino acids that are involved in the structure, function, and regulation of cells.

Psychiatric Genomics Consortium A large group of researchers who are working together to understand the biological risk for developing mental illness.

psychoactive substances Drugs that act in the brain and can affect perception, thinking, motivation, emotion, and behavior.

psychopharmacology The subfield of pharmacology in which the focus is on drugs used to treat mental illness.

pulse song A component of *Drosophila* courtship behavior in which males vibrate a wing in high frequency bursts interspersed with periods of silence. The pulse songs of different species are characterized by different inter-pulse intervals.

Punnett square A useful way to illustrate hybrid crosses to estimate expected genotype and phenotype composition of offspring. Developed by Reginald Punnett.

purines Nucleic acids with a two-ring structure (i.e., adenine and guanine).

pyrimidines Nucleic acids with a one-ring structure (i.e., thymine, cytosine, and uracil).

qualitative traits Traits that vary dimensionally in populations, like height.

quantitative trait loci (QTL) Theoretically QTL represent polygenes. They are identified in so-called QTL studies in non-human animal models, such as mice, in which genetic markers located across the genome are measured in two isogenic parental lines and in their F_2 generation hybrids and subsequently tested for association with behavioral differences.

quantitative traits Traits that vary categorically in populations, like eye color.

racial essentialism The belief that certain physical trait differences between groups of people are true indicators of unobservable and immutable properties for which groups naturally vary in hierarchical fashion.

racial hygiene Perspective that it is important to keep races pure by prohibiting marriages and sexual relations between people of different races.

racism Consists of beliefs, actions, social norms, and laws that assert the superiority of one group over another. The definition of the relevant groups in question (i.e., races) is not fixed, but historically has relied on physical attributes, such as skin color, or country of origin.

rare allele Alleles are typically considered rare if they occur at a frequency of less than 1 percent in a population.

reaction times A basic outcome measure in cognitive psychology. Reaction times can be precisely measured and can index inferred cognitive processing.

reactive aggression Aggression in response to perceived threats or provocation.

realized heritability In a selection study or breeding program, realized heritability can be estimated by observing the actual changes in the trait distribution across generations of selective breeding. It is the ratio of the selection response to the selection differential.

receptor availability An index of the number of receptor sites that can potentially bind a ligand.

receptors Proteins to which ligands, such as neurotransmitters, can bind that produces biological action.

recessive When two copies of an allele are required to produce the phenotype.

reciprocal cross If a cross involves mating males from the first parental line to females from the second parental line (i.e., P1♂ × P2♀), its reciprocal would involve male P2 × female P1 (i.e., P2♂ × P1♀).

recombinant inbred lines Are derived from F_2 generation progeny of parental lines that vary on some phenotype of interest. A single recombinant inbred line is produced by first mating one F2 generation male with an F_2 generation female and then practicing brother–sister matings within that line.

recombinant types Refers to phenotypes of offspring in dihybrid crosses that are combinations of the phenotypes of interest that were not observed in parental lines.

recombination breakpoints The point at which, during meiosis, crossing over results in physical detachment of one chromosomal segment before it can attach to the same point on its homologous chromosome.

recombination rate Can be estimated by calculating the percentage of recombinant types observed in backcross progeny.

ref SNP Naming convention for human single nucleotide polymorphisms that includes the prefix "rs" with a unique identification number. The "rs" stands for reference SNP.

refractory period After an action potential, the period during which a subsequent action potential is either impossible (i.e., absolute) or would require greater than normal depolarization (i.e., relative).

regression analysis A standard statistical method to estimate relationships between predictive factors and an outcome.

reification When an abstract idea becomes thought of as a real biological entity. For example, diagnostic categories may be useful for identifying and treating people who have mental illness, but they may not represent distinct biological conditions.

reliable A concept in research methodology that indexes the capacity of a measure to provide repeated, accurate assessments.

research consortia Groups of researchers who work together to conduct large-scale studies, such as genome-wide association studies, that require sample sizes too large to be collected by a single researcher.

Research Domain Criteria (RDoC) The National Institute of Mental Health effort to understand mental illness risk by studying endophenotypes.

resident-intruder test A commonly used, standardized experimental design to assess aggression in rodents. A "resident" is housed in an enclosure for sufficient time to establish it as its "home cage," and then an unknown "intruder" rodent is introduced into the cage.

response to selection The difference in the mean score of the first selected generation (S1) individuals from the overall population mean in generation 0. It indexes phenotypic change across generations.

resting potential The difference in electrical charge between the inside and the outside of a neuron when the neuron is not being stimulated or transmitting an action potential.

restriction endonucleases Enzymes that cut double-stranded DNA at specific target sequences. These restriction enzymes can be used to cut PCR products to distinguish between alleles when one allele contains the restriction site and the other does not.

restriction fragment length polymorphisms (RFLPs) When one allele of a PCR product contains a restriction site that enables cutting by a restriction endonuclease and the alternative allele does not. The allele that is cut will migrate differently than the uncut allele in gel electrophoresis.

reuptake The removal of neurotransmitter from a synapse via presynaptic transporter proteins.

ribonucleic acid (RNA) A class of molecules involved in gene expression and many other biological processes. It is single-stranded. RNA is the genetic material of some organisms like viruses.

risk allele When one allele is associated with a higher likelihood of a condition than an alternative allele it is labeled a risk allele.

risk indicators Traits that are predictors of a disorder.

RNA polymerase An enzyme involved in copying RNA.

rough endoplasmic reticulum (RER) Organelle in which translation of mRNA to protein occurs.

runner's high After episodes of intense aerobic exercise, such as long-distance running, some people report that they experience feelings of euphoria, relief from anxiety, and reduced ability to feel pain.

running wheel A simple device commonly used to assess voluntary running in rodents. It comprises a wheel suspended by an axel that rotates when the rodent runs while inside.

sampling bias Methodological fault in studies that obtain participants from unrepresentative groups. When unrepresentative samples are studied, the findings may not conform with those from studies that draw participants from a more representative sample.

Sanger sequencing A chain-termination DNA sequencing technique uses special dNTPs (i.e., dideoxynucleotide triphosphate or ddNTP) that once incorporated into the newly copied DNA strand interfere with the addition of more bases. It was the most common method of DNA sequencing for decades.

scientific racism Racism developed into scientific racism when leading academics of the day asserted that traits like feeblemindedness followed Mendelian inheritance patterns in human families. The scientific establishment was explaining the heredity of complex human traits in simple Mendelian terms without carefully considering other potential factors that could influence the traits such as socioeconomic status or acculturation. It represents the misuse of scientific evidence to support the ranking of races.

second filial generation In hybrid crosses between parental lines P1 and P2, the first generation of offspring is called the first filial generation, or F_1. When F_1 generation offspring are mated together, their offspring are called the second filial generation, or F_2.

sedentary Pattern of behavior characterized by much sitting and little physical activity or exercise.

selection differential The difference in the mean trait score between those selected to be parents and the entire population. It illustrates how different those selected to be parents are from the population as whole.

selective breeding An approach used in agriculture or scientific studies with the aim of changing the distribution of a trait in subsequent generations. It involves controlling which individuals mate to produce offspring to make up the next generation. To determine which individuals will become parents, all eligible individuals should first be phenotyped for the trait of interest. Only those who display the desired trait should be allowed to reproduce.

selective permeability A property whereby some substances are capable of crossing membranes, but not others.

selective serotonin reuptake inhibitors (SSRIs) Antidepressant drugs that interfere with the reuptake of serotonin from the synapse.

self-report An approach to collecting data that asks human participants to respond to questions about their own traits or history.

semantic memories Memories of specific facts, such as your home address, or the name of the current President of the United States.

semiconservative replication The copying of double-stranded DNA whereby the new strands each contain one old strand and one newly copied strand.

sense strand During transcription, the double helix DNA is unzipped and it is the sense strand that serves as the template for transcription.

sensitivity alleles Proposed by differential sensitivity hypothesis to be genetic variants that are responsive to both negative and positive exposures.

sex chromosomes The non-autosomal chromosomes that play a role in sex determination (e.g., X and Y).

sex-linked When a phenotype is determined by a genotype found on the X-chromosome, it is known as a sex-linked phenotype.

sexual orientation Characterized by the sex of individuals to whom someone is sexually attracted.

sexual selection The evolution of sexual dimorphism in morphological and behavioral traits can be driven by the choosy sex's preferences when individual differences in traits are at least partially due to genetic differences between them. For example, the male bowerbird's elaborately constructed and decorated bowers have evolved as a result of female bowerbirds preferring to mate with males that construct more attractive bowers.

shared environmental factors When partitioning variance in a population, those non-genetic factors that tend to be associated with increased phenotypic similarity.

shock avoidance Experimental paradigm to study depression-like behavior in non-human animal models that assesses an individual's speed of moving to a safe area after a period in a compartment where they had previously received shocks.

silent mutation DNA sequence variations in a gene's coding region that do not result in a different amino acid in the encoded polypeptide.

sine song A component of *Drosophila* courtship behavior in which males vibrate a wing with varying frequencies that resemble the regular oscillation of a sine wave when viewed on an oscilloscope.

single nucleotide polymorphism (SNP) The most common type of variant in the human genome. It is a DNA sequence difference of one base.

sister chromatids During meiosis, DNA replication produces a copy of the paternally derived chromosome and the maternally derived chromosome. Sister chromatids represent chromosome copies derived from the same parent.

smooth endoplasmic reticulum (SER) Organelle involved in vesicular transport of proteins.

SNP heritability The proportion of variation in a trait in a population that is accounted for by the additive contribution of all observed single nucleotide polymorphisms in a genome-wide association study.

sociability The drive to interact with others.

social behaviors Any behaviors that involve others of the same species.

social cognition Involves thinking about and communicating with others and includes an understanding that other individuals have their own minds.

Social Darwinism The view that providing social supports for the poor impedes the progression of evolution because with such charity the unfit

survive and multiply, and without it they do not. It was only when these artificial supports are removed that natural selection can act to cull the unfit, which would lead to progress toward higher levels. Allowing the unfit to survive and multiply diminishes the overall fitness of the population and leads to its stagnation or degeneration.

social desirability A biased pattern of participant responses to personal questions motivated by the desire to avoid portraying themselves negatively.

social recognition memory Social animals interact with certain individuals on a recurring basis so that the capacity to recognize individuals and have a memory of interactions with them facilitates ongoing social relationships.

sodium potassium pump An integral membrane protein that ejects three sodium ions (Na+) and takes in two potassium ions (K+) each time it operates in neurons. It helps to maintain neurons' resting potential.

somatic Gene edits that are made to somatic cells (i.e., body cells that do not produce gametes) which cannot be passed down to later generations.

specific learning disorder A diagnosis that reflects an impairment in reading, writing, or mathematical skill learning in childhood.

spliced After transcription, the primary mRNA transcript may undergo processing that can include the excision of intron or exon sequence. The remaining exons are then joined, or spliced, together to form a mature mRNA transcript that is ready for translation.

stabilizing selection When extreme expressions of a trait are selected against, the population maintains a stable, intermediate mean.

standard deviation An index of the spread of a distribution. For a normally distributed trait, approximately 68 percent of individuals fall within 1 standard deviation (s.d.) of the population mean, 95 percent of individuals fall within 2 s.d., and nearly everyone falls within 3 s.d.

stigma The structure of a plant where the pollen germinates.

stop codons Three codons that signal the termination of translation, UAA, UAG, and UGA.

stressor Anything that activates the body's stress response system.

strong genetic explanation Requires the identification and characterization of a specific genetic mechanism that accounts for the behavioral differences. Such an explanation necessarily involves biological components other than genes and can be considered causal.

subjective mental state Inner experience that is the product of physical feelings, behaviors, and thoughts.

sympathetic nervous system Component of the autonomic nervous system that prepares the body to deal with challenges (i.e., fight or flight).

symptom heterogeneity When individuals with the same diagnosis have different symptoms. It is a complicating factor in efforts to understand the biology underlying the disorder.

synapse The space between a presynaptic neuron terminal and a postsynaptic cell.

synaptic cell adhesion molecules Protein structures that allow presynaptic and postsynaptic cells to maintain the structural integrity of the synaptic gap.

synaptic integrity Proper synaptic physical conformation to facilitate neurotransmission.

synaptogenesis Formation of new synapses.

synaptopathology Diseases caused by synaptic dysfunction.

syndromic obesity Obesity that is a symptom of a disorder, such as in Prader-Willi syndrome.

synteny The sharing of gene order on chromosomes across species.

tail suspension test Research paradigm in which rodents are suspended by taping their tail to a hook or a rod across the top of a small chamber. The time that the animal spends immobile is the index of behavioral despair.

Taq polymerase A thermostable enzyme derived from bacteria that live in hot springs (*Thermus aquaticus*) widely used in molecular biology.

target sample In a two-stage study design to test the association of genetic variants to behaviors, risk alleles are first identified in a sample of participants (i.e., discovery sample), which is independent of another sample in which they are subsequently tested when combined into a polygenic risk score (i.e., the target sample).

thermalcycler Machines to change temperatures accurately and rapidly that are commonly used in molecular biology labs for polymerase chain reaction.

thrifty genotype hypothesis Hypothesis to explain the increase in obesity across human history, wherein individual differences in preference for high-fat and high-calorie foods, the capacity to eat large meals, and efficiency in storing excess calories as fat were partially due to genetic differences. Thrifty genotypes were hypothesized to be selectively advantageous during periods of feast and famine, but deleterious during times of food abundance.

tolerance A symptom of substance use disorder whereby more of the substance is needed to achieve the same effect than was necessary when use was initiated.

transcription factors A class of DNA-binding proteins that facilitate transcription.

transfer RNAs RNA molecule that carries an anticodon to recognize a complementary mRNA sequence and a corresponding amino acid that will be added to the growing polypeptide chain during translation.

transgenerational When epigenetic regulation is passed across multiple generations (i.e., beyond first-generation offspring). Such inheritance of epigenetic regulation is not thought to be common.

transgenic An organism that carries genetic material from an unrelated organism. For example, transgenic mice can be engineered to carry DNA sequences derived from humans.

translation The process by which mRNA sequence is used to determine sequence of amino acids in a growing polypeptide chain, thereby building proteins.

transporters Integral membrane proteins that facilitate the movement of neurotransporters across membranes.

trauma Any experience that produces significant disturbance and feelings of anxiety or fear to have long-lasting impact on a person's health.

trinucleotide repeat Three-base sequence that is present in multiple copies in a stretch of DNA. For example, CGG is repeated from 6 to over 200 times on the X-chromosome.

triplet repeat expansions Chromosomal regions containing variable numbers of trinucleotide repeats that may produce increased repeat numbers across generations, and are associated with disorders such as Fragile X, Huntington's disease or Friedreich's ataxia.

trisomy Having three copies of a chromosome.

Trisomy 21 Genetic condition that can be identified by karyotype inspection whereby thee copies of chromosome 21 are present. Trisomy 21 causes Down syndrome.

twin study The most commonly used method for estimating heritability in human populations. The basic design assesses phenotypic similarity for pairs of monozygotic and dizygotic twins.

two-bottle choice test Research paradigm to study alcohol preference in rodents that provides access to two drinking bottles, one containing plain water and another that contains an ethanol solution.

typological thinking An assumption that trait variation in a population represents deviation from an ideal type.

valid A concept in research methodology that addresses the extent to which a measurement is appropriate for the intended construct.

variance A statistical term that indexes individual differences in the trait of interest.

varieties Plants of different varieties (or lines) breed true for specific phenotypes.

vesicles A structure within a cell that temporarily stores neurotransmitters for transport to the terminal and eventual release into the synapse.

vivisection The practice of conducting surgery on live animals for research purposes.

weak genetic explanation Refers to the simple observation that genetic differences between people are statistically associated with individual differences in behavior.

wild-type The most commonly occurring phenotype is sometimes called the wild-type, such as red eyes in fruit flies. Whereas white eyes are a mutant phenotype.

Williams syndrome A disorder resulting from a deletion of 28 genes on chromosome 7 characterized by hyper-sociability, including decreased social anxiety.

Williams syndrome critical region A region on chromosome 7 (7q11.23) containing 28 genes, the deletion of which causes Williams syndrome.

withdrawal A suite of aversive effects that occurs sometime after cessation of substance use.

working memory A type of memory for active maintenance of information relevant for current goal or task. Individual differences in working memory capacity exist and are related to capacity for higher level thought, similar to the way that more random-access memory (RAM) in your computer enables you to run more applications at the same time.

X-linked dominant A pattern of inheritance in a pedigree in which affected fathers can pass on the trait to their daughters, but not to their sons. Affected mothers can pass on the trait to children of either sex equally.

X-linked recessive A pattern of inheritance in a pedigree in which the frequency of the trait is higher in males than in females.

zygote An egg fertilized by a sperm produces a diploid cell that is the first stage in development.

Index

Page numbers in bold indicate Glossary items

3q29 microdeletion
  schizophrenia risk factor, 159–160
5-HT, *See* serotonin
23andMe, *See* direct-to-consumer genetic testing

abnormal, **372**
activator proteins, 81, **372**
active genotype–environment correlation, **372**
addiction, 248
  brain structures involved in, 132–135
  diagnosing substance use disorders, 251–252
  heritability of substance use disorders, 264
  lay understanding of, 248
  prevalence of substance use, 248–250
  prevalence of substance use disorders, 249–252
  psychoactive substances, 248, 250
  withdrawal syndromes, 251
addiction neurobiology
  activation of the brain reward system, 254
  anhedonia and risk of relapse, 254
  binge/intoxication stage, 254–255
  compulsive drug-seeking behavior, 256–257
  craving, 256–257
  development of tolerance, 254–255
  downregulation of the brain reward system, 254–255
  homeostatic neuroadaptation, 254–255
  negative reinforcement, 255–256
  nucleus accumbens and the reward pathway, 255
  positive reinforcement, 254
  preoccupation/anticipation stage, 256–257
  stages of, 254
  withdrawal/negative affect stage, 255–256
additive genetic effects, **372**
additive genetic variance, 52
adenine, 79
adenosine triphosphate (ATP), 119, **372**
adoption studies, **372**
  estimating heritability in humans, 63
affiliation, **372**

affiliation and attachment
  autism spectrum disorder, 317–319
  definition of affiliation, 314
  definition of attachment, 315
  individual differences and variation in oxytocin genes, 315–316
  oxytocin knockout mice, 316
  oxytocin system variants as candidate genes, 316–317
  Research Domain Criteria (RDoC) construct, 314
  role of oxytocin, 314–319
aggression, 324–326
  Brunner syndrome, 324
  genes associated with human aggression, 326
  genetic variation and individual differences, 324–326
  measuring aggressive behavior, 324–325
  proactive aggression, 324
  range of aggressive behaviors, 324
  reactive aggression, 324
  stabilizing selection, 324
aggressive behaviors, **372**
agonistic behavior, 308–309, **372**
agonists, 136, **372**
agricultural revolution, 352, **372**
alcohol dehydrogenases (ADHs), 265
  alcoholism risk and protective mutations, 266
alcohol dependence (ICD-11), 253
alcohol flushing response, **372**
  alcoholism risk and, 265–267
alcohol use
  prevalence of, 249–250
alcohol use disorder
  alcohol dependence (ICD-11), 253
  alcohol flushing response and alcoholism risk, 265–267
  brain structures involved in addiction, 263
  candidate gene studies, 270–271
  diagnosing, 251–252
  ethanol metabolism, 265

familial nature of alcohol problems, 262–264

genetically engineered mouse models, 261

genome-wide association studies, 271–272

heredity and alcohol-related behavior in fruit flies (*D. melanogaster*), 261–262

heritability estimate, 264

high- and low-drinking rat lines, 267–269

influence of alcohol metabolizing genes, 265–269

large number of genes contribute to risk, 269–272

measures of family history, 262–263

non-human animal models, 257–262

prevalence of, 249–252

prospective longitudinal studies of alcoholism risk, 263

QTL (quantitative trait loci) mapping in rodents, 259–261

risk and protective mutations in ADH, 266

rodent strain comparisons for alcohol preference, 257–259

withdrawal syndrome, 251

aldehyde dehydrogenases (ALDHs), 265

alexithymia, 196, **372**

all-or-none action potentials, **372**

alleles of a gene, 33, **372**

alloparental care, **372**

alternative splicing of mRNA, 82, **372**

Alzheimer disease, 119, 180, **372**

age at onset, 184–190

amyloid plaques, 185–187, 189

burden of disease, 185–190

cause of neurocognitive disorder, 184

dementia due to Alzheimer disease (ICD-11), 185

diagnosis, 185–187

early and late onset variants, 187–189

genetic variants associated with risk for, 187–189

neurofibrillary tangles, 185, 189

non-human animal models, 189

prevalence, 184

risk related to apolipoprotein E (APOE) variants, 187–189

role of APP (amyloid precursor protein) processing, 185–188

role of the KIBRA protein in memory formation, 180–182

signs and symptoms, 185–187

tau protein, 189

Trisomy 21 (Down syndrome) risk factor, 174–175, 185–187

using genetic information in diagnosis, 185–187

Alzheimer disease risk

direct-to-consumer genetic testing, 333

amino acids, **372**

chemical structures of, 81

effects of altered amino acid sequences, 100–101

how DNA nucleotide bases code for amino acids, 83–84

process of constructing proteins, 81–84

sequence in proteins is specified by DNA sequence, 81–84

types of, 81

amnion, **372**

amygdala

genetic differences in activation in response to threat, 197–198

role in processing emotional information, 197–198

role in response to threats, 223

amyloid plaques, 185–187, 189, **372**

ancestral reference populations, **372**

ancestry reports

direct-to-consumer genetic testing, 334–336

aneuploidy, 99, **373**

Angelman syndrome, 87

anhedonia, **373**

animal models. *See* non-human animal models

animalculists, 26–27, **373**

annealing (in PCR), **373**

anorexia nervosa. *See* eating disorders

antagonists, 136, **373**

anticodons, 82, **373**

antisocial alcoholism, **373**

antisocial personality disorder, 264

anxiety, **373**

behaviors associated with, 223–225

defensive circuits provide information about potential threats, 223

defensive response to threat, 222–223

definition of, 222–223

effects of domestication, 228–229

genetics of fear and anxiety in mice, 225–226

individual differences in public-speaking anxiety, 222

anxiety (cont.)
    research paradigms, 223–225
    role of HPA axis components, 227–228
    role of the GABA neurotransmitter system,
        226–227
    role of the serotonin transporter system, 227
anxiety disorders, 174
    anxiety and fear-related disorders (ICD-11),
        232
    candidate gene association studies, 234–235
    familial inheritance, 234
    generalized anxiety disorder, 232
    genome-wide association studies, 235–236
    Million Veteran Program, 235–236
    obsessive-compulsive or related disorders
        (ICD-11), 237
    polygenic nature, 234
    prevalence of, 231–233
    types of, 231–232
anxiety-related personality traits
    candidate gene association studies and GWAS,
        230–231
    heritability estimates, 229–230
    phenotypes for genetic analysis, 229–231
    study of neuroticism, 229–231
apolipoprotein E (APOE) variants
    Alzheimer disease risk, 187–189
apoptosis, 126, **373**
applied research, **373**
appraisal, **373**
Aryans, **373**
ataxia, **373**
attachment, **373**
attachment styles, 308, **373**
        See also affiliation and attachment
attention bias, 225, **373**
attention-deficit/hyperactivity disorder (ADHD), 172,
    174, 203
autism spectrum disorder, 162, 172, 174–175, 203,
    317–319, **373**
    genetic influences, 317–319
    heritability estimates, 317
    ICD-11 diagnosis, 319
    potential genetic risk factors, 126–128
    prevalence, 317
autonomic nervous system, 196, 223
autosomal dominant inheritance, 42–43, **373**
autosomal recessive inheritance, 43–44, **373**
autosomes, 37, 73, **373**

Avery, Oswald, 77
axon, **373**
axon hillock, **373**
axon terminal, **373**

backcross, 38–41, **373**
Bakewell, Robert
    strategy for breeding sheep, 28
basal metabolism, 281, **373**
basic research, **373**
Bateson, William, 46
BDNF (brain-derived neurotrophic factor)
    role in depressive disorders, 216
BDNF (brain-derived neurotrophic factor) gene, 135
behavior genetics, **373**
    applied research, 331
    approach to mental illness research, 149–153
    avoiding oversimplification of effects of
        genetic variation, 15
    basic research, 331
    caution about the interpretation of heritability
        estimates, 369
    combination of genetic and environmental
        variations, 12
    defining a gene, 91–92
    essential role of non-human animal models,
        16–20
    ethical limits with human participants, 16–17
    ethical oversight of research, 20–22
    focus on individual differences, 10
    identifying gene–behavior associations, 14–15
    importance of genetic variation, 94
    influence of genomic sequence variation on
        behavior, 91–92
    levels of analysis, 13–15
    molecular mechanisms of pathways from gene
        to behavior, 14–15
    population thinking versus typological
        thinking, 12–13
    racial differences are not the focus, 369
    real-life applications, 331
    reliable and valid measures of behavior, 10–11
    research findings and future developments,
        345–348
    responsibility to respect human rights, 369
    role in eugenics, 351
    role of genes in behavior, 14–15
    shared evolutionary history across species,
        17–19

strong genetic explanation, 346–347

testing for genetic differences between individuals, 11–15

three basic types of questions for researchers, 14–15

use of convergent evidence, 16

weak genetic explanation, 346–347

behavior genetics studies

emotions, 198–199

behavioral studies, **373**

emotions, 198

behaviorism, 8–9

bell curve. *See* normal distribution

Bell, Alexander Graham, 358

Belyaev, Dmitri, 228

benzodiazepines, 226

Big Science, 198

binding affinity, 136, **373**

Binet-Simon test, 363

binge drinking, **374**

bioavailability of drugs, 137, **374**

biomedical research

impact of the Human Genome Project, 113–115

Biometricians, 46–47, **374**

bipolar and related disorders

characteristics, 201

diagnosis of Bipolar type I disorder (ICD-11), 202

familial inheritance, 202

genetic correlation across psychiatric disorders, 202–203

genetic risk factors, 202–203

heritability, 202

ICD-11 diagnosis, 201

polygenic traits, 202–203

prevalence of, 202

private damaging mutations, 163

black-backed jackal (*Canis mesomelas*), 309

blending inheritance, 32, **374**

blood alcohol concentration, **374**

Bloomington Drosophila Stock Center, 41–42, 183

body dysmorphic disorder, 237

body mass index (BMI), 284–285, **374**

body-focused repetitive behavior disorders, 237

bonobo (*Pan paniscus*), 170

brain

structures involved in addiction, 263

brain development

apoptosis process, 126

impact of genetic variations on neurological functions, 126–128

neurogenesis, 126

synaptogenesis, 126

brain reward system, **374**

brain structure

impacts of genetic variation, 132–135

bred true, **374**

breeding true, 31

Bridges, Calvin, 41

broad sense heritability, **374**

Brunner syndrome, 324, **374**

Buck v. Bell eugenics test case (1927), 360–362

Buck, Carrie, 360–362

bulimia nervosa. *See* eating disorders

Burbank, Luther, 358

calories, **374**

cancer risk reports

direct-to-consumer genetic testing, 334

candidate gene association studies, 108, 132, **374**

candidate genes, **374**

Canis lupus familiaris, *See* dog

Capecchi, Mario R., 111

Carnegie, Andrew, 357–358

carrier screening

direct-to-consumer genetic testing, 333

Celera Genomics, 113

Celexa, 137

cell division

producing diploid cells by mitosis, 76–77

producing haploid gametes by meiosis, 74–76

cells

basic cellular functions, 117–119

cytoplasm, 117

Golgi apparatus, 119

lysosomes, 119

membrane, 117–118

mitochondria, 119

nucleus, 119

organelles, 117

rough endoplasmic reticulum, 119

smooth endoplasmic reticulum, 119

centimorgans (cM), 41, **374**

central nervous system, **374**

centromere, **374**

Chase, Martha, 78

childhood maltreatment, **374**
  risk factor for negative outcomes, 307–308
chorion, **374**
chromatids, 74–75, **374**
chromatin, 86, **374**
chromatin remodeling, 81, **374**
chromosomal theory of inheritance, 37
chromosomes, **374**
  aneuploidy, 99
  autosomes, 73
  centromere, 74–75
  chromatids, 74–75
  chromosomal theory of inheritance, 73
  dosage compensation, 87
  homologous pairs, 74
  human karyotype, 74
  imprinted inactivation, 87
  making copies by DNA replication, 80
  mapping relative positions of genes on, 36–41
  meiosis (producing haploid gametes), 74–76
  mitosis (producing diploid cells), 76–77
  nature of human chromosome 21, 175
  non-allelic homologous recombination, 314
  physical basis of Mendelian inheritance, 73
  prevalence of chromosomal abnormalities in
    humans, 174
  recombination (crossing over) during meiosis,
    75–76
  role of DNA, 77–79
  sex chromosomes, 73
  structure and functions, 73–77
  X-chromosome inactivation, 87
citalopram, 137
civil rights movement
  impact of eugenics, 368
classical conditioning, 254
ClinVar database (NCBI), 332
codons, 83–84, **374**
Cold Spring Harbor Laboratory, 358
Collins, Francis, 113
color vision deficiency
  X-linked recessive inheritance pattern, 44
comorbidity, **374**
complementary base pairing, **374**
complementation test, 282, **375**
compulsions, **375**
compulsive behavior, **375**
COMT (catechol-O-methyltransferase) gene, 135
concentration camps, **375**

concordance, **375**
conditional knockout techniques, 111, **375**
conservative mutations, **375**
convergent evidence, 16, **375**
  role in understanding heredity–behavior
    relations, 101
copy number variants, 98, **375**
  detection and measurement, 106–107
  schizophrenia risk, 159–160
corticotrophin hormone receptor gene (*CRHR1*)
    variants, 231
courtship behavior, 308, **375**
COVID-19
  rapid development of mRNA vaccines, 115
CpG islands in DNA, 86, **375**
craving, **375**
Crick, Francis, 78
CRISPR-Cas9 technique, 111–112, **375**
cross-fostering designs, **375**
cross-sectional studies, **375**
crossing over, **375**
crossover events during gamete formation, 39–41
crossover interaction, 54–56, **375**
culture
  differences in emotions, 194
cystic fibrosis, 333
cytochrome P 450 enzymes, **375**
  genetic variability, 139–140
cytoplasm, **375**
cytosine, 79

Darwin, Charles, 4, 6, 195, 228
  natural selection in human populations, 352–353
  theory of evolution, 4–5, 354
Davenport, Charles, 358, 364, 366
de novo mutations, **375**
declarative memories, 179, **376**
decreasing alleles, 47, **376**
defensive circuits, **376**
degenerate characterisic of the genetic code, **376**
demand characteristics, **376**
dementia due to Alzheimer disease (ICD-11), 185
dementia risk
  Trisomy 21 (Down syndrome), 174–175
denaturation (in PCR), **376**
denature (protein), **376**
dendrites, **376**
deoxyribonucleic acid, *See* DNA
depolarizing input (neuron), **376**

depression-like behavior, **376**
in mice, 49–50
selective breeding in rats, 63–64
depressive disorders
burden of disease, 204–206
candidate gene association studies, 208–210
characteristics of, 201–202
DALYs caused by, 204–206
family and twin studies, 206–208
genetic correlation across psychiatric disorders, 202–203
genetic epidemiology, 206–208
genome-wide association studies (GWAS), 210
heritability estimates, 206–208
ICD-11 diagnosis, 201, 204
individual differences in response to SSRIs, 212
linkage studies, 208
monoamine hypothesis of depression, 211
non-human animal models of depression, 212–216
polygenic risk scores, 210–211
prevalence, 204–205
question of adequacy as a phenotype, 206
response to antidepressant medications, 211–212
role of 5-HTTLPR variants, 208–210
role of BDNF, 216
role of the HPA axis, 215–216
studies of genetic mechanisms, 208–212
symptom heterogeneity, 204–206
symptoms, 204
designer babies, 343–345
genetically engineered human babies, 344–345
pre-implantation genetic screening, 343–344
sex selection, 320–323
views on human genetic engineering, 343
developmental learning disorder (ICD-11), 177
diabetes
in obese mice, 281
Diagnostic and Statistical Manual of Mental Disorders. *See* DSM
diathesis-stress model, 148, **376**
diazepam, 226–227, **376**
differential sensitivity hypothesis, 148–149, **376**
differentiation of cells, **376**
diffusion process, **376**
dihybrid cross, **376**
backcross, 38–41
independent assortment of traits, 37–38
linkage, 38–41
Punnett square, 36
recombinant types, 38–41
work of Gregor Mendel, 35–36
diploid (2n), **376**
direct-to-consumer genetic testing
ancestry reports, 334–336
availability of, 331–332
cancer risk reports, 334
carrier screening, 332–333
ClinVar database (NCBI), 332
concerns about, 336
genetic weight reports, 334–335
health risk reports, 333
interpretation of reports, 336
miscellaneous features and traits reports, 334
pharmacogenetic reports, 333–334
potential for unexpected information about relatives, 336
privacy of personal genetic information, 336
types of reports provided, 331
wellness reports, 334–335
disability-adjusted life years (DALYs), 145–147, **376**
leading causes worldwide, 204–206
DISC1 gene
schizophrenia studies, 164
discovery sample, **376**
disorders of intellectual development (ICD-11), 171
dizygotic twins (DZ), **376**
DNA, **376**
codon sequence specifies amino acid sequence in proteins, 81–84
codons, 83–84
complementary base pairing, 78–79
confirmation as the genetic material, 77–79
CpG islands, 86
discovery of, 77
discovery of the structure of, 65
double helix structure, 78–79
epigenetic marks, 87
exons, 82
forensic DNA phenotyping, 341
four bases, 77
histone modifications, 86–87
histone packing, 81

DNA (cont.)
  how four nucleotide bases code for amino
      acids, 83–84
  introns, 82
  methylation and demethylation, 86–87
  nucleotide bases, 78–79
  process of constructing proteins, 81–84
  replication process, 80
  transcription (making mRNA), 73–81
  translation into proteins, 82–84
DNA fingerprinting, 340, **377**
DNA polymerase, 80, 102–103, **377**
DNA profiles, 340
DNA sequencing, 103–105
  gel electrophoresis, 104–105
  Next generation sequencing, 105
  Sanger sequencing, 104–105
dNTPs (deoxynucleotide triphosphates), 103, **377**
Dobzhansky, Theodosius, 17, 41, 94
dog (*Canis lupus familiaris*)
  as model organisms, 18
  concept of the dog breed, 6–7
  genes associated with human-directed
      sociability, 314
  genome, 94–95
  morphological and behavioral diversity, 6–7
  prevalence of genetic disorders in dog breeds, 8
  selective breeding for certain traits, 6–8
  similarity of dog and human diseases, 8
  use in behavior genetics studies, 9
dog (*Canis lupus familiaris*) model
  neurobiology of fear and anxiety, 239–240
dog breed, **377**
domestication syndrome, **377**
  silver fox (*Vulpes vulpes*) study, 228–229
dominance genetic variance, 52–53
dominance hierarchies, 308, **377**
dominance variance (V_D), **377**
dominant allele, **377**
dominant traits, 32–33
dopamine hypothesis of schizophrenia, 156, **377**
dopamine receptor D2 (DRD2), 210
dosage compensation, **377**
dosage sensitive genes, **377**
dose dependent effects, **377**
double crossovers, 41, **377**
Down syndrome, 99, 174–176, **377**
  characteristics of, 174–175
  dementia risk, 174–175

  incidence of trisomy 21, 174
  mouse models of Trisomy 21, 175–176
  risk factor for Alzheimer disease, 185–187
drinking in the dark assay, 259, **377**
Drosophila melanogaster, See fruit fly (*Drosophila
    melanogaster*)
drugs
  agonists, 136
  antagonists, 136
  bioavailability, 137
  full agonists, 136
  genetic variations moderate effects on neural
      activity, 138–140
  impacts on neural activation, 136–137
  inverse agonists, 136
  monoamine oxidase inhibitors (MAOIs), 137
  partial agonists, 136
  SSRIs (selective serotonin reuptake inhibitors),
      137–139
DSM, **376**
DSM-5, 149
DSM-5 diagnosis
  specific learning disorder, 177
DTNBP1 gene
  schizophrenia studies, 164
dyscalculia, 177
dysgraphia, 177
dyslexia, 177, **377**
  genes involved in neuronal migration, 178
  non-human animal models, 178

early onset Alzheimer disease (EAOD), **377**
early onset disorder, **377**
early onset forms of disorders, 238
eating disorders
  anorexia nervosa, 203
  anorexia nervosa diagnosis, 292
  bulimia nervosa diagnosis, 292–293
  candidate gene association studies, 294
  diagnosis, 292–293
  endophenotypes and, 295
  feeding or eating disorders (ICD-11), 290
  genetic correlations with other disorders,
      295
  genome-wide association studies, 294–296
  heritability estimates, 293
  mortality rate for anorexia nervosa, 292
  prevalence of, 290
  role of puberty in disordered eating, 293–294

tendency to run in families, 293
types of, 289
eating habits
appetite control circuits, 283–284
body mass index (BMI) and obesity, 284–285
energy balance, 281
evolutionary forces, 279–281
food availability and, 279–280
health impacts of being overweight or obese, 287
nutrition transition, 279–281
obesity in mice with defective leptin signaling, 281–283
rates of obesity, 284
role of leptin in appetite control, 281–283
susceptibility to obesity, 279–281
thrifty genotype hypothesis, 279–281
weight control, 279
electrodermal response, 225, **377**
electroencephalograms (EEG), 196–197
electrostatic pressure, **377**
elevated mazes, 224, **378**
elongation (in PCR), **378**
emotion regulation, **378**
difficulties may lead to psychopathology, 199–201
emotional problems, 199
externalizing disorders, 200
heritability of emotion regulation traits, 200–201
internalizing disorders, 200
mental illness and, 201
process model, 200
strategies, 200
emotional problems, 199, **378**
emotions, 194
alexithymia, 196
autonomic nervous system, 196
behavior genetics studies, 198–199
behavioral studies, 198
cognitive appraisal component, 194–195
communication of, 195
cultural and language differences, 194
defining, 194–195
distinction from feelings, 194
genetic differences in amygdala activation in response to threat, 197–198
heritability of neuroticism trait, 199
in animals, 195

interoception, 194
listing all human emotions, 194
measuring brain activity associated with, 196–198
methods for measuring, 196–199
neuroticism personality trait and, 196
physiological measures, 196
preparation for action, 195
role of the amygdala in processing emotional information, 197–198
schadenfreude, 194
self-report questionnaires, 196
SNP heritability estimates, 198–199
Enclosure Acts, 352, **378**
endocannabinoid system, **378**
role in "runner's high," 300–301
endophenotypes, 151–153, **378**
genetic correlations between different disorders, 295
schizophrenia, 160–161
Enhancing NeuroImaging Genetics through Meta-Analysis (ENIGMA) Consortium, 198
environmental effects, **378**
environmental factors, **378**
environmental risk, **378**
environmental variance, **378**
contribution to phenotypic variance, 48–51
genotype–environment correlations, 56
genotype–environment interaction, 54–56
influence on genotypes, 54–56
measurement error as source of, 53–54
non-shared environmental factors, 54
potential to increase or decrease similarity, 54
shared environmental factors, 54
sources of, 53–56
epigenetic marks, **378**
epigenetic processes
DNA methylation and demethylation, 86–87
effects of life experiences on gene expression, 88
effects of maternal behavior in early life, 88
epigenetic marks, 87
histone modifications of DNA, 86–87
imprinted inactivation, 87
imprinting (parent-of-origin dependent gene expression), 87–88
influence on gene expression, 85–88
transgenerational epigenetic inheritance, 88–89
X-chromosome inactivation, 87

epigenetics, **378**

episodic memories, 179, **378**

epistasis, 52–53, **378**

equal environments assumption, **378**

escitalopram, 137

ethical implications of genomic research, 114

ethical issues

    use of non-human animal models instead of human subjects, 16–17

    use of non-human animals for research, 19

ethical oversight of research, 20–22

    history of unethical research practices, 21

    human research participants, 21–22

    Institutional Animal Care and Use Committees (IACUCs), 20–21

    Institutional Review Boards (IRBs), 21–22

    non-human animal subjects, 20–21

ethics committees, 21

ethyl methanesulfonate (EMS), 110

euchromatin, 86, **378**

eugenics, 6, 8–9, 12, 46, 67, **378**

    American Breeders Association, 358–359

    Buck v. Bell test case (1927), 360–362

    case of Carrie Buck, 360–362

    Cold Spring Harbor Laboratory, 358

    Darwin and natural selection, 352–353

    Darwin's theory of evolution, 354

    decision of Supreme Court Justice Oliver Wendell Holmes, Jr., 361

    Eugenics Records Office, England, 355

    Eugenics Records Office, United States, 356–359

    exported from America to Nazi Germany, 364–366

    extending the reach of American eugenics, 358–359

    funding by philanthropists in the United States, 357–358

    Galton Professorship of Eugenics, University of London, 355

    Galton's theory of eugenics, 354–355

    Goddard's work on IQ tests, 363

    Harry H. Laughlin and the ERO, 358–359

    Hitler's inspiration from American eugenics, 364–365

    impact on the civil rights movement, 368

    in post-WWII United States, 367–369

    influence of Laughlin on compulsory sterilization law, 360–361

    influence of Madison Grant, 364

    influence of the Kallikak family study by Goddard, 356–357

    influence on immigration policy in the United States, 362–363

    institutionalization in the United States, 356–359

    institutionalizing eugenics in England, 355

    International Federation of Eugenic Organizations, 364

    involuntary sterilization laws in the United States, 359–362

    Laughlin's influence on immigration policy, 363

    laws banning interracial marriage, 367

    Lebensborn Program in Nazi Germany, 365–366

    Malthusian argument, 352–353

    master race notion originated in the United States, 356

    Nazi Germany, 364–366

    notions of superiority and inferiority, 366–367

    opposition to support for the poor, 352–353

    origins in the eighteenth century, 352–353

    promotion by Charles Davenport, 358

    promotion of racism by Jensen, 368

    promotion of racism by Shockley, 367–368

    push for legalization by Albert Priddy, 360–361

    racial classifications, 367

    racial differences are not the focus of behavior genetics, 369

    racial focus, 366

    racism and, 351

    rediscovery of Mendel's work, 354

    role of behavior genetics in, 351

    scientific racism, 352–353

    Social Darwinism, 351–353

    support from Andrew Carnegie, 357–358

    support from leading academics of the day, 366–367

    survival of the fittest (Spencer), 353

    Terman's work on IQ tests, 363

    use of IQ testing to promote discrimination, 362–363

    Victims of Eugenics Sterilization Compensation Program (Virginia, 2015), 362

    views of Herbert Spencer, 353

views of Madison Grant, 356
Virginia Sterilization Act of 1924, 360–362
euploidy, **378**
Evans, Martin J., 111
evocative genotype–environment correlation, **378**
evolution, **378**
  behavior as a driving force, 5
  role in behavioral differences, 4
  shared evolutionary history across species, 5,
    17–19
  theory of, 5
exercise, **378**
  candidate gene association studies for physical
    activity, 298–299
  definition of, 296
  definition of physical activity, 296
  effects of the endocannabinoid system, 300–301
  energy balance, 281
  evolution of sedentary lifestyles, 279–281
  familial association with physical activity,
    297–298
  genome-wide association studies for physical
    activity, 299–300
  health benefits of regular physical activity, 297
  heritability estimates for physical activity,
    297–298
  leptin-deficient mice, 300
  rates of insufficient physical activity, 297–298
  recommended levels for health, 297
  reinforcing effect of "runner's high", 300–301
  thrifty genotype hypothesis, 296
  voluntary physical activity in rodents, 300–301
exocytosis, **378**
exons, 82, **378**
extermination camps, **379**
externalizing behavior, **379**
externalizing disorders, 200
externalizing psychopathology, 264

F₁ (first filial generation), 31
F₂ (second filial generation), 31
familial inheritance
  autosomal dominant inheritance pattern, 42–43
  autosomal recessive inheritance pattern, 43–44
  linkage studies, 107–108
  rare single-gene disorders in humans, 42–44
  use of pedigrees, 42–44
  X-linked dominant inheritance pattern, 43
  X-linked recessive inheritance pattern, 44

familial obesity, 287
familial resemblance, **379**
  contribution of genetic variance, 52–53
  historical awareness of, 3–4
  work of Francis Galton, 5–6
family history
  measures of, 262–263
fear, **379**
  behaviors associated with, 223–225
  defensive circuits provide information about
    potential threats, 223
  defensive response to threat, 222–223
  definition of, 222–223
  effects of domestication, 228–229
  genetics of fear and anxiety in mice, 225–226
  research paradigms, 223–225
  role of HPA axis components, 227–228
  role of the GABA neurotransmitter system,
    226–227
  role of the serotonin transporter system, 227
fear conditioning, 213, **379**
fear-related disorders
  anxiety- and fear-related disorders (ICD-11),
    232
feeblemindedness, **379**
feeding or eating disorders. *See* eating disorders
first filial (F₁) generation, **379**
Fisher, R. A., 355
  polygenic inheritance model, 46–47
Five Factor Model of personality traits, 229
five-trial habituation-dishabituation test, 316, **379**
fluoxetine, 137
fluvoxamine, 137
FMR1 gene
  mutation in Fragile X syndrome, 172–173
  trinucleotide repeats, 173
  triplet repeat expansions, 173–174
forced sterilization, 67
forced swim test, 11, 49–50, 213, **379**
  depression-like behavior in rats, 63–64
forensic DNA phenotyping, 341, **379**
Fragile X syndrome, 172–174, **379**
  comorbidities, 174
  FMR1 gene mutation, 172–173
  pattern of inheritance, 172–173
  trinucleotide repeats in the *FMR1* gene, 173
  triplet repeat expansions in the *FMR1* gene,
    173–174
frameshift mutations, 101, **379**

Franklin, Rosalind, 78
fraternal twins, **379**
Friedreich's ataxia, 174
fruit fly (*Drosophila melanogaster*), 8–9, 16, 18, 73
 aggressive behavior, 325
 Bloomington Drosophila Stock Center, 41–42
 courtship behavior, 321–322
 doubling of X-linked gene transcription in
  males, 87
 dunce mutation, 183
 genome, 94–95
 mapping relative positions of genes on
  chromosomes, 36–41
 mutagenesis using ethyl methanesulfonate
  (EMS), 110
 mutagenesis using transposable elements
  (transposons), 110
 mutations affecting learning and memory,
  183–184
 role of heredity in alcohol-related behavior,
  261–262
 rutabaga mutation, 183
 sex-linked white eye mutation, 37–38
 shared biology with humans, 17–19
 testing learning and memory, 182
 X-ray mutagenesis, 110
full agonists, 136, **379**
full mutation, **379**
functional magnetic resonance imaging (fMRI), 133,
 196–198, **379**

GABA neurotransmitter system
 role in fear and anxiety, 226–227
Galton, Francis, 5–6, 8, 11, 25, 230, 358, 363, 366
 support for eugenics in England, 355
 theory of eugenics, 354–355
gametes, 73, **379**
 producing haploid gametes by meiosis, 74–76
garden pea (*Pisum sativum*)
 Mendel's choice for hybridization experiments,
  30–32
Gaucher disease, 119
gel electrophoresis, 104–105, **379**
gene editing
 CRISPR-Cas9 technique, 111–112
gene expression, **379**
 altered gene expression caused by mutations,
  101
 effects of life experiences, 88

 influence of epigenetic processes, 85–88
 process of constructing proteins, 81–84
general cognitive ability, **379**
generalized anxiety disorder, 232
generalize (findings), **379**
generation, **379**
 animalculist view, 26–27
 early thinking on, 26–28
 focus in nineteenth-century farming, 25–26
 ovist view, 26–27
 preformationist theory, 26–27
 qualitative versus quantitative traits, 27
 sheep breeding strategies in the eighteenth and
  nineteenth centuries, 28
 view that heredity derives from only one
  parent, 26–27
genes, **379**
 avoiding oversimplification of effects of
  genetic variation, 15
 conceptualizing a gene, 89–92
 defined by function, 91–92
 defined by phenotype, 90
 epigenetic marks, 87
 for behaviors, 90
 identifying gene–behavior associations, 14–15
 imprinting (parent-of-origin dependent
  expression), 87–88
 mapping relative positions of genes on
  chromosomes, 36–41
 quantitative genetics, 73
 role in behavior, 14–15
 role of DNA, 77–79
 structure and functions of chromosomes, 73–77
genetic architecture, **379**
genetic code, **380**
 how DNA nucleotide bases code for amino
  acids, 83–84
genetic correlation, **380**
genetic determinism, **380**
 lack of scientific support for, 67
genetic differences
 testing for, 11–15
genetic disorders
 genetic mapping of Mendelian traits in
  humans, 42–44
genetic effect, **380**
genetic engineering
 germline genetic changes, 344
 homologous recombination technique, 111

humans, 343–345
knockout and knock-in mutations, 111
somatic cell genetic changes, 344
genetic essentialism, **380**
avoiding, 66–67
genetic genealogy, 340–341, **380**
Genetic Information Nondiscrimination Act of 2008, 336
genetic markers, 107–108, **380**
genetic risk, **380**
genetic testing, *See* direct-to-consumer genetic testing
genetic variability
generation by sexual reproduction, 76
generation during meiosis, 74–76
genetic variance, **380**
additive variance, 52
contribution to phenotypic variance, 48–51
dominance variance, 52–53
heritability, 58–59
interaction variance (epistasis), 52–53
non-additive genetic variance, 53
sources of, 52–53
genetic variation
altered amino acid sequences, 100–101
altered gene expression or splicing caused by mutations, 101
aneuploidy, 99
copy number variants, 98
de novo mutations, 95
effects of differences in brain structure, 132–135
effects on neural activation patterns, 131–135
frameshift mutations, 101
genes for formation and maintenance of synapses, 126–131
Genome Data Viewer (NCBI), 97–98
genome-wide association studies (GWAS), 109
genomes, 94–95
impact on brain development and function, 126–128
indels (insertion/deletion), 98–99
inversions, 99
large deletions, 99
missense mutations, 100
mobile element insertions (MEIs), 99
moderation of drug effects on neural activity, 138–140
mouse models of neurotransmission, 131–132

neural components, 122–126
nonsense mutations, 101
potential mechanisms of synaptopathology, 126–128
role in evolution, 94
role in phenotype differences, 99–101
role of convergent evidence in understanding, 101
serotonin receptor genetics, 124–126
silent mutations, 100
SNPs (single nucleotide polymorphisms), 95–96
structural variants, 98–99
types of, 94–99
genetic variation measurement, 102–107
candidate gene association studies, 108
components used in molecular genetics, 102–103
copy number variants, 106–107
DNA sequencing, 103–105
effects of population stratification on statistical associations, 109–110
experimental methods, 110–112
genetic markers, 107–108
indels (insertion/deletion), 106–107
limitations of research methods, 109–110
linkage analysis, 107–108
methods for generating genetic variation (mutagenesis), 110–112
microarray methods, 106–107
non-experimental methods, 107–110
polygenic risk scores, 108
polymerase chain reaction (PCR), 105–107
quantitative trait loci (QTL) studies, 108
SNPs (single nucleotide polymorphisms), 106–107
testing associations between genetic variants and behavior, 107–110
using familial inheritance patterns, 107–108
Genome Data Viewer (NCBI), 97–98
genomes, 94–95, **380**
cost of sequencing, 114
Human Genome Project, 113–115
mitochondrial genome, 94
nuclear genome, 94
online genomics databases, 97–98
species important in behavior genetics, 95
twins, 95
genome-wide association studies (GWAS), 109, **380**

genotype–environment correlations, 56–58, **380**
    active correlations, 57
    evocative correlations, 57
    passive correlations, 56–57
genotype–environment interaction, 54–56
    crossover interaction, 54–56
genotypes, 33–34, **380**
    influence of environmental context, 54–56
genotyping, 140
germ cells, 73, **380**
germline cells, **380**
germ-plasm, **380**
ghrelin, **380**
    role in appetite stimulation, 287–288
Goddard, Henry H., 172, 356–357, 363
Golden Gate Killer (Joseph James DeAngelo, Jr.), 341
Golgi apparatus, **380**
Grant, Madison, 356, 364
Griffith, Frederick, 77
guanine, 79
G×E interaction, **380**

Hall, G. Stanley, 363
haploid (n), **380**
haplotype block, 317, **380**
Harriman, Mary, 358
health risk reports
    direct-to-consumer genetic testing, 333
helicase, 80, **380**
hemizygous, 44, **380**
heredity
    early thinking on generation, 26–28
    focus on generation in nineteenth-century
        farming, 25–26
    preformationist theory, 26–27
    qualitative versus quantitative traits, 27
    sheep breeding strategies in the eighteenth and
        nineteenth centuries, 28
    state of knowledge in the nineteenth century,
        25–26
heritability, 58–59
    broad sense heritability, 58
    narrow sense heritability, 58
    realized heritability, 63, 65
    understanding that traits are not inherited, 66
heritability estimation
    avoiding genetic essentialism, 66–67
    in selective breeding of livestock, 60
    lack of support for genetic determinism, 67

methods, 59–64
    potential for misunderstanding and bias,
        66–67
    twin studies to estimate in humans, 61–62
    use of phenotypic similarity and genetic
        relatedness, 59–60
    using adoption studies to estimate in humans, 63
    using selective breeding, 63–64
heritable, **380**
Hershey, Alfred, 78
heterochromatin, 86, **381**
heteromeric, **381**
heterozygosity, 49, **381**
heterozygous genotypes, 33, **381**
Hirsch, Jerry, 41
histones, 81, 86–87, **381**
history of behavior genetics
    awareness of familial resemblance, 3–4
    behavior as a driving force of evolution, 5
    blank-slate view of John Locke, 4
    contribution of Francis Galton, 5–6
    dog breeding for certain traits, 6–8
    establishment of behavior genetics in the
        twentieth century, 8–9
    eugenics, 6, 8–9
    evolutionary view of Charles Darwin, 4
    familial resemblance, 5–6
    influence of Gregor Mendel, 8–9
    lessons from, 3
    nature-versus-nurture debate, 4–6
    origins of the field, 3
    scientific racism, 8–9
    theory of evolution, 5
    twin studies, 6
    use of non-human animal models, 5, 9
    work of Thomas Hunt Morgan, 8
hoarding disorder, 237
Holmes, Oliver Wendell, Jr., 361
Holocaust, 67
homeostasis, **381**
homeostatic neuroadaptation, **381**
homologous chromosomes, **381**
homologous pair, **381**
homologous recombination, 111, **381**
    non-allelic, 313–314
homomeric, **381**
homosexual behavior
    changing views on, 170
homozygosity, 49

homozygous genotypes, 33, **381**
homunculus, 27
honeybee (*Apis mellifera*), 9, 18
 aggressive behavior, 325
 genome, 94–95
Human Genome Epidemiology (HuGE) Navigator, 269
Human Genome Project, 42
 impact on biomedical research and technology, 113–115
humanized mouse lines, 111, **381**
humans (*Homo sapiens*)
 genes associated with violence and aggression in humans, 326
 genome of, 95
 human genetic engineering, 343–345
 human karyotype, 74
 sex determination, 323
 sexual orientation, 323
Huntington's disease, 43, 119, 174
hybrid cross, 31, **381**
hyperphagia, **381**
hyperpolarizing input, **381**
hypochondriasis, 237
hypofrontality, **381**
hypomanic episode, **381**
hypothalamic-pituitary-adrenal (HPA) axis
 role in fear and anxiety, 227–228
 role in stress and depression, 215–216
 role in the stress response, 88, 223
hypothalamus
 role in response to threats, 223

ICD-11, 149
ICD-11 diagnosis
 alcohol dependence, 253
 anorexia nervosa, 292
 anxiety and fear-related disorders, 232
 autism spectrum disorder, 319
 Bipolar type I, 202
 bulimia nervosa, 292–293
 dementia due to Alzheimer disease, 185
 depressive disorders, 204
 developmental learning disorder, 177
 disorders of intellectual development, 171
 disorders specifically associated with stress, 240–241
 feeding or eating disorders, 290
 obsessive-compulsive or related disorders, 237
 schizophrenia, 154–155

identical twins, **381**
imprinted inactivation, **381**
inbred strains, 49, **381**
increasing alleles, 47, **381**
indels (insertion/deletion), 98–99, **381**
 detection and measurement, 106–107
individual differences, **381**
 among school children, 169
 combination of genetic and environmental variations, 12–15
 contribution of genetic variance, 52–53
 focus of behavior genetics, 9–10
 population thinking (diversity approach), 12–13
 testing for genetic differences, 11–15
 typological thinking (categorical approach), 12–13
industrial revolution, 352, **381**
inebriometer, 261, **381**
Institutional Animal Care and Use Committees (IACUCs), 20–21, **382**
Institutional Review Boards (IRBs), 21–22, **382**
intellectual disability, **382**
 developmental disorder with multiple causes, 171–176
 disorders of intellectual development (ICD-11), 171
 DSM-5 definition, 171
 environmental and genetic causes, 172–176
 Fragile X syndrome, 172–174
 learning disorders not considered as, 177–178
 mouse models of Trisomy 21, 175–176
 prevalence of, 172
 previous terminology for, 172
 Trisomy 21 (Down syndrome), 174–176
intelligence, **382**
 changing views on what is normal, 170–171
 defining, 169
 standardization of IQ tests, 169–170
 testing, 169–170
intelligence quotient (IQ), **382**
 See also IQ
interaction genetic variance (epistasis), 52–53
interaction variance, **382**
intergenerational modification, **382**
intermediate allele, **382**
intermediate phenotypes, 152, **382**
internalizing behavior, **382**
internalizing disorders, 200

International Classification of Diseases, **382**
See also ICD
International Human Genome Sequencing
Consortium, 113
interoception, **382**
introns, 82, **382**
inverse agonists, 136, **382**
inversions in chromosomes, 99, **382**
ionotropic receptors, **382**
ions, 120, **382**
IQ testing
use by eugenicists to promote discrimination,
362–363
use by the US Army, 362–363
IQ tests
standardization of, 169–170
isoforms, **382**
isogenic lines, **382**
isogenic strains, 49

Jensen, Arthur, 368
justice system
DNA fingerprinting, 340
DNA profiles, 340
forensic DNA phenotyping, 341
identification of the Golden Gate Killer
(Joseph James DeAngelo, Jr.), 341
use of genetic information in the courtroom,
342
using genetic genealogy to identify suspects,
340–341

karyotypes, **382**
human karyotype, 74
KIBRA protein
role in memory formation, 180–182
Klinefelter syndrome, 312
knockout and knock-in mutations, 111

large deletions, 99, **382**
late onset Alzheimer disease (LOAD), **382**
Laughlin, Harry H., 358–361, 363–364
Law of Independent Assortment, **382**
Law of Segregation, **382**
learning
changing views on what is normal, 46–48
defining intelligence, 169
individual differences among school children,
169

intelligence testing, 169–170
learning and memory mutations in *Drosophila melanogaster*, 183–184
testing learning and memory in *Drosophila melanogaster*, 182
learning disorders
developmental learning disorder (ICD-11), 177
dyscalculia, 177
dysgraphia, 177
dyslexia, 177
dyslexia and genes involved in neuronal
migration, 178
non-human animal models of dyslexia, 178
not considered intellectual disability, 177–178
specific learning disorder (DSM-5), 177
Lebensborn Program, **382**
leptin, **383**
leptin-deficient mice, 300
levels in people with Prader-Willi syndrome,
287
obesity in mice with defective leptin signaling,
281–283
role in appetite control, 281–283
level of analysis, **383**
levels of analysis, 13–15, **383**
Lexapro, 137
life experiences
effects on gene expression, 88
lifetime prevalence, **383**
light-dark box, 224, **383**
linkage, 38–41, **383**
linkage analysis, 107–108, **383**
linkage groups, 37
liver
ethanol metabolism, 265
Locke, John, 4
locus, **383**
longitudinal studies, **383**
loss, **383**
Lutz, Frank, 37
Luvox, 137
lysosomal storage disorders, 119
lysosomes, **383**

magnetic resonance imaging (MRI), 133, **383**
major allele, **383**
Malthus, Thomas, 352–353
manic episode, **383**
map distance, **383**

maternal care, **383**

mean, **383**

measurement error
    environmental variance caused by, 53–54

measuring behavior
    forced swim test for rodents, 11
    measures used for humans, 10
    measures used for non-human animals, 10
    methods used for humans, 10–11
    methods used for non-human animals, 11
    reliable and valid measures, 10–11
    resident-intruder test for rodents, 11
    running wheel for rodents, 11
    self-report measures, 10

meiosis, **383**
    producing haploid gametes, 74–76
    recombination (crossing over) during, 75–76

meiosis I, **383**

meiosis II, **383**

membranes, **383**

memory
    declarative memories, 179
    episodic memories, 179
    learning and memory mutations in *Drosophila melanogaster*, 183–184
    role in cognitive ability, 179–180
    semantic memories, 179
    testing learning and memory in *Drosophila melanogaster*, 182
    types of, 179–180
    working memory, 180

memory dysfunction
    causes of, 179
    impairment and distress caused by, 180
    post-traumatic stress disorder (PTSD), 180
    testing episodic memory, 180
    See also Alzheimer disease

memory formation
    role of the KIBRA protein, 180–182

Mendel, Johann (Gregor), 25, 29, 73
    choice of the garden pea (*Pisum sativum*) for hybridization experiments, 30–32
    dihybrid cross, 35–36
    dominant traits, 32–33
    early life and health problems, 29
    experimental hybridization work, 30–32
    influence on behavior genetics, 8–9
    interest in understanding the mechanism of heredity, 30–32

Law of Independent Assortment (inheritance at multiple loci), 35–36
    Law of Segregation (inheritance at a single locus), 32–34
    life as an Augustinian monk, 29–30
    monohybrid cross, 32–34
    recessive traits, 32–33
    rediscovery of his work in 1900, 354
    success and failure at teaching, 30
    theoretical model of particulate inheritance, 33–34

Mendelian genetics
    crossover events during gamete formation, 39–41
    linkage, 38–41
    mapping relative positions of genes on chromosomes, 36–41
    recombinant types, 38–41

Mendelian inheritance
    autosomal dominant inheritance pattern, 42–43
    autosomal recessive inheritance pattern, 43–44
    chromosomes as the physical basis of, 73
    mapping of genetic disorders in humans, 42–44
    normal distribution of a trait within a population, 46–48
    polygenic inheritance model, 46–47
    problem of dimensional (quantitative) traits, 46–48
    use of pedigrees, 42–44
    X-linked dominant inheritance pattern, 43
    X-linked recessive inheritance pattern, 44

Mendelians, 46, **383**

mental health services, 146–147, **383**

mental illness, **383**
    behavior genetic research, 145
    behavior genetic research approach, 149–153
    characteristics of, 145
    comorbidity, 145
    diagnostic systems, 149–150
    diathesis-stress model, 148
    differential sensitivity hypothesis, 148–149
    disability-adjusted life years (DALYs), 145–147
    emotion dysfunction and, 201
    endophenotypes, 151–153
    environmental risk and protective factors, 147–148
    genetic correlation across psychiatric disorders, 202–203

mental illness (cont.)
    genetic risk and protective factors, 147
    levels of analysis of genetic effects, 150–151
    negative impacts on length and quality of life,
        145–146
    potential mechanisms of synaptopathology,
        126–128
    prevalence of, 145
    Research Domain Criteria (RDoC), 151–153
    risk factors for, 147–149
    treatments provided by mental health services,
        146–147
    variation in genes for serotonin synthesis and
        metabolism, 123–124
mental retardation, **384**
messenger RNA. *See* mRNA
meta-analysis, **384**
metabotropic receptors, **384**
methylation and demethylation of DNA, 86–87
Michigan Longitudinal Study (MLS), 263
microarray methods, 106–107
mid-parent value, **384**
Miescher, Friedrich, 77
Milgram's Obedience Study, 21
Million Veteran Program, 235–236
minor allele, **384**
miscegenation, **384**
missense mutations, 100, **384**
missing heritability, **384**
mitochondria, 119, **384**
mitochondrial DNA, 119
mitochondrial genome, 94, **384**
mitosis, **384**
    producing diploid cells, 76–77
mobile element insertions (MEIs), 99, **384**
molecular genetics
    basic components used in, 102–103
    DNA collection and processing, 102
    DNA polymerase, 102–103
    DNA sequencing, 103–105
    gel electrophoresis, 104–105
    nucleotides (dNTPs), 103
    oligonucleotide primers, 102–103
    oligonucleotide probes, 103
    polymerase chain reaction (PCR), 105–107
    schizophrenia, 159–163
    Taq polymerase, 102
molecular mechanisms, **384**
    pathways from gene to behavior, 14–15

molecules of heredity, 73
monkeys
    use in behavior genetics studies, 9
monoamine hypothesis of depression, 211, **384**
monoamine oxidase inhibitors (MAOIs), 137, **384**
monoamines, **384**
monohybrid cross, 31–32, **384**
    Mendel's classic experiments, 32–34
    Punnett square, 33–34
monosomy, 99, **384**
monozygotic twins (MZ), **384**
mood disorders, 201
    ICD-11 diagnosis, 201
Morgan, Thomas Hunt, 8, 36–41, 73, 110
morphological feature, **384**
mosaicism, **384**
mouse (*Mus musculus*), 9, 18
    aggressive behavior, 325
    behaviors studied in, 51
    description, 51
    development of knockout lines, 111
    forced swim test for depression-like behavior,
        49–50
    genetics, 51
    genetics of fear and anxiety, 225–226
    genome, 94–95
    humanized mouse lines, 111
    partitioning trait variance, 49–50
    shared biology with humans, 17–19
mouse (*Mus musculus*) models
    alcohol use disorder, 261
    Alzheimer disease, 189
    knockout model of obsessive-compulsive
        disorder, 239–240
    neurotransmission, 131–132
    obesity related to defective leptin signaling,
        281–283
    oxytocin knockout mice, 315–316
    serotonin system genes knockout mice,
        324–325
    serotonin transporter (SERT) knockout, 132
    serotonin transporter gene *Slc6a4* knockout
        mice, 215
    transgenerational epigenetic inheritance, 89
    Trisomy 21, 175–176
mRNA, **384**
    processing of the primary transcript, 73–81
    transcription of DNA, 73–81
    translation into proteins, 82–84

mRNA vaccines for COVID-19, 115
Muller, Herman J., 110
multiple comparisons, **384**
mutagenesis, 17, 110, **384**
    conditional knockout techniques, 111
    CRISPR-Cas9 technique, 111–112
    ethyl methanesulfonate (EMS), 110
    homologous recombination technique, 111
    knockout and knock-in mutations, 111
    methods for generating genetic variation,
        110–112
    transposable elements (transposons), 110
    X-ray mutagenesis in *Drosophila*
        melanogaster, 110
mutations
    altered gene expression or splicing caused by, 101
    frameshift mutations, 101
    missense mutations, 100
    nonsense mutations, 101
    point mutations, 110
    private damaging mutations, 162–163
    silent mutations, 100

Napp, Cyrill, 29–30
narrow sense heritability, **384**
National Center for Biotechnology Information
    (NCBI)
    ClinVar database, 332
    Genome Data Viewer, 97–98
National Center for Human Genome Research, 113
National Epidemiologic Survey on Alcohol and
    Related Conditions III, 249
National Human Genome Research Institute, 114
National Survey on Drug Use and Health (NSDUH),
    249
natural, **385**
natural selection, 5, **385**
nature-versus-nurture debate, 4, **385**
    work of Francis Galton, 5–6
Nazi Germany, 67
    breeding more Aryans (Lebensborn Program),
        365–366
    concentration camps, 364–365
    eugenics policy inspired by the United States,
        364–366
    experimentation on concentration camp
        prisoners, 21
    extermination camps, 365
    forced sterilization laws, 364

    Hitler's inspiration from American eugenics,
        364–365
    Nuremberg Laws on race, 367
negative symptoms, **385**
negatively reinforcing behavior, **385**
neural activation patterns
    effects of genetic variation, 131–135
neural activity
    drug effects moderated by genetic variations,
        138–140
neural activity patterns, **385**
neural function
    impacts of drugs on, 136–137
neurexins, 127–128, **385**
neuroadaptation, 131–132, **385**
neurodegenerative diseases, 119
neuroendocrine cells, **385**
neurogenesis, 126, **385**
neuroimaging genetics, 133–134
    functional magnetic resonance imaging
        (fMRI), 133
    magnetic resonance imaging (MRI), 133
    positron emission tomography (PET), 133
neurolaw, **385**
neuroligins, 127–128, **385**
neurological function
    impact of genetic variation during brain
        development, 126–128
neurons, **385**
    action potential, 121
    activity underlying behavior, 117
    axon, 120
    basic cellular functions, 117–119
    basic structure of an interneuron, 120
    cell cytoplasm, 117
    cell membrane, 117–118
    cell nucleus, 119
    cell organelles, 117
    communication process, 120
    dendrites, 120
    diffusion pressure, 121
    electrostatic pressure, 121
    genes for formation and maintenance of
        synapses, 126–131
    genetic variation in neural components, 122–126
    genetic variation in neurotransmitter binding at
        synapses, 128–131
    Golgi apparatus, 119
    interneurons, 120

neurons (cont.)
  ion channels, 121
  lysosomes, 119
  mitochondria, 119
  motor neurons, 120
  movement of ions during neurotransmission, 120–121
  neuroadaptation, 131
  neurotransmitter receptors, 120
  perikaryon, 120
  potential mechanisms of synaptopathology, 126–128
  receiving and transmitting information, 119–121
  resting potential, 120–121
  rough endoplasmic reticulum, 119
  sensory neurons, 120
  serotonin synthesis and metabolism pathway, 123–124
  similarities across the animal kingdom, 120
  smooth endoplasmic reticulum, 119
  synapse, 120
  synaptic activity, 121–122
  types of, 120
neuroticism personality trait, 196, **385**
  candidate gene associations studies and GWAS, 230–231
  heritability estimates, 229–230
  heritability of, 199
  study of genetic differences in anxiety, 229–231
neurotransmission
  effects of genetic differences in brain structure, 132–135
  mouse models of genetic effects, 131–132
neurotransmitter receptors, 120
  serotonin receptor genetics, 124–126
neurotransmitter systems, 122–123
neurotransmitters, 120, **385**
  genetic variation in binding to receptors at synapses, 128–131
Next generation sequencing, **385**
niche specialization, 5, **385**
non-additive genetic variance, 53, **385**
non-allelic homologous recombination, 313–314
non-conservative mutations, **385**
non-human animal models, **385**
  alcohol use disorder, 257–262
  Alzheimer disease, 5
  behavioral measures, 10–11
  consideration in convergent evidence, 16

contribution to human well-being, 16
controlled matings, 16–17
depression, 212–216
dyslexia, 178
essential role in behavior genetics, 16–20
ethical oversight of research, 20–21
ethics of using animals for research, 19
fear-conditioning paradigm, 213
forced swim test, 213
limitations of, 19–20
model organisms, 17–18
mutagenesis, 17
problem of generalization from one species to another, 19–20
PTSD, 243
range of animals used in behavior genetics, 8–9
recombinant inbred lines, 259–261
schizophrenia genetic models, 42, 163–164
shared evolutionary history across species, 5, 17–19
shock avoidance paradigm, 213
similarity of dog and human diseases, 8
tail suspension test, 213
two-bottle choice test, 214
where ethical issues prevent using human subjects, 16–17
  See also particular species
nonsense mutations, 101, **385**
non-shared environmental factors, **385**
non-sister chromatids, **385**
non-synonymous mutations, *See* missense mutations
normal, **385**
  changing definitions of, 170–171
normal distribution, **385**
  polygenic inheritance model, 46–48
norms, **386**
NRG1 gene schizophrenia studies, 164
nuclear genome, **386**
nucleic acids
  discovery of, 77
nucleus, **386**
Nuremberg Laws, **386**
nutrition transition, **386**

obesity, **386**
  body mass index (BMI) and, 284–285
  burden of disease, 287
  candidate genes associated with, 288–289
  contributing factors, 287

familial obesity, 287
health impacts, 287
in mice with defective leptin signaling,
   281–283
in Prader-Willi syndrome, 287–288
rates of, 284
susceptibility to, 279–281
syndromic obesity, 287–288
obesogenic environments, **386**
obsessions, **386**
obsessive-compulsive disorder, 203
candidate gene association studies, 238–239
characteristics of, 237
early onset form, 238
familial inheritance, 237–238
genome-wide association studies, 239
heritability estimate, 238
ICD-11 diagnosis, 237
knockout mouse model, 239–240
olfactory reference disorder, 237
oligonucleotide primers, 102–103
oligonucleotide probes, 103
oligonucleotides, **386**
one drop rule, **386**
operational definition, **386**
organelles, **386**
outbred strains, 49, **386**
ovists, 26–27, **386**
oxytocin, **386**
role in affiliation and attachment, 314–319
variation in genes for, 315–316
oxytocin knockout mice, 316
oxytocin system variants as candidate genes, 316–317

pangenesis, **386**
Parabon Nanolabs, 341
parasympathetic nervous system, 223, **386**
parental generation, **386**
parental types, 39, **386**
paroxetine, 137
partial agonists, 136, **386**
passive genotype–environment correlation, **386**
paternal care, **386**
Paxil, 137
Pearson, Karl, 46, 355
pedigrees, 42–44, **386**
penetrance, **386**
pentameric protein, **386**
perikaryon, **386**

personality traits
Big Five, 229
heritability of neuroticism trait, 199
neuroticism, 196
pharmacodynamics, 136–137, **386**
pharmacogenetic reports
direct-to-consumer genetic testing, 333–334
pharmacogenetics, 136, 138–140, **386**
pharmacogenomics, 138, 140, **386**
pharmacokinetics, 136–137, **386**
pharmacology, 136, **386**
phenotypes, 33–34, **386**
forensic DNA phenotyping, 341
role of genetic variation, 99–101
phenotypic variance, **387**
genetic and environmental sources of, 48–51
genotype–environment correlations, 56–58
heritability, 58–59
partitioning into genetic and environmental
   components, 49–50
sources of environmental variance, 53–56
sources of genetic variance, 52–53
phenylketonuria (PKU), 43–44, 368
phospholipid bilayer, **387**
physical activity, 296, **387**, 387
   See also exercise
physiological measures, **387**
pleiotropy, 160–161, **387**
Ploetz, Alfred, 364
point mutations, **387**
point prevalence, **387**
pollen, **387**
polygenes, 73, **387**
polygenic inheritance
additive genetic variation, 57–58
polygenic inheritance model, 46–47
polygenic risk scores, 108, **387**
polymerase chain reaction (PCR), 9, 105–107, **387**
population stratification, **387**
effects on genetic variation statistical
   associations, 109–110
population thinking, 12–13, **387**
positive symptoms, **387**
positively reinforcing behavior, **387**
positron emission tomography (PET), 133, **387**
post-traumatic stress disorder (PTSD), 180, 241–243
candidate gene association studies, 242
characteristics of, 241
estimates of heritability of risk, 242

post-traumatic stress disorder (PTSD) (cont.)
    family and twin studies, 241–242
    genome-wide association studies, 242–243
    non-human animal models, 243
    prevalence of, 241
    risk factors and protective factors, 241–242
Prader-Willi syndrome, 88
    obesity in people with, 287–288
precision medicine, 337, **387**
    All of Us study (Precision Medicine Initiative),
        337–338
    in psychiatry, 338–340
    serotonin transporter 5-HTTLPR variants and
        SSRI response, 339–340
Precision Medicine Initiative, 337–338
preference ratios, **387**
preformationist theory, 26–27, 32, **387**
premutation, **387**
Priddy, Albert, 360–361
primary investigators, **387**
primary transcript, **387**
primers, **387**
private damaging mutations, 162–163, **387**
proactive aggression, **387**
proband, **388**
probes, **388**
process model of emotion regulation, **388**
proteins, **388**
    amino acid sequence specified by DNA
        sequence, 81–84
    construction process, 81–84
    description and functions of, 81
    role of tRNA in protein construction, 82–84
Prozac, 137
Psychiatric Genetics Consortium, 109
Psychiatric Genomics Consortium, 160, 202, **388**
    Cross-Disorder Group, 203
psychiatry
    precision medicine, 338–340
psychoactive substances, 248, 250–251, **388**
psychopharmacology, 136, **388**
pulse song, **388**
Punnett square, 33–34, **388**
    dihybrid cross, 36
purines, 79, **388**
pyrimidines, 79, **388**

qualitative traits, 27, 31, **388**
quantitative genetics, 58, 73
    Fisher's polygenic model of inheritance, 46–47
    origins of, 46

quantitative trait loci (QTL), **388**
quantitative trait loci (QTL) studies, 108
quantitative traits, 27, 31, **388**
    dominance genetic variance, 52
    problem of dimensional traits, 46–48

racial essentialism, 366, **388**
racial hygiene, **388**
racism, 351, **388**
    scientific racism, 8–9
rare alleles, **388**
rat (*Rattus norvegicus*), 9, 18
    Fawn Hooded (FH) strain, 214
    Flinders sensitive line (FSL), 214
    genome, 94–95
    Learned Helplessness (LH) line, 214
    selective breeding for depression-like behavior,
        63–64
    Wistar-Kyoto (WKY) line, 214
reaction times, **388**
reactive aggression, **388**
realized heritability, **388**
receptor availability, 136, **388**
receptor binding affinity, 136
recessive traits, 32–33, **388**
reciprocal cross, 31, **388**
recombinant inbred lines, 259–261, **389**
recombinant types, 38–41, **389**
recombination breakpoints, **389**
recombination rate, **389**
ref SNP, **389**
refractory period, **389**
regression analysis, 60, **389**
reification, 150, **389**
reliable measures, 10, **389**
RELN gene
    schizophrenia studies, 164
reproductive strategies
    influence on parental care, 307
research consortia, **389**
Research Domain Criteria (RDoC), 151–153, 206,
        295, 314, **389**
resident-intruder test, 11, **389**
response to selection, **389**
resting potential, **389**
restriction endonucleases, 106, **389**
restriction fragment length polymorphisms (RFLPs),
        106, **389**
Rett syndrome, 43
reuptake, **389**
Revised Stanford-Binet IQ test, 363

ribonucleic acid. *See* RNA
ribosomes, 84
risk alleles, 108, **389**
risk indicators, **389**
RNA, **389**
    discovery of, 77
    four bases, 77
RNA polymerase, 81, **389**
rough endoplasmic reticulum, **389**
roundworm (*Caenorhabditis elegans*), 9, 16, 18
    genome, 94–95
Rüdin, Ernst, 364
runner's high, **389**
running wheel, 11, **390**

sampling bias, **390**
Sanger sequencing, 104–105, **390**
Satin Bowerbird (*Ptilonorhynchus violaceus*), 321
schizophrenia, 203
    3q29 microdeletion risk factor, 159–160
    age of onset, 154
    burden of disease, 154
    copy number variants risk factor, 159–160
    DISC1 gene studies, 164
    dopamine hypothesis, 156
    DTNBP1 gene studies, 164
    endophenotypes, 160–161
    enlarged ventricles associated with, 155–156
    environmental risk factors, 158
    heritability, 157–159
    hypofrontality associated with, 156
    ICD-11 diagnosis, 154–155
    in populations with African ancestry,
        162–163
    molecular genetics, 159–163
    neurobiological features associated with,
        155–156
    non-human animal genetic models, 163–164
    NRG1 gene studies, 164
    pleiotropy among associated genes, 160–161
    polygenic risk score, 161
    polygenic trait, 159
    positive and negative symptoms, 155
    prevalence, 154
    private damaging mutations, 162–163
    RELN gene studies, 164
    risk associated with familial relatedness,
        157–159
    symptom heterogeneity, 155
    symptoms, 154–155
    treatment, 154

scientific racism, 8–9, 352–353, **390**
sedentary behavior, **390**
selection differential, **390**
selective breeding, **390**
    depression-like behavior in rats, 63–64
    dog breeding for certain traits, 6–8
    domestication syndrome, 228–229
    using to estimate heritability, 63–64
selective breeding of livestock
    use of heritability estimation, 60
selective permeability, **390**
selective serotonin reuptake inhibitors. *See* SSRIs
self-report measures, 10, **390**
semantic memories, 179, **390**
semiconservative replication, 80, **390**
sense strand of DNA, 81, **390**
sensitivity alleles, **390**
serotonergic system, 122–123
serotonin
    variation in genes that code for synthesis and
        metabolism, 123–124
serotonin receptor 5-HT1B
    genetic variation in neurotransmitter binding at
        synapses, 128–131
serotonin receptor 5-HTR1A, 134–135
serotonin receptor 5-HTR2C, 139
serotonin receptor genetics, 124–126
serotonin transporter (SERT)
    mouse knockout models, 132
serotonin transporter 5-HTTLPR variants, 138–139
    anxiety and, 230–231
    effects on SSRI response, 339–340
    role in depressive disorders, 208–210
    role in individual differences in SSRI response,
        212
serotonin transporter gene *Slc6a4* knockout mice,
    215
serotonin transporter system
    role in fear and anxiety, 227
sertraline, 137
sex chromosome number
    impact of alterations on social cognition, 312
sex chromosomes, 73, **390**
sex determination in humans, 323
sex-linked inheritance
    white eye mutation in fruit flies, 37–38
sex-linked phenotype, **390**
sexual behavior circuits, 320–323
sexual orientation in humans, 323, **390**
sexual reproduction
    generation of genetic variability, 76

sexual selection, 320–323, **390**
  courtship in *Drosophila melanogaster*,
    321–322
Shakespeare, William, 4
shared environmental factors, **391**
sheep
  Bakewell's New Leicester sheep (New Dishley
    sheep), 28
  breeding strategies in the eighteenth and
    nineteenth centuries, 28
shock avoidance, **391**
Shockley, William, 367–368
sickle cell anemia, 333
silent mutations, 100, **391**
silver fox (*Vulpes vulpes*)
  domestication study, 228–229
sine song, **391**
single nucleotide polymorphisms. *See* SNPs
sister chromatids, **391**
Smithies, Oliver, 111
smooth endoplasmic reticulum, **391**
SNP heritability, **391**
SNPs (single nucleotide polymorphisms), 95–96, **391**
  detection and identification, 106–107
  heritability estimates, 198–199
  missing heritability problem, 198–199
sociability, **391**
  definition of, 311
  genetic variation and individual differences,
    311–314
  people with Williams syndrome, 312–314
social behavior, **391**
  affiliation and attachment, 314–319
  agonistic behavior, 308–309
  attachment styles, 308
  brain circuits involved in, 310
  caregiving, 306–308
  challenge of studying the effects of genetic
    variation, 306
  courtship behavior, 308
  deficits associated with autism spectrum
    disorder, 319
  definition of, 306
  development in childhood, 307–308
  dominance hierarchies, 308
  dynamically reciprocal nature, 309–310
  effects of childhood maltreatment, 307–308
  genetic variation and individual differences in
    social cognition, 311–314

influence of reproductive strategies, 307
neurobiology of, 309–310
parental care, 306–308
role of oxytocin, 314–319
social cognition, 308
social cognition, 308, **391**
  genetic variation and individual differences,
    311–314
  impact of sex chromosome number alterations,
    312
  people with Turner syndrome, 311–312
Social Darwinism, 351–353, **391**
social desirability, **391**
social psychology, 306, 308
social recognition memory, 316, **391**
sodium potassium pump, **391**
somatic gene edits, **391**
specific learning disorder (DSM-5), 177, **391**
Spencer, Herbert, 353, 363
spliced mRNA, **391**
SSRIs (selective serotonin reuptake inhibitors),
    137–139, 208, 211–212, **390**
  influence of 5-HTTLPR variants on response
    to, 339–340
stabilizing selection, 324, **391**
standard deviation, **391**
Stanford Prison Experiment, 21
Stanford-Binet Intelligence Scales, 363
statistics, 46, 58
stigma (of a plant), **391**
stop codons, **391**
stress-related disorders, 240–241
  disorders specifically associated with stress
    (ICD-11), 240–241
  post-traumatic stress disorder (PTSD),
    241–243
stress response
  effects of maternal behavior in early life, 88
  role of the HPA axis, 88
stressors, **392**
strong genetic explanation, **392**
Sturtevant, Alfred H., 41
subjective mental state, **392**
Sutton, Walter S., 73
sympathetic nervous system, 223, **392**
symptom heterogeneity, **392**
synapses, **392**
  genes for formation and maintenance of,
    126–131

genetic variation in binding of
neurotransmitters, 128–131
potential mechanisms of synaptopathology,
126–128
synaptic cell adhesion molecules, 127–128, **392**
synaptic integrity, **392**
synaptogenesis, 126, **392**
synaptopathology, **392**
syndromic obesity, **392**
synonymous mutations, *See* silent mutations
synteny, **392**

tail suspension test, 213, **392**
Taq polymerase, 102, **392**
target sample, **392**
Tay-Sachs disease, 333
Terman, Lewis M., 363
The Institute for Genomic Research (TIGR), 113
thermalcyclers, 102, **392**
Thermus aquaticus
source of Taq polymerase, 102
thrifty genotype hypothesis, 279–281, 296, **392**
thymine, 79
tolerance, **392**
Tolman, Edward Chace, 8
Tourette syndrome, 203
transcription factors, 81, **392**
transgenerational epigenetic inheritance, 88–89, **392**
transgenic organisms, **392**
translation, **392**
transporter proteins, **392**
transposable elements (transposons), 110
trauma, **392**
trauma-related disorders, 240–241
disorders specifically associated with stress
(ICD-11), 240–241
post-traumatic stress disorder (PTSD),
241–243
tricyclic antidepressants, 211
trihybrid backcrosses, 41
trinucleotide repeats, **393**
triplet repeat expansions, **393**
FMR1 gene, 173–174
trisomy, 99, **393**
Trisomy 21, 99, 174–176, **393**
characteristics of, 174–175
dementia risk, 174–175
incidence, 174
mouse models, 175–176

risk factor for Alzheimer disease, 185–187
trisomy X, 312
tRNA (transfer RNA), **392**
role in constructing proteins, 82–84
Trut, Lyudmila, 228
Tryon, Robert Choate, 8
Turner syndrome, 99
impact on social cognition, 311–312
Tuskegee Syphilis Experiment, 21
twin studies, **393**
equal environment assumption, 62
estimating heritability in humans, 61–62
heritability of neuroticism, 196
types of twins, 61
work of Francis Galton, 6
twins
genomes, 95
two-bottle choice test, 214, 257, **393**
typological thinking, 12–13, **393**

UBE3A gene, 87
unfolded protein response (UPR) genes, 119

valid measures, 10, **393**
variance, **393**
definition of, 48–49
partitioning into genetic and environmental
components, 49–50
varieties, 31, **393**
Venter, Craig, 113
vesicles, **393**
Virginia Sterilization Act of 1924, 360–362

Watson, James, 78, 113, 358
weak genetic explanation, **393**
weight
genetic weight reports, 334–335
weight control, 279
Weldon, W. F. R., 46
wellness reports
direct-to-consumer genetic testing,
334–335
wild-type, 37, **393**
Wilkins, Maurice, 78
Williams syndrome, **393**
sociability, 312–314
Williams syndrome critical region, **393**
withdrawal syndromes, 251, **393**
working memory, 180, **393**

X-chromosome inactivation, 87
X-linked dominant inheritance, 43, **393**
X-linked recessive inheritance, 44, **393**
X-ray crystallography, 78
X-ray mutagenesis
    fruit fly (*Drosophila melanogaster*), 110
XYY syndrome, 312

Yerkes, Robert, 362

zebra fish (*Danio rerio*), 9, 18
    aggressive behavior, 325
    genome, 94–95
Zoloft, 137
zygotes, **393**